LANGUAGE AN

C000132403

Language and Style

In Honour of Mick Short

Edited by

Dan McIntyre

and

Beatrix Busse

palgrave
macmillan

First published 2010 by
PALGRAVE MACMILLAN

Palgrave Macmillan in the UK is an imprint of Macmillan Publishers Limited,
registered in England, company number 785998, of Houndmills, Basingstoke,
Hampshire RG21 6XS.

Palgrave Macmillan in the US is a division of St Martin's Press LLC,
175 Fifth Avenue, New York, NY 10010.

Palgrave Macmillan is the global academic imprint of the above companies
and has companies and representatives throughout the world.

Palgrave® and Macmillan® are registered trademarks in the United States,
the United Kingdom, Europe and other countries

ISBN: 978–0–230–23156–6 hardback
ISBN: 978–0–230–23157–3 paperback

This book is printed on paper suitable for recycling and made from fully
managed and sustained forest sources. Logging, pulping and manufacturing
processes are expected to conform to the environmental regulations of the
country of origin.

A catalogue record for this book is available from the British Library.

A catalog record for this book is available from the Library of Congress.

10 9 8 7 6 5 4 3 2 1
19 18 17 16 15 14 13 12 11 10

Printed and bound in Great Britain by
CPI Antony Rowe, Chippenham and Eastbourne

Contents

AFTERWORD

Acknowledgements

A book of this scope necessarily relies on the goodwill and professionalism of its contributors, and in this respect we have been very fortunate indeed. Everyone we approached to contribute a chapter agreed enthusiastically as soon as they learnt that this was a book in honour of Mick Short. Our grateful thanks go to all our authors for their willingness to meet strict deadlines, to respond to reviewers' comments, and for their patience as we resolved issues such as copyright permissions and the other small problems that go along with putting together a book such as this.

We are especially grateful to Kitty van Boxel at Palgrave Macmillan for commissioning the book, for believing in it from the word go, and for demonstrating vast reserves of patience as we took longer and longer to finish it.

Susanne Lachat-Haney and Roman Pfäffli did an excellent job of proofreading the chapters and collating the references. Brian Walker went far beyond what we required of our authors by also compiling the index for the book. Their sterling efforts saved us many hours of work and we thank them for it.

We are also grateful to the Research Committee of the School of Music, Humanities and Media at the University of Huddersfield, and the English Department of the University of Bern, for providing financial support towards the cost of copyright fees for quoted material.

Finally, our greatest acknowledgement is, of course, to Mick Short himself. Both of us have benefited greatly from his support over the years and we hope that this book goes some way towards recording our thanks to him.

The authors and publishers would like to thank the following for permission to reproduce material:

Anvil Press Poetry, for 'Public House Confidence', from *Norman Cameron: Collected Poems and Selected Translations*, edited by Warren Hope and Jonathan Barker. Published by Anvil Press Poetry, 1990.

Craig Raine, and David Goodwin Associates as his representative, for permission to use 'A Martian Sends a Postcard Home', by Craig Raine © Craig Raine, 1979.

Faber and Faber Ltd, for 'Hawk Roosting', by Ted Hughes, from *Lupercal* (1960) and 'Broadcast', by Philip Larkin, from *The Whitsun Weddings* (1964).

Methuen Publishing Ltd, for 'One leg too few', from *The Complete beyond the Fringe* by Bennet, A., Cook, P., Miller, J. and Moore, D. (1987) pp. 148–50, London: Methuen.

Pearson Education Ltd, for the diagram on p. 226 from *Exploring the Language of Poems, Plays and Prose*, by Mick Short (1996) London: Longman.

Pressdram Ltd, for permission to reproduce ten *Private Eye* covers. Each cover is reproduced by kind permission of PRIVATE EYE magazine.

Rosie Bailey, for kind permission to reproduce 'The Unprofessionals', by Fanthorpe U. A., from *Safe as Houses* (1995) Calstock: Peterloo Poets.

The Literary Trustees of Walter de la Mare and the Society of Authors as their representative, for 'The Listeners', from *The Listeners and Other Poems* by Walter de la Mare (1912) London: Constable & Co.

The Random House Group, for 'Circle of Prayer', from *The Progress of Love*, by Alice Munro, published by Chatto & Windus. Reprinted by permission of The Random House Group Ltd.

Every effort has been made to trace the copyright holders but if any have been inadvertently overlooked the publishers will be pleased to make the necessary arrangement at the first opportunity.

Contributors

Marc Alexander is the linguistics research assistant for the JISC enroller repository at the University of Glasgow. His research interests include the cognitive manipulation of readers in narratives (particularly the detective fiction of Agatha Christie), and the semantic-stylistic interface in scientific popularizations. He has worked on the Historical Thesaurus of English for the past four years and is currently investigating its use in stylistic and lexicological studies.

Dawn Archer is Reader in Corpus Linguistics, and Research Lead for Linguistics, at the University of Central Lancashire, Preston, UK. She is interested in the discursive practices of the English historical courtroom and her 2005 monograph explored *Questions and Answers* during the period 1640–1760. More recently, she has begun to investigate the nineteenth-century English courtroom and facework within the context of the courtroom (historical and modern). Her work in this area draws upon her other areas of expertise: (historical) pragmatics and corpus linguistics. She is also involved in the development of content analysis tools and corpus annotation schemes for historical texts, and the promotion of the use of such tools/schemes across linguistics, including stylistics, and other disciplines: see, for example, her recent edited collection, *What's in a Word-list?* (Ashgate, 2009).

Tom Barney has a PhD from Lancaster University on the rhythm and intonation of recited poetry. He now researches and writes on metre and rhythm in poetry, and all aspects of form in literature. He is especially interested in the ways the formal patterns of works of literature represent their underlying themes.

Derek Bousfield is head of the Division of Linguistics, English Language, Literature and Culture at the University of Central Lancashire, Preston, UK. His main research interests are pragmatics, stylistics, context, and linguistic approaches to understanding and accounting for aggression, conflict and conflict resolution. His major publications include *Impoliteness in Interaction* (John Benjamins, 2008) and the co-edited *Impoliteness in Language* (Walter de Gruyter, 2008). He is editor-in-chief (with Karen Grainger) of the *Journal of Politeness Research*.

Joe Bray is Senior Lecturer in the School of English Literature, Language and Linguistics at the University of Sheffield. He has research interests in stylistics, the eighteenth-century novel and book history and textual culture. Among his publications are *The Epistolary Novel: Representations of Consciousness* (Routledge, 2003) and *The Female Reader in the Eighteenth-Century Novel* (Routledge, 2008).

Beatrix Busse is Associate Professor of English (historical) linguistics at the English Department of the University of Berne, Switzerland. She has been a visiting researcher in Birmingham (UK), Stratford (UK), and Lancaster (UK), and a visiting fellow of the British Academy. Her scholarly interests include the history of English, (historical) pragmatics, systemic-functional grammar, Shakespeare studies, stylistics and corpus linguistics. One of her major publications is on *Vocative Constructions in the Language of Shakespeare* and was published by John Benjamins in 2006. One of her current research projects is on speech, writing and thought presentation in nineteenth-century English.

Ronald Carter is Professor of Modern English Language at the University of Nottingham. He has written and edited more than 50 books in the fields of literary-linguistics, language and education, applied linguistics and the teaching of English. He has taught and lectured in over 30 countries worldwide and published over 100 academic papers. Recent books include: *Language and Creativity* (Routledge, 2004); *The Cambridge Grammar of English* (Cambridge University Press, 2006, with Mike McCarthy); *From Corpus to Classroom* (Cambridge University Press, 2007, with Mike McCarthy and Anne O'Keeffe); and *The Language and Literature Reader* (Routledge, 2008, with Peter Stockwell). Professor Carter is a fellow of the Royal Society of Arts, a fellow of the British Academy for Social Sciences, and was chair of the British Association for Applied Linguistics from 2004 to 2007.

Jonathan Culpeper is Senior Lecturer in the Department of Linguistics and English Language at Lancaster University, UK. His work spans pragmatics, stylistics, and the history of English, and his major publications include *Exploring the Language of Drama* (Routledge, 1998, co-edited with Mick Short and Peter Verdonk), *Language and Characterisation: People in Plays and Other Texts* (Longman, 2001), *Cognitive Stylistics: Language and Cognition in Text Analysis* (John Benjamins, 2002, co-edited with Elena Semino), and *English Language: Description, Variation and Context* (Palgrave, 2009, co-edited with Francis Katamba, Paul Kerswill, Ruth Wodak and Tony McEnery). He has recently completed a three-year ESRC fellowship studying impoliteness.

Catherine Emmott is Senior Lecturer in the Department of English Language at the University of Glasgow. Her publications include *Narrative Comprehension: A Discourse Perspective* (Oxford University Press, 1997) and articles on narrative, cognitive stylistics and anaphora. She is assistant editor of *Language and Literature* and was the stylistics and text analysis editor for the

Encyclopedia of Language and Linguistics (Elsevier, 2006). She is on the editorial/advisory boards of *English Text Construction, Narratologia* and *Storyworlds: A Journal of Narrative Studies*, and is Director of the STACS Project (*Stylistics, Text Analysis and Cognitive Science: Interdisciplinary Perspectives on the Nature of Reading*).

Monika Fludernik is Professor of English at the University of Freiburg in Germany. Her publications include *The Fictions of Language and the Languages of Fiction* (Routledge, 1993), *Towards a 'Natural' Narratology* (Routledge, 1996) and *An Introduction to Narratology* (2009). She has edited several special issues of journals (on second-person fiction, *Style* 1994; on metaphor, *Poetics Today* 1999; on voice, *New Literary History* 2001; and on German narratology, *Style* 2004) as well as a number of collections of essays including *In the Grip of the Law: Prisons, Trials, and the Space Between* (2004, with Greta Olson); *Diaspora and Multiculturalism* (2003); *and Hybridity and Postcolonialism* (1998). Her essays have appeared in, among others, *Anglia, Arial, Diacritics, English Literary History, English Studies, Narrative, New Literary History, Poetica, Semiotica, Style* and *Textual Practice*.

Joanna Gavins is Senior Lecturer in English Language and Literature at the University of Sheffield, where she teaches courses in stylistics, cognitive poetics, and contemporary literature. She has been at the forefront of the development of text world theory for the last ten years. Her major publications include *Cognitive Poetics in Practice* (Routledge, 2003, co-edited with Gerard Steen) and *Text World Theory: An Introduction* (Edinburgh University Press, 2007).

Geoff Hall is Senior Lecturer in the School of Arts and Humanities at Swansea University. His research interests include stylistics and applied linguistics, and he is the author of *Literature in Language Education* (Palgrave, 2005). He is the current editor of the journal *Language and Literature*.

David L. Hoover is Professor of English at New York University, where he has taught since 1981. His research interests include the digital humanities, computational stylistics, corpus stylistics and authorship attribution. His most recent books are *Stylistics: Prospect and Retrospect* (Rodopi, 2007; with Sharon Lattig) and *Language and Style in* The Inheritors (University Press of America, 1999). He is active in the Association for Computers and the Humanities, the Association for Literary and Linguistic Computing, the MLA and the Poetics and Linguistics Association, and serves on the editorial boards of *Language and Literature, Digital Studies/Le champ numérique* and the book series *Linguistics Approaches to Literature*.

Lesley Jeffries is Professor of English Language at the University of Huddersfield and a former chair of the international Poetics and Linguistics Association (PALA). Her most recent books include *Textual Construction of the*

Female Body (Palgrave, 2007), *Critical Stylistics* (Palgrave, 2010), *Opposition in Discourse* (Continuum, 2010) and *Stylistics* (Cambridge University Press, 2010, with Dan McIntyre). At Huddersfield she is director of the Stylistics Research Centre and is currently working on a corpus-based study of poetry, as well as numerous projects on language in conflict. With Dan McIntyre she edits the Palgrave series *Perspectives on the English Language.*

Geoffrey Leech is Professor Emeritus of English Linguistics at Lancaster University, where he has taught for 40 years. He has written, co-authored or co-edited 29 books in the areas of stylistics, English grammar, pragmatics, computational linguistics and corpus linguistics. In the area of stylistics he has written *A Linguistic Guide to English Poetry* (1969), *Style in Fiction: An Introduction to English Fictional Prose* (with Mick Short; 2nd edition 2007) and *Language in Literature: Style and Foregrounding* (2008). All three books were published by Longman. He is an honorary fellow of Lancaster University, a fellow of the British Academy and a member of the Academia Europaea.

Michaela Mahlberg is Associate Professor in English Language and Applied Linguistics at the University of Nottingham. She is the author of *English General Nouns: A Corpus Theoretical Approach* (John Benjamins, 2005) and *Text, Discourse and Corpora. Theory and Analysis* (Continuum, 2007, jointly with Michael Hoey, Michael Stubbs, and Wolfgang Teubert), and she is the editor of the *International Journal of Corpus Linguistics* (John Benjamins) and co-editor of the series *Corpus and Discourse* (Continuum). Her main research interests are in corpus linguistics and its applications. Currently she is working on a book on corpus stylistics and Dickens's fiction.

Dan McIntyre is Reader in English Language and Linguistics at the University of Huddersfield. He is the author of *Point of View in Plays* (John Benjamins, 2006), *History of English* (Routledge, 2008) and *Stylistics* (Cambridge University Press, 2010, with Lesley Jeffries), and co-editor of *Stylistics and Social Cognition* (Rodopi, 2007, with Lesley Jeffries and Derek Bousfield). Dan edits the book series *Advances in Stylistics* for Continuum, and with Lesley Jeffries is co-editor of the Palgrave series *Perspectives on the English Language*. He is also reviews editor for the journal *Language and Literature.*

Marga Munkelt teaches English Studies at the University of Münster and has repeatedly taught as a visiting professor at the University of New Mexico (Albuquerque). Her teaching experience includes all fields of English literature and selected aspects of anglophone studies such as American and (post) colonial literature. Her main research interests are Shakespeare studies (with emphases on editing, theatre history and performance criticism), Mexican-American studies, drama, and editorial theory and practice. She has edited Shakespeare and has published widely in all her research fields.

Nina Nørgaard is Associate Professor of Applied Linguistics at the Institute of Language and Communication, University of Southern Denmark. She has published various articles on stylistics and multimodality as well as the monograph *Systemic Functional Linguistics and Literary Analysis. A Hallidayan Approach to Joyce – A Joycean Approach to Halliday* (University Press of Southern Denmark, 2003). She is currently working on a monograph, *Multimodal Stylistics*, as well as the reference book *Key Terms in Stylistics* (Continuum, forthcoming 2010).

Lisa Lena Opas-Hänninen is head of English Philology at the University of Oulu, Finland. She is a long-term member of both PALA and the Association for Literary and Linguistic Computing. She has research interests in many aspects of digital humanities and has published widely in this area.

Elena Semino is Senior Lecturer in the Department of Linguistics and English Language at Lancaster University. She is interested in stylistics, corpus linguistics and metaphor research. She is the author of *Language and World Creation in Poems and Other Texts* (Longman, 1997) and *Metaphor in Discourse* (Cambridge University Press, 2008), co-author of *Corpus Stylistics: Speech, Writing and Thought Presentation in a Corpus of English Writing* (Routledge, 2004, with Mick Short) and co-editor of *Cognitive Stylistics: Language and Cognition in Text Analysis* (John Benjamins, 2002, with Jonathan Culpeper).

Tapio Seppänen is Professor of Biomedical Engineering at the University of Oulu, Finland. His research interests in linguistics include multimedia signal processing, specifically the prosodic analysis of speech, text prediction, digital watermarking, and content-based information retrieval, and he has published widely in these areas.

Dan Shen is Changjiang Professor of English and Director of the Center for European and American Literatures at Peking [Beijing] University. She is on the editorial boards of *Language and Literature* and *JLS: Journal of Literary Semantics*, and is a consultant editor of *The Routledge Encyclopedia of Narrative Theory*. In addition to numerous books and essays published in China, she has published widely in North America and Europe, in journals including *Style*, *Narrative*, *Poetics Today*, *JNT: The Journal of Narrative Theory*, *Comparative Literature Studies* and *Nineteenth-Century Literature*.

Paul Simpson is Professor of English Language in the School of English at Queen's University, Belfast. His publications have ranged from studies of the sociolinguistic features of pop singing styles to the pragmatics of advertising discourse, although he is best known for his work in stylistics, critical linguistics and the linguistics of verbal humour. He is a former editor of the journal *Language and Literature* and his books include *On the Discourse of Satire* (John Benjamins, 2003), *Stylistics* (Routledge, 2004), *Language, Ideology and Point* *of View* (Routledge, 1993) and *Language through Literature* (Routledge, 1996). He is co-author of the recent *Language and Power* (Routledge, 2009).

Catherine Smith is a Research Fellow at the University of Nottingham where she is currently working on a project on adolescent health communication through the internet. With a background in biblical studies, systemic functional linguistics and computer science, she previously worked on various projects at the universities of Birmingham and Liverpool. Her main research interests are the application of corpus linguistic methods within sociolinguistics and literary stylistics, and the development of software tools for corpus linguistics.

Peter Stockwell is Professor of Literary Linguistics at the University of Nottingham where he teaches and researches in stylistics, particularly cognitive poetics. His book publications in stylistics include *Texture* (Edinburgh University Press, 2009), *Cognitive Poetics* (Routledge, 2002), *The Poetics of Science Fiction* (Longman, 2000) and the co-edited *Language and Literature Reader* (Routledge, 2008), *Contemporary Stylistics* (Continuum, 2007), *Contextualised Stylistics* (Rodopi, 2000) and *Impossibility Fiction* (Rodopi, 1996). In the field of English language teaching and research, he is the author of *Sociolinguistics* (Routledge, 2007) and *Key Concepts in Language and Linguistics* (Routledge, 2007), and the co-author of *Introducing English Language* (Routledge, 2010), *The Routledge Companion to Sociolinguistics* (Routledge, 2007), *Language in Theory* (Routledge, 2005) and *Investigating English Language* (Stanley Thornes, 1996).

Michael Toolan teaches courses in language, stylistics and narrative at the University of Birmingham, where he is currently head of the Department of English. His books include *The Stylistics of Fiction* (Routledge, 1988), *Total Speech* (1996), *Language in Literature* (1998), *Narrative: A Critical Linguistic Introduction* (2nd edition, 2001) and most recently *Narrative Progression in the Short Story: A Corpus Stylistic Approach* (John Benjamins, 2009).

Peter Verdonk is Emeritus Professor of Stylistics at the University of Amsterdam, where he started teaching in the early 1970s, after a career in maritime law. His research interests are stylistics, rhetoric, literary criticism, discourse analysis, ekphrastic poetry and cognitive poetics. His books include *Twentieth-century Poetry* (Routledge, 1993), *Literature and the New Interdisciplinarity* (Rodopi, 1994, with Roger D. Sell), *Twentieth-century Fiction* (Routledge, 1995, with Jean Jacques Weber), *Exploring the Language of Drama* (Routledge, 1998, with Jonathan Culpeper and Mick Short) and *Stylistics* (Oxford University Press, 2002). He is an honorary member of the Poetics and Linguistics Association (PALA). On his retirement, he was honoured with a festschrift entitled *Contextualized Stylistics*, edited by Tony Bex, Michael Burke and Peter Stockwell (Rodopi, 2000).

Katie Wales is Special Professor in the School of English, University of Nottingham. Formerly she was Research Professor in English at the University of Sheffield; Professor of Modern English Language at the University of Leeds; and Professor of English Language at Royal Holloway, University of London. She is a founder member of the Poetics and Linguistics Association, and a past editor of the journal *Language and Literature*. Her research interests and related publications cover a wide range: English language and literature from Old English to the present-day, with particular enthusiasms for stylistics, rhetoric, and the social and cultural history of northern English: the latter being the subject of a book for Cambridge University Press (2006). One current project is a stylistic and rhetorical study of 'conversations with the dead'; another is revising the *Dictionary of Stylistics* for a third edition (2nd edition 2001, Longman). Other books include *The Language of James Joyce* (Macmillan, 1992) and *Personal Pronouns in Present-day English* (1996).

Brian Walker is a research student in the Department of Linguistics and English Language at Lancaster University, and a research assistant in corpus linguistics at the University of Huddersfield. His PhD thesis combines stylistic and corpus-based approaches to investigate the characters in Julian Barnes's novel *Talking It Over*. By using a combination of these two different approaches his research explores how stylistics and corpus linguistics can work together in the analysis of literary texts.

INTRODUCTION

Language, Literature and Stylistics

BEATRIX BUSSE AND DAN MCINTYRE

This book has two purposes. It is a collection of essays demonstrating the state of the art in stylistics, and it is a tribute to Professor Mick Short and his contribution to stylistics over the course of his long and distinguished career. Such books are often called festschrifts, though we have deliberately not used this word in the title of the book for reasons we will explain below.

To anyone even vaguely familiar with stylistics, Mick Short will be an immediately recognisable name. Indeed, one of the reviewers of our proposal for this book described him as 'perhaps the most influential stylistician of the latter part of the twentieth and first part of the twenty-first century'. We would concur entirely, save for the word 'perhaps'. Since 1996 Mick has been Professor of English Language and Literature in the Department of Linguistics and English Language at Lancaster University, where he has taught since 1973. His connection with Lancaster extends back even further, as he was an undergraduate student at the university before moving to the University of Birmingham for his MA. Following a short spell teaching in Birmingham, Mick Short returned to Lancaster, subsequently gaining a PhD for his work on the stylistics of drama. Professor Short's work at Lancaster has focused primarily on stylistics, and it is in this area that he has developed a truly international reputation. Of course, many academics achieve such status, but what sets Mick Short apart is the extent to which he has influenced his discipline, his colleagues and his students.

Nowadays, anyone interested in learning about stylistics has myriad opportunities open to them. There is a worldwide organization to join – the *Poetics and Linguistics Association* (PALA). There are international journals to read – PALA's own *Language and Literature*, as well as others such as the *Journal of Literary Semantics*. There are textbooks to consult, and research monographs available. And there is an increasing number of stylistics courses on offer at universities the world over. It is no exaggeration to say that Mick Short has had a significant hand in establishing this current state

3

of affairs. He is, for example, responsible for PALA, which he founded in 1979, with the support of his colleagues Ron Carter, Roger Fowler and Katie Wales, and for which he acted as chair from 1990 to 1993. He was the founding editor of PALA's journal, *Language and Literature*, from 1992 to 1996, and of its predecessor, *Parlance*. Through his teaching and lectures at universities and conferences worldwide, he has played a leading role in establishing stylistics as an area of serious academic research both in the United Kingdom and overseas, particularly in China where he taught from 1983 to 1984.

Additionally, Mick is the author of many books and articles which have contributed to the development of stylistics as a discipline. He established his reputation with *Style in Fiction* (Longman, 1981) which he wrote in collaboration with his colleague Geoffrey Leech. This book is notable for the systematic and detailed account it gives of the language of narrative fiction, as well as for its introduction of a stylistic 'tool-kit' for the literary critic. *Style in Fiction* also includes the original model of discourse presentation (i.e. speech, thought and writing presentation) that has been so influential both within and beyond stylistics. Since the publication of *Style in Fiction*, Mick has continued his work on discourse presentation with other colleagues, elaborating and extending the model through meticulous corpus-based research (see Semino and Short 2004). The importance of *Style in Fiction* is also apparent by the fact that in 2005 PALA members voted it the most influential stylistics book published in the preceding 25 years. Furthermore, Mick Short's textbook *Exploring the Language of Poems, Plays and Prose* (1996) has become a classic introduction to stylistics, demonstrating its potential for the systematic, retrievable and rigorous investigation of (literary) texts. He has been influential in almost all areas of stylistics, and was one of the first stylisticians to apply pragmatic findings to the analysis of drama (Short 1981). Most recently, he has illustrated the usefulness of the stylistic approach to the analysis of film.

Mick Short's work as an editor is also significant, and demonstrates his commitment to the academic community. In addition to his own edited collections (Short 1989; Thomas and Short 1996; Culpeper *et al.* 1998) he was also responsible for editing *Text Worlds: Representing Conceptual Space in Discourse* (1999) from an unfinished manuscript by the late Paul Werth. Werth's work has, of course, gone on to have tremendous influence on the recent development of cognitive stylistics.

What makes this enviable reputation for research all the more impressive is that it has not been achieved at the expense of his primary role as a university teacher. Throughout his career Professor Short has been committed to sharing his knowledge and to educating the next generation of stylisticians. For many years at Lancaster he has taught a first-year introduction to stylistics called *Language and Style* (the title of this book is a direct tribute to the success of this course). This is a course famed (some would say notorious) for its innovative pedagogical techniques, which include, *inter alia*, cross-dressing to perform extracts from featured plays and sketches, having students stand hand-in-hand at the front of the lecture theatre to illustrate the concept of syntactic co-ordination, and hitting students over the head with an inflatable hammer to remind them of the arbitrariness of sound symbolism (see Short and Breen 1988; Breen and Short 1988; Short 1993; and McIntyre 2003 for serious scholarly accounts of this outlandish behaviour). For this innovative teaching, Mick was awarded a UK National Teaching Fellowship in 2000. Typically, he used his award of £50,000, granted to him for his fellowship, to try and improve his students' learning experience by developing a web-based interactive version of the *Language and Style* course, which in 2005 he made freely available on the internet.[1] And in a perfect demonstration of the symbiotic nature of teaching and research, he edited a special issue of the journal *Language and Literature* (Short et al. 2006) in 2006, reporting on the findings from various investigations of the efficacy of the web-based course.

This interest in the pedagogy of stylistics is what led us to abandon the idea of a traditional festschrift in favour of a book that students as well as researchers would benefit from. In view of his interests, this seems a far more fitting tribute to Professor Short's contribution to stylistics. In a further break with tradition, we are presenting this book to Mick not as a valedictory gift to mark his retirement, nor in honour of a significant birthday, but to mark the 30th anniversary of PALA. We have done this because stylistics has always been a forward-looking discipline and nowhere is this more apparent than in the activities of PALA. We want Mick to enjoy using the book with his own students and we present it to him in gratitude for the knowledge, advice, support and time that he has given to us and to all his students, colleagues and friends over the years.

Aims of this collection

As explained above, *Language and Style* is intended to demonstrate current thinking at the cutting edge of the discipline, as well as to convey the practical means by which stylistic analysis can be carried out. To the researcher or student new to stylistics, however, the sheer volume of work now available can be bewildering. What links corpus-based analysis to the more qualitative endeavours of the past? How is cognitive stylistics related to literary criticism more generally? What are the foundational principles of stylistics, and how are these reflected in current research? It is an awareness of the historical development of stylistics that provides the answers to these questions. To understand where we are heading we need to know where we have come from.

A brief history of stylistics

Stylistics in its most general sense is the study of style in language and how this results from the intra-linguistic features of a text in relation to non-linguistic factors such as author, genre, historical period, and so on. It is also about making meaning inferences based on the linguistic framework of the text. While stylisticians have engaged with a wide variety of text-types, it remains the case that the most popular object of study for stylistics is literature. Indeed, this is the primary concern of most of the chapters in this collection. The history of stylistics sheds some light on why literary texts have remained core to the analytical concerns of stylisticians.

Even from its beginning we can see that stylistics embraces much more than the rhetorical notion of literary embellishment or 'elocutio'. Stylistics as a discipline can trace its roots to the formalist tradition that developed in Russian literary criticism at the turn of the twentieth century. Of particular interest is the work of the Moscow Linguistic Circle. Its most famous member and the most well known exponent of Russian Formalism was Roman Jakobson (1896–1982), whose work in this area focused on defining the qualities of what he termed 'poetic language'. According to Jakobson (1960), the poetic function of language is realized in those communicative acts where the focus is on the message for its own sake (as opposed, say, to a communicative act focused on conveying the emotions of the speaker). Jakobson's work was to have tremendous influence on the development of stylistics, not least as a result of his varied academic career and the opportunities it afforded for the cross-fertilization of ideas. Following his emigration to Czechoslovakia in 1920, Jakobson began collaborating with Czech literary scholars such as Jan Mukařovský (1891–1975), establishing the Prague Linguistic Circle in 1926 which was to become famous as the birthplace of structuralism. Like Jakobson, Mukařovský was interested in identifying the formal and functional distinctions between literary and non-literary writing, noting that literary texts deviate from what he termed the 'standard language' (Mukařovský 1964). According to Mukařovský, the consequence of such deviation is the creation of a defamiliarizing effect for the reader, something he claimed to be one of the hallmarks of literature. In turn, Jakobson (1960) suggests that defamiliarization also results from structural patterning in texts, or, to give it its later name, parallelism. Shklovsky's (1917, 1925) notion of defamiliarization ('estrangement') or 'making strange' also entailed a political notion because he stressed that the function of art is to make people look at the world from a new perspective. These concepts – deviation, parallelism, and foregrounding – are the foundations of contemporary stylistics.

Jakobson's work with the Prague structuralists was interrupted by the Second World War, which forced him into an extended period as an itinerant scholar. After several years in Denmark, Norway, and Sweden he finally settled in America in 1941. This move to the US was crucial to the spread of his ideas to scholars in Europe and America, and to the later development of the New Criticism and Practical Criticism movements, in America and Britain respectively.

This, though, is to get ahead of ourselves. Almost in tandem with the work of the formalist and structuralist movements, developments in the linguistic study of literature were being made by continental European scholars. Chief among these was Leo Spitzer, an Austrian philologist interested in the literature of the Romance languages. In Spitzer's work (e.g. Spitzer 1948) we see an approach that will be familiar to any modern stylistician; namely, the concept of starting with an interpretation of a literary text and then using a linguistic analysis to validate or invalidate that initial hypothesis. Spitzer rejected purely impressionistic criticism and his work may thus be seen as a forerunner to later work in stylistics which embraced the scientific notion of objectivity in analysis. Alongside Spitzer, other important scholars working in this tradition included Auerbach (1951), Bally (1909), and Guiraud (1954), whose work was to have an influence on the development of the French tradition of *analyse de texte*. While this approach is more intuitive than would be accepted by today's stylisticians, there is undoubtedly a relation here to contemporary stylistics.

Of these two groups of scholars – characterized by Jakobson on the one hand and Spitzer on the other – it was the former which was to have the most immediate impact on the development of modern stylistics. Russian Formalism influenced the development of the two movements we have already mentioned – New Criticism in America and Practical Criticism in Britain. Both of these approaches were characterized by a focus on the language of the text, though New Criticism (exemplified in the work of Brooks and Warren, 1976) was concerned with the description of the aesthetic qualities of a literary text, while Practical Criticism (developed in the work of I. A. Richards, 1929) was interested in the psychological aspects of how readers comprehend texts. Both essentially proceeded by means of techniques of close reading, and while this approach is viewed by today's stylisticians as too imprecise in analytical terms, West (2007) points out that the concern of Practical Criticism with readers' processing of texts makes it a direct precursor of contemporary cognitive stylistics.

While the formalist and structuralist work of Jakobson and others is not without problems, it should be clear that its value is in the insights that it generated and the later approaches it inspired. Indeed, insights from formalism have proved essential for modern stylistics, with the concepts of deviation, parallelism, and foregrounding still acting as the linchpins of contemporary approaches to the discipline. Van Peer (1986) has provided empirical support for Mukařovský's notion of foregrounding, while Leech (1969) demonstrates convincingly that foregrounding in texts is intrinsic to literary interpretation. The connection between analysis and interpretation is strengthened by Leech's concepts of congruence and cohesion of foregrounding, which goes some considerable way towards refuting accusations of interpretative positivism often levelled at stylistics by its critics and robustly defended by stylisticians like Mick Short (see, for example, Short *et al.* 1998). And in recent work in cognitive stylistics, foregrounding has been related directly to the cognitive concepts of figure and ground.

Nonetheless, for a while New and Practical Criticism's formalist tendencies could still be observed in stylistics as it developed. Since stylistics draws so heavily on linguistics, a history of its development would not be complete without some reference to the work of Noam Chomsky. Although Chomsky's concerns were never with literary texts and their effects, his influence on the development of linguistics inevitably impacts on stylistics. Semino and Culpeper (1995) cite the work of Thorne (1965), Halle and Keyser (1966) and Ohmann (1964) as exemplars of early stylistics that proceeds on the assumption that literary texts constitute instances of linguistic transformations of some underlying structure. To these we can add the work of Levin (1962) on linguistic structures in poetry. Indeed, Hough (1969: 103) notes that the contribution of linguistics to literary study is 'virtually confined to semantics and syntax', therein reflecting the dominance of Chomskyan linguistics at the time he was writing.

While stylistics had so far concentrated on using linguistic tools to explain literary effects, it had also been the subject of criticism for its eclecticism, its lack of a methodological and theoretical foundation, and its alleged base in literary criticism. A major focus on poetry also caused some suspicion in linguistic circles. In the 1960s and early seventies these criticisms were addressed in part through the development of a branch of stylistics that focused particularly on style in non-literary language. The work of Crystal and Davy (1969) and Enkvist (1964, 1973) is particularly important here. Crystal and Davy's concern was how particular social contexts restrict the range of linguistic options open to speakers, while Enkvist proposed that this could work the other way too: that is, that a speaker's stylistic choices could affect the context for his or her addressees (think, for instance, about the informal lexis and grammar often used in adverts for high street banks, and how this is designed to create a context of informality for customers). Work in non-literary stylistics, however, appeared to stall at this point, and it was not until much later that it picked up again. The reasons for this are perhaps the lack of linguistic frameworks able to deal with the contextual issues at the heart of Crystal and Davy's and Enkvist's work.

The basis of stylistics in linguistics has always meant that an advance in the latter inevitably impacts on the former, and so it was in the 1970s and early eighties. Some of the attacks levelled at stylistics were circumvented by its becoming particularly practical and by the movement of stylistics into the areas of language teaching and pedagogical stylistics. Furthermore, Halliday's work on systemic functional grammar (Halliday 1971, 1978, 1985) related form to function within the context of the language system as a whole and had particular influence on the study of prose fiction. Here, Hallidayean-style transitivity analysis was used to uncover point-of-view patterns in text (see, for example, Fowler 1977, 1986, whose own *Essays on Style and Language*, 1966, is a seminal work in early stylistics). The influence of Halliday's work can also be seen in Leech and Short's now famous *Style in Fiction* ([1981] 2007).

During the late seventies and early eighties, advances were also made in the developing field of pragmatics, where the focus was on how context affects meaning. Carter and Simpson (1989) is an exemplar of how this work influenced the development of stylistics in the 1980s. These advances enabled for the first time the serious stylistic study of drama. Burton (1980) is an early attempt at using pragmatic and sociolinguistic insights in the study of dramatic discourse, and Short's (1981) article on discourse analysis applied to drama is a groundbreaking study of how such insights can be used to uncover aspects of characterization. Advances in pragmatics and their concern with context also facilitated a renewed interest in non-literary stylistics (Carter and Nash, 1990) and the ideology-shaping nature of texts (Fowler, 1986). There is a crossover here, of course, with work in Critical Discourse Analysis (CDA), though CDA-inspired work that is unremittingly stylistic in approach continues today and is exemplified in the work of Lesley Jeffries (2007, 2009, 2010).

Into the 1990s there was a growing concern with the cognitive elements involved in comprehending and processing texts, and this movement gave rise to the branch of the discipline now generally known as cognitive stylistics or cognitive poetics (see, for example, Emmott 1997; Stockwell 2002; Semino and Culpeper 2002; and Gavins and Steen 2003). Of course, all forms of stylistic analysis have always considered text comprehension to a certain extent, and in this respect current work in cognitive stylistics can be seen as directly related to earlier investigations into the ways in which readers process texts. Among such earlier work is the Practical Criticism of Richards (1929) and the later reader-response work of, for example, Fairly (1988) and Alderson and Short (1989). Advances in computer technology in recent years have also had a significant impact on the direction in which stylistics is heading. The construction and analysis of large-scale linguistic corpora is easier than ever before and this has enabled a return to some of the original concerns of stylistics – namely, the extent to which foregrounding is quantifiable and whether authorial style really is as distinguishable as critics have claimed. These were questions that were largely unanswerable before the development of corpus linguistics. Nowadays, the ease with which it is possible to analyse a text computationally means that there is almost no excuse not to use evidence from corpus studies to support qualitative analysis. Beyond such corpus-assisted stylistics, of course, lies the more sophisticated use of corpora for the study of style (see, for example, Semino and Short 2004, Mahlberg 2007a, and Hoover, this volume).

Stylistics, then, has come a long way since its beginnings. Its primary concern with literary texts is a direct result of the early interests of the formalists and structuralists, though it is by no means exclusively focused on literature any more. In addition to current work in non-literary stylistics, a developing interest in multimodal texts is taking stylistics in yet another direction. In addition, other branches, such as historical stylistics, draw on a variety of approaches mentioned here in order to investigate the style of a particular historical period or text, or to investigate the ways particular styles change over time. The chapters in this volume all draw on the rich traditions of stylistics outlined in this section and represent the current research concerns of stylisticians. Since stylistics has always prided itself on clarity of expression, these chapters are also intended as exemplars of how to go about doing stylistic analysis. In this respect, a brief explanation of the structure of the book will be useful.

Language and Style

There are many introductory stylistics books available that demonstrate how insights from linguistics can be applied in the analysis of literary texts, in order to explain how texts mean and what interpretative effects such texts have on readers. Among such books is Mick Short's own bestselling *Exploring the Language of Poems, Plays and Prose* (1996), in which he demonstrates how to analyse stylistically the three main literary genres.

Correspondingly, *Language and Style* also has three carefully balanced broad sub-sections in which each chapter is intended to demonstrate a particular analytical technique and how this might be applied to a text from one of the literary genres (in many cases, the insights revealed are also applicable in the analysis of non-literary texts). These are preceded by an introductory segment, entitled 'Preliminaries', designed to cover some of the foundational principles of stylistics outlined in the previous section. Each initial chapter in the genre-based sections has an introductory purpose and aims either to survey the field or to provide a general stylistic analysis of a text from the genre in question. The remaining chapters provide exemplars for both students and researchers of the classic and the very latest analytical techniques. Common to all the chapters of the book is that each owes something to the work of Mick Short. They can be read in tandem with his own introductory books on stylistics, or with any other stylistic introductions or linguistics textbooks, but they also stand independently as examples of current research concerns in stylistics. All are based on the original research of their authors.

In Part I, 'Preliminaries', Geoffrey Leech's model stylistic analysis of two famous Shakespearean speeches functions as an exemplar of the kind of analysis that this book is concerned with. This is followed by chapters from Beatrix Busse and Ron Carter, each of which focus on stylistic methodologies: on stylistic methods and their pedagogic potential, both generally and in specific relation to the language classroom (Carter), and on essential parameters for the stylistic analysis of historical texts (Busse). In discussing current work in historical stylistics and by looking at the past, Busse's chapter also suggests that this is an area that will be of increasing concern to stylistics in the future.

Part II of the book focuses on poetry, the literary genre which has been of concern to stylisticians since the inception of stylistics. Katie Wales's opening chapter is a classic stylistic analysis of Walter de la Mare's famous poem 'The Listeners', and illustrates how stylistic analysis can elucidate our response to a literary text. The other chapters in this section demonstrate a wide variety of stylistic approaches to poetry, taking in cognitive stylistics (Verdonk), syntactic iconicity (Jeffries), text worlds (Semino) and sound patterns (Barney).

The focus of Part III of the book is on the stylistics of drama. The move from poetry to drama matches the arrangement of topics in Short's (1996) *Exploring the Language of Poems, Plays and Prose*, and also reflects the increasing complexity of the discourse structures of the three literary genres. Part III begins with a chapter on the universal elements of drama (Munkelt) and continues with a corpus stylistic approach to dialogue and characterization in film (McIntyre), a pragma-stylistic investigation of the language of Shakespeare's *King Lear* (Bousfield and Archer) and an analysis of how activity type theory can shed light on the creation of humour in dramatic texts (McIntyre and Culpeper). Readers will notice that Part III of the book is by far the shortest. In this respect it is representative of the current balance of interest within stylistics, and also reflects the fact that this is the newest of the three main literary genres to have been studied by stylisticians.

Part IV concerns the stylistics of narrative fiction. Its status as the longest section of the book reflects the dominance of prose analysis within stylistics. The section begins with Dan Shen's introductory application of the stylistic tool-kit to a range of extracts from novels. The other chapters in this section

extend the range of topics that Shen discusses and cover such diverse subjects as authorial style (Hoover), stance in popular fiction (Opas-Hänninen
and Seppänen), point of view (Simpson), sentence and clause types (Toolan),
plot construction and reader manipulation (Emmott and Alexander), narrative and metaphor (Fludernik), corpus-based semantic analysis (Walker), discourse presentation (Bray), text world theory (Gavins), texture (Stockwell),
multimodality (Nørgaard), corpus stylistics generally (Mahlberg and Smith)
and the analysis of non-literary language from a stylistic perspective (Busse).
Fittingly, the final chapter of the book is an afterword by Geoff Hall, the
current editor of *Language and Literature*, the journal of the Poetics and
Linguistics Association whose founding editor was Mick Short. In an admirably succinct essay, Hall describes the contribution that Mick Short has made
to stylistics, and the influence that he has had on his discipline and on his
many colleagues and friends.

NOTE

1. See <http://www.lancs.ac.uk/fass/projects/stylistics/index.htm>

Part I
Preliminaries

CHAPTER 1

Analysing Literature through Language: Two Shakespearean Speeches

GEOFFREY LEECH

1. Prologue

Mick Short wrote a classic introductory work on stylistics, entitled *Exploring the Language of Poems, Plays and Prose* (Short 1996), the first chapter of which was called *Who is Stylistics?* Each of these two titles illustrates one of the key features of the creative use of language. The first title contains an example of sound patterning, in this case a kind of phonetic parallelism that has been called 'chiming': this will be evident in the phonetic transcription of the last four words: /pəʊəmz pleɪz ənd prəʊz/. Each of the three nouns in this fragment is a monosyllable beginning with the consonant /p/ and ending with the consonant /z/ – a sound pattern (consisting of variables and constants) that could be represented /p—z p—z ən p—z/. Normally we do not expect such a pattern to crop up randomly by accident in a text. If it occurs, it is probably by design, and if it was an intended pattern, then as interpreters, we ask: 'What was the point of this pattern? Does it have a meaning, a warranty?' In this case, it can be said that the pattern has a point: the phonetic pattern highlights a syntactic pattern of repetition (Noun, Noun, and Noun) and, more importantly, a semantic parallelism: all three nouns refer to the traditionally recognized three major genres of literature. Mick could have called his book *Exploring the Language of Poetry, Drama and Narrative Fiction*, but in that case the parallelism would have been lost. This is a small illustration of how 'literary' modes of writing make extraordinary use of language. In this case, what is extraordinary is the patternedness: literature tends to exhibit regularity of patterning over and above the patterning that one normally expects to observe of a piece of language.

The second title, *Who is stylistics?* illustrates the extraordinary use of language in a more obvious way. Every reader will be able to identify the oddity
here: the framing of a question 'Who is X?' implies that X is a person. But,
however little we know about *stylistics*, we can recognize that it is not the
name of a person, but is an abstract noun. So – what is the point? Mick, at the
beginning of his introduction, plays with the idea that 'stylistics' is a person,
saying 'she is a friend of mine' (Short 1996: 1). But it is difficult to sustain this
idea, unless we re-spell the word with a capital '*S*': *Stylistics*. Then, with a bit
of effort, we can resurrect a hallowed convention whereby abstract qualities
are personified: Fortune, Vanity, Beauty, Love – typically these qualities have
been personified as female deity-like figures. Perhaps Mick was reconnecting
with this classical literary tradition when he conjured up a female stylistics,
his tutelary goddess? But then, at the end of the chapter he comes clean,
and makes it clear that *Who is stylistics?* was his whimsical device to imprint
the subject on our memories: 'even if you forget entirely the content of this
chapter, you are unlikely to forget its title' (ibid.: 28). More important here,
however, is its value as a simple illustration of the concept of foregrounding,
which in Mick's book was a key concept informing the linguist's analysis of
literary language.

Exploring the Language of Poems, Plays and Prose (Short 1996) is a work
about literature, rather than a work *of* literature. Nevertheless, the examples
above will serve to underline that in studying the language of literature we
are studying *extraordinary* uses of language (using *extraordinary* to mean 'out
of the ordinary' generally with a positive evaluation), and moreover that the
artistry of literary language can be found not just in canonical literature,
but in any piece of language, such as a book title or a chapter title, which is
intended to make us take special notice. The interest of this often lies not just
in the form of language used, but in the acts of interpretation or meaning
construction by which we make sense of what is written or said. Those who
have read Mick's book will be familiar with the idea of *foregrounding* in literary
language. This is the positive side of what is more negatively labelled *deviation* or *deviance*. Deviation implies that writers show themselves to be creative
(and not just in literature) by departing from some norm of language use. To
use language creatively, we avoid what is ordinary, routine, normal, expected;
and this can be done by foregrounded regularity (extra patterning) as well as
by foregrounded *ir*regularity, as in breaching a pattern.

The term *foregrounding* (see Mukařovský 1964; van Peer 1986; Douthwaite
2000) refers to the way we register mentally the unusualness of such departures from the norm, and hence seek to interpret them, as already illustrated
in a small way in the examples above. In my earliest attempt to explore the
concept of foregrounding in print, in 1966 (see Leech 2008: 11–27), I distinguished two basic ways of foregrounding: deviation through irregularity

Good Example!

(a breach of the language pattern, as in 'Who is stylistics?') and deviation through regularity – extra patterning in addition to what is required by the language, as in the *Poems, Plays and Prose* example.

Way back in the 1960s, this formulation gave me a way of focusing on the special nature of literary language and literary meaning. But deviation is a far richer concept, far more adaptable for explicating literary language, than has so far been shown. There is not only the obvious kind of deviation illustrated by 'Who is stylistics?' There are many types and degrees of deviation: in addition to external deviation (deviation against the norms of the language) there is internal deviation (deviation against the norms of a particular text) (Levin 1965). There is also deviation against the norms of the literary tradition (Leech 2008: 55–69), and quantitative (or statistical) deviation vs qualitative (or determinate) deviation (Levin 1963). There are also types of foregrounding that cannot be so easily attributed to deviation from linguistic norms: for example, the unexpected effect achieved by a sudden transition from one style into another, or by the sudden perception of an ambiguity – a pun, for instance. I agree with Mick in placing foregrounding at the centre of the analysis of literature from a linguistic point of view.

2. What is style and what is stylistics?

The term *style* occurs in the title of the present book, and I have already cited the term *stylistics* in referring to its subject matter, with which we are concerned in celebrating Mick Short's work. We should now consider the relation between these two concepts. There is no great harm in defining *style*, in line with a common dictionary definition, as 'a way of using language'. It was this general usage of *style* and *stylistics* that informed two classic books on the subject: Crystal and Davy's *Investigating English Style* (1969) and Enkvist's *Linguistic Stylistics* (1973). But the terms as they stand are so vague that we have to narrow them down and to make certain distinctions. First, in the present context, the focus is on literary style – on the way language is used for artistic purposes – which is a common, though more specialised, use of the term *style* (with no implication that we can neatly divide texts into those that are literary and those that are not). Second, when we study style, we talk about 'the style *of X*' – almost inevitably studying the way the language is used in a certain *textual domain* – call it *X*. This *X* may be the corpus, for example, of a particular (sub)genre of writing at a particular time (say, seventeenth-century love lyrics) or of a particular author's literary works (say, the fictional works of Doris Lessing). Most specifically, however, it can be the style of a particular text or text-extract (say, one particular poem or the first act of a drama), and this is a typical domain for the analysis of style, since

Stylistics = Fiction.
CDA = Non-fiction

the text is the most concrete and manageable domain one can choose to show how stylistic analysis can be done. This will be, in fact, the main focus of the present book.

The term *stylistics*, as the name implies, can mean simply the study of style. But in this case the restriction to literary style is conventionalised: it is rather unusual for a *stylistician* (another technical term) to undertake the stylistic analysis of a non-literary text such as a newspaper article or a cookbook.

Nevertheless, people often do undertake stylistic analyses of non-literary texts, and sometimes apply the term *stylistics* to this type of analysis – as in two recent books by Jeffries: *Opposition in Discourse* (2010b) and *Critical Stylistics* (2010a). But others in the same field are inclined to call what they are doing by a different name, such as critical discourse analysis or text linguistics. In practice it is difficult to distinguish between different branches of linguistics that focus on the study of texts.

So let us simply characterize stylistics here as the analysis of literary texts, using linguistic techniques. But we should not let this definition suggest too narrow, too technical a view of what stylistics involves. It might suggest that stylistics confines itself to the application of the 'core' disciplines of linguistics: undertaking phonetic, phonological, morphological or syntactic analysis, for example. This describes the focus stylistics often had in its earlier days of the 1960s, but since that time stylistics, like linguistics, has moved on, expanding its interests in many directions. First, it has become widely accepted that there is no ring-fencing of literary texts: the creatively artistic phenomena typical of literature are found in many 'non-literary' genres, and creativity in ordinary conversation (see Carter 2004) is by no means to be ignored. Second, in recent decades the narrower concern with the formal levels of foregrounding in texts (phonetic, grammatical, and so on) has been widened to embrace functional and interdisciplinary spheres such as pragmatics, discourse analysis, and cognitive linguistics, which provide a bridge between linguistic and other – social and psychological – domains of enquiry. Third, the initial focus on lyric poetry, as the most 'concentrated' mode of literary expression, which was common in the 1960s, soon extended itself to other genres: to prose fiction, to drama, and even to multimedia works such as films. Fourth, the interests of stylisticians have tended to move away from the text, as a material linguistic object manifested in the physical form of words and punctuation on the page, to the mental representation and processing of texts (this has been called 'the cognitive turn'), and to their socio-cultural setting ('the social turn'), broadly conceived. In this volume, that breadth of reach will be celebrated, and the topics I have mentioned will be among those to be explored in various chapters: see for example, Wales, Verdonk, and Barney, this volume.

At the same time, in this introductory chapter there is reason to keep close to the text, since this is the phenomenon that, when all is said and done, stylistics explicates. We will find present-day stylisticians going well beyond text, yet text must be their starting point: not text in the narrow sense of a paper object manifesting visible letters and punctuation on a page, but text in the richer and more abstract sense of a linguistic object, having form, structure, and meaning. (The term 'text' is often misunderstood in literary studies. For my attempt to explain it as a linguistic concept, see Leech 2008: 186–94.)

3. An essay in stylistics: Two speeches in *The Merchant of Venice*

Taking my cue, then, from the last sentence above, I feel it is appropriate to begin this book with a piece of practical stylistic analysis at the textual heart of stylistics. And if stylistics cannot say anything interesting about the greatest name in English literature, it can demonstrate nothing. For these reasons I choose, in this opening chapter, to discuss two famous set-piece speeches in Shakespeare's *The Merchant of Venice*. Shylock's speech containing *If you prick us, do we not bleed?* (III.i.48–66); and Portia's speech beginning *The quality of mercy is not strained* (IV.i.181–99). Another reason for choosing these speeches is that between them they combine the three traditionally recognized genres of poetry, prose, and drama. Portia's speech, with its high-flown rhetoric in blank verse, shows us poetry; Shylock's, with its own vigorous rhetoric, shows us prose, and both, of course, show us drama. But when we combine these three, we also find that the *poems, plays and prose* of Mick's title are ultimately inseparable. As Mick himself points out in the preface of his book (Short 1996: xii–xiii), the same techniques of analysis can apply to all.

But now, some words of apology for 'lifting' passages out of a play for commentary. It is dangerous to separate a famous speech from its context – as Portia's speech has often been – to be inspected, anatomized, learned by rote, or paraphrased and commented on in exam papers. Apart from anything else, the four centuries that separate us from the Early Modern English of Shakespeare's day should invite a careful consideration of how the language reflects its context of Elizabethan England. For example, the allusion to the five senses in Shylock's speech in 3.1 below:

> Hath not a Jew eyes? Hath not a Jew hands, organs, dimensions, senses, affections, passions?

summons up the Elizabethan and Jacobean concept of sensuality (see Brathwaite 1620). Also, the reference to a king's double nature in Portia's speech in 3.2 reflects the two bodies, a *body natural* and a *body politic* which should merge together in the Elizabethan ideal of kingship (Kantorowicz 1957).

Contextualization is particularly crucial for the stylistic analysis of drama, where it will be necessary to see these passages as part of a dialogue, and to spend a little time looking at how they fit into the scene, the act, and the play they belong to: *The Merchant* as a whole. A second danger, in analysing the text of a play, is that thinking of the play as a written text, we do not envisage it as a dramatic performance – and surely no play is alive until it is performed.

Regarding both these dangers, one is reminded of William Empson's joking characterization of the literary critic (Empson 1953: 9) as a dog who, not content with relieving itself on the flower of beauty, scratches it up afterwards – or, changing the metaphor, as someone who examines a living work of art through a microscope, and, having anaesthetized it on a laboratory bench, dismembers it.

With reference to the first charge, that stylistics (or for that matter, close criticism) subjects to intellectually rigorous analysis something that should only be appreciated aesthetically or emotionally, as a thing of beauty, I do not feel apologetic, as my experience is the opposite: that approaching a piece of literature analytically enhances one's appreciation of its value. Only if we *understand* how a poem is working on our ear, on our eye, on our mind, can we fully recognize and enjoy the mastery behind its composition.

With reference to the second charge, more specifically directed against the analysis of plays as written texts, Mick Short (1998) has argued convincingly that to equate a play with a particular performance on stage is a mistake – rather like the error of believing that an orchestral masterpiece does not exist until you hear a top-quality orchestra playing it. There is no doubt that hearing and watching a play – like hearing and watching a symphony – allows the fullest possible experience of it. And yet, the play itself is best seen as a *potential* for performance, a text which the reader can realize through the imagination, as well as in observing its performance. It is in this spirit that I approach the two speeches from *The Merchant*.

The speeches come from different parts of the play (Act III and Act IV), yet are thematically counterpoised. Both are pieces of argumentative rhetoric in which the speakers show remarkable skill in justifying a particular stance and persuasively arguing for the position they take – Shylock arguing in favour of justice, and Portia in favour of mercy. This description makes these speeches seem philosophically abstract and remote from practical life; yet in the play, they are uttered compellingly for and against a particularly painful and imminent piece of butchery: the cutting of a pound of flesh from the body of Antonio, the merchant of the play's title. This is the recompense legally due to Shylock on Antonio's defaulting on a loan; and so Shylock's argument is simple: Give me justice according to the law! Give me my pound of flesh! Portia, speaking in disguise as a young lawyer, presents the opposing argument: those who wield temporal power should allow justice (according to the law) to be outweighed by mercy (which is divine).

3.1. *Shylock's speech*

First, we consider Shylock's speech. Antonio's friend Salerio, implying that the pound of flesh is worthless to Shylock, supposes that he will not enforce his bond:

Salerio   Why I am sure that if he forfeit, thou wilt not take his flesh – what's that good for?

Shylock   To bait fish withal, – if it will feed nothing else, it will feed my revenge; he hath disgraced me, and hind'red me half a million, laugh'd at my losses, mock'd at my gains, scorned my nation, thwarted my bargains, cooled my friends, heated mine enemies, – and what's the reason? I am a Jew. Hath not a Jew eyes? Hath not a Jew hands, organs, dimensions, senses, affections, passions? fed with the same food, hurt with the same weapons, subject to the same diseases, healed by the same means, warmed and cooled by the same winter and summer as a Christian is? – if you prick us do we not bleed? if you tickle us do we not laugh? if you poison us do we not die? and if you wrong us, shall we not revenge? – if we are like you in the rest, we will resemble you in that. If a Jew wrong a Christian, what should his sufferance*
be by Christian example? – why revenge! The villainy you teach me I will execute, and it shall go hard but I will better the instruction.
(III.1.48–66)

[*_sufferance_ = 'suffering hardship/pain']

Shylock answers with a spirited harangue, essentially elaborating on the adage 'What is sauce for the goose is sauce for the gander.' He draws on the history of oppression of Jews by Christians, and in particular on his own disdainful and unjust treatment at the hands of Antonio. But he begins with a highly repulsive image: the idea that a pound of a living man's flesh is good (only) to use as fish-bait. We do not have to take this literally – it is an answer to the question 'What's that good for?' which from the point of view represented by Shylock, demanding the letter of the law, is quite beside the point. Hence Shylock's response is not to be taken seriously – indeed, it could be uttered under his breath, almost as an aside. A pointless question, he seems to say, deserves an outrageous reply. And he goes on to admit that the value of the pound of flesh to him is not material at all, but in the mind: *if it feed nothing else, it will feed my revenge.*

In the line just quoted we have the first instance of a structure of parallelism – to be followed by plenty more examples in the rest of the speech. A lexico-grammatical parallelism such as this consists of part repetition, and part change – or, putting it otherwise, a repetition of a pattern within which there is also variation:

(1)	S	V	O	
	if it	*feed*	*nothing else*	(Phase 1)
	it	*will feed*	*my revenge.*	(Phase 2)

The same pattern S V O (subject – verb – object) is repeated in the second line, with the same subject and main verb, but with a change in the form of the object – from *nothing else* to *my revenge*. The change in the object, however, also enforces a change in the way we interpret the verb *feed*. *Feed* in the first line takes up the most obvious sense required by Salerio's question 'What's that good for?': What material benefit can this flesh be to you? As food? To which Shylock's reply disdains material benefit – and takes the argument to a different level, the psychological level of volition, satisfaction, revenge.

If we stop at this point to consider what *extraordinary use* is being made of language here, we note a combination of features. First, Shylock's answer to Salerio's question is gruesomely unbelievable – an ironic throwaway reply: 'Yes, it is worth cutting a pound of flesh from a man's body to use it as fish-bait'. The unbelievability of the reply leads to an indirect interpretation of the remark, viz. 'Your question is an irrelevance.' Shylock's second answer is more considered, and its foregrounding of a pattern of repetition enacts the argument: 'You ask for material justification; I provide a mental, an emotional one.'

Lexico-grammatical parallelism is in many ways the dominant stylistic device of this speech, in which it is combined with another stylistic device – the rhetorical question. The term 'lexico-grammatical' means that the repetitive part of the pattern consists of both word repetition and grammatical (syntactic) repetition. Each repetition may be called a *phase* of the pattern, as is shown in (1) above, where the first line displays the first phrase, and the second line the second. The variant elements of each pattern point to its function or interpretation, of which we may recognize two main types. Type A is a cumulative pattern working towards an expressive climax, as illustrated in the build-up to the climactic word *revenge* in (1). Type B is the antithetical pattern pointing to a contrast between the phases of a two-phase pattern, of which we will see examples in Portia's speech. Shylock's examples, on the other hand, are entirely of the cumulative type, except where the pattern in (2) below contains Type B as a subpattern: for example *cooled my friends, heated my enemies*, achieving by this insistent juxtaposition of sensual metaphors the emotional heightening of angry protest that characterizes his speech.

As Shylock's speech continues, we can represent this next parallelism in a diagramatic way as follows, as Shylock enumerates his reasons for bearing a grudge against Antonio (^ signals ellipsis):

(2)		S	V		O	
		he	*hath*	*disgrac'd*	*me*	
	and	^	^	*hind'red*	*me*	***half a million***
		^	^	*laugh'd at*	*my losses*	
		^	^	*mock'd at*	*my gains*	
		^	^	*scorned*	*my nation*	
		^	^	*thwarted*	*my bargains*	
		^	^	*cooled*	*my friends*	
		^	^	*heated*	*my enemies*	

And again, the pattern is SVO, but this time more lengthily elaborated than before: it has eight phases. In each case the subject – explicit or implicit – is *he*, and the object is either *me* or *my* N (where N is a noun). The eight phases of the pattern repeatedly underline the multitude of ways in which Antonio has wronged him. The end of the enumeration is not signalled by *and* – as it normally is – so this lack of coordination (technically known as asyndeton) signals that the list is open-ended: more reasons could be given, we are led to suppose, if Shylock wanted to. Another point to observe about this parallel structure is that although it is highly patterned, it sometimes 'exceeds' the pattern by the insertion of extra words, as if Shylock is speaking under the power of spontaneous emotion, and only partly under the control of his rational faculties. The parallelism itself brings vehement emphasis: if you read it aloud, or enact it on a stage, the vehemence will almost certainly be felt in the rhythmic drumbeat pattern of syllables: dum-di-di dum-(di) (/ x x / (x)) repeated several times. Pairs of lines reinforce the pattern through contrast (type B): *laugh'd at my losses* goes antithetically with *mock'd at my gains*, just as *cooled my friends* goes with *heated my enemies*.

Here we note another general characteristic of parallelism: if the parallelism persists for a while with absolute regularity, the result can be tedious. Instead, skilled writers and speakers introduce extra variety or irregularity into the pattern. One type of extra variation is ellipsis – the omission of words that can be mentally retrieved from the context, signalled by ^ in (2) above. This speeds up the enunciation of the pattern, by cutting away what can be understood: the words *he hath* in this case. Another kind of extra variety is the addition of extra words or phrases, as illustrated by the underlined words in *he hath disgrac'd me, and hind'red me half a million*, as if Shylock has not yet got into his stride, yet his deep sense of grievance is welling up to the surface. For a third kind of extra variety, substitution, we will need to look at example (6) below. These typical types of variation help to give effects of spontaneity, variety and emotive colouring to spoken delivery.

The list in (2) ends with a question and answer. The list of grievances seems to require a delivery at speed, in keeping with the heightened emotion, as the pattern becomes insistently predictable, working towards a climax. But then there has to be a marked slowing-down for rhetorical effect in the question-and-answer sequence. The sentence could have ended briefly and dismissively: *because I am a Jew*. But the question *and what's the reason?* begs us to think of an answer (hence a pause is appropriate) and the answer brings a climax of outrage: *I am a Jew*. In slow motion, we can spell out the implications in square brackets as follows: ... *and what's the reason?* ['There must be some reason for this vindictive behaviour, so what is it?']. *I am a Jew* ['But this is no reason!'].

Here we meet the first question (*what's the reason?*) in a speech where the number of questions is remarkable. Shylock's speech is ostensibly answering the question *what's that good for?* and so we expect his answers to be in the declarative form. But instead of statements, questions predominate. The questions, however, serve a declarative purpose: that of showing that Salerio's initial question is totally out of court. Two of Shylock's questions – the first and the last in this passage – are followed by a self-answering response. The rhetorical force of such a question is to challenge one's addressee mentally to seek a reply, and then to supply the reply, with emotive finality, oneself. The brief statement *I am a Jew*, coming after the question, has the effect of emphatic unchallenge-ability. We can imagine Shylock's gesture of dismissal at this point. An even greater effect is achieved in the last question-and-answer sequence *what should his sufferance be? Why, revenge!* The remaining questions in the speech are of the kind traditionally called *rhetorical questions*. These are questions to which no answer is given, but to which the implicit answer seems obvious and is inevitably the opposite polarity of the question. Hence rhetorical questions have the force of emphatic statements. All the rhetorical questions in the passage are negative (*Hath not a Jew eyes?* etc.), and so the implied answer to them all is a resounding 'Yes! A Jew has eyes/hands/organs etc., just as others have.'

The emphasis achieved through piling up reiterative lists is then repeated:

(3)   Hath not a Jew eyes? Hath not a Jew hands, organs, dimensions, senses, affections, passions?

Obviously, the unspoken implication here is 'Jews are just like other people', thereby refuting the implication of the previous question-and-answer sequence: 'I am treated differently (i.e. very badly) because I am a Jew.' As before, the parallel repetition of structure in the first two phases is short-circuited by ellipsis on the remaining five phases, giving the impression that Shylock's mind is racing forward to grasp all the obvious ways in which Jews are human beings just as Christians are.

(4)	V	*not*	S	O
	Hath	*not*	*a Jew*	*eyes?*
	Hath	*not*	*a Jew*	*hands,*
				organs,
				dimensions,
				senses,
				affections,
				passions?

The parallel comparison continues more elaborately (Adj/PP stands for 'adjective or past participle', prep = preposition, NP = noun phrase), with ellipsis, it must be assumed, of *Is not a Jew* before each phase:

(5)	Adj/PP	prep	NP *[the same N]*
	fed	*with*	*the same food,*
	hurt	*with*	*the same weapons,*
	subject	*to*	*the same diseases,*
	healed	*by*	*the same means,*
	warmed **and cooled**	*by*	*the same winter* **and summer as a Christian is?**

Here, a partial breach of the pattern occurs in the fifth and last phase, again signalled by the words in boldface. Then, parallelism continues even more elaborately, in:

(6)	*If you* V *us,* aux *we not* V
	If you prick us do we not bleed?
	If you tickle us do we not laugh?
	If you poison us do we not die?
And	*if you wrong us* **shall** *we not revenge?*

Once again, notice the elements in bold: they show where the pattern established in the first three phases is exceeded (by addition and substitution) in the fourth. These mark the last phase (as is normally the case) as the climactic conclusion of this parallel sequence. The change of auxiliary verb from *do* to *shall* is particularly telling: whereas the previous three sentences have been presented as general truths in the present tense ('If X happens, Y inevitably follows'), the last is presented as a future event, giving it the force of a threat. Shylock's argument is that Jews are like Christians in all these respects – including the law of retribution that follows wrongdoing. This is the principle of universal justice before the law on which he insists.

3.2. Portia's speech

Much more of interest could be said about Shylock's speech, but it is time to move on to the second speech to be examined, Portia's speech at the legal hearing which follows, and at which she impersonates a 'wise young judge':

Portia   Then must the Jew be merciful.

Shylock   On what compulsion must I? Tell me that.

Portia   The quality of mercy is not strained,
               It droppeth as the gentle rain from heaven
               Upon the place beneath. It is twice blest,
               It blesseth him that gives and him that takes.
               'Tis mightiest in the mightiest, it becomes [*becomes* = 'befits']
               The thronèd monarch better than his crown.
               His sceptre shows the force of temporal power,
               The attribute to awe and majesty,
               Wherein doth sit the dread and fear of kings;
               But mercy is above this sceptred sway, [*sway* = power,
                                                    dominion]
               It is enthronèd in the hearts of kings,
               It is an attribute to God himself,
               And earthly power doth then show likest God's
               When mercy seasons justice; therefore Jew, [*seasons* = softens,
                                                    moderates]
               Though justice be thy plea, consider this:
               That in the course of justice none of us
               Should see salvation. We do pray for mercy,
               And that same prayer doth teach us all to render
               The deeds of mercy. (IV.i.179–99)
               [The last three-and-a-half lines of the speech are omitted.]

As before, I partially contextualize the speech by showing a little bit of the dialogue leading up to it. After she has checked the validity of the bond, Portia's 'must' at the beginning of the passage has an epistemic (necessity) force: 'there can be no other solution' but mercy. She apparently regards the execution of the bond too absurdly barbaric for contemplation. However, Shylock takes 'must' in a more personal deontic (obligational) sense: his challenge is: 'What law or rule compels me to be merciful?' Like the beginning of Shylock's speech we have already examined, Portia's opening line argues the preceding question to be on the wrong footing: *The quality of mercy is not strain'd*, that is, 'is not *constrained*'. That is, mercy is a quality not yielding to compulsion.

The rhetoric of this passage, again like that of Shylock's speech, is based on repetition. But in this case, the repetition is mainly lexical, semantic and prosodic, not syntactic. In the following rendering of the speech, I have marked elements of repetition as follows:

- **bold** = lexical repetition, where the same word or base is repeated.
- underscore = semantic repetition, where the same meaning is repeated in a synonymous item.
- broken underscore = partial semantic repetition, in the form of antonyms or opposites (e.g. *give* and *take* are antonyms which share the same meaning of passing something between one person and another).

The items recurring in patterns of repetition are marked by the same superscript numbers.

> The quality of **mercy**[1] is not strain'd[2],
> It droppeth as the gentle rain from heaven[3]
> Upon the place beneath[3]: it is twice **blest**[4],
> It **bless**eth[4] him that gives[5], and him that takes[5],
> 'Tis **might**iest[6] in the **might**iest[6], it becomes
> The **thronèd**[7] monarch[8] better than his crown.
> His **sceptre**[9] shows the force of temporal **power**[6],
> The attribute to awe[10] and majesty,
> Wherein doth sit the dread[10] and fear[10] of **kings**[8]:
> But **mercy**[1] is above this **sceptred** sway[12],
> It is en**thronèd**[7] in the hearts of **kings**[8],
> It is an attribute to **God**[11] himself;
> And earthly[2] **power**[6] doth then show likest **God**[11]'s
> When **mercy**[1] seasons **justice**[12]: therefore Jew,
> Though **justice**[12] be thy plea, consider this,
> That in the course of **justice**[12], none of us

Should see salvation: we do **pray**[14] for **mercy**[1],
And that same **pray**er[14], doth teach us all to render
The deeds of **mercy**[1]. (IV.i.179–99)

Another difference between this and the previous passage is that the patterns
of repetition are chiefly antithetical: they are two-phrase contrastive patterns,
rather than the cumulative multi-phrase patterns of Shylock's rhetoric. In
this passage, however, there are scarcely any patterns of lexico-grammatical
parallelism. The only clear exception is the parallelism of *him that gives and
him that takes*.

As poetry, however, this speech shows the kind of parallelism manifested
in the verse pattern: blank verse adheres to the ideal pattern of alternating
stressed and unstressed syllables, stress being shown as an acute accent in the
following lines:

It blésseth hím that gíves, and hím that tákes,   (x / x / x / x / x /)
[/ = stressed syllable; x = unstressed/weak syllable]

(Notice here how the metrical pattern of repeated iambic feet reinforces the
lexico-grammatical pattern of *[him that gives] and [him that takes]*). Another
example of a perfectly regular iambic pentameter is:

His scéptre shóws the fórce of témporal pówer   (x / x / x / x / x /)

But of course, there are allowable variations on this strict prosodic parallelism, as when the weak syllable -*y* at the end of *quality* fills a 'stress' position
in the first line:

The quálity of mércy is not stráin'd   (a) (x / x x x / x x x /)

In the same line, as shown in (a), there is another instance of filling a 'stress'
position with a weak syllable: *is*. However, the second half of this line could
arguably illustrate a different kind of variation, where the order of stressed
and unstressed syllables is reversed. On this reading the line would be rendered with stress on *not*:

The quálity of mércy is nót stráin'd   (b) (x / x x x / x x / /)

To justify this analysis, we look again at the context: Shylock's *must* in the
preceding line is being denied. Portia takes up the meanings of 'mercy' and

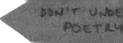

'strain'd' from the two previous lines: this beginning of Portia's reply there-fore contains given information, which will be intonationally placed in the background. But the really important, contrastive piece of new information in this line is the negative particle *not*: the argument of Shylock's appeal to law is being rejected. Hence *not* would most likely be rendered as a strong syllable in this line, although it goes against the flow of the metre.

On the whole, the blank verse of this speech is fairly regular, with few disruptions of the alternating 'strong-weak' pattern of the iambic pentam-eter, and a predominance of end-stopped lines. But superimposed on this superficial regularity, there is the level of the intonation contour which, if we render it in a way to give value to contrasts implicit in the text, is highly expressive. Certain words seem to require more forceful stress-ing, because of their contrastive character. In the following, the prosodic accent (plausibly a falling tone) is placed over the nuclear (most promi-nent) syllables:

> His sceptre shows the force of temporal power,
>
> Wherein doth sit the dread and fear of kings;
>
> But mercy is above this sceptred sway,
>
> It is enthronèd in the hearts of kings, ...
>
> The deeds of mercy.

Portia is celebrating mercy, because mercy is the key to her argument. She is arguing that the outward trappings of monarchy – the sceptre, the crown – are merely symbols of the power kings enjoy and the fear they instil. But the greater attribute of a king – his 'throne', as it were – is the quality of mercy which makes a monarch most like God. It follows that the virtue of justice that characterizes any good monarch is outdone by the higher virtue of mercy. Presupposing the Christian doctrine of original sin, Portia concludes that if we rely on justice, then we will not be saved; but if we rely on God's mercy, then all can be well. The Lord's Prayer enjoins 'forgive us our trespasses as we forgive them that trespass against us': so, if we show mercy, it follows that mercy will be shown to us.[1]

All this argument is played out through antithesis. The repetitive pattern of the iambic pentameter interacts with the superimposed emphases of con-trastive accent. The same interplay of argument and antithesis comes with lexical repetitions. The key noun *mercy* is repeated five times in varying con-texts – and in every case it occurs on its own, as a noun phrase without quali-fication or modification, as if *mercy* is indivisible and inscrutable. Yet *mercy* becomes rich in meaning because of the contrasts into which it enters. This semi-paraphrase is intended to highlight these contrasts:

> mercy comes from *heaven* – it falls on the *earth*
> mercy blesses both the *giver* and the *taker*
> mercy befits a monarch on his *throne* better than his *crown*
> the king's *sceptre* shows *temporal power* and inspires *fear*
> but mercy is *above* the sceptre – its seat is the king's *heart* –
> *earthly* power is most like God's *divine* power when *mercy* mitigates *justice*
> *justice* will not bring salvation; but *mercy* can
> if we pray to *receive* mercy, that prayer teaches us to *act* mercifully to others ...

4. Conclusion

The *Merchant of Venice* is a play beset by controversy – both in the racial theme of the play and in the ways in which it has been interpreted. It is too simple to regard it as a racist enactment of the contrast between Jewish justice-according-to-the-law and Christian mercy, the Old Testament morality and the New Testament morality, although there is no doubt that generations of playgoers sought and found in it an anti-semitic message of this kind. In this chapter, I have simply tried to contrast the two kinds of rhetoric. Shylock's rhetoric predominantly consists of cumulative build-up, repeated variations on the same theme ('causes of grievance'; 'sameness of Jews and gentiles'). Portia's rhetoric predominantly consists of antithesis. Shylock gives us the rhetoric of *samenesses*; Portia gives us the rhetoric of *differences*.

Returning to the three genres of 'poems, plays, and prose', all three are shown to interact in these passages. Much of the meaning of these speeches comes from the dialogue of which they are part, and more broadly from the thematic development of conflict in *The Merchant* as a play. As far as poetry and prose are concerned, Shylock's speech is written as prose, and Portia's as verse, but this difference does not justify separating them into two quite different genres. It is true that Portia, as a member of the aristocracy, is expected to speak in verse in Shakespearean drama, whereas Shylock, of a more lowly if not outcast status, can be expected to 'speak in prose'. But this cannot be the whole story, because there are exceptions, like Shylock's contributions to the judgement scene (as in his line of blank verse preceding Portia's *quality of mercy* speech) which are in verse. One could argue, rather, that Shylock's 'talking in prose' enables his rhetoric to develop a particular emotive power through variations on the repetitious nature of parallelism. And on the other hand, Portia's blank verse form enables her rhetoric to develop in a more controlled and balanced way, more fitting for a judge, and more conducive to the semantic patterns of balance and contrast found in her speech. Emphasizing the thinness of the line between verse and prose, it is worthwhile recalling that biblical Hebrew versification, found above all in the psalms of the Old Testament, rested on the principle of lexico-grammatical parallelism (see Fabb and Halle 2008: 2), as illustrated in these verses from well-known psalms, quoted from the King James Bible:

> The Lord of hosts is with us; the God of Jacob is our refuge.
>   (Psalm 46, verse 7)
> Thy word is *a lamp unto my feet*, and *a light unto my path*.
>   (Psalm 119, verse 105)

Shylock's own Hebrew verse tradition was thus close to the Shakespearean version of his rhetoric. In conclusion, we can agree with Mick Short's statement (1996: 354):

> Although the three genres can be distinguished in general terms from one another ..., there are many texts that have mixed genre characteristics.

The Merchant of Venice is one of those.

NOTE

1. Portia appears here to be on the side of the angels. It has been pointed out, however, that she shows herself signally merciless in the retribution she exacts from Shylock after his plea has failed!

CHAPTER 2

Recent Trends in
New Historical Stylistics

BEATRIX BUSSE

1. Introduction

The last decade has seen a further branching of stylistics into, for example, cognitive stylistics, multimodal stylistics, and corpus stylistics. Comparable to the reaction of stylistics to new trends and findings in linguistics, '*modern historical linguistics*' (Mair 2006; my emphasis) is also a folding fan of different approaches to analysing historical texts. In contrast to traditional historical linguistic approaches where a focus is often on classic linguistic areas, such as historical phonology or morpho-syntactic structures, modern historical linguistics aims at, for example, telling new sociopragmatic or cognitive stories about specific aspects of the history of English and its varieties. *Diachronic* or *historical stylistic* approaches have always focused on the meticulous qualitative investigation of historical texts and on changing or stable styles in literary language. These studies have illustrated, implicitly though, that even on a historical dimension the language-literature divide is a myth.

The dominating influence of the new technologies affects stylistics, modern historical linguistics, and diachronic stylistics. Such technology offers us a wealth of more easily accessible data and new ways of engaging with texts and literature, and it has influenced the ways we investigate texts linguistically. Never have there been such 'facilitated possibilities of searching, browsing, referencing and linking' (Toolan forthcoming). Through computerized text analysis, for example, we are now able to sort and systematically investigate much larger amounts of (historical) texts and corpora and to analyse such phenomena as repetition, foregrounding, and deviation on a much larger scale. The creation of historical corpora immediately followed the compilation of present-day English corpora. Inevitably, literary texts constitute an important part of multi-genre corpora such as Kytö and Culpeper's (2006)

A Corpus of English Dialogues, often because fictional dialogue is the only representation of speech that is available for particular historical periods. With the advent of large corpora, academic interest in the linguistics of older stages of English has increased and entered new dimensions, although it is obvious that number-crunching for its own sake does not comprise a complex historical stylistic framework. Despite growing interest in corpus-based historical linguistics, however, the potential of historical corpora for an *explicit historical stylistic* investigation has only rather tentatively been exploited.

This chapter consolidates new approaches to the stylistic investigation of historical texts with more traditional approaches. It bridges major stylistic, historical linguistic, historical stylistic as well as literary critical approaches, and it describes the methodological, theoretical, and practical challenges involved. The term *New Historical Stylistics* is used as a label here for my focus on outlining what a new diachronic turn in stylistics entails and what its major tenets are. I stress the strength of New Historical Stylistics to explore styles (in the broadest sense of the term) within larger quantitative and qualitative frameworks. At the same time, I explicitly point to the *stylistic* aspects of New Historical Stylistics. I also show that New Historical Stylistics focuses on *how* a historical text contributes to issues at stake in modern historical linguistics. These issues include questions about the validity of data and about aspects of English which are in need of a more functionally oriented interpretation. As such, I promote the linguistic study of historical periods and the history of the English language itself, to help raise the status of a subject area in which students and lay people often seem to have a natural interest. The past influences the present. The past (that is, its history, culture, or the way language was used) also helps us to understand that present-day language/English and its history is not just something of the past, but is ever-present. Within this framework, students' methodological awareness should also be raised. My own teaching experience has revealed that students are very interested in exploring the diverse features of the development of English, but often do not know how to go about it, or are not aware of the various challenges involved.

My view of historical stylistics is outlined with the help of a list of essential parameters. It will then be put into practice via recourse to the analysis of the interplay between thought presentation and narration in nineteenth-century narrative fiction.

2. Who is 'New Historical Stylistics'?

In *Exploring the Language of Poems, Plays and Prose*, Mick Short (1996: 1) begins his first chapter by asking 'Who is stylistics?' Accordingly, I now want to ask 'Who is New Historical Stylistics?' and can similarly reply following

Short's words: 'She is also a friend of mine!' A less personal and more scientific definition of New Historical Stylistics embraces it as the application
of the complex approaches, tools, methods, and theories from stylistics to
historical (literary) texts. One aim is to investigate diachronically changing
or stable and/or foregrounded styles in historical (literary) texts, in a particular situation, in a particular genre, writer, and so on (Leech and Short
[1981]/2007: 11, 200). New Historical Stylistics also includes the synchronic
investigation of particular historical (literary) texts from a stylistic perspective. This New Historical Stylistic perspective may include all areas into
which stylistics has branched out. It is combined with an informed quantitative methodology, and uses the analytical potential recently offered to
us by historical corpus linguistics. At the same time, the interplay with an
informed, systematic, and detailed microlinguistically oriented and qualitative analysis is necessary, which comprises an informed literary critical
analysis in a historical dimension. It embraces an interdisciplinary approach
in order to capture the various contexts that play a role for a historical linguistic analysis. A major focus of a New Historical Stylistic approach is
to explain the questions 'How and why does a text work as it does?' and
'What effects does it have on the reader?' For example, it is possible to
investigate the changing style of discourse presentation in the history of
English (Adamson 1994, 2001; Busse forthcoming) or to investigate the use
of expressive speech acts, such as compliments, across the course of Early
Modern English.

New Historical Stylistics embraces the fundamental characteristics of
stylistics. One is the focus on the text, and on answering the question of why
and how a text means what it does. Taavitsainen and Fitzmaurice (2007:
11) stress how historical linguists need to validate their interpretations and
analyses. As modern historical linguists, we can only reconstruct the past,
because we are not witnesses to the past usages of the English language. The
focus of stylistics on an informed, systematic, retrievable, and contextual
analysis, which aims at describing and explaining how readers derive meaning from the words on the page, meets the need for securing the validation
of data. Aspects of understanding are equally determined by the structure
of the text. Likewise, a New Historical Stylistic approach does not 'think
that literary texts have one and only one meaning, but we do think that the
number of significantly different interpretations texts have is usually pretty
small, whatever some critics might say' (Short, quoted in Plummer and
Busse 2007: 17).

New Historical Stylistics should be seen as an 'interdiscipline' (Leech
2008: 1f.) between linguistic description and (literary) interpretation, which
is formal and functional and provides theoretical investigations with practical
applications, because it is only through a hands-on and close textual analysis

that valid interpretations can be made. As Leech points out

> the proof of the pudding must be in the eating... [and by] choosing to take a
> text as a subject for stylistic analysis, we open ourselves to every possibility of
> establishing the nexus between form and interpretation in the text, and in this
> sense, of seeking its full communicative potential as a literary text.
>
> (Leech 2008: 4)

A New Historical Stylistic analysis of texts from older stages of the English language presupposes a comprehensive knowledge of the period, the context, and the language in which the text was produced. There is a variety of contextual information which guides our reading: generic knowledge, encyclopaedic background knowledge, and knowledge of schemas and scripts and belief systems, which may all lead to what Toolan (2009: 7) calls a 'colouring by the reader'. But our modern assumptions about a historical text can also easily lead us astray. Language change is inevitable. It is visible in such grammaticalized forms as *actually*, which used to be an adverb of time before it changed into a pragmatic epistemic stance marker indicating actuality and reality (Biber et al. 1999: 870). As a further example, present-day English politeness strategies do not show the same realization patterns as those in Early Modern English, and the functions of those realizations may be different. For example, in Early Modern English requests, there was less hedging and less indirectness (Culpeper and Archer 2008). Therefore, a balance is necessary between the analysis of texts and the understanding of processes of and sources for interpretation, as well as language's interrelations (Leech 2008: 179). We do not even have to be whole-hearted integrational linguists to understand the role of context – social, material, cultural, political, or linguistic – to realize that, ultimately, it is context which determines functional import. A historical text is a linguistic object or a 'manifestation of the use of language' (ibid: 186),[1] which has all the various levels of language coded with it. And because of the interplay between all the functions of language, it is multi-levelled and at times may even be ambiguous in its linguistic realizations. In addition, the text as it stands is the guiding force, that is, a corrective to which the attentive reader may add particular significance. However, the choice of representative data to be analysed needs to follow contextual parameters and be in line with the research goals outlined. The question of what constitutes representative data is not trivial because it also includes knowledge of genre conventions, existent editions, copy texts, and spelling variation, and the role of the editor as a mediator (Taavitsainen and Fitzmaurice 2007: 21f.). Modern categories cannot be immediately transferred. For example, a modern edition of Shakespeare's play *Hamlet* usually refers to a copy text, which forms the basis of the textual material that is presented.

In order to find out what a historical text means, it is obviously impossible to test the reaction of contemporary readers to particular styles and stylistic features. Yet, what we can do is to include contemporary sources (Nevalainen and Raumolin-Brunberg 2004: 8f.) in the interpretation process, despite the time and effort it may take. Although historical descriptions of, or comments on, a particular grammatical or linguistic phenomenon are often normative rather than descriptive, they nevertheless show us what was considered to be of importance and can give us vital c(l)ues to the purposes of usage. Contemporary sources, such as dictionaries, grammars, and rhetorical handbooks serve to enhance modern (linguistic) theories and methods. They may not serve as an interpretative agenda but as interpretative help. The same holds true for present-day English studies of a linguistic phenomenon that is to be investigated historically. These studies serve as good starting points for a New Historical Stylistic analysis. For example, in order to investigate stance adverbials in the history of the English language (Busse 2010), it makes sense to systematically research what has been published on this topic for present-day English.

Despite the criticism levelled at the traditional philological or literary critical approaches, for example New Criticism, and their focus on the aesthetic value of texts in their socio-historical, cultural, and political contexts, these historically situated philological approaches (and their reconsiderations through theories from anthropology, history or political history) are of equal value to New Historical Stylistic analysis (Taavitsainen and Fitzmaurice 2007: 22f.). Depending on which theory is construed to be relevant, the theory shapes and constrains the qualitative reading of the text as a communicative and contextual event. New Historicism and Stephen Greenblatt's (1988: 1) famous discussion of what 'to speak with the dead' actually means suggest that this interplay between a text and its context is indispensable for the interpretation process. That is, in order to understand Shakespearean English in its full complexity, for example, it is important to know about the Elizabethan world picture, the Early Modern preoccupations with language, and so on. It is through this interplay and the 'new philology' (Taavitsainen and Fitzmaurice 2007: 22) that even more recent linguistic/stylistic approaches and methods can be further enhanced.

The value of 'older' or 'classic' literary, stylistic, and historical linguistic studies should also be stressed. The interaction between classic studies and more recent approaches in New Historical Stylistics and new historical linguistics help us to see that discourse analysis and interpretation are cultural practices of traditions and histories (ibid: 22). A re-invigoration of the importance of reading the data to be investigated as well as a sound knowledge of the corpora under investigation, and the context in which these were produced, cannot be amiss.

In the process of interpretation of historical (literary) data, the creative interaction between quantitative and qualitative investigations are crucial to the New Historical Stylistic approach. This interplay must avoid circularity and 'number-crunching' for its own sake. However, it cannot rely only on individual and purely subjective readings alone. Cooperation between intuition and corpus linguistic methods (Semino and Short 2004: 8; McIntyre 2007b) is paramount for a New Historical Stylistic approach. Corpus-based investigations aim at identifying forms and repetitive patterns, but we need to situate them within their contexts, otherwise we only establish their frequency (Taavitsainen and Fitzmaurice 2007: 18). It takes a human analyst to make sense of and interpret the discourses at stake (Toolan 2009: 16). Otherwise it is impossible to make our interpretations of historical data valid. Large amounts of data and the linguistic investigation of corpora help us to detect patterns of usage, as well as deviations from those norms in a number of texts. These observations might otherwise go unnoticed (Kohnen 2006: 73). The investigation of large amounts of data also provides us with a framework and a norm against which the results of a New Historical Stylistic investigation can be qualitatively measured, to establish the discourses of a particular genre or stylistic realization of a particular linguistic feature or text, or to establish what constitutes creative language use generally. Leech and Smith (2006) explain, for example, that an investigation of a 30-year period in the twentieth century has revealed a number of crucial linguistic changes.

Establishing norms and irregularities relates to another highly crucial concept within stylistics that is also indispensable for New Historical Stylistics, namely the theory of foregrounding. The interplay between the analysis of a linguistic phenomenon in a historical text and the various contexts in which it occurs is highly complex. It allows the analyst to establish what changes and what remains constant, or, in other words, it allows the establishment of the relationship between the conventional and the innovative (Taavitsainen and Fitzmaurice 2007: 27f.). From a historical perspective, the concept or theory of foregrounding (cf. Leech 2008) lies at the intersection between form and function, because the linguistic code is formally departing, by means of parallelism to or deviation from, what is expected linguistically or socially, that is, from a linguistic and social norm established within the historical context. Functionally speaking, foregrounding conveys a particular effect.[2] Linguistically speaking, foregrounding can be achieved by means of (an overuse of) parallelism and deviation, which has to be determined.

In order to measure and describe (Mahlberg 2007a) the levels of foregrounding (including deviation and parallelism) in a historical dimension, it is impossible to argue on a one-to-one basis that what occurs in a large historical reference corpus constitutes the ordinary or the norm. A more delicate and contextually based analysis is necessary, which deals with context and envisages the notion of 'emergent grammar' or emergent styles (Taavitsainen and Fitzmaurice 2007). Styles in historical texts are not always stable in terms of form-to-function or function-to-form, but may be constantly modulated within a historical framework. What constitutes a writer's motivated choice may, in the course of time, be a norm, and become highly frequent. Hence, it is valid to be more microlinguistically/stylistically oriented and to investigate the styles of a genre, a person or a situation, and then evaluate these results against a reference corpus, which is historically based. In addition, Leech's (1985b) concepts of primary, secondary, and tertiary deviation need to be seen as interdependent in exploring the effects of linguistic processes in historical contexts. Language norms, discourse-specific norms, and text-internal norms all play a role in evaluating stylistic change and stability within a historical dimension. We also need to bear in mind that a bottom-up corpus linguistic approach is very much determined by and focuses on lexis. Hence, complex discoursal frameworks cannot immediately be identified with the help of generally available programs for text analysis.

For historical pragmatics and historical sociolinguistics much has been laudably said and done to illustrate the usefulness of functionally situated approaches for broadening our scope and knowledge of the usage of English in former times. Written data has been accepted to be a valuable and necessary source, and the time-span for the investigation of 'spoken' language has also been broadened. An investigation of the relationship between language form and meaning within a New Historical Stylistics framework uses and enhances methods and terminology from historical pragmatics and historical sociolinguistics in order to discover both change and stability. Both a pragmaphilological and a diachronic approach (Jacobs and Jucker 1995), including a form-to-function and a function-to-form mapping, are seen in New Historical Stylistics as interdependent, and too complex to be set apart from one another. For example, the search for specific historical expressions of attitude or stance needs to define what these functions entail linguistically. At the same time, it is necessary to investigate which forms could have been used, for example, as Early Modern expressions of stance (Busse forthcoming). New Historical Stylistics therefore also includes Brinton's (2001) notions of 'discourse-oriented historical linguistics' and 'historical discourse analysis proper'. These mappings guarantee the systematic rigour of a New Historical Stylistic approach, because it is usually from a specific modern linguistic form or function that the analyst starts his/her explorations. Yet there may be cases when the analyst needs to know about a particular function to discover linguistic realizations, and, in contrast, particular forms may have ambiguous functions in certain contexts. A sociopragmatic framework (Leech 1983) deals with local conditions of language usage, and how speakers exploit the linguistic means and norms at their disposal to make meaning (see also Culpeper 2009a). Local language usage may be described as the immediate speech situation, the immediate text and co-text of interlocutors. Yet the social situation, such as particular norms of speech events, also have to be included and to serve as the major focus of historical sociopragmatics, while it is obvious that the context of culture cannot be underestimated either. Often the description of the relationship between language and context and the theorization of this interplay overlap.

Therefore, the methodology of a New Historical Stylistic approach also has to be cyclic (Leech 2008). We have to work both deductively and inductively: from textual analysis to the formulation of hypotheses, and from the formulation of hypotheses to the linguistic/textual evidence or analysis. In this respect, the approach must also be interdisciplinary (Nevalainen and Raumolin-Brunberg 2004), drawing on historical studies, sociological investigations, and so on. The question also arises to what extent New Historical Stylistics is different from historical pragmatics and historical sociolinguistics, and from other modern historical linguistic approaches. The major potential of New Historical Stylistics results from the focus on a) the notion of (changing and stable) style(s), b) how a text means (rather than what), and c) the reader, and how he or she construes meaning in context. All of this is included in the application of classic, as well as more recent, stylistic approaches to historical texts.

As we have seen, whether there are ways of proving linguistically, textually, stylistically, and statistically what is interesting about those features that are bound to be deviant relies on a balance: between form and function, quantitative and qualitative analysis, and interpretation. A major focus needs to be on the development of statistical procedures to understand and manage non-randomness and statistical representativeness in historical corpus data. Yet from a New Historical Stylistic point of view, low-frequency items have to be seen in relation to those of high frequency, because their interplay is crucial to establish foregrounding. My approach to New Historical Stylistics considers each choice to be meaningful, and low-frequency items to be meaning-making and hence stylistic (when evaluated against the background of, for example, repeated patterns). It is probably here that the New Historical Stylistic approach differs most from (historical) corpus linguistics.

In order to be able to apply some key notions from corpus linguistics, such as prospection (Sinclair 2004: 82–101) or Hoey's (2005) concept of lexical priming, we need to establish historical norms first. For example, lexical priming is dependent upon and sensitive to entrenched repetition of collocational chunks, and in historical texts these must also be both influenced by, and influence, the perception of the mode of discourse, a genre and/or a situation, if we follow Romaine's (1982) 'uniformitarian principle'. Collocation and colligation equally have to be seen within a historical linguistic framework. For example, unlike today, in the Early Modern English noun phrase the adjective did not always follow the determiner but could also precede it, as in 'Dear my lord'. This might also have lead to specific collocations.

For twentieth-century short stories, Toolan (2009) impressively discusses, among other issues, the effect of collocation studies on stylistics and on 'reader progression' and how readers perceive texts. Louw's (2000: 57) concept of 'semantic prosody' sees collocations as 'the expression of the attitude of its speaker or writer towards some pragmatic situation'. He argues that the systematic and bottom-up investigation of collocations helps disclose the phrasings in literary texts, and, at the same time, represents a panacea that rescues stylistics from its base in intuition. There can be no doubt that textual and lexical patterns guide our understanding of literary texts. But what Toolan (2009: 21) points out about how readers are guided in literary texts is even more essential to the stylistic investigations of historical texts: 'This [the identification of collocational patterns] may be a longer-term ambition, but in the meantime a more realistic but still difficult goal is the uncovering of some textual patternings that give rise to critical readings' (ibid). Although, as mentioned, it is much easier and incredibly rewarding today to search for textual patterns with the available programs and tools, for historical investigations in particular there is a danger of considering this technical possibility to be too much in opposition with intuitive readings, and of allowing our programs to guide our research questions just because it is so easy to do. As Mahlberg (2007a: 371) points out, 'A corpus linguistic, bottom-up description of language prioritizes lexis'. Yet other patterns might be missed if we follow only that (Toolan 2009: 22). In addition, although a computer program identifies the significantly deviant features of a text, and how deviant they are from a statistical point of view, it does not tell us which features are foregrounded, because the (historical) stylistician needs to follow up a stylistic analysis in terms of foregrounding (Leech 2008), and relate the different results to one another.

To conclude, and to borrow a pun from Hall (this volume), a 'Short' checklist (see Stockwell, this volume, for more on Mick Short's famous checksheets) of how to go about a New Historical Stylistic analysis would include the following items:

a) Use the main characteristics of stylistic analysis: be systematic and rigorous in your analysis and focus on the questions of how and why a historical text means what it does.
b) As a starting point use present-day linguistic knowledge of the linguistic phenomenon/function you would like to investigate, but then carefully and systematically verify or falsify that knowledge for the historical period and the historical discourse under investigation.

c) Compile state-of-the-art research on that particular topic.
d) Collect information about the contexts of production (social, cultural, linguistic, pragmatic) and work across disciplines.
e) Ensure that the choice of data is informed by knowledge of genre conventions, editorial history, and compilation processes.
f) Use contemporary sources for an informed contextual approach.
g) Combine function-to-form and form-to-function (Jacobs and Jucker 1995) mapping.
h) Combine quantitative and qualitative analyses to establish historical linguistic norms and deviations. There should be an informed cooperation between, for example, corpus stylistics, and more qualitatively oriented stylistic investigation or intuition. High-frequency items and low-frequency items should be carefully discriminated and evaluated within the contexts in which they appear.
i) Determine whether you are following a diachronic or a synchronic New Historical Stylistic investigation of a linguistic phenomenon based on your research question. If a diachronic investigation is included, clearly chart the time course.
j) Be aware that the available contemporary linguistic and non-linguistic sources are not the same for all periods and that they have a sociopragmatic validity that may change within the discourses of time.
k) Raise the level of awareness for methodological problems.

3. Thought presentation and narration in nineteenth-century narrative fiction

Among the parameters of New Historical Stylistics is the necessary interplay between quantitative and qualitative investigation, and the contextualization of respective results within contemporary statements. This section illustrates this complex interplay by analysing thought presentation and stretches of paralinguistic narration in nineteenth-century narrative fiction. The analysis is based on my investigation of speech, writing, and thought presentation in a selected corpus of nineteenth-century narrative fiction (Busse forthcoming), which has been manually annotated for occurrence of the different modes of discourse presentation. The scheme used for the annotation is based on Leech and Short ([1981] 2007) and Semino and Short (2004). The roughly 2000-word stretches from the 23 novels have been chosen according to the-matic, generic, and diachronic parameters. The corpus includes such novels as Jane Austen's (1816) *Emma*, Charles Dickens's (1860) *Great Expectations*, and Elizabeth Gaskell's (1854) *North and South*. I use nineteenth-century statements about vision and the psyche to further exploit the interplay between thought presentation and narration in nineteenth-century novels. My reading of this interplay as foregrounded is a result of the analysis of the systematic annotation of the corpus, and the quantitative as well as qualitative analysis of thought presentation categories and the narrative stretches accompanying it.

A comparison of percentages of thought presentation in my corpus of nineteenth-century narrative fiction with Semino and Short's (2004) results for twentieth-century narrative fiction shows that thought presentation tags were identified only 3 per cent less frequently in the nineteenth-century corpus than in the twentieth-century corpus (Table 2.1). This result may seem surprising considering the fact that it is often claimed that thought presentation in narrative fiction was only in the process of being developed in the nineteenth century.

The use of the term *tag* may be misleading in view of what Genette (1972) calls 'tagged' and 'untagged speech'. Here, a *tag* annotates a stretch of a reporting clause, such as 'he thought', or any category of speech, writing, and thought presentation identified by Semino and Short (2004). For example, in ' "I have buried one friend to-day," he thought: "what if this should cost me another?" ' (Stevenson [1886] 1993: 129) from *Strange Case of Dr. Jekyll and Mr. Hyde*, the stretch 'I have buried one friend to-day' is labelled as a direct thought (DT) tag, while 'he thought' receives the annotation Narrator's Report of Thought (NRT). The percentages of tags attributed to the different stretches in my corpus are hence given in relation to all the annotations made.

The results achieved for thought presentation in general point to the foregrounded status of thought presentation categories in the nineteenth-century corpus of narrative fiction, especially if the number of identified tags is also correlated to the number of words by which thought presentation categories are realized in the corpus.

Table 2.1: Discourse presentation tags in the nineteenth- and twentieth-century narrative fiction corpora

Discourse presentation mode	Nineteenth-century corpus (%)	Twentieth-century corpus (Semino and Short 2004) (%)
Speech	37.0	50.06
Thought	21.4	24.4
Writing	2.4	1.65
Narration	35.2	20.99
Other	4.0	2.9
Sum	100	100

Table 2.2 shows that the percentage of number of words representing the thought presentation categories in the nineteenth-century corpus is slightly higher than that identified for twentieth-century narrative fiction. As Table 2.3 illustrates, the tags for the categories of Narrator's Report of Thought Act (NRTA), Indirect Thought (IT) and Free Indirect Thought (FIT) are the most frequently occurring categories of thought presentation. Hence, there is a levelled distribution between those thought presentation categories that are more character-oriented (FIT) and those that focus more on the narrator (such as NRTA) (Short 2007). Table 2.4 illustrates one reason why Free Indirect Thought has so far been perceived to occur particularly prominently in nineteenth-century narrative fiction. Interestingly, the number of words by which these tags are represented is highest in FIT, although it is not the most frequently occurring category of thought presentation.

In the following, I draw the reader's attention to the narrative stretches that make reference to aspects of vision and that surround the different modes of thought presentation. These reveal that in nineteenth-century narrative fiction,

Table 2.2: Percentages of words under the speech, writing, and thought tags in the nineteenth-century corpus and the Semino and Short (2004) corpus of twentieth-century narrative fiction

Mode	Percentages of words in nineteenth-century corpus (%)	Percentages of words in twentieth-century corpus (%)
Speech	33.8	31.59
Thought	19.8	19.20
Writing	2.2	0.63
Narration	40.1	45.04

Table 2.3: Percentages of thought presentation tags in the nineteenth-century corpus (in symbol)

Thought presentation category	NI	NT	NRTA	IT	FIT	DT	FDT	Sum all
Percentages of tags	3.9	0.7	7.3	5.3	3.7	0.4	0.1	21.4

Table 2.4: Percentages of words under the speech, writing, and thought tags in the nineteenth-century corpus (in symbol)

Thought presentation category	NI	NT	NRTA	IT	FIT	DT	FDT	Sum all
Percentages of words representing the thought presentation tags	2.4	0.6	6.0	3.8	6.7	0.3	0.0	19.8

paralinguistic information is often given by the narrator to create as well as to pre-empt what is going to come, or to encapsulate what has been described (Sinclair [1993] 2004). It also foregrounds a state of mind, or the thought presentation categories that follow or that precede the narrative stretch (see also Mahlberg and Smith, this volume). According to Brown (1996: 112), paralinguistic features 'contribute to the expression of attitude by a speaker', and the meaning contributed by the paralinguistic features is the affective meaning of the utterance, where the feeling and the attitudes of the speaker are to some extent revealed. To my knowledge, Brown (1996) and Person (1999) are two of the few scholars to transfer their observation of paralinguistic features to the analysis of literature. Brown includes such features as pitch span, placing in voice range, tempo, voice setting, lip setting, and pausing.

The annotation of the stretches of discourse presentation, on the one hand, and narration, on the other, has revealed a) an interplay between thought presentation and narrative reference to the thinker's eyes, b) thought presentation and its co-occurrence with a metaphorical expression in which thought is seen as movement and activity, and c) paralinguistic narrative passages which construe or stand for a character's thinking process (and reference is often made to the movement of eyes). These strategies have interpersonal, textual, and experiential function in the Hallidayean (1994, 2004) sense, and address the reader's cognitive abilities of world-building (Oatley 2009). These are activated by linguistically evoking a multimodal and sensual world in which reference is made to the movements or status of the thinker's eyes. This reference functions to announce or summarize a character's introspection, to describe a state of mind which is not overtly expressed or discussed, or to interrupt in order to express the visual role of the blinking of 'eyes' as discourse markers to initiate a turn.

A description of the movement of a character's eyes, or a gazing look, is used to describe a character's state of mind. In the novel *Strange Case of Dr. Jekyll and Mr. Hyde* (Stevenson [1886] 1993), Utterson uses 'the look in the eye' to determine Dr Lanyon's well-being and current state of mind.

> The rosy man had grown pale; his flesh had fallen away; he was visibly balder and older; and yet it was not so much these tokens of a swift physical decay that arrested the lawyer's notice, as a look in the eye and quality of manner that seemed to testify to some deep-seated terror of the mind.
>
> (Stevenson [1886] 1993: 128)

It is a well-worn trope that the expressions of eyes provide a window to the soul. In this example, the connection is directly expressed because Utterson's look and Dr Lanyon's expression 'seem to testify to some deep-seated terror of mind'.

The difference between saying and thinking, on the one hand, and the function of eyes to indicate one's real feelings/thoughts, on the other, is romantically transferred in the following example:

> 'Then I am old Blaize's niece.' She tripped him a soft curtsey. The magnetized youth gazed at her. By what magic was it that this divine sweet creature could be allied with that old churl! 'Then what – what is your name?' said his mouth, while his eyes added, 'O wonderful creature! How came you to enrich the earth?' 'Have you forgot the Desboroughs of Dorset, too?' she peered at him from a side-bend of the flapping brim. 'The Desboroughs of Dorset?' A light broke in on him. 'And have you grown to this? That little girl I saw there!'
>
> (Meredith [1859] 1968: 123)

The reporting clause 'while his eyes added' introduces a stretch of direct thought, beginning with 'O wonderful creature'. It stands in contrast to the narrator's report of speech in 'said his mouth' and the stretch of direct speech in 'Then what – what is your name?' Through a lexical antithesis between 'his mouth said' and 'his eyes added', the narrator obviously underlines the discrepancy between Richard's words and what he is really thinking (and is not allowed to say). In terms of Text World Theory (Werth 1999: 221; Gavins 2007a: 50), this move from the actual words uttered between them to his thoughts represents a move into a deictic sub-world or a world switch in which Richard's thinking is temporarily the deictic centre. Eyes can only speak paralinguistically, but they represent a conventional reference to the mind. As such, the mentioning of his eyes is a key marker which foreshadows a narratological switch to the presentation of his direct thoughts. Reference to the conventional notion of eyes telling the truth adds to the notion of faithfulness to the presentation of the character's thoughts.

In Dickens's *Oliver Twist*, a similar contrast between changing states of minds is expressed by means of the narrator's reference to the movement of Mr Bumble's eyes:

> When Mr. Bumble had laughed a little while, his eyes again encountered the cocked hat; and he became grave. 'We are forgetting business, ma'am,' said the beadle; 'here is your porochial stipend for the month'.
>
> (Dickens [1839] 1993: 120)

Mr Bumble's eye movement causes him to spot his hat, which, in turn, reminds him of the business he has to undertake. This foreshadows the change of mood that takes place in him, and he switches from laughing to becoming 'grave'.

In Jane Austen's *Emma*, Emma is cunningly described as satisfied with Frank Churchill's assertion that he is still willing to arrange the ball. Her gratefulness is not presented through discourse, but – entertainingly – through narration. This strategy portrays Emma giving feedback on Frank Churchill's turn, before he is given a voice again in direct speech.

> 'If I can come again, we are still to have our ball. My father depends on it. Do not forget your engagement.' *Emma looked graciously.* 'Such a fortnight as it has been!' he continued; 'every day more precious and more delightful than the day before! – every day making me less fit to bear any other place. Happy those, who can remain at Highbury!'
>
> (Austen [1816] 1985: 264; my emphasis)

The short, three-word narratological insertions of contextual and paralinguistic information in 'Emma looked graciously' focuses on the expression on Emma's face, and especially her eyes. The omission of the presentation of a proper turn uttered by Emma foregrounds Emma's state of mind and her emotional reliance on what Frank says. Also, the reader experiences a rather swift move to Emma's thoughts before Frank's text world is presented again in direct speech. The fact that her turn-taking is not verbal but paralinguistic shows that these types of narrative stretches surrounding speech and thought presentation function as markers of turn-taking. They represent an attempt to faithfully and in detail describe the verbal and non-verbal characteristics of conversation. The reference to her facial expression is attitudinal because the foregrounding of her facial expression as 'Emma looked graciously' foregrounds her attempt at being cordial. It also gives the reader an understanding of the narrator's ironic comment on the stereotypical atmosphere between two people who are almost in love.

In Oscar Wilde's *The Picture of Dorian Gray*, Dorian is described as utterly embarrassed when he mistakes Lady Harry's entrance in the salon for that of Lord Harry. Here the focus of the interrupting narratological section is on Dorian. The description of his eyes 'glancing quickly round' and of his bodily movement project as well as encapsulate Dorian's insecurity.

> 'I'm afraid it is not Harry, Mr. Gray,' answered a shrill voice. *He glanced quickly round and rose to his feet.* 'I beg your pardon. I thought –' 'You thought it was my husband. It is only his wife. You must let me introduce myself. I know you quite well by your photographs. I think my husband has got seventeen of them.'
>
> (Wilde [1890] 1994: 55f; my emphasis)

Following Mrs Fairfax's verbal announcement in Charlotte Brontë's *Jane Eyre* that Jane has entered the room to finally be introduced in person to

Mr. Rochester, Mr Rochester flouts Grice's (1975) maxim of quality (do not say what you believe to be false) and is impolite by not replying to Mrs Fairfax's statement or welcoming Jane. Instead he takes a paralinguistic turn – bowing – which signifies his acknowledgement of Jane's arrival. Yet he does not move his eyes towards them, and therefore does not grant her a polite look at her face.

> 'Here is Miss Eyre, sir,' said Mrs Fairfax, in her quiet way. He bowed, still not taking his eyes from the group of the dog and child.
>
> (C. Brontë [1847] 1985: 152)

The negative polarity in 'still not taking his eyes from the group of the dog and the child' implies the positive, namely, that he should have done so (Nørgaard 2007). His persistent look at the dog and the child questions his apparent lack of interest in Jane's arrival.

Utterson's sadness about Dr Lanyon's death is reinforced by a letter he receives after the funeral. His stretch of direct thought mentioned above – ' "I have buried one friend to-day," he thought: "what if this should cost me another?" ' – is then followed by a descriptive passage of him opening the seal of Lanyon's letter:

> And then he condemned the fear as a disloyalty, and broke the seal. Within there was another enclosure, likewise sealed, and marked upon the cover as 'not to be opened till the death or disappearance of Dr. Henry Jekyll'. *Utterson could not trust his eyes.* Yes, it was disappearance; here again, as in the mad will which he had long ago restored to its author, here again were the idea of a disappearance and the name of Henry Jekyll bracketed. But in the will, that idea had sprung from the sinister suggestion of the man Hyde.
>
> (Stevenson [1886] 1993: 129; my emphasis)

The narrator describes Utterson's astonishment at Lanyon's words – hinting at Dr Jekyll's possible disappearance – through reference to Dr Lanyon's eyes: 'Utterson could not trust his eyes.' This foreshadows a shift and world switch back to Utterson's feelings. It also presents a shift back to his eyes, because it could be seen as a stretch of free indirect thought which refers back to the reading process.

The visual movement of eyes is stereotypically used to announce a character's introspection. This strategy is employed in the following example from *The Picture of Dorian Gray*, where Lord Henry, after his conversation with Dorian about love and marriage, is left alone to think. The narrator's report of thought in 'he began to think' is used to frame the reader's mind towards the presentation of Lord Henry's thought in free indirect thought. But before that, reference is also made paralinguistically to the movement of his eyes in 'his heavy eyelids drooped':

> As he left the room, Lord Henry's heavy eyelids drooped, and he began *to think*. Certainly few people had ever interested him so much as Dorian Gray, and yet the lad's mad adoration of some one else caused him not the slightest pang of annoyance or jealousy. He was pleased by it. It made him a more interesting study.
>
> (Wilde [1890] 1994: 68f.; my emphasis)

The description of what a character does with his or her eyes not only introduces the observer's or observed's thought presentation or embeds it, but also represents a means of depicting detail and prompts a world switch from the narratological description to the observed and what he might be thinking. The visual stands for a thought process that is going on in the observer's mind.

In Gaskell's *Cousin Phillis*, the first-person narrator uses the reporting clause 'I felt' to introduce his indirect thought. Yet embedded in his thoughts is also a description of what Phillis does with 'those deep grey eyes [...] upon me':

> Her daughter Phillis took up her knitting – a long grey worsted man's stocking, I remember – and knitted away without looking at her work. I felt that the steady gaze of those deep grey eyes was upon me, though once, when I stealthily raised mine to hers, she was examining something on the wall above my head.
>
> (Gaskell [1863] 2006: 379)

The narrator's ongoing thinking process is enhanced by the embedded speculation of what Phillis might be thinking. Here the paralinguistic reference to the 'steady gaze' and 'those deep grey eyes' illustrates to the reader that Phillis is both observing and, at the same time, thinking about him. In text world theory terms (Werth 1999: 221), the move from the narrative description of her knitting to his thoughts introduced by the reporting clause 'I felt' is a world switch in which paralinguistic descriptions are mixed with his thought presentation. This is done in an embedded and multi-modal way, with Phillis's thought process alluded to by the way she directs her visual camera.

In the following example from *Jane Eyre*, Jane's answer to Mrs Rochester's question about whether Jane is fond of presents should further elicit a turn from her. This is described by a paralinguistic narratological intervention that refers to what Mr Rochester does with his eyes: 'and he searched my face with eyes that I saw were dark, irate, and piercing':

> 'Who talks of cadeaux?' said he gruffly. 'Did you expect a present, Miss Eyre? Are you fond of presents?' and he searched my face with eyes that I saw were

dark, irate, and piercing. 'I hardly know, sir; I have little experience of them: they are generally thought pleasant things.'

(C. Brontë [1847] 1985: 152)

The pronounced focalization on Mr Rochester's paralinguistic movements portrays him as a vigilant observer and underlines his interest in Jane's psyche. At the same time, the narrator immediately shifts back to Jane's thoughts, because the way she perceives those eyes as 'dark, irate, and piercing' is described. Mr Rochester attempts to see with his eyes what Jane is thinking and, at the same time, to visually ask her to reply to his question. The prepositional phrase 'with eyes that I saw were dark, irate, and piercing' is chosen by the first-person narrator to foreground the colour and force of Mr Rochester's eyes.

If Oatley (2001, 2009) is correct to argue that literature offers its readers a simulation of everyday situation and experience, the qualitative narratological reference to the eyes serves at least as a trigger to announce a state of mind or thought process within the intra-textual frame or the text world. Readers may experience within themselves the emotion that is announced via recourse to the eyes, or they may have experienced the qualitative force of this paralinguistic movement, which leads to the question whether this is a form of what Toolan (2009) has aptly called narrative progression. Yet it is impossible for us to test the reactions of a nineteenth-century reader, even though the uniformitarian principle (Romaine 1982) may allow us to transfer modern cognitive linguistic findings to the informed interpretations of earlier stages of the English language. Reconstructing some of the contextual frameworks that might have lead to this precise and detailed narratological description of the complex interplay between paralinguistic narration and thought presentation in nineteenth-century literature leads us to nineteenth-century psychological, biological and literary statements about vision and the psyche. This endeavour seems especially valid because, in the nineteenth century, the humanities as well as the sciences were not as fragmented as they seem today (Zwierlein 2005).

The nineteenth century saw a preoccupation with research into psychological consciousness and the effect of optical inventions, coupled with literature's reaction to these developments. The rising interest in psychology, illustrated, for example, in pre-Freudian physiological psychology (ibid: 3) and works like Spencer's (1855) *Principles of Psychology* or Lewes's (1874–79) *Problems of Life and Mind*, also finds its expression in explicit and implicit inclusion in literature of issues such as consciousness, agency, cognitive processes, and depictions of the mind. For example, George Eliot ([1871–2] 1986: 784f.) describes the famous 'web of connection' in *Middlemarch* and expresses the social nature of a human being, which also affects the mind: 'There is no creature whose inward being is so strong that it is not greatly determined by what lies outside.' In George Eliot's ([1876] 1998: 235) *Daniel Deronda*, it is stressed that the mysteries of the human psyche – like the mysteries in the sciences (Zwierlein 2005: 5) – are still to be explored: 'There is a great deal of unmapped country within us which would have to be taken into account in the explanation of our guts and storms.' In 'The Critic as Artist', Oscar Wilde also generally muses about the potential of literature for presenting human thought and consciousness but, like Eliot, concedes that so far literature has not yet managed to explore the intricacies of the human psyche:

> He who would stir us now by fiction, must either give us an entirely new background, or reveal to us the soul of man in its innermost workings. [...] People sometimes say that fiction is getting too morbid. As far as psychology is concerned, it has never been morbid enough. We have merely touched the surface of the soul, that is all. In one single ivory cell of the brain there are stored away things more marvelous and more terrible than even they have dreamed of, who, [...] have sought to track the soul into its most secret places, and to make life confess its dearest sins. Still, there is a limit even to the number of untried backgrounds, and it is possible that a further development of the habit of introspection may prove fatal to that creative faculty to which it seeks to supply fresh material. [...] There are always new attitudes for the mind, and new points of view.
>
> (Wilde [1890] 1969: 402)

Despite these statements of acknowledged deficiencies in the portrayal of the human psyche, the presentation of thought discovered in my corpus, the number of words by which it is presented, and its interplay with paralinguistic narration, all give apt linguistic testimony of and allows us to construe a nineteenth-century discourse with concepts of introspection and the psyche. Furthermore, narrative stretches that refer to vision and perception seem to be authorial efforts at presenting the minds of characters. They are therefore also directed at the reader as encouragements to create his or her own spaces, and to apply the textual to the real world.

This idea of vision, introspection, and seeing, which can be related to the well-known metaphor that UNDERSTANDING IS SEEING, also corresponds to nineteenth-century research into the perception of colours and optical inventions, as well as to literary reactions to such progress (Kern-Stähler 2005: 108). For example, Berkley's (1732) 'New Theory of Vision' conceptualized the act of vision and the activity of the mind. These notions of agency, perception, and looking find their complex pragmatic expression in the interplay between narrative and discourse presentation, and provide the fictional narrator with a means of presenting cognitive processes. Hence, as we have seen, the focalized characters' eyes play a crucial role as a marker of stance (Biber et al. 1999: 967), indicating an additional attitudinal comment on the part of the narrator, and projecting introspection to the reader.

Henry James's concept of the 'house of fiction', outlined in his Preface to the 'second edition' of *A Portrait of a Lady*, serves as a theoretical description of the interplay between the mind, language, and emotion. James sees the novel as a literary form 'to range through all the differences of the individual relation to its general subject matter, all the varieties of outlook on life' (James [1905] 1975: 7). He uses the image of a 'house of fiction' to portray the complexity of life described in the following way:

> The house of fiction has in short not one window, but a million – a number of possible windows not to be reckoned, rather; every one of which has been pierced, or is still pierceable, in its vast front, by the need of the individual vision and by the pressure of the individual will. These apertures of dissimilar shape and size, hang so, all together, over the human scene that we might have expected of them a greater sameness of report than we find. They are but windows at the best, mere holes in a dead wall, disconnected, perched aloft; they are not hinged doors opening straight upon life. But they have this mark of their own that at each of them stands a figure with a pair of eyes, or at least with a field glass, which forms, again and again, for observation a unique instrument, insuring to the person making use of it an impression distinct from every other. He and his neighbours are watching the same show, but one seeing more where the other sees less, one seeing black where the other sees white, one seeing big where the other sees small [...]. The spreading field, the human field, is 'the choice of subject'; [...] but they are, singly or together, as nothing without the posted presence of the watcher – without, in other words, the consciousness of the artist.
>
> (James [1905] 1975: 7)

Like Thomas De Quincey's (1845) notion of the human brain functioning as a palimpsest outlined in *Suspiria de Profundis*, James describes how the various facets of the human condition can both be seen in the 'house of fiction' and described by the author or narrator who uses – with his eyes and his consciousness – the various and multi-shaped windows to watch what is happening. James's reference to the watcher's eyes in, for example, 'stands a figure with a pair of eyes, or at least with a field glass [...] insuring to the person making use of it an impression distinct from every other' alludes to the narrator's means of introspection, for which the presentation of discourse in its interplay with narration can be seen as one linguistic means of achieving the variety of shapes of these windows, of the presentation of the multi-layered voices, and of characterization.

Richter (2009) sees narrating in nineteenth-century novels as an evolutionary adaptation, and as a creation of a room of imagination in order to preserve what Darwin destroyed in his theory of natural selection outlined in *The Origin of Species* (1859). Darwin's theory of natural selection has a synchronic and a diachronic dimension, with species slowly evolving over centuries and struggling for existence at a particular point in time. Terminology from cell biology was used to metaphorically describe human communication, social fragmentation, and identity. It is through the use of the mode of speech, writing or thought presentation that, on the one hand, the alleged superiority of the human being, and his/her ability to communicate, can be presented, while, on the other hand, discourse presentation is also a means of meticulously describing social fragmentation and the complexities of human communication, as well as the relation between language and power.

To further underline the activity of thinking as well as the complexity involved in the human psyche, I refer to the fact that in nineteenth-century narrative fiction thought is presented by means of a metaphor where it is conceptualized as movement and the thinker is seen as active. In the following example, Emma's thoughts are presented as direct thought:

> And Mrs. Weston! – Astonished that the person who had brought me up should be a gentlewoman! Worse and worse. I never met with her equal. Much beyond my hopes. Harriet is disgraced by any comparison. Oh! what would Frank Churchill say to her, if he were here? How angry and how diverted he would be! Ah! there I am – thinking of him directly. Always the first person to be thought of! How I catch myself out! *Frank Churchill comes as regularly into my mind!'*
>
> (Austen [1816] 1985: 280f; my emphasis)

Emma's thoughts are then summarized as follows:

> *All this ran so glibly through her thoughts*, that by the time her father had arranged himself, after the bustle of the Eltons' departure, and was ready to speak, she was very tolerably capable of attending.
>
> (Austen [1816] 1985: 280f; my emphasis)

The narrator's summary in 'all this ran so glibly through her thoughts', which could be seen as a presentation of a Narrator's Report of a Thought Act (NRTA), serves as an encapsulation of Emma's thoughts because, through the deictic demonstrative pronoun 'this', it summarizes, and hence anaphorically refers back to, her emotional outburst. At the same time, the narratological intervention ridicules her elaborated fit of rage. Furthermore, through the quantitative clash between the words used to report her direct thoughts and those used in the encapsulating NRTA/NI, her real feelings for Mr Knightley are foregrounded. *Glibly* usually collocates with speech (*OED* 1), but here the transference is made to stress the speed of her active mind illustrated by the verb *run*. The mind is often seen as a physical object, and thinking is presented in terms of a physical movement of an entity.

When Emma almost theatrically reveals to herself that she and Mr Knightley should be married, indirect thought presentation co-occurs with: 'It darted through her, with the speed of an arrow, that Mr Knightley must marry no one but herself' (Austen [1816] 1985: 398). The verb *dart* as well as the appositively positioned prepositional phrase, which functions as an adverbial ('with the speed of an arrow'), stresses the speed with which she realizes that she is in love with Mr Knightley. The reader, however, who is aware of the length of the novel, at this stage immediately realizes how long it really took her to make this discovery. Hence, the irony is reinforced by a foregrounded and overdone emphasis on the speed of her thoughts: she is a quick thinker, but not when it comes to her own feelings. We can refer to Lakoff and Johnson (1980; Semino and Short 2004: 129) who argue, as described above, that the mind is often seen as a physical object, and thinking presented in terms of a physical movement of an entity. Here it is the force and the speed of an arrow, which evokes the image of the Cupid story.[3]

4. Conclusions

This chapter has established major tenets of what I have called New Historical Stylistics, and has situated the stylistic investigation of historical texts within a framework of recent approaches in stylistics, historical linguistics, and literary criticism. I have further outlined two of the main characteristics of New Historical Stylistics in relation to an analysis of nineteenth-century narrative fiction. I have shown the interplay between contextual and corpus-based analysis and corpus-stylistics investigation, and also contextualized my findings with nineteenth-century statements about vision, the psyche, and literary reactions. The historical realisation of discourse presentation has so far only been pursued qualitatively, and often the focus is more literary-critical. But we have seen that these areas are linguistically construed and that it is a field that depends highly on, and is suggestive of, a functional interpretation, and has repercussions on nineteenth-century modes of thinking in general. In addition, the linguistic features identified to announce, for example, thought presentation may not only be seen as markers of narrative progression (Toolan 2009), but also as features that could be searched for in an automatized retrieval of thought presentation.

The analytical usefulness of New Historical Stylistics results from the fact that its methodology and foundations are based on general stylistics. It therefore includes linguistic approaches and theories beyond those used in, for example, pragmatics or sociolinguistics. My label New Historical Stylistics also results from the fact that it is now possible to exploit the advantages of a quantitative and qualitative stylistic investigation within a broader framework. In addition, new directions in stylistics can be used in New Historical Stylistics, which in turn will inevitably influence historical linguistic methodology and theory in general, as well as views on language change and stability.

NOTES

1. See Leech (2008: 187) for other approaches to text and his reasoning why he follows the basic linguistic notion of a text.
2. See also van Peer (1986) and Douthwaite (2000).
3. There is a controversy about when and how metaphors like THINKING IS MOVEMENT are processed, because not all metaphors activate underlying cross-domain mappings in people's mind, but are rather too conventional and therefore processed by (simple) lexical disambiguation. But reference to thinking being conceptualized as movement can be found in the nineteenth-century corpus of narrative fiction. As further examples can serve: 'But so active were her thoughts' (Austen [1817] 1985: 150), 'The multitude of feelings that crowded into my mind' (Shelley [1818] 2003: 76), 'Mary's heart began to beat more quickly', or 'Various ideas rushed through her mind as to what the burning of a second will might imply. She had to make a difficult decision in a hurry' (Eliot [1871] 2006: 234).

CHAPTER 3

Methodologies for Stylistic Analysis: Practices and Pedagogies

RONALD CARTER

1. Introduction

This chapter explores a selected range of methodologies used in stylistic analysis with a particular focus on applications to stylistics in the classroom. Methodology is very important in any form of text analysis, and analysts themselves also have a responsibility to say what they are doing and how they are doing it. This makes the analysis transparent to others and enables readers to retrieve how analysts have reached their interpretive decisions. Necessarily, too, the introduction discusses stylistics itself as a methodology. The chapter begins with some theoretical background to issues of curriculum design and development, and then illustrates the different pedagogic possibilities that different methodologies for stylistic analysis entail.

2. Literature, language, and education: Some background

The past 20 years have seen significant advances in linguistics, education, and literary and cultural theory, a development that has provided a strong basis for exploring texts using a diverse range of methodologies (see Hall 2005 for a comprehensive survey). Literary theory has embraced many topics, including the nature of an author's intentions, the character and measurement of the responses of a reader, and the specific textuality of a literary text. In particular, there has also been a continuing theorization of the selection of literary texts for study which has had considerable resonance for the teaching of literature and for its interfaces with the language classroom. On the one hand, there is a view, widespread still internationally, that the study of literature is the study of a select number of great writers judged according to the enduringly serious nature of their examination of the human condition. On the other hand, there is the view that the notion of literature is relative and that ascriptions of value to texts are a transient process dependent on the given values of a given time.

How tastes change and evaluations shift as part of a process of canon formation are therefore inextricably bound up with definitions of what literature is and what it is for. In this respect, definitions of literature, and of literary language, are either *ontological* – establishing an essential, timeless property of what literature or literary language *is* – or *functional* – establishing the specific and variable circumstances within which texts are designated as literary, and the ends to which these texts are and can be used. Recent work on creativity and language play has reinforced this awareness of both continuities and discontinuities in degrees of literariness across discourse types (Crystal 1998; Cook 1994, 2000; Carter 2004; Pope 2005). One outcome has been the introduction into language curricula, for both first and for second or foreign language learners, of a much greater variety of texts and text-types so that literary texts are studied alongside advertisements, newspaper reports, magazines, popular song lyrics, blogs, internet discourse, and the many multimodal texts to which we have become accustomed.

In parallel with these developments methodologies for analysis of texts have evolved. In a wide-ranging survey of trends over the past century of literature in foreign language education, Kramsch and Kramsch (2000) underline how, in the early part of the twentieth century, learning a foreign language meant a close study of the canonical literature in that language (indeed, in some parts of the world the language course book still consists of canonical literary extracts). In the period from the 1940s to the 1960s literature was seen as extraneous to everyday communicative needs and as something of an elitist pursuit. However, in the 1970s and 1980s the growth of communicative language teaching methods led to a reconsideration of the place of literature in the language classroom, with recognition of the primary authenticity of literary texts and of the fact that more imaginative and representational uses of language could be embedded alongside more referentially utilitarian output. Kramsch and Kramsch (2000: 567) term this the 'proficiency movement' and underline how it saw in literature 'an opportunity to develop vocabulary acquisition, the development of reading strategies, and the training of critical thinking, that is, reasoning skills'. They point out how awareness dawned that literature, since it had continuities with other discourses, could be addressed by the same pedagogic procedures as those adopted for the treatment of all

texts to develop relevant skill sets, especially reading skills, leading in particular to explorations of what it might mean to read a text closely (see Alderson 2000 and Kern 2000 for further valuable surveys).

3. Stylistics as methodology

As a methodology, the pedagogic value of stylistics in the teaching of literary language and of how such language works within a text, in both native-speaker and non-native-speaker contexts, has resided in an explication of how texts are understood and interpreted by readers, mainly in terms of their interaction with the linguistic organization of the text. Stylistics has therefore served to make explicit and retrievable how interpretation is formed, or new aspects of interpretation revealed (see Short 1995: 53).

The adoption of stylistic approaches is not without its problems, however. Many literature specialists feel that stylistics is too mechanistic and too reductive, saying nothing significant about historical context or aesthetic theory, eschewing evaluation for the most part in the interests of a naïve 'objectivity' and claiming too much for interpretations that are at best merely text-immanent (see Fowler 1986 and Verdonk 2002 for further discussion). And some language teachers and language researchers feel that it is only appropriate at the most advanced of levels (Gower 1986) and lacks proper empirical research support for its claims (Edmondson 1997).

A more considered view is that stylistics has contributed in diverse ways to methodology in the teaching of literature and that by turns, developments in pedagogy in both L1 and L2 contexts have become embedded in stylistics. Among the most striking developments have been those that focus on 'textual transformations' using comparative text analysis by means of processes of rewriting from different angles and positions that 'translate' the text from one medium to another along an axis of spoken to written, verbal to visual, or textual to dramatic (see Pope 1994; Widdowson 1992; Carter and Long 1987, 1991; Durant and Fabb 1990). Once again the emerging value of such work is its concern with guiding learners through *processes* of reading and engaging with what such a process reveals for understanding the meanings of texts, not in order to disclose any one single universal meaning but for what it may reveal to the reader in different social and cultural contexts in and out of the classroom.

4. Critical Discourse Analysis

A further aspect of textual analysis with which some stylisticians concern themselves, and about which others have reservations, is the study of the extent to which interpretation is influenced by tensions between the text and its reception in the wider context of social relations and sociopolitical structures (see Mills 1995; Fairclough 1989). In some contexts stylistic analysis has become embedded within a framework of Critical Discourse Analysis (CDA). In this way, explorations of ideology and social power feature as part of a stylistic analysis with attention paid both to the formal features of the text and to its reception within a reading community. This development has been the subject of some controversy, not least because *all* texts chosen for analysis may generate ideological considerations and interpretations according to the disposition of the individual analyst (see Widdowson 1995, 2004; Fairclough 1989, 1992; Toolan 1997 for further discussion). Nevertheless, despite such criticisms, CDA has been the first attempt so far to formalize a methodology that seeks to articulate the relationship between a text and the context in which it is produced, received, and interpreted, thus moving beyond a concern with wholly text-immanent interpretation and considering wider social and cultural issues.

Thus what has emerged in both theory and classroom practice is the view that, although there are not an infinite number of possible interpretations and although it would be wrong to suggest that anything goes, there is no single 'correct' way of analysing and interpreting text, nor any single correct approach. In this sense, the appropriate method is very much a hands-on approach taking each text on its own merits, using what the reader knows and what the reader is aiming for in his or her learning context, and employing all of the available tools, both in terms of language knowledge and methodological approaches. It is a process-based methodology which encourages learners to be active participants in, and explorers of, linguistic and cultural processes both with an awareness of and an interest in the process itself, including the development of a metalanguage for articulating responses to it. Beginnings have emerged in work in stylistics reported above and in a range of texts for both students and teachers during the past 20 years or so (see Collie and Slater 1987; Maley 1999; Maley and Moulding 1985; McRae and Vethamani 1999; Paran 2006).

5. Methodologies: Practical stylistics

Having considered some background to stylistics we now embrace more closely the range of methodologies available to and utilized by practitioners of stylistics. *Practical stylistics* involves close reading of the verbal texture of texts. Deriving as it does from practical criticism and from the practice of making uses of language a 'way in' to the meaning of texts, practical stylistics is the basic practice of stylistics (Widdowson 1975, 1992). The basic assumption is that literature is made from and with language, that language is the medium of literature, and that beginning with the very textuality of the text is a secure foundation for its interpretation. The following extract from Dickens's *Bleak House* (the opening paragraphs of the novel) illustrates some of these basic analytical and interpretive assumptions and practices:

London. Michaelmas Term lately over, and the Lord Chancellor sitting in Lincoln's Inn Hall. Implacable November weather. As much mud in the streets, as if the waters had but newly retired from the face of the earth, and it would not be wonderful to meet a Megalosaurus, forty feet long or so, waddling like an elephantine lizard up Holborn Hill. Smoke lowering down from chimney-pots, making a soft black drizzle with flakes of soot in it as big as full-grown snowflakes – gone into mourning, one might imagine, for the death of the sun. Dogs, undistinguishable in the mire. Horses, scarcely better; splashed to their very blinkers. Foot passengers, jostling one another's umbrellas, in a general infection of ill-temper, and losing their foothold at street-corners, where tens of thousands of other foot passengers have been slipping and sliding since the day broke (if this day ever broke) adding new deposits to the crust upon crust of mud, sticking at those points tenaciously to the pavement and accumulating at compound interest.

Fog everywhere. Fog up the river, where it flows among green aits and meadows; fog down the river, where it rolls defiled among the tiers of shipping, and the waterside pollution of a great (and dirty) city. Fog on the Essex Marshes, fog on the Kentish heights. Fog creeping into the cabooses of collier-brigs; fog lying out on the yards, and hovering in the rigging of great ships; fog drooping on the gunwales of barges and small boats. Fog in the eyes and throats of ancient Greenwich pensioners, wheezing by the firesides of their wards; fog in the stem and bowl of the afternoon pipe of the wrathful skipper, down in his close cabin; fog cruelly pinching the toes and fingers of his shivering little 'prentice boy on deck. Chance people on the bridges peeping over the parapets into a nether sky of fog, with fog all round them, as if they were up in a balloon, and hanging in the misty clouds.

Gas looming through the fog in divers places in the street, much as the sun may, from the spongey fields, be seen to loom by husbandman and ploughboy. Most of the shops lighted two hours before their time – as the gas seems to know, for it has a haggard and unwilling look.

The raw afternoon is rawest, and the dense fog is densest, and the muddy streets are muddiest, near that leaden-headed old obstruction, appropriate ornament for the threshold of leaden-headed old corporation: Temple Bar. And hard by Temple Bar, in Lincoln's Inn Hall, at the very heart of the fog, sits the Lord High Chancellor in his High Court of Chancery.

Very basic and preliminary interpretation of this text would need to take due account of the following stylistic features.

The role of verbs

in the opening paragraph alone there are verbs such as 'retired', 'waddling', 'splashed', 'jostling', 'slipping', 'sliding', and so on. The verbs all serve to create an atmosphere of constant action and movement in the big city. Yet there are no finite verbs in main clauses in the text. There is thus a difference between the following two sentences, the first of which (1) contains a main finite verb, the second of which (2) does not:

(1) Foot passengers jostled one another's umbrellas and lost their foothold at street-corners.

(2) Foot passengers jostling one another's umbrellas and losing their foothold at street-corners.

Main finite verbs provide, as it were, a kind of anchor for the action. It is clear when something took place and that the action was completed. In sentence (2) above from *Bleak House* the reader is left suspended, knowing that the action is ongoing, but awaiting a main verb to get his/her bearings. A sentence such as (3) provides that kind of 'anchor' for the action in the verb *arrived*, which is the finite verb in the sentence:

(3) Foot passengers jostling one another's umbrellas and losing their foothold at street corners *arrived* at the bank.

The finite verb is thus a verb which tells us when something happened (past or present), how many were/are involved (singular or plural), and who the participants are ('you'/'we'/'I', and so on). Sentence (2) above is a kind of model for many of the sentences in the first three paragraphs. Sentences such as the following therefore serve to create a sense of both disorientation and dislocation.

London.
Implacable November weather.
Smoke lowering down from the chimneypots.
Dogs undistinguishable in the mire.
Foot passengers jostling one another's umbrellas.
Fog in the eyes and throats of ancient Greenwich pensioners wheezing by the firesides.
Gas looming through the fog in divers places.

The reader feels that all the activity of London is confused and directionless; and no-one knows what timescale they are in. Furthermore, the present participles in particular ('lowering', 'jostling', 'wheezing', 'looming') convey a feeling of continuous action which could almost be timeless. Given this timeless character which is imparted to these descriptions it is perhaps not surprising that Dickens can suggest that London has an almost prehistoric feel to it – 'and it would not be wonderful to meet a Megalosaurus, forty feet long or so, waddling like an elephantine lizard up Holborn Hill'.

This kind of preliminary practical stylistic analysis is the cornerstone of close reading. It seeks iconic equations between observed linguistic choices and patterns and the enactment of meaning. It links linguistic form and literary meaning. The forms that are identified as significant are largely based on intuition and observation and may vary from one analyst to another, but no stylistic account of the text can omit some treatment and interpretation of such features. Practical stylistics operates in a systematic manner (sometimes drawing on checklists; see Short 1996) but in an otherwise relatively informal way with no specific technological support: just the reader, a knowledge of how the language works, and a willingness to seek explanation of the effects produced by the language. The difference between practical stylistics and the looser, more discursive accounts found in practical criticism is one of degree, along a continuum with the stylistic account seeking above all else to be made retrievable and recoverable by other readers. It accords, in other words, with a basic principle of stylistic analysis that others need to be able to see how you have reached the interpretive account that is offered. It is this process which makes an account of the text retrievable and recoverable, allows others to agree or disagree, and makes it possible for different interpretations to be compared transparently and objectively in the sense defined by Wales (2001: 373), who qualifies the extremes of this debate by saying that '[s]tylistics is only "objective" (and the scare quotes are significant) in the sense of being methodical, systematic, empirical, analytical, coherent, accessible, retrievable and consensual'.

It is, however, the analyst's analysis and does not derive from others. It is a basic form of stylistic analysis. It is steam stylistics; stylistics by candle-light, stylistics before the age of electricity. It is an improvement on horse power but exists in a world relatively untroubled by subsequent developments in literary theory, before the advent of computer power and corpus stylistics, or the subtleties of cognitive poetics. It is a naïve practice. It requires, in pedagogic terms, quite a bit of practice to gain confidence in. It is not easy, especially for native speakers of a language, to convert knowledge *of* the language into knowledge *about* the language. It is, however, a practice without the mastery of which no subsequent stylistic analysis can easily take place.

6. Transformative text analysis

It will be seen that the 'reading' of the opening to *Bleak House* took place largely by means of a process of reading and re-reading that involved consideration of how particular linguistic features operate in the text compared with more normal uses and functions. In terms of pedagogy, what are the methodologies that best develop those kinds of skills of observation, comparison, and analysis?

Transformative text analysis is built on similar assumptions to those of close reading but is augmented by a methodology of *active reading* (Knights and Thurgar-Dawson 2006). Transformative analysis is built on a pedagogic assumption that close reading has tendencies toward a more passive reception of the text, and that putting the reader into a more active role by forcing the text into a different linguistic or generic design will lead to more active engagement with its specific textuality.

Transformative text analysis assumes that noticing is more likely to take place if features of language and textual organization are drawn to a reader's attention as a result of the text having been deliberately manipulated in some way. The process here is one in which the reader compares the original text with one which has been rewritten, transformed, re-registered. *Rewriting* involves making use of a different range of linguistic choices; *transformation* is the manipulation of some key design feature of the text such as its narrative organization; and *re-registration* involves a more distinctive shift so that the same content is conveyed in a different genre. Thus: rewriting the Dickens passage might involve some extension of a process that has already been undertaken, that of comparing the effects of the presence or absence of particular verbal structures. Textual transformation involves relatively more radical interventions such as a change in the point of view from which the text is narrated. For example, the opening paragraph to *Bleak House* would be transformed to narration in the first or third person. And yet more radical textual surgery would see a re-registration of the text from a novel to a travelogue or a tourist guide to the city of London, with readers invited to comment on how the different genres invite and prompt different kinds of reading practice and interpretation alongside consideration of the nature of literary and non-literary language functions (see also Pope 1994).

The notion of re-registration means that no single word or stylistic feature will be barred from admission to a literary context. This is not to say that certain stylistic or lexical features are not regarded as more conventionally 'literary' than others. However, re-registration recognizes that the full, unrestricted resources of a language are open to exploitation for literary ends. As studies of novelistic discourse by Bakhtin (1984) suggest, not simply single words, but the characteristics of other discursive genres, may be represented in a literary context. According to Bakhtin, the effects of re-registration, of appropriating the characteristics of another discourse as an object for representation, are often deliberately parodic and travestying, highlighting through a process of imitation the core qualities of the object being investigated.

To illustrate: in the final paragraph of this opening to *Bleak House*, main finite verbs are restored to the sentences of the text. In particular the main verb 'to be' is repeated: 'The raw afternoon is rawest, and the dense fog is densest, and the muddy streets are muddiest ...' The presence of a main verb is most noticeable in the final sentence:

> And hard by Temple Bar, in Lincoln's Inn Hall, at the very heart of the fog, sits the Lord High Chancellor in his High Court of Chancery.

Here the main finite verb is *sits*. The action and location of the Lord High Chancellor is thus clearly situated. Indeed, the sentence is structured so that the location of the main subject of the sentence ('the Lord High Chancellor') comes first in the sentence. He sits:

> hard by Temple Bar, in Lincoln's Inn Hall, at the very heart of the fog ...

Structured differently, the sentence might have read:

> The Lord High Chancellor sits hard by Temple Bar, in Lincoln's Inn Hall, at the very heart of the fog.

This structure would be more normal and would follow the conventional word order for sentences in English in which the subject ('The Lord High Chancellor') occurs first and is then followed by a main finite verb ('sits'). But one of Dickens's purposes may be to delay the subject so that it has more impact as a result of its occurrence in an unusual position. It also has a very particular impact as a result of being in the simple present tense ('sits') when readers of a novel or of any kind of narrative might expect verbs to be in the simple past tense ('sat'). 'Sits' suggests, however, that the Lord High Chancellor always sits there and is a permanent landmark in this landscape. The simple present tense in English carries this sense of a permanent, general, unchanging truth.

In this final paragraph one of the main effects which Dickens creates may be to imply that the legal system of the country is in a state of permanent confusion, or even creates states of confusion which cannot be changed. And both in these opening paragraphs and in the novel as a whole, *fog* assumes symbolic importance, reinforcing a sense both of general confusion and of not being able to see clearly. The Lord High Chancellor is always 'at the very heart of the fog' and nothing will alter this position. For this reason perhaps, choices of language and of the structure of the sentence position 'the Lord High Chancellor' and 'the heart of the fog' together.

7. Reader responses and the role of the reader

The various forms of textual manipulation described here are designed to impact on the nature of the reading process undertaken by the reader, with the pedagogic aim of fostering more active and engaged reading on the part of individual readers. It is, however, in the nature of stylistic analysis to ask to what degree responses to texts are shared and to explore the extent to which variant readings might be accounted for. In part, this kind of inquiry is stimulated by an underlying belief that interpretations should not vary markedly if texts are analysed with due care and appropriate linguistic rigour. As a consequence, there have been numerous attempts in recent times by practitioners of stylistics to go beyond the individual reader and to try to account for multiple reader responses (see Kintgen 1983; van Peer 1986; Hanauer 1999 and others). The underlying impulse is to provide real empirical evidence and a quantitatively rooted support for investigative processes which, it is felt, may otherwise be deemed unduly impressionistic.

Such stylistic methodologies are less targeted at approaches to teaching and learning, but there are interesting possibilities nonetheless for group reading and group interpretations of texts. Alderson and Short (1989), for example, develop the interesting practice of revealing a text line by line in a gradual unfolding of meaning, and invite readers to undertake a step-by-step interpretation and reinterpretation of features of the language of a text as it emerges. The responses of readers may be collected in the form of protocols (written during and after the analytical process) or recorded orally as readers talk out their responses in varying degrees of immediacy of engagement. In the case of the *Bleak House* passage reader response approaches would *inter alia* be interested in measuring the kind of attention a reader gives to the text as he or she reads it, at what points exactly such attention is drawn more or less powerfully by particular foregrounded features, and what the effects are that such foregrounding has on the reader. For example, just *how* do readers respond to all those repetitions of the word 'fog'? Are they surprised, unsettled, overwhelmed? What are the precise points at which such feelings set in? Can effects of disorientation be precisely located in the process of reading? How cumulative are they? How exactly do readers feel when reading sentences without main verbs? What other effects are produced and how can they be described? Such data is commonly elicited by questionnaires, by verbal protocols collected as the readers individually audio-record their responses as they read, or in a process of post-hoc group discussion. Each of these strategies for collecting the data are different and they need to be disentangled, but the aim is to get closer to the linguistic particulars, the actual 'texture' (Stockwell 2009a) of the reading experience, and to build theories that are based both on theoretical speculation and on empirical evidence of what readers (from various backgrounds and reading positions of course) actually *do*.

8. From steam to broadband: Corpus stylistics

Corpus stylistics makes use of computer-driven searches of the language of large, multi-million word databases to help identify particular stylistic features. The use of corpus linguistic techniques and strategies is a necessary methodological advance in stylistics as it allows the power of computational analysis to identify significant linguistic patterns that would not be identifiable by human intuition, at least not over the extent of a novel the size of *Bleak House*. Significant here are: the size of language corpora these days and the ease with which written text (including textual examples from different historical periods) can be collected and stored; the speed with which data can be retrieved; the advances in ease of analytical software use such as Wordsmith Tools (Scott 2008); and the range of search tools available including sophisticated programmes that allow searches not just on individual words but on word patterns and clusters, as well as on particular syntactic and discoursal forms. Most relevantly, too, software advances also now generate comparison between different corpora, allowing a novel by a contemporary writer to be stylistically compared and benchmarked with a multi-million-word standard language corpus, and providing whole new vistas on issues of norms and deviations, foregrounding and parallelism of the kind that in previous generations, however rigorous the analysis, would rely more on individual responses and judgements and were built, inevitably, on shorter texts and extracts.

In a basic sense, corpus linguistic description of language prioritizes lexis. Whereas stylistics pays more attention to deviations from linguistic norms that lead to the creation of artistic effects, corpus linguistics focuses on what can be identified computationally – which tends to be on lexical patterns, especially patterns that are frequently repeated. Corpus linguistics identifies words that habitually co-occur, with a particular emphasis on the significance of collocation recently extended in Sinclair's (2004) concept of the lexical item with the categories of 'collocation', 'colligation', 'semantic preference', and 'semantic prosody' to describe patterns of lexical partnership around a fixed core. Innovative descriptive categories that have been developed in the field of corpus linguistics can also be used in literary stylistics. Whereas general corpus studies may want to disregard idiosyncrasies of individual texts, corpus stylistic studies can pay closer attention to the individual qualities of a specific text, as Stubbs (2005) and Fischer-Starcke (2006) illustrate by concentrating on lexical clusters in Conrad's *Heart of Darkness* and in Austen's *Persuasion* respectively.

In terms of our focus in this chapter on the opening to *Bleak House*, a corpus stylistic methodology would search the whole novel for what is revealed to be of significance in its lexical population: for example, the word *fog* is frequent and a computer search on what in the field of corpus linguistics is called a 'keyword' would reveal the extent to which *fog* remains salient across the whole novel, the nature of its other collocates, the words that surround it in lexical partnerships across the whole novel, and their repetition in different parts of the novel and the parts of the novel where they congregate with a particular lexical density. Mahlberg (2007a,b) notes the significance of lexical clusters in Dickens and explores by means of corpus stylistic analysis the significance of particularly frequent and prominent lexical clusters in a corpus of novels by Dickens, comparing the novels with a general language corpus of nineteenth-century texts and with one another. One cluster she notes to be of significance is the structure *as if* and *as if it were*, a cluster or bundle of words that, alongside modal expressions such as *would not be*, structures a hypothetical extension of meanings, the introduction through the indeterminacy of the fog of a textual world, so that the reader is not altogether sure where the real world stops and another world of *irrealis*, a more fantastical and improbable world, begins:

> As much mud in the streets, **as if** the waters had but newly retired from the face of the earth, and it would not be wonderful to meet a Megalosaurus, forty feet long or so, waddling like an elephantine lizard up Holborn Hill.
>
> Chance people on the bridges peeping over the parapets into a nether sky of fog, with fog all round them, **as if** they were up in a balloon, and hanging in the misty clouds.

Here is a table as illustrated by Mahlberg which shows in this case the regularity of extensions to this structure (with a personal pronoun) in several of Dickens's novels relative to other common nineteenth-century texts.

Types of structure	Dickens	Nineteenth-century texts
as if he would have	41	2
as if he were a	45	7
as if he were going	32	3
as if it were a	72	23
if he were going to	26	3

Of course, corpus stylistic analysis is an essentially quantitative procedure and involves an assessment of significance drawn statistically from a corpus-informed count. The actual application of corpus stylistics to texts necessarily involves, as we have seen, qualitative decisions and interpretive acts made by the analyst in the light of and to some degree in advance of the results from the assembled data-bank. Corpus stylistic analysis is a relatively objective methodological procedure that at its best is guided by a relatively subjective process of interpretation. Its full potential for literary stylistics is yet to be exploited and, as Semino and Short (2004) and Wynne (2005) point out, both philosophical and practical barriers need to be overcome, but it has emerged as a major methodological feature of any future stylistics landscape.

9. Methodological futures: Linking the cognitive and the social

Recent developments in cognitive poetics, particularly text world theory (Hidalgo-Downing 2000; Stockwell 2002; Gavins 2007b), have underlined another key methodology for capturing the integration of more or less subjective and objective accounts of texts. Here the stylistic focus is often on the deictic properties of a text that highlight these relationships between subjectivities, on the basis of locating person, time, and place, and also in terms of social and textual positioning. As Stockwell (forthcoming) puts it:

> A world, in this model, is a deictically-defined space with participants. At the top, discourse world level, readers and authors create a text world on the basis of the literary text. This text world is built in the reader's mind as a rich world representation that is used as the medium of the literary experience. ... Within the text world, further departures from the deictic location can be made, creating one or several embedded world-switches. These switches are triggered by modalizations, negatives, metaphors, flashbacks, flashforwards, speculative or hypothetical states, direct speech and other narrative switches, or reorientations in spatial location. ... All of these shifts are enacted stylistically.

The deictic texture of the opening to *Bleak House* reinforces the potential of this more cognitive dimension to ally with the more social interpretation framed by the 'position' of Lord High Chancellors, obtuse and socially disadvantaging legal systems, and a world that is as primitive as it has always been. In the four opening paragraphs to the novel, innumerable deictic expressions evidencing 'world-switches' can be seen across the passage, in fact so many that the images of confusion and chaos are compounded in the lack of any clear deictic centre: that is, a clear vantage point from which the position of the different locational references and prepositional phrases of place (*up Holborn*

Hill, at street-corners) can be seen. Specific places and topographical features in and around London are mentioned (*the Essex Marshes, the Kentish heights, Lincoln's Inn Hall, Temple Bar, Holborn Hill*) but the world which is invoked is unstable, with constant shifts in spatial location. Modalizations, negatives, and hypothetical conditionals (*it would not be wonderful, if this day ever broke, one might imagine, may be seen to loom*) compound the disorientation.

Up and down the Thames text worlds, fictional worlds, and real worlds, literal and metaphorical, socially and cognitively embedded, blur and slip and slide and accumulate only more accretions of confusion, accompanied as they are by 'flashbacks and flashforwards, speculative and hypothetical states'. And key financial and banking metaphors also emerge through the fog to create a mental mapping that underlines that in *Bleak House* London is a capital of capital, a text world where the dirt of money and wealth and privilege sits static and permanent: *adding new **deposits** to the crust upon crust of mud, sticking at those points tenaciously to the pavement and **accumulating** at **compound interest***.

A cognitively oriented linguistics and poetics add extra dimensions to stylistic analysis. We could go on, anchoring more interpretive suggestions to deictic reference, metaphoric constellation, and lexico-syntactic pattern. We could explore the extent to which the patterns identified here underscore key themes in the novel where legal obfuscation and inequities of power are discussed. We could look for further stylistic features using other tools and methodologies. There is no necessary stopping point to stylistic analysis; only a sense that sometimes less may be more, and this chapter aims to do no more than introduce the outlines of key approaches and methods which, as I hope we have seen, have the power to deliver in the classroom, empowering readers with an equipment that, above all else, allows them to take it further for themselves.

10. Conclusion

The methodologies employed to advance the study of style are united by a determination to better account for the processes of meaning construction which are the basis for our understanding and interpretation of texts. In pedagogic terms, the aim is to provide a systematic set of analytical tools, drawn from linguistics, that can foster insights into the patterning of literary texts in ways which allow those insights to be open, evidenced, and retrievable. It is, as Toolan (1986) points out, the work of *bricoleurs*, not engineers. Considerable progress has been made over the course of the last century, and the start of this century promises many more advances in a field that has become ever more confident and assured of its relevance to literary and language studies, and to its multiple classroom applications.

PART II
THE STYLISTICS OF POETRY

CHAPTER 4

The Stylistics of Poetry: Walter de la Mare's 'The Listeners'

KATIE WALES

1. Introduction

In Ronald Carter and Peter Stockwell's concluding chapter (2008) to their collection of what they see as significant work in stylistics in the past forty years, they state what is almost a truism for teachers and students of stylistics, and certainly obvious from the objectives of this very volume. Stylistic analysis 'shed[s] light on the crafted texture of the literary text, as well as offering a productive form of assistance in completing interpretations, making them richer and more complex'. It is, inextricably, both 'a descriptive tool' and 'a catalyst for interpretation' (Carter and Stockwell 2008: 296–7). For poetry, 'crafted texture' is obviously a well-suited collocation, and the perennial appeal of poems to analysts and readers alike must owe a great deal to the aesthetic satisfaction of such artistic artefacts. Mick Short (1996: xii), however, would see stylistics as having a further goal: to help us understand how we are 'affected' by a text. This again seems particularly important for the full appreciation of poetry: its subliminal emotive triggers, reverberations, echoes, and even after-effects.

In one important sense, then, stylistics offers us a 'way in' to a poetic text, and in this chapter I shall be touching on some of the ways or means, which are dealt with more expansively in subsequent chapters, that are important for the 'shedding of light', such as sound patterns and metre, foregrounding, schemas or scenarios, conceptual metaphor, and particular kinds of textual contexts. It is precisely the notion of context which leads me to propose here that stylistics also offers us a 'way out' to further areas of pedagogical exploration and study; comparisons, re-evaluations, and philosophical, historical,

71

and cultural issues in general. But in focusing on the particular poem I have
chosen, I am also using stylistics to probe a significant aspect of poetic production and reception generally, which is strangely neglected: the power of
poetry to be memorable to 'lay' readers. This, I feel, is not unrelated to the
larger issue for the appeal of literature generally: the continuing popularity
of some texts across the generations. My chosen poem, Walter de la Mare's
(1912) 'The Listeners', nicely renders that last prepositional phrase 'across
the generations' ambiguous: it appeals to children and adults alike; and has
done since it first appeared nearly a century ago. Here is the poem:

The Listeners

'Is there anybody there?' said the Traveller,
    Knocking on the moonlit door;
And his horse in the silence champed the grasses
    Of the forest's ferny floor:
5   And a bird flew up out of the turret,
    Above the Traveller's head:
And he smote upon the door again a second time;
    'Is there anybody there?' he said.
But no one descended to the Traveller;
10   No head from the leaf-fringed sill
Leaned over and looked into his grey eyes,
    Where he stood perplexed and still.
But only a host of phantom listeners
    That dwelt in the lone house then
15   Stood listening in the quiet of the moonlight
    To that voice from the world of men:
Stood thronging the faint moonbeams on the dark stair,
    That goes down to the empty hall,
Harkening in an air stirred and shaken,
20   By the lonely Traveller's call.
And he felt in his heart their strangeness,
    Their stillness answering his cry,
While his horse moved, cropping the dark turf,
    'Neath the starred and leafy sky;
25   For he suddenly smote on the door, even
    Louder, and lifted his head:–
'Tell them I came, and no one answered,
    That I kept my word,' he said.
Never the least stir made the listeners,
30   Though every word he spake
Fell echoing through the shadowiness of the still house

From the one man left awake:
Ay, they heard his foot upon the stirrup,
    And the sound of iron on stone,
35 And how the silence surged softly backward,
    When the plunging hoofs were gone.

2. The popularity of 'The Listeners'

In December 2007 a report appeared in the national press from the English schools inspectorate Ofsted, warning that poetry teaching in schools could be repetitive and dull, with the same few poems chosen time and again for study in primary schools and again at secondary level. These included whimsical or nonsense poems by Lewis Carroll and Edward Lear; poems easy to 'imitate', like Roger McGough's; and poems that told 'a strong story' like Walter de la Mare's 'The Listeners'. The message was, as *The Times*'s (7 December 2007) sub-heading declared, 'Too much lightweight verse taught in schools'. While any attempt to encourage the appreciation of poetry in schools must be praised, there are certain assumptions, even paradoxes, here. De la Mare was certainly a celebrated and prolific writer of poems specifically for children, but this particular poem, 'The Listeners', first published in 1912, was not written for this readership. Moreover, the inspectors do not appear to have been interested in *why* this poem is clearly repeatedly chosen and appreciated by teachers and pupils of all ages, apart from its apparent 'strong story'. It certainly features in the 'hundred best poems for children chosen by children (and teachers)', edited by the self-same Roger McGough in 2002. The poem is unfortunately juxtaposed with the whimsical and naïve, which is interesting (and ironical) in one sense, since de la Mare himself loved the childish nonsense of the nursery rhyme; but the poem, as we shall see, has a sheen of metrical simplicity that belies its actual complexity. Importantly, the metre of the poem aids its memorability.

There is no doubt that the publication of 'The Listeners' in an anthology of the same name made de la Mare's fame. He had published very little, prose or verse, before this of which critics and readers took much note. It was well liked by the poet Robert Frost, who met de la Mare in 1916–17. The strong impression the poem made upon him was still vivid in his eighties, when he talked of de la Mare at London Airport in 1961 (Whistler 2003: 202; 269–70). It was the poem Thomas Hardy most wanted read to him as he lay dying in 1928, believing it to be 'possibly the finest poem of the century' (Whistler 2003: 348) – a century only a quarter of the way through. It was reprinted in four editions in the next 30 years before de la Mare's own death in 1956; and was given Sir Arthur Quiller-Couch's 'seal of approval' in his second edition (1939) of *The

Oxford Book of English Verse, extended in this edition from 1900 until 1918. Its popularity is already implicated in the critical study of de la Mare by a fellow poet, Forrest Reid, in 1929, who writes that 'The Listeners' is 'too well known to require quotation' even (Reid 1929: 157), let alone any critical comments on it. He shows uncanny powers of foresight, however, when he states that 'it has somehow caught the popular taste and there appears to be a danger of its coming to occupy a position among his poems not unlike that of *The Raven* among the poems of Edgar [Allan] Poe' (Reid 1929: 158). The poem was so popular that de la Mare himself actually stopped giving permission for it to be published in anthologies (Whistler 2003: 203).

A very interesting anthology in which it does appear was published in 1944, during the Second World War. Its editor was Field Marshal Earl Wavell, who was Viceroy of India. In his introduction he states that memorizing poetry was for him a mental relaxation, and all the poems in the anthology were at one time or another in his head. The Ofsted report mentioned above makes no mention of memorizing poetry; yet this has been a strong tradition in schools, in the first half of the twentieth century at least. Changes in educational theories since then have led to its unfashionableness in Britain. Recitation of poetry aloud is sadly also unfashionable, killed off by silent reading, but this aids memorizing, and indeed memorability. So popular poems like 'The Listeners', Wordsworth's 'The Daffodils', and Poe's 'The Raven' indeed, have often been recited and learned off by heart in the past; and parts, if not the whole, can still be invoked by older readers.

In 1995 the BBC conducted a poll, to coincide with National Poetry Day, to find the nation's favourite poems. The ensuing anthology (1996) edited by the popular television comedian and presenter Griff Rhys Jones has been reprinted over 40 times since then, suggesting that the appreciation of poetry still has a significant place in contemporary culture. 'The Listeners' appeared in third place, after Rudyard Kipling's 'If' (see Stockwell 2005) and Tennyson's 'The Lady of Shalott' (Wordsworth's 'Daffodils' came fifth). In his Introduction, Rhys Jones makes some interesting and pertinent comments. 'You may be surprised that Walter de la Mare came in ahead of Shakespeare. I was' (Jones 1996: 6). Why, we may ask, should he be surprised? Also, he refers to the influence of school: 'A cynic might be tempted to claim that people voted for what they could remember; cherishing whatever they were forced to cherish at school'; but he adds, and quite reasonably: 'If this is merely a collection of "O" Level standard English primer gems, then we ought to be grateful to the nation's English masters. Personally, I find fragments of what I stuffed in at fourth-form level spinning up, unbidden, in solitary moments, and when it does it's oddly potent.'

The BBC book has inspired other more recent anthologies, for example *Classic FM's One Hundred Favourite Poems* edited by Mike Read (1997). 'The

Listeners' is again in third position, but this time below 'The Daffodils' and, again, Kipling's 'If'.

3. Sound patterns and metre

'The Listeners' is very much a poem for listeners. There are friends of mine who can recite from memory the first half of 'The Listeners' at least, but many more people can recite the first two lines of the poem: they are even more dramatic than the first two lines of Wordsworth's 'The Daffodils', which are equally well known:

> 'Is there anybody there?' said the Traveller,
> Knocking on the moonlit door...

These first two lines are even inscribed on the wall of a travel inn on the out-skirts of Guildford.

The use of a direct question as an opening device is dramatic in itself, occurring rarely at the beginnings of novels, for example (see Wales 1984); but occurring quite frequently to open de la Mare's poems, it has to be said. The interrogative cleverly thrusts the reader into the text-world of the poem, since the implied respondent is not the reader but a character, or characters, in that world. The question, of course, does have distinct reverberations or echoes in itself, to which I shall return, which add to the drama. We are plunged *in medias res*, into a dialogue within a narrative, but we do not know who the Traveller is or where the door is, only that it is night-time. So there is an immediate sense of mystery.

In other contexts the question might be considered quite commonplace, but already the first line sets up a strong, apparently regular, rhythm:

> x   x   / x x /   / x   / x x
> 'Is there anybody there?', said the Traveller

in itself a mixture of anapaests (x x /) and iambs (x /) and, in my reading (but contra Duffin 1949: 37), probably four strong beats. This is then inverted in the second line:

> /   x x x   / \   /
> Knocking on the moonlit door

The emphatic trochaic 'Knocking' (/ x) and the strong beat ending the three strong stressed line almost echoes the loud knocking on the door of the Traveller himself.

These two lines together set up a kind of metrical 'norm' or base for the rest of the poem, and suggest a pace suitable for a story. For while it might be possible to read the metre in other ways (e.g. by suggesting a 'rest' at the end of the second line), a base of four plus three strong beats actually provides a common pattern for the ballad; and the intertextual associations of the ballad are indeed very important for readerly expectations of both a narrative and concrete details, relevant here, as we shall see. So lines three and four, and five and six, repeat the pattern:

```
  x   x   /   x  x  / x         /      x   /   x
And his horse in the silence champed the grasses
  x  x   / x     / x   /
Of the forest's ferny floor:
  x  x   /   /  /  x  x x   / x
And a bird flew up out of the turret
  x  /   x   / x  x      /
Above the Traveller's head
```

The monosyllabic rhyming words so far, the 'masculine' rhymes, and the foregrounded alliteration of 'forest's ferny floor', aid recitation and memorability. Consider the alliteration of Old English poetry, for example, inherited from the Germanic oral tradition of recitation (see Rubin 1995); or spells and counting rhymes. The alliterative phrase is almost tactile, so that there is a strong sense already of the tangibility of the world created. Moreover, in lines three to six the metrical pattern is reinforced by the syntactic repetition of the chronicle-connective *And*, and the semantic and syntactic parallelism of an animal/bird action followed by a line-filling prepositional phrase.

Alliteration occurs frequently in the poem, mostly fricatives and liquids: 'smote...a second time' (line 7); 'leaf-fringed sill/ Leaned over and looked' (10–1); 'where he stood perplexed and still' (12); 'listening in the...moonlight' (15); 'stood...on the dark stair' (17); 'hall/ Harkening' (18–19); 'strangeness/...stillness' (21–2); 'suddenly smote' (25); 'Louder, and lifted ...' (26); 'came.../...kept' (27–8); 'least...listeners' (29). Most noticeably it occurs in the concluding four lines of the poem, where the fricatives appear to symbolize the silence described:

Ay, they heard his foot upon the stirrup,
And the sound of iron on stone,
And how the silence surged softly backward,
When the plunging hoofs were gone.

[margin, rotated text:] OLD POEMS → THINGS DONE TO MID RECITATION.

Here, remarkably, the silence is also a presence capable of movement (surging backward), like a palpable mist or fog; and as significant in the poem as the sounds of knocking, calling and horse hoofs. The Traveller has disturbed the silence at the beginning of the poem, and now the status quo is restored.

In line seven the conjunction *And* occurs again, but the rhythm of the line possibly changes to permit five strong beats:

    x   x   /   x x x   / x /? x / x   /
    And he smote upon the door again a second time

Reading the line aloud we are aware of the knocking, with this emphatic rhythm. A similar effect occurs in lines 25 to 26, as the Traveller knocks at the door a third time:

    x x   /   x x   /   x x   / / x
    For he suddenly smote on the door even
    / x   x / x   x   /
    Louder, and lifted his head

Four beats here, but the unusual enjambement within a phrase makes us want to read 'Louder' louder!

At other points in the poem there is again the possibility of five rather than four strong beats:

    /   / x x   /   x x x   / /
    Leaned over and looked into his grey eyes
    /   / x x   /   /   \ x x   / /
    Stood thronging the faint moonbeams on the dark stair

– two strong stresses at the beginning and end of the line, with matching initial verbs and final adjective and nouns. The syntactic pattern of 'Stood thronging' is picked up in

    /   / x x   x   x / x x x x x   / /
    Fell echoing through the shadowiness of the still house

with the similar pattern of stressed adjective and noun at the end of the line. The effect is to slow down the reading pace, and it is noteworthy that these three lines above precisely concern the 'stillness' of the interior and its possible inhabitants, in the sense both of silence and lack of movement, in contrast to the noisy knocking of the Traveller. It is rather like the surreal effect of slow-motion, as in a dream: of wanting to move, but being unable to. I return below to this suggestion of the subliminal or the subconscious.

Generally speaking, Robert Frost (cited in Whistler 2003: 270) is probably right when he states that in this poem 'the scansion defeats the prosodists, for its actual metric pattern will not fit their formulas'; he himself was a poet who matched in verse the natural rhythms of the speaking voice. But certainly it is the first line of each 'couplet', as it were, which tends to have more strong beats; the second line, with the rhyming word, tends to maintain the three strong beats. As early as the 1920s William Thomson (1923) provided a 'rhythmical analysis' of the poem which emphasized the regular 'musicality' as he saw it of the alternate lines, using actual musical notation; and the varying numbers of unstressed syllables in the other lines: what he therefore called two sets of 'voice tones' (reprinted in Megroz [1924]: Appendix). These, he suggested, enhanced the 'dual' character of the poem, the world of Man versus the world of 'spirits' (see also Pierson 1964: 381). Let us now move closer to the possible symbolic meanings of the poem by way of the (visual) imagery.

4. Imagery and symbolism

So far I have concentrated on the poem's very obvious auditory and related syntactic patterns (about which much more could be said), since these are clearly very important for its impact, memorability, and atmospheric enhancement of the text world itself. Short (1996: 151) speaks very aptly of the general power of metre and rhythm to evoke 'textual magic': and this is a poem very much about enchantment of all kinds. It is not only a poem for listeners, however, but also a poem for viewers. Whistler (2003: 270) happens to be rather dismissive of what she terms the 'stock-property symbolism in which it is dressed for the eye'. But it is the detail which is arresting, drawing the reader into the text world: the forest's ferny floor and dark turf (line 4), the Traveller's 'grey eyes' (11), the leaf-fringed sill (10), the moonbeams on the dark stair (17). These may be conventional dualisms of light and dark, animate and inanimate, but they evoke also intertextually the literary heritage of the ballads of horse and rider, and also the 'Gothic' romantic poems of Coleridge, Keats and the later Christina Rossetti. 'Stock-property' the imagery may be, but these literary frames, scripts or pre-existing generic text worlds are nonetheless significant for our interpretation of the poem. Some readers may well think of Robert Browning's *Child Roland to the Dark Tower Came* (see Ferguson 1945), where a man keeps his pledge in the face of supernatural opposition. As in many other myths and stories, such as the medieval poem *Sir Gawain and the Green Knight*, the hero appears to be arriving at a mysterious place where he finds himself at the mercy of a 'different and complex power', as Punter (2006: 85) would describe it.

Of course, on the level of *histoire* or 'story' we as readers are tantalized: despite the specific concrete details we are given no clues as to who the

Traveller (with a capital 'T') is; where he comes from and where he returns to; where the house is, and when this happened (other than at night). We do not know who the 'phantom listeners' (13) are; and even more mysteriously, who the 'them' (27) are off-stage, so to speak, in the sub-world, who must be 'told' that he came. Clearly the poem raises more questions than it answers; and this mystery, however frustrating, is also part of its appeal. The poem begins with a strong sense of anticipation: a question expects an answer, which the Traveller fails to get. However 'strong' we may feel the story to be in one sense, there is still a potential anti-climax in this failure, and with the Traveller returning whence he came.

Interestingly, there are two lines in the poem (lines 27–8) which both Megroz (1924) and Reid (1929) feel are out of place, even 'out of key':

> Tell them I came and no one answered
> That I kept my word, he said.

Reid (1929: 157) objects to these lines introducing a motive for the visit, the keeping of a tryst, and so interrupting what he sees as the overall 'illogical' dream effect. But one reader I know told me that all her life she had been 'haunted' (her own word!) by these lines, quoting them even in some appropriate context once or twice a year. Emotively they are very poignant, and suggest even the Traveller's bitterness at his wasted journey, which has indeed been compelled by the mysterious 'them' for whom the 'listeners' are gatekeepers. There is also a hint perhaps that he will be compelled again to return.

Underneath the 'stock-properties' is something more basic that we as readers can respond to in cognitive terms. The narrative appears to be a variant of the experiential gestalt or conceptual metaphor (see Lakoff and Johnson 1980, and Fludernik, this volume) of SOURCE–PATH–GOAL: where, to recall Johnson (1987), there is a COMPULSION to proceed in the first instance (the Traveller has made some kind of pledge), but then a BLOCKAGE: the physical door through which he has no right of entry, and the synaesthetic silence of those listening which represents a powerful COUNTERFORCE (see also Burke 2008: 217–20). Frustration is intensified by the fact that the Traveller has to knock three times, and repeat his initial question. By drawing on such a gestalt we can begin to 'make sense' of the poem; and already we can see that the 'meaning' of the poem, any meaning of the poem, and of any poem indeed, is constructed in the interaction between the words of the text and our own knowledge, both intertextual and experiential or schematic.

But there is another important 'under-current', as it were, which contributes to the power of this poem, and indeed literature in general and poetry especially, but which is sometimes ignored in stylistics: that of emotion. There are quite explicit expressions of emotion in the poem: 'where he stood *perplexed* and still' (12); 'the *lonely* Traveller's call' (20); '*And he felt in his heart their strangeness*' (21). These draw the reader or listener into empathetic identification with the Traveller and his frustration; at the same time contributing, like a prosody, to the overall mood of brooding mystery.

I would go further and argue that there are a range of sub(-)liminal emotive effects cued by displacement: triggered by quite specific details, which therefore function as symbols, and drawing upon deep and ancient culturally embedded scenarios or archetypes. Take the apparently ordinary detail of the door, introduced in line two. In our domestic script a door is a liminal barrier, a threshold, between the outer world and the inner private sanctum, keeping out strangers and welcoming friends. 'Knock, knock.' 'Who's there? Friend or foe?' The question of 'who's there?' has traditionally been rendered more acute in the hours of darkness rather than daylight, when visitors are less likely to be expected and when the imagination runs riot and associates darkness with danger, evil, ghosts, and things that go bump in the night. We now talk metaphorically of 'waiting for the knock at the door', and in this poem the intensity of the suspense and even the fear of those listening inside is almost palpable. Not surprisingly, perhaps, Henry Duffin (1949: 19) writes dramatically of the palpable effect on the reader: with skin creeping and hair beginning to rise.

Moreover, the connotations and symbolism of the very act of knocking accord admirably with Freud's (1919) notion of the 'uncanny', the German *unheimlich*. To Freud the 'un-homely' is related on the one hand to the *heimlich* 'homely' or 'cosy' (so we can think of the knock on the door of home), but also on the other hand to what causes dread and horror. *Heimlich* in German also means secret, unrevealed, intimate: so *unheimlich* for Freud is also the name for everything that ought to have remained secret, that has come to light. So what secrets does the house in the poem keep that we should try to guess at? The poem nicely exploits an ambivalence between the 'homely' details of turret, stair, and horse eating the grass; and the intangibility of the 'phantom' listeners whose secret life inside has been disturbed. As Punter (2006: 90) says of Freud's concept generally, the 'homely' serves to 'sharpen or heighten our sense of the *unheimlich*, of *not* being at home; [or rather] of, perhaps, never being able to feel convincingly at home again'. 'The Listeners' remains a deeply unsettling poem, like a dream or even a nightmare. In a Freudian sense the listeners themselves could be seen as the projections of our own hidden apprehensions and anxieties. Who knows what goes on behind closed doors?

The sense of mystery, of course, is apparent from the dramatic first line of the poem, and this initial question again taps into a diversity of scenarios or scripts (Schank and Abelson 1977) which ambiguously colour our further reading of the poem and our interpretation of it, but which also make it so memorable at the same time. It is this question, 'Is there anybody there?', which inevitably provokes the textual ambivalence between narrative and actual allegory (and we may note again in this connection the capital 'T' of Traveller). Interestingly, Burke (2008: 63) argues that in the reading of any literary text we inevitably implicate ourselves at the level of *discourse* and find ourselves asking time and again 'Who are we? Where did we come from? Where are we going?' These questions apply very obviously at the level of *histoire* to the Traveller in this poem, but in consequence it becomes in itself an explicit catalyst for such metaphysical questions. 'Is there anybody there?' becomes a philosophical, existential question.

Another conceptual metaphor comes to mind then, out of which many literary allegories have been made: LIFE IS A JOURNEY. Here, though the journey is thwarted, the Traveller is condemned to leave again: his 'time' has not yet come perhaps, or he is a figure of the 'Eternal Wanderer', another prominent cultural and literary motif. The educated reader perhaps thinks of Coleridge's Ancient Mariner: a phantasmagorical, nightmarish creation.

For some readers, the juxtaposition of 'Is there anybody there?' and 'knocking' might evoke the scenario of a spiritualist séance. Knocking has been associated with spiritualism since the so-called Rochester knockings or rappings of the Fox sisters in New York State in the mid-nineteenth century. No longer fashionable, séances with such noises were still prominent in the early decades of the twentieth century, especially in the years surrounding and including the Great War. One quotation from the Bible that was inscribed in many spiritualist texts was from the book of Revelation, 3.20: 'Behold, I stand at the door and knock'; also the subject of a famous painting of Christ by the Pre-Raphaelite painter Holman Hunt (d. 1910), with the handle on the inside of the door. In this poem the Traveller knocks not just once, but thrice: and three is a mystic number. It was thrice that Christ was denied by Peter before the cock crew at dawn. Other associations, echoes, might come to mind. There was a common trope in medieval literature of the body as a house to be visited by Christ; and also, it has to be said, by the Devil. In both Christianity and other faiths a door can lead to heaven, or to hell, and 'being at death's door' is still a common figure of speech. The door is not only the threshold between the interior and the outside worlds but also between the known and the unknown, the physical and the spiritual. In this poem, clearly, the Traveller does not go inside: Death perhaps is not ready for him yet.

5. Towards an interpretation?

Can we begin to make sense of all these allusions swirling subliminally in our mind? Is there anybody there? Superficially, the poem presents a series

WRITE PURE BS. WHEN
INTERPRETING A POEM.

of negativities: 'But *no one* descended to the Traveller' (9), '*No head* from the leaf-fringed sill ...' (10), 'Tell them I came, and *no one* answered' (27), '*Never* the least stir made the listeners' (29). The door is literally shut in his face; his 'quest' seems fruitless. This suggests even a nihilistic modernist interpretation: there is no one 'out there', whether God or extra-terrestrials. But look again at the framing of the negation: the propositions are predicated on the expectation of the opposite. And within the text world we know that there is someone there. The poem shifts quite explicitly from the perspective of the Traveller outside to the 'host of phantom listeners' inside, in their own space: that 'dwelt in the lone house then' (14); who 'stood listening' (15), 'stood thronging' (17), 'harkening' (19), and who 'heard his foot on the stirrup,/ And the sound of iron on stone' (33–4). Outside, even the Traveller himself feels 'in his heart their strangeness,/ Their stillness *answering* his cry' (21–2). On the basis of these textual clues then, we may wish to deduce that the poem is not entirely nihilistic: that out of its ambivalence and texture of enigma some consolation can be recuperated; and that a resolution can be inferred by us the readers, despite the lack of resolution in the 'story'. And the Traveller, at least, has 'kept his word' (28): his is an ethical victory. For me as a reader the fundamental metaphor would be simply that LIFE IS A RIDDLE; that Truth eludes us, and that the universe itself is enigmatic. This is a poem about uncertainty: philosophically and emotionally.

We should not be surprised that right from its date of first publication the poem has aroused many different interpretations. The Traveller has been identified with the poet as artist, God, Christ, the Holy Ghost, even a spectral ghost or reincarnation himself; the 'listeners' as fairies or house-elves, mice, the memories of school-fellows, the powers of darkness, and obviously ghosts (see Gwynn and Condee 1954; Bentinck 2001: 74). De la Mare himself was always being asked what the poem 'meant', and he usually replied – quite properly – that 'a poem means whatever the individual reader finds in it' (Whistler 2003: 203). When pressed he tended to give quite different interpretations on different occasions; but also of significance is his further, more general statement that 'at every individual encounter a poem is that particular experience and no other'. Such is the stylistic richness and yet vagueness of the poem, and so various the scenarios evoked and emotions aroused, that on each re-reading of the poem further nuances will come to mind.

Time and again ordinary readers speak of the poem as 'haunting' them: an apt choice given the subject matter of the listeners haunting the lone house, and the Traveller himself, literally a *revenant*, forever doomed to return. But is this simply a cliché, a dead metaphor? 'The Listeners' provides a striking example of the emotive 'after-effect' of reading poetry. No wonder that readers have been drawn to memorize it.

6. Conclusion: The way out

The desire to memorize poetry is really a kind of evaluation in the critical sense, and we should not be too dismissive of this. Nor should we be dismissive or condescending about children's poetry, whether literature written specifically for children, or read by children of all ages at school or at home. It is certainly also true, as McHale (2004) notes, that narrative poetry is currently critically undervalued in favour of lyric. The time is right for a re-assessment of de la Mare's poetry in general: it is not just 'The Listeners' that stands the test of time. Too readily today over-shadowed by his so-called Georgian contemporaries like Rupert Brooke, A. E. Housman, Robert Graves, and D. H. Lawrence, de la Mare had a wide range, as what we would now modishly term a 'crossover' poet, like Robert Louis Stevenson or Christina Rossetti, and his output was immense. Surprisingly, there have been very few critical studies of his poetry since his death in 1956. His anthology for children, *Peacock Pie*, first published in 1913, is gloriously inventive, but similar preoccupations or obsessions can be found in his other writings: riders on horseback, moonlight, knocking on doors, empty houses: symbols or metaphors of memory and the imagination. Whistler (2003: 202) aptly writes of the (paradoxical) humanisation of the fantastic and the 'estrangement' of the human in his poetry, and Duffin (1949: 29) similarly notes his blurring of the distinction between the natural and supernatural worlds. Spiritually, his poetry seems closer to the metaphysics of poets like Henry Vaughan and William Blake; intellectually, he appears to blur the boundary between the conscious and the unconscious, the certain and the uncertain, like James Joyce in *Finnegans Wake*.

A stylistic analysis of poetry helps us to probe deep into a poem, but it should also trigger the desire to read beyond the text to appreciate other poems. Moreover, as Leech writes (2008: 303), such activity 'does not rely on the acceptance of this or that theory or ideology; it is open to all who know the language; or who know something of how the language works'.

Acknowledgements

I am grateful to Gillian Brown, Meg Rowley and Ruth Stables for sharing their responses to this poem with me. I also thank the literary trustees of Walter de la Mare and the Society of Authors as their representative for their permission to reproduce 'The Listeners'.

CHAPTER 5

A Cognitive Stylistic Reading of Rhetorical Patterns in Ted Hughes's 'Hawk Roosting': A Possible Role for Stylistics in a Literary Critical Controversy

PETER VERDONK

Rhetoric, in its most basic sense of effective and persuasive communication, may be assumed to be as old as human speech. This is all the more likely because rhetoric has turned out to be a cognitive and emotive drive in people to use language in such a manner as to impress or emotionalize others, and then persuade them to adopt or reject a certain viewpoint. Therefore, in this day and age of cognitive science, I tend to accept the hypothesis that from an evolutionary perspective, the ultimate source of this basic impulse is likely to have been the instinct of self-preservation. As such, rhetoric in its primary sense may be supposed to have contributed to the preservation of the human species and its subsequent sociocultural evolution (Kennedy 1998: 4). Indeed, in these days the word *rhetoric* is on everyone's lips, with President Barack Obama being hailed as the new Cicero (Higgins 2008).

But to pick up the thread of my argument, the persuasive force of this primary or proto-rhetoric was inevitably produced not only by *what* was said, that is, the content, but also by *how* it was said, that is, the form. Now, this formal aspect or manner of expression is the natural predecessor of what via classical Greek and Roman rhetoric subsequently evolved into the present-day notion of style, which, unsurprisingly, has so far proved to be very difficult to define as an abstract concept. All the same, one might say that behind the external features of style one usually suspects some conscious or unconscious intention and significance. Putting it differently, it is generally assumed that style has a phenomenal as well as a conceptual element, which, though they can be distinguished, are at the same time inseparably interconnected. For instance, the dominant rhetorical pattern of present tense forms in Ted Hughes's 'Hawk Roosting' is a clearly recognizable phenomenal aspect of the poem, which, as we shall see, simultaneously conveys a deep conceptual significance. It is precisely with regard to this process of signification that in the last two decades or so, most stylisticians, I think, inspired by the so-called cognitive revolution in the 1970s, have parted company with the ancient rhetoricians about the role of language in meaning-making. Cognitive stylisticians now hold the view that the meaning of style does not primarily reside in its linguistic manifestations on the page but in the conceptual or mental representations of some earlier relevant experience evoked in the mind of the reader. At the same time, it should not be overlooked that these mental representations are also structured and affected by a relevant sociocultural and historical context, with the important reservation, though, that it is not this context as such that influences the language of discourse but rather how it is subjectively interpreted by the participants in a discourse (van Dijk 2008: 16). Summing up, it may be said that as form language serves the purpose of conveying our conceptualized and contextualized knowledge of the world, and thereby facilitates the communication of meaning (Kövecses 2006: 11).

After these preliminaries, I will propose a cognitive stylistic-cum-rhetorical analysis of the poem 'Hawk Roosting' by the late poet laureate Ted Hughes. Here I am using the term *rhetorical* rather loosely, namely in the sense that my stylistic focus will be on features of language which in my view carry literary persuasion (Cockcroft and Cockcroft 2005: 5).

> *Hawk Roosting*
>
> I sit in the top of the wood, my eyes closed.
> Inaction, no falsifying dream
> Between my hooked head and hooked feet:
> Or in sleep rehearse perfect kills and eat.
>
> 5   The convenience of the high trees!
> The air's buoyancy and the sun's ray
> Are of advantage to me;
> And the earth's face upward for my inspection.
>
> My feet are locked upon the rough bark.
> 10   It took the whole of Creation

To produce my foot, my each feather:
Now I hold Creation in my foot

Or fly up, and revolve it all slowly –
I kill where I please because it is all mine.
15 There is no sophistry in my body:
My manners are tearing off heads –

The allotment of death.
For the one path of my flight is direct
Through the bones of the living.
20 No arguments assert my right:

The sun is behind me.
Nothing has changed since I began.
My eye has permitted no change.
24 I am going to keep things like this.
          (Ted Hughes, 1960, To Sylvia Plath)

Before suggesting a possible interpretation of the poem, I wish to emphasize that when using the term 'the reader' or 'readers' I definitely include the readers of this essay as well as myself in that category. At the same time, I am of course well aware that the poem may trigger a lot of different reactions in all kinds of readers, which may all be equally defensible (Lindauer 2009: 54–5). Because of this wide variety of possible readings of the poem, I am highly interested to know what the outcome would be of an empirically based reading. In a recent article on this subject, it is stated that not enough empirical research has been conducted on poetry reading to present a fully worked-out and empirically based description of poetry reading (Hanauer 2001: 116). Therefore, I hope that the following stylistic analysis, and those by other stylisticians, will provide positive encouragement to continue this enterprise with renewed energy.

With these provisos in mind, I think that what will probably strike many readers first of all is that in the discourse situation of the poem it is the hawk who thinks and speaks throughout, which is why I use the personal relative pronoun 'who' instead of 'which'. The poet, or rather his persona, is conspicuous by his absence from a scene he has obviously created himself. There is nothing in the text that gives away the poet's own voice, except, it seems, in the poem's title 'Hawk Roosting', which is remarkably, perhaps ironically, peaceful compared with the violence expressed in the poem itself. Indeed, apart from this single indication of the poet's presence, there is no hint at all of his perspective on the hawk's megalomaniac claims. In other words, no distinction is made between the observing, human intelligence and the creature observed (Walder 1987: 40). I wish to add here that in my view the poet has deliberately hidden behind a mask for rhetorical reasons, leaving readers entirely to their own devices to come up with an emotional and/or moral response to the hawk's self-revelatory monologue. Yet another effect of the poet's absence as an omniscient commentator appears to be that the hawk's total lack of self-irony and lack of a sense of perspective are in no way held up to ridicule or subject to irony.

Actually, this mask that the poet has put on is a typical example of personification, with the hawk being represented as if it had human qualities. In the persuasive toolbox of the classical rhetorician it is a figure of speech or a trope known as prosopopoeia, which originates from a Greek word literally meaning 'to make a face or a mask'. Generally speaking, this figure of speech enables the orator to shift the responsibility for an unpleasant event or situation onto some personified abstraction or animal. Just like the hawk in our poem, who is saddled, unduly I think, with all kinds of nasty streaks of human behaviour!

However, as I said earlier, the meaning of style, in this case in the form of personification, does not reside in its linguistic manifestation, but in the mental representation of some earlier relevant experience stored in our mind. Therefore, most readers will not be too much surprised by this anthropomorphic hawk because in our early childhood we played with toy animals which often had human-like faces, arms or legs, and so on, and we listened to, and later on read ourselves, fables, fairy-tales and allegories, and, not to forget, saw films featuring speaking and thinking animals.

All these memories were stored as highly adaptable images in the knowledge structures of our minds, which in different branches of cognitive science are referred to as schemata, frames, domains, or idealized cognitive models. Anyway, it is adjustable experiential knowledge which enables us to grasp the idea of a hawk vested with human qualities. Actually, this is also the reason why, in cognitive metaphor theory, personification is primarily treated as a type of ontological metaphor, in which non-human creatures are talked about, or more formally are constructed, in terms of human knowledge and experience (Semino 2008: 38, 101). In this case it seems that the battleground of human life is considered to be not unlike that of the hawk.

I will now look at the poem's main formal structure, which appears to be built up by various linguistic patterns of foregrounded regularity. Such patterns were the favourite persuasive tools of the ancient rhetoricians and are traditionally referred to as schemes, which should not be confused with the earlier-mentioned mental schemata. In cognitive psychology it has been hypothesized that the intuitive ease with which we recognize symmetries of all kinds, as well as our inclination to structure things symmetrically, are a projection of our embodied understanding of the symmetries and repetitive patterns of all kinds of categories, that is, mental representations for objects and events in the world around us (Turner 1991: 68–98). Not surprisingly,

this ingrained disposition is also maximally stimulated by symmetric structures in various art forms such as film, music, dance, painting, and, of course,
architecture. Interestingly, in a very recent publication the case has been made
that art-making and art appreciation are an integral part of our evolutionary-
biological heritage (Lindauer 2009: 34).

The earlier-mentioned phenomenon of foregrounding also brings to mind
the theory of figure-ground organization, which is crucial to cognitive linguistics. The figure-ground phenomenon may be defined as our mental faculty
to distinguish a perceived object (the figure or trajector) from its background
(the ground or landmark). For the purpose of this analysis of Ted Hughes's
poem, it is interesting to know that the figure-ground theory also relates to
our cognitive ability to mentally structure or *construe* situations and texts in
all sorts of ways, for instance by selecting or omitting specific circumstances,
by describing participants in various degrees of detail, by providing different
perspectives, and by creating conspicuous stylistic features that stand out
as figures against the background of the rest of the text (Taylor 2002: 11).
In point of fact, it may be concluded that, in addition to all the other cognitive motivations I suggested, or will suggest further on, the theory of figure-
ground organization provides yet another rational explanation for all the foregrounded patterns of sound, syntax, grammar, and diction that captivated my
attention when reading this poem. By the way, our hawk also makes use of the
very same faculty when, in full flight, it targets its prey (the figure) in a large
open field (the ground).

While working on this essay, I read in a recent research report on sensory
physiology, that is, the study of the normal functions of living things, the following information, which may throw an interesting light on the theories of
foregrounding and figure-ground organization. Our eyes collect an enormous
amount of information about our visual environment, but much of it is not
transmitted to the brain. The retina, a very compact network of neurons lin-
ing the inside of our eyes, selects which information is important and which
is not. But the underlying selection principles and the neuronal mechanisms
responsible for this selection are poorly understood. However, there appears
to be one general principle in this process of selection, namely that unpredictable information is transmitted to the brain more readily than predictable
information. This is as it should be, because if we were not able to perceive
the unexpected, evolution would have got rid of us long ago (Kamermans
2009: 5).

The first foregrounded pattern, then, that is likely to grab the reader's
attention is formed by the pronoun *I*, and its related forms *my*, *mine*, and
me, occurring in nearly every line. Having concluded that the anthropomor-
phized hawk is the only speaker in the discourse-world of the poem, we look
for somebody being spoken to. We do so because, prompted by our cognitively

stored real-world experience, we know that written and spoken discourses are, in principle, interpersonal, that is, if there is an *I*, there must be a *you*. Guided by the same experience, we also know that in ordinary conversation, people usually take turns in their roles of speaker and addressee, and as a result become sometimes *I* and sometimes *you*. Obviously, together with this deictic shift, the point of view changes as well. It is therefore quite significant that this turn-taking does not happen in the poem because the *you* does not show up. Prompted by this rhetorical manipulation of the text and our socio-cognitive consciousness, we are drawn into the discourse-world of the poem and intuitively fill this vacuum, though counter-intuitively the perspective remains all the time with the speaker, that is, the hawk, holding us spellbound. The hawk keeps referring to himself rather obsessively by means of the pronouns 'I', 'my', 'me', and 'mine', which actually occur no less than 21 times and stand out as a conspicuous rhetorical pattern, with the first-person 'I' opening the first and the last lines. To top it all, the reader may spot the phonetic pun in the last line: 'My eye has permitted no change' (24).

The second rhetorical pattern that is likely to affect the reader is an extensive series of present tenses. It is a well known fact that in English the present tense as a grammatical category does not always signify present time in the strict sense of the word (Quirk *et al.* 1985: 175). This semantic discrepancy also occurs in the poem, where the present tense forms do not primarily signify present time. Let us look at the hawk's abrupt statements, which give the reader a pretty good idea of what metal our hawk is made of:

  (1) 'I sit in the top of the wood'
  (4) 'Or in sleep rehearse perfect kills and eat'
 (6/7) 'The air's buoyancy and the sun's ray / Are of advantage to me'
  (9) 'My feet are locked upon the rough bark'
(12/13) 'Now I hold Creation in my foot / Or fly up, and revolve it all slowly'
 (14) 'I kill where I please because it is all mine'
 (15) 'There is no sophistry in my body'
 (16) 'My manners are tearing off heads'
(18/19) 'For the one path of my flight is direct / Through the bones of the living'
 (20) 'No arguments assert my right'
 (21) 'The sun is behind me'.

In all these brusque utterances, the dominant present tenses can be construed as signifying a state or a habit without reference to a specific time. The present tenses in the poem often sound like a kind of conceited self-focused commentary, which even seem to imply a rejection of time. It is as if time stands still. There is not really a sense of the passing of time in human terms.

Therefore, there also seems to be no real sense of the past with its potential for personal reflection, repentance, and self-improvement.

As a result, the single past tense in lines 10–11, 'It took the whole of Creation/ To produce my foot, my each feather', appears to denote an event cut off from now. It refers to a one-off action of Creation ending in total submission to the hawk, who triumphantly claims in lines 12–13 'Now I hold Creation in my foot/ Or fly up, and revolve it all slowly –', like the earth revolving around the sun! The reader is made to believe that the hawk has in fact created his own universe.   God-like?

Nor will there be a future time with its potential for change: 'Nothing has changed since I began./ My eye has permitted no change./ I am going to keep things like this' (22–24). At this point, the reader might notice that there is bitter irony involved here. It is even dramatic irony because the hawk's words carry an implied extra meaning that the reader is aware of but he himself is not. If indeed the hawk is 'going to keep things like this', and sees nature as a cycle only servicing himself, that cycle inevitably also includes his own death, which ironically will then be nature's last service to him.

The first line of the poem is the beginning of the third rhetorical pattern in which nature is represented as completely subservient to the hawk. His bold statement 'I sit in the top of the wood' does not only refer to his natural habitat, but may also be read as a metaphor for his position of absolute power. He can even afford to be off his guard and close his eyes! Nature serves merely as a convenient context for him. The high trees offer him comfort (5), the air's buoyancy, that is, the upward current of warm air, keeps him afloat (6), the sun is always behind him, blinding his victim when he attacks (6–7 and 21), and the face of the earth turns itself upwards for his inspection, no doubt revealing at the same time the hiding places of potential prey (8). This graphic account of the submissive attitude of nature, with the hawk being its permanent focus of attention, is reinforced by the obsessive pattern of the earlier-discussed self-directed personal referents *I*, *my*, and *me*. Indeed, it is extremely striking that none of the normally free elements of nature are independent (Cluysenaar 1982: 304).

As to the hawk's relation to other creatures around him, there can be no doubt about his utter ruthlessness. Even in his sleep he practises hunting and swallowing other animals: 'Or in sleep rehearse perfect kills and eat' (4). He kills where and when he pleases because he thinks the existence of other animals as his prey is part of the purpose of Creation: 'I kill where I please because it is all mine' (14). Jokingly one might say that the hawk is a kind of secret agent like 007 having a licence to kill, as it is put bluntly in line 17. Lines 16 to 17, 'My manners are tearing off heads –/ The allotment of death', show that the allotment of death is his prerogative: he, and only he, decides who is going to die. Considering that in the world of humans

ACTUALLY MAKES SENSE

the word *manners* is usually described as 'behaviour that is considered to be polite', readers may feel that the phrase 'My manners' in line 16 in relation to its complement 'tearing off heads' is deliciously ironic, particularly so if the word 'table manners' comes to mind.

From the boastful statements in lines 10 to 13, 'It took the whole of Creation/ To produce my foot, my each feather:/ Now I hold Creation in my foot/ Or fly up, and revolve it all slowly –', it may well be concluded that the hawk thinks he has turned the tables on Creation, in that he now takes the position of strength and advantage that was formerly held by Creation. The reader may well wonder whether this is a classical case of hubris, of excessive self-confidence and pride, which will be followed by its appropriate nemesis, that is, divine revenge and punishment. Perhaps it is significant that the proud boast in line 12, 'Now I hold Creation in my foot', occurs conspicuously right in the middle of the poem.

The fourth rhetorical pattern stands out because of its contrasting lexical make-up. Native speakers of English intuitively know that their language has almost a double lexicon, in which, ever since the Norman Conquest in 1066, words from the original Germanic/Anglo-Saxon word-stock are often paired with words from Norman French, a Latinate language spoken by the power elite after the invasion of England. Latinate words are generally associated with greater formality, abstraction, and emotional neutrality, whereas English words of Anglo-Saxon origin are generally associated with things which are fundamental, familiar, concrete, or emotional in our lives. Taking this distinction into account, it is remarkable that within his relatively short monologue, the hawk uses such a high proportion of Latinate words. Examples include 'inaction' (2), 'falsifying' (2), 'rehearse' (4), 'perfect' (4), 'convenience' (5), 'buoyancy' (6), 'advantage' (7), 'inspection' (8), 'Creation' (10) and (12), 'revolve' (13), 'allotment' (17), 'arguments' (20), 'assert' (20), 'permitted' (23), and a few others. This Latinate affectation makes the style of the hawk's speech cold, self-possessed, distanced and abstract. Notice in this connection also the pattern of negatives: 'no falsifying dream' (2), 'There is no sophistry in my body' (15), 'No arguments assert my right' (20), 'Nothing has changed since I began' (22), and 'My eye has permitted no change' (23). These negative phrases appear to reinforce the complete domination that the hawk maintains.

On the other hand, there are the no-nonsense words of Anglo-Saxon stock, which the hawk prefers with regard to his weaponry, plumage and predatory killings: 'my hooked head and hooked feet' (3), 'kills and eat' (4), 'My feet are locked upon the rough bark' (9), 'my foot, my each feather' (11), 'body' (15), 'tearing off heads' (15), 'death' (17), 'the one path of my flight' (18), 'through the bones of the living' (19), 'my right' (20), and the ominous, all-out Anglo-Saxon, statement in the last line: 'I am going to keep things like this' (24).

Considering his varied vocabulary, we may perhaps conclude that there is more than one side to the hawk's character. It is intriguing that both words in the poem's title are of Germanic, that is, Anglo-Saxon stock. Dutch speakers will recognize in them the words 'havik' and 'rusten'. In his monologue, the hawk prefers the Latinate 'inaction' to 'roosting'. As I said earlier, the title is the only locus where the reader might sense the presence of the poet's persona.

Lastly, we have to look at the poem's versification, that is, its metre, its sound, and its syntactic structure, which may well reinforce the rhetorical patterns we have discussed just now. The verse pattern is regular (six verses of four lines), though the rhyme and metre are free (three to six stresses and six to eleven syllables per line), which only befits a bird of prey on the wing. Readers scanning the poem's metre will find, or rather hear, that at the end of several lines there are two successive heavy stresses, which appear to reinforce the sense. For example: 'eyes closed' (1), 'hooked feet' (3), 'high trees' (5), 'sun's ray' (6), 'rough bark' (9), 'all mine' (14), and 'no change' (23).

Most verse lines are made up of relatively short sentences reinforcing the hawk's syntax of unshakeable conviction, culminating in the last stanza in which each of the four lines is made up of one full sentence so that metre and syntax run parallel. Furthermore, there are relatively few instances of enjambment or run-on lines, in which the syntax goes beyond the metrical boundary at the end of the line. I have marked these with an arrow in lines 2, 6, 10, 12, 16 and 18. It is at these places that the effects of the interplay between syntax and metre may have a marked semantic impact. We might say that in the case of enjambment, readers get two conflicting prompts: the metrical line-boundary tells them to pause, be it ever so shortly, while the unfinished syntax pulls them into the next line. Therefore, however brief it may be, the resulting wavering is bound to cause some tension, which, on the one hand, heightens our awareness of the last word in the run-on line and, on the other, causes us to wonder about the first word in the next line. Any interpretation of enjambment is highly speculative, but I think that poetry readers cannot resist having a try. Thus, the enjambment or leap from line 2 to 3 seems to emphasize that the hawk does not allow any ambivalent thought to come between his killer instinct and his deadly weapons. Perhaps the hawk is mocking our squeamishness or human conscience in general, which is sup-posed to distinguish us from the beasts. The enjambment in line 6 may be felt to emphasize the total subservience of nature to the hawk's existential needs. Perhaps the rush of enjambments in lines 10, 12 and 16, of which those in lines 12 and 16 even run over the verse boundaries, are perhaps a reflection of the hawk's fierce excitement about having gained control over Creation (Cluysenaar 1982: 305). Finally, the enjambment in line 18 appears to catch the reader unprepared for the horrible image in the next line: 'through the bones of the living'.

[handwritten annotation: Subordinate clause = Subordinating conjunction or relative pronoun + subject + verb. Not a complete thought]

While still on the matter of syntax, it may strike the reader that there are only three subordinate clauses: 'where I please' (14), 'because it is all mine' (14), and 'since I began' (22). Particularly in relation to the hawk's fierce statement 'No arguments assert my right' (20), these sub-clauses must have escaped from the hawk's 'hooked head' unintentionally because they seem to come near to a grudging argumentation for his absolute authority (ibid.).

My attempt at a stylistic analysis cannot do justice, of course, to a poem which has gained great admiration for its verbal artistry, and justly so, I think. At the same time it has aroused considerable controversy between two fundamentally different readings. Because this dispute is spread across a great many books and articles, it is impossible to discuss all its ins and outs within the scope of this essay. Therefore, I must limit myself to a few heavily summarized points ranging from the allegation that the hawk's state of mind is that of a ruthless dictator to the enlightened point of view that it is the hawk's natural function that defines his violent nature.

First, some points of adverse criticism:

1. Because the absurdity of this single-minded concern with violence is not challenged from within the poem, the consciousness of violence comes to us unmediated (Lucas 1986: 193–7).
2. It is a disturbing thought that Hughes appears to recommend the hawk's violent behaviour to his human readers (Williams 1985: 68–71).
3. The whole world in the poem is defined in ruthlessly egocentric terms (Smith 1982: 155–69).

Then a moderate view:

4. The hawk's natural function defines its nature, and the poem reveals it glorying in what it is. The crucial question is: are we, too, invited to glory in what it is? Critics have taken this as the essential meaning of the poem, extending it to include a glorification of totalitarianism (Walder 1987: 39–41).

[handwritten annotation: the Hawk = top of hierarchy]

And finally, the view that the violence is in the mind of the reader:

[handwritten annotation: So much wit can't cope OMG.]

5. The wit of the poem is that no hawk has the self-realization here described. Only human beings have this moral awareness of their place in the world and their actions. The hawk does not need to be absolved from behaving as it must (Spurr 1997: 283–90).

Considering this wide and perhaps even unbridgeable gap between these two literary critical views, the question arises whether stylistics can help readers, especially student readers, in taking up an academically defensible stance in this matter. I really think it can, and for the following reasons. But first I wish to make the obvious point that the way in which stylistics and literary criticism approach a literary text exemplifies a particular perspective, namely a perspective on the study of literature. Thus, very generally speaking, literary criticism directs attention to the larger-scale significance of what is represented by a product of verbal art. On the other hand, stylistics tends to focus on how this significance can be related to specific features of language, that is, to the linguistic texture of a literary work. Following this argument, I think the literary critical and stylistic perspectives are complementary, or perhaps the poles of a dialectical process. Obviously, this complementarity does not provide the means of arriving at a definitive interpretation, which, of course, does not exist anyway. But a stylistic analysis does enable readers, especially student readers, to obtain textual evidence for a particular literary critical view of a poem and, not least, to heighten their own sense of what a literary text means to themselves (Rubik and Widdowson 2000: 6). In sum, stylistics brings literary critical appreciation into clearer focus.

CHAPTER 6

'The Unprofessionals': Syntactic Iconicity and Reader Interpretation in Contemporary Poems

LESLEY JEFFRIES

1. Introduction

In my first attempts to apply linguistic description to poems (see, for example, Jeffries 1993), I noticed that something interesting seemed to be happening in relation to their syntax. Whilst some poetic movements and individuals in the twentieth century (e.g. the L-A-N-G-U-A-G-E poets) used extremely deviant and thus clearly foregrounded syntax, to reflect their concerns and the themes of their times, others (e.g. Larkin, Hughes) seemed on the surface to be using fairly standard sentence and clause structure which made the reading process relatively straightforward and did not cause obvious resistance amongst readers. Nevertheless, these more approachable poets appeared to be using syntax in subtle and possibly iconic ways. It is important to note here that I am using the word 'iconic' in its semiotic or linguistic sense. That is, I am referring to the occurrence of linguistic forms which more or less *directly* reflect their meaning and which have been seen as the exception, rather than the rule, by modern linguistics. Most typically, this iconicity is illustrated at the phonological level by words which are onomatopoeic ('baa', 'moo', and so on), though in this chapter I am referring to the direct representation of meaning in syntactic structure rather than phonology. In the next section, I will link my observations to some of the most relevant recent linguistic work on iconicity, which addresses the question of degrees of directness, among other things. Having initially noticed this phenomenon, I began to realize

95

THIS SHIT MAKES MORE SENSE! Gooood.

that it might link into a level of understanding and appreciation which was, perhaps perversely, more emotionally immediate and less cerebral than the explicit syntactic challenges of, for example, some modernist or avant-garde writers. I say _perversely_ because I believe that many practitioners of syntactic deviation in poetry have used this technique with the intention of getting directly to emotion, by-passing what they see as the stale conventions of the language. I believe it works exactly the other way round.

At the risk of repeating myself, I would like to introduce this subject by returning to an example of this phenomenon that I first noticed in a poem called 'Broadcast' by Philip Larkin (see Jeffries 1993 for a fuller analysis of this poem). The poem recounts a radio broadcast of a concert, which in those days would have been aired _live_. The poet describes the sounds of the audience settling into their seats, getting up again as the National Anthem, 'The Queen', is played, and having to sit back down again afterwards. Then, the audience's anticipation of the music starting is interrupted again, this time by the tuning up of the instruments on stage. Here are the opening lines:

Giant whispering and coughing from
Vast Sunday-full and organ-frowned-on spaces
Precede a sudden scuttle on the drum,
'The Queen', and huge resettling. Then begins
A snivel on the violins:

What struck me here was that the narrator's anticipation and his frustration with all the fuss of people settling in their seats before the concert begins is mirrored in the syntax. It turns out later that he isn't really impressed by the music itself, but wants to use the broadcast to think about his lover who he knows is in the audience. His irritation at the pre-concert noises, then, becomes linked with his desire to settle down and think of her. The first sentence lasts for almost four lines, and we only get to the predicator (verb) of the main clause, 'precede', at the beginning of the third line. Thus, the first two lines consist of one very long grammatical subject, which for English speakers is an uncomfortable length. Since we normally expect to find reference to given information (i.e., information that is already shared) in subject position, and thus arrive fairly quickly at the main verb-phrase, any delay in doing so may produce a sense of frustration or irritation directly in the reader/hearer of the sentence. I argued then, and still maintain, that this entirely natural reaction to an unusual if not excessively deviant sentence structure may – and often does – directly correspond to the emotions being evoked in the content of the poem. This is the phenomenon that I have been labelling _syntactic iconicity_.

Until recently, I had not taken this observation much further, though I have collected very many examples of similar syntactic effects in poems that I believe work in similar ways. However, in working on the question of reader-involvement in poems (see, for example, Jeffries 2001, 2008), I became more interested in how syntactic iconicity operates in relation to the reading process, rather than simply seeing it as just another type of foregrounded feature like alliteration or unusual collocation. In the rest of this chapter I will discuss the concept of iconicity in language, and review some of the writing on this topic. This will be followed by a detailed analysis of a single poem, 'The Unprofessionals' by U. A. Fanthorpe, which will enable us to explore the kind of syntactic iconicity introduced above. Finally, I will draw some tentative conclusions about the cognitive aspects of this phenomenon.

2. Iconicity

The amount of similarity between the symbol + the idea being portrayed. Onomatopeias are iconic.

Although much of modern linguistics, particularly from Saussure onwards, has been predicated on the notion that the linguistic sign has an arbitrary connection to its referent(s), the existence of iconicity in language has always been recognized minimally in the form of onomatopoeia and sound-symbolism more generally, and has recently been studied extensively as a property of language as a whole, including possible universal iconic features. Much of the impetus for this work has come from literary studies, and particularly from those working in this field from countries where English is not the dominant language, who often do not see a gap between literary and linguistic approaches to text. As Müller (1999: 394) says:

> The study of iconicity provides an ideal field of research for linguists and literary critics alike and may thus help to bridge the gulf between the two disciplines which has steadily widened in the course of the twentieth century.

Those working in this field have drawn distinctions between iconicity which has a direct link to referents, in some way straightforwardly mimetic of the 'real world', and iconicity which is more indirect in its linking to referents. These have been labelled *imagic* and *diagrammatic* iconicity respectively, initially by Peirce (1960) and Jakobson (Jakobson and Halle 1956; Jakobson 1963) and later by Haiman (1985b), amongst others. Fischer explains:

> ... only in imagic iconicity, is there a straight iconic link between the verbal sign and the image or object (the 'signans' and the 'signatum'), as for instance in onomatopoeia. Diagrammatic iconicity is more like a topographic map, where the relation between objects or concepts in the real world (as we see it) can be deduced from the relations indicated on the map ... (1999: 346)

If we think in terms of phonology, then, the fact that speech sounds can (directly) mimic other sounds such as whistles (through fricative consonants), high pitches (through close vowels) or gunshots (through plosive consonants) would be seen as *imagic*, since there is a direct correlation between the sign and its referent. Sound-symbolism, such as the use of close vowels to signify small size and open vowels to signify large size, would then be *diagrammatic*, since there is a correlation, but not a direct mimesis.

However, there is not an absolute distinction between these two kinds of iconicity, as Fischer explains:

> But even within diagrammatic iconicity, there are differences in terms of concreteness. It is interesting to observe, for instance, when Max Nänny applies the various types of diagrammatic iconicity distinguished by Haiman (1980) to poetry, that the use made of it there is more concrete than the examples that Haiman gives from the more conventional syntax of everyday speech. (ibid.)

It seems, therefore, that there is at least a single-dimension cline between directly iconic and less concretely iconic signs in language. It is possible, too, that this gradation falls away in more than one direction, as we will see when we discuss the kind of syntactic iconicity observed in poetry, and specifically in 'The Unprofessionals'. Notice that those concerned with iconicity make no qualitative distinction in general between the iconicity of literary works and the language more generally. Müller (1999: 393–4), for example, makes the explicit assumption that literary language works in much the same way as other language:

> Now if iconicity is always a latent possibility of aesthetic or poetic language and, further, if we take it for granted that aesthetic or poetic language exploits, develops and heightens possibilities already inherent in ordinary, non-poetic discourse, the massive presence of iconic forms of expression in literature can be regarded as lending support to the theory of the iconic potential of language in general.

This assumption is one that is now taken for granted in stylistics, which treats all text processing by readers as essentially the same. This will be an important point in the analysis of iconicity later in this chapter, since I want to argue that iconicity in poetry of the kind I am interested in is both dependent on and deviant from the norms of English.

For now, let us consider some of the iconicity that has been proposed at the syntactic level of language. One of the more influential writers on this topic in recent years has been Haiman, who is among those postulating a universal link between the tendency for languages to order their syntax in SVO order,

and the centrality of the action in linking the participants in any process. Here is an explanation of this idea from Conradie (2001: 230):

> Given that entities/things and actions/activities are conceived of as a basic distinction in perception, two universal but complementary strategies of sentence construction come to mind as possible ways of dealing with the relationship between them: (i) a classificatory strategy of grouping together elements similar in status, viz. the entities vs the action, as would be exemplified by SO–V or V–SO structures, and (ii) an activity-based strategy with the action in the centre (not only figuratively, but also literally) and entities relegated to the periphery. Though it is to be expected that any universal trait of language is iconically motivated in some sense, the present claim in regard to iconicity does not apply to the former or other conceivable strategies, but only to the latter, i.e. the relation between SVO structures and activity.

This relation between the SVO order and a proposed arrangement of process/action and participants is part of the argument some put forward for a 'natural' iconicity which reflects the point-of-view of the producer, rather than an objective link to something in the real world. Thus, it is argued, human beings perceive the events that they see unfold as processes linking the various participants and circumstances, with the result that it seems most natural to have the verb in the *middle* of a clause, linking the subject with the object or other participants. Note here that the use of point-of-view refers to the natural, and possibly universal, perceptions of any speaker or writer in any (SVO) language. However, in the case of many specific texts, including literary ones, there is also the potential to exploit this underlying (possibly universal but at least generalized) point-of-view and present a *specific* point-of-view of a character, the narrator or the author. I will return to this point later, but here we should note that even early semiotics (as put forward by Peirce 1960 and others) never really claimed that linguistic signs linked to any *objective* reality; rather, the whole of linguistic signification, from the arbitrary to the iconic, is always a question of point-of-view. Nöth (2001: 20) explains:

> The object of a sign, according to Peirce, is no object of an external reality, no object that exists independently of the sign. Peirce says nothing about the 'reality' of this object at all and describes it as something 'perceptible, or only imaginable or even unimaginable in one sense' (CP 2.230). He even goes so far as to speculate that 'perhaps the Object is altogether fictive' (CP 8.314).

So, iconicity in language is the direct (imagic) or indirect (diagrammatic) or even mediated (metaphoric) representation of perceived objects, events, actions, and processes. If we think in terms of the more concrete (direct) end of this spectrum being a little like looking at a film of a person, then the experience is similar to actually seeing this person, even though it is a two-dimensional image which cannot interact with us, rather than the three-dimensional interactive image we see if we actually encounter her/him. At the other extreme, but still within the non-arbitrary range, we have something like the stylized map of the London Underground, which represents the relationship between stations in terms of their links but has no direct relationship to distance, as anyone who has tried walking overground using a Tube map in London will testify! Some of the stations that look close together on the map are actually very far apart indeed. So, the Tube map is like a code, but it is not completely arbitrary. We can work out routes in the real world from the logic of the system, without being able to directly translate from the map to the lines themselves.

How can we see the iconicity of syntax in relation to this range of iconicity in visual phenomena? We may, perhaps, assume that any direct connections between language and the bodily senses are at the concrete end of the spectrum. Since language cannot be smelt or tasted, and only in relatively rare cases (including of course braille) can it be felt, we are left with the sound and the look of language as the main possibilities for imagic iconicity. These bring us back to the classic case of onomatopoeia in the case of sound, and perhaps concrete poetry, where the layout and font can be made to look like the meaning, in the case of the written language (see Short 1999 for discussion of this phenomenon). As we saw earlier, one step away from direct iconicity might be the sound-symbolism which relies on some kind of indirect relationship, such as the relation between pitch of vowels and size, or the use of fonts in emails to SHOUT at your addressee. Once we move to syntax and higher-level structures, it is the linearity of language which leads us to the most direct kind of syntactic iconicity. Thus it is the linear form of language which can most directly be mapped onto the (perceived) world either in space or in time. Sentences and sequences of sentences often tend to address events and process in the order they happened, leading to the common view that chronology is the default order of a narrative and that this is direct (imagic) iconicity. Similarly, it would be possible for the linearity of a sentence or sequence of sentences to represent relationships in space, though as space is multi-dimensional and time is more clearly experienced as linear, time tends to take precedence in linking to structure.

Whilst this kind of link between syntax or discourse structure and the world may *seem* to be direct, we are reminded by various researchers that the link is between the linguistic form and the norms of human cognition and perception, rather than being simplistically a mirror to reality. Here is

Müller (2001: 305) on this subject:

> What the linguistic structure imitates is not external reality, but a subjective perception or, rather, conception of reality, a mental structure which is related to external reality but does not merely imitate or copy it. Rhetorical features, for instance, schemes like asyndeton and climax or different forms of word-order, are structuring and ordering devices, which point to the structure and activity of the mind and to cognitive and epistemological processes. The categories, which Earl Anderson relates to syntactic 'iconisms' – 'chronology, hierarchy, preference, direction, length or duration, and complexity versus simplicity' (Anderson 1998: 265) – belong to the sphere of the mind or consciousness and not to that of external reality.

This argument appears to take iconicity beyond the purely physical and into the emotional and cognitive field. Directly evoking emotion, as opposed to evoking sensory effects in the visual or auditory domains, seems nevertheless to retain something of the more concrete, imagic form of iconicity since no key is required to unlock the iconicity. However, since it is presented in the quotation above as a version of universal iconicity, which by its nature will be backgrounded, it is being presented as not choice-based and therefore can have no particular stylistic effect. Nevertheless, there do appear to be syntactic choices, in English at least, whereby if we take the basis of syntax and discourse construction to be a case of working with the grain of natural iconicity, authors can produce otherwise syntactically acceptable texts which foreground deviation from this iconic norm. This property of text construction points to what could be seen as a secondary kind of iconicity, producing an iconic reaction in readers as a result of deviating from universal iconicity and leading to effects that I will discuss in relation to the poem in the next section.

Some scholars of rhetoric have argued that there is a relation between the tropes and schemes of rhetoric on the one hand and natural iconicity on the other. Here, Müller (2001: 308) makes this point:

> Citing evidence from the entire tradition of rhetoric, Brian Vickers argues that in writing 'schemes and tropes are basically stylizations or records of man's natural emotional behaviour as expressed in language' (Vickers 1970: 105). Thus rhetorical figures of omission, unusual word order or repetition are held to be imitative of actual disturbances of language in emotional contexts, which, in turn, reflect feelings and emotional states such as anger, grief, indignation or consternation.

This kind of argument is often made, not just in relation to rhetorical figures, but also in relation to the style, for example, of Modernist writing, where the disintegration of syntax was seen as a direct reflection of the apocalyptic views often taken in the literature of the early twentieth century (see Sherry 2004 for a discussion of this subject). What I want to argue here goes beyond the simple reflection of the subject matter of a text in its syntax. I would make the case that the reader is invited to directly experience some of the meaning of the text, triggered by the structures of the text. This is achieved most readily when there is some kind of foregrounding, as explained by Müller (2001: 319):

> In this as in many other cases in rhetorical speech it is just the deviation from the iconic norm which manifests iconicity most conspicuously. This is iconicity, to be sure, on a level different from the mere miming of external reality. It is non-objective or, to use Tabakowska's term once more, 'experiential iconicity'.

Though Müller seems to be arguing that iconicity is foregrounded by being deviant, this foregrounding is normally still within the bounds of syntactic acceptability (unlike some of the more radical syntactic deviation I have mentioned above). Thus, although the reader may be marginally aware of things not being quite 'normal', this will be less salient than, say, an invented word or a string of alliterative words. We will return to the question of salience later. What is clear, from those approaching iconicity from the viewpoint of rhetoric, is that some rhetorical figures are seen as naturally iconic and others seem to be deviant, and thus foregrounded, to achieve their effect.

The closest example I have found to my own observations is from Müller (2001: 406), who describes in detail the way in which Wilkie Collins manages to produce suspense in his most famous novel, *The Woman in White*. The commentary is long, and the following begins about halfway through:

> It is only then that the grammatically required temporal clause is reached which resolves the syntactic and semantic suspense of the construction. But even then Collins uses protracting syntactic devices, an adverbial phrase and a passive construction which shifts the agent of the action to a prepositional phrase: 'when, in one moment, every drop of blood in my body was brought to a stop by the touch of a hand ...'. But, owing to Collins' point-of-view technique, even now the entire event is not yet brought into focus. The following one-sentence paragraph describes the protagonist's physical reaction to the event, before the whole situation is depicted in the last of the quoted sentences, yet again not without the use of suspense-increasing syntactic devices (inversion of the word order, the use of adverbial elements, parenthesis): 'There [...] stood the figure of a solitary Woman ...'. This is indeed a supreme example of the art of creating suspense. The syntax with its many

retarding, i.e. suspense-heightening devices, makes the passage examined a suspense plot in miniature, an analogue to the novel's overall structure with its step-by-step revelation of the central mystery.

Interestingly, the commentary itself acquires something of the same technique of slow revelation as it describes each clause and delaying tactic that is used to produce a sense of anticipation in the reader. What Nöth (2001) does not do, however, is to take the reader's perspective in this description. If he had done so, he would have used this commentary to explain how the reader is drawn into the viewpoint of the narrator and how s/he therefore feels some of the anticipation directly, as a result of the syntactic suspense. It is this direct experience of the reader which interests me here, and which I would argue cuts across some of the distinctions made by other researchers into iconicity.

3. Reading poems

In order to explore the phenomenon of syntactic iconicity a little further, this chapter will focus on the style of a single poem by U. A. Fanthorpe called 'The Unprofessionals'. In it, she describes people (probably relatives and friends) who arrive at your house when something awful happens, and the things they do. Here is the whole poem for you to read before I continue:

The Unprofessionals

When the worst thing happens,
That uproots the future,
That you must live for every hour of your future,

They come,
Unorganized, inarticulate, unprofessional;

They come sheepishly, sit with you, holding hands,
From tea to tea, from Anadin to Valium,
Sleeping on put-you-ups, answering the phone,
Coming in shifts, spontaneously,

Talking sometimes,
About wallflowers, and fishing, and why
Dealing with Kleenex and kettles,
Doing the washing up and the shopping,

Like civilians in a shelter, under bombardment,
Holding hands and sitting it out

Through the immortality of all the seconds,
Until the blunting of time.

(U. A. Fanthorpe, 1995)

When I introduced this poem to second-year undergraduates studying stylistics, I was surprised by their almost unanimous view that the poet (or narrator) did not approve of the 'unprofessionals', since I had personally responded to it as a very *affectionate* account of the support that people give each other when they are in trouble. This led me to wonder whether there was a right answer, and if so, whether it was me or my students that was/were correct. The question of what constitutes a right answer, of course, is contentious and does not indicate a return to the notion of the supremacy of some kind of intentional authorial meaning. However, the orthodoxy that holds sway in some fields of literary theory, which states that meaning is infinitely open and fluid and depends almost entirely on the reader, is also an extreme which is called into question by text analysts, including many stylisticians. Though there is certainly a level at which readers may well take away *different* interpretative impressions from a text, particularly a poem, linguists would also argue that the text itself does close off *some* options, and only the most transgressive or inexperienced readers will be able to read certain meanings into texts. There are at least three possible answers, then, to the problem that my students posed for me in class. Firstly, my interpretation of 'The Unprofessionals' may have been based on textual cues which my students missed. Secondly, they (and I) may have been reacting to an unambiguous narrative from their (my) own experiential perspective. Finally, there may be textual cues to *both* interpretations, which we reacted to differently *because of* our age, experience or background. This question will be revisited later, but it may be worth noting here that other readers of my age and similar background have reacted in the same way as me, which may seem on first sight to favour the final option presented above.

Before I address this question by exploring the syntactic iconicity in the poem, let us consider the other, more commonly noted, stylistic features of this poem. I will concentrate on those features which might be described as the 'traditional' stylistic features, pointing out those which are in some sense foregrounded either by deviation or by parallelism at the different linguistic levels.

Fanthorpe is not generally a poet to exploit the musicality of language. She doesn't depend on strict form and doesn't use rhyme or half-rhyme in any amount. For this reason, where there *are* moments of phonological patterning, such as consonance (alliteration), they are foregrounded. So, line 12's 'Kleenex and kettles' stands out because the two words beginning with the velar plosive /k/ are noticeable, not only because there are two of them, but also because their context is populated with the softer-sounding fricatives (e.g. /f/, /s/) and semi-vowels (e.g. /w/) than with plosives. Whilst this is the kind of feature that makes a poem pleasant to read, and it may possibly be argued that the alliteration and the contrasting context is meaningful in some way, there is nothing in the phonology of this poem that seems to inform our quest for the deeper interpretation.

Similarly, Fanthorpe does not seem to exploit the possibilities of morphology (word formation) very often and therefore, when she does it is more prominently foregrounded than in poets who use inventive morphology more frequently (e.g. Hopkins). The main morphological effect in this poem is the invented noun, the 'Unprofessionals' of the title, which will be discussed in detail below. Line 5 is also morphologically foregrounded with three adjectives being listed, each of which has a negative prefix ('Unorganized, inarticulate, unprofessional'). There is a phonological effect here too, of course, since the profusion of syllables (four in the first and five in the second and third) adds to the impression of fussiness of these people who have arrived, perhaps chaotically in the middle of the loneliness of the person in crisis. One could argue, perhaps, that these syllables iconically reflect the empty chatter of the people who arrive with no specific purpose other than to be of support. The effect of the morphological negation lends some support to the interpretation of my students in thinking that these people are not entirely welcome, hopeless as they seem to be. I will argue later that the syntax of this poem contradicts the negative morphology, and that perhaps the ambivalence that results for the reader is one of the strengths of this as a poetic experience.

Semantically, there are a number of features in the poem which depend on lexis (word choice, word combination, and so on) in this poem. These include, for example, the metaphor which is created in line 2 by combining the verb 'uproots' with an abstract object ('the future'), though it normally requires a concrete, animate (but not animal) object (uproot the tree, the shrub, and so on). This type of collocational feature is sometimes described as breaking the 'selectional restrictions' of the verb. The term *selectional restrictions* was created by generative grammarians to capture what they saw as a generalized semantic restriction on the combining potential of lexical items. Thus, their version of the dictionary attached to a grammar would list alongside words (particularly, but not only verbs) any restrictions of this kind (e.g. 'spill' has to be used with a liquid). Metaphors which depend in this way on breaking the normal rules of lexical combination are foregrounded and may cause the reader to pause and take in the effect of, in this case, comparing the future with a tree. Another semantic effect in the poem is found in the use of nouns from very different semantic fields in the list of topics that are discussed by the visitors ('wallflowers and fishing and why'). The listing of such different items, and in particular the inclusion of the significant third item, which is the question on everyone's mind, demonstrates the changing topic of the conversation, skirting around, and finally settling on, the big question of why this crisis has happened.

Comprehensive stylistic analysis is important, because a poem works as a whole and stylistic features will inevitably form part of the experience of the reader in processing this poem. Many poetic effects are produced by a combination of features from different linguistic levels. Thus, the effect of the line 'From tea to tea, from Anadin to Valium' depends on a range of features, including the following:

- the semantico-syntactic expectation that the frame *from X to Y* expects time nominals, either repeated (e.g. 'time to time') or contrasted (e.g. 'morning to night');
- the musical effect of the assonance of front open vowel /æ/ in 'Anadin' and 'Valium' and its contrast with the /i:/ of 'tea to tea';
- the consonance of the nasals in 'A**n**adi**n**' and 'Valiu**m**';
- the construction of unconventional opposites ('Anadin' and 'Valium') in this frame, echoing the usual collocations of morning and night;
- the underlining of this created opposition sense relation by the almost alphabetical A to V (A to Z) of the brand names of the drugs taken to get up in the morning and go to sleep at night.

The agony of this crisis for the unnamed protagonist (hidden behind the 'you' of the opening line) is reflected in many of these features, even, possibly in the range of vowels and the nasality of the consonants which might be argued to reflect the various sounds of crying. What none of these features does, however, is to throw any light upon the central question of the poem: what does the poet (what should the reader) think of the 'unprofessionals'?

Another typically foregrounded feature is found in line 9 ('Coming in shifts, spontaneously') where the noun 'shifts' semantically includes notions of organization and cooperation, and therefore clashes with the adverb 'spontaneously' because the latter usually collocates with individual and unforeseen activities rather than intrinsically organized and group-based activities like taking on shifts. The comma between the main part of the clause and the adverb almost seems to embody the clash between these two – the organized versus the impulsive – and creates one of the smaller, localized riddles of the poem which the reader is forced to work out. This creation of textual 'problems' which cause the reader to make some effort of understanding is a common result of many lexical and syntactic features in contemporary poems. In this case, responding to the apparent semantic mismatch may cause the reader to think along one or both of the following lines:

- the 'unprofessionals' have indeed organized themselves into shifts to make sure that the person in trouble is not left alone for too long, but they are

THINK LIKE THIS! ↓

pretending that they have arrived spontaneously, to save that person from
feeling too indebted;
- the 'unprofessionals' do in fact arrive at different times from each other,
  which looks as though they have arranged themselves in shifts, but in fact
  this is an accident which could be the result of the concern and care that
  these people are taking, which means they are aware of other likely visitors
  and time their own visits accordingly.

Either or both of these would be appropriate in the context, and each makes
sense of the apparent clash of semantics. Both of them produce a richer
meaning than either 'shifts' or 'spontaneously' would have done in isolation,
since they produce the impression that the person in crisis is attempting to
understand what seems like a strange and alien world, and the people visiting
are, in either scenario, making an effort to be considerate. This example *is*
one that seems to favour my initial argument that the poem is an affectionate appreciation of the unprofessionals' visits. I will return to the question
of individual responses to the poem in the final section, but here it is worth
noting that stylistic analysis of this kind can help readers reach a consensus
about the major interpretative meanings of a poem, even where the text leaves
some problems to be solved.

Perhaps the most foregrounded, and thus the most striking, feature of
the poem is in the title, in the neologism (invented word) 'unprofessionals'.
Whilst there exists an established negated adjective in English, 'unprofessional', there is not, to my knowledge, an equivalent negated countable *noun*
except in this poem. One of the possible reasons for the differing reactions of
myself and my students on reading this poem could be traced to the two different ways of reading this invented word, depending on the order in which
the bound morphemes are added. These options can be represented diagram-
matically in the following way:

- professional (aj) → unprofessional (aj) → unprofessional (n) + {Plural} =
  unprofessionals
- professional (aj) → professional (n) → unprofessional (n) + {Plural} =
  unprofessionals

The first option reads the word as a noun derived from the (already derived)
adjective, 'unprofessional'. This would result in the assessment of these people in negative terms, because the adjective is certainly semantically negative
in its evaluation. A search of the collocates of 'unprofessional' in the British
National Corpus yields only one significantly common collocate, which is
'conduct': thus 'unprofessional conduct'. The referents thus seem to be people who embody the quality of being not very good, and possibly carelessly

slack, in their professional capacity. Although this may well be the *first* thing that springs to mind when encountering the noun, it seems less appropriate to the context than the other possible meaning of the word, which could be seen as a negation of the noun, 'professional', rather than a nominalization of the (already negated) adjective. Note that both understandings of the resulting countable noun originate from the adjective 'professional', so it is the *order* of addition of the morphemes that creates the different meanings. The subtle difference is that these people are then seen less negatively as those visitors to a person in crisis who are not the professionals, but others. Thus, we may surmise, they are not the doctors, social workers, police officers, or whoever is officially involved in the crisis itself, but the friends, family, and neighbours who do not have a specific job to do, but who turn up nonetheless. Note that there is still scope for being irritated by them when they seem not to know how to behave ('Unorganized, inarticulate, unprofessional') and I will return to this issue later, but the important issue here is to recognize that they are being defined by the word *unprofessionals* in the title not as incompetent people, but as non-professional people. This may even lend them a positive air, the professionals so often in such situations being seen as somewhat cold as a result of their smooth professionalism. In reading the poem aloud, one might even make a slight difference in the pronunciation of the word to recognize this difference, with the *un-* morpheme given more emphasis than would be normal, to foreground its effect as the negator of the noun and indicate that it was the last morpheme to be added.

Though there are other aspects of the style of this poem which a literary appreciation may want to take into account, I am concentrating here on those aspects which most clearly link to the interpretative issues that the poem raises. In the remainder of this chapter, I will consider the syntactic aspects of its style which appear to exemplify very well the phenomenon that I call syntactic iconicity.

4. Syntactic deviation and foregrounding

The first thing to note about this phenomenon is that it depends, as many stylistic features do, on a notion of the linguistically *normal*. Thus, there is a range of ways in which the syntax of a poem in English can deviate from the normal English clause and sentence structure; from subtle differences of emphasis to complete 'ungrammaticality'. This range, I would suggest, also represents the range of reactions that an English speaker will feel on encountering deviant syntax of different types. Thus, a slightly over-length noun-phrase in subject position might produce a subtle and probably subconscious effect of waiting (for the verb to appear) whereas a completely odd word-order lacking usual agreements (e.g. between number or person in subject and verb) might produce a more adverse reaction of frustration. Most of the syntactic deviation I will explore here is not at the extreme verging on ungrammaticality and may well not be noted by readers, except subconsciously. The lack of *conscious* awareness of syntactic deviation, though, does not necessarily mean that these features are not foregrounded. Without particular training in grammatical analysis, speakers and readers may react less consciously to such features, but I would argue that they remain affected by such deviation in the same way as they are by more obvious stylistic features such as alliteration or unusual collocation.

Much early work on stylistics emphasized the importance of choice in appreciating the effects of textual features. This may sound as though a stylistic feature is in a sense separate from its meaning, and able to be appreciated purely linguistically, in contrast with the other options that the author may have had for saying essentially the *same* thing. Of course, there is a question in the case of poetry in particular (and the more poetic of prose literature in general) whether there *really* is a choice, since the language of a poem is often seen as being an intrinsic part of the message itself. So, the question of linguistic choice is not always separate from the question of effect or literary interpretation, but is simply a device that stylistics uses to demonstrate that the style of a literary (or other) text is at least partly the source of its meaning and effect.

The syntactic iconicity that I wish to investigate in 'The Unprofessionals', then, may be ascribed to a particular set of choices that writers have to make when constructing clauses and sentences. This is the question of how to structure the information within the confines of English syntax. The basic issues relating to information and clause structure can be summarized as follows:

1. English information structure is connected to clause structure;
2. The predicator (verbal element) is pivotal to the sense of the clause;
3. Earlier clause elements normally contain given information;
4. Later clause elements normally contain new information;
5. There is therefore normally a correlation between given information and short clause elements, and between new information and longer clause elements;
6. If default clause structure is used, this means that grammatical subjects will be shorter on the whole than objects and complements;
7. Optional adverbials (adjuncts, disjuncts, and so on) will occur more readily towards the end of a clause, particularly if they are lengthy;
8. The predicator (verbal element) will occur relatively early in the clause;
9. Deviations from default syntax (such as fronting, passivization, cleft structures) will tend to uphold the principles of information structure as listed in 1–7.

The stylistic assumption, given the principles above, is that readers would have these principles as expectations in their reading and any deviations from this norm will cause them to react, consciously or unconsciously, depending on the extent of deviation, to the differences of emphasis and flow of reading that will result.

Let us now consider, in order, the syntactic effects in this poem, and whether they are iconic in the sense that I have described above. The opening of the poem is a three-line stanza made up entirely of an adverbial subordinate clause which is therefore syntactically optional – the sentence would be perfectly grammatical without it – and is also unusually long for an optional initial clause element. This, I would argue, may cause the reader to feel slightly uneasy, since it is not clear what the sentence is actually about (theme) or what happens in it (rheme or focus). All we know at this stage is that the context is when 'the worst thing happens'. This adverbial clause is itself also complex, as it has two relative clauses expanding on the nature of 'the worst thing', so that we learn that it changes life irrevocably ('That uproots the future') and that it affects your whole life ('That you must live for every hour of your future'). Note that what we have so far in this stanza is a generalized context ('When'), relating to an unknown or generalized person, at this stage with the second-person pronoun being assumed to apply to anyone. This context doesn't state what the 'thing' is, leaving the reader to identify it as the 'worst thing' they are most familiar with. In addition, the double relative clause modification of this unknown event is no more explicit than the adverbial clause itself, leaving us none the wiser, nineteen words, three lines, and some incomplete syntax down the line.

So, the reader may be made to feel uneasy about what could happen to anyone, though note that this is achieved by a hypothetical adverbial clause which is not in fact modal, but categorical: 'When' indicates that 'the worst thing' will indeed happen. The reader is also told that it changes everything, and this will continue for the whole life, in the two relative clauses which by being subordinate to the adverbial clause are also effectively categorical. In all this time, the reader does not get a syntactic resolution of a grammatical subject and verb until line 4, in the second stanza. At that point, 'They come'. Although it is not stated who 'they' might be, the relief of finally arriving at the subject may incline the reader to pass over the lack of explicitness about referents, as we almost don't care who 'they' are, as long as *something* relieves the frustration. The fact that when the main clause elements do finally arrive they are so short and direct is in contrast to what has gone before. The result is that readers may feel that the problem, whatever it is, is thereby solved, the syntax now being complete. Note also that 'come' is spatially deictic and indicates movement towards the deictic centre of the person suffering the crisis. We as readers are positioned in that space too, which may make us empathize more. After the long wait for the relief of some company, there is no adverbial following the verb. 'They' don't come to do anything specific; they just come.

The main clause elements, then, occupy a line on their own, which reinforces the apparent effect of the syntax being complete at this point. However, there is no punctuation and it turns out that there *are* further optional elements of the sentence to follow on line 5 ('Unorganized, inarticulate, unprofessional'). These adjectives are difficult to analyse grammatically, as they could be seen as reduced relative clauses (i.e., 'Which are ...') or they could be seen as postponed modifiers, delayed because they cannot premodify a pronoun (*'Unorganized they'). Either way, they may produce the effect of undermining the relief which was felt as someone ('They') arrived to take charge of the awful situation both by their semantics (these people are not capable) and also by their syntax, as they extend an already long clause with three multisyllabic and syntactically repetitive words. The reader, then, may feel, along with the person at the centre of this crisis, that after an apparently interminable wait, help arrives at last, but is unable, of course, to undo the crisis, instead just being present, as represented in the three long adjectives.

The third stanza begins with a variant of the first main clause, 'They come sheepishly', which is immediately followed by another main clause ('they sit with you'). These two main clauses are the last ones in the poem, as we shall see shortly. So, unlike in the first clause, where there is a long wait for the main clause elements, here the syntax gets quickly to the point ('They come') but this time the manner of their coming is appended ('sheepishly') and the reader is then told the first real piece of information about what happens in the following clause ('sit with you'). This central part of the poem is a turning point, since the 'unprofessionals' have now arrived, and all of their activities fill the rest of the poem's syntactic structure with subordinate clauses, mostly non-finite clauses with the progressive participle (-ing form) indicating repeated actions across a length of time. Stanza three, then, continues after the main clauses with four non-finite adverbial clauses:

- holding hands, / From tea to tea, from Anadin to Valium,
- Sleeping on put-you-ups,
- answering the phone,
- Coming in shifts, spontaneously,

These activities, strung out as they are across the time-frame of the crisis, seem both pointless and also comforting. The 'unprofessionals' fill time and space with activity, and the build-up of these non-finite clauses continues into stanza four with three further similarly structured clauses:

- Talking sometimes,/ About wallflowers, and fishing, and why
- Dealing with Kleenex and kettles,
- Doing the washing up and the shopping,

Note that the first of these three clauses uses a slightly unusual ordering, with the adverbial ('sometimes') appearing to finish the clause, and then the topics of discussion ('wallflowers, and fishing, and why') being appended almost as an after-thought. This syntactic arrangement takes the reader in and out of syntactic security, almost seeming to represent iconically the experience of the person in the poem who is alternately comforted and then reminded of the crisis. In a way, the addition of the three-part list of topics discussed retrospectively changes the nature of the verb 'talk'. In the online reading process, the apparently complete (albeit non-finite) clause 'Talking sometimes', constructs the verb as an intransitive verb with no objects, and only an adverbial to tell us when the talking might happen. After the comma, however, the addition of the prepositional phrases seems to alter the sense of the verb to one which requires adverbial completion, supplying what is being talked *about*. This change, from just talking to talking about things, echoes the talking itself, with the talking itself being the whole point initially, to break the silence (remember these people are 'inarticulate') and once the silence has been broken, the subjects move from random subjects with no connection to the crisis ('wallflowers and fishing') to the big question, 'why' this has happened. The iconicity here, I would argue, is in the sequencing, the gaps, and the change of tone, from talking for its own sake to talking about the issue on everyone's mind. The comma after 'sometimes' creates a pause that the reader, like the 'unprofessionals' themselves, has to span in order to progress with the reading process, and it acts like an awkward moment in a room of grief.

After this slightly longer subordinate clause, we return to the busyness of the earlier clauses, when the visitors perceive that after touching upon the big question ('why') they can now get active, with practical measures of help such as running the household. The fact that there are no further main clauses lends an air of unreality to the situation. These activities are endless and ongoing, and they do not move things forward, though they fill up time.

The final stanza continues the pattern, though with a single long adverbial clause based on another pair of non-finite progressive clauses ('Holding hands and sitting it out'). This time, though, there are further adverbials both before and after the main elements of the clause:

Like civilians in a shelter, under bombardment,
Through the immortality of all the seconds, / Until the blunting of time.

The first of these produces a simile, where the visitors are likened to people in a war, and as in the first clause of the poem, this adverbial extends the waiting time for the reader, who will not know yet whether there is going to be a final, resolving, main clause, or whether the long string of -ing clauses will continue. The next line, of course, confirms the latter, and it is followed by two final lines of adverbial prepositional phrases, each emphasizing the length of time that healing can take. By this stage, even the verbs have disappeared, and they are phrases with nominals expressing time ('immortality', 'all the seconds', 'time') and a nominalization of a verb ('the blunting') expressing the process by which time heals. By the end of the poem, then, it has been eleven-and-a-half lines since the reader encountered a main verb, and though the potential frustration for the reader of the earlier subordinate clauses is less evident in the long list of adverbial clauses after the main verb, it nevertheless may affect the reader by producing a resigned feeling that time is not moving on and that there will be no further syntactic relief.

The iconicity that I would suggest is produced in reading this poem is a direct reflection of the dynamics of the situation in the structure of the syntax. Through the juxtaposition of subordinate clauses and main clauses, the poet may cause the reader not just to perceive but to actually *experience* some of the same feelings of frustration and resignation that are being described. The ongoing presence of the vacuously active 'unprofessionals', against such a bleak background, is, perversely, rather comforting, and this tension between what they actually do and the fact that they are there, endlessly and continuously, seems to reflect both sides of the discrepancy that I noted in the reactions of my students and myself when we read this poem in class.

Of course, personal experience and local or cultural knowledge often has some kind of influence on a reader's interpretation of a poem. In the case of my teaching 'The Unprofessionals', for example, the student who ran crying from the room had recently had experience of caring for, and losing, a close relative. The other students, particularly those with least sympathy for the unprofessionals themselves, seemed to be more distant from recent tragedy or personal crisis.

Apart from the extensive interpretative possibilities that individual experience accounts for, and which cannot be part of a theory of stylistics or interpretation, there are other types of shared knowledge or cultural experience which can be included in such a theory. Schema theory, for example, has been increasingly used in stylistics (see, for example, Cook 1994; Semino 1997 and 2001; Jeffries 2001) to explain some of the means by which readers access textual meaning. Schema theory claims that much of our experience is stored cognitively as patterns (schemata or scripts) which produce our expectations of the situations we find ourselves in. Thus, a schema for what happens after a death in mainstream society in Britain will include much visiting of the bereaved household by family and friends, many of whom have no specific role to play, but try to help (often ineffectually) in practical or emotionally supportive ways. In more highly structured societies (e.g. religious communities or rigid hierarchies), where roles and activities are laid down in an explicitly or at least well-understood codified form, this poem might not be as accessible as it is to those who share the underlying assumption: this is a terrible crisis, and no one knows what to do to help.

The discussion of schema theory in relation to literature has centred on the argument, first produced by Cook (1994), that one of the functions of literature is to defamiliarize (make strange) the familiar. This idea was taken in another direction by Semino (1997), who used schema theory to help explain how readers deal with the oddness of poems which mix unlikely schemata or which seem to pull the familiar schemata out of shape in some way. Jeffries (2001) made the case that not all literary experience involves a change to the reader's schemata, but that the explicit description of familiar, but perhaps relatively hidden, schemata might be one of the functions of poetry. In this case, it could be argued that (particularly in a non-religious society) we have no clear way of dealing with grief and crisis, and that the 'unprofessionals' are a result of this lack of ritual. The ambivalent feelings that a reader or a group of readers may have towards them is thus a reflection on both the unprofessionals' ineffectiveness, and also the fact that this incompetence is the result of a cultural vacuum and is therefore not their fault.

5. Conclusions

The exploration of syntactic iconic effects in the last section depends on the expectation that relatively competent readers of English (it is not yet clear to what extent this iconicity extends to other languages) may experience directly, but not necessarily consciously, the frustration of a long or late grammatical subject, or the timelessness of a minor sentence, or an overly long series of subordinate clauses, and so on. In other words, I am arguing that competent readers of Standard English at least will be accustomed to certain typical lengths of clause elements, early topics (subjects) and predicators (verbs), and right-branching structures where the longer elements represent new information and are later in the clause; in short, that the regular information structure is expected, and diversions from this structure have consequences.

In the context of the iconicity debate more generally, we may ask whether this is more similar to the imagic iconicity of direct mimetic effects such as onomatopoeia, or the diagrammatic iconicity of Haiman and others who argue that, for example, the linear ordering of events in a narrative is iconic of the chronology of the narrative. The fact that language is experienced in time, whether in silent reading or in listening to speech, is support for the iconicity of this default tendency in narrative to be chronological. It also, perhaps, supports the notion that there are levels of concreteness (i.e., directness) which would place chronological ordering somewhere between directly mimetic and less direct effects such as sound symbolism or the use of symmetrical syntax to reflect balance.

Because syntax is less salient for language users than, say, word choice, I would suggest that one of the consequences of altering the expected norms in subtle (i.e., not ungrammatical) ways is to gain access directly to the reader's subconscious, thus producing in them reactions that may not be quite as salient as reactions caused by, say, unusual collocations or novel metaphors, but which nevertheless influence their interpretation of the poem. Thus, in 'The Unprofessionals', the reader will probably make a relatively conscious effort to understand the title, and may note and even revel in the unusual way of marking out day from night in 'from Anadin to Valium'. S/he will probably be relatively aware of the apparent contradiction in 'Coming in shifts, spontaneously' and may think about the simile and to what extent s/he agrees that the people concerned are like 'civilians in a shelter'. What is less likely is that the reader will think consciously about the delayed first main clause elements in line 4 ('They come') or about the fact that the subordinate -ing clauses start in line 6 and continue to the end, though s/he will possibly feel slightly uneasy as they build up without further main clause resolution.

CHAPTER 7

Text Worlds in Poetry

Elena Semino

1. Introduction

Within stylistics, the study of poetry has a long and rich tradition. The analysis of phenomena such as alliteration, rhyme, metre, verse structure, metaphor, and other foregrounding devices has gone a long way towards explaining how we understand and appreciate poems (e.g. Leech 1969; Widdowson 1992; Short 1996). In this chapter, I consider another important aspect of the interpretation of texts, including poetic texts, namely the mental construction of a 'text world' – the sets of scenarios and the type of reality that the text is about.

I discuss different approaches to the study of text worlds by applying them to a well known poem by Craig Raine (1977): 'A Martian Sends a Postcard Home'. More specifically, I consider the contributions made by possible worlds theory (Ryan 1991), text world theory (Werth 1999; Gavins 2007a), and schema theory (Schank and Abelson 1977; Cook 1994) (for a similarly eclectic approach, see also Semino 1997, 2002, 2009). My aim is to show how a stylistic analysis of the poem can be enriched by a consideration of the characteristics and complexities of the 'world' that readers are invited to imagine, and of the processes that may be involved in imagining such a world.

2. The poem and its discourse worlds

Craig Raine's 'A Martian Sends a Postcard Home' was first published in the Christmas issue of the *New Statesman* in 1977. It is reproduced in full below.

A Martian Sends a Postcard Home

Caxtons are mechanical birds with many wings
and some are treasured for their markings –

116

they cause the eyes to melt
or the body to shriek without pain.

I have never seen one fly, but
sometimes they perch on the hand.

Mist is when the sky is tired of flight
and rests its soft machine on the ground:

then the world is dim and bookish
like engravings under tissue paper.

Rain is when the earth is television.
It has the property of making colours darker.

Model T is a room with the lock inside –
a key is turned to free the world

for movement, so quick there is a film
to watch for anything missed.

But time is tied to the wrist
or kept in a box, ticking with impatience.

In homes, a haunted apparatus sleeps,
that snores when you pick it up.

If the ghost cries, they carry it
to their lips and soothe it to sleep

with sounds. And yet, they wake it up
deliberately, by tickling with a finger.

Only the young are allowed to suffer
openly. Adults go to a punishment room

with water but nothing to eat.
They lock the door and suffer the noises

alone. No one is exempt
and everyone's pain has a different smell.

At night, when all colours die,
they hide in pairs

and read about themselves –
in colour, with their eyelids shut.

The theory of text worlds proposed by Werth (1999) and further developed by Gavins (2007a) includes a distinction between the 'discourse world' and the 'text world'. The discourse world is the immediate situation in which communication takes place; the text world is a mental representation of the situation(s) evoked by the text. In this section, I am concerned with the former.

The most prototypical discourse world is an instance of face-to-face communication, where the 'participants' are a speaker and a hearer who share the same physical space. Some aspects of this shared physical space can be selected as the topic of communication (e.g. the size or temperature of the room), and hence become part of the text world. In the case of written communication, however, the writer and readers are typically located in separate discourse worlds, and these discourse worlds may be more or less distant from each other in terms of space and time. On the one hand, this means that the most immediate physical contexts occupied, respectively, by the writer and the reader are often unimportant, as well as inaccessible for the purposes of criticism or linguistic analysis. On the other hand, the more general characteristics of these separate discourse worlds (the identity of the writer, the background and characteristics of the reader, the broader historical and cultural contexts) are crucial to an understanding of the text and its reception, and are indeed a major concern of reviewers, critics, linguists, reader response scholars, and so on.

In the case of 'A Martian Sends a Postcard Home', we have no information about the immediate discourse world in which it was composed, except that Craig Raine was, at the time, a still unknown English poet in his early thirties. Similarly, the immediate discourse worlds in which readers have processed the text are primarily private and inaccessible, but they are likely to have become more varied with each of the many reprints and reproductions of the poem in different types of publications.

As I mentioned earlier, the original audience of the poem were the readers of the *New Statesman* in 1977, who were presented with a rather unusual text by a new author. In October 1978, the poem was reprinted in the same magazine, as the joint winner (with Chistopher Reid's 'Baldanders') of the Prudence Farmer Award for the best poem published in the *New Statesman* in 1977. The prize was awarded by James Fenton, who worked as a critic for the *New Statesman* and who coined the term 'Martian School' to capture the new kind of poetry represented by Raine's and Reid's poems. The readers of the *New Statesman* who (re-)read the poem in 1978 would therefore have been aware both of the prize and of Fenton's view of what the joint winners represented.

Although it is generally acknowledged that the term 'school' applied rather loosely to the group formed by Raine, Reid and a handful of other poets (e.g. Hamilton 1994: 343, Carter and McRae 2001: 450), Craig's poem has enjoyed considerable success, and has come to be regarded as a classic example of texts that provide an estranged view of a familiar reality. After appearing twice in the *New Statesman*, it provided the title for a collection by Craig Raine published in 1979, where it appeared as the first poem. Since then, it has been included in a large number and variety of publications, from high-brow collections of contemporary poetry (e.g. Morrison and Motion 1982) to poetry collections aimed particularly at children (e.g. McGough 2001). In addition, the poem has been discussed and quoted (as a whole or in part) by literary critics and stylisticians (notably Short 1996: 284), and has been included in textbooks aimed at teachers and/or students of language and literature (e.g. Barton 1998). In some of these publications, the poem is accompanied by illustrations, commentary, activities, and exercises.

This brief overview begins to suggest the variety of the discourse worlds in which the poem has been, and continues to be, interpreted. In the discussion that follows, I will point out how this variety may result in partly different processes and products of interpretation, especially as far as the imagined text world is concerned (see also Gavins 2007b). In the rest of this section, I will limit myself to a brief overview of the critical reception of the poem.

By and large, Raine's poem has been praised for the way in which the projection of a 'Martian' viewpoint affords an unpredictable, humorous, and affectionate perspective on some aspects of a familiar, everyday reality (books, cars, telephones, dreaming, etc.). The terms 'defamiliarization' and 'estrangement' are often used to describe the overall effect of the poem. More specifically, the style of Raine's and Reid's poetry has been likened to that of the Metaphysical poets because of the way in which the two poets 'share a delight in outrageous simile and like to twist and mix language in order to revive the ordinary' (Morrison and Motion 1982: 18). However, what some critics positively describe as 'an optimistic emphasis on the richness of life made possible by the inventive reading of signs' (Corcoran 2007: 246), is for others a fatal shortcoming in Raine's poem (and others like it): the absence of a cultural and political critique of the aspects of contemporary reality that are viewed from the Martian's perspective (e.g. Falck 2003: 83).

Interestingly, in discussing discourse worlds, Werth describes as 'non-participants', and specifically as 'voyeurs', the literary critics and 'all those who take a professional interest in language from some sort of outside perspective' (e.g. myself and, quite possibly, many readers of this book) (Werth 1999: 17–18). This is because, in his view, the role that the members of these groups may have as participants in the discourse world is pushed into the background by their other goals in reading a text. While I see Werth's point, I am rather uneasy with this distinction when it comes to literature, not just because it would probably relegate many different groups of people into the role of non-participants (e.g. students), but also because writers may well have reviewers and critics in mind when they write their works. Be that as it may, I will return to the critics' contrasting views in what follows, as they are potentially relevant to how 'ordinary' readers may perceive the overall significance of the poem's peculiar representation of reality.

3. The title and (im)possibility

Titles are important, by definition. The title of Raine's poem, 'A Martian Sends a Postcard Home', is particularly important, as it frames the poem as a whole, by outlining a very specific and bizarre situation.

In Werth's (1999) and Gavins's (2007a) terms, the title sets up a 'text world', that is, 'a deictic space, defined initially by the discourse itself, and specifically by the deictic and referential elements in it' (Werth 1999: 180). The text world is a conceptual construct, which is mentally developed by the reader in interaction with the text. The noun-phrases 'A Martian' and 'a postcard' provide the 'world-building' elements: they refer to the entities (animate or inanimate) that populate the text world. The verb 'sends', and its relationship with 'A Martian', 'postcard', and 'home', provides the 'function-advancing' elements, that is, the action that takes place within the text world. The use of the present tense in 'sends' projects the Martian's action as deictically close, while the combination of 'sends' and 'home' suggests that the location of the text world is *other than* the Martian's home. By default, this location is likely to be identified with some place on earth.

What makes the poem's title interesting and captivating, however, is the nature of the situation it projects, and particularly the reference to a 'Martian' in an apparently earthly setting. The projection of fictional text worlds that contrast in obvious ways with the world we call 'actual' is a central concern within an approach known as possible worlds theory (see Eco 1990; Doležel 1998; Pavel 1986; Ronen 1994; Ryan 1991). Possible worlds theory shares with text world theory a concern for the nature and structure of the 'worlds' we imagine when interpreting texts. However, the two approaches also differ in some important respects. Text world theory is concerned with *verbal* texts, and attempts to account in detail for how linguistic choices enable us to form particular mental representations as we read. Possible worlds theory is concerned with semiotic objects more generally (i.e. not just verbal texts, but also multimodal texts such as films and operas), and with general issues posed by fiction.

The notion of 'possible worlds' was originally used in logic to refer to sets of states of affairs that can be conceived as alternatives to the 'actual' world. Logicians introduced this notion in order to deal with a number of logical problems that had previously proved to be intractable (see Bradley and Swartz 1979). The idea of possible worlds as alternative sets of states of affairs was, however, adopted and substantially developed in narratology and literary theory, in order to account for the status and characteristics of the rich and complex 'worlds' that are projected by fictional texts. Ryan (1991), in particular, has applied the notion of possible worlds in order to (a) define fiction, (b) propose a typology of (im)possibility that is relevant to generic distinctions, and (c) account for the internal structure of fictional worlds. Both (a) and (b) are relevant to the title of Raine's poem.

The relationship between poetry and fictionality is rather complex, and has been the subject of some debate (see Ryan 1991: 83–6). In the case of the poem under analysis, however, the reference to a 'Martian' in the title signals the need for an interpretative move that Ryan (1991: 21f.) describes as the hallmark of fictionality: a process of 'recentering', whereby the frame of reference for the interpretation of the text is shifted from a system of worlds revolving around our 'actual' world to a system of worlds revolving around an alternative possible world:

> For the duration of our immersion in a work of fiction, the realm of possibilities is thus recentered around the sphere which the narrator presents as the actual world. This recentering pushes the reader into a new system of actuality and possibility.
>
> (Ryan 1991: 22)

In the case of Raine's poem, the readers' frame of reference needs to be recentered around a world in which Martians exist and have landed on earth. This world counts as actual for the purposes of the interpretation of the text (Ryan calls it the 'text actual world'), but is an alternative possible world with respect to the 'actual' world in which Raine has written the poem and you or I read it.

While, in Ryan's terms, the process of fictional recentering applies in the same way to Raine's poem as to any other example of fiction (e.g. Orwell's *1984* or *Little Red Riding Hood*), there is of course considerable variation in the degree of overlap and contrast between different fictional worlds and the world we call 'actual'. Ryan therefore sets out to:

> ... address the question of what makes a world possible by exploring the various types of accessibility relations through which APWs [alternative possible worlds] can be linked to the actual world AW.
>
> (Ryan 1991: 31)

More specifically, she goes beyond the restricted sense in which 'possibility' was intended in logic and proposes a typology of fictional worlds based on the following wider set of accessibility relations: *identity of properties, identity of inventory, compatibility of inventory, chronological compatibility, physical compatibility, taxonomic compatibility, logical compatibility, analytical compatibility,* and *linguistic compatibility* (Ryan 1991: 32f.). The worlds projected by non-fictional texts are expected to overlap completely with the actual world, and hence fulfil all these criteria. In contrast, the worlds projected by fictional texts break one or more accessibility relations, depending, in part, on the genre the text belongs to.

The presence of a Martian in the text world that is set up by the title of Raine's poem breaks the relation of taxonomic compatibility, which is defined as follows (in the quotation below, TAW stands for text actual world, and AW for actual world):

> *Taxonomic compatibility* (F/taxonomy): TAW is accessible from AW if both worlds contain the same species, and the species are characterized by the same properties. Within F, it may be useful to distinguish a narrower version F′ stipulating that TAW must contain not only the same inventory of natural species, but also the same type of manufactured objects as found in AW up to the present.
>
> (Ryan 1991: 33)

This rule is broken in the text world set up by the title of Raine's poem, as, in the dominant view of the world we call 'actual world', Martians (i.e. living beings originating from Mars) do not exist. This taxonomic impossibility is central to the poem, as it allows for the Martian's view of the 'actual' world which is conveyed by the rest of the poem. It is also possible for readers to flesh out the poem's text world further, so that, for example, it includes spaceships for interplanetary travel (a further violation of F/taxonomy), and is set in the future (a violation of the rule of chronological compatibility, which stipulates that TAW cannot be 'older' than AW).

Apart from the presence of the Martian, however, readers are likely to assume that the text world is the same as their view of the earthly 'actual' world. This is a central aspect of (fictional) text processing, which Ryan (1991: 48f.) calls the 'principle of minimal departure':

> This law [...] states that we reconstrue the central world of a textual universe [...] as conforming as far as possible to our representation of AW. We will project upon these worlds everything we know about reality, and we will make only the adjustments dictated by the text.
>
> (Ryan 1991: 51)

The operation of this principle is evident in the critics' comments I mentioned earlier, and in all the readings of this poem I have come across in discussions with my students: the world described in the poem is perceived to be the same as our 'actual' world. What is characteristic of the poem is that it seems to convey the perspective of the Martian mentioned in the title. I will now consider this perspective in more detail.

4. The poem's text world and the Martian's perspective

Both expert and non-expert readers of the poem seem to agree that the poem consists of descriptions of the following aspects of our contemporary 'actual' world: books (stanzas 1–3), mist (stanzas 4–5), rain (stanza 6), cars (stanzas 7–8), watches (stanzas 9), telephones (stanzas 10–12), going to the toilet (stanzas 13–14), and dreaming (stanzas 15–16). The idiosyncrasy, and relative obscurity, of the way in which these objects and phenomena are described is justified by the title: what we are reading is the text of the postcard written by the imaginary Martian, and the language used reflects the Martian's peculiar view and understanding of things. Arguably, therefore, as we read the poem we need to distinguish between the Martian's apparently bizarre world view and the aspects of our own mundane reality he is describing (NB: I treat the Martian as male due to the fact that the author of the poem is male, but the poem contains no specification of sex or gender, which may be perceived as appropriate for the representation of an extraterrestrial creature).

Both text world theory as developed by Werth (1999) and Gavins (2007a), and the possible-worlds approach to fiction proposed by Ryan (1991), recognize that the 'worlds' we imagine when reading (fictional) texts often have complex internal structures. This is not just because the story may involve different places and times, but also because we are often presented with hypothetical scenarios, and with characters' beliefs, wishes, dreams, and so on. I cannot discuss in detail the way in which the internal structure of text worlds is handled in each approach, but I will focus on the parts that are relevant to the analysis of Raine's poem.

Ryan (1991: 109f.) makes a distinction between the 'text actual world' or 'factual domain' on the one hand, and the alternative possible worlds that exist in the characters' minds. These alternative possible worlds are versions of the factual domain which correspond to the characters' beliefs, wishes, obligations, or fantasies, and which may differ from the text actual world in a variety of ways. The title of Raine's poem, and the language used in the rest of the text, suggest that we are exposed to the voice of the imaginary Martian, and hence are given access to what Ryan calls his 'knowledge world': what the Martian knows about and believes to be the case in the text actual world he describes. As readers, we 'see through' his descriptions (with more or less difficulty), and conclude that the text actual world the Martian describes is the same as our 'actual' world, apart from the presence of the extraterrestrial observer.

In terms of text world theory, the move from the title of the poem to the first stanza involves the same kind of deictic shift that applies to direct speech presentation, which is typically associated with effects such as vividness and dramatization: if we imagine that we are reading the Martian's postcard, we have moved to a position where the Martian's here-and-now is the deictic centre. In Werth's version of the theory, this results in the creation of a new deictic sub-world, while Gavins would talk of a 'world switch' (Gavins 2007a: 50; Werth 1999: 221). What matters in this poem, however, is not so much the shift in deixis, but the fact that this shift leads to the projection of the Martian's perspective. Werth does not explicitly discuss point of view in a way that directly applies to the issues posed by the poem. His approach does, however, include 'attitudinal sub-worlds' that are described as 'notions entertained by the protagonists' (Werth 1999: 216). The category of attitudinal sub-worlds includes 'belief worlds' as a sub-type (ibid.: 233f.), and Werth uses this notion to account for those cases where a particular state of affairs is explicitly presented as someone's belief (e.g. 'John believes that ...').

Gavins (2007a, 2007b) considers focalization and point of view more explicitly. She relabels Werth's 'attitudinal sub-worlds' as 'modal worlds', and talks about 'epistemic modal-worlds' for cases such as Raine's poem, where we are presented with a character's beliefs (Gavins 2007a: 110). In her book *Text World Theory*, Gavins considers several texts where readers are consistently presented with a single focalizer's world view and suggests that, in such cases, readers can only construct the narrator's or focalizing character's epistemic modal-world while the text world is relegated into the background and left empty (ibid.: 133–4). This seems rather counterintuitive, as readers normally make inferences about the main text world (Ryan's factual domain), even when presented with an entirely subjective, or even unreliable, point of view (e.g. in the case of Ken Kesey's novel *One Flew Over the Cuckoo's Nest*). This is recognized by Gavins in a different study:

> [I]n a fixed focalization no other narratorial voice is present and the reader has no choice but to accept the world-building and function-advancing elements presented to him/her by the focalizer as reliable if the text-world is to be constructed at all. Many prose fiction texts, of course, take advantage of the trust the reader must necessarily place in the focalizer in order to facilitate narrative tricks, deceptions and twists in the tale. The effectiveness of these tricks is entirely dependent on readers conceptualizing what is in fact an example of a remote *modal world* [...] as if it were a text world.
>
> (Gavins 2007b: 139)

With Werth's and Gavins's approach, the scenarios described in the poem involve a series of deictic shifts within the Martian's belief/epistemic world.

Although the situations described in the poem are general rather than specific, they can be described in terms of world-building elements and function-advancing propositions in the way I briefly demonstrated in my analysis of the poem's title.

5. Opaqueness and the Martian's world view

The presentation of the imaginary Martian's perspective in Raine's poem does not simply mean that familiar entities and phenomena are described in unusual ways, but also that readers may not always immediately recognize what is being talked about. This gives the poem a riddle-like quality that probably plays a part in the poem's appeal to younger readers. In terms of the poem's text world, the fact that we are presented with what Ryan would call the Martian's knowledge world may sometimes impede, at least on a first reading, the successful construction of the poem's factual domain. This phenomenon has been discussed in stylistics in relation to deviant mind styles such as that of Lok in Golding's *The Inheritors* and Benji's in Faulkner's *The Sound and the Fury* (Leech and Short 1981: 187f.; Fowler 1986: 147f.), and has been linked particularly to the phenomenon of 'underlexicalization': the absence, in a character's or narrator's verbal repertoire, of fairly common lexical items, which readers are likely to expect to be familiar to a competent language user. This absence is typically interpreted as evidence that the relevant character or narrator lacks the corresponding concepts, or has difficulties accessing them (Fowler 1986: 152). The opposite phenomenon, 'overlexicalization', can also partially impede comprehension and project an idiosyncratic world view.

As I have suggested elsewhere (e.g. Semino 2007), some notions from schema theory can be used to explain the way in which linguistic choices may make it difficult for readers to recognize a familiar scene. Schemata (also known as frames, scripts, or scenarios) are long-term mental representations that contain our background knowledge of people, objects, actions, situations, and so on (see Bartlett 1932; Schank and Abelson 1977; Schank 1982; Cook 1994). Their importance in the mental construction of text worlds is recognized both in text world theory and in possible-worlds approaches: we can only successfully comprehend a text, and construct the relevant text world, if we possess the background knowledge that is assumed by the text. More specifically, cognitive psychologists have shown how comprehension requires not just the *availability* of relevant schemata, but also their *activation* while interpreting a text (Bransford and Johnson 1972). The activation of relevant schemata is facilitated by linguistic items in the text that function as 'headers', that is, references to elements of a schema (Schank and Abelson 1977: 49–50). When a text does not include headers that are sufficiently explicit for a particular reader, that reader may have difficulties recognizing a situation that is in fact familiar to them. Margolin has considered this phenomenon in relation to literature in particular, and has labelled it 'frame-blocking':

> ... the author has *to prevent (block) the reader from activating his or her pertinent categories of world or literary knowledge* and applying them to the textual fragment in question in order to identify the persons, situations, or events portrayed in it.
>
> (Margolin 2003: 277; emphasis in original)

This arguably applies to Raine's poem, as a result of what, in my view, is best described as a combination of underlexicalization and overlexicalization.

The poem's imaginary Martian does not use some rather frequent, everyday lexical items such as 'books', 'cars', 'telephone', 'toilet', or 'dream', which would very clearly function as headers for the activation of the schemata that are relevant to some of the scenes described in the poem. This can be interpreted as an indication that he does not understand these entities in the ways that human beings do. The words he does use, however, may not always immediately trigger the activation of the relevant schema, depending, in large part, on the reader's background knowledge.

In a few cases, the expressions used in the poem can be seen as fairly straightforward instances of underlexicalization that reflect limited or mistaken understanding. This applies, for example, to 'room with the lock inside' in the description of the car in stanza 7, and to 'a punishment room with water but nothing to eat' in the description of the toilet in stanza 13. More frequently, however, the words used by the Martian as a result of his underlexicalization can also be seen as rather unconventional metaphorical descriptions of the relevant objects or phenomena. This applies, for example, to the description of books as 'mechanical birds' in stanza 1, of the telephone as a 'haunted apparatus' that 'sleeps', 'snores', and 'cries' in stanzas 10–11, of dreaming as 'read[ing] about themselves' in stanza 17, and so on. In a few further cases, familiar objects are referred to via what can be described as metonymies. This applies to the reference to books as 'Caxtons' in stanza 1, and to the car as 'Model T' in stanza 7. These examples can in fact be seen as instances of overlexicalization, as the terms used by the imaginary Martian reflect more specialized knowledge than may be available to some readers, that is, that Caxton established the first printing press in England in 1476, and that the Model T was the first car produced by Ford in 1908 for a mass market.

Metonymy and metaphor are often combined in the same description (e.g. stanza 1), so that readers are exposed to multiple cues as to what is being talked about. Nonetheless it is likely that comprehension may be slowed down or even impeded for some, or even most, first-time readers.

6. An ambiguous and inconsistent text world?

As I mentioned above, Raine's poem allows us to imagine that we are directly exposed to the world view of an imaginary Martian observer of our contemporary reality. In this section, I consider in more detail the nature of this world view, which can also be described as the Martian's knowledge world (Ryan 1991), belief world (Werth 1999) or epistemic modal-world (Gavins 2007a).

Firstly, the frequent use of expressions that could be regarded as metaphorical raises some issues for how confidently we can establish the Martian's understanding of things. One of the functions that metaphorical expressions can perform is that of filling lexical gaps, that is, providing ways of naming or describing entities for which no appropriate 'literal' term is available (Goatly 1997: 149). We can readily imagine that this explains the Martian's description of books as 'mechanical birds' and of crying as eyes 'melt[ing]'. It is, however, difficult to establish whether all of the descriptions that can function as metaphors for the reader are also metaphorical for the Martian. Consider, for example, the line 'they cause the eyes to melt', which is part of the description of books. The reference to 'melting' can be interpreted as a metaphorical description of crying, based on a concrete, visual similarity: the physical process of melting involves solids turning into liquids, while crying involves liquid being produced by a physical entity. The (potential) interpretative issue here is whether the Martian uses the verb 'melt' literally or metaphorically. In the former case, the Martian would possess the concept crying (the target domain of the metaphor) as distinct from concept melting (the source domain of the metaphor). He would therefore use the word 'melt' to describe metaphorically a process for which he has no available literal expression. In the latter case, the Martian would have no concept for crying or, minimally, no distinction between the concepts crying and melting, so that the word 'melt' in line 3 of the poem would not be metaphorical for the Martian. The matter is even more complicated in the case of expressions such as 'mechanical birds', where the adjective and the noun potentially realize different source domains (that is, machines and birds) (for a discussion of the complex relationship between metaphor and underlexicalization, see Black 1993).

In some cases, textual evidence does give us some indication one way or the other. The fact that the Martian points out that he has never seen a 'Caxton' 'fly', suggests that he had expected them to do so, and hence that he has no concept of books that is separate from birds. On the other hand, the line

'Rain is when the earth is television' may suggest that the Martian is explicitly making a comparison, and hence lead us to attribute to him the ability to distinguish between the concepts rain and television. A further possibility is that the Martian's descriptions are guided by his awareness of the background knowledge of the imaginary receivers of the postcard, which would make it even harder for readers to be confident about what the Martian knows and how he understands things.

At this point, you may well be thinking that, by pursuing these matters in such detail, I am beginning to spoil the poem for you, and missing the point altogether. In fact, I raised these issues partly to make some important points about how we imagine text worlds. As readers, and especially as readers of literature and fiction, we tend to be tolerant of indeterminacy, and may even enjoy it, at least to some extent (e.g. see Iser 1971). In the case of our poem, what matters is that we can imagine a Martian with a world view that is interestingly unusual. It does not matter than we cannot pin down precisely what exactly that world view is. In fact, we may even appreciate the poem more for the way in which it defeats our attempt to establish exactly what the Martian understands and what he does not.

This 'tolerance' (whether conscious or not) also applies to the presence of potential incongruities and inconsistencies in fictional text worlds. Eco (1990: 78–9) has mentioned that the construction of fictional text worlds requires some degree of 'flexibility and superficiality' on the part of readers. For example, when reading *Little Red Riding Hood*, we accept that the wolf can talk without wondering how this affects the course of evolution in the world of the story. The same attitude is needed in order to make sense of and enjoy the world of 'A Martian Sends a Postcard Home'. The scenario set up by the title potentially raises questions that the text does not answer, such as: How did the Martian get to Earth? What does it look like? And so on. On the other hand, the information that *is* provided in the text raises some more fundamental issues that cannot be resolved: for example, if the Martian has come from Mars (or, at any rate, another planet), why does he use ordinary mail to communicate with other Martians at home? If we consider the poem as the text of the Martian's imaginary postcard, and as a reflection of his world view, further issues may arise, even after we have accepted that the Martian speaks English, and uses it to communicate with other Martians.

As I have already mentioned, the vocabulary used in the poem can be described as involving both underlexicalization and overlexicalization. This leads to potential incongruities: how can the Martian know about Caxton and the Model T, and not know the words 'book' and 'car'?

Similar inconsistencies are revealed by the Martian's use of expressions that can be seen as metaphorical. In cognitive linguistics, metaphor is seen as a tool that we use to think and talk about abstract, complex, and unfamiliar areas of experience (target domains) in terms of more concrete, simpler, and familiar areas of experience (source domains) (e.g. Lakoff and Johnson 1980, 1999). As I have shown elsewhere, a fictional character's mind style and world view can sometimes be conveyed via their overreliance on familiar areas of experience as metaphorical source domains (see Semino and Swindlehurst 1996; Semino 2002, 2007). A close look at the poem, however, does not reveal any consistent patterns in the choice of source and target domains. Rather, it seems to reflect a conscious attempt to defeat our ability to discover such patterns. For example, the word 'book' is not used, and the Martian seems not to understand what books are and how they affect people. However, the adjective 'bookish' is used in stanza 5 to describe the visual effects of mist, and the verb 'read' is used to describe dreaming. In addition, in some cases the source domain of machinery is used to describe non-mechanical entities, such as books ('mechanical birds') and the sky ('its soft machine'). This is consistent with the reasonable assumption that a Martian who has made it to earth is more familiar with machinery and technology than with other aspects of life on earth. On the other hand, however, the Martian does not seem to fully understand cars, or telephones, and repeatedly describes inanimate entities in animate terms (e.g. time, the telephone, etc.). The use of personification assumes intimate knowledge of human beings, as does the Martian's insight into dreaming at the end of the poem. This obviously contrasts with the external, incomprehending description of crying and laughing in stanza 2.

In other words, it is not just the poem's factual domain that seems rather incongruous (a Martian using ordinary mail): the knowledge world through which we view our own reality is also difficult to make internally consistent, if one tries. At a general level, we can probably explain some of the 'inconsistencies' I have mentioned as a result of the difficult enterprise Craig Raine set himself: he had to provide a fresh perspective on the 'actual' world that made it momentarily unrecognizable, but not to an extent that made the poem entirely incomprehensible. Expressions such as 'Caxtons' and 'Model T', or the personification of the telephone as a baby, work well as riddles that different readers will 'solve' with more or less speed and difficulty.

More specifically, however, the text's indeterminacy and potential inconsistencies may play different roles in different readers' interpretations of the poem. As a result of what Eco calls 'flexibility and superficiality', many readers will not consciously notice any of the issues I have mentioned: they will not ponder on why a Martian writes a postcard, nor worry about the apparently 'uneven' nature of his knowledge world. This probably applies to younger readers, but also to many adult readers, including myself on my first few readings of the poem. Other readers may notice at least some of the poem's incongruities, and conclude that the text world is hopelessly inconsistent and the text badly written. If such readers exist, however, they are probably a small minority. Yet other readers may become consciously aware of (some of) the complexities I have described, and incorporate them within their interpretation and appreciation of the poem. This is my own current view of the poem, and one that I often see developing in my students. Noticing the oddities of the poem's text world (including both the factual domain and the Martian's knowledge world) increases the potential humour of the text, as we are not just presented with a Martian, but with an *implausible* Martian. This may reveal a tongue-in-cheek attitude on the part of the author, and may make his presence and voice more 'visible' behind the flimsy screen of the imaginary Martian. In other words, we may become more aware of how the Martian is in fact a humorous pretext for the poet to give us a defamiliar-ized, affectionately humorous view of some of the things we take for granted in our everyday lives. This does not mean that the Martian no longer 'exists' in the text world imagined by these readers, but that it is less of a full-blown character and more of a device that serves the author's purpose. The pos-sibility of at least these different attitudes to the poem and its text world may be part of the reason why it has been anthologized and discussed to the extent that it has.

7. Metaphor, 'double vision', and schema refreshment

Both the text world theory approach and the possible-worlds approach to fictional worlds provide compatible accounts of the role of metaphor. It is recognized that the literal meanings of metaphorical expressions *appear* to outline scenarios that could be regarded as 'worlds' in their own right. However, these scenarios have a peculiar status, in that they are outlined in order to provide a particular view of some aspect of another 'world'. Ryan (1991: 82–3) acknowledges that metaphorical expressions may out-line 'remote possible worlds' via a literal interpretation of their meanings. However, she points out that metaphors do not require a move to a different system of worlds, but rather relate directly to a text's factual domain (or, I would add, to an alternative possible world that revolves around it) (see also Eco 1990: 149f.):

> The meaning that originates in the metaphor world is reflected back toward AW. This world is not created for its own sake, but as a point of view allowing us to rediscover AW from a new perspective.
>
> (Ryan 1991: 82)

Werth (1999: 313f.) relates metaphors primarily to the discourse world, where the author uses a particular area of experience (the source domain) to describe the topic of the discourse in a particular way. Importantly, he adds that metaphors can afford what he calls 'double vision', namely

> that its special quality is that we see both [the literal and metaphorical meanings] simultaneously, or one through the other. Metaphor does not merely substitute one area of experience for another; it combines the two kinds of experiences into a third new way of seeing.
>
> (Werth 1999: 317)

This notion of combining separate experiences into something new is at the centre of Fauconnier and Turner's (2002) theory of conceptual blending, which is integrated by Gavins into her version of text world theory (Gavins 2007a: 148f.).

What is peculiar about Raine's poem is that the adoption of the voice and point of view of an imaginary Martian licenses the exploration of the literal meanings of metaphorical expressions more than is normally the case in the processing of metaphorical expressions. As I mentioned earlier, it is possible to imagine that all of the language of the poem literally reflects the Martian's knowledge world, or to opt for a more nuanced interpretation of potentially figurative expressions. In any case, the poem provides considerable potential for double vision: we have to construct both the imaginary Martian's knowledge world and a factual domain which contains some aspects of everyday reality, so that we see the latter through the former.

What are the consequences of this particular kind of double-vision for how readers may view their 'actual' world after reading the poem? As I mentioned earlier, the critics have expressed different opinions. Most critics praise the poem's freshness and inventiveness, and the way in which it provides a humorous, affectionate, and optimistic view of reality. Other critics berate the poem for the fact that the perspective it adopts is not situated politically or culturally. What all commentators seem to agree on, however, is that our world view is unlikely to be deeply challenged by the poem.

In an earlier reference to Raine's poem (Semino 1997: 216–7), I expressed this general view by suggesting that the poem has a low potential for what Cook (1994) calls 'schema refreshment' – a change in one's existing schemata as a result of reading a text. This low potential for schema refreshment is primarily due to the fact that the Martian's perspective is expressed through (potential) metaphors that, although striking and novel, are unlikely to result in a reconceptualization of the entities or phenomena in question. Rather, these metaphors suggest wonder, or, at best, amusement at the peculiarities of the world we live in.

Today I would provide a slightly more positive assessment of the poem than I did in 1997. The poem does not propose a critique of our contemporary world by encouraging a particular kind of schema refreshment (e.g. by expos-ing the negative consequences of technological advances, or the hypocrisy of some of our everyday conventions). Nonetheless, it provides an opportunity for readers to have their schemata challenged, to experience defamiliariza-tion for its own sake, and to realize that in our daily lives we often lose a proper awareness of what surrounds us. Crucially, it does this in a way that is accessible to and enjoyable by a wide readership (including children), which is not the case for more sophisticated, highbrow poetry. The creation of a Martian observer is central to this broad appeal, as it justifies the estranged perspective, and provides an individual, concrete character whose difficulties and misunderstandings we may sympathize with. Margolin (2003: 287) has recently noted a 'preference of much literature for nonstandard forms of cog-nitive functioning, be they rare or marginal, deviant, or involving a failure, breakdown, or lack of standard patterns'. His comment on this tendency to project minds that work in unusual ways is relevant to 'A Martian Sends a Postcard Home':

> [t]he fictional presentation of cognitive mechanisms in action, especially of their own breakdown and failure, is itself a powerful cognitive tool which may make us aware of actual cognitive mechanisms, and, more specifically, of our own mental functioning.
>
> (Margolin 2003: 278)

In this sense, the processes involved in coming to terms with the world of Raine's poem can indeed be both valuable and powerful.

Overall, I hope to have shown that the study of text worlds in poetry is a use-ful addition to the more well-established analytical techniques of stylistics.

CHAPTER 8

'Public-House Confidence': The Indispensability of Sound Patterns

TOM BARNEY

1. Introduction

'Poets are not much in demand these days –' wrote Cecil Day Lewis in the dedicatory stanzas to his translation of Virgil's *Georgics*: 'We're red, it seems, or cracked, or bribed, or hearty' (Day Lewis 1940: 9). Prosodists, who perhaps are no more than poets turned wrong side up, know this feeling well enough too. We find ourselves the only one of our kind at conferences, or we organize conferences of our own where we discuss matters of metricality as if they were mathematical problems. This is sad, because there are poems which would not 'work' – would not convey the burden of their meaning – without their significant patterns of sound. From this it follows, of course, that they cannot be adequately analysed stylistically without attention to these patterns.

Any example of sound symbolism contributes something to the style of a poem, so is worth analysing for this reason alone. Yet sound patterns are often something like herbs: without them the flavour would be different in kind, but one still feels that they are something of an embellishment. What we admire is the rightness of a metrical, rhyme, or alliteration pattern for the meaning of the words. This is probably the best-known kind of sound symbolism, and some examples of it are very well known indeed:

A needless Alexandrine ends the song,
That, like a wounded snake, drags its slow length along.
(Pope: *An essay on criticism* I, 356)

133

Pope himself, a few lines further on, equally famously claims no more for sound symbolism than that 'The sound must seem an *echo* to the sense.' There are poems, however, in which the sound is the very stuff of the sense, or at least part of it. These, I suggest, are especially worth the attention of stylistics, with its concern for linguistic building blocks and structures, and its belief that it is these that account for our interpretations and emotional responses. It is one such poem – Norman Cameron's 'Public-House Confidence' (1990) – that I want to examine closely in this chapter in order to demonstrate, I hope, the indispensability of sound to poetry and of its analysis to stylistics.

Public-House Confidence

Well, since you're from the other side of town,
I'll tell you how I hold a soft job down.
In the designing-rooms and laboratory
I'm dressed in overalls, and so pretend
To be on business from the factory.   5
The workmen think I'm from the other end.
The in-betweens and smart commission-men
Believe I must have some pull with the boss.
So, playing off the spanner against the pen,
I never let the rumour get across   10
Of how I am no use at all to either,
And draw the pay of both for doing neither.
                                        (Cameron 1990)

Norman Cameron (1905–53) was described by his friend Robert Graves (1957: 23) as 'a divided character'; Graves added that Cameron's poems often 'joke about the equivocal task of being Norman'. This, clearly, is such a poem. We are presented with an entire existence which is built on a division. There is everything here (this is how a man lives, and lavishly) and there is nothing (he does no work). He achieves this by fooling the technical and scientific staff that he is a factory-floor worker, and vice versa. These are polar opposites but the poem appears to reconcile them. It seems to make perfect logical sense yet one feels that it is impossible: *could* such a life be lived? Because the speaker is a passing stranger we have to take his story on trust, or not. He sums up his way of life, but at the same time gives us no more than a fragment of it. The poem – with a mere 12 lines – is itself a fragment, but it has a formal and prosodic integrity which plays a large part in making the story the speaker tells seem both bizarre and logically inevitable.

The poem consists of 12 lines of iambic pentameter, rhyming *aabcbcdedeff*. It consists, in other words, of an initial rhyming couplet, two *abab* quatrains, and a final couplet, the whole forming a mirror image. Now the argument of the poem begins with a preamble, then moves on to create some confusion as the speaker describes his scheme of work: as he begins to do the latter we wonder 'how' precisely he manages to 'hold a soft job down'. This is followed by clauses which summarize the scheme of work in more abstract terms ('playing off the spanner against the pen...draw the pay of both for doing neither') which by being both concise and all-encompassing draw the threads together. Prosodically too the poem moves from the regular beat and exact, monosyllabic rhymes of the initial couplet; through the less regular, more open and colloquial structure of the quatrains, where the alternation of beat and offbeat is challenged, and where the syntax runs across the line divisions, for example 'In the...laboratory / I'm dressed in overalls, and so pretend / To be on business ...'; and back to the regularity of the final couplet, where the steady alternation of beat and offbeat reasserts itself, especially in the last line, and where co-ordinated clauses divide neatly at the line boundary (*either,* / *And*).

It is not just, though, that the rhythm is a fitting one for the argument, mimicking the latter's progress from clarity to confusion and back. The argument is not of the kind where we perceive the essential point early, the rest then consisting of elaboration or detail or example. The essential point – that the speaker's mode of existence is to do no work for double pay – comes only at the very end, like the punch-line of a joke. It is the form and prosody of the poem which allow this measured unfolding of the argument and narrative. Because the regularity of the initial couplet gives way to a middle section in which, as I shall show, we become uncertain of the rhythm and the rhyme scheme, we feel a confusion about the argument which we would not feel so strongly without these formal devices, and likewise the return of regularity at the end gives a stronger sense of clarification of the argument, and of full closure of the poem. Discord and harmony are reinforced: the prosody actually works on the mind to produce these qualities.

For the form to work on us satisfactorily, then, we need to read the whole poem (compare this with longer poems of many stanzas, where the same pattern of lines and rhymes is repeated stanza after stanza for perhaps many pages); and since reading is a linear process the form is capable of springing surprises on us as it unfolds. The extent to which an idea can be sustained through a formal scheme has been called by the composer Vincent Persichetti (1970: 180) the 'projectional capacity' of a work of art. While in a long poem or novel or symphony there will be many such ideas, each having a local projectional capacity but joined together into a larger whole, the projectional capacity of 'Public-House Confidence' is the entire poem: both rhetorical and formal closure must wait for the very end, and neither would work properly without the other. In the remainder of this chapter I shall show how the complex prosodic patterns operate, and how they interact with the structure of the argument and narrative to produce this final harmony.

2. From regularity to irregularity

A metre most commonly consists of a recurring pattern of beats and off-beats grouped into lines containing a set number of these patterns. In the iambic pentameter of 'Public-House Confidence', for example, the recurring pattern consists of an offbeat followed by a beat; this pattern occurs five times in each line (notice, in particular, line 10). Certain deviations from the offbeat-beat patterns are permitted to occur (see Attridge 1982; Carper and Attridge 2003). Our sense that the rhythm of any particular poem, or line within a poem, is more or less regular or irregular is mainly caused by a combination of three things. One is how far the recurring pattern of beat and offbeat is kept to or deviated from. Another is how far the ends of syntactic components – phrase, clause, sentence – coincide with the ends of lines and so reinforce our sense of the line as a higher metrical unit; if a line ends with a syntactic component incomplete this sets up what Roger Fowler (1966: 87) calls a 'tension between the metre, wanting to make a break, and the grammar, wanting to be continuous'. Rhyme provides a third influence in rhyming verse: we are likely to think the rhythm more regular the closer together the rhymed words are, for example a rhyming couplet will seem more regular than verse in which rhymes are separated by one or more lines; and we are likely to think the rhythm more regular the more exact the rhymes are. All these factors work on us simultaneously, in different degrees at different times. Our perception of regularity and irregularity in rhythm is, then, a complex matter.

The initial rhyming couplet of 'Public-House Confidence' –

Well, since you're from the other side of town,
I'll tell you how I hold a soft job down.

– establishes a formal regularity. It does this partly because it *is* a rhyming couplet, where the rhymes come close together, and partly because of the syntax, which forms what Sinclair (1966, 1972) calls an *arrest-release* structure. That is, at the end of a line some syntactic unit such as a phrase, clause, or sentence is clearly incomplete, but because we are at the end of a line – a metrical unit – we are inclined to pause. This sets up a tension because, though we are impatient for completion, it does not come until the following line, after the pause. In this couplet an adverbial clause, 'Well, since you're from the other side of town' (line 1), occupies the whole of the first line so that, as we pause at the line-end, we expect a main clause to follow. It duly does, and occupies the whole of the second line: 'I'll tell you how I hold a soft job down' (line 2). Couplet and sentence are completed together and a strong partial closure achieved.

The regularity of these two lines sets up an expectation that the regularity will continue, but the poem at once frustrates this expectation, in three ways. One of these ways is obvious: the first of the *abab* quatrains occurs instead of another couplet. This does not simply give a different pattern of rhyme from what has gone before, but begins with two lines which do not rhyme. Since we are expecting a couplet, and so we are anticipating a rhyme at the end of the second line of this pair, the internal deviation constituted by the absence of such a rhyme jars.

The second way in which our expectations are frustrated is that the rhymes that do occur in the quatrain are somewhat oblique. The normal principle on which words rhyme is that, except for any initial consonants, the words should have an identical form from the last stressed syllable onwards. The 'laboratory'/'factory' (lines 3 and 5) rhyme violates this principle, since *laboratory* from its last stressed syllable (-*bo*-) onward consists of a stress and two non-stresses, *factory* of a stress and a single non-stress (assuming that -*tory* is elided into a single syllable in each case). The stressed syllables themselves have different vowels. Then, the different stress patterns are in their turn aligned differently with the metrical beats. Lines 3 and 5 both end with a stressed beat, followed by an offbeat, followed by what Attridge (1982) calls a 'promotion', that is, a beat which falls on a normally unstressed syllable. The alignment of the metrical beat and offbeat with the stress patterns of the words in these lines is as follows (I here use / for a stressed and x for an unstressed syllable, and the notation of Carper and Attridge [2003] where **B** stands for a stressed beat, **b** for a promotion, **o** for an offbeat, and **-o-** for a double offbeat, one realized by two syllables):

```
x  x   x  /  x    /    x  x  / x  x
In the designing-rooms and laboratory
b   -o-  B  o    B     -o-  B o  b
```

```
x  x  x  /    x   x   x   / x
To be on business from the factory.
o  b  o B     o   b   o   B o b
```

Look now at how the two words under discussion align with the B-o-b pattern:

```
laboratory              factory
  B o  b                 B o  b
```

How are the words to be pronounced? If we elide the *-tory* element in both, then *-borat'ry* can carry the B-o-b pattern but *fact'ry* cannot. If we elide it in neither the result – *la-bo-ra-to-ry, fac-to-ry* – is grossly unidiomatic. If we elide it only in *laboratory* this does not solve the problem as a beat will naturally fall at the end of the word, on either *-to-* or *-t'ry*, whether the elision takes place or not, and if we elide it only in *factory* we still lack a syllable on which to place the final, unemphasized beat. In short there is no solution to this problem: *laboratory* and *factory* will differ to the point where our sense of a rhyme is hazy at best. The *pretend / end* rhyme of lines 4 and 6 is also oblique, although in a less extreme way. Because the line boundary after *pretend* comes in the middle of a clause, the accent on *pretend* is unlikely to be the most prominent accent in the clause. (This, commonly known as the *nucleus* or *nuclear accent*, normally comes close to the end of a major syntactic constituent and is commonly characterized by its greater length and/ or a movement from one pitch to another.) This is especially so as there is almost certain to be a substantial prosodic discontinuity (a pause, or a large jump up or down in pitch, or both) accompanying the caesura after *overalls*; the short distance between *overalls* and the line-end increases the strength of run-on between lines 4 and 5. The accent on *pretend* will therefore probably be high-pitched (the incomplete clause will be signalled by the 'up in the air' pitch) and level in tone. [E]*nd*, on the other hand, being at the end of a sentence, will either carry a nuclear accent or, if the accent is placed on *other*, lose its accent altogether; either way, it will have, or glide to, low tone. [P]*retend* and *end* will almost certainly differ in both pitch pattern and relative emphasis.

The third way in which our expectations of regularity are frustrated is that there is some disturbance in the regular alternation of beats and off-beats. In line 3 we have an initial inversion (the line begins beat, double offbeat instead of the strict iambic pattern offbeat, beat), plus a double offbeat inserted later in the line. But in practice the line is likely to travel further than this from a regular iambic alternation. The three syllables 'In the de-' (line 3) belong syntactically to the prepositional phrase *In the designing-rooms* (line 3), which also functions as a rhythmic unit: all the other syllables of the phrase cluster round the main stress on *-sign-*. The syllables *In the de-* (line 3), which precede and look forward to this stress, are known as *proclitics*. Knowles (1974: 126) observes that 'As a general impression, proclitics are rushed over on the way to the peak [i.e. the main stress], while enclitics [the syllables which follow the main stress] are lingered on.' The speed of this rush is likely to blur the sensation of a beat on *In* even if *In* has an accent (which is not inevitable). Add to this the compound *designing-rooms* in which, as in all compounds, greater emphasis will normally be given to the stress (*-sign-*) of the first element than to that of the second, and we lose a good deal of the sensation of an alternating strong and weak pulse in this line. The other lines of the quatrain maintain this effect with a number of promotions – '-alls', 'so', 'be', 'from' – which ensure that the beat is often unemphasized, the latter two especially thanks to the run of proclitics 'To be on' and 'from the'. The regularity, both of metre and of rhyme, is strongly challenged.

3. Form and content

This move from prosodic regularity to irregularity reinforces a mismatch throughout between the formal and discourse structure of the poem. Each of the formal subdivisions of the poem (the two couplets and the two quatrains) has an internally consistent rhyme scheme of its own which marks it off as a subdivision. The story the speaker tells has three stages: the preamble (lines 1 and 2), an account of how he works his employment trick, and some commentary on its result for him. These narrative sections do not coincide with the formal sections. We can tabulate the alignment of the two schemes of organization thus:

Narrative section	Preamble	The employment trick	Commentary
Formal section	Initial couplet	1st quatrain and 1st half of 2nd quatrain	2nd half of 2nd quatrain and final couplet
No. of lines	2	6	4
Rhyme scheme	aa	bcbcde	deff

The poem's formal organization is symmetrical (couplet, quatrain, quatrain, couplet), but the organization of the narrative is asymmetrical: unequal amounts of space, and differently organized sections of the rhyme scheme, are devoted to each narrative section. This narrative organization pulls against the form, counteracting and so weakening our sense of the latter. When, as in the lines immediately following line 2, the form has its own local asymmetry affecting metre and rhyme (the move from couplet to quatrain discussed above) our sense of any scheme in the poem is doubly out of kilter.

Let us now look more closely at the middle narrative section – the account of the employment trick. The speaker practises a different deception on each of three groups of staff:

(1) the staff of 'the designing-rooms and laboratory' (line 3),
(2) the 'workmen' (line 6), and
(3) the 'in-betweens and smart commission-men' (line 7).

The account of each one of these takes up a single sentence, but the sentence recounting (1) spreads over three lines, that for (2) a single line, and that for (3) two lines. (1) and (2) together are co-terminous with the first quatrain (lines 3–6), but they offset the structure of this quatrain by the imbalance between them in sentence length, and by the very fact that line 6 is detached from the other three by a sentence boundary which, by detaching line 6 syntactically, partly obscures its place in the rhyme scheme (thus de-emphasizing still further the *pretend* / *end* rhyme). The sentence recounting (3) (lines 7 and 8) occupies the first half of the second quatrain, with the result that no rhymes occur within this sentence itself; the integrity of the sentence as a syntactic unit reduces further our felt sense of the rhyme scheme. There is also, here, the heavy metrical irregularity of line 8. The alternation between beat and offbeat is challenged in this line, which has juxtaposed beats and a double offbeat. There is some ambiguity about whether the metrical pattern is:

Believe I must have some pull with the boss.
  o B o B   B   o   B   -o-   B

or:

Believe I must have some pull with the boss.
  o B o B   o   B   B   -o-   B

or even:

Believe I must have some pull with the boss.
  o B   -o-   B B B   -o-   B

although any of these will disrupt the regular beat. And it is also quite likely that someone reciting this line would give it a pattern of stressed and unstressed syllables such as:

  x / x x   /   x   /   x x   /
Believe I must have some pull with the boss.

or:

  x / x /   x   x   /   x x   /
Believe I must have some pull with the boss.

which would make it difficult to perceive five metrical beats at all.

4. Closure: The return of regularity

With line 9 the 'commentary' section of the narrative begins and with it the preparation for rhetorical and poetic closure. The words *pen* and *across* provide the rhymes for *men* and *boss*, so counteracting retrospectively the sense we have as we read it that the sentence *The in-betweens...boss* is isolated from the rhyme scheme. The metre of lines 9 and 10 is comparatively regular, especially line 10, which is an undeviating iambic pentameter. At the same time the poem starts to refer less to what the speaker *does* and more to the abstract ideas behind this which are the theme of the poem: *spanner* and *pen* are concrete enough things in themselves and not necessarily opposed in spirit, but here they are metonymies for the opposed ideas of hand- and brain-work.

It is the final couplet, however, which does the most towards giving us a sense of rhetorical and prosodic closure – and perhaps the least important reason for this is that it comes at the end of the poem, and so literally closes it. Obviously, being a couplet, it brings the final rhyming words close together and so 'seals' the poem when compared with the *abab* quatrains we have had. But the rhyme itself is between two words whose lexical meanings are opposite, *either* and *neither* (= not either). Thus the prosodic closure is another manifestation of the opposition, summarized by *spanner* and *pen*, upon which the poem is founded, but at the same time the auditory harmony of the rhyme itself joins the words so that we think of them together as if they were semantically compatible. This trick is then played again in the last line with the close association of another pair of opposites, *both* and *neither*. The opposition here is as stark as it could be: the speaker receives double pay for doing no work at all. But if we read this line without a pause, so elliptical in context are the meanings of *both* and *neither* – we need to think to work out what they refer to here – that comprehension may well lag behind delivery, and what will immediately strike us is the formal symmetry of the opposition; as if, because at the formal level we require both words to create the effect, their meanings weren't in fact incompatible, and a means of making a living which would surely be impossible in real life made perfect sense.

Lines 9–12 consist of a single sentence, the longest in the poem, which drapes across all of the final three line boundaries. The first two of these boundaries, *pen, / I* and *across / Of,* are arrest-release structures: by delaying completion twice while also making clear we have not reached it, they give us a sense of a gradual but inexorable movement towards a close. The final line boundary, *either / And,* is an example of Sinclair's (1972) extension structure. In an extension structure, in contrast to an arrest-release, a syntactic component appears to be complete at a line end: we naturally pause, to mark the completion of the metrical unit of the line and the apparent completion of the phrase, clause, or sentence; there is no tension between the two. Then, as we begin the next line, we see that the syntactic component was not complete after all: more material is added to it, and this springs a surprise. Here the sentence up to and including 'Of how I am no use at all to either' could stand complete on its own. *And draw...* then adds an additional, co-ordinated clause. Line 12 nonetheless does have a completive effect, like the 'release' of an arrest-release structure. It supplies the rhyme for *either* and, as the poem ends, it summarizes and clarifies its theme, this sudden clarification giving it its surprise effect. Syntax and prosody work together here to complete the design of the poem.

5. Conclusion

Langer (1953) argues that the essence of poetry is not that it *describes* experience but that it symbolically *re-creates* it. It is this that gives point to such phenomena as sound patterns since, when they reinforce the meaning of the words, they give us as readers a stronger sense of vicarious experience than we would have if they were not there. In *Public-House Confidence* there is an integrity of formal and sound patterning which constitutes the framework of the poem; it is what guides the narrative and argument of the poem in and out of clarity and confusion. It is not until we have read to the end of the poem that we can apprehend the shape of the formal design. When we do, we see that the formal and prosodic patterns have organized the shape of a rhetorical design. The opposites at the heart of the poem are carefully balanced, and so reconciled – but opposites they remain. Without the form and sound patterns this ambivalence would not have its force.

PART III
THE STYLISTICS OF DRAMA

CHAPTER 9

The Stylistics of Drama: Universal Elements

MARGA MUNKELT

1. Introduction

In Aristotle's *Poetics* (trans. Hubbard 1972; rpt. 1989) the six elements that characterize 'virtually every play' are 'spectacle, the *mimesis* of character, plot, verbal expression, song, and the *mimesis* of intellect', with *mimesis* meaning people 'doing things' (Aristotle 1989: 52–3; my emphasis) in order to represent (i.e. imitate) life (ibid.: 59). Aristotle thus differentiates clearly between the effects that are either achieved through actions or through words (as actions). Whereas, on stage, actions as such can be intelligible without words, the intended effect of speech acts (i.e. 'rhetoric') goes beyond the mere support of action, because 'the speaker would be quite unnecessary if the desired result were obvious without his saying anything' (ibid.: 75). Aristotle's sense of 'rhetoric', therefore, distinguishes 'verbal expression' from mere 'sound' (ibid.: 76). He thus establishes action and speech as elements of equal significance in a play, but indirectly claims that they could also exist without each other.

In Shakespeare's *The Winter's Tale*, a third component is touched on – the role of the spectator. At the end of the play, an eye-witness describes the reunion between the King and his son as follows:

> There was speech in their dumbness, language in their very gesture. [...] A notable passion of wonder appear'd in them; but the wisest beholder that knew no more but seeing could not say if th' importance were joy or sorrow.
>
> (*WT* 5.2.13–19)

Here the 'beholder' is required to form an opinion about the action that may be ambiguous. The dumb show in *Hamlet*, which anticipates the play-within-the-play performed by Hamlet's travelling players, further illustrates the point. It supports the thesis that although enactment, that is, the presentation of action on stage, is the essence of drama, the evaluation of this enactment in terms of characterization depends on the active intellectual and emotional participation of the audience. The standard version of the dumb show in the second quarto edition (Q2)[1] reads:

> The trumpets sounds. Dumb show follows.
> Enter a King and a Queen, the Queen embracing him and he her. He takes her up and declines his head upon her neck. He lies him down upon a bank of flowers. She, seeing him asleep, leaves him. Anon comes in another man, takes off his crown, kisses it, pours poison in the sleeper's ears, and leaves him. The Queen returns, finds the King dead, makes passionate action. The pois'ner with some three or four come in again, seem to condole with her. The dead body is carried away. The pois'ner woos the Queen with gifts; she seems harsh awhile, but in the end accepts love.
>
> (*Ham.* 3.2.135)

This action without words is, obviously, not entirely clear, because Ophelia asks Hamlet: 'What means this, my lord?' (*Ham.* 3.2.136) and assumes: 'Belike this show imports the argument of the play' (*Ham.* 3.2.140). The spectators' uncertainty is further demonstrated by the exchange between Hamlet and his mother: Gertrude says, 'The lady doth protest too much, methinks' (*Ham.* 3.2.230), countered by Hamlet's 'O but she'll keep her word' (*Ham.* 3.2.231) – a more than ambiguous statement, because it leaves open which part she will 'keep' – the double killing of her husband or the fact that 'never come mischance between' them. Ophelia finds Hamlet 'as good as a chorus' (*Ham.* 3.2.245).

The example from *Hamlet* not only illustrates the interdependence of speech and action but also the necessity of additional analysis and commentary, when motivations and emotions are relevant. It suggests that there are, indeed, three indispensable elements of drama – action, speech, and their perception, with the spectators' task being to find meaning in them. If 'verbal expression' is missing, 'mimesis' may require choric explanation, although of course an actor's performance can turn action metaphorically into 'visible speech' (Meisel 2007: 51–6).

Among the three universal and uncontroversial elements – action, speech, and perception – one or the other characteristic can be foregrounded in varying degrees and for varying effects. Thus, the two most extreme forms of drama are plays without spoken words as opposed to plays consisting only and exclusively of spoken words. The general distinction is between physical actions without words that have a general or universal significance, and dialogic actions that have the potential for individuality and can express unique emotional and intellectual conflict. Although Manfred Pfister's study of drama weights action with speech (Pfister 1993: xv) and elevates dialogue to the 'fundamental mode of presentation' (Pfister 1993: 6), because the speech situation is what distinguishes drama from narrative fiction, the provocative thesis at the beginning of the following examination is that language is less important than enactment and performance in the genre that has been called 'conversational genre' (Short 1996: 168f.), that the generic function of action is superior to that of speech, but that speech and language lend depth to action and character in a play.

2. Transforming the familiar: Narrative into speech

According to general knowledge, English drama has evolved from two traditions: the classical, on the one hand, and the native medieval liturgical, on the other. Both are religiously motivated and both relied, in their earliest forms, on the audiences' familiarity with the respective myths and stories on which they were based. The early religious activities that are negotiated as the origins of drama ritualize action and movement as expressions of religious devotions. Similarly, the presentation of biblical scenes in front of the altar primarily adds physical action to the well known narratives from the gospel. This can be achieved either in ritualized shows, dances, movements, and processions, or in the transformation of narratives into speeches.

The medieval liturgical plays are very short (all fewer than 200 verse lines) and consist of only a few characters who render declamatory speeches one after the other. The absence of real interaction does not allow the classification of those speeches as dialogue.[2] There is no attempt at presenting an evolving action or a character development. The quality that makes these texts plays is their transformation of a narrative into speeches. Thus, the play *The Creation, and the Fall of Lucifer* begins with God praising himself:

> I am gracious and great, God without beginning;
> I am maker unmade, all might is in me;
> I am life and way into wealth-winning;
> I am foremost and first, as I bid shall it be
> 　　　　　　　　(ed. Cawley 1956: 3, lines 1–4).

Similarly, Lucifer's first speech reveals his association with light as well as his ambition and wish to rise:

> Oh certes, what I am worthily wrought with worship, iwis!
> For in a glorious glee my glittering it gleams.

[...]
I shall be like unto him that is highest on height.
                  (ed. Cawley 1956: 6, lines 81–91)

The creation of the world followed by Adam and Eve's temptation by Satan
and their ensuing expulsion from Paradise, and Cain's banishment after
his murder of Abel, as narrated in Genesis 1–5 is covered by four medieval
plays, *The Creation, and the Fall of Lucifer* (York Cycle), *The Creation of Adam
and Eve* (York Cycle), *The Fall of Man* (York Cycle), and *Cain and Abel* (N.
Town Cycle).[3] Only the fall of Lucifer is not part of Genesis and thereby
illustrates the equal status of myth and Scripture as possible material for
drama. Standardized characteristics of these mythical characters are revealed
through their speeches that touch on their generally known features.

Although in *The Fall of Man* and *Cain and Abel* tentative signs of insight into
some of the characters' thoughts are noticeable – as in Satan's opening soliloquy in hell, including his intention to tempt Eve (ed. Cawley 1956: 19, lines
1–22), Abel's offerings to the invisible God (ed. Cawley 1956: 29–30, lines
62–91), with which he soliloquizes about his personal devotion, and Cain's
soliloquy lamenting his isolation with an anticipation of his future suffering
(ed. Cawley 1956: 33, lines 183–95) – these passages do not lose their quality
as set speeches; the transformation of narrative into dialogue and even into
occasional soliloquies is not utilized for an in-depth presentation of the characters' minds. The main function of these speeches is to convey the action
that is already known to the spectators and to verbalize expected attitudes.

3. Provoking the unfamiliar: Individuality through language

The transition from medieval to Renaissance drama and its further development can be described as moving from the general to the personal. Whereas
in medieval and early classical plays on the Renaissance stage one speaker
might read out loud a narrated action, in later, fully fledged plays the use of
spoken language endows characters with emotions; the presentation of the
'conflicts of wills and passions' requires the use of dialogue (see McIlwraith
1961: vii–viii) and other speech forms, and even more so an individualized
use of language that – rather than presenting all-human experiences – highlights character and individuality. A look at a twentieth-century play, covering the same material as the four liturgical plays discussed, supports this
statement. In Arthur Miller's play *The Creation of the World and Other Business*
(1972), no expectations are confirmed, but the spoken language in this play
surprises the spectators: apart from rare exceptions, when short passages from

the King James Bible are transmitted literally, the speeches endow the mythical characters with unexpected emotions and thoughts. The play is by no
means a 'dramatic paraphrase of part of Genesis' (Richardson 1973: 89). The
clash between the myth as known and its possible reinterpretation is intensified by a juxtaposition of language varieties from different historical phases.
The combination of Early Modern English (the language of the Authorized
Version of the Bible) with the American vernacular of the 1970s (the language
of the play's composition) calls attention, on the one hand, to the universal
validity in the Western world of the creation of the world, but foregrounds, on
the other hand, the power of language, which can turn figures into characters
by means of individualized speech acts, and which avoids the oversimplifica-
tion of action. Drama as the imitation of life in general versus drama as the
presentation of specific characters' lives is illustrated by Miller's play.

Miller uses direct and indirect intertextual references to other biblical narratives as well as to contemporary (American) myths – like that of the happy
American family – and also to controversies concerning these myths. God is,
for example, the great Creator who knows beforehand of his Creation 'that it
was good', but he is also the great experimenter when he admits to Adam:

> Now and then I do something and, quite frankly, it's only afterwards that I dis-
> cover the reasons. [...] In your case it was extremely experimental. I had just
> finished the chimpanzee and had some clay left over. And I – well, just played
> around with it, and by golly there you were, the spitting image of me.
>
> (Miller 1972: Act 1, pp. 5–6)

God here reduces man's significance as the crown of the Creation to the result
of leftovers. Not only does he irreligiously advocate Darwin's theory of evolution, but he also questions his own significance, whose 'spitting image' man
has become. The interjection 'by golly', a popular belittling and euphemiza-
tion of 'by God' (see *Webster's Third*) with which he, strictly speaking, abuses
his own name and thereby violates the first of his own Ten Commandments,
shifts God's greatness to another level and endows him with a great sense
of humour. Moreover, it invites comparison with Eve's direct use of 'Oh
my God' during her orgasm, on which God comments: 'I have never heard
my name so genuinely praised' (Miller 1972: Act 1, p. 31). Other linguistic
games consist of Miller's regular allusions to his own Jewish background by
inserting Yiddish vocabulary – such as God addressing Adam as 'schmuck'[4]
(Miller 1972: Act 1, p. 27) – into passages of Early Modern English and
American slang. Anachronistically, he also lets Adam state that God said 'in
plain Hebrew' (Miller 1972: Act 1, p. 23) that Eve and he are not allowed to
eat from the Tree of Knowledge. The juxtaposition of the vocative *schmuck*
for Adam with the direct quotation from Genesis 4.17–18, 'cursed is the

ground [...] forth to thee', and the Americanized version of the curse, 'No more going around just picking up lunch' (Miller 1972: Act 1, p. 27), transposes the biblical myth into a contemporary context. This strategy is, again, applied when God prefers Abel's food to Cain's and is interested in the recipe (Miller 1972: Act 3, pp. 90–1).

In Miller's play, it is the use of verbal expression and speech forms which distances the play from its biblical origin, but simultaneously creates an alienating pattern of intertextuality. Dialogues between God and Lucifer suggest an overall reference to the Book of Job by presenting God and Lucifer as partners, however competitive they may be; they discuss the degree of, respectively, innocence and ignorance, of Adam and Eve throughout the play. Also, life in Paradise as a variant of the (wrong) American Dream (particularly in Act 2, pp. 44 and 50) is conveyed by language. Moreover, not only does Lucifer tempt Eve in a dream, but also the later dialogues between Adam, Eve, Cain, and Abel are conducted like everyday conversations among members of a typical American family (especially in Act 3, p. 83) and thereby emphasize the metaphoric relationship between individual dreams and the myth of the American Dream. The supernatural/suprahuman aura of the Creation and God's greatness are reduced by references to human creations of art, when the angels, for example, praise God by singing Händel's 'Hallelujah' (Miller 1972: Act 1, p. 12).

Miller attacks the American society and the Americans frequently implied claim that they are God's chosen people, and questions their belief in the Creation and its textual source. To do so, his linguistic and thematic emphasis is on sex and biological multiplication (Miller 1972: Act 1, p. 13f.) as well as on verbal puns and double-entendres (Miller 1972: Act 1, p. 15). By linguistic means Miller retells Genesis. His reinterpretation of Scripture retains all the recognizable elements of the Creation myth, but through language he changes its meaning.

4. Crossing genre elements: Epic within drama

Language in drama has been shown to be primarily used for the presentation of the characters' thoughts and emotions.[5] However, the development of plays from religious rituals and processions to declamatory renditions of known religious myths, to a revelation of characters' minds by means of linguistic interaction, does not continue as an inevitable sequence. The hierarchy of the universal elements of drama discussed here – action (mimesis), speech (rhetoric/verbal expression), and perception (understanding/comment) – is in no way stable, and their received emphasis in drama has been varied in plays across centuries and cultures. It was particularly in the 1950s that what is generally called modern American drama began to turn this hierarchy upside down[6] by a demonstration of the failure of language in drama as an analogy for life. A quality shared by practically all American plays since the 1950s is experimentation with drama as a literary genre and an innovative utilization of theatre as its medium. Its crossing of genre boundaries has had a world-wide impact. It is no exaggeration to call Tennessee Williams the precursor for this process of innovation. His play *The Glass Menagerie* (1944), though written in the mid-forties, is the main influence on playwriting in the fifties and also the sixties; a critic has called it the motor for postwar American drama (Hughes, 1976: 16). The genre element 'perception' is elevated to the same rank as speech. Thus, epic and dramatic elements are juxtaposed.

Williams's plays often begin with extensive 'production notes' in which he describes his ideas about the scenery, lighting, music, props, and other ingredients of performance achieved by the 'collaboration in the theatre' between playwright, production team, and audience. In his *Memoirs* Williams says: 'Poetry doesn't have to be words. [...] In the theatre it can be situations, it can be silences,' and he goes on to explain this idea of what he calls the 'plastic theatre' which 'must take the place of the exhausted theatre of realistic conventions' (Williams 1969: 229).

The emphasis in Williams's plays is on the characters' inner lives and it takes further elements of his 'plastic theatre', such as music and lighting, to make them noticeable. Thus, in *The Glass Menagerie*, the stage directions that are integrated in the play's text do not always coincide in style and terminology with ordinary stage jargon. When Laura and Jim meet we are told, for example, that '*while the incident is apparently unimportant [to Jim], it is to Laura the climax of her secret life*' (Williams 1969: Scene 7, p. 291). Thus the result of the performance is described, and not the way in which the actors are supposed to achieve it. Similarly, after she learns that Jim is engaged to be married, '*The holy candles in the altar of Laura's's face have been snuffed out. There is a look of almost infinite desolation*' (Williams 1969: Scene 7, p. 307). Both phrasings emphasize how much Williams gives priority to emotions over spectacular actions by making visible the inner lives of the characters. In order to support the presentation of thoughts Williams originally created 'screen images' as headlines for the scenes. Their purpose is also to keep the audience attentive (Williams 1969: Scene 1, p. 230). The religious allusion, 'the altar of Laura's face', quoted above, is anticipated by a 'screen image' entitling the scene 'Annunciation' (Williams 1969: Scene 5, pp. 264, 266). Williams's 'screen images' illustrate how differently the characters evaluate one and the same incident. This concept relies on the paradox of using visible images in order to present the 'invisible'. Moreover, in *The Glass Menagerie*, Williams integrates a narrator into his play: Tom Wingfield is present in a dual function as narrator and commentator, on the one hand, and as a speaking and acting character, on the other. The choice of this genre-exceeding role in the play is made necessary because the play is the re-enactment of Tom Wingfield's memories. The material presented on stage is a subjective experience. Williams himself talks of the 'poetic licence' of memory (Williams 1969: Scene 1, p. 233), but also of the necessity to take 'whatever licence with dramatic convention is convenient' (Williams 1969: Scene 1, 234) for the purpose of the presentation of an entire mind – not only of individual thoughts.

Tom Wingfield steps into and out of his varying roles continuously. In a way he is also director and stage manager of the play, when, for example, he orders the musicians to play, or asks for a particular kind of lighting, or orders the curtain to come down to end a scene. From time to time the other characters ignore Tom's absence when he is involved in activities outside the dramatic action of the play. Amanda, for example, continues talking to Tom as if he were still at the dining table with them: '[Amanda] addresses Tom as though he were seated in the vacant chair at the table though he remains by portières. He plays this scene as though he held the book' (Williams 1969: Scene 1, p. 238). Sometimes the characteristics of Tom's varying roles are intentionally not kept apart. Details enhance the fusion, if not confusion, of character, stage manager, narrator, and even playwright or poet. We witness Tom improvising his creation of a double life as 'Killer Wingfield' who is also called 'El Diablo' (Williams 1969: Scene 3, p. 252). 'The metatheatrical element in Williams's work is central,' says Christopher Bigsby. 'The theatre was not only Williams's avocation, it was his fundamental metaphor. His characters tend to be writers and actors, literal or symbolic, who theatricalise their world in order to be able to survive in it' (Bigsby 1992: 41–2).

As John Lennard and Mary Luckhurst (2002: 51) have pointed out, 'it is vital to remember that genres are not mutually exclusive: that any two (or ten) genres can combine within the same work in parallel, in series, or in fusion', and that, accordingly, elements from narrative fiction as well as from lyric poetry can be embedded in a play. The most innovative feature in Williams's concept of drama is, however, the transformed inclusion of medieval genre characteristics that are put into tension with his 'plastic theatre'. Thus, in addition to having his narrator introduce episodes from the present as well as from the past, moments of the current unique action alternate with repeated incidents and typical situations. The stage set supports this procedure: thus the dining room is reserved for the performance of repeated/typical situations, whereas the living room is the place for current unique experiences. The episodes are revived on the basis of Tom's associative memory, and further associations of other characters are enacted. In this episodic feature, the play deviates from Aristotle's description, but in its inclusion of repeated and typical experiences the play corresponds with it, as well as with the nature of medieval morality plays.

The merging of innovative and experimental elements of drama with the origins of the genre are likewise maintained in Arthur Miller's *A View from the Bridge* (1955).[7] Although the play shares with *The Glass Menagerie* its episodic character and the use of flashbacks, unlike them it shifts the focus from characterization to an emphasis on an onlooker's perception of and response to this character's experience, which can be used for didactic purposes. The narrator, the Carbone family's lawyer Mr Alfieri, is in the play but not personally involved in the emotional crises, and he observes the action from Brooklyn Bridge (hence the play's title). Alfieri's presence is used by Miller to give unity and continuity to the play. His perception with an outsider's eyes is shared by the audience so as to not let them be caught up in details, but to learn and be taught instead.

The conflict presented in *A View from the Bridge* – Eddie's sexual obsession with his niece and the family's immigration problems – is, despite its specific geographical, sociological, economical, and historical contexts, tied up with general moral and ethical concerns. Miller's device of using Mr Alfieri is vital in this respect: as a character in the play, because of his profession as a lawyer, he represents moral principles as well as law and order; as witness and commentator on the entire play – and especially because he is looking from a raised position on the bridge down into the dock area – he represents the kind of superiority and objectivity which is characteristic of the chorus in Greek tragedy. His guiding of the audience is also similar to that of an authorial or intrusive narrator in a novel.

In the Epilogue at the end of *A View from the Bridge*, Alfieri evaluates his own response:

> ... even as I know how wrong he [Eddie] was, and his death useless, I tremble
> [...] he allowed himself to be wholly known and for that I think I will love him
> more than all my sensible clients. [...] And so I mourn him [...] with a certain
> [...] alarm.
>
> (Miller 1970: Act 2, p. 85)

He is made the mouthpiece of those who learn from what they have seen. His *trembling* and feeling *alarmed* coincide with meaning and purpose in Aristotle's definition of *catharsis*, that is, the audience's cleansing from and through *pity* and *fear*. Not only does *A View from the Bridge* invite the spectators to participate in an event of major moral dimensions, but its performance functions as a mirror for them to see their own responses. Both effects are achieved by the device of giving to Mr Alfieri the multiple functions of witness, commentator, chorus, lawyer, and character. His presence guarantees the goal of tragedy in Aristotle's sense – though not by Aristotle's means.

5. Scaling down the world: Allegory and absurdity

The paradox of genre innovations as means of recalling the most basic genre elements and origins is illustrated by what is usually categorized as the Theatre of the Absurd. According to Martin Esslin, 'the convention of the Absurd springs from a feeling of deep disillusionment' (Esslin 1985: 311). In his absurdist plays, Edward Albee, for example, uses a virtually empty stage that is physically similar to both the medieval *simultaneous stage* and the Shakespearean stage. Albee does not, however, try to utilize the flexibility caused by the absence of scenery and does not make up, so to speak, for the lack of visual illusion. Instead, he reinforces the aspect of bareness on a thematic level by exposing the failure of language. The universal elements of drama, speech, and mimesis are foregrounded by Albee. He does not, however, do so by making any of them particularly intelligible, but rather by exposing their failure. The main procedure is reduction: characters, events, topics of conversations, relationships – everything is made small and narrowed down. Albee criticizes the lack of mutual understanding and the absence of humanity in the American society of the late fifties by letting the spectators experience a severe lack of comprehension: the characters in the plays are unable to reach each other, nor does the audience understand their (problems of) communication. Language in Albee's plays is exposed as an impediment to – not as a means of – direct understanding, and in order to make the audience aware of this his use of language likewise remains unclear (one critic even talks of a 'puzzle'). In performances of Albee's plays, actors and spectators seem to be busy with the same activities, but there is no correspondence between them (Paolucci 1986: 14–15).

In his play *The American Dream* (1959–1960) Albee converts the American values of the 1950s into clichés, and exposes them in the form of allegory. The dramatis personae are not characters but types, and instead of having proper names they are called Mommy, Daddy, Grandma, and Young Man. Varying the personified vices and virtues of medieval morality plays, *The American Dream* allegorizes family relationships. Apparently, in contrast to medieval drama, the play's concern is not a journey via the temptations and dangers of life on earth to heavenly salvation, but the search for the right image. The all-embracing world of allegory is reduced by Albee to minimal size and limited to a framework of acceptable social behaviour. This is done by further specifying the functions of family members as father and mother – not husband and wife. Unfortunately, Mommy's and Daddy's fulfilment of the American ideal is impaired by the lack of an appropriate child. Several allusions in the play indicate that once there was a child, but because it did not meet the image-requirements it had to be removed.

The man-made quality of the world is ever-present in the reduction of moral to physical values and the exaggeration of manners whose origin is forgotten.

According to Esslin, 'the American dream of the good life is still very strong. [...] Edward Albee comes into the category of the Theatre of the Absurd precisely because his work attacks the very foundations of American optimism' (Esslin 1985: 311–12). The theme of emotional insincerity, sterility, and emptiness in *The American Dream* is emphasized by repeated references to surgical operations. Daddy's emotions, 'qualms', and 'misgivings' (Albee 1995: 82) are confused with physical pain, and we are told that he is able to feel something only near the stitches and scars. Figurative meanings and metaphors have obviously disappeared, and everything is taken literally. Also the Young Man, whom Grandma recognizes to be the embodiment of the 'American Dream', consists exclusively of externals: his outward appearance is beautiful although his inside is hollow and he lacks intelligence, but he is available for money. He admits: 'I have no talents at all, except what you see' (Albee 1995: 113). As the Young Man lacks emotions (Albee 1995: 114–15), language lacks meaning and depth, and communication is converted, if not perverted. Similarly, the other foregrounded element of drama, mimesis, is transformed: Unlike self-explanatory actions on stage that present universal experiences, Albee (as do other playwrights of the Absurd) calls attention to the deceptiveness of what is visible. Grandma in the American Dream, for example, is 'disposed of' by Mommy and Daddy but turns out to be indisposable and even superior to those who think otherwise. Although she is now no longer meant to be present, she has the last word in the play and explains to the audience:

> [T]his is a comedy, and I don't think we'd better go any further. [...] So, let's leave things as they are right now – while everybody's happy – while everybody's got what he wants – or everybody's got what he thinks he wants. Good night, dears.
>
> (Albee 1995: 127).

By applying the convention of a character's being invisible on stage Albee questions the happiness of the ending. This is also why he calls his play 'a comedy, yet' (Albee 1995: Preface).

In Albee's *The Sandbox* (1959), Grandma is done away with by Mommy and Daddy in a sandbox in order to make her die. Grandma buries herself in the sand with a child's shovel and thereby enacts her death. Thus, in a strongly abbreviated form, she performs the phases of human life and lets childhood in a sandbox coincide with death in a coffin (see Zinman 2008: 30). The simultaneous use of a stage property as a metaphor for the beginning of life and its end symbolizes the similarity of childhood and old age, and the cyclic nature of human life, with one's inevitable return in old age to childishness. A critic calls Grandma an 'aged, abandoned child' (Gabbard 1982: 28). As with the telescoping of the phases of human life, language, in this play, is reduced to only a few striking characteristics. Grandma's utterances are inarticulate sounds – the lack of verbal coherence in early childhood and old age are made identical. Aristotle's distinction between 'verbal expression' and 'sound' (Aristotle 1989: 76) has nearly disappeared.

Albee meets Aristotle's requirement that the action of a play should not exceed the time-span from sunrise to sunset. In his method of minimizing life, these 24 hours are, however, not a day and a night, but represent an entire human life. Grandma is the personification of humanity – although unfortunately a dying representative – but she is not a tragic protagonist. Death is not considered to be tragic, for two reasons: firstly, it only finishes a life which is, according to Albee, so small and insignificant that it fits into a sandbox; and secondly, it marks the ending of an empty life – as represented by Mommy and Daddy: a life that can be performed in 14 minutes.

The length of Albee's play is roughly the same as that of the medieval liturgical plays. Whereas, however, the ingredients of the early plays focus on the greatness of the Creation, in the plays of Absurd theatre they are modified so as to expose its insignificance. Again, whereas the subject matter of religious medieval plays is self-explanatory and does not need length, the brevity of the plays of Absurd theatre is based on a reduction of action and speech in order to reveal their meaninglessness. Centuries ago, the belief in God's power, in the stability of the universe, and in a firm and stable hierarchy of values made their dramatic reproduction easy and intelligible. Drama was readily accepted as a mirror of life, and the stage as an image of the entire world. Since then, the horizon of humankind has expanded considerably due to new discoveries and the confrontation with other world views in the process of globalization. However, instead of one big world, the twenty-first century offers a variety of small worlds. Therefore the life of one human being can no longer be considered exemplary; the reduced stature of the characters is enhanced on stage by the presentation of limited locations like residential areas, apartment buildings, parks, hotel rooms, shops, or sandboxes. We do not observe God or Satan or a good or bad Christian, but we get glimpses of an individual's meaningless life. This is why the presentation of continuous actions and accepted values in five-act plays has been abandoned in favour of individual, psychological experiences. However, the original classical and native origins of drama have not altogether disappeared but are still recognizable in their metamorphoses: moral values are narrowed down to clichés, and the so-called three unities survive mostly in the unity of place; but the former unity of action gives way to episodic and cyclic scenes because they correspond more to the presentation of the human mind. Moreover, the tasks and functions in the theatre of actors, directors, characters, and spectators likewise seem to lose their distinctive qualities because they become more and more interchangeable. And, finally, the main function of language – communication and information – is changed.

6. Varying languages: Ethnicity and linguistic (con-)fusion

The metamorphosis of language reaches yet another dimension in plays of the so-called ethnic theatre. Only a glimpse of the range of linguistic (and other) experiments can be offered here, and Mexican-American/Chicana(o)[8] drama has been chosen as one of many examples of those kinds of playtexts that belong to at least two cultures and two languages. Texts by Chicana(o) writers composed in English 'can be compared to the literatures of other colonized peoples who have sought to reveal the evils of an oppressive colonial system and simultaneously to illuminate positive elements of a native culture and its spiritual and philosophical struggles with the dominant culture' (Gonzales-Berry and Gynan 1989: 306). As those Mexican-American writers who compose plays for political purposes tend to write in English rather than Spanish, in order to reach as many people as possible (Thelen-Schaefer 1992: 78–85), the intended spectators are outsiders who must be informed, educated, and, if possible, made interested in the goals of the 'minority'.[9]

Particularly in the literature of the 1970s and 1980s, this use of English is thematized as being necessary for professional advancement, and, of course, the price is the gradual loss – even in the private sphere – of one's native language (Thelen-Schaefer 1992: 82–3); bilingualism is still considered a deviation from the established system (despite several attempts at introducing bilingual education to the American school system). This hierarchical weighting of the languages that represent the two cultures to which Mexican Americans belong, is often foregrounded in their literature. Not infrequently, the writers operate with three linguistic codes: Chicano-English, Chicano-Spanish, and a mixture of both, a form of code-switching (Gonzales-Berry and Gynan 1989: 306). The function of code-switching has, above all, changed from an emergency device originally intended to overcome vocabulary shortage, into a literary tool for the deliberate demonstration of cultural and political conflict.

In his play *Zoot Suit* (1978), Luis Valdez utilizes this 'bilingual idiom' (Gonzales-Berry and Gynan 1989: 306) in order to expose how the English language is used as an instrument of power in a questionable legal system, but also how other non-verbal 'languages', such as the languages of stereotypes or of clothes, are likewise used by those in power. They suppressed the linguistic versatility and other forms of strength of the defendants accused of murder in the 'Sleepy Lagoon Murder Trial' of 1942.[10] *Zoot Suit* is partly a documentary play. Utilizing the genre potential, Valdez, however, surmounts the limitations inherent in one political event.[11] He favours drama as an instrument of (political) education, and as an admirer and follower of Bertolt Brecht's epic theatre, he uses epic elements, especially narrative stage directions, and a character as narrator and commentator. This character stepping into and out of his role is El Pachuco, who also recalls and symbolizes Mexican Americans' Aztec past. In addition to operating with forms of alienation, the play, with El Pachuco as motor, uses show elements like singing, dancing, and choruses – all of which cross the standard boundaries between 'serious' drama and 'popular' entertainment – but meet Aristotle's requirement of 'spectacle' (Aristotle 1989: 52–3). *Zoot Suit* is, thus, a play rebelling against various conventions – including the conventions of linguistic variety and register.

In this play, language is used to expose cultural bias and wrong assumptions about characters' origins on the basis of their appearance – when, for example, the lawyer George Shearer confronts the gang's silent prejudice that he might be a non-Spanish-speaking American cop by exposing their stereotypical thinking:

> The problem seems to be that I look like an Anglo to you. What if I were to tell you that I had Spanish blood in my veins? That my roots go back to Spain, just like yours? What if I'm an Arab? What if I'm a Jew?
>
> (Valdez 1992: 43)

But language is also either a barrier or a bridge in personal relationships. On a private level, the Jewish-American journalist Alice, who establishes a friendship with the gang-leader Henry Reyna, begins to learn Spanish to be able to communicate with him in depth. Absence of language, the refusal or inability to speak, is used for purposes of rebellion when El Pachuco, during the trial, disobeys and squats or stands, although he is ordered by the judges to do the opposite. However, the lawyer's statement in favour of tolerance and against racism (Valdez 1992: 62) is made monolingually and unequivocally in American English in order to be intelligible to the intended audience within the courtroom – in the play, and in the theatre. The personal realm, however, cannot survive without a mutual understanding created through language. Thus, George's and Alice's Spanish vocabulary expands in the course of the play so as to render them capable of understanding their clients' and friends' personally expressed moods, feelings, and thoughts, as well as their publicly voiced opinions.

Language is, thus, foregrounded in a play whose theme is the implementation of civil rights, tolerance, and humanity as well as the extinction of racism and ethnic prejudice. It is vital, to cause intelligibility through the use of English but simultaneously to interrupt the show of what is easy to understand by means of defamiliarization – in most cases a foreign language, that is, the language of the 'minority'. Ethnic drama deprived of linguistic devices would become meaningless.

7. Conclusion

An evaluation of the universal elements of drama discussed here – action, speech/language, and perception – cannot be final. As has been shown, their functions and the possible dominance of one over the other are varied and keep changing, because their role is dependent on the connection between the world and its mirror on stage. However, a preliminary conclusion of the investigation is that plays without words are a greater challenge than plays without physical action. The spectator must think more actively and intensively about meaning than in plays with words – unless plays with language distort language to such a degree as to become unintelligible. Plays without words are examplified by Samuel Beckett's *Act Without Words I* (first performed 1957), *Act Without Words II* (first performed 1960), and, probably the most famous example, *Breath* (written and performed 1969). Examples of plays without action other than speech are Edward Albee's *Box* and *Quotations From Chairman Mao Tse-tung* (both first performed 1968), about which the author himself says that they are simple plays with the condition that the audience 'be willing to approach the dramatic experience without a preconception of what the nature of the dramatic experience should be' (Albee 1971: 123). Not surprisingly, these texts are representative of what is generally called the Theatre of the Absurd, which reached its climax in the 1960s. This was a highly experimental phase in the development of drama, characterized by an emphasis on the failure of human communication.

Often, the meaninglessness of speech can be shown either in a reversal of the functions of language, when it is not used for communication but forms an obstacle to communication; when language ceases to exist and is replaced by other signals, such as sounds and/or lights; and, most notably, when plays stop representing human beings but feature objects and apparently unmotivated chains of reaction, as in Beckett's *Breath*. In this play, the only feature with any connection to a living creature is a human cry (*vagitus*) and breath. Although the main sign of a human being's 'existence' is his/her breathing, the distinction between just existing and living is expressed: a life that consists only of breathing is a vegetable life, whereas human life means communicating with other human beings, sharing thoughts, and understanding each other through language.

Plays do not need language to convey actions that reflect general experiences of mankind, or myths that are familiar to their audience. However, language is indispensable for the presentation of traditions or rituals, or even conventions whose frameworks or contexts are unknown to the spectators. Consequently, political or other messages cannot be understood without linguistic means unless the symbolic actions from which they can be inferred are embedded in well known cultural and historical contexts.

Moreover, as has been shown, language is superior to action for the presentation of unique situations and of individual emotional and/or intellectual conditions. A presentation of a human being's mind is dependent on the use of linguistic expression – even if it is not always semantically meaningful and consists of incomplete morphemes or phonemes, as in the case of Grandma in *Sandbox* – and an image of the subconscious needs additional verbal interpretation by other human beings in order to become intelligible to the audience, as is the case of the dumbshow in *Hamlet*.

NOTES

1. Of the three extant texts of *Hamlet*, Q2 (1604–1605) has generally been accepted as copy-text/ control-text.
2. A dialogue is more than a series of monologues, that is, 'a colloquy' and a 'literary work in the form of a conversation between two or more persons' (see *OED*, Dialogue 1 and 2).
3. These anonymous plays were composed and acted in the late fourteenth century by the trade guilds as part of the Corpus Christi celebrations. They have survived in manuscripts of the fifteenth and sixteenth centuries (Cawley 1956: x–xi). As is known, 'the cycles at Chester, York, and Wakefield were acted processionally, probably under the influence of the Corpus Christi procession', and 'each guild performed its pageant on a wagon which was moved from one station [...] to another' (Cawley 1956: xii).
4. *Schmuck* = Yiddish *shmok* for 'fool', meaning 'jerk' (see *Webster's Third*, s.v. *schmo* or *schmoe*).
5. This fact holds true also for the so-called discussion play, a category of drama flourishing in the nineteenth century and particularly associated with George Bernard Shaw (examples are *Major Barbara* and *Mrs Warren's Profession*), in which different intellectual positions cannot but be expressed through speech acts.
6. For a survey and analysis of the influence of drama in the 1950s on drama in general, see Lennard and Luckhurst (2002: 245–60).
7. *A View from the Bridge* exists in two versions, an early verse-drama in one act, and a later prose-play in two acts (which is discussed here).
8. In this analysis, Mexican-American and Chicana(o) are used as synonyms.
9. The development of Mexican-American literature since the 1970s has shown attempts at operating with both linguistic practices – writing, on the one hand, in Spanish for those Mexican Americans with a higher education who are able to read, write, and understand the language of their ancestors, and writing, on the other hand, for those who were raised speaking English, the language of those in power and of assumed success. See Thelen-Schaefer (1992: 78–85) and Gonzales-Berry/Gynan (1989: 306). Other minority literatures seem to be intended for insiders rather than outsiders. See Berkowitz (1992: 203–8).
10. The Sleepy Lagoon Trials gained a world-wide reputation in 1942, when 17 young Mexican-Americans were arrested by the Los Angeles Police, accused, and convicted of murder without sufficient evidence (Thelen-Schaefer 1992: 74). The authorities (also in the play) denied the accused Mexican Americans their right to present themselves as, and be treated like, American citizens. They did so by forcing them to wear clothes and hairstyles that speak the stereotypical language of second-class citizens.

The so-called zoot suit was an outfit chosen as a form of protest by the criminalized young adults to emphasize that they were stereotyped, and to protest against this atti-tude. The Pachuco is the 'urban prototype of Chicano defiance' (Sanchez-Tranquilino and Tagg 1992: 569). There was, accordingly, a Pachuco Movement associated with the trials, which was revived in the 1970s as part of the Chicano Movement.
11. Valdez was the founder of El Teatro Campesino in the 1960s, an amateur farmwork-ers' theatre 'dedicated to the exposure of socio-political problems within the Chicano communities of the United States' (Huerta 1992: 7).

CHAPTER 10

Dialogue and Characterization in Quentin Tarantino's *Reservoir Dogs:* A Corpus Stylistic Analysis

DAN MCINTYRE

1. Introduction

Quentin Tarantino's directorial debut, *Reservoir Dogs*, exploded on to cinema screens in 1992. Lauded by film critics, this story of a diamond heist gone wrong is innovative in its non-linear narrative structure and its sharp and witty dialogue. Indeed, Tarantino is widely acknowledged to be a master at writing film dialogue that is both naturalistic and distinctive (Smith 2007) and for creating characters that, despite being rooted in stereotypes (e.g. the gangster, the drug dealer, the priest) somehow transcend the archetypes of which they are born. Thomson, for instance, summarizes Tarantino as:

> ... a real, weird writer, a conduit for swinging, hardboiled talk which, if it is gangsterese for the moment, might one day end in inspired comedy. For all the much-copied riffs and routines, sometimes Tarantino's characters are eloquent and human in their talk[.]
>
> (Thomson 2002: 859–60)

Since Tarantino is one of the few directors who is equally famous for his screenwriting, it may seem surprising that barely any attention has been paid by film critics to the dialogue in his films. Certainly there has been no linguistic analysis of Tarantino's character dialogue.

In fact, this neglect of an important aspect of Tarantino's films is representative of an almost complete lack of concern in film studies for dialogue generally. Instead, work on dramatic speech is concentrated almost exclusively within stylistics, where the tools of pragmatics have been employed to considerable effect in analysing and interpreting dialogue in drama and its consequences for characterization (see, for example, Herman 1991 and Culpeper *et al.* 1998). Much of this early work on the stylistics of drama tended to be qualitative in nature and focused on representative sections of a text, rather than complete scripts. More recently, however, stylisticians have begun to apply the techniques of pragmatics and corpus linguistics in the analysis of much larger samples of dramatic texts than was previously possible. Busse (2006b), for example, draws on a range of analytical tools and methodologies, including corpus linguistics, in a study of vocative constructions in Shakespeare. Culpeper (2009b) further shows how keyword analysis can elucidate our understanding of Shakespeare's plays. There is, of course, no reason why such techniques should not be applied to contemporary dramatic texts, and in this chapter I demonstrate the potential of corpus linguistics software for contributing to our understanding of the relationship between dialogue and characterization in film scripts. I analyse Quentin Tarantino's screenplay *Reservoir Dogs* (1994) using Wmatrix (Rayson 2008), a software package for corpus linguistic analysis (see also Walker, and Archer and Bousfield, this volume). The focus of my analysis is on what makes each character distinct. To this end I compare each character's total speech against the remainder of the character dialogue from the screenplay, and investigate keywords and key semantic domains; that is, words and semantic fields that are statistically over-represented in particular characters' speech when compared against that of the others. In this way I am able to isolate distinctive features of character dialogue. I also briefly consider n-grams – repeated sequences of dialogue – and relate these to characterization triggers, drawing on Mahlberg's (2007a,b) work on n-grams in prose fiction and using Culpeper's (2001) model of dramatic characterization as a theoretical guide. My analysis demonstrates how the corpus stylistic methodology can provide insights into the mechanics of film dialogue, and sheds some interpretative light on what makes Tarantino's characters so distinctive. The value of this type of analysis for film studies is that it facilitates a far more detailed understanding of character behaviour than that drawn only from observing the propositional content of character dialogue. Furthermore, it gives the critic more evidence with which to make objective generalizations about character, thus removing the need to argue through force of rhetoric alone. It is also the case that only with this very meticulous analysis of dialogue is it possible to move towards exploring the relationship between dialogue and camera angles, and other aspects

of *mise-en-scene*. In this respect I suggest that corpus stylistics has much to
offer film criticism.

I begin with a synopsis of the plot of *Reservoir Dogs* and follow this with a
discussion of my methodology and the pre-processing work involved in pre-
paring the screenplay for corpus analysis. I then discuss theoretical work on
characterization and corpus stylistics before going on to present my analysis
of character dialogue in Tarantino's film.

2. A plot synopsis of *Reservoir Dogs*

Reservoir Dogs tells the story of a group of eight crooks who together plan and
carry out a robbery of a jewellery store. In order to avoid the potential for any
member of the gang to betray the others, Joe Cabot, the gang leader, gives each
member a pseudonym. The gang members are thus Mr White, Mr Pink, Mr
Brown, Mr Blue, Mr Blonde, and Mr Orange. The only member of the team
besides Joe who is not given a pseudonym is Joe's son, Nice Guy Eddie.

Unbeknownst to the gang, Mr Orange is an undercover cop and tips off the
police about the time and place of the robbery. Consequently, when the gang
carry out their crime, they are surprised by a large squad of police officers.
The robbers, though, have no intention of surrendering quietly and instead
shoot their way out of the store. The whole event turns into a bloodbath. Mr
Brown and Mr Blue are killed by the police, Mr Blonde and Mr White shoot a
number of cops, and Mr Orange is shot by a member of the public, following
which his involuntary response is to shoot the woman who has just shot him.
For both sides – cops and robbers – the heist is a disaster. The only mitigating
factor for the gang is that Mr Pink has managed to hang on to the diamonds.

Following the robbery, the gang make their individual ways back to their
hideout in an abandoned warehouse. Mr White and the injured Mr Orange are
the first to arrive, followed by Mr Pink. As Mr Pink and Mr White discuss the
possibility that they have been set up, Mr Blonde arrives. Mr White is furious
with Mr Blonde for acting like a psychopath during the robbery. In response to
Mr White's anger, Mr Blonde reveals that he has taken one of the cops hostage.
Mr Blonde's audacity calms the situation and he, Mr White and Mr Pink fetch
the cop from the trunk of Mr Blonde's car, tie him up in the warehouse and
begin to beat him. During this beating, Nice Guy Eddie turns up. Fearful of
what Joe's reaction will be if he arrives to find so many cars parked outside the
hideout, Nice Guy Eddie instructs Mr White and Mr Pink to go with him to
drop the cars off elsewhere and to recover the diamonds. Mr Blonde is left alone
with the cop, Marvin Nash. Marvin tells Mr Blonde that he doesn't know anything about a set-up and that, consequently, even if Mr Blonde tortures him,
he won't be able to reveal anything. Mr Blonde responds by saying that he will

torture him anyway, simply because it amuses him. In a grimly comic scene, Mr Blonde then cuts off Marvin's ear with a razor blade, to the soundtrack of Gerry Rafferty and Joe Egan's 'Stuck in the Middle with You'. Mr Blonde then drenches Marvin in gasoline. However, just as he is about to set light to him, Mr Orange somehow finds the strength to shoot Mr Blonde dead. Mr Orange tells Marvin that he is a cop and Marvin reveals that he knew this all along. At this point Mr White, Mr Pink, and Nice Guy Eddie return. Finding Mr Blonde dead, Nice Guy Eddie demands to know what happened. Mr Orange makes up a story, saying that Mr Blonde went crazy and planned to burn Marvin, shoot Mr Orange, murder the others when they returned, and make off with the diamonds. Nice Guy Eddie refuses to believe this, on the basis that Mr Blonde has previously taken the rap for a crime that Joe Cabot committed, and has proved his loyalty to Joe and Eddie by serving time in prison for them.

At this point Joe arrives at the warehouse. Joe tells Eddie that everything Mr Orange has said has been a lie, and that Mr Orange is actually an undercover cop. Mr White refuses to believe this, especially when Joe's 'evidence' for this turns out to be nothing more than gut instinct. The arguments intensify and escalate into a Mexican stand-off involving Joe, Nice Guy Eddie, and Mr White. Mr Pink's efforts to defuse the situation fail. Joe shoots Mr Orange, Mr White shoots Joe, Mr Orange shoots Nice Guy Eddie, and Nice Guy Eddie shoots Mr White. As the gang members lay dying, Mr Pink quietly slips out of the warehouse with the diamonds. Moments later, the police arrive. Mr White crawls over to Mr Orange and tells him that it looks like they will both have to do some time. In response to this, Mr Orange reveals that he really is a cop. At this point the police arrive on the scene, screaming for Mr White to drop his gun. As the screen goes blank, shots are heard, and we can assume that Mr White has shot Mr Orange and that he himself has been killed in retaliation by the police.

It will be apparent from this synopsis that the plot of *Reservoir Dogs* is not a complicated one. What makes the film tense and surprising is the way that Tarantino plays around with the narrative structure. For example, it is only part way through the film that the audience learns, through a series of flashbacks, that Mr Orange is a cop. And what keeps the pace of the film alive is the sparkling dialogue as the characters joke, argue and fight with each other. It is the aspects of characterization inherent in the dialogue that the corpus analysis below aims to capture.

3. The corpus stylistic methodology applied to drama

My analysis focuses on the dialogue of the crooks: Joe Cabot, Nice Guy Eddie, Mr White, Mr Pink, Mr Brown, Mr Blonde, and Mr Orange. I have disregarded Mr Blue since he speaks only 61 words. In the analysis that follows

I compare each character's speech against the speech of the other criminal characters. So, for example, Mr White's speech is compared against a reference corpus consisting of the speech of Joe Cabot, Nice Guy Eddie, Mr Pink, Mr Brown, Mr Blonde, and Mr Orange.

In order to do this, it was first necessary to create individual text files for each character's dialogue. This involved retrieving all the words spoken by a particular character from an electronic version of the screenplay. The means by which this was achieved was to mark up the screenplay in such a way as to separate out each individual character's dialogue and to distinguish it from screen directions. Below is an example of the mark-up used (tags are in bold):

```
<screen>Mr Pink rubs two of his fingers together.</screen>
<char id="Mr Pink">Do you know what this is? It's the world's smallest violin,
playing just for the waitresses.</char>
<char id="Mr White">You don't have any idea what you're talking about. These
people bust their ass. This is a hard job.</char>
```

This mark-up allowed the extraction of particular characters' dialogue using Scott Piao's *Multilingual Corpus Toolkit* software (freely available on the web). Once extracted, each character's dialogue was stored as a separate plain text file (.txt) and a reference corpus created for that character consisting of the speech of all the other criminal characters. The files and their related reference corpora were then uploaded to Wmatrix.

Once the files have been tagged for part-of-speech and semantic categories by Wmatrix, n-grams – repeated sequences of words – are easily extracted. To calculate keywords and key semantic domains it is necessary to compare a file containing a character's dialogue against its relevant reference corpus. A key word is one which is either over- or underused by that character when compared against the speech of the characters in the reference corpus. A key semantic domain is a semantic field that is either over- or underused in relation to the reference corpus (see Walker, this volume, for more details on how Wmatrix operates). The reason for calculating these is that keywords and key domains can give us an insight into dramatic characters and how they are perceived by the reader and by other members of the *dramatis personae*, since they often act as stylistic markers (Culpeper 2009b). In the section that follows, I discuss some of the recent work in this area in order to demonstrate how this works.

4. Dialogue, corpora and characterization

In his book *Language and Characterisation* (2001), Culpeper presents a model of the characterization process which suggests that when we read dramatic texts we engage in both top-down and bottom-up processing in order to construct mental representations of characters. Top-down processing involves the application of pre-exisiting schemas as we read, drawn from our real-life experiences and from fiction. For example, in Priestley's (1947) play *An Inspector Calls*, our initial assessment of the Inspector character is likely to be driven by our existing background knowledge of police officers and how they stereotypically behave (and this background knowledge does not have to have been developed through first-hand experience; fiction can give us equally well-developed schemas). Bottom-up processing, on the other hand, involves taking linguistic cues from the text itself in order to build up a conception of a character. To refer back to the same example, as we continue to read the play we may well find ourselves reassessing the character of the Inspector on the basis of his aggressive linguistic behaviour, perhaps to the extent that we retune our schema for police officers to make sense of this (see Short 1996 for a fuller discussion of the relevance of schema theory to stylistics). In practice, the process of generating a mental representation of a dramatic character is likely to involve a combination of top-down and bottom-up processing.

In order to systematize the process of analysing the bottom-up component of the characterization process, Culpeper (2001: 163–324) draws together a checklist of typical linguistic indicators of character. In doing this he makes a distinction between explicit and implicit characterization. The former refers to instances where characters make direct statements about themselves or others. The latter refers to the kind of characterization that comes about through the process of the reader/audience making inferences about characters from their linguistic behaviour. Of the various kinds of triggers of implicit characterization, Culpeper (2001: 199) explains that keywords can be strong indicators of particular character traits, noting that they can act as what Enkvist (1973) calls 'style markers': that is, words whose frequency in particular contexts differs from their frequency in the language generally.

There are a variety of available computer programs that will calculate 'keyness' – the extent to which the frequency of lexical items in one corpus differs from their frequency in a larger reference corpus. I used Wmatrix (Rayson 2008) to do this. With regard to reference corpora, Scott (2009) suggests that so long as they are over a certain size in relation to the target corpus, it is not a major issue what kind of texts are contained within the reference corpus; that is, the same core of keywords will be generated whatever reference corpus is used. In calculating the keywords of the criminal characters in *Reservoir Dogs*, I compared each character's speech against a reference corpus containing the speech of all the other criminal characters. This is because, as Culpeper (2009b: 35) notes, '[t]he closer the relationship between the target corpus and the reference corpus, the more likely the resultant keywords will reflect something specific to the target corpus'; that is, something specific to the particular character under observation.

Keywords and key domains have the potential to act as characterization indicators, as Walker (this volume) demonstrates in relation to prose fiction. Mahlberg (2007a) has demonstrated that the same can be true of n-grams. In a study of the novels of Charles Dickens, she shows how the identification of repeated patterns can 'relate to themes and characters' (2007a: 31). As she explains, '[e]xact repetitions of sequences of words are not very common' (2007a: 25). In this respect, n-grams – like keywords and key semantic domains – may be seen as constituting foregrounded elements of a text, deserving of special analytical attention.

5. Criminal characters in *Reservoir Dogs*

In this section I present the results of my corpus-based analysis. Wmatrix calculates keywords and key semantic domains using the log-likelihood statistical test. For keywords, I used the critical value of 10.83. Scores above this indicate 99.9 per cent confidence of statistical significance ($p < 0.001$); that is, we can be 99.9 per cent confident that a word with this score or higher is genuinely over-used in comparison to its frequency in the reference corpus, and that the result is not just due to chance. For key domains, I used a lower critical value of 6.63 ($p < 0.01$), indicating 99 per cent confidence of statistical significance, in view of the fact that the small amount of data meant that fewer semantic domains were available for keyness comparison.

One caveat to any analysis of keyness is that statistical significance does not necessarily equate to interpretative significance. That is, just because a word or semantic domain is marked as being over- or underused in comparison to the reference corpus, this does not mean that it automatically has a special interpretative effect. While Wmatrix carries out statistical analysis, it is up to us to interpret the results of that analysis. As an example, one of Mr Orange's keywords is *Joe Cabot* (Wmatrix treats this as one lexeme). However, this is explained by the fact that it is a proper noun and an unusual one at that. Unsurprisingly, therefore, it is marked as key in Mr Orange's speech. When we look at a concordance of the lexeme we find that Mr Orange uses it when talking to the cop, Marvin, who at this point does not know the gang-leader's name. It is apparent, then, that there is little interpretative significance to this key word, since Mr Orange uses it only to inform Marvin of the gang-leader's identity. However, this is not to say that all personal names have no interpretative significance. For example, Mr White's top key word is also *Joe*, and when we look at *his* use of the name in context we find that it has a much greater interpretative significance. It is always used in reference to Joe's organization of the heist (e.g. 'Joe could help him', 'when Joe gets here', 'Joe's gonna get you a doctor'). In this respect, it seems that Mr White's use of the name indicates his confidence in Joe as an organizer, as opposed to it simply being used to identify the character to others. The degree of trust that Mr White has for Joe makes his refusal to believe Joe's explanation that Mr Orange is a cop all the more poignant, since we know that Mr White would not normally disagree with his boss. The irony, of course, is that Joe turns out to be right. Working out the interpretative significance of a key word or domain thus involves looking at its use in context, and interpreting lists of key items involves filtering out those words/domains on the list that we would intuitively expect to see. It is, for instance, no surprise to find character names as key if we are comparing our target text against a general reference corpus. In such cases it is only by looking at concordances that we can determine whether they have interpretative significance. In cases where a proportion of a text is compared against the text as a whole (as is the case here, where I compare a character's dialogue against all the other characters' speech), we may be less inclined to expect character names to turn up as key. Where they do, this gives rise to a number of possibilities. For instance, a particular character name may be key because it is only used by one character. Alternatively, the interpretative significance of a character name being key may lie not so much in the name itself as in the fact that it is used in place of a pronoun.

Of course, character names are not the only stylistically revealing items to be found in a keyword list. Of particular interest are words and semantic domains that our intuitions would not necessarily predict. While we might expect to find words and domains relating to the text's overall theme to be key, we are less likely to predict statistically significant grammatical words or semantic domains that are not explicitly theme-related. Summarizing Scott's work on keywords, Culpeper (2009b) notes that some will relate to what is often called the text's 'aboutness'. That is, we will expect some words to be key because they reflect/create particular characteristics of the text's genre. *Reservoir Dogs* is a crime thriller, therefore we will expect to see words related to crime (and, indeed, we find *cop, parole, jail,* and so on), some of which may well work to trigger the schemas we need to interpret the action in the film. In this respect, while 'aboutness' keywords may be important in establishing schematic aspects of genre and the fictional world, they will not necessarily be indicative of specific elements of characterization. Determining those keywords that are markers of character style thus involves filtering out those proper nouns and aboutness keywords which have no bearing on characterization, and focusing on those that we might be less inclined to predict through intuition.

In the analysis that follows, I take each character in turn and discuss how their positive keywords and key semantic domains (those words and domains which are overused) might be indicative of aspects of their character (see Table 10.1). Following this, I also provide a brief discussion of n-grams and how these too can act as characterization cues.

Mr Blonde

Table 10.1: Keywords and key semantic domains in
Mr Blonde's speech

Mr Blonde	
Keywords (no. of instances)	*Log-likelihood score*
vic (4)	19.60
blah (3)	14.70
guy (3)	14.70
Key semantic domains (no. of instances)	*Log-likelihood score*
SENSORY: TOUCH (3)	10.38
EVALUATION: AUTHENTIC (3)	10.38
LIVING CREATURES: ANIMALS, BIRDS, ETC. (9)	7.04

Mr Blonde has just three keywords, only one of which appears to have interpretative significance. This is *Vic*. While Culpeper (2009b) notes that proper nouns often have little interpretative significance, in this case *Vic* is Mr Blonde's own first name, and it seems unusual that he should use it to refer to himself. A concordance reveals that Mr Blonde uses this name when reporting Joe's speech to Eddie. The importance of the name *Vic* for Joe and Eddie seems to be that it encodes the close social relationship that the two men have with Mr Blonde. That Mr Blonde also uses the name in his report of Joe's speech perhaps suggests that he himself recognizes his own importance to Joe and Eddie. Mr Blonde's other keywords – *blah* and *guy* – seem to be aboutness keywords, typical of the informal dialogue in the film.

Of Mr Blonde's three key semantic domains, the last one – LIVING CREATURES: ANIMALS, BIRDS, ETC. – seems to reflect a particular aspect of his character (N.B. two of the nine items in this domain are mistagged and have been disregarded here). All of these animal references are used to refer to other characters, and are abusive (notwithstanding the fact that some of these terms are used in banter). This perhaps suggests a contemptuous aspect of Mr Blonde's character:

erve what they got . You gon na	**bark**	all day , little doggie , or are
ou gon na bark all day , little	**doggie**	, or are you gon na bite ? I sai
na bite ? I said Are you gon na	**bark**	all day , dog , or are you gon n
d Are you gon na bark all day ,	**dog**	, or are you gon na bite . Well
little fun finding out who the	**rat**	is . It 's a change . Sure . A g
Nice Guy , but I 'd make you my	**dog**	's bitch . You 'd be suckin the
nd going down on a mangy T-bone	**hound**	. Seymour Scagnetti . He is a mo

Mr White

Table 10.2: Keywords and key semantic domains in
Mr White's speech

Mr White	
Keywords (no. of instances)	*Log-likelihood score*
joe (22)	20.55
next (5)	15.15
guy (4)	12.12
're (37)	11.59
Key semantic domains (no. of instances)	*Log-likelihood score*
IF (18)	8.48
WARFARE, DEFENCE AND THE ARMY: WEAPONS (15)	8.22
MEDICINES AND MEDICAL TREATMENT (12)	8.20

Of Mr White's key semantic domains, WARFARE, DEFENCE AND THE ARMY: WEAPONS is explained by Mr White's repeated references to Mr Orange having been shot, as is the domain of MEDICINES AND MEDICAL TREATMENT (see Table 10.2). These, then, are domains related to aboutness. More revealing interpretatively is the top key semantic domain, IF, indicating that conditionals are a key feature of Mr White's speech:

```
know what you 're talking about . So if   you 're through giving me your amateu
sed out . He will be dead fer sure ,  if  we do n't get him to a hospital . Wit
reams in pain . Joe could help him .  If  we can get in touch with Joe , Joe co
e turning him over to the cops , but  if  we do n't , he 's dead . He begged me
t fucking patronize me . Of course .  If  I have to tell you again to back off
 you are gon na go round and round .  If  we do n't , he 'll die . That fucking
e . You almost killed me , asshole !  If  I had any idea what type of guy you w
hit , he 's gon na fucking die on us  if  we do n't get him taken care of . </s
e this guy 's a fucking psycho . And  if  you think Joe 's pissed at us , that
ight difference . Okay , Mr Expert .  If  this is such a truism , how come ever
 cares what your name is ? Who cares  if  you 're Mr Pink , Mr Purple , Mr Puss
give you any resistance whatsoever .  If  you get a customer or an employee who
t . Watch her shut the fuck up . Now  if  it 's a manager , that 's a different
know better than to fuck around . So  if  one 's givin you static , he probably
s break that son-of-a-bitch in two .  If  you wan na know something and he wo n
 's next . After that he 'll tell ya  if  he wears ladies underwear . I 'm hung
istake I ca n't let you make . Joe ,  if  you kill that man , you die next . Re
l that man , you die next . Repeat ,  if  you kill that man , you die next ! Go
```

From this we might suppose that Mr White is a character who makes a habit of hypothesizing about the future. This is further reflected in his use of the key word *next*:

```
t those sick assholes are gon na do  next  . I mean , Jesus Christ , how old do
ou 're gon na smash her in the face  next  . Watch her shut the fuck up . Now i
```

```
ne . Then you tell 'im his thumb 's next . After that he 'll tell ya if he we
oe , if you kill that man , you die next . Repeat , if you kill that man , yo
at , if you kill that man , you die next ! Goddamn you , Joe , do n't make me
```

If and *next* work to convey a specific aspect of Mr White's character that sets him apart from the other criminals. He appears calculating – able to consider the consequences of his own actions. This establishes him as someone not likely to act impulsively, which arguably foregrounds his behaviour at the end of the film when he does, on impulse, refuse to believe Joe's statement that Mr Orange is the rat. This is made all the more striking by the fact that Mr White has, throughout the film, expressed his loyalty to and belief in Joe. This much is conveyed by the key word *Joe* which, as I explained earlier, appears to reflect Mr White's loyalty to his boss and his capacity for solving the gang's problems. Of the other keywords, *guy* seems unremarkable by virtue of its being an 'aboutness' key word, while *'re* is a contraction of *are* (e.g. *you're, we're, they're*). Mr White appears partly to be characterized by his propensity for issuing assessments of other characters and their actions (e.g. 'you're hurt', you're right', 'you're hot', 'you're super-fucking pissed', 'they're insured up the ass'), and of the situations that he and they find themselves in (e.g. 'We're already freaked out'). All of these structures are what Halliday (1994) terms intensive relational processes in the attributive mode, and this grammatical patterning serves to foreground this aspect of Mr White's character. Establishing this tendency towards evaluation as a character trait only serves to intensify Mr White's mistaken assessment of Mr Orange at the end of the film.

Mr Pink

Table 10.3: Keywords and key semantic domains in
Mr Pink's speech

Mr Pink	
Keywords (no. of instances)	*Log-likelihood score*
were (20)	21.19
blonde (7)	18.64
blue (6)	15.97
they (33)	15.85
Key semantic domains (no. of instances)	*Log-likelihood score*
OPEN; FINDING; SHOWING (11)	8.33

Mr Pink's top key word is *were* (see Table 10.3), and an examination of the concordance for this item reveals that it is used to reflect on what went wrong during the robbery (e.g. 'We were fucking set up!'). This works to characterize him as someone more concerned with what happened in the past than what might happen next. While Mr White speculates on the likely outcomes of his actions, Mr Pink focuses on events that have already happened, often in order to apportion blame. Related to this is Mr Pink's only key semantic domain, OPEN; FINDING; SHOWING. Many of the instances of this category suggest that Mr Pink attributes considerable importance to the demonstration of particular points (e.g. 'You show me a paper says the government shouldn't do that', 'They ain't gonna hafta show him a helluva lot of pictures for him to pick you out', 'I'll show you who you're fucking with!'). Taken together with the key word *were*, I would suggest that this characterizes Mr Pink as reflective, anxious, and insecure. Of his other keywords, *blonde* is key because of Mr Pink's unwavering belief that it is Mr Blonde who has set them up. *Blue* refers both to Mr Blue and to the Madonna song 'True Blue' that the crooks talk about over coffee at the beginning of the film, as well as being a metonym for the police. Finally, *they* appears to reflect Mr Pink's obsessive concern with other people and how their actions impact on him. While *blonde* and *blue* are aboutness keywords, *they* seems more likely to be indicative of character. Here again is a possible indicator of his insecure personality.

Mr Brown

Table 10.4: Keywords and key semantic domains in Mr Brown's speech

Mr Brown	
Keywords (no. of instances)	*Log-likelihood score*
guy (4)	29.00
hurts (4)	29.00
virgin (4)	24.05
whoa (3)	17.30
blind (2)	14.50
machine (2)	14.50
like (7)	13.35
Key semantic domains (no. of instances)	*Log-likelihood score*
DISEASE (7)	17.23
UNSEEN (2)	14.50
RELATIONSHIP: INTIMACY AND SEX (7)	10.00
OTHER PROPER NAMES (5)	9.97

Mr Brown is a minor character in the film who only appears in two scenes. Unsurprisingly, then, Mr Brown's keywords and semantic domains are related to aboutness (see Table 10.4). All of Mr Brown's keywords and key semantic domains except for *blind* and UNSEEN relate to the story he tells to the other criminals at the beginning of the film about why the Madonna song 'Like a Virgin' is so called. These words and domains function to establish crude conversation and banter as typical of the criminal characters, but they are not indicative of Mr Brown's character specifically. *Blind* and UNSEEN relate to the event during the robbery when Mr Brown is shot and can no longer see. Again, these are aboutness keywords. After this event Mr Brown dies, hence playing no further part in the story.

Joe

Table 10.5: Keywords and key semantic domains in Joe's speech

Joe	
Keywords (no. of instances)	Log-likelihood score
vic (6)	21.85
Sid (5)	18.21
Eddie (9)	16.29
crowd (4)	14.56
juicy (4)	14.56
more (4)	14.56
Toby (7)	14.33
way (7)	14.33
come_in (3)	10.92
parole (3)	10.92
two (8)	10.87
Key semantic domains (no. of instances)	Log-likelihood score
MENTAL OBJECT: MEANS, METHOD (8)	15.27
BUSINESS: GENERALLY (6)	11.45
THE MEDIA: BOOKS (4)	9.91
SUBSTANCES AND MATERIALS: LIQUID (4)	9.91
PLANTS (4)	9.91
PERSONAL NAMES (48)	8.44
TOUGH/STRONG (2)	7.28

The first three of Joe's keywords are personal names (see Table 10.5). *Vic* and *Eddie* reflect two particularly close personal relationships, while *Sid* perhaps reinforces the notion that Joe is a character for whom personal relationships are important (Sid is a character to whom Joe lends money) – not least for the fact that someone indebted to him on a personal level is highly manipulable. While these are proper nouns, it seems that in this case they do have some stylistic import. *Crowd* is used in relation to the customers at the jewellery store whom the crooks will have to control during the robbery. This suggestion of 'crowd control' trivializes the violent crime that the gang carry out, and hints at a lack of concern on the part of Joe that belies his genial exterior. The negative traits of Joe's character are further pointed at by the word *juicy*, which Joe uses on numerous occasions to describe the profits of the robbery. In this sense, the word has clear connotations of greed. The remaining keywords appear to have no interpretative significance, being related instead to aboutness.

Of Joe's key semantic domains, MENTAL OBJECT: MEANS, METHOD contains words related to organization and reflects Joe's status as the gang leader and brains behind the robbery:

```
tones from Israel . They 're like a  way   station . They are gon na get picked
e like hell for you to hear it this  way   . But when Vic asked me how 's busin
on a certain day . They 're like a   way   station . It 's gon na get picked up
is what you 're going to do . This   way   the only ones who know who the membe
Eddie and myself . And that 's the   way   I like it . Because in the unlikely
. I ai n't worried . Besides , this  way   you got ta trust me . I like that .
ng ! Listen up Mr Pink . We got two  ways  here , my way or the highway . And y
Mr Pink . We got two ways here , my  way   or the highway . And you can go down
```

The next domain, BUSINESS: GENERALLY refers both to the business hours during which the gang will carry out the robbery, and the 'business' that Joe engages in. This latter use is euphemistic and suggests an attempt to legitimize the means by which Joe makes his money. THE MEDIA: BOOKS is an aboutness domain, pointing to an incident in the first scene where Mr White takes Joe's address book and refuses to return it. SUBSTANCES AND MATERIALS: LIQUID contains the four occurrences of the key word *juicy*, PLANTS refers to weed (i.e. cannabis), PERSONAL NAMES has some stylistic significance, as outlined in the discussion of proper nouns above, and TOUGH/STRONG contains just two instances of the evaluative adjective *tough*, used in relation to Joe's description of the planned robbery.

Freddy and Mr Orange

Table 10.6: Keywords and key semantic domains in Freddy's speech

Freddy	
Keywords (no. of instances)	Log-likelihood score
guy (10)	41.88
weed (7)	20.31

Continued

Table 10.6: Continued

Keywords (no. of instances)	Log-likelihood score
connection (4)	16.75
pot (4)	16.75
had (8)	13.43
barking (3)	12.56
buyin (3)	12.56
sell (3)	12.56
smoking (3)	12.56
worth (3)	12.56
friends (3)	12.01

Key semantic domains (no. of instances)	Log-likelihood score
SMOKING AND NON-MEDICAL DRUGS (6)	19.65
BUSINESS: SELLING (12)	15.39
PLANTS (7)	14.33
TELECOMMUNICATIONS (4)	9.64
WEATHER (2)	8.38
SENSORY: SMELL (2)	8.38
MONEY: COST AND PRICE (3)	8.33
OBJECTS GENERALLY (15)	7.82
PERSONAL RELATIONSHIP: GENERAL (8)	7.73

Table 10.7: Keywords and key semantic domains in
Mr Orange's speech

Mr Orange	
Keywords (no. of instances)	Log-likelihood score
Marvin (4)	23.23
'm (16)	19.42
I (42)	15.00
look (5)	14.56
me (17)	13.43
jail (3)	13.04
cop (5)	12.62
die (5)	11.80
doctor (5)	11.80
Joe_Cabot (2)	11.62
burn (2)	11.62
in_my_eyes (2)	11.62

Continued

Table 10.7: Continued

Key semantic domains (no. of instances)	Log-likelihood score
MEDICINES AND MEDICAL TREATMENT (7)	13.03
DEAD (9)	7.96
SEEM (5)	7.37
NEGATIVE (27)	6.77

The character of the undercover cop is referred to in the script as both Mr Orange and Freddy, and for this reason I have treated these as two separate characters. Tarantino's use of two names for this character generates a point-of-view effect. At those points in the screenplay where the character name is given as Freddy, we are more likely to view events from his point-of-view and see the other characters for the crooks that they are. Freddy's keywords are all related to the story that he tells Joe and the others when he first meets them, to convince them that he has previous form as a criminal. His invented story concerns a drug-deal in which he came close to being discovered by a group of cops carrying a large amount of cannabis whilst in a lavatory. The way he avoids their suspicion is by brazening it out and acting as normally as he can, taking his time washing and drying his hands and ignoring the incessant barking of the cops' Alsatian dog. It is perhaps significant that all of Freddy's keywords are related to a story that he tells to convince the crooks that he is genuine (see Table 10.6). This seems symbolic of the consistency with which he inhabits his invented persona and the extent to which he is able to convince the crooks.

The keywords for Mr Orange, however, generate a very different characterization (see Table 10.7). *Marvin* is clearly key because it is a personal name and Mr Orange is the only one to address the cop in this way. The keywords *i* and *'m* (e.g. 'I'm'), however, appear to reflect a degree of egotism on Mr Orange's part, that perhaps stems from a desire to come across as confident and brash in order to convince in his role as an undercover cop. *Me* has obviously similar effects. *Look* too has a related effect, being used in a series of imperatives. Mr Orange uses the word *jail* when he expresses his lack of concern about being imprisoned if Mr White were to take him to a hospital ('I don't give a fuck about jail', 'Fuck jail!', 'I don't give a shit about jail'). Once the reader/viewer has realized that Mr Orange is actually working undercover, these lines can be interpreted very differently; of course, Mr Orange is unconcerned by the prospect of jail because he knows that he will not be going there. However, the fact that Mr Orange overuses *jail* in comparison to the other criminals perhaps indicates that at this point in the film his cover is slipping.

There is no clear interpretative significance to Mr Orange's other keywords since they all relate to aboutness. Of his key semantic domains, however,

NEGATIVE contains 27 instances of *not*, which might suggest that negativity is a key aspect of his invented persona.

Nice Guy Eddie

Table 10.8: Keywords and key semantic domains in Nice Guy Eddie's speech

Nice Guy Eddie	
Keywords (no. of instances)	*Log-likelihood score*
daddy (9)	30.87
Elois (6)	20.58
black (5)	17.15
Vic (4)	13.72
blue (4)	13.72
Key semantic domains (no. of instances)	*Log-likelihood score*
KIN (2)	31.02
EXCESSIVE DRINKING (6)	12.38
WITHOUT CLOTHES (2)	6.86
SCIENCE AND TECHNOLOGY IN GENERAL (2)	6.86

Turning to Nice Guy Eddie, his top key word is the vocative *daddy* which he uses to address and refer to his father, Joe (see Table 10.8). *Daddy* is proximally deictic in social terms and thus indicates a close relationship between Eddie and his father. However, this usage is deviant (and, hence, foregrounded) since it is unusual for adults to refer to their parents using diminutive forms. What this perhaps suggests is that Eddie as a character is infantilized. Despite being a violent criminal, he still feels in thrall to his father. His infantilization perhaps explains his inability to empathize with the victims of the crimes he carries out, since he has never developed an adult view of the world. It is striking too that KIN is Eddie's top key semantic domain, and of the 20 words in that domain, 12 are references to Joe Cabot. Familial relationships seem important to Eddie, particularly the relationship he has with his father.

Of Eddie's other keywords, *Elois* and *black* are related to a sexist and racist story that Eddie tells to amuse Mr White, Mr Pink and Mr Orange. The keyness of these words perhaps explains Smith's (2007: 29) comment that, in *Reservoir Dogs*, '[h]ighly noticeable is the use of homophobic and racist language'. *Blue*, on the other hand, refers to Mr Blue and to the song 'True Blue'. *Vic*, however, appears to be significant interpretatively, despite being a proper noun, because it indicates a close relationship between Eddie and Mr Blonde; *Vic* is another proximal social deictic term. Moreover, it is Mr Blonde's real name. Eddie does not refer to any of the other characters by their real names, despite knowing these. Unsurprisingly, then, Eddie refuses to believe Mr Orange's claim that he shot Mr Blonde because he was going to double-cross the others by making off with the diamonds; Eddie's loyalty to his friend is consistent with the naming convention he uses to address him.

Eddie's other key semantic domains are EXCESSIVE DRINKING and WITHOUT CLOTHES, relating to the story referred to above that Eddie tells to the others. SCIENCE AND TECHNOLOGY IN GENERAL turns out to refer only to an acronym that Eddie uses for 'parole officer', and to a single instance of the word *technology*. It seems, then, that only his top key semantic domain has interpretative significance.

N-grams

While keywords and semantic domains seem intrinsic to the characterization of the criminals in *Reservoir Dogs*, n-grams provide further support for the arguments made above. N-grams are sequences of words that are repeated in a corpus. They are also referred to as clusters or lexical bundles, the N in n-gram simply standing for any number. So, a 4-gram is a four-word sequence, a 5-gram a five-word sequence, and so on. Mr Blonde's 5-grams are all related to the same statement, namely his claim that his parole officer will not let him leave the halfway house in which he is staying:

5-gram	Frequency
me leave the halfway house	3
let me leave the halfway	3
won t let me leave	3

We might presume from the repetition that this is something that concerns him and, indeed, this is the impetus for his getting involved with the robbery.

Mr White's 5-grams are all related to his efforts to reassure Mr Orange that he is not going to die of the gunshot wound he received in the aftermath of the robbery. This works to characterize Mr White as considerate in a way that the other characters are not, which again sets him apart from them and, I would argue, increases the likelihood of our empathizing with his character. For this reason, we are likely to view Mr White's eventual fate as more tragic than that of the other criminals.

5-gram	Frequency
you re gonna be okay	4
I don t know what	3
just hold on buddy boy	3

Mr Pink has only one 5-gram – 'I didn't tell him' – which is repeated three times. Of his three 4-grams, 'didn't tell him' and 'I didn't tell' are reduced forms of the 5-gram, though the remaining 4-grams seem interpretatively significant. 'I don't know' is repeated three times and this, in conjunction with the 5-gram, provides further support for the notion that Mr Pink is a character who is unwilling to accept any responsibility for his actions and for what has gone wrong during the robbery.

Mr Orange's 5-gram is 'take me to a doctor', repeated five times. Clearly this is related to his distress from his injuries, which is in contrast to the cool exterior he has previously portrayed to the gang. Of his three 4-grams, two are reduced forms of the 5-gram while the other, 'I won't tell', is again related to his plea to be taken to a hospital. This pleading seems at odds with the brash exterior he exudes in the lead-up to the robbery, indicating a different – and possibly more genuine – facet of his character.

Finally, Nice Guy Eddie has just one 4-gram which is repeated four times. This is 'I don't know', which reflects the confusion he feels at the end of the film when confronted with the possibility that Mr Blonde has betrayed him.

6. Conclusion

The analysis of keywords, key semantic domains and n-grams indicates some of the differences of character among the criminals in *Reservoir Dogs*, and suggests which particular aspects of their speech work as characterization cues. Such cues begin to explain why we react to the characters in the way that we do. Notice that this is distinct from the kind of analysis that simply asserts the characteristics of a given dramatic character on the basis of impressionistic observation. A corpus stylistic approach to characterization enables the analyst to see objectively what aspects of character dialogue contribute to the construction of character generally, and by doing this we are able to avoid the basic claim-and-quote strategy typified in the kind of film studies analysis that disregards linguistic analysis. Of course, this is not to say that we would not reach the same conclusions about a character through impressionistic observation. In such a case, we might ask why a corpus stylistic analysis is necessary. An answer to this is provided by Spitzer (albeit in relation to authorial style), whose work on the analysis of literature was among that which laid the foundations for modern stylistics (see Busse and McIntyre, this volume):

> Sometimes it may happen that this etymology leads simply to a characteriza-
> tion of the author that has long been accepted by literary historians (who have

not needed apparently to follow the winding path I chose), and which can be summed up in a phrase which smacks of a college handbook. But to make our way to an old truth is not only to enrich our own understanding: it produces new evidence of objective value for this truth – which is thereby renewed. (Spitzer 1948: 38)

Furthermore, impressionistic analysis often lacks the specific detail which a stylistic approach can provide. Smith (2007: 29), for instance, picks up on the racist and homophobic dialogue in the film but fails to mention that this comes primarily from Nice Guy Eddie. And in some cases, corpus stylistic analysis can invalidate subjective observations. Smith (2007: 27) asserts, for example, that '[t]he absolutely key word for the film and several of its protagonists however is "professional"'. This observation is not borne out in the analysis of keyness provided above.

What I hope to have shown is how Wmatrix can uncover aspects of character that are foregrounded by virtue of their statistical significance, but which would be unlikely to be consciously noticed while reading the screenplay of *Reservoir Dogs* in the conventional manner (though, of course, I am arguing that we are likely to respond to these characterization cues unconsciously). This appears to be a different kind of foregrounding from that commonly associated with deviation from linguistic norms, and for that reason is perhaps better described as salience; at the very least, we need to make clear that we are talking about statistical deviation rather than deviation from linguistic norms.

With regard to *Reservoir Dogs* particularly, the corpus analysis described above is able to account for the distinctions between characters and, potentially, why we react to them in the way that we do. Mr White, for example, is distinguished from Mr Pink by his tendency to hypothesize about future events. Mr Pink, on the other hand, is a character more focused on apportioning blame for what he perceives as events that have gone wrong in the past. Those characters whose keywords, key semantic domains, and n-grams are not solely content-related (i.e. in terms of aboutness) appear to be the more fully developed characters.

The corpus methodology provides a means of assessing dramatic character from an objective standpoint, which is a key methodological principle of stylistics. What such an analysis can also provide is an indication of which aspects of the text are likely to be worthy of further qualitative investigation. As Rayson (2008) points out, part of the value of Wmatrix is its capacity for finding candidate research questions. For example, the evidence presented above that Mr White is a character well aware of the consequences of his actions might provide a starting point for an analysis of how this aspect of his character is revealed pragmatically. What should also be apparent from the above analysis is that interpreting the results of an investigation of keyness is not a simple mechanistic process. Corpus software will provide statistical analysis, but it is up to the stylistician to interpret the qualitative significance of those results. Keywords, key semantic domains, and n-grams are simply additions to the stylistician's tool-kit, to be used in conjunction with the wealth of other analytical tools available, a comprehensive survey of which can be found in Short (1996).

CHAPTER 11

'See Better, Lear'? See Lear Better! A Corpus-Based Pragma-Stylistic Investigation of Shakespeare's *King Lear*

DAWN ARCHER AND DEREK BOUSFIELD

1. Introduction

Shakespeare's *King Lear* tackles a number of central (Early Modern) themes, including: sight and blindness (literal and metaphorical), love and hate, honour and betrayal, duty and responsibility, person and state, state and family, sanity and madness, justice (and the lack of justice) and, ultimately, life and death. As this chapter will reveal, many of these themes can be traced, in turn, to Shakespeare's initial characterization of Lear in the 'state division scene' (Act I, scene 1). Drawing on a combination of linguistic approaches (pragmatics, stylistics, and corpus linguistics), we investigate Lear's interaction(s) with his daughters and with the Earl of Kent in this important opening scene (Sections 4-5.3). Specifically, we use the characters' keywords and key semantic domains – as identified by the web-based annotation tool, Wmatrix (see Section 3) – as a 'first step' for our analyses of the characters' relational work (and our interpretations of those characters, based on that relational work), paying particular attention to Shakespeare's depiction of Lear's eccentricity and the other characters' responses to that eccentricity. By relational work, we mean the actions Shakespeare allocates to respective characters which reflect their level of investment in/attendance to each other during their interactional exchanges (see, for example, Locher and Watts 2005). By keywords and key domains, we mean those lexical items in a target text (e.g. Lear's speeches in Act I, scene 1) that – when compared to a reference text or corpus (e.g. the full play minus Lear's utterances throughout the play) – are found to be frequent or infrequent, *statistically speaking*, and thus indicative of what it is that makes the target text (i.e. Lear's utterances) *distinctive* from the reference text (i.e. the speech of all the other characters from *King Lear*). We begin by detailing some of the studies that have explored Shakespearean texts using a combination of pragmatics, stylistics and corpus linguistics.

2. Pragmatic, stylistic and/or keyness studies relating to Shakespearean works

Studying the nature, role, and reasons for Shakespeare's (depictions of) relational work is not new (see, for example, Brown and Gilman 1989; Calvo 1992; Culpeper 1998; Kopytko 1995; Rudanko 2006; Bousfield 2007; Busse 2006a, 2007; Munkelt and B. Busse 2007; U. Busse 2008; see also Spevack 1963; Crystal and Crystal 2002). Four of the aforementioned studies – Koptyko (1995), B. Busse (2007), Munkelt and B. Busse (2007) and U. Busse (2008) – are particularly relevant (to our study) and are thus discussed below:

- Koptyko (1995) has drawn from both Brown and Gilman's work, and also the strategies identified by Brown and Levinson ([1978], 1987), to investigate linguistic politeness strategies evidenced in four tragedies (*Hamlet, Macbeth, Othello*, and *King Lear*) and four comedies (*The Taming of the Shrew, A Midsummer Night's Dream, The Merchant of Venice*, and *Twelfth Night*). His purpose in so doing was to argue that variables other than *power, social distance* and *ranking of impositions* need to be accounted for if one is to fully capture the politeness strategies utilized by Shakespearean characters. The most interesting of the additional variables suggested – in respect to *King Lear* – and thus the most interesting for our purposes seems to be that of *cunning*, which captures the 'premeditated act[s]' that characters undertake as a means of deceiving the hearer (H) – by making him/her 'believe' that their relational work is 'sincere, unselfish or simply for the benefit of H' (Kopytko 1995: 534).
- B. Busse (2007) focuses on the characters' use of address forms (e.g. vocatives and the personal pronouns *you* and *thou*) in Shakespeare's *The Reign of King Edward III*. She also discusses the links between address forms, metaphor and other foregrounding processes (see also B. Busse 2006b). In earlier work (see, for example, Munkelt and B. Busse 2007), B. Busse and her co-author focused on the king's tension resulting from the incompatibility of being both a fully fledged human being and a successful monarch, something that we will also be pursuing in this chapter. In B. Busse (2007) she further suggests that, through the Countess, Shakespeare makes use

of the metaphors THE BODY IS A HOUSE and UNDERSTANDING IS SEEING, as a means of establishing how the Countess's 'body and soul are peacefully united in a moral shell of her being a loving wife. She is therefore able to see through and understand the King's moral and political failures' (B. Busse 2007: 241). As U. Busse (2008) has shown (and we will also demonstrate), Shakespeare's Lear does not possess the kinds of perceptive abilities exhibited by the Countess in *The Reign of King Edward III* – until, that is, a change in his circumstances forces him to 'see better' (Kent to Lear, I.1.158).

- Although U. Busse's (2008: 85) stated aim was 'to arrive at an ideally complete inventory of the linguistic forms which were available [...] for carrying out directive speech acts' at that time, his study could be seen as an analysis of Lear's transformation from 'a self-assured person, free of doubt, to somebody who has very painfully learnt to pay consideration to other person's feelings' (ibid.: 113). For example, U. Busse (2008: 111) identifies how, 'at the beginning of [*King Lear*], Lear issues directives and expects everybody to execute his will without exception'; this is due, as we will argue (Section 5), to the nature of the relationship between King Lear's *body natural* and *body politic*, that is, Lear's human side and his (divinely appointed) role as head of state (Kantorowicz [1957] 1997; see also B. Busse 2006a, b, 2007; Munkelt and B. Busse 2007; Nostbakken 1997). However, as Lear's circumstances change for the worse, following his own insistence on the separation of the body natural from the body politic, his empathy for others – especially those he has wronged – grows. This is signalled, linguistically, by Lear's directives becoming less frequent as the play progresses 'and [by] more questions occur[ring] in-between' (U. Busse 2008: 112). Moreover, when his directives are analysed more closely, 'their form and, even more so, their communicative function changes from commanding and ordering to inviting, offering and pleading' (U. Busse 2008: 112). The latter tend to be associated with the relatively powerless when engaging with the relatively powerful in traditional approaches to politeness (see, for example, Brown and Levinson 1987): the adoption of more explicitly indirect directives can be taken as an indication of Lear's growing appreciation of his declining position.

A number of Shakespearean-related studies (Archer *et al.* 2009; Culpeper 2002; Scott and Tribble 2006) have also utilized keyword and/or key domain analysis. As highlighted in the introduction, keyness analysis involves comparing word, semantic domain and/or parts-of-speech lists of one's target text(s) with a *reference* word/domain (or part-of-speech) list, as a means of identifying those linguistic items that – because of their statistical (in)frequency – distinguish the target text from the reference text(s). Culpeper's (2002) study of

Romeo and Juliet's Romeo, Juliet, Mercutio, Benvolio, Capulet, Friar Lawrence and the Nurse is particular relevant for our purposes as he shares our interest in the extent to which keyword analyses can be utilized to determine character traits in addition to a literary text's *aboutness*: that is, what a given text conveys (see, for example, Phillips 1989). Culpeper (2002) points out, for example, that Juliet is characterized by keywords that suggest she is 'the anxious target of love' (e.g. **if**,[1] **or** and **yet**), whilst the Nurse is characterized by keywords that suggest she is the emotional thermometer of the play (e.g. **warrant, faith, marry, ah, o, well**, and **god**). In Hoover *et al.* (forthcoming), Culpeper also goes on to suggest that the characters' keywords can be labelled according to their ideational, textual, and interpersonal functions, and gives the examples of Romeo (whose keywords include **beauty** and **love**) for ideational keywords, Juliet (and even more so Mercutio) for textual keywords, and the Nurse for interpersonal keywords. In this study, we will also be utilizing keywords and key domains to investigate Shakespearean characterizations. Specifically, we will use the keyness items as a quantitative 'first step' into the respective utterances of Lear, his daughters, and Kent. Our qualitative investigations will then pick up on the extent to which our quantitative findings tell us something about the relational work undertaken by the respective characters – and also the consequences of that relational work.

3. Explanation of our dataset and the annotation tool utilized in this study

For our study, we have prepared five texts which capture the interactional contributions of *King Lear*'s Lear, Cordelia, Regan, Goneril and Kent in the first scene only, and five texts which capture their interactional contributions in the full play. We have also prepared specific reference texts against which to compare each of the latter, using Wmatrix (for details of which see below). These reference texts equate to the full play minus the words/utterances of the specific characters under investigation. The Shakespearean edition of *King Lear* that we have utilized, the *New Penguin* edition edited by G. K. Hunter, is a modern spelling edition.

The UCREL Semantic Annotation System (henceforth USAS) enables the automatic analysis of texts at three levels: word (including multi-word units), semantic field, and part-of-speech. Texts are initially uploaded into *Wmatrix* (the web interface to USAS), and then grammatically and semantically annotated using two programs: CLAWS and SEMTAG. The tagset behind SEMTAG was originally based on the *Longman Lexicon of Contemporary English* (McArthur 1981) but has since been revised in the light of tagging problems met in the course of previous research dating back some 15 years. The current semantic classification has a hierarchical structure with 21 top-level domains, which capture 232 semantic field tags, signalling a broadly Westernized conception of the modern world. It should be noted that, although there are plans to redevelop the current tagset (drawing, for example, on Spevack 1993) as a means of making it more appropriate to an Early Modern English context, that work is as yet incomplete. Therefore, the results we report here – and any results reported by others using similar tools – must be carefully scrutinized as to their actual validity. This is not as problematic as it may seem, however, since we (as analysts) are more likely to keep in mind the limits of automatic annotation tools in such contexts, and thus seek to combine our quantitative analyses with more detailed qualitative analyses – as we do in this chapter (see also Archer 2007; Archer 2009; Archer *et al.* 2009).

4. The keywords of Lear, his daughters, and the Earl of Kent

Table 11.1 captures both (a) Lear's keywords and key domains in the opening scene when compared to the full play (minus his contributions), and (b) Lear's keywords and key domains for the full play when compared to the full play (minus Lear's contributions). The figures in brackets represent the Log Likelihood (LL) scores for each keyword and key domain. We have opted to focus on keyness items assigned an LL score of 7-plus, so that the possibility of words/domains occurring by 'chance' is kept to a minimum (statistically speaking): for example, an LL score of 6.63+ is deemed to have a 1 per cent chance of occurring accidentally, and an LL score of 15+, a 0.01 per cent chance.

Table 11.1: Lear's keywords and key domains

	Keywords	Key domains
Act 1, sc. 1	Our (83.24), Burgundy (44.52), France (38.16), we (27.33), king (25.44), dower (19.08), her (18.74), with (13.23), Kent (12.72), cares (12.72), dowers (12.72), Goneril (12.72), pride (12.72), stranger (12.72), daughter (12.22), be (11.26), thine (8.98), on (8.71), third (8.13), nothing (7.79), kingdom (7.46), cease (7.34), hers (7.34)	*Linear order* (12.26) – first, second, third, last, then, turns, tenth, following *No knowledge* (11.06) – mysteries, stranger. *Kin* (8.53) – son, daughters, dowers, daughter, wife, sisters, dower, paternal, father, marry, sons

Continued

Table 11.1: Continued

	Keywords	Key domains
Full play	Kent (42.64), Regan (42.64), Gloucester (39.59), king (39.59), Goneril (36.55), Cordelia (33.50), her (33.3), thou (30.00), France (27.41), Burgundy (21.32), daughter (18.35), me (17.87), with (15.85), no (14.67), ha (12.95), weep (12.77), boy (12.24), pride (12.18), 'll (11.77), our (11.46), justice (10.31), ashamed (9.14), cheeks (9.14), dower (9.14), felt (9.14), grave (9.14), money (9.14), philosopher (9.14), prithee (9.14), we (9.04), kill (8.87), look (8.60), art (8.55), daughters (8.30), nature (7.83), dinner (7.67), howl (7.67)	*No knowledge* (10.58) – mysteries, stranger, forget, forgot, mystery *Hot/on fire* (8.78) – hot ('hot tears', 'hot duke'), fiery ('fiery duke'), flames (blinding flames), warm (), fires ('thought-executing fires'), fire, blanch, burning, scalding, scald *Dead* (8.06) – death, execution, pestilent, murder, tomb, drown, die, mortality, kill, dead, murderers *Anatomy and physiology* (7.82) – eyes, heart(s), flesh, hand(s), blood, body, tears, arm(s), breath, cheeks, back, head(s), beard, mouth, (a)sleep, face, lips, heads, skin, hairs, waist, ear(s), brains, tongue(s), bosom, frown, waking, womb, organs, spleen, brow, tooth, visage, bones, nimble, knee

Key items relating to the opening scene that are worthy of brief note, here, include the keywords **kingdom** and **daughter** and the key domain **kin**. For example, although **kingdom** is a keyword for Lear in the opening scene, it is not key for him in the full play (when compared to the usage of 'kingdom' by the rest of the characters). Possible reasons for these findings are that, in dividing his kingdom and in attempting to divide his *body politic* from his *body natural* (see Section 5, below), Lear ultimately loses his power over the land. In direct contrast to **kingdom**, **daughters** (plural) is key for Lear in the full play only. **Daughter** (singular), however, is key for Lear in both the full play *and* the opening scene.

When viewed together with many of the remaining keywords in Lear's opening speech, Lear's use of **daughter** captures the *aboutness* of his utterances (Phillips 1989) as well as pointing to individual character traits/flaws (cf. Culpeper 2002). For example, **Burgundy** and the **King** of **France** are Cordelia's potential suitors as the play begins. However, when Lear acts to disown his youngest **daughter**, **Burgundy** changes his mind about marrying Cordelia – and, in so doing, he intimates that her **dower** (dowry) is more important to him than **her** companionship/love. The astute Cordelia is keenly and explicitly aware of this when she bids Burgundy farewell:

> Peace be with you Burgundy! Since that respect and fortunes are his love, I shall not be his wife.

(I.1.247–9)

Several of Lear's keywords also (in)directly refer to his dissolving relationship with Cordelia, thereby highlighting her pivotal role in the play (even though Lear seems not to call Cordelia by name sufficiently often in the opening scene for 'Cordelia' to be one of Lear's keywords). Lear intimates that Cordelia's **pride** will prevent her from finding a suitor, for example, and calls on '**pride**, which she calls plainness, [to] marry her' (I.1.129). Interestingly, Lear also refers to 'strain'd **pride**' when Kent pleads with him (i) to 'see better' with respect to Cordelia and her sisters (I.1.158), and (ii) not to rush to 'hideous rashness' (I.1. 150–1) – for, like Cordelia, Kent recognized that Goneril and Regan's 'large speeches' were covertly (and, hence, deceitfully) insincere (I.1.184).

Some readers might want to claim, at this point, that the above (content) analysis only tells us what we already know. We would suggest that this, in itself, is not a bad thing; indeed, it could be taken as 'proof' that the current version of Wmatrix works – even on Early Modern English texts (cf. Section 3). Moreover, some of the keywords (for the full play, in particular) are not as predictable as we might imagine: notice, for example, that **Kent** is Lear's most statistically frequent keyword in both the opening scene and the full play – suggesting that Kent is as pivotal a character to Lear as are Cordelia and her sisters. We therefore document Kent's keywords/key domains in Section 4.2, and outline Lear's interaction with Kent in more detail in Sections 5.3–5.4 of this chapter. Before doing so, however, we will focus on the keywords of Lear's daughters as a 'first step' into our analyses of their relational work (which follows in Sections 5–5.2).

4.1. Lear's daughters

Table 11.2 captures the keywords and key domains of Cordelia:

Table 11.2: Cordelia's keywords and key domains

	Key words	Key domains
Act I, sc. I	love (26.45), richer (17.41), faults (13.62), I (11.24), our father (10.76), tongue (10.76), since (10.64), my (10.63), shall (9.68), majesty (9.17), want (9.17), according (8.71), action (8.71), blot (8.71), bosoms (8.71), derides (8.71), dishonour (8.71), foulness (8.71), glib (8.71), heave (8.71), hides (8.71), husbands (8.71), jewels (8.71), loath (8.71), lost (8.71), me (8.71), oily (8.71), plaited (8.71), prefer (8.71), professed (8.71), respects (8.71), still-soliciting (8.71), unchaste (8.71), unfold (8.71), wash (8.71), wed (8.71), sisters (8.06), am (7.77), half (7.61), sure (7.61), lord (7.48)	*Like* (15) – love, liking, loved, favour, prefer *(No) respect* (7.21) – dishonour, derides

Continued

Table 11.2: Continued

	Key words	Key domains
Full play	love (20.57), king (13.83), richer (13.83), weeds (13.83), sisters (13.69), majesty (10.48), faults (10.08), short (8.41), those (7.34), our father (7.29), stood (7.29), tongue (7.29), am (7.09), father (7.08)	*Like* (12) – love, dear, loved, liking, favour, prefer *Wanted* (7.09) – want, wants, ambition, will, fain, purpose, intend

If we compare the above findings with those of Regan (Table 11.3) and Goneril (Table 11.4), we notice that Cordelia is the only sister to be characterized by **love** throughout the play. Many of the items in Table 11.2 (i.e. **love, tongue, glib, oily, sure**) also point to Cordelia's refusal to engage in the type of (insincere) politeness associated with the '**glib** and **oily** art ...' (I.1.224–33). Cordelia's asides following her sisters' speeches during the love contest are particularly revealing: 'What shall Cordelia speak? Love, and be silent' (line 61); 'Then poor / Cordelia! / And yet not so; **since I am sure my love**'s/ More ponderous than **my tongue**' (I.1.77–8) – and effectively 'encourage' the audience to interpret Goneril's and Regan's speeches through Cordelia's eyes, whilst also providing them with an interesting contrast to Lear, for Lear's egotistical needs initially blind him to the sisters' scheming (see Sections 5–5.2 for a more detailed discussion).

When contrasted with Cordelia's, Regan's keywords and key domains point to her use of hyperbole – especially when seeking to deceive Lear in the opening scene's love contest (see, for example, 'an enemy to all other **joys**', 'I am made of that self **metal** as my sister, / And **prize** me at her worth', '... she names my **very deed** of love' (I.1.69–71)) – and, as such, appear to corroborate Cordelia's and Kent's summations of Lear's oldest daughters (Section 4; see also Sections 5.2 and 5.4):

Table 11.3: Regan's keywords and key domains

	Key words	Key domains
Act 1, sc. 1	Kent (10.70), deed (10.70), felicitate (10.70), joys (10.70), metal (10.70), next month (10.70), prescribe (10.70), slenderly (10.70), square (10.70), starts (10.70), unconstant (10.70), find (10.04), infirmity (7.94), possesses (7.94), prize (7.94), self-same (7.94)	*Exclusivizers/particularizers* (10.69) – only, alone *Detailed* (8.02) – certain, very

Continued

Table 11.3: Continued

	Key words	Key domains
Full play	sister (44.22), her (18.55), Gloucester (11.85), Kent (11.85), messengers (11.85), needful (11.85), being (11.59), bosom (11.26), you (10.79), pray (9.58), convenient (8.14), dispatch (8.14), followers (8.14), sojourn (8.14), the old man (8.14), she (7.58)	*Pronouns* (15.62) – You, I, my, her, your, that, him, he, our, his, me, she, what, it, us, we, 't, they, which, thee, them, thou, thy, himself, this, thine, one, themselves, their, hers, itself, myself, whom, yourself, these
		Danger (11.86) – danger, dangerous, treacherous
		Easy (7.72) – convenient, simple

That said, Goneril does speak of love sufficiently for **loved** to be one of her keywords and to have a key domain that includes 'love' in the opening scene. Unlike Cordelia, however, Goneril's love appears to be motivated by deceitful, selfish ambition:

Table 11.4: Goneril's keywords and key domains

	Keywords	Key domains
Act 1, sc. 1	beyond (18.81), our father (12.14), hath (10.30), all manner of (9.41), alms (9.41), appertains (9.41), changes (9.41), choleric (9.41), dispositions (9.41), eyesight (9.41), grossly (9.41), hit (9.41), I think (9.41), imperfections (9.41), leavetaking (9.41), look to (9.41), loved (9.41), nearly (9.41), observation (9.41), rare (9.41), soundest (9.41), surrender (9.41), therewithal (9.41), unable (9.41), unruly (9.41), wanted (9.41), waywardness (9.41), wield (9.41), age (8.55)	*Like* (8.65) – love, loved *Wanted* (7.51) – want, wanted, look to, will
Full play	Gloucester (23.06), knights (20.00), dotage (17.29), wrongs (17.29), hundred (12.43), Oswald (11.53), beyond (11.53), disorder (11.53), dispositions (11.53), fancy (11.53, hasten (11.53), on the way (11.53), each (9.32), sister (9.24), you (9.13), command (7.82), dislike (7.82), fellows (7.82), particular (7.82), still (7.61)	*Wanted* (8.38) – want, will, wanted, look to, purposes, desired, choice, purposed, wishes

Indeed, immediately following Lear's division of his kingdom between her and Regan, Goneril discusses with her sister how they 'must do something, and i' th'heat' (immediately) if they are not to lose out to Lear's increasingly unpredictable and unstable **disposition** (see the interaction in I.1.283–306).

4.2. Kent's keywords and key domains

Table 11.5 captures Kent's keywords in the opening scene and the full play (when compared with the full play, minus his contributions). The table also documents Kent's key domains in the full play (Kent did not utilize any statistically significant semantic domains in the opening scene):

Table 11.5: Kent's keywords and key domains

	Keywords
Act I, sc. I	King (26.18), doom (17.45), thy (13.86), wilt (9.20), adieu (8.73), approve (8.73), blank (8.73), bows (8.73), consideration (8.73), deeds (8.73), empty-hearted (8.73), fee (8.73), flattery (8.73), fork (8.73), freedom (8.73), held (8.73), invade (8.73), motive (8.73), physician (8.73), rashness (8.73), region (8.73), reverbs (8.73), reverse (8.73), revoke (8.73), shelter (8.73), speeches (8.73), stoops (8.73), sue (8.73), throat (8.73), undone (8.73), unmannerly (8.73), vent (8.73), Lear (7.75)
Full play	King (78.37), master (20.34), rogue (18.44), plain (13.10), rascal (11.22), sir (10.27), hard (10.24), heels (9.54), Albany (9.22), Cornwall (9.22), approve (9.22), broken (9.22), doom (9.22), mate (9.22), open (9.22), raised (9.22), speeches (9.22), draw (7.90), their (7.53), stars (7.52), whoreson (7.52), letters (7.13)

	Key domains
Full play	*In power* (29.62) – Sir, king, lord, master, power(s), highness, influence, mistress, commanded, earl, dukes, force, oppressed, queen, govern, sovereign, princess, royal, princes, royalty, lords, masters
	Sound (inc. volume) (9.54) – whistle, loud, groans
	Unexpected (9.22) – amazed, wonder
	Worry (7.13) – affliction, unsettle, trouble, distressed, care, finical
	Fear (7.06) – fear, coward(s), dread, lily-livered, cowardly

As we might expect, given Kent's role, **master** represents one of Kent's keywords in the full play. However, **king** is also a keyword for Kent: indeed, it is Kent's most statistically significant keyword in the opening scene and the full play. These keyness items, when viewed in conjunction with Kent's (statistically significant) key domains relating to *In power*, *Worry* and *Fear* in the full play, seem to point to the character's loyalty to Lear – in spite of the treatment Kent receives from Lear in the state division scene – as well as to Kent's concerns for Lear and the state of the kingdom as the play unfolds. Indeed, such are his concerns that, after being banished, Kent disguises himself so that he can continue to 'shape his old course [of looking after Lear] in a country new' (i.e. in the 'country new' where Goneril and Regan effectively share joint power/custody of the land). Note, in addition, that those keywords that USAS classified as 'key' in the opening scene and which have a negative semantic prosody (i.e. **doom, blank, empty-hearted, invade, rashness, undone, unmannerly, vent**) relate to Kent's attempts to persuade Lear to 'see better' (and to his resulting banishment). These and other findings captured by Table 11.5 will guide our necessarily brief pragma-stylistic analysis of Kent's interactions with Lear (see Sections 5.3–5.4). Our relational analyses begin, however, with Lear's interactions with his daughters.

5. A pragma-corpus-stylistic analysis of the state division scene (I.1.33–266)

The main argument we propose here, is that the state division scene centres upon Lear's own initial deceit and his explicit (yet pragmatically tacit) request and desire for *reciprocal deceit*. Put simply, Lear encourages Goneril, Regan, and Cordelia to compete for a larger share of his kingdom, by professing their love for him – but in ways that are overtly *face-enhancing*:

> ... Tell me, my **daughters** ...
> Which of you shall **we** say doth love us most?
> That **we our** largest bounty may extend ...
>   (I.1.48–52)

However, the love contest is itself a deceit, or 'a sham and not really meant to determine who gets what share' (Halio 1992: 95, footnote), for Lear has decided upon the likely divisions in Cordelia's favour. Indeed, Lear informs his self-professed 'joy' (I.1.82) that her share will be 'more opulent than [her] **sisters**' (I.1.85–6) – as long as she *plays his game*. The issue, of course, is that Cordelia does not share her sisters' propensity for (false) flattery (i.e. deceit is a familial trait that Lear shares only with Goneril and Regan: Section 4.1; see also Section 5.2), and she therefore refuses to state more than 'according to [her] bond' (I.1.93). We will argue (below) that Cordelia's dominant 'bond' with Lear, at this point, is that occasioned by their *father-daughter* relationship as opposed to their *king-subject* relationship; Lear is explicitly in the process of divesting himself of the cares of kingship, after all. For Lear, however, the latter is still as important to him if not more important (for he still intends to retain the title of 'King', and the benefits that this brings). Consequently, his role-as-king wins out over his role-as-father in this scene: he disowns Cordelia and divides the remainder of his kingdom between Goneril and Regan (cf. B. Busse 2006a).

5.1. The 'two body' nature of kingship

Lear's deceit over the real motivation(s) for the love contest provide us with useful evidence regarding the king's egotistical characteristics. Indeed, U. Busse (2008: 97) suggests Lear 'stage-managed' the love contest because he 'want[s] to be in the limelight and expect[s] that all participants [will] follow his orders'. Whilst we agree with U. Busse, we would also point (as do Munkelt and B. Busse 2007) to the importance of the 'two body' nature of kingship (see also B. Busse 2007; Kantorowicz 1997) and to its affinity with the notion of a *public* and a *private* face (Goffman 1967). To elucidate, the body politic is seen as divinely ordained, and hence inviolate. It is, by its very nature, primarily a 'public' aspect of kingship (and therefore closer to the notion of a publicly constructed 'face'). In contrast, the body natural is a *body mortal*. It is therefore

> subject to all [the] infirmities that come by Nature or Accident, to the imbecility of Infancy or Old Age, and to the like defects that happen to the natural Bodies of other people.
>
> (Kantorowicz 1997: 7)

As such, the private aspect to kingship is commensurately closer to the notion of 'private face'. With this in mind, let's return to the love contest at this point: Lear's elevated social position, the formal setting at his court, and his expectation that his 'fast intent' (I.1.38) will be executed meant that Lear – wrapped in the cloak of the body politic – did not feel compelled 'to pay any attention to other people's face wants' (U. Busse 2008: 97). The fact that he was more attentive to Cordelia's face than he was to the faces of Goneril and Regan – at least initially – is thus a sign of Lear's deep affection for his youngest daughter (see, for example, line 82, 'our joy'; see also the discussion of this vocative in B. Busse 2006b). It may also help to explain why, although 'her honest but blunt reply' of 'nothing' completely stuns him (see, for example, U. Busse 2008: 97), he is initially prepared to explain to Cordelia that '[n]othing will come of nothing' (I.1.90). As Table 11.1 reveals, **nothing** is a keyword of Lear's in the opening scene, and this is primarily because it is used by Lear in *response* to Cordelia's refusal to exaggerate the extent of her love for him (see, for example, the interaction in I.1.87–107). As U. Busse (2008: 99) goes on to explain, Lear also invites Cordelia (albeit with an imperative) 'to correct her answer', by 'speak[ing] again'. However, her second answer only serves to irritate Lear further (lines 91–4):

| **Cordelia** | Unhappy that **I** am, **I** cannot **heave My** heart into **my** mouth: **I love** your **Majesty According** to **my** bond; no more nor less. |
| **Lear** | How, how, Cordelia! Mend your speech a little ... |

This and other contributions by Lear suggest that negative face (Brown and Levinson 1987: 129) – that is, the want to have freedom of action – and hence negative face-oriented politeness is an important feature of *King Lear* (at least in the opening scene but arguably beyond too), even though Early Modern English society is said to have preferred positive face-oriented politeness (see, for example, Kopytko 1995). For example, Lear does not allow for the possibility of Cordelia remaining silent, which impinges on her negative face as well as signalling his disregard for her (face) 'wants'. Nevertheless, despite Lear's best commanding efforts, Cordelia will not be drawn into the deceit of (false) flattery (see lines 91–2, above). Moreover, when Cordelia does speak, her (albeit overtly polite) utterance confirms that which her earlier responses had intimated (lines 95–104):

> ... Good **my Lord**,
> You have begot **me**, bred **me**, **loved me**: **I**
> Return those duties back as are right fit,
> Obey you, **love** you, and most honour you.
> Why have my **sisters husbands**, if they say
> They **love** you all? Happily, when I **shall** wed,
> That **lord** whose hand must take **my** plight **shall** carry
> Half **my love** with him, half **my** care and duty:
> Sure **I shall** never marry like **my sisters**,
> To **love my father** all.

There are a number of points that need to be made here. For example, we must recognize that Cordelia *is* attempting to use positive politeness with Lear in lines 95–8. That is to say, she is attempting to attend to:

> ...his perennial desire that his wants (or the actions / acquisitions / values resulting from them) should be thought of as desirable. Redress consists in partially satisfying that desire by communicating that one's own wants (or some of them) are in some respects similar to the addressee's wants.
>
> (Brown and Levinson 1987: 101)

In lines 96 and 103 especially, Cordelia shows approval of Lear *as a father*. However, her attempt at positive politeness ('you have begot **me**, bred **me**, **loved me**' [line 96]) does not *specifically* show deference to him *in his role as king*, and, as such, does not seem to satisfy his perennial desire that his 'kingly' face wants (i.e. those relating to the body politic) be enhanced, maintained or 'appropriately' constructed *according to Lear's expectations*. It would seem, then, that Lear wanted his daughters to flatter both his body natural (his physical being/private face) and his body politic (his royal being/ public face) at the point of his *very public* division of state. As such, Cordelia's attempt at politeness – which is directed only at Lear's body natural – appears to be interpreted by Lear as being wholly disrespectful of his (and her) role and station and their (public) relationship. There is an obvious but grim irony here, of course: Lear is meant to be seeking to 'shake all cares and business from [his] age' (line 39) in a way that separates the 'inseparable' (see, for example, the crown lawyers' 1550 position that 'the Body natural and the Body politic are not distinct, but united and as one body', as noted in Kantorowicz 1997: 12). Yet, Lear fails to appreciate Cordelia's sincere, deferential *father-oriented* politeness (i.e. her attempts to appropriately construct Lear's private positive face in a way that appeals to his body mortal). Instead, he withdraws his affection and, ironically, his paternity too – and, by so doing, underlines his utter inability to separate the two aspects of his being (body politic and body natural). Note, in particular, the occurrence of the keywords **dower** and **cease**, as well as the occurrence of **stranger** and **paternal**, which are captured by the key domains *no knowledge* and *kin* respectively (lines 108–16):

> Let it **be** so; thy truth, then, be thy **dower**:
> For, by the sacred radiance of the sun,
> The **mysteries** of Hecate, and the night,
> By all the operation of the orbs
> From whom **we** do exist, and **cease** to **be**,
> Here I disclaim all my **paternal** care,
> Propinquity and property of blood,
> And as a **stranger** to my heart and me
> Hold thee, from this, for ever.

According to U. Busse (2008: 99), Lear's speech acts during the state division scene 'were carried out so as to please him. The speech acts of his two elder daughters met his expectations, but those of Cordelia did not'. This position is unsurprising given what we have argued hitherto. As highlighted above, however, what is marked is Lear's inability to separate the bodies politic and natural, despite his professed 'darker purpose' (line 36). Note, in particular, how the key items **paternal**, **cease to be**, and **stranger** (in relation to 'my heart and me') signal the private/body natural and public/body politic aspects respectively and, of course, how the royal **we** signals that Lear is operating as the indivisible, dual-bodied King – but in a way that supports Kantorowicz's (1997: 11) claim that the body politic (always) commanded the 'greater' weight.

Given the greater import of the public body politic over the private body natural, readers will not be surprised to learn that the face issues relating to this aspect of Lear's character are themselves greater. U. Busse (2008: 103) notes, for example, that 'non-compliance or uninvited pieces of advice are regarded as signs of disobedience, which raise anger and even wrath'. As well as being important in terms of Lear's characterization (and, potentially, *mind style*, i.e. the *oddness* of his world view, as constituted by his logical reasoning; cf. McIntyre 2005), they act as further signs of Lear's inability to separate his bodies natural and politic – despite his apparent, ill-conceived attempt to do so. We will explore this aspect further in Section 5.3, when we discuss Lear's dealings with Kent. Before that, we briefly turn our attention to Goneril and Regan.

5.2. *Goneril and Regan's cunning during the love contest*

As we argue above, Lear's decision to divide his kingdom between his daughters was apparently motivated by a firm desire ('fast intent') to live the remaining years of his life as king, but without the cares of state (see lines 36–9). As Shakespeare intimates to the audience at the close of the opening scene, however, Goneril and Regan conspire together primarily because they are concerned that Lear will continue to control them, 'If [Lear was to continue to] carry authority with such **disposition** as he/ bears' (lines 383–4). We should note, in particular, the sisters' characterization of their father as someone who is 'full of **changes**', that is, as someone whose behaviour can be dangerously 'rash' and/or erratic even during 'the best and soundest of his time' (lines 283–98):

Goneril	Sister, it is not little I have to say of what most nearly appertains to us both. **I think our father** will hence tonight.
Regan	That's most certain, and with you; **next month** with us.
Goneril	You see how full of **changes** he is. The **observation** we have made of it **hath** not been little. He always **loved** our sister most; and with what poor judgement he **hath** now cast her off appears too **grossly**.
Regan	'Tis the **infirmity** of his age. Yet he hath ever but **slenderly** known himself.
Goneril	The best and **soundest** of his time **hath** been but rash. Then we must look from his **age** to receive not alone the **imperfections** of long-ingraffed condition, but therewithal the unruly waywardness that infirm and **choleric** years bring with them.

In stark contrast to their earlier claims of love and devotion to Lear (which we discuss below), this exchange between Goneril and Regan suggests that their relationship with their father is not one primarily characterized by 'affection' – and not only because they were effectively planning to break their promise to Lear (to continue to honour and look after him and his entourage in his dotage). Notice, for example, that the scene points to the sisters' awareness that Lear, their father, 'loved' Cordelia 'most', and that his actions (in banishing Cordelia) demonstrated 'poor judgement' on his part (lines 290–1) – despite the fact that his 'poor judgement' directly benefits them. This alone suggests that the sisters, themselves, note and recognize the utter impossibility of dividing the kingdom by separating Lear's body politic from his body natural. This scene, then, points to an incisiveness/shrewdness – that is, a high degree of cunning – on the sisters' part and a willingness to *play the (love) game* only when it suits their purposes. With this in mind, let us turn our attention (albeit briefly) to the sisters' performances during the infamous 'love contest'.

We are made aware, from the outset of the love contest, that Lear *displays* little outward affection towards any of his daughters (even his beloved Cordelia). Indeed, he initially addresses Goneril using a simple imperative preceded by a form of address: 'Goneril, Our eldest-born, speak first'. We would agree with Kopytko (1995: 518) that Goneril's response at this point (see, for example, lines 55–61) is best understood as an attempt to 'exaggerat[e] sympathy [and/or] approval' as a means of deceiving Lear – and, as such, is akin to 'cunning':

Goneril (to Lear)   Sir, I love you more than words can **wield** the matter,
Dearer than **eyesight**, space and liberty,
Beyond what can be valued, rich or rare,
No less than life, with grace, health, beauty, honour;
As much as child e'er **loved**, or father found;
A love that makes breath poor and speech **unable**.
Beyond all manner of 'so much' I **love** you.

According to Kopytko (1995: 518, 520), acts of cunning relate to S (the speaker) undertaking behaviour that (superficially) appears to satisfy H (i.e. the hearer's wants) in some way – because it exaggerates S's sympathy for and/or approval of H, for example. Alternatively, it may 'assert common ground' or 'assert S's knowledge of and concern for H's wants' (ibid.: 520–1). However, the primary motivation of such behaviour is S's desire to induce 'H to satisfy S's wants' (ibid.: 520). For 'cunning' to be successfully performed, it is therefore important that H remains oblivious (at least, temporarily) to S's real motivations. And this is the situation that we have with Lear and his two older daughters during the love contest. Indeed, the fact that Goneril and Regan's 'exaggerated approval' of Lear equates to cunning, on their part, is not explicitly obvious (to the audience/reader nor to Lear, as yet) until the end of the opening scene (see above) – even though the audience/reader is made suspicious, through Cordelia's asides during the love contest, that all may not be as it seems (see Section 4.1). Consequently, Goneril's abundant praise of her father achieves its aim: Lear assigns his eldest daughter her (pre-determined) portion of land: 'To thine and Albany's issue/ Be this perpetual' (line 66–7). Similarly, when Regan makes reference to Goneril's response, so that she might emphasize how it came 'too short' when asked 'What says our second daughter/ Our dearest Regan, wife of Cornwall?' (lines 67–8), Lear accepts the (false) flattery unquestioningly:

Regan	I am made of that self **mettle [metal]** as my sister,
	And price me at her worth. In my true heart
	I find she names my very **deed** of love;
	Only she comes too short, that I profess
	Myself an enemy to all other **joys**
	Which the most precious square of sense **possesses,**
	And find I am alone **felicitate**
	In your dear highness' love.

And he accordingly confers a (pre-determined) portion of land onto Regan and Cornwall:

Lear	To thee and thine hereditary ever,
	Remain this ample third of our fair kingdom,
	No less in space, validity, and pleasure,
	Than that conferred on Goneril.

(Lines 69–82)

Cordelia, of course, recognizes her sisters' cunning from the outset. However, she fails to make her feelings explicit to the other characters until she is exiting the opening scene. Indeed, it is in her final addresses to Goneril and Regan (after being banished by Lear) that she assures her sisters she 'know[s] what [they] are' (line 269), and warns them to 'Love well [their] father' (line 271). Tellingly, she also points to the tragedy that will unfold with time: 'Time shall unfold what plighted cunning hides' (line 280). In Section 5.3 (following) we continue our discussion of Lear and Cordelia, whilst also discussing the Earl of Kent's attempts to calm 'the dragon [being Lear] and his wrath' (line 122) in the opening scene.

5.3. *Kent's interaction with Lear*

As we highlighted above, **Kent** appears as one of the statistically significant keywords in Lear's utterances (for both the opening scene and the play as a whole), thereby signalling his continuing importance to the king (albeit at a mostly subconscious level, on Lear's part). Yet, as will become clear, Kent's attempts to defend both the face and position of Cordelia ultimately result in his banishment from Lear's kingdom – and render highly tenuous his place in the successor states to Lear's kingdom, the 'country new' (I.1.187). Due to length constraints, our focus in this section relates to lines 120–87 of the opening scene – for these lines, in particular, highlight many of the main themes of the play whilst also having an important role in regard to (the development of) Kent and Lear as characters. By way of illustration, Kent initially adopts the traditional (and expected) line of attempting to use (positive) politeness to (a) enhance Lear's face and (b) excuse the fact that he is speaking 'out of turn'. However, when interrupted, he adopts the dangerous, power-contesting, and wholly unprecedented line of using increasingly challenging, intense, and direct forms of impoliteness (see Bousfield 2008) in his interactions with Lear. However it is with 'appropriate' levels of politeness that Kent begins – in the sense that he publicly and politely addresses Lear's body politic (see, for example, 'Good my liege –' (line 120) and 'Royal Lear, whom I have ever honoured as my **king**... thought on in my prayers –' [lines 139–42]).

Lear's responses of 'Peace Kent! Come not between the dragon and his wrath' (lines 121–2) and 'The bow is bent and drawn; make from the shaft' (line 143) are particularly interesting: by way of illustration, line 143 can be interpreted as an impatient directive instructing Kent to 'get to the point' or, alternatively, as a (milder) instruction to 'get away from the firing line' (see, for example, Halio 1992; Muir 1994). Notice, however, that both of these interpretations serve to depict Lear as someone who is dangerous and unforgiving and whose tolerance levels are fast diminishing and, as such, can be captured by the LEAR IS A DANGEROUS ENTITY/WORDS ARE WEAPONS conceptual metaphors (see Bousfield 2008, for a discussion of the potency of off-record strategies). Kent, showing his acute and incisive mind, not to mention his bravery in his struggle between duty (to his king) and responsibility (to protect Lear), goes on to manipulate Lear's bent-bow metaphor, with an indirect criticism: 'Let it fall rather, though the **fork invade** / The regions of my heart' (a suitable interpretation might be 'your stance saddens and wounds me to my very core'). Kent's next move of 'Be Kent **unmannerly** when **Lear** is mad' (lines 145–6) is also pertinent: we take **unmannerly** (a key word for Kent) to mean both less-than-polite and less-than-politic in this context. In addition, the follow-up line, 'What wouldst thou do, old man?', shows disrespect towards Lear (by calling him an old man): indeed, Halio (1992: 103, foot-note) argues that 'the appellation, *old man*, when viewed in conjunction with his direct, blunt address, using the familiar second person, appropriate only to subordinates and children...is stunning in its impudence ...'. Kent's turn also contains an impolite implicature, of course, which flouts the Gricean (1975, 1989) maxims of manner and possibly relation, to insinuate that Lear must be (temporarily) insane to be acting in this way (cf. U. Busse 2008; see also Leech 1983).

5.4. *The dichotomization of duty and responsibility*

Lines 147–54 (I.1.147–54) are also worthy of brief mention here, for at least two reasons. First, they appear to act as the trigger point in the 'offending event' (Bousfield 2008: 183) which ultimately leads to Kent's banishment. Second, by directing his impoliteness towards Lear's public and private faces, and the positive and negative aspects of those faces, the character of Kent points to one of the key themes of the play – the dichotomization of duty and responsibility in interplay with Lear's attempt to separate the bodies natural and politic. Indeed, Kent explicitly makes reference to his duty to protect Lear in the face of his daughters' false flattery and deceit:

> Think'st thou that duty shall have dread to speak
> When power to **flattery bows**? To plainness honour's bound
> When majesty **stoops** to folly. Reserve thy state,
> And in **thy** best consideration check
> This hideous **rashness**. Answer my life my judgement,
> **Thy** youngest daughter does not love thee least,
> Nor are those empty-hearted whose low sounds
> Reverb no hollowness.

Like Cordelia, Kent is able to see that it is Goneril's and Regan's words which are truly hollow. However, Lear repays Kent by (indirectly) threaten-ing his life: 'Kent, on thy life, no more!' (line 154). And when Kent pursues the matter, Lear orders him 'Out of [his] sight!' (line 157). It is at this point that Shakespeare allows Kent to echo Lear in what must be one of the most pertinent lines of *Lear*: Kent urges his king to 'see better...and let [him] still remain/ The true blank of [his] eye' (lines 158–9), and thus reminds the audience of another important theme within *Lear* – metaphorical blind-ness (cf. B. Busse 2006a). But it is to no avail. A frustrated Kent thus resorts to the most direct means of criticism: '... whilst I can **vent** clamour from my **throat** / I'll tell thee thou dost evil' (lines 174–75). It proves to be a step-too-far for Lear, who banishes Kent amidst accusations, threats (to life) and criticisms.

6. Using keyness analyses as a 'way in' to relational work and characterization

In this chapter, we have sought to demonstrate the benefits to be gained by adopting a combination of linguistic approaches when exploring (characters from) *King Lear*: specifically, a pragmatic, a corpus linguistic and, to a lesser extent, a stylistic approach. In particular, we have shown how keyness analyses can be used as a valuable 'way in' to understanding characterizations, especially if we pay particular attention to the relational work that the characters undertake with one another (cf. Culpeper 2002). Indeed, the combined approach we adopt here has enabled us to uncover – and briefly explore – a number of themes that are introduced in the play's opening scene (and which prove crucial to the play's development). These include (i) *person and state*, (ii) *duty*, (iii) *the (in)ability to see* (metaphorically speaking), (iv) the links between *love, flattery* and *deceit*, and finally, (v) *erratic behaviour* – which, for Lear, becomes *literal madness* as the play progresses. By way of illustration, the theme of *person and state* is ably demonstrated by Goneril's and Regan's insistence that Lear (repeatedly) reduce his retinue to nothing as the play unfolds. Goneril and Regan also demonstrate the consequences of *blind* ambition. In fact, as the play progresses, they become so void of mercy that they use the (literal and metaphorical) *blindness* of other characters to their advantage. In this respect, Goneril and Regan are mirrored by Edmund, who seeks to undermine both his father, Gloucester, and his brother Edgar (i.e. he seeks to 'top the legitimate' so that he might 'grow... [and] prosper': I.2.20–1). In addition, Gloucester is a mirror of Lear (see, for example, Gloucester's initial *blindness* to Edmund's scheming to destroy and supplant him). Unlike Lear, however, Gloucester's ability to 'see better' (Kent to Lear, I.1.158) arises once he is made *literally blind* (see B. Busse 2006a). In contrast, it is Lear's *madness* which ultimately allows him to *see* some of his mistakes: our use of 'some' is deliberate, here, for, whilst Lear seems to come to comprehend his ill-treatment of Cordelia, he remains incapable of (re-)establishing meaningful relationships with Goneril and Regan. In fact, Lear curses Goneril with barrenness when he becomes aware of her treachery. As such, *King Lear* (the play) seems to particularly problematize the *love* between a parent and a child – a feature that researchers may wish to pursue in the future, drawing from existing studies of *mind style* (see, for example, McIntyre 2005; Semino 2002) – as well as problematizing the relationship between the body natural and the body politic (see, for example, Munkelt and B. Busse 2007).

We would reiterate a message, in closing, that we have voiced consistently throughout this chapter: keyness analyses are at best a 'way in' to a text. That is to say, they provide the researcher with a 'means of uncovering lexical salience/([statistical] frequency) patterns that invite – and frequently repay – further qualitative investigation' (Archer 2009: 15). Indeed, when used intelligently/in combination with other approaches, they can help us to *confirm* what established researchers have already noted about (classical) texts, and/or cause us to see connections between words and/or semantic domains (and even parts of speech) which are not initially apparent – even to experts. We would add, further, that our teaching experience has shown us that students new to the fields of language and literature especially benefit from being provided with such a 'way in' to the texts that they study: indeed, it allows them to develop a knowledge-base that we all too often assume they already have. For such research needs, and for pedagogically based reasons, we see our work as being very much in the spirit of the 'tool-kit' approach advocated by Short (1996).

NOTE

1. To help the reader, we are emboldening characters' lexical items that have been found to be key by Wmatrix – at the word and/or semantic domain level – from this point onwards.

CHAPTER 12

Activity Types, Incongruity and Humour in Dramatic Discourse

DAN MCINTYRE AND JONATHAN CULPEPER

1. Introduction

Although stylistics as a discipline is not restricted to the analysis of literary texts, it is certainly the case that literature has been the primary object of study for most stylisticians. Of the three main literary genres, poetry and prose have received the most attention. Compared against these text-types, the amount of research into dramatic texts pales substantially. The apparent reason for this comparative lack of concern with drama is that prior to the advent of pragmatics and discourse analysis stylisticians did not have the tools with which to analyse dramatic texts. It was Mick Short's ground-breaking article 'Discourse Analysis and the Analysis of Drama' (1989) that systematically demonstrated how the style of play-texts could be analysed and what was specific to the stylistics of that genre (notably, its relationship with performance). Since the growth of pragmatics, research into the stylistics of drama has picked up (see, for example, Culpeper *et al.* 1998), but drama is woefully neglected as a genre in light of the amount of research carried out into poetry and prose. To illustrate, of the 135 pieces (articles and book reviews) published in the journal *Language and Literature* since 2005, a mere seven – or about 5 per cent – concern drama, itself a disconcertingly broad term encompassing the analysis of play scripts (e.g. Hunter 2005), screenplays (Mandala 2007), multimodal aspects of performance (McIntyre 2008) and audience responses to these (Hakemulder 2007). Our focus in this chapter is on the dramatic text, that is, the written play script. Our aim is to suggest a means of resolving one of the issues with much extant work on dramatic texts, namely that it has tended to be fragmented and atomistic;

that is, individual studies have usually focused exclusively on the analysis of a specific aspect of the text from one particular perspective. Such studies can be seen in Culpeper *et al.* (1998), in which individual chapters orient to conversation analysis, speech acts, inferencing, and so on. While such analyses are revealing, it is also the case that focusing on one discourse area to the exclusion of others can result in a skewed or incomplete analysis.

In this chapter we will show that an approach to the stylistic analysis of drama based on the notion of 'activity types' (Levinson 1992) offers a principled means of avoiding this atomistic approach by replacing it with something altogether more holistic. In a previous chapter (Culpeper and McIntyre 2010), we explored how activity type theory can help us better understand the characterization process in drama. Here we extend this work to explore how activity type theory might be used to account for audience entertainment, particularly incongruity as a source of humour in dramatic discourse. (We use the term 'dramatic discourse' to emphasize our focus not just on the structural aspects of fictional dialogue but also on the dynamic processes of meaning-making involved when we read dramatic texts.) Specifically, we analyse the activity type of the audition. We begin by noting some features of 'real-life' auditions, both standard auditions and exploitative ones. This sets up the background for the main part of this chapter, which focuses on a sketch by the late British satirist Peter Cook called 'One leg too few'. The sketch concerns a one-legged actor's attempt to audition for the part of Tarzan in an up-coming film, and was first performed in the popular 1960s satirical revue *Beyond the Fringe*. Our analysis explains how the linguistic behaviour of the interviewer is incongruous with the 'audition' activity type invoked at the outset of the sketch. Key to this are the interviewer's politeness strategies, which deviate considerably from the norms of the audition activity type. We suggest that incongruity arising in this way generates much of the humour that derives from the sketch. We begin by introducing activity type theory as conceptualized by Levinson (1992), Sarangi (2000), and others, and then clarifying its cognitive and interactional dimensions.

2. Activity type theory

According to Levinson ([1979] 1992), an activity type is a collection of speech acts (e.g. commands, threats, offers) which stand in some particular pragmatic relationship to each other, and that in so doing form some kind of culturally recognized activity. Prototypical activity types include a wide variety of events, such as lectures, telephone calls, job interviews, political rallies, sports commentaries, pub quizzes, and many more. Levinson himself says:

> I take the notion of an activity type to refer to a fuzzy category whose focal members are goal-defined, socially constituted, bounded events with *constraints* on participants, setting, and so on, but above all on the kinds of allowable contributions.
>
> (Levinson [1979] 1992: 69)

The conventionalized nature of activity types means that there are restrictions on the functions that particular speech acts are assumed to fulfil within them. For example, a bank robber who jumps into a getaway car and shouts 'Let's go!' is likely to have his utterance interpreted as a command. Alternatively, 'Let's go' when said by one of a group of friends in a pub is more likely to be interpreted either as a statement (of boredom perhaps) or as a suggestion to move on. In both cases, the particular activity type influences the range of likely functions of the speech act. As Levinson puts it: 'The structural properties of an activity constrain the verbal contributions that can be made towards it' (1992: 71). Participating in and/or understanding activity types thus relies on a certain amount of schematic information concerning the activity type in question. Levinson acknowledges this, noting also that 'The structural properties of specific activities set up strong expectations' (1992: 79). Activity types thus help participants to determine the likely inference behind particular implicatures.

It should be clear that activity types involve both a linguistic and a cognitive dimension. With regard to the latter, participants in any kind of communicative activity invoke particular schemas in order to make sense of the interaction. The term *schema* is simply a generic label for a package of background knowledge about a particular aspect of the world. So, for example, university students quickly develop a lecture schema which allows them to make sense of this particular activity type. In fact, Schank and Abelson's (1977: 41) cognitive notion of a *script*, a specific kind of schema, is ideally suited for the cognitive dimension of activity types, given that it concerns stereotyped action sequences:

> A structure that describes appropriate sequences of events in a particular context [...] scripts handle stylised everyday situations [...] [a] script is a predetermined, stereotyped sequence of actions that defined a well-known situation.
>
> (1977: 41)

Schank and Abelson (1977) note that schemas (which they prefer to call *scripts*) are composed of numerous *slots*, which are filled with different elements depending on the schema in question. A lecture schema, for instance, might include slots for props (rows of seats, a front desk, a projector screen, a projector, and so on), roles (lecturer, students, technicians possibly), scenes (entering the lecture theatre, picking up a handout, sitting down, taking notes), and entry conditions (being a member of the university perhaps, or being a student on a particular course), among others (see Semino 1997 for a full discussion of schema theory in relation to stylistics, and Jeffries and McIntyre 2010 for a more concise summary). Schemas are triggered by headers, linguistic cues which relate to particular elements of the schema in question. So a sentence such as 'The students were waiting in the corridor for the lecturer to arrive' is likely to trigger the reader's lecture schema because it works as what Schank and Abelson call a precondition header. These headers refer to necessary preconditions for a particular scenario. Naturally, the presence of a lecturer is required for a lecture, and reference to this presence is likely to cause readers to invoke this schema (empirical evidence for schemas and their invocation can be found in Steffensen and Joag-Dev 1984).

Instrumental headers, on the other hand, are those that refer to actions that are likely to trigger a particular schema: for example, 'The students shuffled along the banked rows of seats.' Locale headers refer to locations likely to trigger the schema in question (e.g. 'The acoustics in Canalside West were appalling'), while internal conceptualization headers refer to actions and roles within the schema, reference to which is likely to cause its invocation (e.g. 'Professor Short switched on the overhead projector'). The relation between schemas and activity types is that schematic knowledge helps us to recognize and shape particular activity types. Invoking a particular schema also helps us to interpret and make sense of the linguistic activities that occur within it. For example, finding ourselves within a lecture situation we are likely to invoke our lecture schema, which will help us to understand that if a lecturer asks a question such as 'Can you tell me the grammatical structure of this sentence?', he or she intends this as an opportunity for the student who answers it to demonstrate his or her knowledge. It is not a simple request from the lecturer for information that he or she does not know (i.e. it would not be appropriate to answer 'yes' or 'no').

In addition to this cognitive dimension, activity types also have an interactional facet. Thomas (1995: 190–2) suggests that the interactional elements of a given activity type are likely to include the following:

- The goals of the participants
- Allowable contributions
- The degree to which Gricean maxims are adhered to or are suspended
- The degree to which interpersonal maxims (cf. Leech's Politeness Principle, 1983) are adhered to or are suspended
- Turn-taking and topic control
- The manipulation of pragmatic parameters (e.g. power, social distance)

In order to solve the problem of distinguishing between activity types when the list of potential interactional elements is so wide-ranging, Sarangi (2000) suggests that it is profitable to characterize the forms of talk that occur within specific activity types as *discourse types*. For Sarangi, the term *discourse type* refers to structural, sequential and stylistic forms of talk, while *activity type* refers to the contextual factors that govern the interpretation of discourse types.

At this point, it is perhaps useful to summarize the discussion so far and make clear the value of activity type theory for stylistics. Activity type theory posits that context can be created and shaped by language use in conjunction with prior world knowledge. Meaning is generated through the interaction between language and context, including the context one constructs in one's mind. As an example, imagine that a student makes an appointment to see a tutor to talk about his/her dissertation. The tutor suggests meeting in a coffee shop on campus to discuss this. Despite the fact that the external contextual elements of the meeting place are not suggestive of a dissertation supervision scenario, this particular activity type can be generated by the linguistic behaviour of the participants. In effect, schematic knowledge of dissertation supervisions allows the participants to generate the relevant context. The discourse types they employ shape this context and override those other elements that are not stereotypically associated with a supervision activity type. Activity types are not fixed but are created in discoursal interaction. However, once a participant assumes a particular activity type to be relevant, a normative backdrop is provided for the interaction. The relevance of this for the stylistic analysis of play scripts is that when the norms for an activity type are deviated from, foregrounding arises. The kind of foregrounding we have in mind is that developed in relation to schema theory, where the notion of deviation is not restricted to the linguistic fabric of the text but extended to the extra-linguistic knowledge that people deploy in making sense of texts (see in particular Cook 1994 and Semino 1997, and their discussion of 'schema refreshment'). Such foregrounding becomes a focus for our interpretation of the text, as we will demonstrate.

3. The audition activity type

In order to tap into some of the constituents that make up the activity type of an audition, we reviewed numerous guidelines and advice sheets concerning how to audition, most of which are available on the internet. We will not attempt, for reasons of space, a full elaboration of what constitutes an audition, but instead concentrate on aspects that involve verbal interaction, particularly verbal interaction concerning feedback from the assessors.

The first point to note is that feedback on a candidate's performance cannot be expected. One website advising candidates on their audition for a musical warns: 'Due to the volume of applicants, we are not able to provide feedback on unsuccessful auditions' (www.alra.co.uk/documents/Auditions/Audition%20Guidelines.doc). Auditions are always subject to pressing time constraints, something which will minimize the possibility for non-essential interaction. In fact, a book on short films advises directors and producers to keep an open mind until the end of the auditions and not give feedback which may give the candidate the impression that they have got the part (Rea and Irving 2001: 117). In the event of feedback, advice on turn-taking is clear:

> Don't…
>
> • Say nothing. If you don't interact with a casting director how will s/he be able to work with you?
> • Not let the casting director speak! You've had your time now let them have theirs.
>
> (http://www.theactingwebsite.com/audition-toad-c640.html)

> If the auditioners comment on your performance, don't answer back or be rude in return.
>
> (http://www.vocalist.org.uk/audition_advice.html)

Clearly, the casting director has power over the conversational floor. The auditioner must not hog the conversational floor, but on the other hand must respond to elicitations of talk (indeed, it is in the interests of the auditioner to do so). Note that the quality of those responses is prescribed: 'don't answer back or be rude in return'. Directors are licenced in this activity type to damage the faces (cf. Goffman 1967) of the auditioners, but the auditioners are not allowed to retaliate. In fact, even defence is not advised; it is more a matter of the graceful acceptance of the result:

> **Accept rejection gracefully – remember the Audition Panel want you to be successful.**
> Do not ask for this feedback if you are unable to take constructive criticism.
>
> (http://www.simads.co.uk/Audition%20Guidelines.htm)

However, it is important to note here that these guidelines specify 'constructive criticism'. Obviously, what exactly counts as constructive criticism is likely to be the subject of dispute, but uncalled for, gratuitous criticism is clearly ruled out. Auditioners can expect to hear their faults plainly pointed out, but may also expect to hear how they might rectify them.

Generally, auditioners are advised to stick with Gricean efficiency:

> **DO NOT** outstay your welcome, argue if you are cut off in mid-note, or be evasive about your head voice, chest voice, legit experience, range or dance

expertise. Answer questions in a straightforward manner that expresses your individuality. 'Well, I can move!' ranks as the most often heard evasion in answer to a question about previous dance training.

(http://www.ccm.uc.edu/musical_theatre/dos.htm)

On the other hand, Gricean efficiency must be balanced against personal goals and interpersonal maxims relating to politeness (cf. Leech 1983). It is a recognized part of the audition that the auditioner is seeking to 'sell' themselves and consequently the activity type allows for some relaxation of the maxim of modesty (Leech 1983). But this should not be excessive:

DO consider your deportment. [...] Ask intelligent questions, exude confidence as you enter the room, say your name with authority, answer questions in a provocative way, look your best, thank the faculty for their attention and leave with the air of a job well done. And if you are really interested in pursuing the program, write a note to the faculty on your return home. You may do a brilliant audition and ruin your chances by appearing obnoxious. If you seem to have 'attitude,' are a 'diva' or possess an ego the size of Manhattan, you are unlikely to be accepted into a first rate program. On the other hand, you may be a good performer but slink in and out of the room, appear as confident as a Jello on the San Andreas fault and miss your chance. Find a happy medium!

(http://www.ccm.uc.edu/musical_theatre/dos.htm)

Today, it is reasonable to suppose that most people's notion of an audition is shaped, at least to some degree, by auditions they see as part of exploitative talent TV shows, such as *Britain's Got Talent* and *X Factor* (for a discussion of exploitative TV shows, impoliteness and entertainment, see Culpeper 2005). Exploitative TV show auditions contain some clear differences from standard auditions. The participants and the roles they play are different. The assessors, whilst they might be directors or producers, as is typical of standard auditions, primarily play a role of 'judge', and this is typically the label used to designate them. But the crucial difference is that, whereas standard auditions are typically held in private, exploitative auditions are a public spectacle: they involve the entertainment of an audience, whether that be the immediate audience in the auditioning venue or the remote audience behind a TV screen, or indeed both. Let us briefly look at a short extract from an audition on the show *X Factor*:

1. **Simon Cowell**   Hello.
2. **Robert Unwin**   Hello.
3. **Simon Cowell**   What's your name?
4. **Robert Unwin**   Robert Unwin.

5.	**Simon Cowell**	And what do you do?
6.	**Robert Unwin**	Er, I work in a chicken factory.
7.	**Simon Cowell**	Good. Do you think you've got the X factor?
8.	**Robert Unwin**	I dunno 'cos I'm not quite sure what the X factor is.
9.	**Simon Cowell**	All right.
10.	**Robert Unwin**	Ready?

[Robert Unwin sings]

11.	**Simon Cowell**	All right. Is this a joke?
12.	**Robert Unwin**	No.
13.	**Louis Walsh**	Oh, I think it was funny.
14.	**Simon Cowell**	You're winding me up.
15.	**Robert Unwin**	I ain't.
16.	**Simon Cowell**	I think we've heard enough.
17.	**Sharon Osbourne**	I'm very confused.
18.	**Robert Unwin**	When, when people hear me at a different karaoke that I've never been to I get, erm, applause and that. And it's genuine. Obviously when you're on a karaoke machine you've got the music in the background, plus you've got a bit of echo and that which does help in a way. So ...
19.	**Simon Cowell**	Oh, right. So we're missing the echo? Robert, I can honestly say you are the worst singer I've ever heard in my life.
20.	**Robert Unwin**	Thank you.
21.	**Sharon Osbourne**	Were you trying to ...
22.	**Simon Cowell**	Well, not 'thank you'. You are absolutely useless. All right Robert, well, look, it is a unanimous no.
23.	**Robert Unwin**	I know, yeah.
24.	**Sharon Osbourne**	Bye.
25.	**Robert Unwin**	Bye.
26.	**Sharon Osbourne**	Oh, bless him.
27.	**Louis Walsh**	Ah, God help him.

The goal of the auditioner is to persuade the judges to vote in favour of putting him or her through to the next round of the competition. The goal of the judges is ostensibly to convey to the auditioner their decision as to whether he or she has been successful, although of course there are additional goals relating to providing entertainment for the audience. Note the kind of speech acts that characterize these auditions – questions, answers, and evaluative statements, framed by greeting and parting sequences. In both extracts the judges control the talk, the initiation of topics, and the turn allocational component of the dialogue by asking questions of the auditioner and giving feedback. In fact, evaluative feedback is key, as it is here that there is potential for entertainment, as the judges exploit both general norms of politeness behaviour and the specific norms of 'standard' talent shows (see Culpeper 2005). Similarly, 'One leg too few', analysed in the following section, exploits the social norms of auditions, often through the evaluative comments of the interviewer, in order to generate satirical humour. In contrast, the auditioners in *X Factor*-style shows only contribute in response to the judges' comments. The institutional power of the judges is reflected in their linguistic behaviour, and the auditioners' relative weakness in theirs.

As with standard auditions, with regard to the Gricean maxims, we can assume that competitors in the audition will not fully uphold the maxim of quantity (and perhaps quality) in that they will not reveal everything about themselves, but just those elements that place them in a good light. In contrast, there are no restrictions on the maxims of quality and quantity for the judges when providing critical feedback. According to Leech (1983) people often trade Gricean cooperativeness for the maintenance of politeness, but this does not accurately characterize what happens here. Even in the standard audition activity type, judges, as we pointed out, are licensed to damage face, and so there is no need to sacrifice Gricean cooperativeness for the sake of politeness. In fact judges are distinctly uncooperative in exploitative auditions. Gricean cooperativeness is sacrificed in order to trigger and/or exacerbate impoliteness. Consider the following comment by the judge Simon Cowell: 'I can honestly say you are the worst singer I've ever heard in my life' (extract 2, turn 19). Regarding the comment clause 'I can honestly say', it is highly dubious as to whether Cowell can 'honestly' – upholding the maxim of quality – 'say' that this is the worst singer (he has made similar statements in the past; it seems unlikely that each time he is carefully comparing the current case with *all* previous cases). This is not pitched as a statement of empirical truth; by saying something obviously untrue, he implies, by flouting the maxim of quality, that the contestant sings as if he were the worst singer he has ever heard. A feature of auditions in exploitative TV shows is that both politeness and Gricean cooperativeness are sacrificed for the purposes of entertainment. Note that the contestant Robert's response is a polite 'thank you'. Robert sticks to the standard audition activity type; he does not engage in retaliation but delivers a gracious politeness response. But he does this despite the fact that Simon Cowell's criticism is far from constructive; and unconstructive, gratuitously impolite criticism licenses some kind of defence. Part of the entertainment comes about because Robert seems oblivious to what Simon Cowell is doing. Exploitative auditions are parasitic on the norms of standard auditions.

4. An activity type analysis of 'One leg too few'

Despite *Beyond the Fringe*'s reputation as a satirical show, many of Peter Cook's contributions to it were rooted more obviously in absurdist drama than straight satire. 'One leg too few' is such a sketch:

1. Peter	Miss Rigby! Stella, my love! Would you send in the next auditioner, please. Mr Spiggott I believe it is.	

Enter Dudley, hopping energetically on one leg.

2. Peter	Mr Spiggott, I believe?
3. Dudley	Yes – Spiggott by name, Spiggott by nature. (*Keeps hopping*)
4. Peter	Yes ... if you'd like to remain motionless for a moment, Mr Spiggott. Please be stood. Now, Mr Spiggott, you are, I believe, auditioning for the role of Tarzan.
5. Dudley	Right.
6. Peter	Now, Mr Spiggott, I couldn't help noticing almost at once that you are a one-legged person.
7. Dudley	You noticed that?
8. Peter	I noticed that, Mr Spiggott. When you have been in the business as long as I have you come to notice these little things almost instinctively. Now, Mr Spiggott, you, a one-legged man, are applying for the role of Tarzan – a role which traditionally involves the use of a two-legged actor.
9. Dudley	Correct.
10. Peter	And yet you, a unidexter, are applying for the role.
11. Dudley	Right.
12. Peter	A role for which two legs would seem to be the minimum requirement.
13. Dudley	Very true.
14. Peter	Well, Mr Spiggott, need I point out to you where your deficiency lies as regards landing the role?
15. Dudley	Yes, I think you ought to.
16. Peter	Need I say with over-much emphasis that it is in the leg division that you are deficient.
17. Dudley	The leg division?
18. Peter	Yes, the leg division, Mr Spiggott. You are deficient in it – to the tune of one. Your right leg I like. I like your right leg. A lovely leg for the role. That's what I said when I saw you come in. I said, 'A lovely leg for the role.' I've got nothing

	against your right leg. The trouble is – neither have you. You fall down on your left.
19. Dudley	You mean it's inadequate.
20. Peter	Yes, it's inadequate, Mr Spiggott. And, to my mind, the British public is just not ready for the sight of a one-legged ape-man swinging through the jungly tendrils.
21. Dudley	I see.
22. Peter	However, don't despair. After all, you score over a man with no legs at all. Should a legless man come in here demanding the role, I should have no hesitation in saying, 'Get out, run away.'
23. Dudley	So there's still a chance?
24. Peter	There is still a very good chance. If we get no two-legged actors in here within the next two months, there is still a very good chance that you will land this vital role. Failing two-legged actors, you, a unidexter, are just the sort of person we shall be attempting to contact telephonically.
25. Dudley	Well ... thank you very much.
26. Peter	So, my advice is, to hop on a bus, go home, and sit by your telephone in the hope that we will be getting in touch with you. (*Showing Dudley out*) I'm really sorry I can't be more definite, but as you realise, it's a two-legged man we're after. Good morning, Mr Spiggott.

Dudley goes off.

| **27. Peter** | Now, Miss Rigby, perhaps you'd show Mr Stanger in. (*Enter Mr Stanger*) Ah, good morning Mr Stanger. Now I believe you are applying for the role of Long John Silver. |

(Cook 1963)

The crux of the sketch is that Peter as the interviewer must tell Dudley, the auditioner, that he is unsuitable for the role of Tarzan. This constitutes a major threat to Dudley's positive face (Brown and Levinson 1987) and Peter attempts to mitigate this through indirectness.[1] This is in tune with the constructive criticism of the standard audition. The activity type is such that we would expect Dudley to make the relevant inferences from Peter's implicatures; in this activity type, implicit messages are likely to count as negative feedback. Dudley's failure to do this means Peter makes repeated attempts to carry out the face-threatening act (FTA) and his attempts to mitigate this go beyond what we would normally expect of the activity type.

   The audition activity type is initially generated through Peter's utterance in turn 1: 'Would you send in the next auditioner, please.' This amounts to an internal conceptualization header where 'the next auditioner' constitutes a schematic role that triggers the activation of an audition schema for the reader. With this schema invoked, we have certain expectations concerning the characters' linguistic and non-linguistic behaviour. Where these are not met – that is, where the sketch deviates from our expectations – a foregrounding effect is generated. It appears to be the case that while the audition activity type is invoked for the reader/audience, the characters themselves are unaware or have a different conception of the interactional constraints that it demands. Both Peter's and Dudley's linguistic choices deviate from what we would expect of the activity type, thereby creating an incongruity between our expectations and their actual behaviour.

4.1. Schematic deviations from the audition activity type

The first clash of expectations is non-linguistic in nature and occurs with Dudley's entrance. The stage direction indicates that Dudley enters 'hopping energetically on one leg'. As we read on, it transpires that the reason for this is that Dudley only has one leg. (In a stage performance of the sketch, this fact would be immediately apparent to the audience, since Dudley enters with one leg strapped up underneath a long mackintosh; various versions of the sketch are available on YouTube.) At this stage, it is not the fact that Dudley has only one leg that is absurd, but the fact that he is not using any aid such as a prosthetic limb or a wheelchair. The incongruity of this schematic clash is made more prominent when we learn from turn 4 that Dudley (or 'Mr Spiggott' to give him his character name) is here to audition for the part of Tarzan. Our schematic knowledge of the Tarzan character is of a muscular and fit athlete (cf. the classic Johnny Weissmuller interpretation of the role), and Dudley's character simply does not fit this stereotype. Note that this clash is reinforced in performance by Dudley's short stature and the shabby raincoat he is wearing; a further aspect of our audition schema might be that actors turn up having dressed in a style appropriate to the role they are auditioning for.
   The schema clash above is undoubtedly significant in our interpretation of the sketch, but it is arguably one that the characters themselves do not treat as particularly odd. Peter's surprise is that Dudley should be auditioning for the role of Tarzan when he has only one leg, not that Dudley enters the audition hopping. Here, it is useful to refer to Short's (1996) conception of the discourse architecture of prototypical dramatic texts, which he notes are comprised of two discourse levels (see Figure 12.1). The first concerns the message conveyed by writer to reader (or audience, if we are discussing theatrical

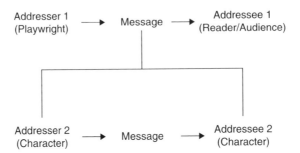

Figure 12.1: Discourse architecture of a prototypical dramatic text

performance). The second and embedded level refers to the message(s) conveyed from character to character.

In the sketch it would seem that the clash of expectations regarding Dudley's lack of a prosthetic limb or wheelchair is one that is recognized only at level one of the discourse structure diagram in Figure 12.1. The characters themselves do not appear to recognize any absurdity in the situation. Indeed, this is one of the hallmarks of absurdist drama. We might thus note a further clash: that of the reader's and the characters' conception of the audition activity type.

In addition to this level-one schematic deviation, we might observe a further potential schematic deviation at the writer-to-reader level. This is the fact that there is only one interviewer present, which might not necessarily accord with our schematic expectations for auditions (especially if our schema is based largely on the kind of exploitative auditions described earlier). Notice, though, that this schematic inconsistency is overridden by the internal conceptualization header in turn 1.

4.2. Interactional deviations from the audition activity type

In our discussion of the audition activity type, we noted that the interviewers may not give feedback at all, and in fact generally keep interaction to a minimum. We also noted that although they are licensed to damage the face of auditioners, the norms of standard auditions orient to constructive criticism, destructive criticism being a characteristic of exploitative auditions. Peter's attempt to inform Dudley of his unsuitability for the role is prolonged to the point of absurdity. 'Real' auditions, as we commented, are subject to time pressures. In this respect, Peter's behaviour is incongruous with the audition activity type, since his strategies for achieving his goal vary from the norm – prolonged indirectness from the director/judge about a fault or inadequacy is not at all normal. Moreover, Dudley fails to interpret Peter's meaning and Peter becomes increasingly indirect in an effort to mitigate the FTA. Neither character gives any indication that he considers the interaction odd, whereas at the writer-to-reader level of the text the extreme politeness is likely to be seen as incongruous with the audition activity type, thereby creating the potential for humour. The fact that the characters show no sign of reacting to the oddity is one of the features that give the sketch its absurdist flavour: they seem to be operating with a different set of assumptions.

Whether Peter's politeness is genuine is debatable. An argument might be made that Peter is at certain points being sarcastic. For example, in turn 24 the suggestion that Dudley does, in fact, stand a small chance of being offered the role if no other actors apply seems highly unlikely. However, that Peter apparently does not recognize anything odd about Dudley's hopping suggests that the absurdity of the situation is not recognized by the characters. Consequently, we cannot be sure that sarcasm is Peter's intention. At a surface level, Peter is certainly polite from the outset. The first instance of this is in turn 4, when Peter says 'Yes ... if you'd like to remain motionless for a moment, Mr Spiggott. Please be stood.' Here Peter flouts the Gricean maxim of manner in an effort to imply that Dudley should stand still. What is notable here is the extreme indirectness. Rather than using a conventional modalized question (e.g. 'Can you stand still?'), Peter generates his implicature via an unfinished conditional ('if you'd like to remain motionless for a moment, Mr Spiggott'), a more indirect (and in this context more polite) structure. The phrase that follows – 'Please be stood' – is also indirect. Compare this with 'Please stand'. Here the action is in the main verb (it is an instruction to perform the action of standing); in our case the action is made more remote by being placed in the past participle (it is an instruction to attain the state of being stood). Moreover, 'Please be stood' is clearly modelled on the conventionally polite formula 'Please be seated'. In this it appears to be quite creative; 'be stood', where 'be' is an imperative, fails to appear in the two-billion-word *Oxford English Corpus*. This creative oddity (particularly in view of the fact that Dudley is already standing, just not standing still) foregrounds it further and adds to our view of Peter as a strange character.

Peter's comment in turn 6 continues his efforts at politeness ('Now, Mr Spiggott, I couldn't help noticing almost at once that you are a one-legged person'). Here, the absurdity arises from the negative verb-phrase (via a further flouting of the maxim of manner) which generates the implicature that Peter would not have noticed Mr Spiggott's lack of leg if he could have avoided doing so. While this kind of redressive comment clause is commonly used as a politeness strategy (flagging the speaker's observation as accidental), the absurdity in this case arises from the fact that Mr Spiggott's lack of a leg could never in reality go unnoticed. This is in contrast with more normal cases – for example, 'I couldn't help noticing that you're wearing odd socks' – where the detail observed is relatively insignificant and could plausibly not have been noticed by the speaker. Peter follows this up by saying in turn 8: 'When you have been in the business as long as I have you come to notice these little things almost instinctively.' Peter's utterance downplays the significance of Dudley having only one leg by referring to it as a little thing. Of course, given the role Dudley wants to play, it is not. Peter clearly recognizes this (indeed, this is the impetus for the whole sketch). Nonetheless, the absurdity of Peter's behaviour so far is such that we are likely to interpret his utterance in turn 8 as something more akin to a boast than sarcasm. His implicature appears to be that not everyone notices little things but that he does. But, of course, at the writer-to-reader level of the discourse structure diagram, the fact that Dudley has only one leg is not a little thing at all. There is, then, another clash between Peter's beliefs and those of the reader/audience.

In turn 10, having established that the role of Tarzan is traditionally played by a two-legged actor, Peter says to Dudley: 'And yet you, a unidexter, are applying for the role.' The utterance itself flouts the maxim of manner in order to create the implicature that Dudley is not suitable for the part. The lack of clarity associated with a flout of this maxim is here generated through the neologism *unidexter*, a noun composed of two morphemes – *uni* (Latin for 'one') and *dexter* (meaning 'on the right'). The noun is a euphemistic reference to Dudley's only having one leg, and in politeness terms works as a means of obfuscating the FTA. Unfortunately, Peter's strategy is too successful, since Dudley fails to pick up on the implicature. Generally, indirectness and implicitness mean loss of pragmatic clarity. However, here we might note a further deviation from the activity type expectations: in the context of the audition activity type we would not expect such implicitness from the auditioner and we would expect the person being auditioned to be readier in understanding that repeated implicit messages mean that all is not well.

Peter again flouts the maxim of manner in turn 12, and, in turn 14, asks a rhetorical question: 'Well, Mr Spiggott, need I point out to you where your deficiency lies as regards landing the role?' Because of its status as a rhetorical question, Dudley's answer, 'Yes, I think you ought to', is a dispreferred response and is thus foregrounded. Peter tries the same strategy in turn 16 only to be met with further confusion from Dudley. In turn 18, Peter flouts the maxim of quantity as a result of pursuing a tactic of flattery. This is in line with Brown and Levinson's (1987) positive politeness strategy of giving 'gifts' to the hearer; in this case the gift is positive assessment. Peter's strategy here is to downplay the FTA he is carrying out by reinforcing Dudley's positive characteristics, thereby attending to his positive face needs. This, in fact, is the turn in which Peter succeeds in conveying his message, via a pun which forces the reader to reinterpret Peter's eighth sentence in turn 18. Peter's statement, 'I've got nothing against your right leg', seems on first reading to be a metaphorical assertion that Peter has no problem with the state of Dudley's right leg. When he follows this up by saying, 'The trouble is – neither have you. You fall down on your left', we realize that Peter is also speaking literally. Now that Dudley has finally realized his inadequacy, Peter at last observes the maxim of quality, this time in line with our expectation for the activity type (see turn 20: 'Yes, it's inadequate, Mr Spiggott.'). However, Peter then follows this up with a statement in turn 22 that is patently absurd ('After all, you score over a man with no legs at all.'). From the point of view of the audience, this looks unlikely to be serious politeness, but may be interpreted as mock politeness on Peter's part. The same might be said of turn 24, where Peter's politeness strategy extends to violating the maxim of quality ('There is still a very good chance'), given that by any normal assessment Dudley is completely unsuited for the role. Here again we might see this as Peter using mock politeness for sarcasm. However, by now the audience is likely to realize that the world of the sketch involves different assumptions, and this is supported by the conclusion of the sketch. The sketch closes with a two-legged man entering to audition for the role of Long John Silver, the irony being that this part (a one-legged pirate) would have been perfect for Dudley. That Peter seems not to have realized supports the idea that what we might have viewed as mock politeness is simply some peculiar functioning of politeness in this world.

There are, then, a number of incongruities when the audition activity type in the sketch is set against normal 'real-life' assumptions. While the reader/audience's audition activity type schema is invoked by the internal conceptualization header in turn 1, neither Peter nor Dudley seem to have an audition schema closely matching our own. Possession of a similar schema would arguably have prevented Dudley from applying for the role in the first place, and would have helped Peter to end the audition quickly if he had. With regard to the characters' deviations from the interactional elements of the activity type, we can note that Peter flouts and violates the maxim of quality in his efforts to mitigate his FTA, and uses extreme politeness. In doing this Peter weakens his institutional role as interviewer. Dudley, for his part, fails to pick up on Peter's implicatures for some considerable time. The two characters deviate considerably from the norms of the activity type, and their behaviour is incongruous with it, and therefore foregrounded. Nonetheless, the reader/audience's schema for auditions is likely to fit sufficiently strongly to maintain the activity type (e.g. to prevent a switch to another activity type), thereby preserving the norms from which the characters' linguistic behaviour deviates.

5. The effects of activity type incongruities

Having established how Peter's and Dudley's linguistic behaviour deviates from the audition activity type, we can now consider the effects of their incongruous behaviour. 'One leg too few' has a reputation as a classic comic sketch, though we cannot attribute this solely to incongruity. Incongruities do not necessarily trigger humour. The reason for this, according to Attardo (2009), is twofold. Firstly, it is important to note that whether people find something funny can be affected by a range of external factors; these include whether they are tired, distressed, or unhappy, whether they have the relevant schematic knowledge to be able to appreciate the incongruity in question, and so on. There is, then, no direct link between incongruity and humour. Rather, the experience of humour is a result of the perception of a stimulus for humour, the appreciation of this, and a reaction to it (Hay 2001, cited in Attardo 2009). Secondly, while incongruities can work as stimuli for humour, they can also generate other effects. Attardo cites the example of detective stories, wherein incongruities may be set up such that the reader cannot reconcile an event in the story with his or her knowledge of the fictional world. An example is Agatha Christie's novel *The 4.50 from Paddington*, in which a character called Mrs McGillicuddy is convinced she has witnessed a murder on a train travelling parallel to hers, despite the fact that no body is found on the train in question. For the reader, the lack of a body after a murder in a confined space is incongruous with his or her knowledge of the textual actual world. Nonetheless, the result is suspense rather than humour.

Attardo (2009) suggests that for a text to be perceived as humorous certain elements need to be in place. The reader needs to be in the right state of mind to pick up on the stimulus for humour, and the incongruities that provide that stimulus need to be of a certain type. Attardo summarizes these, saying that the following are features of incongruities which result in humour:

- Non-threatening
- Not too complex or too simple
- Based on available scripts/knowledge
- Unexpected, surprising
- Occurs in playful mode: the situation must be framed or keyed as humour (in the Goffmanian sense). Particularly, it should reflect suspension of disbelief in the factuality of information (fictionality).
- Occurs in the co-presence of opposed scripts: the two scripts should be available at the same time, or at least be activated closely.

(Attardo 2009: 166)

If we consider 'One leg too few' in relation to these criteria it becomes possible to explain why the incongruities contained within the sketch are likely, under the right circumstances, to lead the reader to perceive the sketch as humorous. First of all, the sketch is in what Attardo calls 'playful mode' and is keyed for humour because it occurs as part of a satirical revue, *Beyond the Fringe*. When the sketch is read or seen in the context of the show as a whole, the reader/audience is set up to expect it to be humorous. The incongruities themselves are non-threatening (cf. the incongruities in a detective or science-fiction novel) and are unexpected given the norms of the audition activity type. Furthermore, the incongruities are based on schematic scripts that have been activated for the reader via the internal conceptualization header in turn 1, thereby fulfilling Attardo's requirement that incongruities should be available scripts. Finally, with regard to the notion that 'the two scripts should be available at the same time', we can note that the odd audition activity type possessed by the characters exists simultaneously with the standard and/or exploitative activity type possessed by most readers, creating a schematic clash. Taken together, these factors begin to explain how the sketch is perceived as humorous, and, with respect to the clash, absurd.

6. Conclusion

We hope to have shown that taking an approach to the stylistic analysis of drama that is rooted in activity type theory pays dividends in terms of its explanatory potential. By analysing 'One leg too few' in these terms we have been able to posit an explanation for the sketch's humorous potential. A conventional, atomistic analysis would not have been able to achieve this fully. For instance, a simple analysis of turn-taking is not in and of itself revealing of the characters' deviant behaviour. Nor is an analysis of implicature or politeness. It is only when taken in the context of what is normal for the activity type that such analytical approaches bear fruit. In the sketch the audition activity type is invoked by Peter's initial request for his secretary to send in the auditioner, Mr Spiggott. While the characters' subsequent linguistic behaviour is incongruous with the audition activity type, the norms of the activity type are maintained as a result of our own schema as readers having been activated. We thus perceive the characters' behaviour against our own particular schematic knowledge. That we experience a clash between our conception of the activity type and that of the characters generates the incongruity that itself is a stimulus for humour and the creation of absurdist drama.

NOTE

1. Searle (1975) articulates a very restrictive notion of (in)directness which essentially relies on whether the illocutionary point matches the syntactic form. Weizmann (e.g. 1985, 1989) points out that (in)directness also involves reference and propositional content.

We take indirectness to be a matter of pragmatic explicitness. Pragmatic explicitness involves the transparency of (1) the illocutionary point (this accommodates Searle's insights); (2) the referents (e.g. a passive structure allowing agent deletion); and (3) propositional content (e.g. ambiguities and obscurities of expression concerning word-meaning and grammatical structure).

PART IV
THE STYLISTICS OF NARRATIVE FICTION

CHAPTER 13

The Stylistics of Narrative Fiction

DAN SHEN

1. Introduction

Like poets, writers of prose fiction make various choices of language to convey literary significance. But traditionally, stylistic analysis focused on poetic style, very much neglecting prose style. The publication of the highly influential *Style in Fiction* ([1981] 2007) by Geoffrey Leech and Mick Short played a key role in directing attention to style in novels and short stories, and the second edition of the book finds itself in a good position to celebrate the rapid developments in the stylistic analysis of prose fiction over the past two or three decades (Leech and Short [1981] 2007: 298–303). In terms of Mick Short's own investigation of narrative fiction, two areas have received most attention: (i) point of view in relation to discourse structure, and (ii) speech and thought presentation (Short 1996: 255–325; see also Semino and Short 2004). As a follow-up to Short's investigation, this chapter will first offer a theoretical discussion of the two areas in question, a discussion that aims at extending the scope of concern and clarifying certain issues involved. Based on the theoretical framework, the chapter will make an analysis of different versions of a mini-narrative, focusing on point of view and speech/thought presentation, while touching on related stylistic and narratological issues of interest.

2. Complex discourse situation and point of view

Compared with poetry and drama, prose fiction is marked by a more complex discourse situation (Short 1996: 255–63), whose basic structure

225

can be diagramed as:

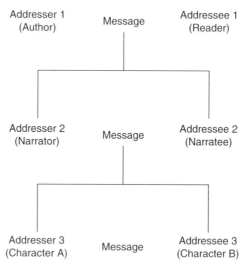

(Short 1996: 257; I have replaced 'Writer' by 'Author')

As for the author, Short (1996) follows Booth (1961) in making a distinction between 'the real author' and 'the implied author'. The former is the author in everyday life and the latter is the author who writes the text in a particular manner and whose image is implied by the text for the reader to infer (Booth 1961, 2005; see also Shen 2007: 173–4). While we can construct the image of 'the real author' by reading biographies, autobiographies, letters, diary, interviews, and so on, we can only infer the image of 'the implied author' from the specific text itself, that is, from 'the sum of his own [textual] choices' made in the writing process (Booth 1961: 75). Distinguishing the implied author from the real author can help get rid of the fetters of the fixed image of the author, whose stance may vary from work to work. While trying to infer the implied author's image from the text itself, we should be aware of the connections between the implied author's textual choices and the real author's life experiences, since one's (earlier) experiences may bear on his or her textual choices. On a broader scale, we should pay attention to the relation between the implied author's textual choices and the relevant sociohistorical factors or influences.

If the author can be divided into the real author and the implied author, the 'narrator' is marked by a different kind of complexity. In many works of narrative fiction, there is more than one level of narration (such cases would involve an extra level to be added to the discourse structure diagram). In Joseph Conrad's *Lord Jim* (1900), for instance, there is an omniscient narrator outside the story, in whose narration is embedded Marlow's narration, in which is again embedded the narration by some other characters. Moreover, the narrator can be either reliable (who gives a factual report of events and makes correct interpretations and judgements) or unreliable (who consciously or unconsciously distorts the facts or makes wrong evaluations) (see Booth 1961; Phelan 2005; Shen and Xu 2007: 50–5). In terms of grammatical person, narrators can be divided into the first-person narrator (who is a character in the story and refers to himself or herself in the first person), the second-person narrator (who uses 'you' to refer to the protagonist or another main character) and the third-person narrator (who is outside the story and who uses third-person pronouns to refer to the characters). Traditionally, implied authors prefer third-person and, to a lesser extent, first-person narration, seldom choosing second-person narration.

Both first-person narration and third-person narration can employ different modes of point of view or focalization (Wales 2001[1990]: 306–7; Prince 2005: 442–3; Genette 1980[1972]: 185–211; Jahn 2005: 173–7). In terms of first-person narration, the 'I' can either be the protagonist in the story (e.g. Pip in Charles Dickens's *Great Expectations*, 1861) perceiving the events from the centre, or an observer (e.g. the anonymous 'I' in Sherwood Anderson's 'Death in the Woods' observing the farm woman) at the periphery of the events. But, of course, the *I*-as-observer can also be at the centre of the events, such as Marlow in Joseph Conrad's *Heart of Darkness* (1902). No matter whether the 'I' is a protagonist or an observer, in first-person narration, there can appear two different perspectives of the 'I'. If a 40-year-old man is narrating what happened 20 years ago, one is the 40-year-old man's (or the *I*-as-narrator's) present perspective, looking back on the past happening, and the other the man's younger self's (or the I-as-character's) perspective, observing the event at the very moment 20 years ago. Compare the following two versions:

Example 1

We were sitting at a table with *a man* of about my age... I was enjoying myself *now*... I turned again to my new acquaintance. 'This is an unusual party for me. I haven't even seen the host. I live over there —' I waved my hand at the invisible hedge in the distance, 'and this man Gatsby sent over his chauffeur with an invitation'. For a moment he looked at me as if he failed to understand. 'I'm Gatsby', he said suddenly. 'What!' I exclaimed.

> (Scott Fitzgerald, [1925] 1993: 31, *The Great Gatsby*, my emphasis)

We sat at a table with *Gatsby*, who was about my age. *At that time* I had no idea that the man beside me was no other than Gatsby... I was enjoying myself *then*...

> (My rewriting)

Although the first-person narrator Nick knows the identity of the man sitting beside him on that past occasion, he temporarily keeps the reader in the dark by adopting his younger self's perspective for the sake of creating a dramatic effect. The difference between the indefinite or vague referential expression 'a man' in the original and the definite 'Gatsby' in the paraphrase reflects the difference between the younger Nick's limited viewpoint and the older Nick's more knowledgeable viewpoint. And compared with the 'remote' deictic adverbs 'then' and 'at that time' in the paraphrase, the 'close' deictic adverb 'now' in the original brings the reader to the very moment of the happening, generating much immediacy. If in the paraphrase the speaker and perceiver are unified in the *I*-as-narrator, in the original the speaker is the *I*-as-narrator but the perceiver is the *I*-as-character. The separation of the narrating voice and the observing eye enables the retrospective narration to lead the reader to discover the identity of Gatsby together with the younger Nick, sharing his shock when the unexpected identity of the man is suddenly revealed.

In first-person narration, the narrator can also borrow other characters' perspectives in telling the story. The following is a case in point:

Example 2
I steamed up a bit, then swung downstream, and two thousand eyes followed the evolutions of the splashing, thumping, fierce river-demon beating the water with its terrible tail and breathing black smoke into the air.

(Conrad 1902: 56, *Heart of Darkness*)

Compare:

I steamed up a bit, then swung downstream, and two thousand eyes of the natives followed the movement of our boat, which they took to be a splashing, thumping, fierce river-demon, mistaking its stern for the terrible tail and its smoke for the black breath of the demon.

(My rewriting)

In the original version, the first-person narrator Marlow temporarily gives up his own perspective and adopts the African natives' viewpoint in presenting the movement of the boat. In contrast to example 1, the viewpoint here is not a matter of temporal or spatial position, but a matter of 'a generalized mind set or outlook on the world' (Short 1996: 277). The value-laden expressions 'fierce river-demon' and 'terrible tail' bring out the primitive fear of the African natives, who have never seen a boat and who therefore mistake the boat's movement for the evolutions of a river monster. Significantly, the primitive outlook appears without any explicit signals on the level of Marlow's narration. This is a case of the narrator's use of language to imitate implicitly the structure of the character's mental self, a technique referred to as 'mind-style' (Fowler 1977; Short 1994; Shen 2005b). Interestingly, this technique presents a challenge to the traditional distinction between content and style. Compare:

(a) the fierce river-demon beating the water with its terrible tail
(b) the boat with its stern moving in the water

The difference between (a) and (b) can only be located at the level of sense, which is traditionally regarded as 'the invariant factor of content rather than the variable factor of style' (Leech and Short [1981] 2007: 26–7). But actually, the two versions constitute two different ways of presenting the same thing, which should be regarded as a variation in style. To account for such stylistic differences, we may borrow the narratological distinction between 'story' and 'discourse' (Shen 2005c, 2002), which corresponds to the Russian formalist distinction between *fabula* (the basic story stuff) and *sjuzhet* (the story as actually told in artistic presentation and arrangement). Versions (a) and (b) may be viewed as two different discourse presentations (i.e. two different styles) of the same story happening (i.e. the same content). At least in narratives where the events of the narrative can be distinguished from the way of presentation, the distinction between 'story' and 'discourse' offers a convenient means to discuss such stylistic variations at the level of sense.

In first-person narration, apart from the shift in point of view, there sometimes occurs the transgression of the chosen mode of point of view (Shen 2001), where the first-person narrator typically assumes the more knowledgeable perspective and the more objective stance of a third-person omniscient narrator. In Sherwood Anderson's 'The Egg' (1921), for instance, the adolescent first-person narrator describes, with implicit transgression of the chosen mode, the climactic scene in which his ambitious yet inept father tries to entertain a guest by doing tricks with eggs, but ends up in total failure:

Example 3

On that evening ... Joe was left alone in the restaurant with father. From the moment he came into our place the Bidwell young man must have been puzzled by my father's actions. It was his notion that father was angry at him for hanging around. He noticed that the restaurant keeper was apparently disturbed by his presence and he thought of going out ... A fire with the showman's passion and at the same time a good deal disconcerted by the failure of his first effort, father now took the bottles containing the poultry monstrosities down from their place on the shelf and began to show them to his visitor. 'How would you like to have seven legs and two heads like this fellow?' he asked, exhibiting the most remarkable of his treasures ... His visitor was made a little ill by the sight of the body of the terribly deformed bird floating in the alcohol in the bottle

and got up to go ... Father grinned and winked at his visitor. Joe Kane decided
that the man who confronted him was mildly insane but harmless ...

(Anderson 1921)

In this piece of first-person narration, there appear many linguistic choices
pointing to the mode of third-person omniscient narration. The contrast
between the epistemic modal auxiliary *must* in '[Joe Kane] must have been
puzzled' and the unmodalized straightforward report 'It was his notion
that ... Joe Kane decided that ...' is a contrast between the limited first-person
perspective and a God-like perspective characteristic of the omniscient narrator. Indeed, epistemic modality is 'possibly the most important regarding
the analysis of point of view in fiction' (Simpson 1993: 48), since the limited
point of view of a character or a first-person narrator is often brought out by
epistemic words like *must, may, possibly* or *likely*, expressing uncertainty about
the perception or judgement involved. Apart from the scope of perception,
the contrast in referring expressions between 'my father' and 'the restaurant keeper' (compare: 'He noticed that my father was apparently disturbed
by ...') also constitutes a contrast between the first-person and the third-
person mode. Moreover, the lexical choice 'the poultry monstrosities' subtly
betrays the viewpoint of the more objective third-person omniscient mode. In
the father's eyes, the misshaped chicken bodies are valuable artistic treasures,
and as a loving son, *I* shares, at least to a certain extent, his father's feelings.
Before the transgression takes place, *I* regards the deformed chickens as 'the
poor little things' and 'the little monstrous things' with the adjectives 'poor'
and 'little' exhibiting his own tender feeling, and with the bad connotations of
the term 'monstrous' significantly played down by its neighbouring words. In
the above passage, by contrast, the lexical choices 'the poultry monstrosities'
and 'the terribly deformed bird' point to a very detached viewing stance typical of omniscient narration, which is notably out of harmony with the father's
view as reflected in 'the most remarkable of his treasures', an expression that
is made to take on a strong ring of irony in this context (other 'detached'
expressions like 'afire with the showman's passion' also add to the irony).
The implicit transgression into the third-person omniscient mode makes it
possible for the first-person narrator to convey better the misunderstandings
between his father and Joe Kane and to produce strong comic effects with his
father as the butt, which contributes greatly to the success of the narrative as a
tragi-comedy. In narrative fiction, that is to say, significant stylistic effects
may arise from the subtle transgression of the chosen mode of point of view as
reflected in the contrastive linguistic choices pointing to another mode.

Now, let us turn our attention to point of view in third-person narration.
Traditionally, third-person narration is mostly in the omniscient mode, where
the God-like narrator can view events occurring at any time (past, present,

future) or in any location, and can penetrate into any character's mind. But to avoid over-transparency and to create various dramatic effects, the omniscient narrator often refrains from peering into certain characters' minds. In Jane Austin's *Pride and Prejudice* (1813), for instance, the omniscient narrator, while frequently revealing the inner activities of Elizabeth, seldom penetrates into the mind of Darcy and never into that of Wickham. So at first the reader is as ignorant as Elizabeth in terms of the true nature of the two characters. The reader's prejudice against Darcy and wrong impression of Wickham are put right almost at the same time as those of Elizabeth's. Only in this way can the reader fully understand and appreciate Elizabeth, who is clever and intelligent and whose temporary wrong opinions are very much due to her perceptual limitations as a human being, limitations shared by her readers. The success of *Pride and Prejudice*, that is to say, lies to an extent in the narrator's keeping certain characters' minds in the dark.

Moreover, the omniscient narrator may sometimes adopt a character's limited perspective in observing events, for instance:

Example 4
Tess still stood hesitating like a bather about to make his plunge, hardly knowing whether to retreat or to persevere, when *a figure* came forth from the dark triangular door of the tent. It was that of *a tall young man*, smoking. He had an almost swarthy complexion, with full lips, badly moulded, though red and smooth, above which was a well-groomed black moustache with curled points, though his age *could not be* more than three- or four-and-twenty. Despite the touches of barbarism in his contours, there was a singular force in *the gentleman's* face, and in his bold rolling eye. 'Well, my Beauty, what can I do for you?' said he, coming forward. And perceiving that she stood quite confounded: 'Never mind me. I am Mr d'Urberville. Have you come to see me or my mother?'

(Hardy, [1891] 1892: 46, *Tess of the d'Urbervilles*, my emphasis)

Compare it with the paraphrase:

Tess saw Mr d'Urberville come forth from the dark triangular door of the tent but she did not know who it was. She noticed that Mr d'Urberville was a tall young man, with a swarthy complexion...she sensed a singular force in Mr d'Urberville's face and his bold rolling eyes.

In the original, the indefinite and vague referential expressions 'a figure', 'a tall young man', coupled with the epistemic modal auxiliary *could* (in 'could not be') indicate that here the narrator, who knows the young man's identity and age, has given up his omniscient perspective and is using instead

Tess's limited viewpoint in representing the happening. The psychological sequencing from 'a figure' to 'a tall young man' to 'the gentleman' subtly imitates the process of Tess's gaining an increasingly clear perception of the person, creating much vividness and immediacy. Norman Friedman in his influential essay 'Point of view in fiction', makes the following comment on the passage:

> Now, although Tess is standing there and observing, Alex is described as seen by Hardy and not by his heroine ... I have rewritten the passage by placing this description more directly within Tess's sensory frame: 'She saw a figure come forth from the dark triangular door of the tent. It was that of a tall young man, smoking. She noticed his swarthy complexion, his full lips ... Yet despite the apparent touches of barbarism in his features, she sensed a singular force in the gentleman's face and in his bold rolling eyes.'
>
> (1967: 123–4)

However, if we compare Friedman's version with the paraphrase immediately following the original, we will discover that the perception verbs or *verba sentiendi* (verbs denoting perception, belief, opinion, and so on) actually have no power in determining or changing the mode of point of view: although 'Tess saw', 'she noticed', 'she sensed', are used in that paraphrase, the point of view is still the omniscient narrator's since only he knows that the man coming out of the tent is Mr d'Urberville. That is to say, the *verba sentiendi* has not affected the omniscient viewpoint – Tess's perception processes only form the object of the omniscient narrator's observation. In other words, we are observing Tess and Mr d'Urberville through the omniscient narrator's perspective, rather than observing Mr d'Urberville through Tess's perspective. In Hardy's version, although there is no *verba sentiendi* to describe Tess's perception, the point of view in effect resides in Tess, who, in contrast with the omniscient narrator, is ignorant of the identity of the young man coming out of the tent. And the reader, now observing the event through Tess's eyes, shares that ignorance. Thus momentary suspense is created and the reader's curiosity is aroused, adding to the dramatic impact of the work. It should be noted that using *verba sentiendi* as the sole criterion is a frequently occurring error in works on narrative point of view.

In third-person narration, if the narrator consistently uses a character's (usually the protagonist's) point of view in rendering the events, then the omniscient perspective will be consistently replaced by the character's limited perspective, such as in Henry James's *The Ambassadors* (see example 10), and the mode will become 'consistently limited third-person point of view' (also called 'third-person centre of consciousness'). Friedman (1967) calls this mode 'selective omniscience', but the very nature of this mode lies in the replacement of the omniscient perspective by a character's limited perspective. There is in effect a different mode befitting the label 'selective omniscience': the omniscient narrator only penetrates into the mind of the protagonist (or another main character) while keeping all the other characters' minds in the dark. Here the perspective remains omniscient, but the narrator has selected only one character's mind to reveal (see example 12).

If the third-person narrator shifts from one character's limited point of view to another character's limited point of view, then we will have the mode of 'shifting limited' point of view (Chatman 1978: 215–9). Virginia Woolf's *To the Lighthouse* (1927) and Henry James's *The Golden Bowl* (1904) are typical cases in point. Stream-of-consciousness novels are usually in the limited mode – either of the consistent kind or of the shifting kind, where the viewing position, located in the character, is *internal* to the story (hence Genette [1980: 189–90] classifies such modes as fixed or variable 'internal focalization'). If, in a narrative, different characters' limited (internal) viewpoints focus on the same event, then we will have the 'multiple' limited (internal) mode.

In third-person narration, if the narrator uses his own point of view to render the story, the viewing position will be *external* to the story. Apart from the 'omniscient' mode, there are the 'dramatic' mode and the 'camera' mode, where the external narrator functions almost as a camera (see example 13) or as a spectator in the theatre (such as Hemingway's 'The Killers' and 'Hills Like White Elephants', 1927).

In discussing point of view, it is important to see the difference between two dichotomies: (i) 'internal' point of view (the viewing position is inside the story) versus 'external' point of view (the viewing position is outside the story), and (ii) 'inside' view (penetrating into a character's consciousness) versus 'outside' view (observing a character's outward behaviour). In the omniscient mode, if the narrator perceives a character's thoughts or feelings, the viewpoint is 'external' (the narrator is outside the story) but we are given an 'inside' view of the character. In first-person retrospective narration, if the narrator uses his present viewpoint in revealing his past thoughts or feelings, the viewing position is likewise 'external' and we are likewise given an 'inside' view of the 'I' as an experiencing character.

The author, the narrator and the viewpoint adopted by the narrator in presenting the story all belong to the addresser side of the narrative communication. As for the addressee side, we may distinguish two kinds of readers. Corresponding to 'the implied author' is 'the implied reader' (or ideal reader) who is supposed to understand fully the implied author's message. By contrast, there is 'the real reader' or 'flesh-and-blood reader', often with various biases and limitations associated with individual experiences that stand in the way of a good understanding of the implied author's message. Although we are all 'real readers' with diversified experiences, in doing a stylistic analysis of a novel or a short story we have to try to get as close as possible to the implied reader's position if we want to understand the message sent out by the implied author. But, of course, the stylistician can set store by personal experiences and investigate individual readers' different responses to the text. Traditionally, stylistic analysis is concerned with shared understandings of the effects produced by the implied author's choices of language. But recent cognitive stylistic investigations sometimes direct attention to readers' different responses as influenced or determined by unique personal experiences or different interpretive frames (see, for instance, Gavins 2007b; Semino and Culpeper 2002).

Moreover, on the addressee side, the direct audience of the narrator is 'the narratee' (Prince [1987] 2003: 57), a textual construct which can either be overt (such as Mallow's audience aboard a ship in Joseph Conrad's *Heart of Darkness*) or covert (when the narrator makes no mention of the audience in the whole text). Interestingly, in one narrative, the narrator can address different types of narratee. In William Thackeray's *Vanity Fair* ([1847–8] 1961), for instance, the narrator addresses, in different parts of the text, 'ladies', 'kind friends', 'any respected bachelor', 'fair young reader', 'poor parasite and humble hanger-on' and 'the observant reader'.

In the discourse structure diagram given at the beginning of this section, the lowest level is character-to-character communication. And this brings us to a consideration of the means used by the narrator to present characters' words.

3. Speech and thought presentation

In contrast with drama and film, where we always hear characters' speech directly, in prose fiction characters' speech is reported to the reader by an intermediary narrator. And as distinct from drama and film, where characters' thoughts cannot be made known unless expressed by themselves, in prose fiction the omniscient narrator can reveal any character's inner thoughts. The narrator may edit a character's speech/thought by making use of a range of reporting modes, which differ in communicative and expressive functions and which therefore may constitute effective means of conveying various artistic or thematic effects (Leech and Short [1981] 2007: 255–81; Short 1996: 288–325; Short 1988).

In English, the traditional dichotomy of direct speech (DS) and indirect speech (IS) has been found inadequate to give a satisfactory coverage of the diversified types of speech presentation. Free indirect speech (FIS) and free direct speech (FDS), which have been developing in English fiction at least since the nineteenth century, were added around the 1960s (following the earlier practice of French stylisticians) to the categorical framework. FDS differs from DS in the omission of the inverted commas and the reporting clause; and FIS differs from IS in according the character's speech independent syntactic status, which makes it possible to preserve all the linguistic features indicating character's subjectivity as in DS, although the speech is reported in third person and past tense as in IS.

DS: She said/exclaimed, 'What a nice day it is today!'
FDS: What a nice day it is today!
IS: She said/exclaimed that it was a very nice day that day.
FIS: What a nice day it was today!

If the narrator merely reports the speech act in a form like 'She made a comment on the good weather' or 'She praised the good weather', we would have Narrator's Representation of Speech Act (NRSA). Short (1996: 293) made a further distinction between NRSA and Narrator's Representation of Speech (NRS, for example 'We talked for an hour'). If speech and thought (T) are considered separately, we have the following modes:

| Speech Presentation: | NRS | NRSA | IS | FIS | DS | FDS |
| Thought Presentation: | NRT | NRTA | IT | FIT | DT | FDT |

This diagram is based on Short (1996) and Leech and Short ([1981] 2007) instead of Semino and Short (2004), where NV (Narrator's Representation of Voice) rather than NRS is used for cases like 'We talked for an hour'. Semino and Short (ibid.) introduce a new category for thought presentation, namely, 'NI' (Internal Narration, or Narration of Internal States, for example 'I was immediately filled with alarm'). But since NI refers to character's internal states 'without any indication that he or she engaged in anything that could be described as a specific thought act' (Semino and Short 2004: 46), we will not include it in the 'Thought Presentation' scale and we will use NRT (Narrator's Representation of Thought) for cases like 'She thought for a while'. In the above diagram, from left to right, the modes form a cline or continuum with a gradual decrease in the narrator's intervention and a progressive increase in the character's autonomy or subjectivity.

Leech and Short ([1981] 2007: 270) observe that the representation of the thoughts of characters, like the use of soliloquy on stage, is a licence or an artifice since we cannot see inside the minds of other people. But unlike in daily life and stage performance by real human beings, in fictional prose characters are created by the implied author who is supposed to know all their inner activities. Thus, in contrast with the unnatural soliloquy on stage, it is quite 'natural' for a God-like omniscient narrator to report any character's thoughts, and stream-of-consciousness novels achieve much authenticity by directly revealing characters' mental activities in third-person narration. But as pointed out by Leech and Short ([1981] 2007: 274–5), DT and FDT, which create the impression that the character is 'talking' to himself or herself, make the thought take on a conscious quality. It should, however, be noted that DT, with the inverted commas serving as an invitation to an auditory experience, tends to result in a stronger sense of the character's being conscious. Compare:

> It's a good chance, he thought, but I cannot take it.
> 'It's a good chance,' he thought, 'but I cannot take it.'

It should also be noted that whether the thought involved appears conscious or subconscious very much depends on the degree of cohesion and coherence of the thought itself. If the thought is incohesive and incoherent, even if it is presented in the free direct mode, it will appear to be subconscious.

The elliptical, incohesive, and incoherent verbal structure, which conveys the free association of ideas, points to the subconscious quality of the thought presented in the free direct mode. Not surprisingly, FDT is frequently used in stream-of-consciousness novels, where DT is hardly in evidence. When it comes to speech presentation, however, if a character's words appear incohesive and incoherent, it will not point to the subconscious state unless the character is drunk or not fully awake, and it may form a symptom of some kind of mental disorder or emotional agitation. Moreover, in speech presentation the contrast between the direct and the free direct mode usually does not bear on the degree of being conscious, since speech is usually consciously uttered. But the contrast between these two modes may produce some other literary effects. The following is a case in point:

Example 5
I said, I hope you slept well.
  'Where is this, who are you, why have you brought me here?'
I can't tell you.
She said, 'I demand to be released at once. This is monstrous.'
We just stood staring at each other.
'Get out of the way. I'm going to leave.'
I said, you can't go yet. Please don't oblige me to use force again.
                                        (Fowles 1963: 12, *The Collector*)

Compare:

> I said, I hope you slept well.
>   Where is this, who are you, why have you brought me here?

I can't tell you.
She said, I demand to be released at once. This is monstrous.
We just stood staring at each other.
Get out of the way. I'm going to leave.
I said, you can't go yet. Please don't oblige me to use force again.

This is a dialogue between Miranda, an upper-class art student, and Clegg, an ordinary clerk who is hopelessly obsessed with Miranda and kidnaps her in a vain attempt to win her love. The mode of DS, with the inverted commas signalling auditory impact, appears louder and more forceful than the mode of FDS (given, of course, the same lexical and syntactical choices). Thus the contrast between DS and FDS, which is quite consistently used in the former part of the novel, functions to reinforce Miranda's sense of superiority and her challenging, dominating tone.

In speech and thought presentation, there sometimes appear mixed cases. Leech and Short ([1981] 2007: 265–6) take issue with Norman Page (1973: 32) in classifying impure cases like the following:

He said that the bloody train had been late.
He told her to leave him alone!

Page takes syntactic subordination to be the determining criterion in judging IS versus FIS (see Banfield 1982). Thus, such cases are IS 'coloured' by lexical and graphological features ('bloody' and '!') associated with the original DS. But Leech and Short ([1981] 2007: 266) treat such cases as FIS since they believe that 'features from any of the three major linguistic levels might be instrumental in indicating that a particular sentence is in FIS'. Let us have a look at the following cases (the non-asterisked ones are from *Mrs Dalloway*):

    * She said (that) what a nice day it was today!
       What a nice day it was today!
    * He asked that was it a good book?
       Was it a good book?
    * Clarissa insisted that absurd, she was.
       Absurd, she was – very absurd.
                (Woolf 1925, *Mrs Dalloway*)

When a character's words are subordinated to the narrator's reporting clause in IS, many linguistic features associated with (F)DS cannot be preserved, but they can all be preserved in FIS (the exclamatory, interrogative, and colloquial syntactic structures and graphological features). It is the suppression

of subordination that enables FIS to retain all the features indicating a character's subjectivity except for tense and person, and subordination is therefore
the determining criterion of FIS/T. Interestingly, speech colouring can occur
not only in IS but also in NRSA:

He complained about the bloody train.

Apparently, the lexical feature associated with FDS (*bloody*) only functions to
add subjective colouring to the NRSA, without involving a change in mode.

Although the different presentation modes are usually distinguished from
each other by linguistic features, sometimes contextual factors may also have
a role to play. Consider the following sentence:

Example 6
How Miss Sharp lay awake, thinking, will he come or not to-morrow? need
not be told here.
(Thackeray, 1961: 37, *Vanity Fair*)

Linguistically, 'will he come or not to-morrow?' seems to be the character's
original thought, but contextually it also seems to be the narrator's summary
of the character's mental activity. In this ambiguous mode, the words implicitly take on certain narratorial interference and are more or less distanced
from the readers.

Of all the modes of speech/thought presentation, the free indirect form has
attracted most critical attention. In particular texts, FIS or FIT may play various thematic functions, 'contributing or being analogous to the governing thematic principle(s) of the work under consideration' (Rimmon-Kenan [1983]
2002: 1–13; see also McHale 1978). The two most important functions are
associated with irony and sympathy. It has been widely noticed that the free
indirect form is a vehicle for irony. Yet, as a mode in itself, free indirect speech
or thought cannot automatically produce irony; irony arises only when the
content or possibly the context of the speech/thought contains some element of
absurdity or incongruity. But to attribute the ironic effect solely to the content
or context is to deny unwarrantably the potentially greater usefulness of the
free indirect form in conveying irony. Then the question arises: how and why
FIS/T is more effective than other modes in terms of conveying or reinforcing the ironic effect? First, the *identity* in grammatical form between the free
indirect mode and narratorial statement may serve to highlight the *discrepancy*
in opinion between the author and the character, for example:

(i) He said/thought, 'I'll become the greatest man in the world.'
(ii) He would become the greatest man in the world.

If accorded by the author to a commonplace character, the speech/thought – both (i) and (ii) – will generate irony. But the ironic effect in (ii) is at once more subtle and striking. For, on the one hand, the (authorial) narrator's reporting of the character's speech/thought in partially indirect form makes the irony more implicit while, on the other hand, something of the impression that the narrator is saying (mimicking the sense of) what he apparently takes to be false adds to the speech/thought a ring of mockery, and makes the irony all the more penetrating. As Cohn (1978: 117) puts it, casting 'the language of subjective mind into the grammar of objective narration' can 'throw into ironic relief all false notes struck by a figural mind'. Closely related to this, the remote-shift in person and back-shift in tense in FIS/T helps generate an ironic distance between the reader and the words of the character, enabling the reader to appreciate better the narrator's implicit comment of irony or mockery.

If the content of the character's speech or thought invites sympathy, the free indirect mode can provide a vehicle for reinforcing empathy:

Example 7

She couldn't go home; Ethel was there. It would frighten Ethel out of her life. She couldn't sit on a bench anywhere; people would come asking her questions... Oh, wasn't there anywhere where she could hide and keep herself to herself and stay as long as she liked, not disturbing anybody, and nobody worrying her? Wasn't there anywhere in the world where she could have her cry out – at last?

(Mansfield 1921, 'Life of Ma Parker')

The protagonist, a widowed charwoman, has endured an extremely hard life and finally wants to cry out at the loss of her loving grandson – her only comfort in life – but she cannot even find a place to cry. Compared with the indirect mode, the free indirect thought brings the reader closer to the character, thus making the emotive concern of the character more immediately felt. Moreover, by fusing the narrator's voice with that of the character (thereby involving the narrator and derivatively the reader), and by preserving the emotive force of the original thought (syntactic features and some choices of words which are often sacrificed in the indirect mode), the free indirect mode presents a powerful means for sympathetic identification. It is of interest to note that the two somewhat converse functions of irony and empathy can, in a single instance of free indirect mode, either be coexistent (Pascal 1977: 42) or indistinguishable (McHale 1978: 275).

The limitation of space does not permit this chapter to carry out a theoretical discussion of other stylistic aspects in narrative fiction, many of which will be dealt with in detail in the following sections. With the theoretical discussion of point of view and speech and thought presentation paving the way, we now proceed to practical analysis to illustrate the functions of various stylistic and narratological features in narrative fiction.

4. Analysing different versions of a mini-narrative

Stylistic analysis is comparative in nature. To see the different functions of different modes of point of view and S/T presentation, as well as other stylistic contrasts, we will make an analysis of different versions of a mini-narrative.

Example 8

I [Alice] knew as I watched Harry mindlessly burrowing into the sports section of the News that the moment had come to make a break for freedom. I had to say it. I had to say 'Good-bye'. He asked me to pass the jam, and I mechanically obliged. Had he noticed that my hand was trembling? Had he noticed my suitcase packed and beckoning in the hallway? Suddenly I pushed back my chair, choked out a rather faint 'So long, Harry' through a last mouthful of toast, stumbled to my suitcase and out the door. As I drove away from the curb, I gave the house one last glance – just in time to see a sudden gust of wind hurl the still-open door shut.

This mini-narrative and the following versions of the same story (except for example 10) are provided by Seyler and Wilan in their *Introduction to Literature* (1981: 159–160). They characterize the above version as 'first-person' point of view. But in first-person narration there are usually two different kinds of point of view: that of the retrospective 'I' (*I*-as-narrator recalling what happened in the past), and that of the experiencing 'I' (*I*-as-character at the moment of happening). Compare:

i. At that moment I asked myself, 'Has he noticed that my hand is trembling now?'
ii. At that moment I wondered if Harry had noticed that my hand trembled (or: was trembling).
iii. Had he noticed that my hand was trembling now?

In (ii), the remote deictic adverbial 'at that moment' and the edited, mediated syntax indicate the narrator's retrospective distance, but the FIT in (iii), with the impulsive appearance of the character's thought, the original interrogative syntax, and the deictic adverb *now*, points to the fact that the narrator has given up the retrospective viewpoint and is using instead the experiencing viewpoint at the very moment of happening. Interestingly, the first-person experiencing point of view is essentially similar to the character's limited point of view in third-person narration. Compare:

Example 9

She knew as she watched Harry mindlessly burrowing into the sports section of the News that the moment had come to make a break for freedom. She had to say it. She had to say 'Good-bye'. He asked her to pass the jam, and she mechanically obliged. Had he noticed that her hand was trembling? Had he noticed her suitcase packed and beckoning in the hallway? Suddenly she pushed back her chair, choked out a rather faint 'So long, Harry' through a last mouthful of toast, stumbled to her suitcase and out the door. As she drove away from the curb, she gave the house one last glance – just in time to see a sudden gust of wind hurl the still-open door shut.

Traditionally, the first-person mode and the third-person mode were regarded as two contrastive modes of narration and point of view. But in the latter half of the twentieth century, narrative theorists have increasingly come to realize the essential similarity in point of view between the third-person limited mode and the first-person mode, to the point of putting the two completely on a par with each other (see, for instance, Rimmon-Kenan [1983] 2002: 74–5). However, there are still in effect some differences between the two. For instance, in first-person narration, the retrospective viewpoint constitutes the norm and the use of the experiencing viewpoint therefore forms a rhetorical device (see the comparison between the original and the paraphrase in example 1), while in the third-person limited mode, the experiencing viewpoint is the only viewpoint available (for a comprehensive discussion, see Shen 2003). Interestingly, since example 10 begins with the anaphoric pronoun *she*, the narrative takes on the effect of beginning *in medias res*, an effect not shared by example 9 beginning with the non-anaphoric *I*. But of course, the most important thing is to realize the essential similarity between the two modes – both adopting the character's internal perspective in rendering the story. So by analysing example 9, we can also get to know the essential features and effects of example 10.

The character's viewpoint, no matter whether it is first-person or third-person, is marked by limitation of perception. So Alice is in the dark as to what Harry thinks. As readers see things only from Alice's perspective, they tend to be more sympathetic towards Alice. But the character's view is subjective, and may be partial and biased. Thus readers are invited to play an active role in the meaning-making process, which makes reading at once more challenging and more interesting.

The first, long, periodic sentence conveys tension and a sense of irretrievable loss, as well as the determination to take a positive action. The derogatory adverb *mindlessly* and the verb *burrow* indicate that Alice is quite irritated by Harry's reading the newspaper. Different readers may react differently to Alice's irritation. Female readers, especially those who have suffered from the indifference of self-centred husbands, may share Alice's view, but male readers, especially those who are dissatisfied with demanding and grumbling wives, may treat Alice's view as quite unreasonable. In any case, in contrast with the traditional omniscient mode where the narrator provides objective facts and often makes authoritative judgements for readers, the experiencing viewpoint is marked by the character's subjectivity, and readers are invited to make their own judgement. Indeed, perhaps the conflict between the husband and wife is so deeply rooted that conventional behaviour at the breakfast table – reading a newspaper – becomes unbearable to Alice (compare the more neutral observation of the behaviour in examples 11–13). The reader may question whether Alice's husband is as mindless as she holds him to be, and may infer that her failure to communicate frankly with her husband and understand him is partly responsible for their marital crisis. The reader may also infer from Alice's point of view her sensitive, delicate personality as well as her strong will. That is to say, this mode can effectively characterize the mind of the viewpoint character.

In this version, the abrupt, impulsive, and hardly mediated FIT ('I had to say it. I had to say "Good-bye". ... Had he noticed that my hand was trembling? Had he noticed my suitcase packed and beckoning in the hallway?') reveals Alice's mental activity in its original agitation, inviting readers to share her concern, agony (*trembling*), and desire for freedom (the personifying 'beckoning'). The repetition of the deontic modal verb 'I *had* to say' conveys Alice's stress and her despairing of the marriage, while the progressive interrogation 'Had he noticed...? Had he noticed...?' indicates, with strong immediacy and dramatic impact, her doubt, anxiety, and sense of urgency. The purpose of the interrogation, however, is ambiguous: Alice might be afraid of being prevented from going or, on the contrary, might subconsciously wish Harry to notice what is happening and ask her to stay. The adverbs *mechanically* and *suddenly*, the verbs *tremble*, *chock*, and *stumble*, and the adjectival 'rather faint', interact to convey Alice's inner struggle, pain, sadness, and helplessness. The description of the wind's hurling the 'still-open door shut' symbolizes the loss of any hope in this marriage, a symbolic meaning reinforced by the repetition of the adjective *last*. Now let us turn our attention to the omniscient mode:

Example 10

Sometimes an apparently insignificant moment brings to a head all of those unresolved problems we face in our daily lives. Such was the case with Harry and Alice that morning as they sat at breakfast over their coffee and toast. They seemed perfectly matched, but in reality, they merely maintained marital harmony by avoiding bringing up anything unpleasant. Thus it was that Harry had not told Alice he was in danger of being fired, and Alice had not told Harry that she felt it necessary to go off on her own for a while to find out who she really was. As he glanced at the Cubs score in the News, Harry thought, 'Damn! Even baseball's getting depressing. They lost again. I wish I could manage to tell Alice about my losing the McVeigh contract – and just maybe my job!' Instead, he simply said, 'Pass the jam'. As Alice complied, she saw that her hand was trembling. She wondered if Harry had noticed. 'No matter,' she thought, 'This is it – the moment of good-bye, the break for freedom'. She arose and, with a half-whispered 'So long, Harry', she walked to the suitcase, picked it up, and went out, leaving the door open. As the wind blew the door closed, neither knew that a few words from the heart that morning would have changed the course of their lives.

This version is characterized by the external narrator's perceiving things from any angle of vision, having access to all the temporal and spatial dimensions of the story. The narration, however, is not based on temporal or spatial order, but proceeds in a systematic fashion from a general statement (a generic sentence) to a specific example, and finally to a moral. The first sentence serves as a topic sentence, round which the following sentences are organized. The main clause of the second sentence 'Such was the case with ...' unequivocally indicates that the following episode of life is used as an illustration – a negative example – of the topic sentence, as well as a means to convey the final moral. Thus considerable narrative distance is generated between the characters and the narrator/author/reader. The narrator takes a balanced view of the two characters and grammatically balances sentences with *he* as subject alternately with those having *she* as subject. The reader is clearly, fully, and impartially informed of what happens between Harry and Alice, including the gap between their inner thoughts and outward behaviour. The narrator observes the characters from above, more or less treating them as puppets, and the reader is invited to join that superior observing position. The verb *seem*, the adverbials *apparently*, *merely*, *simply*, and *in reality* point to the narrator's capability to see through the appearance – to which the characters are confined – and get to the essence of things. The semantic contrast between *insignificant* and *head*, coupled with the assertive *neither knew* and the subjunctive *would have*, also indicates the narrator's superior judgement.

Compared with the first-person narration in example 9, the omniscient narrator is more reliable, and he uses many more neutral and general words, which indicate his impartiality, objectivity, and detachment. Given the difference of the neutral *glance* from the pejorative 'mindlessly burrow', coupled with the inside view of Harry's mental activity, the reader, rather than blaming Harry for his callousness, knows that Harry's insensitivity can be well accounted for by his difficult situation. The contrast between *half-whisper* and *choke out*, and that between *walk* and *stumble*, constitute a contrast between a detached observation and an emotional one, the former making the reader much less involved. Also notice the difference of the neutral *blew* from the emotive *hurl*, as well as the omission of 'sudden gust' in the depiction of the wind. In examples 9 and 10, 'a sudden gust of wind hurl the still-open door shut' is presented as new information, and since it is perceived by Alice, a strong emotional impact on the character is implied. Moreover, this action is not only presented as the major happening in the main clause but also accorded the position of end-focus, both of the sentence and of the whole narrative, which helps to convey the symbolic significance. By contrast, in example 11 the same action is perceived by the narrator, presented apparently as given, and made to appear in a subordinate circumstantial clause with neutral lexical choices ('As the wind blew the door closed'), which greatly reduces the prominence, the emotive force, and the symbolic potential of the action. These stylistic choices lead to a very different effect: instead of having a heavy heart at the departure of Alice, the reader may only think it a pity that Alice and Harry have unwisely failed to achieve understanding.

As for S/T presentation, Alice's agitated questioning in FIT, 'Had he noticed that my hand was trembling?', is replaced by the placid IT with the non-factive cognition verb 'wondered' ('She wondered if Harry had noticed'), which indicates the omniscient narrator's detached observation and reporting. Although the direct mode is used to present Harry's inner thoughts and spoken words, readers still tend to hold aloof from him since they are observing him together with the narrator from a higher position, a superiority indicated, among other things, by words like *thus*, 'had not', 'instead', and 'simply'. It is essentially the same for the DS of Alice. The remote deictic adverbial 'that morning' unequivocally pushes the story to the past, which forms a contrast to examples 9 and 10 where the reader more or less gets a sense that things are happening now. In reading this version, the reader is much less involved and is much less active in imagination since he or she is only required to accept the authoritative judgement made by the omniscient narrator.

This example clearly shows that in the omniscient mode, the character's consciousness is usually the *external* narrator's object of observation, thus forming a contrast with the third-person limited mode (example 10) where the character's consciousness serves as the viewpoint (internal to the story) through which we observe the story happening. As in the case of *verba sentiendi*, confusion often arises since many scholars undiscriminatingly treat a character's consciousness as a determining criterion for an internal viewpoint (see, for instance, Fowler 1986: 134–40). According to Fowler (1986: 135), if the omniscient narrator 'has knowledge of the feelings of the characters', the mode will be an 'internal' point of view. Thus example 11 will fall into this *internal* category. However, we are in effect observing the characters' inner and outer activities together with the narrator from a superior *external* position. The criterion as used by Fowler among other scholars has the following consequences: (i) losing sight of the essential difference between the third-person limited mode (where we see things from the character's internal viewpoint) and the third-person omniscient mode (where we see things from the narrator's *external* viewpoint) – both modes are classified by Fowler (1986: 134–5) as being internal; (ii) It becomes impossible to distinguish between the *I*-as-narrator's *external* perspective from the *I*-as-character's internal perspective in first-person retrospective narration (see example 1) – first-person narration is invariably regarded by Fowler (1986) as having an internal point of view; (iii) It becomes impossible to distinguish between the narrator's using his own viewpoint (external to the story) and the narrator's using a character's viewpoint (internal to the story, as in example 4) in omniscient narration.

We now proceed to a different kind of omniscience.

Example 11
Harry glanced quickly at the Cubs score in the News only to be disappointed by another loss. They were already writing, 'Wait till next year'. It was just another bit of depression to add to his worries about the McVeigh contract. He wanted to tell Alice that his job was in danger, but all he could manage was a feeble 'Pass me the jam'. He didn't notice Alice's trembling hand or hear something faint she uttered. And when the door suddenly slammed he looked up, wondering who could be dropping by at seven in the morning. 'Now where is that woman,' he thought, as he trudged over, annoyed, to open the door. But the emptiness had already entered, drifting by him unnoticed, into the further reaches of the house.

Seyler and Wilan characterize the viewpoint of this version as 'limited omniscient' (1981: 159). But since the adjective 'limited' is conventionally used for a character's confined viewpoint as distinct from omniscience, it is better to use 'selective omniscience' instead. Although Harry's mind is revealed, we are, for most of the time, not seeing things from his internal perspective but are observing him together with the external narrator, so we can see things beyond his perception ('He didn't notice ... drifting by him unnoticed'). In contrast with example 10, most of the syntactic subjects in this version are 'Harry' or 'he' rather than 'she' (Alice). The all-knowing omniscient narrator purposefully keeps Alice's mind in the dark, leaves some details unreported, and refrains from commenting, so there is room left for the active play of the reader's imagination. Since readers are given a inside view of Harry alone and since Harry serves as the deictic centre, especially in the latter part of the passage, readers tend to be more sympathetic towards him.

In contrast with examples 9 and 10, where we are offered the female protagonist's thoughts and feelings in their original agitation, here the narrator analyses and summarizes the male protagonist's state of mind and reports it with general labels like 'disappointed', 'depression', 'worries', and with the mediated indirect mode ('He wanted to tell Alice that...wondering who could be ...'), thus notably undercutting the immediacy, urgency, and vividness of the inner activities. However, in the former part of the narrative, amidst heavy narratorial interference, the abrupt appearance of 'They were already writing' sounds like FIT. This suggests that the narrator is perhaps temporarily adopting the character's viewpoint and mimicking his inner voice, thus giving rise to a sense of immediacy. A certain degree of immediacy can also be found in the short DT 'Now where is that woman', where the socially deictic expression 'that woman' seems to register the social and psychological distance between the husband and wife. This expression echoes 'that man' in 'Now why should that man have fainted?' used by the wife in referring to her husband at the end of Charlotte Perkins Gilman's (1892) famous story 'The Yellow Wallpaper', a referring expression that indicates, among other things, the psychological and social distance between the wife and husband. In the present narrative, the marital gap is also reflected in the textual gap before the words 'And when the door suddenly slammed'. Harry is so absorbed in his own worries that he is oblivious to all external happenings until the noise of the door jerks him out of his insulated personal world. Alice's departure before the door's slamming produces no effect on him, hence this action is omitted by the narrator who is obviously adopting Harry's viewpoint here. The blank deliberately left by the narrator through using the character's perspective needs to be filled in by the reader.

In this version, the symbolic meaning of the shutting of the door is totally lost in the replacement of 'shut' by 'slam', with the emphasis falling on the non-symbolic onomatopoeic effect. But some words chosen are less neutral than in example 11, including the verb 'trudge', the adjective 'feeble', and the emphatic 'all he could manage', which interact to convey vividly Harry's depression and helplessness. This, coupled with the personification of emptiness (symbolizing Harry's loneliness) in the last sentence among other places, leaves the reader with a heavy heart. However, as in example 11, the external narrator is superior to and somewhat distant from Harry, thus creating, through the contrast between two perceptual and reasoning systems, some elements of irony. In 'He didn't notice...or hearing...wondering who could be dropping by ...', Harry's insensitivity to his wife's feeling and behaviour, and his slowness in taking in the situation, are ironically presented by the narrator. So there is effected a secret communication between the knowledgeable narrator and reader at the expense of the ignorant character. The reader, that is to say, while maintaining a certain degree of sympathy with Harry, also enjoys some comic delight at the expense of this anti-hero. Now we come to the final version:

Example 12

A man and a woman sat at opposite sides of a chrome and vinyl dinette table. In the centre of the table was a pot of coffee, a plate of toast, some butter, and some jam. Near the door stood a suitcase. The man was half hidden by the sports section of the morning paper. The woman was sitting tensely, staring at what she could see of her husband. 'Pass the jam,' he said. She passed him the jam. Her hand trembled. Suddenly, she pushed back her chair, saying almost inaudibly, 'So long, Harry.' She walked quickly to the suitcase, picked it up, and went out the door, leaving it open. A sudden gust of wind slammed it shut as Harry looked up with a puzzled expression on his face.

Seyler and Wilan designate this mode 'objective' point of view, but 'objective' is too general a term (as we have seen in example 12, the omniscient narrator can also be covert and objective), not able to characterize this mode. To be more precise, we had better follow Friedman (1967) and call it the 'dramatic' mode or, to capture the camera quality of the viewpoint, call it 'camera' mode. At the very beginning of this version, the indefinite referring expressions 'a man' and 'a woman' indicate that the characters are strangers to the narrator like an external spectator or 'camera', who does not know their past or future and can only observe what they are doing now. We get to know that the man is Harry only through the words uttered by the woman. The story elements are presented in the camera's neutral perceptive order. First, we are given a general shot of the central part of the scene including the things on the table: 'A man and a woman ... some jam'. Then the lens moves toward the door and presents the suitcase. This part of narration sounds very much like stage direction. Then the lens is focused on the man 'half hidden by the sports section of the morning paper'. As compared with 'burrow', 'look at', and 'glance' in the other versions, the verbal choice 'be hidden' points to the spatial positioning and the visual effect of the camera. Then the lens moves to the woman 'sitting tensely, staring at what she could see of her husband', with 'what she could see' reinforcing the visual effect associated with 'hidden'. The adverbial 'almost inaudibly', in contrast with the adjectival 'a rather faint', points on the other hand to the recording function of the camera.

This kind of point of view generates great tension and suspense. The breakfast table at the beginning suggests a comfortable and pleasant family atmosphere, but the suitcase by the door gives rise to an element of suspense. Tension increases with the words 'tensely', 'stare at', and 'tremble', and it is intensified by a series of shots of the wife's suddenly and hastily leaving the house. But the husband does not seem to have noticed anything unusual and he looks puzzled after his wife has left. The lens-based narration-focalization generates a strong sense of mystery and presents an enigma to the reader, who may ask questions such as: 'What is happening between the man and the woman?' 'Why is the woman sitting tensely?' 'Why is her hand trembling?' 'Why is she leaving all of a sudden?' 'What is the man hidden by the newspaper thinking?' It is difficult to find answers from the actions and words presented, and the reader has to resort to imagination to try to puzzle out in his or her own way what is going on. As regards the woman's tense state and trembling hand, divergent inferences may arise. Perhaps the woman is feeling nervous because she has made up her mind to do something, even sacrifice her life to save her husband. Or perhaps the woman is nervous because she has put some poison in the jam to murder her husband. Or perhaps she has done something seriously wrong and is afraid that her husband will find it out. This mode thus gives rise to much indeterminacy and bewilderment, forming a direct contrast with the omniscient mode in example 11.

Although this mode takes on the strongest sense of immediacy as we are watching the scene directly with the camera, it generates a big psychological distance between the characters and the narrator/reader, since the former remains an enigma to the latter, and the latter therefore finds it hard to empathize with the former. The distance between the narrator/reader and the characters interacts with that between the characters themselves, contributing to the theme of the lack of communication and understanding among people. But this mode also has its limitations. As touched on above, compared with drama and film, a notable advantage of prose fiction lies in its capability of revealing naturally characters' inner world (drama has to resort to the awkward form of monologue, and film has to use such clumsy means as the aside). The viewpoint of the present version is purely dramatic or cinematic, completely giving up the advantage of prose fiction in revealing character's mind. This may not be wise in the present case since it is concerned with the psychological relationship between husband and wife, and the short space does not permit a character's psychology to be indirectly revealed by lengthy dialogue, as in Hemingway's 'Hills Like White Elephants'. The purely 'camera' viewpoint may lead to unwanted misunderstanding and too much puzzlement. But given the advantage of this mode in creating unmatched suspense, it seems suitable for representing action plots concerned with events like murder or big-game hunting.

Of the modes of point of view in third-person narration, the omniscient one dominated in the eighteenth and nineteenth centuries; the 'limited' mode came into being, and has become very popular, in modern times; and the 'dramatic' or 'camera' form is also a modern invention. This indicates the shift in emphasis from moral-oriented clarity to aesthetic-oriented opacity. As we have seen, each mode of point of view has its advantages and limitations.

Which one is the best choice for a text very much depends on the fit between the characteristics of the mode and the particular theme to be conveyed, as well as on the taste of the current readers.

Before ending this chapter, it should be noted that stylistics and narratology are complementary to each other in investigating narrative fiction, the former being concerned with verbal techniques and the latter with structural techniques largely going beyond linguistic features (see Shen 2005a,c). Interestingly, point of view (a structural technique, but indicated by linguistic features) and S/T presentation (variation in narrative distance through the change of linguistic features) happen to be two areas where the two approaches converge. In terms of many other areas, however, the two approaches differ greatly. For instance, in terms of 'rhythm', narratology's concern with narrative 'rhythm' (e.g. whether to use ten pages to narrate what lasted for one hour [deceleration] or to use one sentence to summarize what happened in ten years [acceleration]) is essentially different from the verbal rhythm that stylistics is concerned with – the latter being about the features of words and their combination (e.g. the alternation between stressed and unstressed syllables, the use of punctuation, and the length of words, phrases, and sentences). Indeed, to a narratologist, no matter what words describe an event, the narrative speed will remain unchanged as long as those words take up the same textual space. A stylistician, on the other hand, will concentrate on what words are used to describe an event, while hardly paying attention to the narrative 'rhythm' involved. Mick Short is among those stylisticians who have consciously drawn on narratology. In investigating the style of Irvine Welsh's *Marabou Stork Nightmares* (1995), for instance, Short (1999) first offers a discussion of the novel's plot structure, temporal arrangement, and levels of narration. With this narratological investigation paving the way, he goes on to explore the linguistic features of the text. Short's aim is to show how the novel's narratological innovation and stylistic invention interact with each other. This points to the fact that to gain a comprehensive picture of the techniques used by the author in a text of narrative fiction, we need to carry out both stylistic and narratological investigations.

CHAPTER 14

Authorial Style

DAVID L. HOOVER

1. Introduction

Authorial style can be studied in many ways, using any of the methods or approaches of stylistics. Here, I concentrate on the distinctiveness of authorial style, mainly in the area of lexis, using the methods of computational stylistics. This approach will emphasize the comparative nature of style, while at the same time providing an opportunity to explore the styles of the four authors in a context in which the subject matter, plot, characters and themes remain constant for each pair of authors. This exploration will also suggest further directions for investigating authorial style, both in these two cases and more generally.

Authorial style is chiefly linguistic, though a description of the styles of some authors might also invite attention to punctuation and other graphological features, or to illustrations. In some cases, even the page size and layout and the physical characteristics of the text, such as the weight and colour of the paper, may be considered stylistic features. An author's characteristic philosophy, world view, themes, tones, topics and characters are all expressed linguistically, as are the more obviously linguistic elements of grammar, lexis, morphology, phonology, figures of speech, cohesion and collocation (for an excellent checklist of features, see Leech and Short 1981: 75–82). Style, and especially prose style, is also distributed and patterned. Although there are obviously quite local and striking stylistic effects, it is difficult to know how to deal with a truly isolated effect: when Dickens opens *A Tale of Two Cities* with 'It was the best of times', consider the effect of following it with 'it was the worst of times', and the importance of the pattern of opposites that loads the first half of his sentence. Style is also essentially, if not always explicitly, comparative. Any remark on a stylistic characteristic implies a comparison, even if it does not state one. To comment on the 'staccato effect of Hemingway's short sentences' implicitly asserts that his sentences are shorter than 'normal'.

Otherwise, how would the effect arise? The vexed question of the appropriate norm for any given text remains vexed, but the widespread availability of electronic texts now allows a much wider range of defensible answers.

The linguistic, distributed, patterned and comparative nature of style lends itself naturally to computational methods. While I do not suggest that stylistic analysis *must* be computational, I hope to show here that computational methods can reveal stylistic features and characterize authorial style in ways that would be practically impossible in any other way, and that statistical analysis is 'an essential and important tool in stylistic description' (Leech and Short 1981: 71). I concentrate here on words, for reasons of both convenience and principle. Words are easily identifiable and countable, compared with figures of speech or syntactic patterns. They are also very frequent, which makes computational methods both necessary and appropriate. In addition, unlike sequences of letters, which some recent work suggests may more effectively differentiate authors (Clement and Sharp 2003), words are clearly, if not unproblematically, meaningful.

Although 'word' seems an intuitively simple concept, various definitions are defensible. For my purposes, a word (type) is a unique sequence of alphanumeric characters not broken by a space or by any punctuation except the hyphen or the apostrophe. (A *type* is a unique form, a *token* is an instance of a type: the previous sentence contains two tokens of the type *by*.) This definition treats contractions as single words. In some cases, one might be particularly interested in modal verbs or negatives, and so might want to separate contractions; however, in the late nineteenth and early twentieth centuries (the period of the texts I will be analysing here), contracted forms were increasing in frequency, so that they seem likely to be stylistically meaningful. My definition also treats hyphenated words as single words, which seems the simplest choice, though in some analyses one might well want to analyse the elements of such words separately. Unfortunately, my definition does not distinguish homographs, such as the verb and noun meanings of *bear*, but the corpora I analyse are too large to make such distinctions feasible, and I will be analysing very large numbers of words, so that these relatively rare words are unlikely to be problematic. Finally, in some cases one might want to treat inflected or variant forms of a word as equivalent (*go/went/gone, book/books*), but, as we will see, different forms of a word often behave quite differently, so that it seems safer, as well as much simpler, to treat them as different (see Sinclair 2003, task 18, for a discussion of the different behaviour of *eye* and *eyes*).

Most of the methods of computational stylistics have their origins in the field of authorship attribution, where the focus is on classification, on searching for the linguistic equivalent of the fingerprint. These methods capitalize on the linguistic, distributed, patterned and comparative nature of style.

There are more cases of unsolved literary attribution than is often realized; in the Victorian era, for example, many novels and even more periodical fiction was published anonymously, including many texts by canonical authors. My own practice, however, is to apply the methods of literary attribution to the analysis and exploration of individual authorial style. Here I focus on Wilkie Collins's *Blind Love* (1890, 1900, 2003) and Steven Crane's *The O'Ruddy* (1903, 1971) two novels left unfinished at the authors' deaths and completed, respectively, by Walter Besant and Robert Barr.

2. *Blind Love*

Wilkie Collins, friend of Charles Dickens, inventor of the detective novel, and one of the most widely read and successful of Victorian novelists, did not live to complete his final novel, *Blind Love*. When he realized that he would not be able to meet the demanding schedule of the serial publication of the novel, he asked Walter Besant, another prolific, though less important and now little-read novelist, to finish it for him, and furnished an extensive synopsis of the part of the novel he had not finished. In this case we have letters, manuscripts and other records that indicate Collins had completed a long prologue and chapters 1 to 48 of the novel, and that Besant wrote chapters 49 to 64 and an epilogue (referred to below as chapter 65) (Collins 2003).

2.1. *The most frequent (function) words: Cluster analysis*

Among the most widely used variables for authorship attribution are the frequencies of the 30 to 50 most frequent function words. The popularity of these words as authorship indicators is based largely on the reasonable assumption that an author's use of such high-frequency and low-content words is likely to be habitual and ingrained, and that authors are unlikely to alter their use of such words intentionally. These words are extremely frequent and, unlike nouns, adjectives and verbs, are relatively free from the effects of theme, setting, tone and other literary characteristics that often vary widely among an author's works. As Figure 14.1 shows, the frequencies of the 50 most frequent function words easily distinguish Collins from Besant.

The cluster analysis that produces Figure 14.1 begins with a list of the 50 function words that are the most frequent in all of the texts combined (*the, to, of, and, i, in, a, you, he, her, was, that, it, she, my, his, had, me, on, with, at, as, for, is, have, him, be, not, which, by, this, what, if, your, from, no, but, there, will, we, are, an, were, been, they, who, out, do, so, or*). It works in such a way that the further to the left that two texts or groups of texts join into

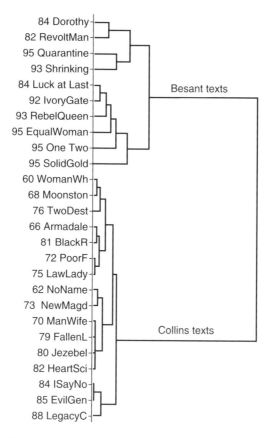

Figure 14.1: Cluster analysis of Besant versus Collins: 50 MFW

one cluster, the more similar they are in terms of the frequencies of all 50 of the words considered simultaneously (see <https://files.nyu.edu/dh3/public/ClusterAnalysis-PCA-T-testingInMinitab.html> for detailed instructions for doing cluster analysis). Thus, Collins's novels are generally more similar to each other in their use of these 50 words than Besant's are, and Collins's three latest novels (at the bottom of the graph) are least like his other novels. Although the frequency of words like *the*, *to*, and *of* do not seem likely to be very interesting to a student of style, John F. Burrows (1987) has shown that frequent function words can yield significant stylistic insights. Nevertheless, recent work (Hoover 2001, 2004b, 2007) has shown that, however reasonable the assumption that the most frequent function words are the most appropriate words to use for authorship attribution, in practice, increasing the size of the word list to include all of the 600 to 1200 of the most frequent words, regardless of type, almost invariably increases the accuracy of an analysis of novel-sized texts. For the set above, for example, an analysis based on the 990 MFW, which together account for more than 80 per cent of all the words of the texts, not only keeps the two authors distinct, it also groups the Collins novels neatly into an early group, 1860–76, and a late group, 1879–88. (Minitab [2005], my preferred statistical software, has a practical limit of about 990 words, which accounts for the odd-seeming use of 990 words.) Fortunately, computational stylistics provides methods for identifying the characteristic vocabulary of writers that extend beyond the most frequent words of the text, and *Blind Love* provides an opportunity to examine more closely what such methods can teach us about the styles of Collins and Besant (on cluster analysis and chronological style, see Hoover 2007).

2.2. Student's t-test

Student's t-test is a well-studied method for testing whether or not any difference between two groups is likely to have arisen by chance. (Any introductory statistics text will provide a full explanation; for a classic discussion of the use of t-tests in authorship and stylistics, see Burrows 1992.) In this case, we want to identify words that are used so differently in the writings of Wilkie Collins and Walter Besant that those differences are extremely unlikely to be a result of chance, and therefore are very likely to indicate real stylistic differences between the writers. Other variables, such as sentence length, word length, the frequencies of various word classes, syntactic units, or any other feature that can be counted, can be tested using this method, but I want to concentrate here on words as an obviously meaningful category, and the other variables just mentioned would require a prohibitive amount of manual identification. I begin by collecting substantial samples of writing by the two authors, in this case, four third-person novels by Besant (1882–93) and three by Collins (1883–85):

> Besant: *The Revolt of Man, In Luck at Last, The Ivory Gate, The Rebel Queen,* about 308,000 words
> Collins: *Heart and Science, I Say No, The Evil Genius,* about 358,000 words

The corpus just described provides a kind of norm, here controlled for point of view, genre, and date; as noted above, Collins's novels show signs of chronological differences in style, and genre effects are often stronger than those of authorship.

I first create a word frequency list for these seven texts combined, then delete words that occur only once or twice in the entire set, reducing the word list from more than 18,000 words to about 9000. The t-test favours relatively frequent words, so these rare words, which could hardly be called 'characteristic', can safely be deleted; their distributions will not be statistically significant. I also delete personal pronouns, which are closely related to the number and gender of characters; given that the goal is to examine *Blind Love*, this seems appropriate, though there are so few pronouns that they are unlikely to have a noticeable effect on the analysis. Next, I delete all words for which a single text accounts for more than 90 per cent of the occurrences; these are almost exclusively proper nouns, typically the names of characters and places. Although the character names an author selects clearly have stylistic significance, removing these words prevents the analysis from inappropriately treating a high frequency of, say, *Tom* in two novels as evidence that they are by the same author. Finally, I also delete words that appear only in Collins or Besant; the t-test cannot be calculated when a variable is absent from either group. (I will examine later a method of identifying characteristic vocabulary that includes words like these.) The process just described leaves about 6600 words upon which to perform t-tests.

To produce strong results, the t-test needs a large number of measurements, so I divide the seven novels into 167 sections of about 4000 words each, 90 sections for Collins and 77 for Besant, collect the frequencies of the 6600 words in each section, and perform a t-test for every word. Finally, I sort the results on the p value that results, so that I can select the most distinctive words for further analysis. The normal practice is to retain any variables for which $p < .05$; that is, here, words with distributions that have a probability of less than 5 per cent of occurring by chance. In practice, however, I often select a smaller group of even better marker words with $p < .01$, or even $p < .001$. In this case, among the 6600 words are about 1700 words with $p < .05$, more than 1000 with $p < .01$, and more than 500 with $p < .001$. In all of these groups, the words that Collins favours outnumber those that Besant favours; nearly 1000 of the 1700 are Collins words (see <https://files.nyu.edu/dh3/public/ClusterAnalysis-PCA-T-testingInMinitab.html> for detailed instructions for doing multiple t-tests).

2.2.1. *Student's t-test: Distinguishing Besant and Collins*

This is a large number of very distinctive marker words for Collins and Besant, and, as Figure 14.2 shows, the 993 most distinctive marker words, about 495 for each author, clearly separate new texts by Besant and Collins that had no part in the creation of the list of words. This graph is based on six texts for each author, an additional novel and five short stories for Besant

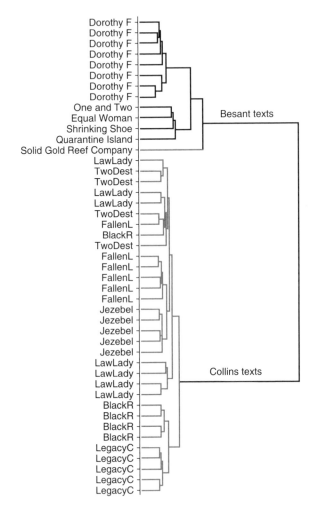

Figure 14.2: Cluster analysis of Besant versus Collins: the 993 most distinctive
t-tested words

and six additional novels for Collins (I began with the 1000 most distinctive words, then deleted those that did not occur in any of the new texts). To
keep the graph readable, I divided the novels into 10,000-word sections and
retained only half the sections for each novel. Including short stories and
first-person novels intentionally makes the task more difficult; nevertheless,
the marker words derived from the authors' third-person novels are obviously
more generally characteristic of the authors, and in this case, at least, limiting
the original corpus to third-person novels seems to have been an unnecessary
precaution.

2.2.2. *Student's t-test and the authorship of the chapters of* Blind Love

With the chapters of *Blind Love* added to this analysis (with the texts divided into 1000 word sections to better match the length of the chapters), the change in authorship after Chapter 48 is starkly apparent, as Figure 14.3 shows, in spite of Besant's use of the long synopsis Collins provided. The graph is based on the sums of the frequencies of the 500 most distinctive Besant words and the 500 most distinctive Collins words in each section. Only a few sections of the novels are shown, and the frequencies of the Collins words are multiplied by -1 to make the graph easier to read. A cluster graph is very crowded with so many texts, but shows essentially the same results.

2.2.3. *Student's t-test and characteristic vocabulary*

These marker words are not simply useful in distinguishing the authors from each other, they can also help to characterize the authors' styles, though it is important to remember that the t-tested words are selected in such a way as to bring out the differences between Collins and Besant. (The method can be modified by testing one author against a group of other authors, which produces a more comprehensive characterization.) Consider the 20 most distinctive words for each author:

> Besant: *upon, all, but, then, and, not, or, very, so, because, great, thing, things, much, every, there, man, everything, is, well*
> Collins: *answered, to, had, Mrs, on, asked, in, Miss, mind, suggested, person, resumed, excuse, left, at, reminded, creature, inquired, reply, when*

The relative banality of the Besant marker words compared to Collins's is quite striking. Most Besant words are frequent function words: 12 of the 20 rank in the top 100 most frequent words in the entire corpus; only 1, *everything*, ranks above 200, and the average rank is 106. In the Collins list, only 8 words rank in the top 100, 7 rank above 300, and the average rank is 262. Also striking is the heavy concentration of Collins words related to speech presentation (*answered, asked, inquired, resumed, suggested*; possibly also *reply* and *reminded*). This concentration is partly a result of a somewhat higher proportion of dialogue in Collins than in Besant – as measured very crudely by calculating the ratio of quotation marks to the total number of words – but that difference is small enough that further research seems necessary to discover more interesting causes. The presence of *added, begged, declared, exclaimed, explained, expressed, muttered, rejoined,* and *said* as likely speech markers among the other Collins marker words, compared with only *gasped, groaned, murmured, replied,*

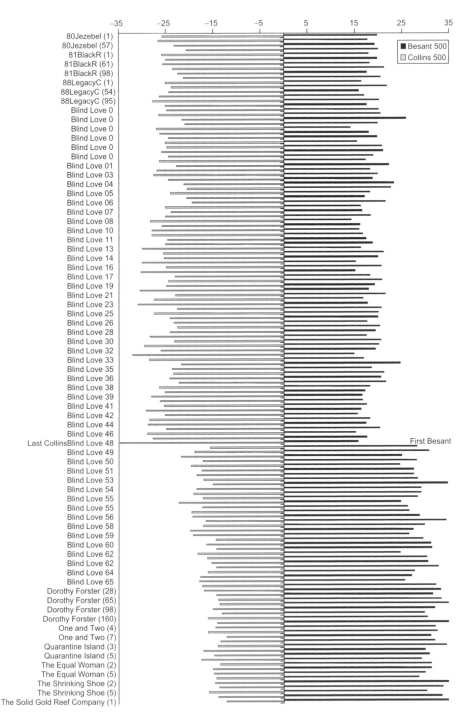

Figure 14.3: 1000-word sections of Besant, Collins, and *Blind Love*: The 1000 most distinctive t-tested words

and *stammered* for Besant, suggests that the two authors present speech in very different ways. A brief examination of the beginnings of Collins's *The Evil Genius* and Besant's *In Luck at Last* suggests that, while both authors frequently leave out speech markers entirely, Besant is more likely than Collins to replace a reporting word with a phrase like 'he turned a beaming and smiling face upon the assistant', or 'Mr James's cheek flushed.' Here, as elsewhere below, I can only suggest further avenues of investigation.

Although these 40 most distinctive words are fascinating in themselves, it is more instructive to sort all 1700 of the p < .05 words alphabetically, along with the scores that show which author favours each word. It is immediately apparent that these distinctive words tend to group in morphologically related families, and that each family strongly tends to be favoured by one of the authors, as can already be seen by the presence of *thing, things,* and *everything* among the 20 most distinctive Besant words. These are joined by *anything* and *nothing* further down his list (*something* is not distinctive for either author). In addition, *every* and *everything* are joined by *everybody* and *everywhere*, and *anything* is joined by *any* and *anywhere*, so that the families are related to each other. The same could be said of *nothing* and *not*, which are joined by *never, no, nobody, none,* and *nor.* (Not all of these families are equally cohesive; I have tried to err on the side of inclusiveness because it gives more chances for the group to fail to cohere.) Finally, *much* is joined by *more, moreover, most,* and *mostly.* For Collins, *answered* is joined by *answer, answering,* and *unanswerable*, and 5 more of his 20 most distinctive words are joined by two other words: *ask, asked, asks; inquired, inquiries, inquiry; leave, leaving, left; person, personally, persons; suggest, suggested, suggestion* (there are some additional two-word families, including one, *reply* and *replied*, in which the second is a Besant marker word).

Among the 1700 distinctive words, about 600 form morphologically related groups, nearly 400 for Collins and more than 200 for Besant. Only about 175 words form groups that contain members from both authors; these form 73 groups that fall into several intriguing patterns. One large pattern shows us that Collins uses more contractions, so that, for example, while *did* and *does* are Besant words, *didn't, doesn't,* and *don't* are Collins words. The same is true for *must, need, should,* and *would* and their negative contractions. This pattern is one reason for the corresponding frequency of *not* in Besant, though it does not explain his distinctive use of the other negative words. In another interesting pattern, partly semantic and partly morphological, the singular and possessive forms of *brother, friend, sister,* and *son* are Collins words and the plural forms are Besant words. The singular Collins vs plural Besant pattern is continued in 32 more nouns; the only exception is that *troubles* is a Collins word and *trouble* is a Besant word. Obviously, some of these words, including *trouble,* are complicated by the fact that some of their occurrences are verbs.

Some other plurals are also Collins markers and some singulars are Besant markers, but in these cases all forms of the words are Collins or Besant markers. Another strong pattern is Collins's use of the -*ing* forms of verbs and Besant the third-person singular present forms, and Besant's plurals and verb forms in -*s* obviously overlap and reinforce each other. A more thorough examination of some of the groups would clearly require part-of-speech disambiguation, but automated tagging is still too inaccurate for my taste, and manual tagging of such a large corpus is impractical.

One of the most surprising patterns is that all 19 of the distinctive words that refer to cardinal numbers are strong Besant markers: all of the numbers from *one* to *ten, twelve, eighteen, twenty, twenty-one, five-and-twenty, thirty, forty, fifty,* and *sixty.* These are joined by *hundred, thousand* and *thousands,* and perhaps one might add *dozen, half,* and *quarter.* The pattern is reversed to some extent in the ordinal numbers; *fourth* is a Besant marker, but *first* and *second* are Collins markers. Naturally, this pattern is related to the preference for plural nouns, which are one of the most common word classes to follow numbers, and which less frequently follow ordinals. Other less consistent patterns exist, but authors' characteristic words are obviously highly patterned, and many more families could be found or made larger by including words that are more frequent in either author, but not significant at the $p < .05$ level. The existence of morphological and semantic families among authors' characteristic words may not seem particularly surprising, but so little research has been done into the nature and character of literary vocabulary that it is difficult to know what *should* seem surprising, and it is unlikely that the number or extent of such patterns would be discovered without a computational analysis. The strong patterns for plurals and number words cry out for more investigation, and further examination of the lists of distinctive words would undoubtedly reveal other semantic and possibly even phonological families, and families of families (for more on word-families, see Hoover 2007).

2.2.4. Student's t-test and the density of authorial style

Another way that t-tested words can be used to investigate style is simply by highlighting them in a text. Doing so reinforces the distributed nature of style and visually emphasizes just how densely patterned style is. In the passages below, I have highlighted just the 500 most distinctive marker words for each author:

> **This** has made a race of **men quick** to **fight** and careless of life, since, willy nilly, they **went daily** in peril; and **many** families **there are** whose **men**, until a **hundred years ago**, **never knew** what it was to die in their beds.
>
> (*Dorothy Forster:* 44 words, 15 **Besant markers**, 0 Collins)

Confronted **by** the **serious** responsibility that he had undertaken, he **justified** what he had **said** to me. **Still** pale, **still distressed**, he was now **nevertheless** master of himself. I **turned** to the **door** to **leave** him alone with the Prisoner. She called me **back**.

(*The Legacy of Cain:* 44 words, 12 **Collins markers**, 0 Besant)

The density of marker words obviously varies throughout each text, but passages as densely marked as these and without any marker words for the opposing author are not difficult to find. The high density of words with distributions in the two authors that are statistically significant (for these 1000 words, the weakest p value is .016) helps make comprehensible the fact that many readers can recognize the style of an author they know well, even in a short passage they have never read before (see also Hoover 2007, 2008).

2.3. Zeta analysis

One drawback of the t-test as a method of characterizing an author's vocabulary is that it privileges high-frequency words: words that occur in many of the sections of one author's texts but fewer sections of the other. These words clearly characterize the authors with respect to each other, but words like *are*, *back*, *by*, *said*, *there*, and *this* are not usually very interesting stylistically. Another drawback is that, as noted above, it cannot measure the importance of words that do not occur at all in one of the authors. Other statistical methods can cope with zero frequencies, but here I would like to present Zeta, a simpler, less technical, and more pragmatic method that is very effective in identifying characteristic vocabulary without requiring formal statistical testing. Zeta was invented by John F. Burrows, but the specific form I will be using here was developed by his colleague Hugh Craig (Craig and Kinney, forthcoming). Like the t-test, Zeta identifies words that are much more frequent in one author than in one or more other authors, but Zeta words are substantially less frequent than those identified by the t-test (for more on original Zeta, see Hoover 2007, 2008).

Calculating Zeta is very simple. Here I use the same seven novels as were used for the t-test and prepare the word list in the same way, retaining only words with a minimum frequency of three, and removing words for which a single text supplies more than 90 per cent of the examples. For this analysis, I have not deleted the personal pronouns and have retained words that are present only in Besant or Collins. Next, I again divide the 7 novels into 167 sections, and then compare how consistently each word appears in the texts of each author. This is done by dividing the number of sections by the first author in which the word appears by the total number of sections for that author, then dividing the number of sections by the second author in which the word does *not* appear by the total number of sections for that author. (This method ignores the word's frequency in each section.) The two ratios are added together to get a composite measure of affinity: a score for how much one author favours the word plus how much the other avoids it. A word that appeared in all Collins segments and no Besant sections would have a score of 2.0; conversely, one that appeared in no Collins segments and all of Besant's would have a score of 0.0. In practice, such words are vanishingly rare, and in the present analysis, *answered* is the most distinctive Collins word, as it was in the t-tests, with a Zeta score of 1.8. It is present in 89 of the 90 Collins sections and is absent from 65 of the 77 Besant sections. Likewise, *upon* is again the most distinctive Besant word, present in all 77 Besant sections and absent from 25 of the 90 Collins sections, with a score of 0.28.

2.3.1. Zeta and characteristic vocabulary

A comparison of the 20 most distinctive Zeta words with those that the t-test identifies is instructive. In the lists of Zeta words below, those that are also identified by the t-test are in bold type:

> Besant: **upon**, *fact, presently, therefore, however,* **everything**, *real, whole, cannot, though, rich, none, thousand, except, fifty, ago,* **because**, *papers, also, twenty*
>
> Collins: **answered, Mrs, Miss, excuse, suggested, resumed, reminded**, *doctor,* **inquired, creature**, *notice, circumstances, tone, idea, temper, object, sense, feeling, governess, impression*

Because Collins's t-tested marker words are much less frequent than Besant's, the overlap is much greater for his Zeta words than for Besant's. Of the 20 t-tested marker words for both authors that ranked in the top 100 in frequency in the corpus, only two are left *(Mrs* and *Miss)*, and the average ranks for the Zeta words are 445 for Besant and 473 for Collins (the average ranks for the t-tested markers were 106 and 261, respectively). For Collins, 372 of the 500 most distinctive t-test words are also among the 500 most distinctive Zeta words; for Besant, the figure is 361. Of the 500 Collins Zeta words, 37 are not found in Besant; of the 500 Besant Zeta words, 50 are not found in Collins.

An examination of all 2000 Zeta words reveals 153 Besant-only words and 122 Collins-only words. One of the benefits of the inclusion of these words is that they augment the morphological families discussed above. Of these 275 words, 59 form new families favoured by a single author; another 27 join the single-author families of the t-tested words. Only 21 words join into families split between the authors. Among the most interesting additions are the following new number words for Besant: *sixteen, twenty-first, one-and-twenty, two-and-twenty, seventy-five, millions,* and possibly *multitude, quantity,* and *several.* Most of these number words collocate with *o'clock, pounds, thousands,* and *years,* depending on the size of the number, suggesting that money and the passage of time are strong thematic elements in Besant's fiction. Again, I can only scratch the surface. Another Besant word-family, *somehow, sometimes,* and *somewhere,* is augmented by the Besant-only word *somewhat.* The Collins-only words *alluding, consultation,* and *excitable* augment the *allude, alluded, allusion, allusions* family, the *consult, consulted, consulting* family, and the *excite, excited, exciting* family.

One final Besant-only word that deserves a brief comment is *thou.* As noted above, I retained the personal pronouns in this Zeta analysis; *herself, myself,* and *yourself* are Collins marker words and *themselves, ourselves, ours,* and *thou* are Besant marker words; note that the pattern of the singular for Collins and the plural for Besant recurs, and no forms of the simple personal pronouns are distinctive. All of these words except *ours* (p = .051) and *thou* (not present in Collins, so that the t-test is impossible) would have been significant at the p < .05 level if they had been included in the t-test analysis. There are, however, too few of them to have had a discernable effect on the analyses presented above, and an argument could be made that they should be excluded in spite of their distinctiveness because the kind of preferences they mark are intimately linked to the nature of the novel, which was determined by Collins.

2.3.2. Zeta and the density of authorial style

Highlighting the 1000 most distinctive Zeta words for each author rather than the 500 most distinctive t-tested words in the same passages reveals a similar density of marker words, though fewer function words and more meaningful words are highlighted:

This has made a **race** of **men quick** to **fight** and careless of life, since, willy nilly, they **went daily** in peril; and **many families** there are whose **men**, until a **hundred years ago**, never **knew** what it was to **die** in their beds. (*Dorothy Forster:* 44 words, 14 **Besant markers**, 0 *Collins*)

Confronted by the **serious responsibility** that he had undertaken, he **justified** what he had said to me. Still pale, still **distressed**, he was now

nevertheless master of himself. **I turned** to the **door** to **leave** him *alone* with the Prisoner. She called me **back**. (*The Legacy of Cain:* 44 words, 11 **Collins markers**, 1 *Besant*)

2.3.3. *Zeta and the authorship of the chapters of* Blind Love

Graphing the frequencies of the Zeta words as the t-tested words were graphed in Figure 14.3 gives similar results. Rather than duplicating them, Figure 14.4 presents a scatter graph in which the vertical axis is the percentage of all the word types (unique words) in the section that are Besant marker words (longer texts are divided into 4000-words sections) and the horizontal axis is the percentage of all word types in the section that are Collins marker words. To make the graph more readable, I have removed the labels for the even-numbered sections 2 to 44 of *Blind Love*, and have included only a few sections of other novels.

Note how distinct Besant's chapters of *Blind Love* are from Collins's. Clearly Zeta marker words are capturing distinctive stylistic vocabulary characteristics. I have also included an additional text in this analysis, *The Case of Mr Lucraft*, a long story jointly written by Besant and James Rice, just to see what

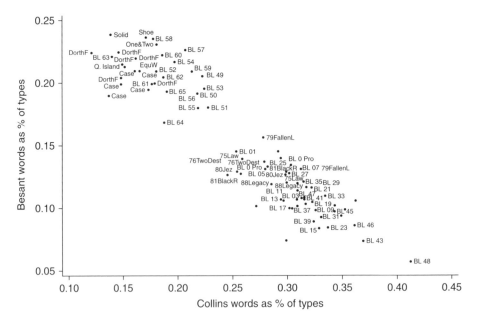

Figure 14.4: 4000-word sections of Besant, Collins, and *Blind Love*: 2000 Zeta words

would happen (the segments of this story are indicated as *Case* in bold type). Figure 14.4 suggests that, as has been argued, Besant did most of the actual writing of the large number of co-written stories and novels that the pair produced from 1872 to 1882, a period during which Besant published nothing on his own (Boege 1956: 251–65). Further research would likely clear up this question, but probably neither Besant nor Rice is important enough to make such research very compelling from a literary point of view.

3. *The O'Ruddy*

I turn next to a discussion of Stephen Crane's posthumously published novel *The O'Ruddy* (1903), completed by Robert Barr. Though Crane was only 28 and lacked the stature of Collins, he was more highly regarded than Barr, who, like Besant, was a popular novelist whose works are now little read. I was initially drawn to this novel by a fascinating short book (O'Donnell 1970) that investigates its authorship, using a small group of variables that includes sentences, words, clauses, clause types, metaphor, parts of speech, and punctuation. O'Donnell reports that, at the time of Crane's death, he had written a manuscript of 65,000 words, of which only Chapter 24 is known to exist, but that Barr at one point claimed to have written three-fourths of what came to be a 33-chapter novel of about 100,000 words. Given the uncertainty about the relative contributions of Crane and Barr, O'Donnell analyses the entire novel paragraph by paragraph (apparently limiting himself to paragraphs of about 100 words or longer). His analysis identifies chapters 1 to 24 as Crane's, chapters 26 to 33 as Barr's, and 25 as a borderline case. To test his findings using frequent words and without preconceptions, I first divided the novel into 37 sections of 2500 words each (about the size of the average chapter) and performed several cluster analyses of the novel and some other texts by Barr and Crane based on the most frequent words. Sections 1 to 24 and 25 to 37 cluster separately and consistently over the entire range of analyses, which suggests, as O'Donnell concludes (1970: 76), that the change of authorship was abrupt, without much joint authorship, except perhaps for Chapter 25. When I divided the novel into chapters, however, I found that cluster analysis divides the novel consistently after Chapter 25, not Chapter 24.

These findings prompted me to further research, and a reference in *A Stephen Crane Encyclopedia* (Wertheim 1997: 251–4) led me in turn to the University of Virginia's authoritative edition of Crane's works. There I discovered that a complete manuscript of the novel exists for chapters 1 to 25 (first recorded in 1969, and unknown to O'Donnell), and that Crane's text was not extensively revised (Crane 1971: xv–lxxiv, 271–98). An independent comparison of chapters 17 and 18 of the original text and the Virginia edition (which is based on the manuscript) confirms that there are only a handful of differences on a typical page, many of which are matters of hyphenation (compound words that are written as one word in the 1903 edition are often hyphenated in the Virginia edition). I might have wished that this information had not come to light until after I had completed my analysis, but it was encouraging that my initial attempts were accurate, even more accurate than O'Donnell's much more labour-intensive methods. (One often overlooked benefit of computational work is that it frequently pushes the analyst toward further research.) The case now appears remarkably similar to that of *Blind Love*, and a further comparison of the results for the two novels is instructive.

3.1. *The most frequent (function) words: Cluster analysis*

After assembling a large set of texts for Barr and Crane, I performed a cluster analysis without including *The O'Ruddy* and discovered that Crane and Barr are much more difficult to distinguish than Collins and Besant. All analyses based on the 200 to 990 MFW attribute Crane's *Active Service* to Barr, and all those based on the 500 to 990 MFW also attribute Crane's *Third Violet* and *The Second Generation* to Barr. Here, the only analyses with just one error are ones based on the 300, 100, and 70 MFW, with errors for three different texts, one by Barr and two by Crane. The variability of the analyses based on small numbers of words and the close similarity of the analyses based on the 500 to 990 MFW both suggest that Crane's and Barr's lexical styles are quite similar.

When *The O'Ruddy* is included, typically from one to three Crane texts are attributed to Barr in the most accurate analyses, but Crane's chapters of *The O'Ruddy* almost universally cluster together, though within the same large cluster that contains Barr's texts, as shown in Figure 14.5.

Note that, though it confirms the division point in the novel, this graph suggests that all of *The O'Ruddy* is more similar to Barr than to Crane, presumably reflecting the fact that this first-person comic novel is considered very uncharacteristic of Crane. Barr himself described it in a letter as 'different from anything he ever wrote before' (quoted in Crane 1932: 18; see also Wertheim 1997: 254; O'Donnell 1970: 33–5; Sorrentino 2008: 61).

3.2. *Student's t-test, zeta, and the authorship of the chapters of* The O'Ruddy

To make my analysis of *The O'Ruddy* comparable to the analysis of *Blind Love*, I collected a similar-sized corpus of texts by Crane and Barr, about 315,000 words each. In this case, because Crane only wrote a few relatively

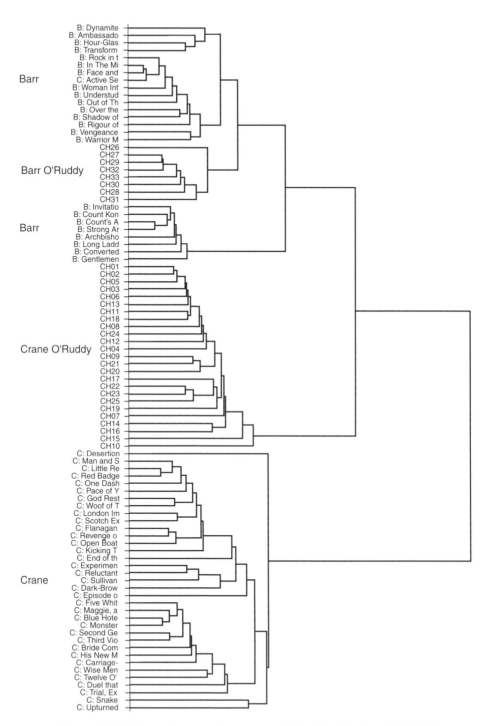

Figure 14.5: Barr, Crane, and chapters of *The O'Ruddy*: The 990 MFW

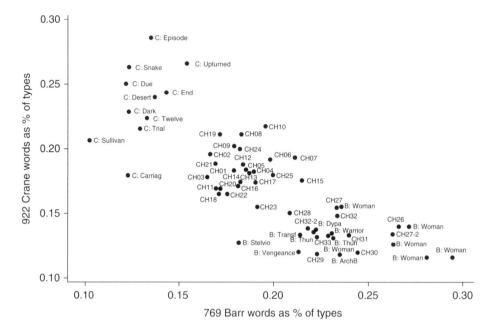

Figure 14.6: Barr, Crane, and *The O'Ruddy*: 1691 t-tested words p < .05

short novels, many of the texts are stories or novellas. I created word lists and collected the t-tested words, just as for Collins and Besant: in this case, 1691 words p < .05, 769 for Barr and 922 for Crane, and 1,000 Zeta words for each author. Analyses based on the two sets of words are remarkably similar, and they confirm the clear distinction between Crane's and Barr's chapters of *The O'Ruddy*. A graph based on the t-tested words is shown in Figure 14.6. Note that Barr's chapters are much more similar to his other texts than Crane's chapters are to his other texts, showing just how uncharacteristic this novel is for Crane.

3.2.1. Student's t-test and characteristic vocabulary

There is only space here for a brief examination of the vocabulary differences between Crane and Barr, but consider the 30 most distinctive marker words for Crane and Barr:

Barr: *have, than, will, for, is, my, so, your, has, may, or, before, am, although, not, shall, own, on, I, that, me, put, should, taken, our, myself, cannot, are, therefore, next*

Crane: *suddenly, they, a, upon, presently, great, turned, began, at, manner, arose, toward, gesture, moved, faces, finally, were, like, went, seemed, eyes, their, black, near, fro, he, obliged, kind, rage, stared*

Barr's list, like Besant's, is quite banal and much less revealing than Crane's. Both lists also again suggest word-families. For example, *my, your, I, our,* and *myself* show Barr's preference for first- and second-person pronouns, a preference that is continued by *mine, yours, yourself, you,* and *we,* among his other marker words. Crane's greater use of contractions (not evident here), however, places *we'll* and *we've* among his marker words. It may also help to explain the presence of the auxiliary verbs in Barr's list above, by reducing the frequency of the full forms in Crane, though the presence of seven lexical verbs in Crane's list and only two in Barr's suggests that contraction is not the full explanation. Crane favours the third-person pronouns, as *they, their,* and *he* suggest, and as is confirmed by the presence of *his, them, 'em,* and *it'll* among his other marker words (note the reinforcement of the contractions). Crane and Barr both typically write in the third person, yet first- and second-person pronouns and contractions all suggest dialogue, so that more research would be needed to explain these patterns. The presence of *faces, eyes,* and *stared,* along with *black,* suggests that Crane is more interested in the visual, and this is confirmed by the presence of *stare, staring, face, faced, apparent, appear, appeared, appearing, glance, glanced, glances, look, looked, looks, resemble, resembled, scene, scenes, shade, shadows, shadowy, shine, shining,* and *shone,* among his other marker words. Among Barr's marker words are only *evident, evidently, recognize, recognized, notice,* and *noticed,* a list that, besides being much shorter, is also less clearly visual. Finally, the contrast between Barr's *is, am,* and *are* and Crane's *were* is completed by *was* among Crane's other maker words; and Crane's other past-tense verbs above, *turned, began, arose, moved, went, seemed,* and *stared,* compared with only *taken* and possibly *put* for Barr, suggest a more general preference for past tense.

Among the 1691 t-tested markers are about 300 morphological families, containing about 730 words: about 130 Crane families, 120 Barr families, but only 50 families with at least one marker word for both Barr and Crane. Among the mixed families, 20 involve a past-tense and a present-tense verb; 17 of the past-tense verbs are Crane markers and only 3 are Barr markers, confirming Crane's preference for the past tense. Furthermore, although past-tense verbs are about equally prevalent among the Barr and Crane families of words, among the words not in families about 19 per cent of Crane's words are past-tense verbs, compared with only about 9 per cent for Barr. Five of the mixed families involve a contraction for Crane, and a few other minor patterns exist, so that more than half of the mixed families exhibit further patterns. Even families that are not fully consistent are often partially patterned, as with *we* versus *we've* and *we're*, above. Consider the *do* family: *do*, *does*, and *doesn't* are Barr markers, and *don't* and *didn't* are Crane markers, so that the pattern of present-tense and full forms for Barr and past-tense forms and contractions for Crane are still visible in spite of the partial exceptions of *doesn't* and *don't*. Forms of *any*, *every*, and *some* present another interesting mixed pattern (Barr markers in bold type):

any	**anyone**	anybody	anyhow	anyway
every	**everyone**	everybody	everywhere	
some	**someone**	somebody	sometimes	
	somewhat			

Within this somewhat confused situation it is clear that the *-one* vs *-body* words form a strong pattern of the kind that is often important for authorship attribution, and the absence of any of the *-thing* forms as marker words is intriguing.

Finally, there are interesting semantic groups of words among the Barr and Crane markers that are not morphologically based. The word *black* within Crane's 30 most distinctive markers is joined by all the other colour words among the marker words: *blue*, *gray*, *grey*, *green*, *pink*, *purple*, *red*, *white*, and *yellow*. Crane also monopolizes the semantic field of swearing, with *cursed*, *curses*, *damn*, *damned*, *hell*, *swearing*, and *swore* among his marker words (many of Crane's texts were originally bowdlerized). Barr, in turn, monopolizes the field of time, with *day*, *days*, *hour*, *minutes*, *moment's*, *moments*, *month*, *year*, and *years* among his marker words. Finally, Crane overwhelmingly favours words related to speed or quickness, with the following among his marker words: *abrupt*, *abruptly*, *flurry*, *gallop*, *galloped*, *galloping*, *hastily*, *hurried*, *immediately*, *presently*, *prompt*, *ran*, *rush*, *rushed*, *shortly*, *sudden*, *suddenly*, *swift*, and *swiftly*. For Barr, in contrast, there are only *runs*, *speedily*, and *suddenness*. Again, I can only point in the directions that this kind of analysis makes possible, and further examination of the word lists would undoubtedly uncover additional patterns of interest.

4. Conclusion

Computational stylistics is neither a substitute for nor an alternative to other kinds of stylistic and literary analysis. Rather, it provides additional tools that can serve as discovery procedures, and it can augment and enhance other methods. Computational stylistics provides a practical way of elucidating the extensive and richly-patterned nature of style, of coping with the dense yet widely-distributed linguistic phenomena which constitute the stylistic features that both make an authorial style distinctive and characterize its nature. Cluster analysis effectively measures the similarity and difference of authors, texts, or parts of texts by taking into account large numbers of features simultaneously, emphasizing and facilitating the comparisons upon which style so intimately depends. T-tests and Zeta analysis are also effective methods of measuring difference and similarity, but they go beyond or beneath this to provide access to patterns too subtle, extensive and numerous to be readily accessible to traditional stylistic analysis, especially where the texts in question are whole sets of novels. They allow the analyst to uncover morphological and semantic families of words, and to investigate the relationship between those families and larger issues of authorial style. They can uncover extraordinarily consistent patterns and puzzling inconsistencies and aberrations that point the way toward more minute and searching literary and stylistic analysis, while also providing a measure of objectivity and consistency that can bolster and support other kinds of argument and analysis. Computational stylistics has earned a place in the expanding stylistics toolbox, and is an especially effective method for analysing authorial style.

CHAPTER 15

2D and 3D Visualization of Stance in Popular Fiction

Lisa Lena Opas-Hänninen and Tapio Seppänen

1. Introduction

Stance is the expression of attitude and it has been studied in both spoken and written language. Since different speakers express their attitudes in different ways, it is also likely that different kinds of texts and different authors will do the same. This chapter investigates how stance has been portrayed in popular detective and romance fiction, using statistical methods and paying particular attention to the visualization of the results.

When using statistical methods to help us look at style in literature, we often show our results by plotting graphs of various types, for example scatterplots, histograms, and dendrograms. While these help us to understand our results, these graphs always necessarily 'flatten' the data into a two-dimensional format. For the purposes of visualization of complex data, we might be better off trying to look at it three-dimensionally if a suitable vector representation of the data is found first. This chapter investigates stance in three types of popular fiction written in the 1990s, namely romance fiction, detective fiction written by female authors, and detective fiction written by male authors, and presents the results using both two-dimensional and three-dimensional visualization. The study shows that when the results of multidimensional statistical analysis are presented three-dimensionally, rather than in the traditional two-dimensional form, we can explain them better.

Romance fiction and detective novels with a murder are both characterized by the fact that they all have the same basic story (Radway 1984: 198; Salgādo 1969, cited in Scaggs 2005: 11–12). In romance fiction it is the story of how the hero and heroine meet, how their relationship develops, and how the happy ending is achieved. In detective fiction involving murders it is the story of the murder, the unravelling of the case, the misleading clues, and the final solution. The same story is being retold over and over again, just as in the oral storytelling tradition (Radway 1984: 198). Although the reader is not left in suspense about the final outcome, each story is different from the others in the details of the events and the way the story is told. Through this the reader becomes involved in the story and is affected by the emotions, attitudes, and thoughts of the protagonist. These feelings, emotions, and moods are marked by syntactic and semantic features often referred to as markers of stance.

Linguists have increasingly investigated the ways in which speakers and writers convey their feelings and assessments, and a number of different labels have been used to describe this phenomenon, including *evaluation, affect, evidentiality, hedging* and *stance* (Barton 1993; Beach and Anson 1992; Biber and Finegan 1988, 1989; Biber et al. 1999; Chafe and Nichols 1986; Conrad and Biber 2000; Holmes 1988; Hunston and Thompson 2000; Hyland 1996; Levorato 2009; Martin 2003; Ochs 1989; Simon-Vandenbergen 2008; White 2003). These studies have looked at the lexical and grammatical devices used to express feelings and assessments, some of them concentrating on one text type and others looking at more general patterns in corpora. For example, the marking of evaluation and stance in academic writing has been a focus of interest and has included such areas as the use of hedging devices, the function of reporting verbs in expressing stance, and various ways of expressing evaluation (Hyland 1996; Lindemann and Mauranen 2001; Mauranen 2003; Poos and Simpson 2002; Swales and Burke 2003; Thompson and Ye 1991). Other studies have concentrated on stance in conversation (Kärkkäinen 2003; Precht 2003; Scheibman 2002). Overall, they support the idea that there are differences between registers in the ways in which stance is expressed, the types of markers used, and even the extent to which stance is expressed.

Biber and Finegan (1989: 93) define stance as 'the lexical and grammatical expression of attitudes, feelings, judgements or commitment concerning the propositional content of a message'. Following this, we use stance here to refer to the expression of attitude and it consists of two different types of expressions of attitude: evidentiality and affect (Biber and Finegan 1989). Evidentiality means that the reader becomes privy to the speaker's attitudes towards whatever knowledge the speaker has, the reliability of that knowledge, and how the speaker came about that knowledge. Affect refers to the personal attitudes of the speaker, that is, his/her emotions, feelings, moods, and so on. Biber and Finegan (1989) investigated 12 different categories of features deemed to mark stance: certainty/doubt adverbs, certainty/doubt verbs, certainty/doubt adjectives, affective expressions, hedges, emphatics, and necessity/possibility/predictive modals. They showed that different text types are likely to express stance in different ways. Opas and Tweedie (1999) studied stance in romance fiction and showed that three types of romance fiction can be distinguished by their expression of stance. In a later study they (Opas and Tweedie 2000) concluded that the detective stories seem to mark evidentiality, that is, the characters express their certainty and doubt. The romance stories, on the other hand, seem to mainly mark affect, that is, the characters express their emotions and moods. In Biber and Finegan's terms (1989), the detective fiction texts show 'interactional evidentiality' and the romance fiction texts show 'emphatic expression of affect'. This chapter continues these studies, paying special attention to the visualization of the results.

2. Data

The data was taken from three main groups of popular fiction: romance fiction, female-authored crime fiction, and male-authored crime fiction, all published in the 1990s, and comprises approximately 780,000 words. The romance fiction comprises a total of 246,283 words and consists of three types, namely the Harlequin Presents series, the Regency Romance series, and Danielle Steel's novels, which are often classified as women's fiction or 'crossovers'. Ten novels from each of these categories were chosen (see Appendix 15.1). The Harlequin Presents series are set in the present, whereas the Regency Romance series are set in the eighteenth or nineteenth centuries. It was assumed that this might lead to slightly different means of expressing stance, since social customs and expressions of feelings were more subdued in the past.

The female-authored detective fiction comprises 313,587 words and includes novels by Patricia Cornwell, Sue Grafton, P. D. James, Donna Leon, Ellis Peters, and Ruth Rendell. They were chosen because they had all been on the bestsellers list within the last few years and were thus likely to have been picked up by the casual reader. For the same reason, the male-authored fiction was chosen to comprise novels by Colin Dexter, Michael Dibdin, Quintin Jardine, Ian Rankin, and Peter Tremayne. They make up 220,107 words. The fact that the detective novels comprise texts written by both American and British authors was not considered to be of interest in the first instance, and indeed did not seem to be significant when looking at the results of the analysis.

The data was chosen using random sampling methods. Each novel was sampled to include enough passages of 2000 words to make up 10 per cent of the novel as a whole. These passages were then scanned, using OCR software, and marked up with metadata including author, title, year of publication, and page numbers. The features analysed were then retrieved using concordancing software, in this case WordSmith (Scott 2004–6).

3. Methodology and results

This chapter follows Biber and Finegan's (1989) investigation of stance, where they looked at a large number of features that they deemed to mark stance and grouped them into 12 categories: certainty/doubt adverbs (definitely, possibly), certainty/doubt verbs (know, doubt), certainty/doubt adjectives (certain, alleged), affect expressions (love, fear, glad, upset, luckily, sadly), hedges (almost, maybe, sort of), emphatics (for sure, really, so+ADV, such a) and possibility/necessity/predictive modals (can, may, might, could; ought, should, must; will, would, shall). In this study, stance attributed to a third person was also taken into account, since many of the novels are written in the third person and Opas and Tweedie (1999) showed that there was no significant difference in the results with romance fiction when including the third person. The number of occurrences of each of the markers of stance listed in the Appendix to Biber and Finegan (1989) were calculated for each text, retaining the grouping into the 12 categories of features. No distinction was made on the basis of the speaker, nor on whether the marker occurred in direct speech or not, since neither of these two features had been marked up in the texts.

The final number of occurrences of stance markers in each of the categories for each text were then standardized. Finally, principal components analysis was used to investigate how the 12 groups of stance markers interact and enable us to see the variation in the data more clearly.

Principal components analysis is a statistical dimension-reducing technique, which helps us to see the way many variables interact by showing which are the most important ones and how they behave in conjunction with each other. This means that we can see which features interact with each other, helping to differentiate between the different texts under scrutiny, and which features really only constitute 'noise' and need not be considered further, because they do not make much of a difference. In other words, what we are looking for are those features which have a high positive or negative loading on each of the principal components (see Figure 15.5) because these are the important features, that is, those which best differentiate between the texts. We want to separate these features from those features which have a very small loading, that is, have little or no impact in drawing the texts apart. In this study the statistical package PAST (paleontological statistics) was used.

The scree plot in Figure 15.1 shows how important each of the principal components is. When looking at the scree plot it is useful to bear in mind that principal components analysis will always produce as many principal components as there are features in the data. In this case, since there are 12 categories of features, that is, certainty verbs, doubt adjective, emphatics, necessity modals, and so on, the analysis will produce 12 components, as can

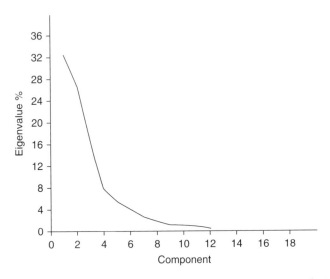

Figure 15.1: Scree plot for the principal components analysis

be seen on the x-axis of the scree plot. These are, in a sense, 12 different ways of grouping the features together to differentiate between the texts.

This figure shows each of the 12 principal components on the x-axis, and the y-axis shows how much of the variation in the data (in percentages) each of the components explains. Normally, one looks for the first levelling off after the initial drop and cuts the plot just above it, looking at those components; in this case the first step is at PC4 and we need to cut above it, looking at the first three components.

The information shown in the scree plot can also be seen in Table 15.1. It shows for each principal component how much of the variation in the data is explained by the component. Together the first three components explain about 75 per cent of the variation between the texts in the three data sets.

Statistical packages, such as PAST, produce scores for each text on each principal component (see Appendix 15.2) and show which of the features under scrutiny help pull the data in different directions on each component. These can be seen plotted two-dimensionally in Figures 15.2 to 15.4. The first of these, Figure 15.2, shows principal component 1 plotted against principal component 2.

The results in Figure 15.2 show that the female-authored detective stories are basically situated above the thick black line drawn diagonally across PC2 and the male-authored detective stories are below it (with a few exceptions which could be seen as 'outliers'). With respect to their use of stance expressions the romance stories, that is Danielle Steel, Regency Romance, and Harlequin Romance stories, are intermingled with the detective stories

Table 15.1: Variance explained by each
component

PC	Eigenvalue	% Variance
I	6.39495	32.348
2	5.22769	26.444
3	3.16245	15.997
4	1.5517	7.8491
5	1.07863	5.4561
6	0.780294	3.9471
7	0.519067	2.6257
8	0.361691	1.8296
9	0.231288	1.17
10	0.207191	1.0481
11	0.162078	0.81986
12	0.0919907	0.46533

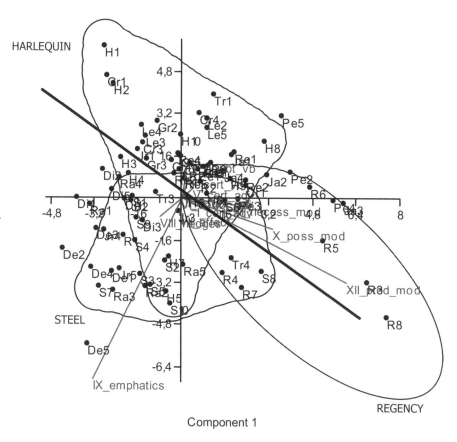

Figure 15.2: Principal components I and 2

and also overlap each other, although some of the Harlequin texts (H1, H3, H4, H10, and H8) and some of the Regency texts (R8, R3, R5, and R6) stand out as different from the other romance texts. This essentially means that the male-authored and the female-authored detective stories express stance in different ways. What it also implies is that some of the romance stories express stance much in the same way as the male-authored detective texts, while other romance texts resemble the female-authored detective texts in their expression of stance.

If we look at principal components 2 and 3, as shown in Figure 15.3, we see a similar situation.

In this figure we can once again separate the female-authored detective stories from the male-authored ones, the two groups being clearly marked here. If we look closely, we can also see that the uses of stance expressions in the

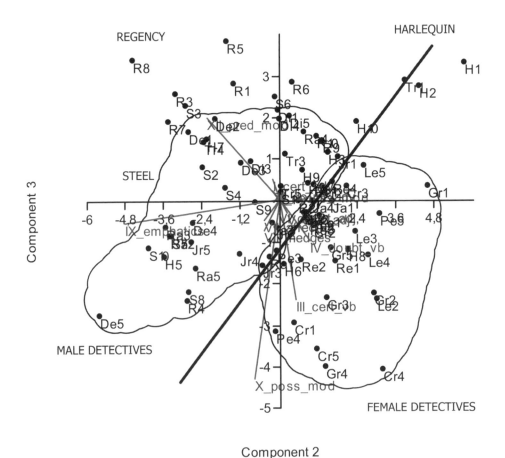

Component 2

Figure 15.3: Principal components 2 and 3

romance texts not only overlap each other, but this time both the Steel and the Harlequin texts overlap more of the male-authored detective texts than in the previous figure.

Finally, if we look at components 1 and 3 (Figure 15.4), we note that it becomes more difficult to say much about the different groups of texts. The male- and female-authored detective texts now overlap significantly and can no longer be separated from each other. Having said that, some of the male-authored texts, however, stand out as different from the female-authored detective texts, notably Colin Dexter's and Michael Dibdin's texts, and conversely, some of the female-authored detective texts are clearly different from the male-authored ones, in particular some texts by Patricia Cornwell, Ellis Peters, P. D. James, and Ruth Rendell. In this figure, we can also see that some Regency texts stand apart.

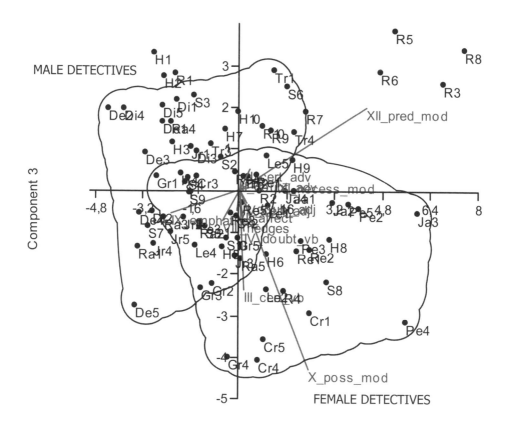

Figure 15.4: Principal components 1 and 3

From these figures it now seems clear that principal component 2 seems to be the decisive one between male- and female-authored texts, since in combination with both of the other two components it clearly teases the text types apart. We need to investigate what features of stance characterize the male- and female-authored detective texts and what, if any, features are characteristic of the romance texts that seem to stand apart.

The twelve categories of stance features are marked in the figures themselves, albeit only the strong features are clearly visible, that is, X_poss_mod (feature group X, possibility modals), III_cert_vb (feature group III, certainty verbs), and XII_pred_mod (feature group XII, predictive modals), and their reach from the 0,0 point indicates their strength. However, we can see how each of the features works on each of the principal components far more clearly when we look at the figures that PAST has drawn showing the feature loadings (Figure 15.5).

The strongest features, that is, those which separate the texts most significantly, on principal component 1 are emphatics (−0,41), possibility modals (0,42), and predictive modals (0,76). On principal component 2 they are emphatics (−0,87) and predictive modals (−0,40), and on principal component 3 they are certainty verbs (−0,43) and possibility modals (−0,78).

Looking back at Figures 15.2, 15.3 and 15.4, we can see that what really sets the male-authored detective stories apart is their use of emphatics. These pull the male-authored texts to the lower left-hand side of Figure 15.2, being a negative feature on both PC1 and PC2, to the left-hand side of Figure 15.3, being a negative feature on PC2, and somewhat to the left-hand side of Figure 15.4, although less strongly so. This can also be seen in the texts:

> Yes, she **did** remember, and very clearly, the man coming out of the Gentlemen's lavatory **just** before the New Years' Eve party was due to begin;
>   (De3: Dexter, *The Secret of Annexe 3*, p. 204, our emphasis)

> 'Awkward, sir,' replied Rebus, '**just** as you say.'
> 'I **do** say. I **do** say.' Watson thrust a finger out towards Rebus. 'It's up to you, John, to make sure the media don't make a meal of this, or of us.'
>   (Ra3: Rankin, *Hide and Seek*, p. 182 , our emphasis)

The female-authored detective stories, on the other hand, are being pulled to the lower right-hand side of both Figure 15.3 and Figure 15.4 by possibility modals and certainty verbs, both negative forces on PC3. This can be seen in the following extracts:

> 'You **could** dive around this sub and **realize** the torpedo tubes, for example, are not sealed. You **might** even be able to tell that the screw was not welded.'
>   (Cr4: Cornwell, *Cause of Death*, p. 291, our emphasis)

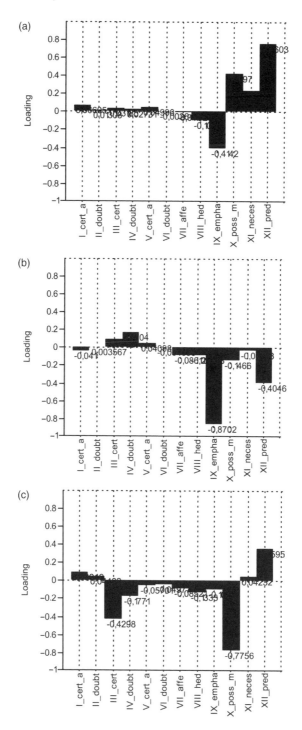

Figure 15.5: Feature loadings on principal component 1 (a), principal component 2 (b), and principal component 3 (c)

Insulation in an old safe **might** be something as basic as natural cement. A more modern safe **might** rely on vermiculite mica or diatomaceous earth, particles of which **can** often be traced back from a burglary suspect's tools and clothing to the specific safe manufacturer.

(Gr4: Grafton, *L is for Lawless*, p. 58, our emphasis)

Finally, it seems that at least some of the Regency texts can be separated from the other categories of text. In all three figures the texts R3, R5, R6, R7, and R8 stand out and they are characterized by predictive modals, as the examples below show:

'I personally **shall** scour the city for the right musicians,' Monsieur Levec promised. 'These floors **shall** shine! The chandeliers **will** be taken down and scrubbed so that they sparkle! The light of a thousand candles **shall** reflect the jewels of the ladies present! The orchestra **will** play the waltz, people **will** dance! It **will** be a night to remember!' He sighed in rapture.

(R3: Baldwin, *A Lady of Fashion*, p. 152, our emphasis)

But on the road back, something inside her rebelled. She **would** not be rushed into a hole-and-corner wedding. She **would** have a grand society affair and –yes – her dear friends, Annabelle and Matilda, **would** be her maids of honor.

(R5: Chesney, *The Scandalous Lady Wright*, p. 178, our emphasis)

There **would** be some initial embarrassment, but she **would** soon see he had changed.

(R8: Smith, *The Notorious Lord Havergal*, p. 118, our emphasis)

These results seem to suggest that male-authored detective fiction expresses stance emphatically, female-authored detective fiction seems to express stance in terms of possibilities, and in the somewhat deviant Regency texts the characters seem to make assertive predictions of what the future will hold.

Although, as we have just seen, it seems that we can separate between the male- and the female-authored detective stories fairly well (Figures 15.2 and 15.3), it seems that the romance texts as a whole express stance in the same ways in which detective stories do, covering a large part of the same areas of the figures, which is quite surprising. Perhaps there is something more complex at work here. To help us understand these phenomena better, we would suggest it is helpful to visualize the workings of the markers of stance in a three-dimensional model.

4. 3-dimensional modelling

To this end, we have built a tool that takes the principal components analysis data, reduces dimensionality down to the three components with the most energy, and presents the data with these components. The software tool is implemented in the MATLAB® environment (The MathWorks, Inc., Massachusetts, USA), utilizing its 3D graphical functions. The tool is an interactive one, allowing the researcher to turn the 3D model and look for the angles that best show the clustering structure and the differences between the texts. It significantly improves the researcher's ability to visualize the research results and to interpret them better.

Our tool reads the data from an excel file and plots it three-dimensionally, grouping it according to whatever groups are in the first two columns, in this case the text number or the text type, that is, female-authored or male-authored detective fiction, or romance. The results are shown in Figures 15.6a to 15.6d.

Needless to say, because the results shown in Figure 15.6 are three-dimensional but are presented here on the two-dimensional page, they are not as clear as they are when actually seen three-dimensionally. However, we can see the main points. Figure 15.6a is the angle that the program thinks best discriminates among the texts. In a three-dimensional space it clearly shows that the female-authored detective fiction texts stand apart from the other texts. However, it does also show that the romance texts are not quite as jumbled together with the detective fiction texts, as they might have seemed on the two-dimensional plots in Figures 15.2 to 15.4. When turning the three-dimensional cube around and looking at it from other angles, as in Figures 15.6b, c and d, we can see perhaps more clearly how the three different groups differ from each other. The female-authored detective fiction stands apart, which is best seen in Figures 15.6b and 15.6d. Figure 15.6d also shows that the romance texts are indeed quite different from the female-authored detective texts, and seemingly only partly in the same space as the male-authored detective texts. If, however, we look more closely at Figures 15.6b and 15.6c, we notice that the male-authored detective texts are actually located around the edges of the areas where the romance texts are. In fact, three-dimensionally, they are clearly set apart from each other.

To confirm what we can see visually in Figures 15.2 to 15.4 and 15.6a to 15.6d, we can turn to the results of the principal components analysis and look at the scores for all the texts (Appendix 15.2). On principal component 1 the male-authored detective fiction lies on the negative side of the component, as do most of the Harlequin and Steel texts. The female-authored detective fiction texts, on the other hand, score mostly on the positive side of the component, as do the Regency texts. On principal component 2, the bulk of the male-authored detective fiction texts are on the negative side of the component, as are most of the Regency and the Steel texts, whereas the female-authored detective fiction texts are on the positive side of the component,

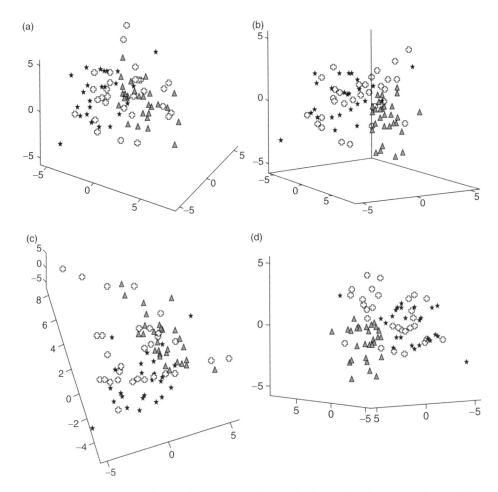

Figure 15.6: Results of the PCA analysis plotted 3-dimensionally, grouped according to text type (legend: ▲ female-authored detective fiction; ✻ male-authored detective fiction; ⬡ romance fiction)

along with most of the Harlequin texts. Finally, on principal component 3, the male-authored detective fiction texts are fairly equally divided on both sides of the component, whereas the female-authored texts are on the negative side and many of them have far higher negative scores than the male-authored texts, placing them further away from the centre than the male-authored texts are. All the romance texts are either on the positive side of the component (the Regency and the Harlequin texts) or fairly near the centre, that is, zero (the Steel texts). The question remains, however: what does this mean in terms of how the texts express stance?

To answer this, we have to go back to Figure 15.5 and the features that separate the texts. As has already been noted, the male-authored texts clearly express stance through emphatics. This puts them on the negative side of PC1 and PC2. On PC3 they are half-negative and half-positive. The features pulling on this component are certainty verbs and possibility modals to the positive side, and predictive modals to the negative side. These texts cannot have too many of the modals, however, since they would have pulled the texts in the opposite direction from where they are on PC1. In fact, what seems to be pulling them to the positive side of this component are the certainty verbs, which these texts do have, just not to the same degree as the female-authored texts, the average for them being 1.97 and 2.76 respectively. These results suggest that the male-authored detective fiction expresses emphatic opinions, in particular emphatic certainty.

The female-authored detective fiction, on the other hand, seems to express stance through possibility modals and certainty verbs, as has been noted earlier. The possibility modals account for these texts being on the positive side of PC1, and together with the certainty verbs they pull the texts to the negative side of PC3. On principal component 2, the female-authored detective fiction texts are on the positive side of the component, but since there is no feature strongly pulling texts in that direction, they are mainly characterized by the absence of the strong negative forces, namely emphatics and predictive modals. It seems then that female-authored detective fiction expresses stance through the weighing of possibilities.

Turning finally to the romance fiction texts, we can note that overall they are characterized by emphatics and predictive modals, although all three categories behave slightly differently from each other. The Regency Romance texts are clearly the ones that have the strongest force from predictive modals; these place the texts on the positive side of PC1 and PC3 and to a large extent on the negative side of PC2. The Harlequin Romance texts seem to have a combination of emphatics and predictive modals, the former placing them on the negative side of PC1 and the latter placing them on the positive side of PC3. However, since they are mostly on the positive side of PC2, they are not as strongly characterized by emphatics as the male-authored detective texts nor as strongly characterized by predictive modals as the Regency Romance texts. Finally, the Danielle Steel texts are clearly characterized by emphatics, since they are mainly on the negative side of both PC1 and PC2, though not as strongly negative as the male-authored detective texts. The Steel texts are also mostly near the zero point on PC3, so do not show any remarkable amount of any of the features pulling texts to either side of the component, that is, certainty verbs, possibility modals, or predictive modals. So while as a whole, we could say that the romance texts express stance through emphatic prediction, it would be better to say that the Regency texts express prediction, the Harlequin texts also express prediction, but more emphatically, and the Steel texts resemble the male-authored detective fiction in that they express emphatic opinions, although less strongly that those texts.

5. Conclusions

It seems then that plotting the results of a principal components analysis three-dimensionally lets us see new angles to the data that simply are not possible on a two-dimensional plot. On the two-dimensional figures (Figures 15.2 to 15.4) the data seem to overlap each other rather heavily. The three-dimensional plot lets us see that, although there is some overlap, as one would expect, the clouds of data seem to lie in succession behind each other, being pulled away from the zero point on the various components more or less strongly. Perhaps Figure 15.6b is the one where it is easiest to visualize three clouds of data, that is, the female-authored detective fiction standing somewhat apart in one area, with the male-authored detective fiction lying in another direction from the zero point and the romance texts more or less lying between these two. Nevertheless, the results are somewhat surprising in the light of previous research.

Opas and Tweedie (2000) concluded that detective stories seem to mark evidentiality, that is, the characters expressing their certainty and doubt. The romance stories, on the other hand, seem to mainly mark affect, that is, the characters expressing their emotions and moods. In Biber and Finegan's terms (1989), the detective fiction texts showed 'interactional evidentiality' and the romance fiction texts showed 'emphatic expression of affect'. What these results seem to suggest is that these three text types can be differentiated on the basis of how they express evidentiality, rather than affect. The female-authored detective texts are clearly fluctuating between certainty and doubt, weighing various possibilities and outcomes. The male-authored detective fiction texts, on the other hand, express certainty in the sense that any opinions are stated emphatically. The romance texts seem to lie in between these two, where some of them, the Steel texts, express strong opinions, though somewhat less emphatically that the male-authored detective fiction, and others, the Regency and Harlequin Romance texts, express certainty in the form of prediction, the latter more emphatically than the former. Thus, the three-dimensional modelling has to some extent helped to explain the rather odd-looking results of two-dimensional analysis, but on the other hand has raised new questions regarding the expression of stance in popular fiction, since these results were not in accordance with previous research.

Appendix 15.1: List of works studied and samples taken

Danielle Steel (Total words: 120,864)

S1: *Accident* (1994). New York: Dell Publishing. Sample: pp. 16–59. Word count: 10,783.

S2: *Heartbeat* (1991). New York: Dell Publishing. Sample: pp. 183–222. Word count: 11,727.

S3: *Jewels* (1992). London: Corgi Books. Sample: pp. 285–331. Word count: 16,286.

S4: *Lightning* (1995). New York: Dell Publishing. Sample: pp. 197–241. Word count: 13,114.

S5: *Message from Nam* (1990). New York: Dell Publishing. Sample: pp. 164–205. Word count: 12,723.

S6: *Mixed Blessings* (1992). New York: Dell Publishing. Sample: pp. 149–91. Word count: 13,264.

S7: *No Greater Love* (1991). New York: Dell Publishing. Sample: pp. 226–63. Word count: 11,631.

S8: *The Gift* (1994). New York: Dell Publishing. Sample: pp. 61–88. Word count: 7671.

S9: *Vanished* (1993). New York: Dell Publishing. Sample: pp. 261–99. Word count: 9508.

S10: *Wings* (1994). New York: Dell Publishing. Sample: pp. 399–443. Word count: 14,157.

Harlequin Presents (Total words: 57,983)

H1: Baird, Jacqueline (1995). *A Devious Desire.* Toronto: Harlequin Books. Sample: pp. 144–61. Word count: 5342.

H2: Charlton, Ann (1994). *Hot November.* Toronto: Harlequin Books. Sample: pp. 22–40. Word count: 5965.

H3: Donald, Robyn (1994). *Dark Fire.* Toronto: Harlequin Books. Toronto: Harlequin Books. Sample: pp. 149–66. Word count: 5972.

H4: Fraser, Alison (1994). *Tainted Love.* Toronto: Harlequin Books. Sample: pp. 69–87. Word count: 5885.

H5: Lamb, Charlotte (1994). *Body and Soul.* Toronto: Harlequin Books. Sample: pp. 109–26. Word count: 5253.

H6: Lee, Miranda (1994). *Scandals and Secrets.* Toronto: Harlequin Books. Sample: pp. 133–49. Word count: 5875.

H7: Marton, Sandra (1992). *A Bride for the Taking.* Toronto: Harlequin Books. Sample: pp. 94–112. Word count: 6049.

H8: Williams, Cathy (1995). *Beyond All Reason.* Toronto: Harlequin Books. Sample: pp. 137–54. Word count: 5928.

H9: Wood, Sara (1993). *Southern Passions.* Toronto: Harlequin Books. Sample: pp. 161–78. Word count: 6015.

H10: Oldfield, Elizabeth (1996). *Fast and Loose.* Toronto: Harlequin Books. Sample: pp. 107–24. Word count: 5699.

Regency Romance Series (Total words: 67,436)

R1: Argers, Helen (1992). *An Unlikely Lady.* New York: Diamond Books. Sample: pp. 21–40. Word count: 8679.

R2: Bailey-Pratt, Cynthia (1991). *The Temporary Bride.* New York: Jove Books. Sample: pp. 146–67. Word count: 8256.

R3: Baldwin, Rebecca (1994). *A Lady of Fashion.* New York: Harper Collins. Sample: pp. 145–65. Word count: 6059.

R4: Benedict, Barbara (1991). *Catch of the Season*. New York: Jove Books. Sample: pp. 114–33. Word count: 5782.

R5: Chesney, Marion (1990). *The Scandalous Lady Wright*. New York: Fawcett Crest. Sample: pp. 167–84. Word count: 4874.

R6: Oliver, Patricia (1995). *An Immodest Proposal*. New York: Signet Books. Sample: pp. 202–24. Word count: 9783.

R7: Robbins, Rebecca (1994). *Lucky in Love*. New York: Avon Books. Sample: pp. 152–73. Word count: 7553.

R8: Smith, Joan (1991). *The Notorious Lord Havergal*. New York: Fawcett Crest. Sample: pp. 112–33. Word count: 6249.

R9: Ward, Rebecca (1991). *Cinderella's Stepmother*. New York: Fawcett Crest. Sample: pp. 20–41. Word count: 5473.

R10: Williams, Claudette (1991). *Lady Sunshine*. New York: Fawcett Crest. Sample: pp. 99–117. Word count: 4728.

Patricia Cornwell (Total words: 51,348)

Cr1: *All That Remains* (1992). New York: Charles Scribner's Sons. Samples: pp. 113–32 and 300–19. Word count: 10,641.

Cr2: *The Body Farm* (1994). London: Warner Books. Samples: pp. 7–26 and 78–98. Word count: 9619.

Cr3: *Body of Evidence* (1991). Avon Books. Samples: pp. 70–90 and 11–31. Word count: 11,121.

Cr4: *Cause of Death* (1996). London: Warner Books. Samples: pp. 285–303 and 194–213. Word count: 10,072.

Cr5: *From Potter's Field* (1995). London: Warner Books. Samples: pp. 94–114 and 314–35. Word count: 9894.

Sue Grafton (Total words: 51,405)

Gr1: *H is for Homicide* (1991). London: Pan Books. Samples: pp. 54–67 and 187–200. Word count: 9,126.

Gr2: *J is for Judgement* (1993). London: Pan Books. Samples: pp. 122–40 and 224–42. Word count: 11,249.

Gr3: *K is for Killer* (1994). London: Pan Books. Samples: pp. 243–57 and 225–40. Word count: 10,195.

Gr4: *L is for Lawless* (1995). New York: Fawcett Crest. Samples: pp. 250–66 and 57–73. Word count: 10,159.

Gr5: *M is for Malice* (1996). London: Pan Books. Samples: pp. 62–80 and 228–47. Word count: 10,676.

P. D. James (Total words: 66,039)

Ja1: *A Certain Justice* (1997). London: Penguin Books. Samples: pp. 2–26 and 234–58. Word count: 16,388.

Ja2: *Devices and Desires* (1989). London: Faber and Faber. Samples: pp. 161–81 and 269–90. Word count: 15,902.

Ja3: *Original Sin* (1994). London: Penguin Books. Samples: pp. 351–78 and 516–44. Word count: 17,506.

Ja4: *A Taste for Death* (1986). London: Faber and Faber. Samples: pp. 30–51 and 301–22. Word count: 16,243.

Donna Leon (Total words: 43,832)

Le1: *The Anonymous Venetian* (1994). London: Pan Books. Samples: pp. 233–50 and 77–94. Word count: 8679.

Le2: *Death at La Fenice* (1992). London: Pan Books. Samples: pp. 202–15 and 23–36. Word count: 8413.

Le3: *Death in a Strange Country* (1993). London: Pan Books. Samples: pp. 183–96 and 168–81. Word count: 10,176.

Le4: *The Death of Faith* (1997). London: Pan Books. Samples: pp. 7–22 and 71–87. Word count: 8254.

Le5: *A Venetian Reckoning* (1995). London: Pan Books. Samples: pp. 47–62 and 200–17. Word count: 8310.

Ellis Peters (Total words: 44,013)

Pe1: *Brother Cadfael's Penance* (1994). London: Warner Futura Books. Samples: pp.: 23–36 and 233–47. Word count: 9464.

Pe2: *The Confession of Brother Haluin* (1988). London: Warner Futura Books. Samples: pp. 62–72 and 105–16. Word count: 7490.

Pe3: *The Heretic's Apprentice* (1989). London: Warner Futura Books. Samples: pp. 57–69 and 178–91. Word count: 9398.

Pe4: *The Holy Thief* (1992). London: Warner Futura Books. Samples: pp. 91–105 and 124–37. Word count: 8661.

Pe5: *The Summer of the Danes* (1991). London: Warner Futura Books. Samples: pp. 80–94 and 202–16. Word count: 9000.

Ruth Rendell (Total words: 56,950)

Re1: *Kissing the Gunner's Daughter* (1993). London: Arrow Books. Samples: pp. 143–63 and 373–94. Word count: 12,624.

Re2: *Road Rage* (1997). London: Hutchinson. Samples: pp. 282–99 and 214–32. Word count: 13,026.

Re3: *Simisola* (1995). London: Arrow Books. Samples: pp. 117–36 and 179–98. Word count: 11,887.

Re4: *An Unkindness of Ravens* (1985). London: Arrow Books. Samples: pp. 146–59 and 111–24. Word count: 9155.

Re5: *The Veiled One* (1989). London: Arrow Books. Samples: pp. 183–97 and 77–91. Word count: 10,258.

Colin Dexter (Total words: 35,972)

De1: *The Way Through the Woods* (1992). London: Macmillan. Samples: pp. 19–32 and 198–214. Word count: 8788.

De2: *The Riddle of the Third Mile* (1984). London: Pan Books. Samples: pp. 183–93 and 77–87. Word count: 5611.

De3: *The Secret of Annexe 3* (1986). London: Pan Books. Samples: pp. 202–12 and 23–33. Word count: 7183.

De4: *The Jewel That Was Ours* (1991). London: Pan Books. Samples: pp. 80–92 and 185–98. Word count: 6466.

De5: *Death Is Now My Neighbour* (1996). London: Macmillan. Samples: pp. 260–76 and 77–94. Word count: 7924.

Michael Dibdin (Total words: 41,471)

Di1: *Blood Rain* (1999). London: Faber and Faber. Samples: pp. 20–35 and 207–22. Word count: 7249.

Di2: *A Long Finish* (1998). London: Faber and Faber. Samples: pp. 250–67 and 57–74. Word count: 7673.

Di3: *Dead Lagoon* (1995). London: Faber and Faber. Samples: pp. 122–39 and 224–42. Word count: 10,604.

Di4: *Cosi Fan Tutti* (1996). London: Faber and Faber. Samples: pp. 243–56 and 225–38. Word count: 6769.

Di5: *Vendetta* (1990). London: Faber and Faber. Samples: pp. 28–41 and 12–26. Word count: 9176.

Quintin Jardine (Total words: 51,162)

Jr1: *Skinner's Festival* (1994). London: Headline Publishing Group. Samples: pp. 226–40 and 268–83. Word count: 10,031.

Jr2: *Skinner's Ghosts* (1998). London: Headline Publishing Group. Samples: pp. 35–54 and 351–71. Word count: 9884.

Jr3: *Skinner's Mission* (1997). London: Headline Publishing Group. Samples: pp. 41–60 and 194–214. Word count: 9692.

Jr4: *Skinner's Round* (1995). London: Headline Publishing Group. Samples: pp. 251–71 and 104–26. Word count: 9806.

Jr5: *Gallery Whispers* (1999). London: Headline Publishing Group. Samples: pp. 14–34 and 150–69. Word count: 11,749.

Ian Rankin (Total words: 45,549)

Ra1: *Black and Blue* (1997). London: Orion. Samples: pp. 111–35 and 197–220. Word count: 13,466.

Ra2: *The Black Book* (1993). London: Orion. Samples: pp. 197–213 and 299–315. Word count: 10,169.

Ra3: *Hide and Seek* (1990). London: Orion. Samples: pp. 76–88 and 178–190. Word count: 7916.

Ra4: *Knots and Crosses* (1998). London: Orion. Samples: pp. 6–16 and 61–72. Word count: 5799.

Ra5: *Tooth and Nail* (1992). London: Orion. Samples: pp. 113–26 and 132–45. Word count: 8199.

Peter Tremayne (Total words: 45,953)

Tr1: *Absolution by Murder* (1994). London: Headline Book Publishing Ltd. Samples: pp. 91–103 and 124–37. Word count: 6455.

Tr2: *The Subtle Serpent* (1996). London: Headline Book Publishing Ltd. Samples: pp. 14–30 and 145–61. Word count: 10,707.

Tr3: *Suffer Little Children* (1995). London: Headline Book Publishing Ltd. Samples: pp. 101–17 and 244–60. Word count: 9238.

Tr4: *The Valley of the Shadow* (1998). London: Headline Book Publishing Ltd. Samples: pp. 232–48 and 254–69. Word count: 9642.

Tr5: *The Spider's Web* (1997). London: Headline Book Publishing Ltd. Samples: pp. 198–214 and 225–41. Word count: 9911.

Appendix 15.2: Scores for all texts on the first three components

TEXT	PC 1	PC 2	PC 3
S1	−1.80	0.03	0.18
S2	−0.58	−2.39	0.78
S3	−1.51	−2.92	2.28
S4	−1.69	−1.66	0.28
S5	−1.11	−3.34	−0.86
S6	1.59	−0.14	2.47
S7	−3.06	−3.36	−0.86
S8	2.95	−2.82	−2.23
S9	−1.67	−0.77	−0.06
S10	−0.42	−4.04	−1.16
H1	−2.87	5.76	3.31
H2	−2.52	4.33	2.74
H3	−2.24	1.52	1.13
H4	−1.92	0.89	0.42
H5	−0.56	−3.57	−1.37
H6	0.91	0.14	−1.54
H7	−0.48	−2.24	1.44
H8	3.05	2.11	−1.21
H9	1.77	0.69	0.72
H10	−0.02	2.39	1.90
R1	−2.12	−1.42	2.80
R2	0.69	0.58	−0.03
R3	6.79	−3.24	2.55
R4	1.48	−2.86	−2.41
R5	5.20	−1.63	3.82
R6	4.68	0.39	2.85
R7	2.21	−3.45	1.87
R8	7.50	−4.53	3.38
R9	1.07	1.32	1.43
R10	0.76	1.15	1.52
Cr1	2.34	0.42	−2.96
CR2	−0.09	1.06	−0.63
Cr3	−1.41	2.06	0.33
Cr4	0.64	3.20	−4.08
Cr5	0.85	1.16	−3.59
Gr1	−2.75	4.61	0.34
Gr2	−0.90	2.90	−2.24
Gr3	−1.27	1.47	−2.35
Gr4	−0.37	1.39	−4.01
Gr5	−0.05	1.58	−1.16
Ja1	1.82	1.63	−0.02
Ja2	3.15	0.86	−0.32
Ja3	5.92	−0.23	−0.55

Continued

Appendix 15.2: Continued

TEXT	PC 1	PC 2	PC 3
Ja4	1.56	1.01	−0.02
Le1	0.96	1.23	−0.37
Le2	0.91	2.99	−2.37
Le3	−1.32	2.32	−0.76
Le4	−1.44	2.72	−1.33
Le5	0.94	2.62	0.82
Pe1	0.59	1.07	0.35
Pe2	4.00	0.94	−0.45
Pe3	2.06	−0.07	−1.23
Pe4	5.56	−0.12	−3.16
Pe5	3.65	3.10	−0.35
Re1	1.92	1.72	−1.48
Re2	2.37	0.66	−1.43
Re3	−0.28	0.92	−0.54
Re4	−0.13	1.65	0.42
Re5	0.10	0.77	−0.32
De1	−2.55	−2.82	1.62
De2	−4.40	−1.97	1.96
De3	−3.14	−1.18	0.91
De4	−3.34	−2.68	−0.55
De5	−3.48	−5.58	−2.79
Di1	−2.11	−0.07	2.18
Di2	−2.89	1.07	−0.51
Di3	−1.43	−0.87	0.92
Di4	−3.86	−0.00	1.94
Di5	−2.58	0.30	2.03
Jr1	−1.62	1.82	1.04
Jr2	−1.86	−0.11	−0.68
Jr3	−0.14	−0.54	−1.59
Jr4	−2.86	−1.24	−1.30
Jr5	−2.28	−2.73	−1.01
Ra1	−3.36	−0.29	−1.36
Ra2	−1.32	−3.38	−0.88
Ra3	−2.51	−3.53	−0.67
Ra4	−2.29	0.76	1.63
Ra5	0.05	−2.59	−1.66
Tr1	1.18	3.89	2.86
Tr2	0.30	1.34	0.34
Tr3	−0.93	0.18	1.10
Tr4	1.81	−2.33	1.40
Tr5	0.17	0.03	0.34

CHAPTER 16

Point of View

PAUL SIMPSON

1. Introduction

In Chimamanda Ngozi Adichie's (2006) novel *Half of a Yellow Sun*, set during the Biafran war of the 1960s, one of the story's central characters, Ugwu, returns to his village after it has been ransacked by the Nigerian federal army. In the following sequence, Ugwu is reunited with his beloved sister, Anulika, but unknown to him (and at this stage, to the readers of the novel); she has been raped by the soldiers ('the vandals') during the attack.

> She didn't answer any of his other questions in the way that he had expected, there were no energetic gestures, no sharp wit in her answers: yes, they had the wine-carrying just before the vandals occupied the village. Onyeka was well; he had gone to the farm. They did not have children yet. She looked away often, as if she felt uncomfortable sitting with him, and Ugwu wondered if he had imagined the easy bond they had shared.
>
> (Adichie 2006: 421–2)

The narrative framework of the passage balances three perspectives: the third-person 'omniscient' narrator who has access to the thoughts and feelings of characters; the voice of the character Ugwu who acts as a reflector of the narrative events; and the voice of Anulika whose speech is merged with and mediated through Ugwu's discourse. The passage abounds in the stylistic markers of narratorial voice and perspective. Notice, for example, how Ugwu's ongoing reflection on unfolding narrative events is relayed through mental processes of cognition: 'expected', 'wondered', and 'imagined'. Unsurprisingly, the transposition of the passage to the first person is simple and straightforward (e.g. 'She didn't answer any of my other questions in the way that I had expected'), showing just how solidly grounded in Ugwu's consciousness the narrative is. This degree of psychological insight and depth is not however accorded to his sister. Instead, Anulika's more 'external' portrayal is relayed through reference to physical gestures and gaze from which Ugwu (and presumably, by imputation, readers) must infer information about this character's attitudinal predisposition: '*as if* she felt uncomfortable'; 'Ugwu wondered *if he had imagined ...*'. Moreover, Anulika's spoken discourse is presented in free indirect speech ('Onyeka was well; he had gone to the farm', as opposed to 'Onyeka is well; he has gone to the farm', and so on), and this strengthens further the sense of her 'voice' being mediated through the perspective of the reflector (see Bray, and Busse, this volume, for more on discourse presentation). It is also interesting that Anulika's speech follows a non-narrated series of questions from Ugwu, with her responses to this narrative 'ellipsis' signalled through polarity devices ('*yes*, they had the wine-carrying'; 'They did *not* have children yet'). The complex weaving and interplay between strands, perspectives, and narrative voices, of the type seen in this passage, forms a key focus in contemporary narrative stylistics, a focus which can be subsumed under the umbrella term *point of view*.

Point of view embraces the 'angle of telling' in a story, and extends from the perhaps limited viewing position of a participating first-person character-narrator to the much broader vantage point of a third-person narrator whose detached 'omniscience' facilitates privileged access to the thoughts and feelings of individual characters. Discussing this aspect of point of view, Short (1996: 256) distinguishes between, on the one hand, what is portrayed in the fictional world and, on the other, the perspective from which it is portrayed. This distinction in viewpoint, he suggests, contributes to making the novel the most complex literary genre in terms of discourse structure. In consequence, the study of the novel in the twentieth century has to a very large extent been dominated by the study of point of view (ibid.).

This chapter will attempt to review, illustrate and consolidate a number of current stylistic frameworks for exploring point of view in narrative. It will develop from the more 'traditional' approaches to point of view, where the emphasis is squarely on linguistic features in the text, and move on to consider more recent approaches which, reflecting contemporary trends in stylistics, are informed by cognitive and sociopragmatic models of analysis. Throughout the chapter, illustrative examples from several works of prose fiction, along with one example from film, are used to exemplify the point-of-view categories surveyed. The approach here is also both cumulative and eclectic, assimilating a range of models in a manner which is intended to be complementary rather than exclusive. Finally, it is argued that the perception of point of view varies with reading experience(s), and so productive use can be made of interpretative paradigms that account for readers' reactions and responses to textual patterning. Thus, as this chapter unfolds, the focus will progressively widen to develop and incorporate a more 'readerly' account of point of view in narrative fiction.

2. Narrative stylistics and point of view

It has long been accepted in stylistics that markers of point of view can be located in certain key indicators in the linguistic fabric of the narrative. An account of these traditional markers will include (but is not restricted to) categories such as the following: *deixis*, which is a set of 'pointing' or 'orientational' words ('this' vs 'that', 'come' vs 'go') that function to attach a speaker/ narrator to a particular context (and see further Short 1996: 269–72); *locative expressions*, which are phrases indicating place, location, and direction ('under the tree', 'around the corner', and so on), and which anchor the spatial position of the reflector of fiction (and see further Fowler 1986: 128–30); and *verba sentiendi*, which are words, such as those used to represent Ugwu's discourse in the extract above, which serve to represent thoughts, feelings, and perceptions of characters or narrators (and see further Uspensky 1973 *passim*).

2.1. Modality and point of view

Other traditional markers of point of view include *modality* which is that part of the system of language which allows speakers to attach expressions of belief, attitude and obligation to what they say or narrate. Simpson (1993) has attempted to build a 'modal grammar' of point of view on the premise that the styles of individual genres of literature, such as the popular romance, the Gothic horror tale, the fairy tale, the 'hard-boiled' detective novel and so on, are in part defined by special and recurrent configurations of modality. For example, Simpson argues that the genre of horror fiction foregrounds certain modal structures to do with knowledge and perception, and these markers of epistemic modality engender a special kind of narrative viewpoint that is not found (to the same extent) in other types of writing. Consider by way of illustration the following fragment from H. P. Lovecraft's (1920) short story 'The Statement of Randolph Carter':

> The place was an ancient cemetery; so ancient I trembled at the manifold signs of immemorial years. It was in a deep, damp hollow, overgrown with rank grass, moss, and curious creeping weeds, and filled with a vague stench which my idle fancy associated absurdly with rotting stone. On every hand were the signs of neglect and decrepitude, and I seemed haunted by the notion that Warren and I were the first living creatures to invade the lethal silence of

centuries. Over the valley's rim a wan, waning crescent moon peered through the noisome vapours that seemed to emanate from unheard-of catacombs, and by its feeble wavering I could distinguish a repellent array of antique slabs, urns, cenotaphs, and mausoleum facades ... My first vivid impression of my own presence in this terrible necropolis concerns the act of pausing with Warren before a certain half-obliterated sepulchre, and of throwing down some burdens which we seemed to have been carrying. I now observed that I had with me an electric lantern and two spades, whilst my companion was supplied with a similar lantern and a portable telephone outfit. No word was uttered, for the spot and the task seemed known to us ....

(Lovecraft [1920] 2002: 8–9)

Although passages of physical description are of course a commonplace of prose fiction, what picks this type of writing out stylistically is the particular type of modal framework in which it is embedded. Notice the number and variety of epistemic modal markers, notably to do with understanding and perception, which signal the first-person narrator's attempts to interpret and make sense of what he sees in the cemetery. The modal verb of perception *seemed* is repeated many times and is supplemented with noun phrases referring to external perception: 'the manifold signs', 'a vague stench', 'the signs of neglect', 'my first vivid impression', 'a certain half-obliterated sepulchre', and so on. The disquieting bewilderment brought about by these 'words of estrangement' (Fowler 1986: 142) is reinforced further with verb phrases detailing the narrator's conscious struggle to reach interpretations: 'my idle fancy *associated* absurdly with rotting stone', 'I *could distinguish* a repellent array of antique slabs', 'I now *observed*', and so on. Overall, in this type of modal framework, the psychological persona of the character-narrator comes to the fore, evidenced through their attempt to draw inferences from external appearances in order to understand the narrative universe they inhabit. Although in no way an exhaustive model, the modal framework can help identify this passage of description as horror writing, in contrast to other genres, because it works on the principle that different 'points of view' typically embody different grammars of modality (see, for example, Simpson and Hardy [2008] for a modal analysis of point of view in a different genre, the 'hard-boiled' American *roman noir*).

2.2. Point of view and speech and thought presentation

The presentation of speech and thought is another aspect of narrative style which intersects naturally with point of view. Clearly, the presentation of the discourse of one character by a narrator (or another character, as in the

Adichie example) has a substantial influence on the 'angle of telling' adopted in the story. At the heart of this interface with point of view is the key speech and thought presentation technique of free indirect discourse (FID), a term which usefully subsumes both its speech (FIS) and thought (FIT) variants. The importance of this narrative technique is evidenced in the existence of numerous other terms for it, such as *erlebte Rede*, 'indirect interior monologue', and *style indirect libre*. What is of special interest to stylisticians is the impression this mode gives of characters and narrators speaking simultaneously, the stylistic force of which (*pace* the Adichie extract) inheres in its seeming merging of different narrative voices.

This coalescence between voices is often located in third-person *heterodiegetic* narratives (Genette 1980), where the use of FID results in an apparent blurring of focus between the speech and thought of a character and that of the external third-person narrator. However, Leech and Short (2007: 264) stress the significance of the technique for first-person narration also, where the reported speech or thought is mediated through the focalizing consciousness of the participating narrator. This often prompts intriguing and complex shifts in perspective and point of view. Consider the following extract from a novel by Roddy Doyle, where the first-person narrator, Paula Spencer, delivers a seemingly unambiguous affirmation of love and commitment to her husband Charlo:

> I had nothing going for me. I was only Paula Spencer because of him. It was the only thing I was. People knew me because of him. We had the house because of him. I was there because he looked at me and proved it. One nice look could wipe out everything. I loved him with all my heart. I could never leave him. He needed me.
>
> (Doyle 1998: 211)

It is only in the last line of the same paragraph that the full import of Paula's pronouncement becomes fully clear:

> ... He told me so, again and again. I was everything to him.
>
> (Doyle 1998: 211)

THIS IS AWESOME.

This final sequence confirms that the narrative 'voice' of the paragraph has not been Paula's, but that of her violent and abusive husband. In other words, all of Paula's previous 'discourse' has been the mediated speech of her husband relayed in the FIS mode, where for example 'I had nothing going for me' is a transformed version of 'You have nothing going for you.' Similarly, 'I was only Paula Spencer because of him' is an FIS rendition of 'You are only Paula Spencer because of me,' and this pattern continues right down to the

disambiguating reporting clause of the penultimate sentence. In the context of
a bleak novel about domestic abuse and the brutalization of women, it seems
that Charlo has invaded and colonized the very voice of his wife, a violation
that means that she can now only express herself through him. She becomes,
in Goffman's (1979: 21) terms, the 'animator' of his discourse because she
articulates a form of language that is no longer her own.

2.3. Point of view and mind-style

The concept of *mind-style* forms another natural intersection with point of
view in fiction. Coining the term over 30 years ago, Fowler (1977: 103; and
see also Semino 2002) defines mind-style as 'any distinctive linguistic presentation of an individual mental self'. Although in its broader sense encompassing the perspectives and values which strongly bias a character's world
view, the concept most productively captures the special and often rather
restricted cognitive perspective of a particular narrator-character. This
sense of a 'consistently restricted' mind-style (Fowler 1977: 105) is important because choices in vocabulary, grammar, and other stylistic markers
effectively limit the narrative to the perspective of the reflector. This 'focal-
ised ignorance' (Hardy 2005: 374) is delivered in such a way as to invite,
or indeed to demand, a 'seeing beyond' by the reader of the limited understanding and world view of the character-narrator. Novels like Faulkner's
The Sound and the Fury or Golding's *The Inheritors* have become familiar
mainstays for the stylistic exploration of mind-style, but here is a telling
instance from a more recent work of prose fiction, Peter Carey's *True History
of the Kelly Gang*:

> But now Ah Fook folded his arms across his chest. I report you b–rs said
> he I report to police you adjectival devils ... Now you hang on a mo said my
> mother you just wait right here. Calmly turning her back on the bristling fel-
> low she walked back to the hut. The Chinaman stayed with his pole held high
> as if about to smite us but we was not scared. I had an axe Jem a mattock and
> when we picked up these implements and made a circle around him he must
> of thought his end were come. Soon after our ma came back from the hut
> holding in her hand a generous jar of grog. This will be after improving you.
> The Chinaman sniffed at the grog. He put down axe said he then I drinkee.
> I laughed then put my axe down as the Chinaman took the jar. When it was
> empty my mother gave him a 10/- note. You would consider that fair but when
> this were all transacted the perfidious celestial walked into Benalla swearing
> to the coppers I had robbed him of £1.
>
> (2000: 118–9 [*sic passim*])

Although Carey carefully interlaces this novel with short fragments from journalism and other media, here, as in the overwhelming bulk of the story, narrative events are located in and mediated through the first-person narrator Ned Kelly's mind-style. A rich assortment of stylistic features consolidate this striking narrative perspective. Features of individual speech style, *idiolect*, abound, as in Ned's archaisms ('celestial' for 'oriental', a term used to describe Chinese immigrants in Australia during the nineteenth century) and his use of biblical vocabulary in expressions like 'perfidious' and 'smite'. An endearing reticence is displayed in his reluctance to use taboo language: 'you b–rs', or 'you adjectival devils'. Patterns of orthography, notably the lack of punctuation for clausal boundaries, create a markedly dysfluent delivery which is suggestive of an uncomfortable transfer from speech into writing by the uneducated though earnest story-teller. The passage is also framed in a kind of quasi-Irish-English 'eye-dialect' through expressions like 'must of' for 'must have', non-standard concord in 'we was not scared' or 'his end were come', and a prospective *after* + *ing* construction in 'This will be after improving you'. I call this 'quasi' dialect because neither prospective *after* + *ing* nor this particular type of non-standard concord are attested features in the Hiberno-English dialect system. That said, Carey locks us into a striking and embodied central narratorial voice which, in contrast to the shorter fragments of journalistic writing positioned around it in the novel, is delineated by a particular and consistent pattern of speech, idiolect, register, and suggested dialect – by a *mind-style* in other words.

2.4. Point of view and 'disnarration'

There is a growing body of research which seeks to align point of view with Prince's (1988, 2006) concept of the *disnarrated*. Broadly understood, 'disnarration' refers to a gap in the onward progression of the narrative, which may be announced, or otherwise inferable from a significant lacuna in the chronology (Prince 1988: 2). The essential point is simply that not all narrative acts need to be related because readers can derive coherence through subtle and complex inferences from absences in the story. Notice how, for example, in the Adichie example at the start of this chapter there was a narrative ellipsis of Uwgu's questions, although the other textual indices in Anulika's replies nonetheless left the content of this 'announced gap' retrievable.

In a series of related studies, Hardy addresses the concept of disnarration by focusing on narrative *gaps* (Hardy 2003, 2005). Rather than considering all 'non-narrated' categories like ellipsis or negation, Hardy deals with narrower and more problematic instances in stories where specific information, a participant, a proposition, or a narrative event, is noticeably absent or delayed.

Concentrating on the prose of Flannery O'Connor, Hardy makes clear the significance of 'unannounced' narrative gapping both to point of view and to mind-style, arguing that the focalized presentation of gapped knowledge is 'a result of limited perception, whether that be on the part of the focaliser, the reader, the narrator, or some combination of all three' (2005: 367–8). Hardy concludes that this technique is stylistically indicative of O'Connor's prose where it may signal an often frustrated intent on a character's part, or it may reflect the writer's concerns with the limitations and possibilities of human knowledge.

Related to the idea of gapping (and point of view) is the notion of *counterfactuality* which is essentially a disnarrated, alternative sequence that has a significant impact on the evaluation of elements of the story. A counterfactual is the representation of an unrealized discourse world, of a world that might have happened, and one or more counterfactual scenarios may run alongside the realized, actual world of events (Dancygier and Sweetser 2005; Fauconnier and Turner 2002). In an important stylistic application of the concept, Riddle Harding (2007) has argued that counterfactuals are an important marker of evaluative stance in fiction, because they enable a series of attitudinal positions to be adopted with respect to both realized and unrealized narrative events. Before exploring this idea more closely, consider the following illustration from another Peter Carey (2006) novel, *Theft*. Here the first-person narrator Butcher Bones imagines a scenario where the fake painting he has just produced is later valued by an influential art dealer:

> ... It took exactly four hours to paint the Broussard, and even then I took more care than Dominique had done. Being Magna, it dried fast and I was soon able to spray it with a solution of sugar and water. I left it on the roof to fake New York grime ...
>
> 'Here's the Broussard, toots,' Milton Hesse would say to Jane Threadwell. 'I know it's crap, baby, but it has some historical value, and anyway the family wants it cleaned.' Something like that ...
>
> Jane Threadwell would not get to the canvas immediately, and then she would be too busy saving a cracking Mondrian and some Kiefer which had aged like a pig farm in a drought. She would give the Broussard to someone in the studio, a little chore, ...
>
> (Carey 2006: 277–8)

Notice how the future hypothetical modal *would* signals the inception of the counterfactual narrative. This counterfactual scenario, which develops over many hundreds of words of text, is imagined as a fantasy outcome for the narrator, an outcome which is preferred over and is at odds with the current predicament of the 'real' narrative situation.

In the Carey extract, the imagined, more positive counterfactual narrative stands in counterpoint to the present reality time. Clearly, other attitudinal variations are possible, and systematizing to some extent Riddle Harding's approach (2007: 264), it is possible to model the different types of counter-factual 'attitude' on a grid thus:

Attitude to present reality	Attitude to counterfactual world
Positive	Positive
Positive	Negative
Negative	Positive
Negative	Negative

The intersection between evaluative position and counterfactual scenario will be returned to shortly, as the discussion now turns to some wider issues per-taining to the study of point of view, and in particular to the sociopragmatic and cognitive dimensions that can help inform the study of focalization in fictional narrative.

3. Point of view: Cognitive and sociopragmatic dimensions

The last two decades have seen an expansion, in both theoretical and ana-lytic terms, of the way stylisticians have approached the concept of point of view. At the forefront of this enlarged focus has been the work of McIntyre, which has extended the concept of point of view to dramatic dialogue (2004, 2006), to poetry (2007a), and to film narrative (2008). Two key aspects of this extension are first that it has preserved the integrity of the central con-cept of point of view (including the distinction between who sees and who tells) even though its range of application has been expanded, and secondly that the tenets of the original model, as sketched in the previous section, have not been jettisoned but rather have been retained and developed in a progressive, cumulative way. Heeding Short's (1999) suggestion that nar-rative viewpoint needs to be grounded in a broader theory of viewpoint in language and communication, McIntyre (2004: 139) demonstrates how indicators of point of view can be found in interactions between characters in drama, adding that these linguistic indicators of viewpoint go beyond those found in prose fiction. A similar rationale underpins McIntyre's (2007a) exploration of poetry, where, using deictic shift theory, he explores Seamus Heaney's 'Mossbawn'. Charting the way in which cognitive proc-esses are influenced by shifts in deictic reference, McIntyre observes how these often dramatic changes in viewpoint move us progressively closer to the spatial and temporal position of the narrator within the poem (2007a: 128–9). More recently again, McIntyre (2008) has examined point of view in film, and although this genre has long had a natural affiliation with narrative stylistics (see Simpson and Montgomery 1995), the approach adopted in his analysis of *Richard III* is multimodal and is concentrated on the linguistic, paralinguistic and non-linguistic elements of Ian McKellen's performance in the film (and see further below). In all, McIntyre's general approach – and that of other recent work in stylistics – has been to open up point of view analysis to a new and more systematic type of exploration, enabling application across different speaker turns in dialogue, different layers in composition and different literary genres.

3.1. Point of view: A sociopragmatic perspective

I want at this stage to develop further the sociopragmatic perspective on narrative viewpoint. McIntyre (2004: 157) has called for future research to capture the 'fluid' quality of point of view within a linguistic framework and to explain how it is that readers are moved from viewpoint to viewpoint within a text. This 'readerly' orientation is important because it is my contention that our perception of what constitutes point of view, as well as other features of creativity in discourse, is constantly open to renegotiation because, for one thing, the interpretative paradigms we employ to understand texts work differently across different historical periods. This point is of course a truism in literary criticism, but there remains much work to be done in stylistics if a coherent, systematic explanation of diachronic shifts in interpretation is to be reached. The short analysis that follows probes some of these issues and, reflecting ongoing research on the pragmatics of ironic discourse (Simpson, in preparation), locates my own responses as a reader of a text within a model of linguistic (socio)pragmatics.

Without further commentary at this stage, consider the following extract, the opening of Frank McCourt's well known book *Angela's Ashes*:

> My father and mother should have stayed in New York where they met and married and where I was born. Instead, they returned to Ireland ... It was of course a miserable childhood ... Worse than the ordinary miserable childhood is the miserable Irish childhood, and worse yet is the miserable Irish Catholic childhood ...
>
> Above all – we were wet.
>
> Out in the Atlantic Ocean great sheets of rain gathered to drift slowly up the River Shannon and settle forever in Limerick. The rain dampened the city from

the Feast of the Circumcision to New Year's Eve. It created a cacophony of hacking coughs, bronchial rattles, asthmatic wheezes, consumptive croaks ...

(McCourt 1996: 1)

There is no doubt that this portrayal is intended to be bleak, and both this and the film version of the novel paint a picture of Irish life that is at once grim and unrelenting. Indeed, critical reaction has made much of the harshness of the tale, acknowledging how its author has depicted the social conditions of the poor people of Ireland in austere and harrowing terms.

On first reading this passage, my own reaction was however very different. To be blunt, I found it so grotesquely inflated a piece of descriptive prose that it rescinded its own claim to seriousness. Particular forms of expression have engendered here a form of unintentional (and hilarious) self-parody such that, borrowing Austin's term (1962), the text's *perlocutionary status* has been altered. It has somehow shifted from a 'straight' text into what the speech act theoreticians have called 'non-serious' discourse, into a text whose claim to sincerity has been revoked (Searle 1971, 1975b).

The reason why, in the face of overwhelming critical response to the contrary, I experience this particular response to the McCourt passage is worth some attention, not least because it can show how stylistic techniques like perspective and point of view often function in harmony and across different levels of textual organization. I isolate three main strands of stylistic organization that seem to activate my own 'problematic' reaction, which are *counterfactuality*, *rhetorical design*, and *intertextuality*. The text opens with a counterfactual (see above), suggesting that the narrator's parents took the wrong option in leaving New York – a course of action upon which the present harrowing tale is now predicated. Commenting on this same counterfactual sequence in McCourt's novel, Riddle Harding (2007: 266) observes that the modal 'should' indicates a positive attitude towards the counterfactual scenario, that is, towards the course of action *not* followed. This evaluative stance corresponds to row three on the counterfactual grid developed in the previous section and although the positive counterfactual scenario casts a shadow over the narrative, it is nonetheless hard to avoid the blunt conclusion that all this misery was in fact avoidable. Moreover, the blame for the present calamity can now be laid somewhere else, as a kind of adolescent 'it was all my parents' fault' complaint.

In terms of rhetorical design, the text to my mind does much to further jeopardize its own claim to sincerity. For instance, the assertion that the story is 'of course' about a miserable childhood signals the predictability and inevitably of the misery. While this intimates at least some awareness of the existence of a complaint tradition in writing about Ireland, the inevitability of the misery makes it, by imputation, hardly worth the relaying. However, the text moves on to do this very thing, to elaborate the theme of unhappiness and to do it within a rhetorical schema which builds up the 'misery' theme through highly stylized parallel clauses. Not only was the narrator's childhood miserable in the 'normal' way, we learn, his was a superlative kind of misery which reaches the very pinnacle of the miserable Irish Catholic childhood. The rhetoric of misery is sustained elsewhere through asyndetic (and partially alliterative) noun phrases ('hacking coughs', 'bronchial rattles', 'asthmatic wheezes', 'consumptive croaks') literally piling on the unhappiness through these indexes of illness.

To my mind, this particular rhetorical-narrative technique is more at home in passages that are intended to be humorous. Witness for instance the technique at work throughout the novels of Charles Dickens, where a very similar style is used for the creation of comically grotesque characters. In their stylistic analysis of the portrayal of the character Mr Bounderby in *Hard Times*, Short and Candlin (1989) note the presence of repeated and heavily stylized parallel sequences, but importantly, they stress that Dickens's stylistic craft is used for exaggerated and comic description (1989: 199). The McCourt sequence displays an unhappy mismatch between on the one hand an attempt to paint a 'straight' picture of poverty and suffering, and on the other the use of a stylistic pattern whose main effect is to engender comic distortion.

Intertextuality, the discourse of allusion, further compounds the problems brought about by the two stylistic patterns highlighted above. Part of (my) problem with McCourt's writing is that it seems to be utterly oblivious to any Irish literary context, and more to the point, to the great tradition of Irish comic writing that precedes it. Unwittingly, the passage resonates across these genres of writing, even echoing particular texts that are similarly patterned rhetorically but yet are meant as anything but serious. Here is a prime example of one such implicit intertext, from Flann O'Brien's *The Poor Mouth*, written half a century before McCourt's novel:

> The night before the *feis* [a Celtic festival] a large gang of men worked diligently in the midst of the rain erecting a platform ... None of these good fellows ever had good health again after the downpour and storm of that night, while one of those who did not survive was buried before that platform was ... I was about fifteen years of age, an unhealthy, dejected, broken-toothed youth, growing with a rapidity which left me weak and without good health ...
>
> Misadventure fell on my misfortune, a further misadventure fell on that misadventure and before long the misadventures were falling thickly on the first misfortune and myself. Then a shower of misfortunes fell on the misadventures, heavy misadventures fell on the misfortunes and finally one great brown misadventure came upon everything ...
>
> (O'Brien [1941] 1996: 60)

Originally published in Irish Gaelic, this comic novel lampoons the rural Gaelic tradition of Ireland in the mid-twentieth century. Note here the same preoccupation with the rain and the weather, and with its 'calamitous' consequences – so bad was one storm that the people were never healthy again. Also in evidence is the piling-up pattern noted in McCourt, but this time used for genuine and superb comic effect: misery falls upon misery, and even in the context of a rural summer festival, there is no escape from misery for the put-upon people of the Irish countryside. The implication of the stylistic profile of the O'Brien text for the McCourt text is that the former makes the latter appear to buy into and elaborate, without either intention or irony, a cheap literary stereotype that (to many Irish readers at least) invites ridicule.

Placing the two passages beside one another in this way simply problematizes, to use another of Austin's terms, the concept of pragmatic *uptake*. Uptake refers to the understanding of the illocutionary force and content of the utterance by its addressee, and to 'the perlocutionary effects on the addressee brought about by means of uttering the sentence, such effects being special to the circumstances of the utterance' (Austin 1962: 116). These 'special circumstances' to my mind inhere in a matrix of stylistic features, shared in part by both texts, but which in McCourt engenders so rhetorically heightened a plaintiff cry that when diachronically situated in context and in literary history it resists being taken seriously. At the point of its delivery, this text attaches what might be termed a 'validity claim of sincerity' (see Habermas 1979: 67–8), but there is nothing within the author's control to preserve this sincerity claim once the text is 'out there' in the public sphere.

As I have attempted to show in this short (self-)analysis, the interpretative paradigms which inform the reception of creativity in writing are subject to variation over time and across readers. And of course, this analysis is not to deny that yet further interpretative possibilities are available for the McCourt passage. Indeed, other readers may find that *neither* the mainstream critical reception *nor* my particular reading of the text are satisfactory; perhaps feeling instead that the passage engenders a kind of grimly comic tone by oscillating between *both* reading positions. Clearly, the reception of creativity is contingent on a number of important sociopragmatic matrices through which individuals interact with texts, and these matrices need to be fully absorbed into the stylistic analysis of point of view.

3.2. Point of View and Cognitive Stylistics

I want to probe the foregoing issues further with a final illustration, which, it has to be said, is more a programmatic suggestion for future work than a fully articulated stylistic analysis of text. In this case, the exploration of point of view moves in a more cognitive direction, drawing directly from work in experimental psychology (more on which shortly). But like much stylistic research, the initial impetus, prompt, and testing ground comes from the language and literature classroom (see Short 1989a: 2–4, 9), and many of the observations below take their cue from this framing pedagogical context.

It is no surprise that an important outcome of the 'cognitive turn' in stylistics has been the discipline's assimilation of important work by psychologists on textual processing and interpretation (a short representative sample of which is Gibbs 1994, Oatley 2003 and Gerrig 1993). Although there is no doubt that further and insightful intersections between the two disciplines will continue to be made, one area of research that to my mind merits systematic exploration is that which marries the stylistic analysis of point of view with experimental work on the psychology of readers' preferences for narrative outcomes. For instance, Egidi and Gerrig (2006) have examined the way readers react to characters' goals and actions, observing, on the basis of quantified informant-response evidence, how readers tend to identify with characters' goals the more 'urgently' those goals are narrated. In a similar vein, Rapp and Gerrig (2006: 66) examine readers' predilections for certain types of narrative outcome, distinguishing between what they call 'moral outcome' and the narrative outcome preferred by a character. Importantly, there are significant 'entanglements' to these outcomes because a reader's moral preference that 'good will out' may be offset by the urgency of a character's preferred narrative outcome – even if that outcome is morally undesirable. In almost all 'heist' movies, for example, we 'root for' the baddie, hoping that the bank robber gets away, and the more eagerly, immediately, or urgently their situation is narrated, the more it seems we identify with *their* preferred narrative ending in the story.

I have been informally exploring these issues in a number of pedagogical contexts with respect to narrative point of view in texts, and especially in film texts. An interesting question is the extent to which a reflector of fiction may establish or invite an empathy from the reader with respect to the reflector's preferred narrative outcome. A broader question is whether or not manipulations of point of view, even through simple textual transpositions between first and third person in prose narration, can have any impact on readers' identification with particular kinds of outcomes in stories. One informal test – carried out with an admittedly very large group of undergraduates – involved charting the students' reactions to a key scene in Alfred Hitchcock's *Psycho* (1960). In this episode, Norman Bates (played by Anthony Perkins) disposes of Marion Crane (Janet Leigh), the murdered visitor to his hotel, whose body is in the boot of the car which Bates attempts to submerge in a nearby swamp. Whereas it is only at the end that Bates is revealed as the eponymous 'psycho' whose disturbed psyche has absorbed the obsessive personality of his late mother, all viewers of the film will know that at this stage he is at least a co-conspirator in Marion's murder. The scene is played out in the following sequence of shots:

'The Car in the Swamp Scene', Chapter 12, Psycho, 2:45 minutes.

Sequence 1: An establishing shot at night of the rear of Marion's car with its number plate clearly visible. The shadowy figure of Bates emerges from the driver's side and pushes the car towards the swamp.

Sequence 2: A series of cuts between (i) the view of the progressively sinking car and (ii) close-ups of Bates, chewing nervously, as he watches the car gradually sink into the swamp.

Sequence 3: A shot back to the rear of the car, which suddenly stops sinking with the boot of the car left in full view. This is quickly followed by a close-up of Bates, who twitches, stops chewing, and looks furtively to his right, then behind, and then back around to his left.

Sequence 4: A return to the shot of the partially submerged car which now begins to sink again, finally disappearing from sight. The final shot of the scene is a close-up of Bates, who, as the car finally disappears into the swamp, begins to chew again and grins in a self-satisfied way.

This is an excellent episode for exploring a number of intersections between point of view and cognitive affect, with the distinction between preferred and dispreferred narrative outcomes at the fore. Even the present informal study of viewers' reactions to the scene – and I stress that this was no more than a show of hands from a large lecture audience – throws up some intriguing issues. For example, all but 10 of the 295 participants, when asked, admitted that they wanted Marion's car to sink into the swamp. (Incidentally, the 10 who did not concur, when asked about their alternative preferences, were not particularly committed to any other narrative possibility, suggesting perhaps a reluctance to engage with the experiment in such a large group.) Those who had seen the film before (the overwhelming majority) were fully aware of Bates's psycho-delusional behaviour and his culpability for Marion's murder, although the few students who had not seen the film still realized that Bates was attempting to cover up the murder of an innocent woman (not quite so bad a baddie, then!). Nevertheless, this moral framework was clearly set aside by the students in favour of an identification with the preferred narrative outcome of the character, suggesting that the evidence from experimental psychology is indeed strong and that the urgency of the character's situation, in the context of his or her preferred narrative outcome, has an important bearing on reader/viewer identification. What is more, follow-up questions to the group as a whole elicited a number of interesting explanations. When asked what made them side with so repugnant a character, a number of respondents replied along the general lines of 'because we see what he is thinking'. This is clearly prompted by the shot/reverse shot pattern developed in sequences 2 and 3.

Commenting on this aspect of Hitchcock's film technique, Bordwell and Thompson single out the director's strategic use of 'eyeline-match' and 'point-of-view cutting' (1990: 227). This, they argue, leads to the intensification of subjectivity because we not only see what a character (in this instance, Bates) sees, but *only* what he sees (1990: 311). Crucially, the technique develops not only subjective depth, but suspense, because viewers (*pace* the stalled sinking of the car and the discomfort shown on Bates's face) share the information that a character learns *at precisely the same moment* in the narrative. The upshot of this is that a kind of narrative empathy is invited. Moreover, as Egidi and Gerrig (2006: 1322) argue, readers, and by implication viewers, are more 'comfortable' with a narrative outcome that is established in a prior 'biasing context': thus, the completion of the action initiated, even though grimly immoral, is easier to integrate psychologically than an action which is inconsistent with a character's goals. There is, so the theory goes, a strong correlation between the urgency of the narrative actions required and the means a character uses to complete them (ibid.: 1323). Hitchcock's rendering of this particular episode through eye-line matching and point-of-view cutting captures a particularly empathetic kind of character reaction, and one wonders indeed how the episode would have been interpreted by viewers had the participating character/reflector not been structurally positioned in this way.

One of the main advantages of this proposed synthesis between stylistic approaches to point of view and psychological investigations of readers' reactions to narrative is that the methodology of one area may enrich the other. A key and obvious pay-off for stylistics is that it offers a more systematic account of readers' interaction with narrative viewpoint. Whereas the psychological studies referred to above are sophisticated in terms of experimental design and informant testing, the conception of narrative structure (especially mind-style, point of view, and related devices) is rather more rudimentary. In the main, consideration of alternative narrative styles and structures is mostly confined to the straightforward transposition of third-person to first-person narration (see, for example, ibid.: 1329). While such transposition is undoubtedly relevant, a much greater range of 'textual intervention' (Pope 1994) could be used to probe informants' reactions to many more, and different, patterns in both film and prose narratives. It is also not entirely clear in the psychological work what aspects of style contribute to the idea of 'urgency' in narration, although stylisticians, for their part, are becoming ever more alert to the multimodal possibilities of narrative analysis and now have useful models for assessing many aspects of performance and delivery (McIntyre 2008: 327–8). In sum, the marriage of stylistic analysis with empirical testing techniques (following, for example, the lead of Zyngier *et al.* 2008) might well lead to the creation of an encompassing and more fully devolved model of narrative point of view.

4. Concluding remarks

This chapter has sought to explore a number of stylistic frameworks for exploring point of view in narrative. Beginning with the more established models of point of view, whose primary point of departure is with linguistic features *in* the text, the chapter has progressively widened its focus to consider approaches to point where the primary emphasis has been on the cognitive and pragmatic features *around* the text. Importantly, the methods outlined here are intended to be inclusive rather than exclusive, incremental rather than autonomous. The chapter has not attempted to be exhaustive, because there are many other recent approaches to point of view that would merit inclusion in a survey like this. For example, Dancygier's study of Jonathan Raban's travel narratives draws on conceptual blending theory to investigate what she terms 'viewpoint compression'. Raban's narratives are interwoven with memories and recollections from his childhood days, such that the present 'now/I' narrator is merged with earlier incarnations. This, according to Dancygier (2005: 124), allows a compression in two points of view without the introduction of any new characters, allowing the narrative to explore situations in greater depth without losing continuity. Exploring point of view in science fiction time-travel narratives, Ryder (2003) has detected similar types of merged viewpoints. Focusing specifically on stories by Robert Heinlein, Ryder draws on Emmott's (1997) work on narrative comprehension in order to explore how the author of the stories both aids and obstructs the reader's identification of characters, noting that time-travel stories pose particular and special challenges to narrative comprehension (Ryder 2003: 230).

Another direction in which point of view study might be taken is in the sustained analysis of a single text, especially a work of contemporary prose fiction that exhibits the sorts of stylistic challenges highlighted by both Dancygier and Ryder. David Mitchell's (2004) *Cloud Atlas* makes for a suitable if exigent candidate. This novel is a veritable stylistician's paradise, or nightmare, depending on the attitude one takes to over 500 pages of exuberant linguistic innovation, intriguing style shifts and embeddings, and astonishingly deft transitions in mind-style and point of view. Mitchell's novel comprises a series of loosely connected narratives, embedded Russian-doll-style within each other, with each narrative world spanning different historical periods (from an early nineteenth-century maritime adventure to a putative futuristic post-apocalyptic world inhabited by automatons). These narratives break at key points in their respective plots to allow the embedding of another story, with the core 'inner-doll' narrative the one set furthest away in the future. Each of the transitions across narrative worlds is delivered in the style of a different genre of writing, including the travelogue, the thriller, the autobiography and the science fiction novel, and each of the generic transitions is marked by the introduction of different reflectors of fiction who deliver their story through complex and remarkably potent projected mind-styles. This is a demanding novel both to read and to study, suffice it to say, where every one (and more) of the features of narrative point of view covered in this short survey is brought into play and pushed to the limits of understanding. The stylistic analysis that would be the basis of such a study, while undeniably insightful, must however be left to another day.

SHOULD PROBS READ CLOUD ATLAS.

V. BIAS, LICKING MITCHELL'S ASS.

CHAPTER 17

The Intrinsic Importance of Sentence Type and Clause Type to Narrative Effect: Or, How Alice Munro's 'Circle of Prayer' Gets Started

Michael Toolan

1. Introduction

In his recent entertaining primer, *How to Read a Poem*, Terry Eagleton regrets the lack of close reading by students today, the reading of poems attentive to their form rather than just their content:

> What gets left out is the *literariness* of the work. Most students can say things like 'the moon imagery recurs in the third verse, adding to the sense of solitude', but not many of them can say things like 'the poem's strident tone is at odds with its shambling syntax'.

> (Eagleton 2007: 3)

This last point he liked so well that he recycled it, lightly altered, in his review in The *Guardian* of Tom Paulin's own primer on *The Secret Life of Poems*:

> Most students of literature can pick apart a metaphor or spot an ethnic stereotype, but not many of them can say things like: 'The poem's sardonic tone is curiously at odds with its plodding syntax.'

Eagleton is firmly of the view that it would be a good thing if students knew and could talk about syntax of the shambling or plodding varieties. But there is a problem here: it is far from clear what 'shambling syntax' is. We might suppose it is syntax that 'shuffles awkwardly along'; but what are the criteria by which we can classify this sentence as shambling or shuffling along, and that one not? Is there a standard or norm of syntactic advance, against which degrees of shambling or plodding could be measured (as a physiotherapist might measure a patient's walking difficulties using normal gait characteristics as a standard?). Or is shambling (plodding, lively, strenuous, etc) syntax another of those things which we cannot quite define, but we know it when we see it? If it is, then it is a flimsy basis on which to build a theory of literariness, and of the importance of form to effect (particular forms, for particular effects) of the kind that Eagleton, like us stylisticians, seeks. In short, Eagleton's 'shambling syntax' does not get us much further than the 'moon imagery' description which, he implies, is inadequate in being all about content to the neglect of form. 'Shambling' is still too contentual, impressionistic, and unverifiable a way of talking about syntax. The essay that follows aims to contribute to the effort to discuss sentential syntactic choices and effects in verifiable ways.

In the penultimate chapter of *Exploring the Language of Poems, Plays and Prose*, a chapter on prose style, Mick Short begins by distinguishing three types of authorial prose style: (i) that style that, regardless of the topic of the passage, prompts us to attribute it to one author rather than any other (e.g. Dickens, and not Hemingway or Lawrence or Austen); (ii) those style features, even less related to text meaning, which are 'tell-tales' or like a particular author's fingerprint, useful for forensic, author-identification purposes; and finally, (iii) text style, style which is 'intrinsically related to meaning' (Short 1996: 330). Like him and most stylisticians, I am rather more interested in this kind of style than the other two: text style is the kind of style that seems most directly motivated by the particular topic or theme of the text in which it occurs, so that we feel there is a 'made to measure' fit between form and content; in the other two kinds of style, by contrast, there is the implication that local content has made little difference to form (see Hoover, this volume).

The discussion that follows is offered as an addition to the line of exploration of a text's broad choices in sentence grammar and what they might entail in the way of meaning and effect, which Short broaches in his chapter on prose style. There, his exemplary (in both senses) commentary is on the famous description in *The Great Gatsby* of the commencement of one of Jay Gatsby's hedonistic parties, held at his fabulous mansion on Long Island Sound. As it happens, there is relatively little of special note to report about clause and sentence structures in the passage (ibid.: 342): while sentences are comparatively long, these use mainly 'trailing' structures (a term I will explain below), and so are still relatively easy to process. By contrast, there is plenty of richness (and absurdity and irony) in the passage's elaborations at the level of phrase structure and in the lexis, and in its sound and rhythmic effects, as Short demonstrates. In something of the same spirit in which Short looked at clause- and sentence-structuring in the Gatsby passage, and in which Leech and Short looked at the opening paragraphs of Henry James's 'The Pupil' (Leech and Short 1981, Chapter 3; especially 100–4), I will discuss the sentence and clause trends in the opening paragraphs of Alice Munro's story 'Open Secrets'. I hope to throw a little new light on what is really an old topic (see, for example, besides Leech and Short [1981] 2007; Sinclair 1966; Dillon 1978; Ceci 1983), sometimes termed 'iconic grammar'. At the least I hope to put new emphases into the interpretation of the relevance of some old, time-tested categorizations.

2. Immediate background

This chapter emerged from one of the most traditional of lessons in an undergraduate degree module on English grammar for students relatively unversed in linguistic matters: a revision class on the three main types of subordinate clauses (nominal, adverbial and restrictive relative) and some of their structural properties. In our language modules at Birmingham University for students whose interests are primarily literary, we teach a relatively simple and traditional constituency grammar, in which the finite clause will contain some of the five elements, subject, predicate, object, complement and adjunct, and these in turn are typically realized by contrasting types of phrase. Thus, subjects and objects are filled in the simplest case by a simple noun-phrase, which comprises a head with optional modifier and qualifier before and after; and predicates are filled by a verb-phrase containing a lexical verb, optionally preceded by up to four 'auxiliaries': modal, perfective, progressive, and passive; and so on.

The three main types of subordinate clause are distinguished structurally as follows. A nominal clause fills the entirety of a noun-phrase (which itself may constitute the S, O or C of a clause. Here, underlined, are some nominal clauses: *What he had done wrong was unclear to him. He decided that he would apologize to her anyway. To be on good terms with her was what he wanted more than anything.* A (restrictive) relative clause fills the qualifier (or 'q') of a noun-phrase, in place of something simpler such as a prepositional phrase (the qualifier or 'q' of a noun-phrase is everything after the head word; thus in *the apple on the desk* and *the apple he brought her, on the desk* and *he brought her* are the q elements). Examples of such relative clauses are underlined in the following sentences: *The apology which he offered to her was not the kind of response that she was looking for.* An adverbial clause is one that fills the

A element of a clause and, when it is finite, it is usually introduced by a sub-ordinating conjunction: <u>*Hiding her disappointment,*</u> *she turned away from him* <u>*until she had regained her composure*</u>.

The above sketch is fairly basic and certainly incomplete, but even this amount of technicality is too much for some literature students, who find talk of restrictive relative clauses 'filling the qualifier' of a noun-phrase rebarbative and bamboozling. I can't really criticize them for feeling alienated and lost. They are not the only ones who have wondered what the *point* is, of being able to distinguish relative clauses from nominal or adverbial ones. For that matter, what is the relevance, to these students' interests and needs, of being able to distinguish compound sentences from complex ones? It is absorbing enough stuff, like being able to identify morphophonemic changes, or to explain the choice among the three allomorphs of the English plural morpheme; but isn't it 'purely' linguistic information, with no real bearing on the students' own reading, writing and analytical understanding (or anyone else's)? To this I want to cry *No, no, no,* that knowing about sentence structure has a bearing on all kinds of understandings and judgements about language (or failings of understanding), near and far. The gaps in understanding are an indirect cause, I believe, of other kinds of weakness in students' writing. Only with an at least implicit grasp of such kinds of linguistic understanding can any of us develop into more proficient writers, more aware of the different potential effects of alternative sentential forms. But I *do* see that we stylisticians need to do more than insist on students learning grammar 'for their own good' ('language doctor knows best'). That is why I have written this chapter: to try to show how knowing about sentence and clause types truly helps us to understand and appreciate fine literary writing 'from the inside'. It also enriches our thinking about distinct kinds of writing, to suit distinct genres and contexts. For these reasons knowing sentence grammar and applying that knowledge is not fuddy-duddy technicality, but permanently relevant. That at least is what I hope to persuade the reader of.

3. The evidence

As a first step in trying to persuade students that spotting the relative clauses or compound sentences in a text does have relevance to the bigger picture, of meaning and effect, I ask them to do their practice grammar analysis (identifying sentence types, and subordinate clause types) not on my own invented sentences, but on sentences invented by a great writer. That is how I came to give my second-year grammar students the opening paragraphs of Alice Munro's story 'Circle of Prayer', asking them first to identify the simple, compound and complex sentences therein, and then all instances of the three main types of subordinate clause. For the relative clauses, I also asked them to indicate whether they were restrictive or non-restrictive. After working through some of their solutions in class, I completed a 'model' answer, for the three types of clausal subordination, using a different kind of underlining for the three types. I told them:

In the text that follows, relative clauses are <u>double underlined</u>, nominal clauses are <u>single underlined</u> and the adverbial ones are <u>wavy underlined</u>.

Here is the text:

Trudy threw a jug across the room. It didn't reach the opposite wall; it didn't hurt anybody, it didn't even break. (1)
      This was the jug without a handle – <u>cement-colored with brown streaks on it, rough as sandpaper to the touch</u> – that Dan made the winter he took pottery classes. He made six little handleless cups <u>to go with it</u>. The jug and the cups were supposed to be for sake, but the local liquor store doesn't carry sake. Once, they brought some home from a trip, but they didn't really like it. So the jug <u>Dan made</u> sits on the highest open shelf in the kitchen, and a few odd items of value are kept in it. Trudy's wedding ring and her engagement ring, the medal <u>Robin won for all-round excellence in Grade 8</u>, a long, two-strand necklace of jet beads <u>that belonged to Dan's mother and was willed to Robin</u>. Trudy won't let her wear it yet. (2)
      Trudy came home from work a little after midnight; she entered the house in the dark. Just the little stove light was on – she and Robin always left that on for each other. Trudy didn't need any other light. She climbed up on a chair <u>without even letting go of her bag</u>, got down the jug, and fished around inside it. (3)
      It was gone. Of course. She had known <u>it would be gone</u>. (4)
      She went through the dark house to Robin's room, <u>still with her bag over her arm, the jug in her hand</u>. She turned on the overhead light. Robin groaned and turned over, pulled the pillow over her head. Shamming. (5)
      'Your grandmother's necklace,' Trudy said. 'Why did you do that? Are you insane?' (6)
      Robin shammed a sleepy groan. All the clothes <u>she owned</u>, it seemed, old and new and clean and dirty, were scattered on the floor, on the chair, the desk, the dresser, even on the bed itself. On the wall was a huge poster <u>showing a hippopotamus, with the words underneath 'Why Was I Born So Beautiful?'</u> And another <u>poster showing Terry Fox running along a rainy highway, with a whole cavalcade of cars behind him</u>. Dirty glasses, empty yogurt containers, school notes, a Tampax <u>still in its wrapper</u>, the stuffed

snake and tiger Robin had had since before she went to school, a collage of pictures of her cat Sausage, who had been run over two years ago. Red and blue ribbons that she had won for jumping, or running, or throwing basketballs. (7)

  'You answer me!' said Trudy. 'You tell me why you did it!' (8)

  She threw the jug. But it was heavier than she'd thought, or else at the very moment of throwing it she lost conviction, because it didn't hit the wall; it fell on the rug beside the dresser and rolled on the floor, undamaged. (9)

(Alice Munro, 'Circle of Prayer')

So what do the passage's trends, in frequent sentence types and scarce ones, and in more frequent subordinate clause types and less frequent ones, show or tell? Before attempting to answer those questions (in Section 6 below), I include two sections. In the first of these I would like to say more about the effect that seems to be achieved by the first few sentences, in the order in which they occur. I do this partly on the grounds that these are what the reader encounters first (the reader does not take even this short span of paragraphs as a simultaneous whole, but rather by increments out of which perceptions of trends and patterns must progressively emerge). But I also want to take this opportunity to fill in some of the story's background and preoccupations (as I see them), relative to which – it may be argued – the teller decided to tell things in the sentence-structuring way she chose, rather than in any of the other ways she could have chosen. In Section 4, a little more commentary is made on sentence types and their impact on reading.

4. The story starts straight away...
and conversationally

The story starts straight away, with 'Trudy threw a jug.' In one sense, concerning the text, it is ridiculous tautology to say that a story 'starts straight away': in that sense, a story starts where it starts and all stories start straight away. But in another sense we are quite used to finding, in the first lines or paragraphs of a story, a preliminary, situation-establishing introduction of the time, the place, the main participants, and some of their habitual activities: these, we understand, are the background set of conditions out of which a destabilizing action or development erupts. There is none of that background here, at the outset; instead, an almost absurdly 'bare' narrative-event clause: 'Trudy threw a jug.' Bare because it lacks any accompanying time or place orientation, no setting of the scene: instead, we get action first, with background perhaps later. So straight away we have been given the answer to the crucial narrative question, 'What happened?'

Well, it emerges that 'Trudy threw a jug' is *one* of the 'what happened?'s, but later we learn of other, not unrelated happenings:

- Trudy's daughter Robin put the jade necklace in her schoolmate's coffin;
- the necklace was bequeathed to Robin by Trudy's mother-in-law some years ago;
- Trudy and Dan divorced (after he took up with a younger woman) a few years ago.

But you've got to begin somewhere, and this story begins with 'Trudy threw a jug.' What else to note about that maximally simple transitive action clause? That in structure it is the kind of sentence someone could easily say, in a slightly shocked tone, in a hushed conversation; so that the sense of voice is projected from the very beginning. Of course someone talking to a friend (it is hard to imagine a natural context – that is, outside fiction – for the opening sentences that is not talk between friends) might not use the name *Trudy*: as likely would be *She threw a jug* or *You threw a jug*; which is why I say the sentence is conversational in structure, rather than wording. Further markers of this 'conversational' tenor is the extensive use of contractions and negation in the narration: *didn't, doesn't, won't* (Biber *et al.* 1999 suggest negation is characteristic of conversation). Yet another indicator is the use of 'even', three times, in the narration of this opening, where it is used for that semantically redundant evaluative emphasis that in appraisal theory (Martin and White 2005) is called graduation (amplification) by focus: 'it didn't even break' [...] 'without even letting go of her bag' [...] 'even on the bed itself'. A fourth linguistic marker one might note – and this does bring us some way back to the question of clause and phrase-combination – is to be found in the oral rather than writerly way in which some clauses or phrases are combined without the ordinarily required coordinating conjunction. The first example of a departure from the norms of formal written English comes in the second sentence, after the semi-colon: linking the two coordinated clauses 'it didn't hurt anybody' and 'it didn't even break' only with a comma does not conform to the standard conventions of written grammar. And when we come to the longer 'item-listing' sentences, such as the penultimate sentence of paragraph 2, beginning 'Trudy's wedding ring', or the final two sentences of paragraph 7, either a subject and main verb or an expectable conjunction (e.g. 'and') is missing, or both are. Does the story continue to be 'conversational' in structure, and how can one evidentially support that claim? This is a subsidiary topic of my chapter.

Despite the series of story happenings listed in the previous paragraph, the heart of the story (I believe) is not so much 'one event' as a tellable situation. That situation is that while Dan left her several years ago, Trudy is still grieving over the loss, and still struggling to understand what she once wished for or indeed now wishes for. Thus midway through the story she learns that a close friend has joined a 'circle of prayer' in which a group of women linked by a phone tree are notified of one member's need for prayer, and all of them privately pray for that person. A sceptical Trudy wonders: if she believed in prayer, what would she pray for, for herself? Time has been a healer, the routines of life and friendship have absorbed her up to a point, but then out of the blue has come this teenage death in a car accident (not to Robin, thankfully), and Robin responding by casually 'donating', for burial or cremation, the precious jade necklace, this material acknowledgement of womanly beauty and connection of the 'matriarchal line' from Dan's mother, through Trudy, to Robin. The necklace has been consigned by Robin, used up, rather than kept forever, for better or for worse, in the way Trudy had thought it should be.

Before moving on to the core of this chapter, let us note something else about the opening lines:

> Trudy threw a jug across the room. It didn't reach the opposite wall; it didn't hurt anybody, it didn't even break.

A story must give us an answer to the simple, sometimes disingenuous, question, 'What happened?' And as already noted, this opening appears to get down to the task, but then doesn't. It tells us one thing that did happen but then three things that did not. As has been variously discussed, use of negation to tell what *didn't* happen is always significant and evaluative, evoking an alternative chains of events (here, one in which the jug *did* break, and/or did *hurt* someone) (Labov 1972; Nørgaard 2007), and sometimes implying some abnormality in the negated events or states that applies here and makes them tellable: if you throw a jug across a room it is more usual for it to at least break, if not to reach the far wall or hit someone, but in this episode none of these reasonably expectable outcomes occurred (Toolan 2009: 148). But what about the sequencing of these negative reports, telling first of the jug's not reaching, then of its not hurting, then of its not breaking? How might this chime with what one might call a painterly or representational preference for iconicity in narration, so stimulatingly discussed in Leech and Short nearly 30 years ago (Leech and Short 1981: 233–43; [2nd edition, 2007: 187–96])? Is this sequencing iconic? The first clause comments on the force and spatial context of the throw, and is purely 'physical' observation, focused on process rather than end point (we are not told where the jug *did* reach or come to rest); the second clause is much more interpretive and complex, addressing immediate effect on other people; the third reports the effect or consequence for the jug itself. There is something implicitly iconic (i.e. mimetic) here, as reflected in the fact that the three statements 'build' to a final one involving *even*. Usually such negative sequences imply a series in which the last is the least, just as positive sequences imply that the last is the most (most valuable, surprising, tellable):

> *They didn't give me dinner, they didn't give me lunch, they didn't even give me coffee and biscuits.*
>
> *They bought me coffee, they bought me lunch, they even bought me dinner.*

I don't wish to say anything more here about 'It didn't reach the opposite wall; it didn't hurt anybody, it didn't even break', but simply cite it as indicative of the kind of careful thought, and regard for iconic effect, that a great artist like Munro puts into the structuring and sequencing of information (here, negated information), of seemingly slight importance.

5. Sentence patterns and inter-clausal processing dependence

Short lists six 'basic sentence patterns' found in English. Types 1 to 3 are: the simple sentence, and the compound sentence, either with coordinator or with paratactic punctuation only. Types 4 to 6 are all complex, with the selected source of complexity, the adverbial clause, variously sited:

    [4]   John loves Mary because Mary loves John. **(trailing structure)**
    [5]   Because Mary loves John, John loves Mary. **(anticipatory structure)**
    [6]   John, because Mary loves him, loves Mary. **(parenthetic structure)**
                                     (Short 1996: 340)

There are numerous alternative terms in the literature for the terms trailing, anticipatory, and parenthetic, such as loose or released structure, fronting or thematizing, and central embedding, respectively, but Short's terms are perfectly adequate. More important are the implications or effects of these different choices (in the case of sentences [4] to [6] above, alternative structures which carry virtually synonymous sentences). Short touches lightly on those effects (1996: 341), but invokes the crucial question of whether 'one clause at a time' is processed by the reader or listener. In the simple and compound types ([1] to [3]) it seems fairly uncontroversial to postulate that processing can be and is conducted one clause at a time (even in those compounds where a pronoun in the second clause co-refers with an antecedent in the first: *John loves Mary and she loves him*). But in all the complex types, there is such a degree of dependence of one clause on another, that we cannot say that one and only one clause at a time can or need be processed. On the contrary a cross- or multi-clausal perspective is required to make sense of the two (or more) clauses involved. This is mildly true in [4], more palpable in [5], and most apparent in [6], where the dependent clause interrupts the sequence of 'inner' higher clause elements, by occurring between the S and the P. It would be only one more step to move the parenthetic clause to the right, to fall between the P and O; but this creates a structure that is both unacceptable and surprisingly hard to process:

[6'] John loves, because Mary loves him, Mary.

As Short notes, anticipatory and parenthetic clause structures are sometimes described as a 'tight' style (1996: 341). And by 'tightness' must be meant this inescapable 'bound-up' interconnection of the clauses involved, so different from the minimal bonding between clauses in structure type 1: *John loves Mary. Mary loves John.* For Saussure, linearity was (with arbitrariness) one of the two fundamental features of language; in the concatenation of simple or compound clauses linearity *at the clausal level* operates in a relatively pure or absolute way, but where complex clauses abound there is clearly substantial compromise of pure linearity. This claim is, I recognize, contentious, and depends on how linearity in reading is understood. Might one dismiss my claims by arguing that, whatever the sentence structure, one reads word by word and thus inescapably linearly? Only if that were the whole story. But is reading/processing truly and only word by word? The most compelling counter-argument relates to sentencehood: the sentence boundary, very clearly marked in modern writing, is a milestone of text-processing of inestimable importance, and it is clear that notwithstanding the linear presentation of writing, we do not process the first word of a new sentence along with the last word of the previous sentence, as word-by-word processing would require. There will be *some* links between these two words, flanking the sentence boundary, but each is made sense of first and extensively within its own sentential envelope. In short, reading is not only and not always word by word, but also and sometimes alternatively sentence by sentence. Space limitations prevent me setting out the subsidiary argument that, between word-by-word and graphological-sentence-by-graphological-sentence processing, clause-by-clause reading is an important intermediate segmentation and processing of text. But again it is crucial to my thesis, and crucial to trying to persuade students that clause-structuring is important to literary understanding. The final step in the reasoning, outlined above, is to argue that by contrast with simple and compound sentences, in complex sentences with a preposed or parenthetically embedded subordinate clause, linear clause-by-clause, proposition-by-proposition processing is disrupted or 'knotted', causing eddies in the dynamic flow of reading.

In the title of this section I have used the term *processing* and it is, I hope, clear that I want to develop an argument about how different patterns of deployment of sentence and clause types can create different effects in readers, since those different types require different kinds of local and contextualized processing. It might be objected that I should not refer to processing and reading without copious reference to the extensive (but often inconclusive) psycholinguistic research on these topics; some would go so far as to say that 'processing' is a matter for psycholinguistics, and mere stylisticians or grammarians should keep away. I disagree with all that, and contend that no elaborate psycholinguistic testing is required for language users to recognize that (all other things being equal) a structurally simple sentence is easier (smoother, without the need to scan backwards or forwards) to process than a complex one, and that parenthetic complexity is slightly more demanding (more disruptive of steady onward incremental reading) than trailing complexity. Indeed it is in part because the 'grammatical' distinctions (simple, compound, complex, fronted, centrally embedded, trailing, nominal, relative, adverbial) have always had some psychological and psycholinguistic validity, some bearing on our processes of text-composition and processing, that they have become so deeply entrenched in our textual descriptions.

Many comments could be made on the analysis of subordinate clauses in the Munro passage, in Section 3 above. I will mention just three. The first concerns verbless subordinate clauses. I emphasized to the students that both finite and non-finite subordinate clauses had been underlined, and that in one or two of the non-finite clauses, no predicate is present so that the clause is quite incomplete ('reduced'). Nevertheless, if there was more than one clause element present, for example if what was present was more than just a prepositional phrase functioning as a single A, then I suggested there were grounds for calling the chunk a reduced clause. Thus, for example in the case of 'a Tampax <u>still in its wrapper</u>', I would analyse this as a reduced version of a relative clause:

```
                         NP
  m    h                      q
   [ S                  P    A        A    ]
 a Tampax [that/which | was | still | in its wrapper]
```

A second point to note is that in focusing on the three main types of subordinate clause, I have neglected other less frequent types; thus the comparative clause in the final sentence in the passage, demarcated by a broken rectangle, is not commented upon. A third point is that some analytical decisions are contestable. In the following sentence, for example, I have underlined the brief relative clause attached to 'clothes' –

> All the clothes <u>she owned</u>, it seemed, old and new and clean and dirty, were scattered on the floor, on the chair...

– but there is a case for saying that 'All the clothes she owned', 'old and new' [...] and 'were scattered on the floor' are all part of a Nominal Clause associated with the 'it' of 'it seemed'. For reasons too lengthy to rehearse here, I have rejected that analysis.

6. What does the sentence- and clause-structural analysis show?

The grammar analysis highlights quite a lot about this wonderful story opening. One thing we can immediately note is *how little* subordination, that is, use of complex sentence structure, there is here, until we get to the section describing Robin's chaotic bedroom. There are very few adverbial clauses, finite or non-finite, and those that occur are without exception sited clause-finally (i.e. in the 'trailing' or releasing position, which we have noted makes low demands on processing effort). Nominal clauses are even scarcer (there are just two), and these too are in that easiest-to-manage clause- and sentence-final position. They are undemanding, also, in that they only encapsulate and repeat ideas that have already been expressed earlier in the text (without subordination). For example, Trudy asks Robin: 'Why did you do that?' and a few lines later says (using an embedded nominal clause): 'You tell me <u>why you did it</u>!' Only relative clauses occur here in any significant number (almost always of the restrictive or defining kind: 'who had been run over two years ago' is one exception). And restrictive relative clauses we can describe as normally 'trailing' in a particular sense: as here, they almost invariably directly follow the modifier and head of the noun-phrase which they specify without even the possibility of separation by a comma. Thus positionally restrictive relative clauses present the reader with no surprises.

At this point it may be useful to distinguish two types of complex sentences (a different distinction from that made in Short's trailing/anticipatory/parenthetic classification, but one that can be combined with the latter). The two types of complex sentence I now want to distinguish are:

i. those involving an adverbial or a nominal subordinate clause, which latter can be said to function on two levels, as clauses in themselves and as full elements in a 'higher' clause; adverbial and nominal clauses are relatively freely moveable (e.g. to an anticipatory position):

The house has a ramp now for wheelchairs, because some of the mentally handicapped may be physically handicapped as well.

Because some of the mentally handicapped may be physically handicapped as well, the house has a ramp now for wheelchairs.

She never really found out what had happened at Genevieve's house.

What had happened at Genevieve's house, she never really found out.

ii. those containing a restrictive relative clause: such a subordinate clause really functions only on one level, by virtue of being embedded as qualifier within a nominal element (S, O or C) of a higher clause. In Short's terms restrictive relatives always 'trail' the head noun, and can never be anticipatory or parenthetic; but because they can attach to any head noun in a sentence and not just the final head noun, they can create parenthetic effects – albeit only local parenthetic effects.

The jug that Dan made one winter was cement-colored with brown streaks on it, rough as sandpaper to the touch.

*That Dan made one winter the jug was cement-colored with brown streaks on it, rough as sandpaper to the touch.

Trudy hated the jug that Dan made in pottery class.

*Trudy hated the Dan made in pottery class jug.

I will argue that the former type involve greater structural complexity and – all other things being equal – tend to be more difficult to process. A sentence labelled complex simply by virtue of containing a restrictive relative clause is more difficult to process than a simple clause –

So the jug Dan made sits on the highest open shelf in the kitchen.

So the jug sits on the highest open shelf in the kitchen.

– but not much. In terms of the two types of complex sentence just described, those sentences in the Munro passage that are complex are overwhelmingly of the cognitively less demanding type, in which a trailing relative clause follows and supplies further information about the head of a noun-phrase.

Where sentences qualify as complex, then, by virtue of the appearance of a subordinate clause somewhere in their structure, still there are varying degrees of delay, complexity, or 'thickening', over and above the trailing/parenthetical/anticipatory alternation. Looking more closely at complex sentences involving an adverbial or nominal clause (my type i), those with a nominal clause normally seem more 'delaying' than those with an adverbial one. Thus an SPOA clause with a clause filling the final adjunct element after a simple noun-phrase object, is arguably less complex than one where the O is filled by a nominal clause while the A is phrasal: *She had known it even before she checked; She had known it would be gone before checking.* And whatever the subordination, movement of that subordinate clause to sentence-initial position ('fronting'), I will assume, invariably introduces a little more complexity (or 'slowed' processing) than the unfronted alternative:

> Even before she checked, she had known it.
> She had known it even before she checked.

A general point can be made, also, about the simple/compound/complex typology of sentence patterns. This implies a three-way contrast, but I would suggest that often the most significant distinction is a binary one, between simple or compound sentences on the one hand, and complex ones on the other. This is because what distinguish compound sentences from simple ones (provided one can tolerate simple sentences introduced by coordinators such as *and* and *or*) are relatively superficial 'diacritical' markers, namely punctuation. Indicative of the smallness of the contrast, it is hard for a listener to distinguish an enunciation of the following actual version of the second graphological sentence of the passage:

> It didn't reach the opposite wall; it didn't hurt anybody, it didn't even break.

from this alternative, sense-preserving presentation, as three simple sentences:

> It didn't reach the opposite wall. It didn't hurt anybody. It didn't even break.

That is to say, a listener cannot easily tell that the first version is a compound sentence, the second version three simple sentences. There is no way of similarly conflating complex sentences, in the hearing of a spoken delivery, with either of the other two types:

> He made six little handleless cups. To go with it.
> She had known. It would be gone.

Thus there is much that unites simple and compound sentences as a single syntagmatic style of steady advance, to be contrasted with the 'thicker' advance, made more complicated by the clausal elaboration at one point or another of the structure, involved in complex sentences.

Even with the relative clauses that feature in paragraphs 2 and 7, the passage remains predominantly one of compound sentences, which means in turn that the passage is a chain of clauses of equal grammatical level, linked by punctuation such as the semi-colon, and *and*s, *but*s and *or*s. It is thus a series of pulses or packets of information that can be taken in order, like beads on a necklace, with very little need to hold one packet in mind while a preced-ing, following, or interrupting packet is processed. This short paragraph, for instance, is typical:

> Trudy came home from work a little after midnight; she entered the house in the dark. Just the little stove light was on – she and Robin always left that on for each other. Trudy didn't need any other light. She climbed up on a chair without even letting go of her bag, got down the jug, and fished around inside it.

What we find here is a series of simple clauses, one after the other, with relatively little cross-clausal linkage, so that each is relatively free-standing. Much of it can be written out *as* free-standing separate sentences, with little change in effect:

> Trudy came home from work a little after midnight.
> She entered the house in the dark.
> Just the little stove light was on.
> She and Robin always left that on for each other.
> Trudy didn't need any other light.

This means that each can be taken in turn, without need for extensive 'hold-ing in mind' of the content of a previous clause *as a clause*; and that structural format is very well suited to a simple, maximally straightforward telling of events. This is not to deny the numerous cohesive links between these clauses (*Trudy → She; came home → entered the house; little stove light → that → any other light*; and so on), but to suggest that clausally each is completed (and read) before the next begins (Sinclair's challenging idea of encapsulation may be relevant here: see Sinclair 2004: 14f. and discussion in Toolan 2007). And by 'straightforward telling' I do not necessarily mean a chronological telling in which events are reported strictly in their order of assumed occurrence: in fact we have already seen that the story departs from that simplest ordering in its first sentence; and besides, even among the five sentences reformat-ted immediately above, we can see that the third reports what was already the case even before Trudy got home, while the fourth reports a habitual or recurrent practice, not tied to any particular evening. By 'straightforward' I mean that in adopting a texture that is predominantly simple sentences, with limited *grammatical* cross-clause linkage, the telling advances by easy steps (easy to compose, easy to process), rather than by this larger kind of 'stride' (difficult to compose, difficult to process):

> She waited, Kate Croy, for her father to come in, but he kept her unconscion-ably, and there were moments at which she showed herself, in the glass over

the mantel, a face positively pale with the irritation that had brought her to the point of going away without sight of him. It was at this point, however, that she remained; changing her place, moving from the shabby sofa to the armchair upholstered in a glazed cloth that gave at once – she had tried it – the sense of the slippery and of the sticky.

(Henry James, *The Wings of a Dove*)

To be sure, the James passage still advances by compound sentences, but there is a depth of embedding in the long extraposed subject noun-phrase 'moments at which she showed herself, in the glass over the mantel, a face positively pale with the irritation that had brought her to the point of going away without sight of him' unlike anything in the Munro opening. The embedding is chiefly a matter of recursive relativization, finite or non-finite ('at which she showed herself ...'; 'a face [that was] positively pale ...'; 'the irritation that had brought her ...'; 'the point of going away ...'). And one of the things we can say about restrictive relative clause constructions is that they invariably supply more information about entities that have *already* been named, so in that sense they are non-dynamic: they add more informative depth to an already reported event or situation rather than reporting a new situation or event. This is very much borne out by paragraph seven of the Munro passage: in this relative-clause-heavy paragraph, there is a strong sense of scenic pause, relative to surrounding paragraphs. We are not told this explicitly, but we infer that Trudy is scanning Robin's entire messy room, like a camera pan, and what is described is what she sees. At first items are reported with some locational specificity (the clothes are on the floor, or on the chair, and so on; the posters are on the wall); but by the fifth sentence we are given a random listing (without a main verb for the sentence), and left to guess quite where the dirty glasses, the school notes, and so on, are precisely situated. In short there is a rhythm and a contrast here, between the steady onward drive of the first six paragraphs (somewhat resumed in eight and nine) and the hiatus, where Trudy takes in the 'primal scene' of Robin's bedroom, in paragraph seven. The grammar and content – and how we are to take the content – all fit.

In the foregoing I have not intended to imply that a sentence that is grammatically simple or compound in structure is inevitably simple to process; I have only wished to suggest that the contrast between simple and complex *in clause structure* is a relevant part of the picture of what makes for ease, smoothness, rapidity, dynamism – and all their opposites – in the reading of literary narrative. A simple sentence could present much complexity of processing, if, for example, it contained elaborate (but non-clausal) phrase-structure within its subject and object noun-phrases. But that would be a matter of phrasal, not clausal, structure; and only the latter has been my focus here.

To give an admittedly extreme example of the emphasis on coordination and compounding and simplicity of narration and processing entailed in the bulk of the extract, I would cite the following:

The jug and the cups were supposed to be for sake, but the local liquor store doesn't carry sake.

It takes a certain kind of literary confidence, about the tone that you wish a passage to project, to write sentences of such seemingly artless inconsequentiality and repetitiveness. What is the tone and effect that is achieved by this and other recyclings ('She entered the house in the dark. Just the little stove light was on. It was gone ... She had known it would be gone')? I have proposed two answers: conversationality of tone, and an emphasis on steady, incremental narration, of one event or fact at a time (even if the facts or events narrated are being reported a second or third time). These in turn may give rise to other broader implicatures, such as that the narration is direct and immediate rather than detached and rehearsed, that it comes *as if* from Trudy's perspective and is expressive of her direct involvement in what is narrated. Little touches of free indirect thought (see Leech and Short, Chapter 10, and Bray, this volume), such as the 'Of course' of paragraph 4, reflect that immediacy and character-aligned involvement. And with the dominant steady onward flow of subordination-free clauses, a sense of urgency and movement is created, entirely congruent with events: you hear about girls putting valuables in another girl's coffin, you bet your daughter has done the same, you get off work, you come home, get up on a chair to grab the jug, the necklace is gone of course, you storm into Robin's room, she shams, you flip and you throw the jug at her. This is Trudy's and Robin's 'danger of death' narrative, of the time Trudy 'could have killed' Robin with that jug, in her anger about the necklace. That's what happened and what needs to be told (or admitted, in conversation), and Munro's clause- and sentence-structure choices do that as effectively as one could imagine. Literature or creative writing students who shut their minds to pondering at least some of this, by deciding that clause- and sentence- analysis is too technical or irrelevant, are missing an opportunity to examine and explore.

Acknowledgement

I am grateful to Nina Nørgaard for helpful comments on an earlier version of this chapter.

CHAPTER 18

Detective Fiction, Plot Construction, and Reader Manipulation: Rhetorical Control and Cognitive Misdirection in Agatha Christie's *Sparkling Cyanide*

CATHERINE EMMOTT AND MARC ALEXANDER

1. Introduction

Detective fiction provides cognitive stylisticians with a prime example of how an author can manipulate readers for plot purposes. Agatha Christie is widely recognized as the 'Queen of Crime' (e.g. Haining 1990: 11f.), and *Sparkling Cyanide* (1955 [1945]) is one of her classic detective stories, serving in this chapter as a case study of the 'whodunit' genre. Psychology research shows readers to be highly selective in focusing their attention on specific aspects of a text and not noticing other aspects (Sanford and Garrod 1981; Sanford and Sturt 2002). We argue that Christie's skill in writing this novel lies in cognitive misdirection, since she focuses attention on a small group of characters as suspects for the crimes, whilst information about the main murderer is presented as background detail which is apparently of no significance to the murder inquiry. Christie also distracts attention by time-consuming and puzzling 'red herrings'.

Christie's technique plays on the cognitive limitations of her readers. Readers who follow her rhetorical lead in *Sparkling Cyanide* may not even consider the main murderer as a suspect, hence being totally surprised by the resolution. The plot of the book is so convoluted that we view it as highly unlikely that readers would be able to guess not only 'whodunit', but also how and why.

In *Sparkling Cyanide*, characters in the story are so mystified by events surrounding one of the murders that they refer to it as a 'conjuring trick' (p. 117).[1] Using cognitive stylistic tools, we will show that the real conjurer is Agatha Christie, who uses her rhetorical skills to control readers' attention, hence cognitively misdirecting readers.

2. Cognitive stylistic tools to analyse reader manipulation

2.1. Contextual frames and character constructs

We draw on contextual frame theory (Emmott 1997) to show how Agatha Christie focuses attention on certain characters and deflects attention from others. Contextual frame theory proposes that we retain knowledge of all the characters mentioned in a novel in a mental representation termed a *central directory*, suggesting that:

> In a detective novel ... each fresh piece of evidence may cause the reader to run through their mental listing of the suspects to determine whether this evidence makes each character more or less likely to be the guilty person.
>
> (Emmott 1997: 220)

In the current chapter we refine this model by distinguishing between the central directory (the full list) and the *suspect list*, a sublist consisting of those characters who are judged to have the personality, motive, and/or opportunity to commit the crime. Christie's trick in *Sparkling Cyanide* is to keep her main murderer off the suspect list, which is the primary source of information for solving the crime, then, at the finale, she reveals that the main murderer was in fact one of the non-suspects. We will see later how Christie rhetorically controls who is on the suspect list and who is a non-suspect.

Contextual frame theory is also relevant in keeping track of who is present at the murder scene, since contextual frames monitor the presence of characters in a specific location. Where characters are known by the reader to be together in a context, they are referred to as being *bound* within that context. Bound characters are sub-classified as follows. Where the reader is currently actively monitoring that context (i.e. observing events unfold), the characters are referred to as *primed*: where they are in another context away from the reader's focus of attention, they are referred to as *unprimed* (ibid.: 125).

The two murders in *Sparkling Cyanide* both take place in the same restaurant and so the issue of who is present or absent at the dinner table is central to the murder investigation in terms of determining the suspect list. However, there is also a broader issue of who is in the general vicinity. Emmott suggests that:

> Our real-world knowledge of spatial constraints also controls our assumptions about how likely it is that other characters will enter the context. Sometimes it will be impossible for characters to enter the current [primed] context because they are bound into a frame set in a distant physical location. Sometimes characters may be sufficiently near that they can be assumed to be able to enter a context easily.
>
> (Emmott 1997: 130)

In this chapter, we will term these assumptions *proximity assumptions*. As a general rule, people are more surprised to meet someone in the street who they believe to be abroad, than someone who they know is currently based in that city, although the exact nature and strength of such assumptions can be modified by circumstances. We will see later that Christie draws on this type of proximity assumption to shield her main murderer from suspicion.

We will also add some additional categorization of contextual frames here. In *Sparkling Cyanide*, there is a series of *replicated contextual frames*. Replicated contextual frames are different but parallel frames (as opposed to *frame replays* which are the same scene shown more than once). As we will see later, the two murders take place at two dinner parties, the latter a deliberate attempt by one of the characters to replicate the first. There is also a later simulation by the murder investigators of the events that occurred at the second dinner party, which is a replication of a more schematic nature. Characters and readers, rightly or wrongly, often draw parallels between events in replicated frames, seeing connections that might or might not actually be there.

Also relevant to this story are *frame reconstructions*, where details are added to a contextual frame after it has occurred. Since we never see the first murder in *Sparkling Cyanide* (it occurs before the story starts), it is created entirely from after-the-event frame reconstructions. The second murder is presented to us first as a primed frame where we 'witness' events ourselves, but then we later acquire extra knowledge of events as eyewitnesses provide additional details, producing frame reconstructions as they give their evidence. Again, the reconstructions are after-the-event as additional evidence is subsequently given by suspects and witnesses in police interviews (the alternative technique would be to provide a replay of the scene with extra details). When we look at this as text analysts, we can see that the initial primed contextual frame that we felt we were 'witnessing' as readers must have been somewhat partial in its presentation, but we may not be aware of this at the time since it is in the nature of text often not to spell out every detail of every action. We suggest that whether information is given in the initial primed frame or in later reconstruction(s) may make a difference to the type and degree of attention readers give to it, and that splitting information between these frames may make it more difficult for readers to understand exactly what has happened. These factors may be significant in cases where a detective story writer is trying to confuse readers.

Contextual frame theory offers another cognitive stylistic tool, that of the *character construct* (Emmott 1997). Character constructs are mental representations storing all the information we acquire about characters as we read a text, including their attributes, their relations to other characters, and a record of the contexts in which they appear. We suggest in the current article that our awareness of characters' attributes may be increased by repetition and also increased/decreased depending on whether information is presented as the main discourse focus or as background information. Information in the character construct can also be presented reliably or unreliably. These points are discussed in Section 2.2.

In addition to drawing on contextual frame theory, we will use the notion of scenario-dependence from psychology, as proposed by Sanford and Garrod (1981, 1998; Anderson et al. 1983) and utilized in our previous stylistic work (Emmott 2003; Alexander 2006, 2008; Emmott et al. [in press]). Sanford and Garrod's scenario-mapping and focus model is an empirically tested psycholinguistic version of schema theory (e.g. Minsky's [1975] frames and Schank and Abelson's [1977] scripts). Sanford and Garrod distinguish between *principal characters*, who are the fully developed characters in a story, and *scenario-dependent characters*, who are simply playing a specific role in an institutional location, such as a waiter in a restaurant. Scenario-dependent characters tend to be taken for granted and may be hardly noticed by readers if performing their stereotypical role with little extra detail being given. This can be exploited by detective writers, since if a murderer is a scenario-dependent character, we may be less likely to notice him/her. However, it has been shown empirically (Sanford and Garrod 1981: 171–2) that if extra detail is given about a scenario-dependent character, it is possible to make readers more attentive to this individual. Both the taken-for-granted nature of scenario-dependent characters and their upgrading by extra information is utilized by Agatha Christie in *Sparkling Cyanide* in relation to different types of waiter at the murder scenes, as we shall see later. Christie also uses other *scenario-background characters*, as we term them here, meaning characters who are (apparently) not principal characters and who are not fulfilling an institutional role, but are simply part of the general background. These are the (initially) unidentified guests at nearby tables in the restaurant, who we would expect not to attract much attention, as will also be discussed later.

2.2. Rhetorical control

Christie uses the following main rhetorical techniques to misdirect readers from the story's eventual solution.

2.2.1. Burying information to encourage shallow processing

Psychologists have shown that readers process text in a very selective fashion (Sanford and Garrod 1981). The term *depth of processing* is used to describe varying levels of attention to different parts of a text (e.g. Sanford 2002; Sanford and Sturt 2002). More specifically, the term *shallow processing* is used when attention is low and details are not properly absorbed (e.g. Sanford and Graesser [eds] 2006; A. J. S. Sanford et al. 2006). In *Sparkling Cyanide*, when plot details have been kept out of the main spotlight of attention, Christie's detectives can claim that all the information for determining the solution was available, even though it had been previously buried. Rhetorical tricks are used, such as embedding plot information grammatically within a subordinate clause or placing it in the middle of a list of unimportant details. Such tricks work because a phrase is 'particularly difficult to challenge, and therefore is particularly effective as manipulation, when it is not the main point of the clause' (Thompson and Hunston 2000: 8; see also Hoey 2000: 33). Psychologists have provided empirical evidence for this in relation to subordinate clauses, since they have shown that readers detect falsehoods less easily in these structures than in main clauses (Baker and Wagner 1987; Cooreman and Sanford 1996).

In addition to grammatical placement in a specific sentence, readers may be encouraged to view details as background description rather than as relevant to the main plot, even though these details subsequently turn out to be plot-crucial. Hence, readers are guided by the local discourse to extract the main *rhetorical point* at the time,[2] but may thereby overlook facts which are drawn on to support a later rhetorical point as the detectives argue for their overall interpretation of the case. In *Sparkling Cyanide* key details about the main murderer's location are repeated many times throughout the story, but this information is presented as if it has no relevance to the murder investigation. Readers may not see the significance of the information as they attempt to solve the mystery themselves, but the repetition may make the information sufficiently memorable for it to be drawn on later by the detectives as they present their solution.

2.2.2. *Using supposedly reliable characters to vouch for the reliability of other characters*

The notions of *reliability* and *unreliability* were used by Booth (1991 [1961]) to describe whether the commentary of a narrator is trustworthy. We will use these terms more generally to describe the trustworthiness of characters.

Zunshine (2006) has employed the notion of 'metarepresentation' (derived from Cosmides and Tooby [2000]) to describe the way in which readers may monitor the sources of information represented in their cognitive models of fictional worlds. Zunshine points out that some information is stored 'under various degrees of advisement' (p. 60), particularly if the source is suspect. As Tamir-Ghez (1979) says, in a narrative 'the different speakers can omit relevant information about characters, events, atmosphere, ideas, etc., and they can distort, misinterpret or misrepresent them' (p. 69).

In detective fiction the trick is to make readers believe untrustworthy information. Normally, we might be dubious about information provided by characters who are suspects in a murder, but we can be guided towards not questioning what they say. One way to do this is to get the detectives, who are assumed to be reliable due to their professional status, to vouch for the reliability of these witnesses and their evidence. This *reliability vouching* takes the form 'A is (supposedly) reliable, A says/thinks B is reliable, therefore B is assumed to be reliable'. Nevertheless, the detectives are in fact fallible until the solution is determined, so their opinions can subsequently be shown to be wrong. In the meantime, readers can be pushed into wrongly evaluating unreliable evidence, or unreliable characters, as reliable.

2.2.3. *Setting false trails as a distraction to readers*

Red herrings are a well known reader-distraction technique. A red herring is a device to confuse readers, providing a false trail for readers to follow and thereby masking the correct solution. Large quantities of text are devoted to information which ultimately has no relevance, and these false trails may draw heavily on the cognitive resources of readers by actively presenting puzzles to be solved. Red herrings can be made additionally plausible by the detectives taking a red herring seriously (another instance of a detective vouching for the reliability of information, as described in 2.2.2).

2.2.4. *Final authentication of the solution*

At the end of the story, readers need to become convinced of the hidden solution presented to them by the detective. Believing this conclusion over any alternatives, and having it cohere with what has been presented earlier in the narrative, is a key part of making the story and its solution acceptable to readers. One option is for detective writers to rely on the mechanics of the fictional world. Hence, they may present events which support the conclusion, such as a convenient full confession by the murderer. In *Sparkling Cyanide*, this type of support comes from the murderer's accomplice being assumed to be guilty due to having tried to commit a further murder. Another option is for the author to manipulate the discourse, resorting to rhetorical tricks to make the solution more palatable to readers (Alexander 2006: 44f., 63f.). So we may be told that the detective's solution is clever or we may see the characters convinced by it. An author may also rely on the fact that readers are unlikely to remember exact details, and then present information in the final summary in a rather different light than it appeared in the main story. In addition, questionable elements in the explanation may be buried in the same way as important information is downgraded in earlier parts of the novel (see 2.2.1).

Sparkling Cyanide's solution is not entirely satisfactory when looked at closely since it fails to account fully for the details of the first murder, and since the events surrounding the second murder are difficult to believe if we stop to think about them. However, the solution is made more acceptable to readers by all the techniques described above.

3. The plot

Although we will present a standard plot summary, there are a number of reasons why no plot summary can be adequate to the task of explaining this novel:

1. Our main argument is that a reader's understanding of plot lies in rhetorical manipulations as much as in the plot events, so the plot summary must be complemented by our subsequent discussion of the rhetorical techniques.
2. The plot requires readers to view events from different perspectives at different stages in the book. Hence, this plot summary relies on retrospective knowledge to highlight events which are later important, but might not seem at all important at the time of reading.
3. Conversely, events which seem important on first reading may have little or no relevance to the murder inquiry. Since the plot is complex, we omit much of the 'red herring' information from the plot summary, but will return to it in the later discussion.

Plot summary

Rosemary Barton has apparently committed suicide, nearly a year before the story commences, by drinking champagne containing cyanide at a dinner party at the Luxembourg restaurant. The case has been closed, but we

later have reason to suspect that it is murder [*Murder I*]. Present at the dinner party were six other people: George Barton (Rosemary's husband), Iris
Marle (Rosemary's teenage sister), Anthony Browne, Stephen Farraday, Lady
Alexandra Farraday, and Ruth Lessing (George's secretary). In the first part
of the book (Book I, pp. 5–63), these six are presented to us in turn and each
appears to have a motive for murdering Rosemary.

Throughout the first half of the book (pp. 5–96), we are given information
that appears to be background detail and it is only at the end of the book that
we realize its significance for the murder inquiry. Rosemary was rich and left
all her money to her sister, Iris. Iris now lives with Rosemary's ex-husband
George, together with Iris's aunt, Lucilla Drake. Lucilla is constantly pes-
tered for money by her son Victor, the 'black sheep' of the family. Victor is
apparently abroad for much of the story, sent there by George as a way of
keeping him out of trouble in Britain.

During the first half of the book, George receives an anonymous letter which
suggests that Rosemary's death was murder, not suicide. He arranges a second
dinner at the Luxembourg, with the remaining guests from the first party.
This is the scene for *Murder II* (Chapter Six of Book II, pp. 97–100). The
party is ostensibly for Iris's birthday, but George plans to shock the murderer
into revealing him/herself. The guests sit round a large table, with Iris next to
George. Nearby sit two couples at smaller tables. After the meal and cabaret,
there is a sequence of events which later mystifies the characters (the so-called
'conjuring trick').[3] George proposes a birthday toast to Iris and the toast is
drunk. Everyone at the table then gets up to dance and the glasses are not
refilled. On their return to the table, George proposes a remembrance toast to
the dead Rosemary. On drinking, George falls dead, poisoned by cyanide in
the champagne. This sequence of events is puzzling because George appears
to drink twice from his glass, only falling dead on the second occasion.

The second half of the book (Book III, pp. 101–87) comprises the investigation of Murder II (with some reference to the parallel Murder I), the denouement and final explanation. The investigation is conducted by Colonel Race
(a former secret service agent), Chief Inspector Kemp (a police officer), and
Anthony Browne (revealed to be a secret service agent who has been working
under cover). Various people give evidence and confirm that no one, except a
junior waiter, approached the table in the period between the two toasts. The
waiters are considered to be above suspicion by the investigators.

The denouement reveals that the 'conjuring trick' was in fact an accident. The intended victim of Murder II was Iris, with George being killed
by mistake. As the couples danced between two toasts, the junior waiter had
picked up Iris's handbag, which had fallen on the floor, and had accidentally
replaced it by the wrong seat, one position round. Consequently Iris unknowingly moved round a seat, as did all the other guests, with George occupying

Iris's seat and drinking from what had been her glass. Iris's glass had in fact been poisoned during the cabaret, not the later dance (making all the evidence about what happened during the two toasts irrelevant). The poisoning of the champagne went unnoticed during the first toast because Iris, being the recipient of the toast, was the one person not to drink. George later drank the poisoned champagne during the second toast.

At the denouement, Anthony Browne performs a simulation of the 'conjuring trick' and reveals that, as Iris was the intended victim, her life is in danger. It becomes apparent that a recent accident, where she was nearly run over, was *Attempted Murder III*. Anthony and the other detectives rush to rescue her as *Attempted Murder IV* is in progress, Iris being found knocked unconscious near the open jet of a gas fire.

Anthony and Colonel Race provide the following explanation of Murder II as follows: Victor Drake, the black sheep, is the main murderer and his accomplice is Ruth Lessing, George's secretary. Victor had not really been abroad at the time of the murders – Ruth had previously claimed to have seen him board the ship but had lied due to having fallen in love with him when sent by George to dispatch him abroad. Victor has in fact been in the restaurant sat at one of the nearby tables, disguised as a middle-aged foreigner, Pedro Morales. During the cabaret, preceding the two toasts, Victor/Pedro has left his table, dressed up as a waiter, and served the poisoned champagne.

Attempted Murders III and IV were committed by Ruth, the former causing her to be suspected and the latter identifying her as guilty. The real circumstances behind Murder I, Rosemary's death, are glossed over by Christie, but it seems that Victor was again responsible, with Ruth again an accomplice. The motive for Victor was money; and for Ruth money, love for Victor, and hatred of Rosemary. When Rosemary died, she left her money to Iris. If Iris had died before marrying, her money would have gone to her aunt, Lucilla Drake, who is her next-of-kin. Since Victor is easily able to acquire money from his mother, the money would eventually have passed to Victor.

4. Cognitive-rhetorical misdirection in *Sparkling Cyanide*

In explaining the plot, our aim is to focus on rhetorical manipulations. There will be points at which readers are tricked by events in the story and thereby cognitively misdirected, but our interest as cognitive stylisticians lies primarily in cases where the language and/or overall text prominence play a major role in the trick, which we will refer to as *cognitive-rhetorical misdirection*.

Sparkling Cyanide is famous for its apparent 'conjuring trick', the accidentally moved dinner places described above. This provides cognitive misdirection by disguising both the intended victim of Murder II (Iris, not George) and the time of the poisoning of the champagne (during the earlier cabaret, not between the toasts). This is a neat twist, but the manipulation owes more to the unusual events than to rhetorical factors. We will therefore focus the majority of our discussion on the presentation of characters, since this seems to be the main rhetorical manipulation, returning to the 'conjuring trick' briefly at the end for the sake of completeness.

4.1. The characters in general: the suspect list, witness reliability, and red herrings

One of the main ways that Christie controls our attention in relation to the characters in *Sparkling Cyanide* is by her rhetorical management of the suspect list, using the following techniques:

i. Text quantity and position – Each of the characters from the first dinner party (Murder I) is introduced in their own chapter at the start of the novel. These introductions take up the whole of Book I (pp. 5–63). At the outset they are not actually suspects since Rosemary's death is thought to be suicide, but they are given main-character status and linked with the night of her death.

ii. Overt narratological statements – These statements emphasize the centrality of certain individuals. The opening sentence of the book is 'Six people were thinking of Rosemary Barton who had died nearly a year ago.' (p. 5). Also, at the start of the Murder II scene we are told, foregrounded in a mini-paragraph, 'They had all come.' (p. 97), and shortly afterwards 'They were all there ...' (p. 97).

iii. Explicit statements about suspects – The characters overtly refer to the suspect list. The police mention 'suspects' (p. 103) and there are several statements by other characters, which limit the suspects to the characters in the dining party, for example:

> '... *If* Rosemary was killed, one of those people round the table, one of our friends, must have done it ...' (pp. 83–4, Christie's italics)[4]

iv. Explicit statements about the number of suspects – The above quotation presupposes that there is only one guilty person, whereas in fact there are two. On other occasions too, we are told that it is 'one of them' (p. 102, see also pp. 133 and 162). Agatha Christie thereby exploits the 'only one murderer assumption'.

v. Explicit exclusion of characters as suspects – We are told that 'no-one – no-one at all came near the table while they were away' (p. 115). Also, as we will see later, the waiters are explicitly stated not to be suspects, but this is a rhetorical strategy rather than due to any real evidence for their exclusion.

Another control strategy is to explicitly tag evidence as reliable or unreliable. The evidence of Pedro's dining partner, Christine Shannon, provides an example. When she gives evidence, the police repeatedly vouch for her reliability:

> '... That girl's the right kind of witness. Sees things and remembers them accurately. If there had been anything to see, she'd have seen it ...'
>
> (pp. 116–17)

Christine gives her evidence in good faith, but she does not notice the crucial fact that Victor/Pedro has disguised himself as a waiter and has poisoned the champagne. This happened during the cabaret when the lights were down and the diners were focusing on the acts (Christine is asked about what she saw during the dancing, not during the cabaret). We have been rhetorically guided here to adopt a particular evaluation of Christine's evidence.

Christie also manipulates readers by introducing red herrings. Two examples of major red herrings in this novel are (i) the possible guilt of all the suspects on the suspect list except Ruth, the murderer's accomplice, and (ii) the puzzle of whether Rosemary's lover was Stephen Farraday or Anthony Browne.[5] An additional distraction is the suspenseful episode in the final chapters as Anthony and the other detectives rush to save Iris's life during Attempted Murder IV. The length, excitement, and strategic placement of this episode might be argued to deflect attention from the somewhat unsatisfactory final explanation of the solution to the murders.

4.2. Victor the murderer: Christie's exercise in burying information

4.2.1. Victor as a background character

Christie's main rhetorical trick in *Sparkling Cyanide* is to bury the fact that Victor is a key character and that he is in the vicinity. At the denouement, Anthony comments on Victor as follows:

> '... And there is nothing difficult about seeing Victor as First Murderer. All along, from the very start of the case, there have been references to Victor, mentions of Victor. He has been in the offing, a shadowy, unsubstantial, evil figure.'
>
> (p. 183)

This is typical of Christie's persuasive method at the denouement, suggesting that the solution has been obvious all along, when actually it has not. We argue that it is difficult even to consider Victor as the first murderer. He is so much in the background, that it is unlikely that readers will suspect him. There are certainly plenty of references to Victor, but he is a minor character from his first introduction:

> In the meantime, the first thing to settle was [Iris's] place of residence. Mr George Barton had shown himself anxious for her to continue living with him and had suggested that her father's sister, Mrs Drake, who was in impoverished circumstances owing to the financial claims of <u>a son (the black sheep of the Marle family)</u>, should make her home with them and chaperon Iris in society. Did Iris approve of this plan?
>
> (p. 12, our underlining)

This introduction is embedded in a chapter devoted to introducing Iris (her name is given as the chapter heading) and the main rhetorical point here is Iris's place of residence, not Victor. Mention of Victor is further embedded by the grammatical structure, by being placed in a relative clause describing Mrs Drake. The question at the end of this paragraph is a focusing device putting the main emphasis on Iris. Victor is incidental here and on many subsequent occasions, being presented simply as a minor nuisance.

Anthony's final explanation, quoted above, states that Victor 'has been in the offing' (which we assume means that he has been presented as potentially involved in the murder). Again, this later representation is a rhetorical distortion of how the earlier text presented events, in this case the earlier handling of frame proximity information. The repeated mentions of Victor reinforce the supposed fact that he is not present, hence eliminating him as a potential suspect. We are constantly reminded that he is abroad by direct statements of characters and by the arrival of cables. In particular, there are several mentions of his supposed overseas location strategically placed immediately before the crucial Murder II scene. He has been sent abroad by ship and any return by the same means of transport would not be rapid, so we might assume him to be beyond consideration (bearing in mind that Christie is writing before the age of mass air travel).

Anthony's final explanation also describes Victor as evil. In one key scene (where he first meets Ruth), there have been comments that he has 'the strength of the devil. He could make evil seem amusing' (p. 34) and that he is (by his own admission) 'Wicked, perhaps' (p. 33). However, the overall presentation is more that of a petty criminal than a potential murderer (e.g. 'damned swindling young crook' [p. 91]).[6] His negative attributes are also apparently mitigated by statements of his charm (e.g. 'an agreeable devilry' [p. 32]) and his mother's descriptions of him as a 'dear boy' (pp. 66, 90, and 137).[7] His negative attributes make him a plausible murderer at the end of the novel, but do not in themselves suggest this during the case.

4.2.2. *Victor in disguise*

Victor disguises himself as Pedro to dine in the restaurant and then disguises himself as a waiter in order to commit Murder II. This physical disguise is facilitated by rhetorical backgrounding.

Pedro appears in the murder scene as an unnamed scenario-background figure, since he is just another guest in the restaurant:

> <u>A middle-aged sallow foreigner</u> and a blonde lovely were at one [nearby table], a slip of a boy and a girl at the other.
>
> (p. 97, our underlining)

We hear nothing more of this character whilst the Murder II frame is primed, only learning his name during the investigation. His companion, Christine, tells us more about him during a later frame reconstruction, when she gives evidence:

> 'But of course someone might have gone to the table without your noticing?'
>
> But Christine shook her head very determinedly.
>
> 'No, I'm quite sure they didn't. <u>You see Pedro had been called to the telephone and hadn't got back yet</u>, so I had nothing to do but look around and feel bored. I'm pretty good at noticing things and from where I was sitting there wasn't much else to see but the empty table next to us.'
>
> (p. 116, our underlining)

Victor/Pedro has left to assume the disguise of a waiter, crucial information that needs to be buried to avoid alerting readers to the correct solution. Pedro is retrospectively bound out of the dinner party frame, meaning that we are told he has left after he has gone, rather than any emphasis being put on his actual exit or the timing of his departure. The information is also embedded within the frame reconstruction, rather than being shown in the original primed murder frame, which might attract more attention to it. Furthermore, the main rhetorical point is that Christine is alone and therefore able to observe events around her, so the focus of attention is not on Pedro's whereabouts.

As far as Victor's character construct is concerned, Christie builds up Victor's attributes so that he is distinct from Pedro. Victor is described as young and handsome, and he is repeatedly referred to as a boy by his mother (see 4.2.1). By contrast, Pedro is presented as middle-aged and unattractive. Victor's 'lean brown face' (p. 32) becomes 'sallow' in the description of Pedro (p. 97). In addition to this, Pedro is presented simply as a witness, with no suggestion that we should consider him as a suspect. After Pedro is interviewed, he intends to leave the country. Our proximity assumptions may then make him a less actively considered central directory character. Of course, being abroad does not mean that he could not have previously committed a murder when in the country, but the issue here is which characters the reader is actively focusing attention on.

We never actually see Victor dressed as a waiter, so his physical attributes are irrelevant then. It is his scenario-dependent status there which disguises him (see the discussion of the waiters below). In the final explanation, Colonel Race claims that only someone who had actually been a professional waiter could successfully fill the part (p. 184). This attribute of Victor has been mentioned previously, but is firmly buried in the middle of a list of occupations:

> 'I enjoy myself immensely. I've seen a good deal of life, Ruth. I've done almost everything. I've been an actor and a storekeeper and <u>a waiter</u> and an odd job man, and a luggage porter, and a property man in a circus! I've sailed before the mast in a tramp steamer. I've been in the running for President in a South American Republic. I've been in prison! ...'
>
> (pp. 33–4, our underlining)

This list culminates with items that are far more likely to gain attention. Also, the main rhetorical point is Victor's enjoyment of life rather than the skills acquired in these jobs. Later Victor's jobs are mentioned again, but the use of narrative report of a speech act (Leech and Short 2007) ('... here followed a list of Victor's varied occupations' [p. 137]) means the exact details are not disclosed.

4.3. Ruth the accomplice – Christie's presentation of an unreliable witness

Ruth has an obvious motive to murder Rosemary since she hates her. However, the police cannot link her to the murder, because her position at the Murder II dinner table would have made it 'practically impossible' (p. 162) for her to commit that crime. Her role is as an accomplice to Victor, lying about his whereabouts so that we believe him to be abroad. She is therefore an unreliable witness, as Anthony reveals at the denouement:

> '... all the evidence for Victor's being in South America depends on Ruth's word. None of it was verified because it was never a main issue! ...'
>
> (p. 183)

As stated here, there was no reason for the characters or readers to suspect Ruth's word because Victor seems to be irrelevant to the murder inquiry. In addition, readers are pushed towards accepting Ruth's word when one of the investigators rather oddly vouches for her reliability shortly before the point at which she gives evidence about sending Victor abroad:

> 'Yes, Miss Lessing? I'm sure your impressions will be accurate.'
>
> (p. 130)

Ruth also lies in her evidence about contacting George's overseas agent about Victor, immediately prior to Murder II. Again there is a comment about her reliability when she is questioned by one of the investigators:

> Ruth [went] over the events of the morning – George's annoyance over Victor's importunity, her own telephone calls to South America and the arrangements made and George's pleasure when the matter was settled. She then described her arrival at the Luxembourg and George's flurried excited bearing as host. She carried her narrative up to the final moment of the tragedy. <u>Her account tallied in every respect with those he had already heard</u>.
>
> (p. 133, our underlining)

The final sentence here may be true where Ruth's account overlaps with those of other witnesses, but as Anthony tells us in his final explanation, we only have her word for the information about the overseas telephone calls, which is therefore unverified.

During the episode in which Ruth gives evidence, Christie not only makes her appear reliable when she is giving unreliable information, but also distracts us by putting considerable emphasis on other evidence. Colonel Race is noticeably surprised when Ruth gives information that could implicate Alexandra Farraday, and he thinks:

> The girl looked placid and unaware of any significance in what she had said. But it *was* significant.
>
> (p. 132, Christie's italics)

This is actually a red herring, unimportant to the eventual solution.

Ruth's meeting with Victor is another episode which has to be handled carefully by Christie because it links the murderer and his accomplice. There is mention that Ruth finds Victor attractive and that she has been affected by the meeting. When we discover at the end of the story that she has fallen in love with him, this is made plausible by this episode. However, Christie distracts us from this by a description of Ruth's devotion to George immediately prior to the episode (p. 29), and by later gossip which assumes that Ruth wants to marry George (p. 65). Also, again, we are unlikely to dwell on the episode because of Victor's apparent irrelevance to the murder investigation. At the denouement, Anthony again attempts to rhetorically manipulate the reader, this time by providing some dubious generalizations in order to justify Ruth's sudden infatuation with Victor and her change in personality ('Those quiet, level-headed, law-abiding women are the kind that often fall for a real bad lot' [p. 183] and 'every murderess was a nice girl once' [p. 185]).

4.4. *The waiters – Christie's handling of scenario-dependent characters*

There are two categories of 'waiters' in the novel; real waiters, and Victor/Pedro, the murderer disguised as a waiter. Those of the first category would normally be typical scenario-dependent characters, which would make them less noticeable and hence less likely to be suspected. However, in this case Christie adds extra attributes, which psychology research has shown to make us more aware of these characters (see Section 2.1). In particular, Giuseppe Bolsano, the waiter pouring champagne during the meal which prefaces Murder II, is given a name, description, personality, background, wife, and children. Christie's strategy here is to present this waiter as being above suspicion by virtue of his lack of motive and high reputation. When the detectives compile the list of suspects, they discount him:

> '... It was one of [the diners] or it was the waiter, Giuseppe Bolsano ... but I can't believe he had anything to do with it ...'
>
> (p. 102, see also p. 162 for a similar statement)

Another real waiter, Pierre (the junior waiter who had moved Iris's bag), is interrogated, but subsequently discounted. He is also given special status as the nephew of the head waiter at the Luxembourg, being described as:

> '... a little waiter who was of the royal line of waiters – a cherubic waiter – a waiter above suspicion. And he's still above suspicion ...'
>
> (p. 175)

Victor is in a different category, because he is not a waiter at the Luxembourg at all, although he has previously worked as a waiter. The entire plot hinges on his perception by the other characters as being one of the staff, and ignored as such due to his scenario-dependence:

> '[Victor] Drake had been an actor and he had been something more impor-tant – a *waiter* ... as a *bona fide* waiter none of you noticed or saw him. You were

looking at the cabaret, not noticing that portion of the restaurant's furnishings – the waiter!'

(p. 184, Christie's italics)

Here the fact that there were several waiters attending the table is partially
addressed by the reference to 'furnishings', which presumes that waiters are
not noticed by the characters and that this is a natural state of affairs. We
only learn of Victor's appearance as a waiter in a reconstructed frame, as the
solution is presented. Victor then occupies the slot of the champagne-pouring
waiter which was previously filled by the above-reproach Giuseppe. In this
way, the eventual murderer is concealed by having his crucial scenario role
slot, his opportunity to commit the murder, occupied and blocked by a character who was never under active suspicion by the investigators.

4.5. The dinner party seat change – the accidental 'conjuring trick'

As we have already pointed out, the accidental 'conjuring trick' is an important event in terms of deflecting attention in the investigation. In his final
explanation, Anthony suggests that the detectives have overlooked a linguistic issue, the possible ambiguity of the phrase 'George's glass'. George drinks
out of 'his glass' before and after the cyanide is added, but afterwards it is a
different glass, the one that was previously Iris's. Anthony labours this point,
making it into a major rhetorical display (lasting over a page in the novel
[pp. 181–2]). However, Christie's trick would have worked just as well if she
had repeatedly used an expression such as 'George toasted Iris/Rosemary'
rather than a possessive, so this designation of the glass is somewhat irrelevant. We might argue that, viewed cynically, this lengthy linguistic analysis[8]
by Christie allows her to distract us from considering how no one at this table
notices that every place has moved round by one.

Of more relevance, perhaps, is the fact that a discourse can lack full detail
when describing a primed context. In the presentation of the scene of Murder
II (Book II, Chapter 6), we are not told that Iris's bag is left by the table
as she dances, or that a waiter picks it up and moves it to a different place.
Indeed we are not even told in this scene that Iris has a bag. This information comes in later witness evidence, in subsequent frame reconstructions.
Splitting the presentation of the details between the primed frame and the
frame reconstructions makes it more difficult for us to piece together events
ourselves. In addition, the fact that the solution to Murder II is presented
to us in a replicated frame, a simulation of the place-switching manoeu-
vre, puts the emphasis on the success of this small-scale simulation rather
than the original dinner-party event. Anthony's self-evaluation of his final

explanation as being clever (p. 181) also pushes us towards accepting its validity.

5. Conclusion

If we were to give guidelines on how to manipulate readers in a 'whodunit' novel such as *Sparkling Cyanide*, we would include the following points:

1. Control the suspect list, keeping the main murderer off it.
2. Keep the main murderer in the background, presenting him/her as a minor character and repeatedly mentioning that he/she is far away.
3. Make a supposedly reliable character, such as one of the investigators, vouch for the reliability of unreliable characters.
4. Utilize the fact that a scenario-dependent character is unlikely to be noticed as the murderer.
5. Bury key information by grammatical embedding, by surrounding it with more interesting material, and by manipulating the overall focus of the discourse so that the buried information is not the main rhetorical point.
6. Overtly tell readers what is and is not significant in order to guide their assumption-making.
7. Distract readers with time-consuming red herrings, making them as puzzling as possible to put a cognitive load on readers.
8. Allow the details of the murder under investigation to be split across a primed frame and later frame reconstructions, hence making it difficult for readers to piece together events.
9. Provide a dramatic and suspenseful denouement, which will distract readers from any inadequacies in the explanation.
10. Demonstrate the solution on a simulation that is much simpler than the real murder situation.
11. Persuade readers to see plot details at the solution stage in a different light to how they were originally presented.
12. Tell readers that the final explanation is extremely clever and that it adequately explains earlier events.

These principles of cognitive-rhetorical misdirection work alongside physical plot features in *Sparkling Cyanide* such as disguises and the death of the wrong victim, serving to baffle readers until the finale. For the cognitive stylistician, these cognitive-rhetorical misdirections provide an indication of the ways in which readers' attention may be manipulated by persuasively upgrading and downgrading information, and selectively controlling cognitive load.

Acknowledgement

The authors are grateful to the Arts and Humanities Research Council for funding for Emmott and Sanford's STACS project (Stylistics, Text Analysis and Cognitive Science: Interdisciplinary Perspectives on the Nature of Reading) and for Alexander's M.Phil. thesis.

NOTES

1. See also pages 170, 174–5, and 182.
2. This bears some similarities to Vipond and Hunt's (1984) notion of point, but we do not make their distinction between point-driven interpretation and story-driven interpretation here. For us, there can be different rhetorical points to a piece of information at different stages of a story.
3. An earlier version of this 'conjuring trick' appeared in Christie's (1999 [1937]) 'Yellow Iris', a Poirot story.
4. See also pages 28, 102, and 162 for similar statements.
5. Other major red herrings are (i) the suggestion that Anthony Browne has a sinister occupation, before he is revealed to be a secret service officer, (ii) the erroneous attribution of an anonymous letter to a maid servant, and (iii) the hiring of an actress to impersonate the dead Rosemary at the second dinner party and the actress's failure to arrive.
6. Also, 'ne'er-do-well son' (p. 19) and 'black sheep' (pp. 12, 20, 30, 130).
7. Also, a 'poor', 'darling', 'clever', and 'affectionate, handsome' 'boy' (pp. 19, 66, 90, 91, and 137).
8. Anthony also provides a linguistic discussion of the use of the definite and indefinite articles for mentions of the waiters. Again, we view this as largely irrelevant to the main rhetorical manipulations in the story.

CHAPTER 19

Narrative and Metaphor

MONIKA FLUDERNIK

In Sir Philip Sidney's *Old Arcadia* (1580), Pyrocles falls in love with Philoclea, of whom he has seen a painting in the house of Kerxenus (Book I; 1994: 10–11):

> But when within short time he came to the degree of uncertain wishes, and that those wishes grew to unquiet longings; [...] then did poor Pyrocles yield to the burden, finding himself prisoner before he had leisure to arm himself, and that he might well, like the spaniel, gnaw upon the chain that ties him, but he should sooner mar his teeth than procure liberty.

Throughout the narrative, Pyrocles' love is figured as madness and excess. In the quoted passage, his succumbing to desire is presented in two ways, that of the warrior surprised into captivity, and of the prisoner struggling bootlessly to rid himself of his chains. The overall trope of the prison of love (*la prison amoureuse*) is here inflected in two ways, as a metaphor ('finding himself prisoner') and as a simile ('like the spaniel'). Whereas the traditional analysis of metaphors based on I. A. Richards's distinctions between the vehicle (*comparandum*), the tenor (*comparatum*), and the ground (*tertium comparationis*) (Richards [1936] 1965) can easily explain how Pyrocles is a prisoner surprised by the enemy (his love) and taken captive, it has more problems with the second image, the simile. The captive now becomes a dog fretting at its chain. Like the metaphor, the simile also focuses on Pyrocles as a captive and figures that state of bondage specifically in the chain; but the narrative imposes another layer of imagery over the chain by metonymically invoking a dog who is thus restricted.

The vocabulary of traditional metaphor studies is not well suited to dealing with this co-occurrence of metaphor proper, simile, and metonymy. Cognitive metaphor theory improves on this situation by two means. In the older version of cognitive metaphor theory (Lakoff and Johnson 1980), the terms *vehicle* and *tenor* were dropped in favour of *source* and *target domain*. Pyrocles in battle with desire is thus reconceptualized in terms of soldiers and warfare, a source domain that is projected on the lover and his emotions (target domain). More importantly, the Richardsonian ground is being dispensed with; instead, a blend (Fauconnier 1997; Fauconnier and Turner 1996, 2002; Turner and Fauconnier 1999) is established in which the common structure of the two domains ('X is overpowered by Y', called the generic space) is preserved and transported into the blend. In the blend, Pyrocles as warrior is captured unawares by an enemy force, that is, desire or love (Figure 19.1).

As one can see in Figure 19.1, there is a generic space which provides a structure linking source and target domain and results in the metaphoric blend. (The equivalences in structure are marked by dotted lines.) The individual elements of the two domains and the blend are metonymically related within a frame of the captured warrior who is imprisoned (or the lover overpowered by his feelings).

The simile can likewise be pictured as a blend. One would see Pyrocles straining against his erotic inclinations in the image of a dog fretfully chafing at his

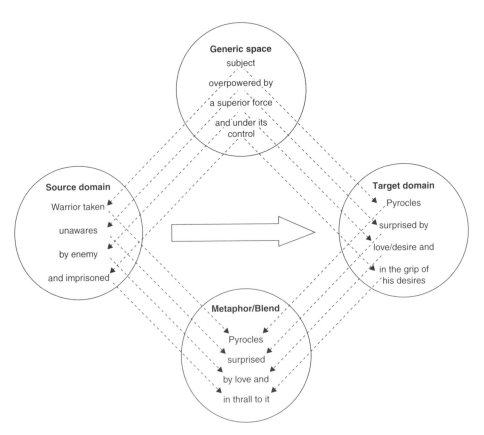

Figure 19.1: Blend for Pyrocles 'finding himself prisoner'

leash. The second major improvement of cognitive metaphor theory (including blending theory) is, therefore, its demonstration of affinities between the traditional figures of simile, metaphor, and metonymy. All three are now analysed as the result of a transfer of structure from source to target domain. In the present case, the simile-cum-metonymy focuses on Pyrocles chafing at his bonds and worrying at the metaphoric leash on which love is keeping him. Whereas the experience of being overpowered lay at the heart of the first image, the focus of the second blend is the fruitless attempt to escape one's ties. Captivity is specified in terms of restraint rather than in terms of containers. Both images focus on an experience, a *verb*, if you will, rather than on the identity of Pyrocles with either warrior or dog, although the frame of the source domain imposes this identification implicitly. Pyrocles, who is a warrior and elsewhere presented in positive heroic terms, by the agency of love behaves like a silly spaniel unable to slip his chain. The simile at least implicitly also hints at Pyrocles' effeminization. Spaniels were ladies' dogs and conceived of as ignominious creatures full of sexual lust (see Braunschneider 2006 and King 2008). Both the subjection of Pyrocles to a woman through his desires, which he cannot control, and his emasculation (inability to bite through the leash on which he finds himself) come out strongly. The double image of before and after captures Pyrocles' lapse from warrior to lapdog as a lesson against loss of control over one's emotions. The metaphorical depiction of Pyrocles fighting against his desires therefore metaphorically leads to his becoming a metaphoric lapdog – desires become leashes and leashes evoke the canine species.

Narrative and metaphor in Sidney's romance combine in exemplary fashion to articulate the moral message of the book, which is a criticism of self-indulgence. The noble pair, the two young warriors who join King Basilius in disguise, install themselves in the good graces of the king and then betray this trust by sleeping with and eloping with, respectively, his daughters. They (the warriors) are guilty of self-indulgence, as is the king himself, and this failing is closely linked to their excessive amatory dispositions (Basilius' assignation with Cleophila, that is, Pyrocles in cross-dressing; Musidorus' wooing of Pamela, Pyrocles' of Philoclea). Love turns Basilius into a being of asinine cowardice and irresponsible laziness; it likewise, as our metaphor already indicates, converts the admirable warrior Pyrocles into a contemptible spaniel and later into a woman (the Amazon Cleophila).

The status of metaphor as a litmus test of truthful prediction is, however, somewhat compromised by its use in the description of Pamela from Musidorus' perspective:

He thought *her fair forehead was a field where all his fancies fought, and every hair of her head seemed a strong chain that tied him.* Her fair lids (then hiding her fairer eyes) seemed unto him sweet boxes of *mother of pearl*, rich in themselves, but containing in them *far richer jewels*. Her cheeks, with their colour most delicately mixed, would have entertained his eyes for somewhile, but that the *roses of her lips* (whose separating was wont to be accompanied with most wise speeches) now by force drew his sight to mark how prettily they lay one over the other, uniting their divided beauties, and through them *the eye of his fancy* delivered to his memory *the lying (as in ambush) under her lips of those armed ranks, all armed in most pure white, and keeping the most precise order of military discipline*. And lest this beauty might seem the picture of some excellent artificer, forth there stake a soft breath, carrying good testimony of her inward sweetness; and so stealingly it came out as it seemed loath to leave his contentful mansion, but that it hoped to be drawn in again to *that well closed paradise*, that did so *tyrannize* over Musidorus's affects that he was compelled to put his face as low to hers as he could, sucking the breath with such joy that he did determine in himself there had been no life to a chameleon's, if he might be suffered to enjoy that food. But each of these having a mighty working in his heart, all joined together did so draw his will into the nature of their confederacy that now his promise began to have but a fainting force, and each thought that rase [*sic*] against those desires was received but as a stranger to his counsel, well experiencing in himself that no vow is so strong as the avoiding of occasions; so that rising softly from her, *overmastered with the fury of delight*, having all his senses partial against himself and inclined to his *well beloved adversary*, he was bent to take the advantage of his weakness of the watch, and see whether at that season he could *win the bulwark before timely help might come*.

(Book III; 1994: 176–7; my emphasis)

This passage starts out with a depiction of Pamela's beauty in terms of the Petrarchan love sonnet. Her beauty (as Philoclea's with Pyrocles) incites Musidorus to criminal action, namely an attempted rape, which – ironically – is only prevented through the arrival of 'a dozen clownish villains' (177), who are part of a rebellious mob. The attractions of Pamela's beauty are rendered in the imagery of precious stones ('mother of pearl', 'jewels'), flowers ('the roses of her lips'), and order (the row of her teeth as serried ranks of soldiers), and the allurement of her breath tempts Musidorus to the conquest of the 'closed paradise' of her mouth, overcoming the 'bulwark' of her virtue. Pamela's beauty, in other words, instigates Musidorus to illicit fantasy. She (literally, her forehead) becomes 'a field where all his fancies fought', and her hair (rather than being figured as gold) becomes a tool of his captivity, mutating into ropes that bind him. Thus, like Pyrocles, Musidorus lapses into sexual incontinence at the sight of a beautiful woman, and sinks into captivity. The metaphors here are clearly subjective since they are linked to what Musidorus sees ('He thought', 'seemed', 'seemed unto him', 'by force drew his sight'). It is 'the eye of his fancy' which incites him to imaginary conquest. Whereas, that is, the metaphors discussed earlier were clearly authorial (linked to the narrator), here they are inflected subjectively so that the text underlines that it is only in the infected (disturbed) mind of Musidorus that Pamela appears thus. Rather than uncovering hidden identities, the metaphors in this passage in Ovidian terms seem to metamorphose what is actually there and cause a disruption of the protagonist's honourable behaviour.

Such is the power of love, the implied message reads, if uncontrolled by virtue and moral restraint. In another passage, the madness of love is figured by Pyrocles as a disease which rationality does not help to cure. Earlier, Musidorus had criticized Pyrocles' infatuation with Philoclea and had urged him 'to purge your head of this vile infection' (Book I, 1994: 22). In response, Pyrocles reproaches his friend for his cruel and illogical behaviour:

> But truly, you deal with me like a physician that, seeing his patient in a pestilent fever, should chide him instead of ministering help, and bid him be sick no more; or rather, like such a friend that, visiting his friend condemned to perpetual prison and loaden with grievous fetters, should will him to shake off his fetters, or he would leave him. I am sick, and sick to the death. I am prisoner; neither is there any redress but by her to whom I am slave.
>
> (Book I, 1994: 22)

Both images, of the patient and the prisoner, which are equated, depict the lover as helpless to free himself and as smitten by a fateful force, unable by his own ability to extricate himself from his hopeless predicament. Pyrocles therefore here accuses Musidorus of hypocrisy and treachery in asking him to love no more – love in both metaphors is imaged as an oppressor and an invader who has caught the lover and put him in thrall. As with a real infection, however, Musidorus is entirely correct in appealing to his friend's powers of resistance. At this early point in the narrative, he takes the role of the wise doctor who is not obeyed or who in any case would be powerless against the forces in whose grip Pyrocles finds himself.

*   *   *

Metaphor in narrative has been discussed in stylistics in two ways. On the one hand, it has been contrasted with metonymy in the wake of Roman Jakobson's distinction between these two tropes as basic cognitive approaches rooted in similarity and contiguity (Jakobson 1956). This is the perspective picked up on by David Lodge (1977) in his *Modes of Modern Writing*. On the other hand, narratologists have been concerned primarily with the question of who is responsible for specific metaphors in a narrative: the narrator, the character, or even the (implied) author? I will discuss both of these approaches in turn.

Jakobson (1956) famously distinguished between two types of aphasia, contiguity disorder and similarity disorder. Thence he concluded that the human brain fundamentally distinguished association by contiguity (frame-internal association or metonymy) and association by means of similarity in metaphor (see Schifko 1979; Goossens 1995; Kövesces and Radden 1998; Panther and Radden 1999; Barcelona 2000, 2002; Dirven and Pörings 2002; and Panther and Thornburg 2004.). In Lodge's fine diagram, reproduced below (a summary of Jakobson's arguments), metaphor and metonymy come to collocate not only with similarity and contiguity, but also with the paradigmatic and syntagmatic axes in language, and even with particularly 'pure' stylistic and historical genres such as surrealism or symbolism (metaphor) and cubism or realism (metonymy).

Lodge was astute enough to visually redesign Jakobson's dichotomy figured as the horizontal and vertical coordinates of the paradigmatic and syntagmatic axes; he sees the relationship of metaphor and metonymy as a scale, with a metaphoric pole (exemplified by T. S. Eliot's poetry) at one end, and a metonymic pole (represented by a newspaper article) at the other (Table 19.1). Lodge thereby underlines the fact that metaphors may occur in prose, although they will not tend to be the dominant mode of writing in narrative. In fact, metaphors in novels tend to get classified as 'lyric' style, as do alliterations, foregrounded repetitions, parallelisms, and playing with sound (assonance, consonance, internal rhyme). Lodge does not spend extensive time on analysing the possible functions of metaphors in prose. Indeed, his emphasis in the book concerns structures of contiguity interfering with similarity, for

Table 19.1: Metaphor vs metonymy (Lodge 1988: 81)

Metaphor	Metonymy
Paradigm	Syntagm
Similarity	Contiguity
Selection	Combination
Substitution	[Deletion] Contexture
Contiguity Disorder	Similarity Disorder
Contexture Deficiency	Selection Deficiency
Drama	Film
Montage	Close-up
Dream symbolism	Dream Condensation and Displacement
Surrealism	Cubism
Imitative Magic	Contagious Magic
Poetry	Prose
Lyric	Epic
Romanticism and Symbolism	Realism

instance in his discussion of Proust's use of corn ears as a source term for two clock towers, and later his figuring of church steeples as fish bodies. In both cases the physical contiguity of, respectively, cornfields and the sea seems to have infected the metaphor chosen (Lodge 1988: 115–16). Even more interestingly, Lodge goes on to consider metonymic style in Wordsworth's poetry (1988: 119–24).

Few of Lodge's instances of the metonymic are actually metonyms of the familiar *pars pro toto* kind. He does, however, very insightfully point to prose which refunctionalizes a basically metonymic structure based on contiguity into a metaphor. Thus, citing Guy Rosolato (1972), he notes that the 'slice of life' metaphor for novelistic realism indeed characterizes realism as implying reality or life as we know it, thus functioning as a metaphor (109–10): the 'extract' of reality in the novel is *like* 'real life'.

This insight can be supplemented by pointing to a complementary strategy of novels employing a key metaphor which, through repetition, implies that the metaphor needs to be taken as appropriate for the text as a whole. Thus, in Samuel Richardson's (1749) *Clarissa*, the protagonist finds herself imprisoned in several locations – her home, her room in her home, in the house that Lovelace takes her to, and ultimately in her body, whence her soul will soar to heaven. Through these recurring scenes, the novel insists on Clarissa's metaphorical imprisonment by patriarchy in this life. The contiguity of scenes of imprisonment results in an overall metaphor.

Students of metaphor are increasingly noting that metaphor and metonymy are interbraided in interesting ways. The entire concept of blending as introduced by Gilles Fauconnier (1997; see also Fauconnier and Turner 1996, 2002, and Turner and Fauconnier 1999) is in fact based on a combination of frame-related contiguity and metaphoric transfer. Thus, in the famous cognitive metaphors MY SURGEON IS A BUTCHER or MY JOB IS A JAIL, the source domains (*butcher* and *jail*) are imposed on the targets (the surgeon and the job) under the rubric of a generic structure that metonymically aligns a key set of elements which become foregrounded in the blend. Improving on the invariance principle (Lakoff 1995: 215–7), the blend sets in relief those associations that help to configure the thrust of the metaphoric transfer. In the case of MY SURGEON IS A BUTCHER, the image of the butcher wielding a cleaver is superimposed on that of the surgeon handling a scalpel, yielding the blend in which the surgeon operates on his patient by means of an axe, and the patient becomes a corpse (like the butcher's dead carcass). While the invariance principle underlines that the 'cognitive topology' of the source domain is preserved in the target domain 'in a way consistent with the inherent structure of the target domain' (ibid.: 215), blends explain how new meaning (incompetence) arises from the transfer.

Likewise, in MY JOB IS A JAIL (Glucksberg and Keysar 1990), the associations with incarceration invoke the workplace as a location to which one is

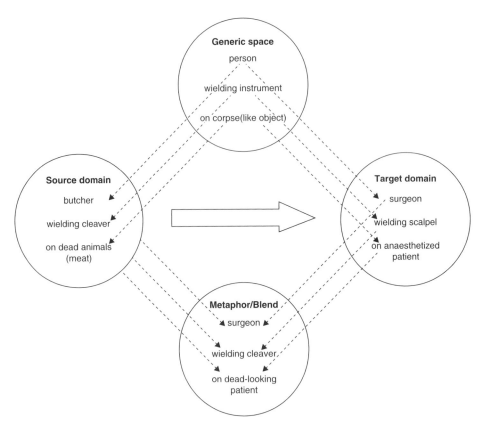

Figure 19.2: Blend for 'My surgeon is a butcher'

tied and in which, possibly, one is under the control of a warder-like boss who is experienced as abusive, unreasonable or strict, and pedantic. A cartoon of this metaphor in action might foreground the worker's office as a tiny dark room with barred windows and add the boss in the posture of a shouting slave-driver, or it might show the employee seated at his desk or standing at his machine in the factory with his ankle chained to a cannonball attached to the desk/machine. Visual narratives (a cartoon of this type could be regarded as a kernel narrative) have a great range of techniques for producing metaphors, frequently also by means of verbal messages in the subscript (see, for instance, the 'Life without parole' cartoon discussed in Swan 2002 and Fludernik 2005). The blend of this metaphor highlights the fact that the employee is confined to the workplace (chained to it) and subjected to the dictates of an irate employer, who either abuses him or makes him work by coercion (in a cartoon version perhaps figured by a boss wielding a whip). Which of the two readings of MY JOB IS A JAIL will be dominant depends on the context or on people's individual associations with imprisonment (as primarily confinement or also as control, abuse, or slave work). In fact, other associations might be developed, given suitable contexts or individual inclination (loneliness, boredom, frustration). One possible visualization of a blend for MY JOB IS A JAIL could be Figure 19.3 as given below.

It is obvious from the above that the associations that emerge from the metaphoric source-to-target transfer are metonymic; they refer to elements of the source frame that in turn activate congenial elements in the target domain. Thus, the cleaver associated with butchers condignly points to the scalpel by way of structural parallel and semantic contrast. Likewise, in MY JOB IS A JAIL, the associations with prison – bars, chains, functional bareness of the cell, windowless walls, cruel warders, and so on – can be utilized to emphasize aspects of the target domain that correspond to these elements. Other than sheer frustration at a job one hates, what precisely in this occupation might be prison-like? Here a series of possibilities open up, and cartoons

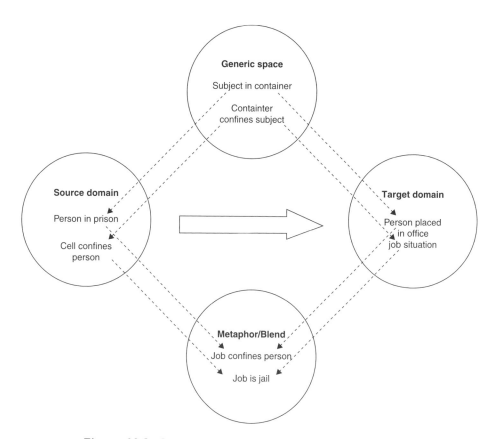

Figure 19.3: Blend for 'My job is a jail' (confinement reading)

are a good way of visualizing them, externalizing the images we produce in our minds.

If this interbraiding of metaphor and metonymy is already observable in common metaphors used in conversation, it becomes even more prominent in literary discourse. Since we are here dealing with narrative rather than poetry, the question is to what extent metaphoric language in narrative combines with metonymy. A good example of this can be adduced by considering a passage from Henry Fielding's *Joseph Andrews* ([1742] 1986). Book II of this novel opens with a meta-narrative chapter entitled 'Chapter 1. Of Divisions in Authors' and discusses – not, as one might have thought, clashes of opinion and lobbies among authors – but the division of the text into chapters, a practice that was a fairly recent innovation in Fielding's time. The chapter opens with a characterization of chapter divisions as one of the 'secrets' of the 'trad[e]' (Fielding [1742] 1986: 99) of writing. This positive view of the author's knack of structuring the text is opposed to the critical opinion of 'common readers', who 'imagine, that by this art of dividing, we mean only to swell our works to a much larger bulk than they would otherwise be extended to' (ibid.). The chapters, viewed from this invidious perspective, are then 'understood as so much buckram, stays, and stay-tape in a taylor's bill, serving only to make up the sum total, commonly found at the bottom of our first page, and of his last' (ibid.). From secrets of the trade of writing, the chapters and books of the literary work are here metamorphosed into the internal props of waistcoats and dresses that are necessary parts of a garment, but perceived as superfluous additions to one's bill. Note that this image actually underlines that 'stays and buckram' are required as scaffolding, without which the edifice of vestment would crumble to inconspicuous formless shape. Chapters and book divisions are therefore claimed to be essential even when they seem merely superfluous additions like ribbons or flounces.

When we go on to the next paragraph, now quoted in full, another image takes centre stage, namely the metaphor READING IS A JOURNEY, which then combines with the argument on chapters:

> But in reality the case is otherwise, and in this, as well as all other instances, we consult the advantage of our reader, not our own; and indeed many notable uses arise to him from this method: for first, those little spaces between our chapters may be looked upon as an inn or resting-place, where he may stop and take a glass, or any other refreshment, as it pleases him. Nay, our fine readers will, perhaps, be scarce able to travel farther than through one of them in a day. As to those vacant pages which are placed between our books, they are to be regarded as those stages, where, in long journeys, the traveller stays some time to repose himself, and consider of what he hath seen in the parts he hath already past [*sic*] through; a consideration which I take the liberty

to recommend a little to the reader: for however swift his capacity may be, I would not advise him to travel through these pages too fast: for if he doth, he may probably miss the seeing some curious productions of nature which will be observed by the slower and more accurate reader. A volume without any such places of rest resembles the opening of wilds or seas, which tires the eye and fatigues the spirit when entered upon.

Secondly, what are the contents prefixed to every chapter, but so many inscriptions over the gates of inns (to continue the same metaphor,) informing the reader what entertainment he is to expect, which if he likes not, he may travel on to the next: for in biography, as we are not tied down to an exact concatenation equally with other historians; so a chapter or two (for instance this I am now writing) may be often pass'd over without any injury to the whole. And in these inscriptions I have been as faithful as possible, not imitating the celebrated Montagne [sic], who promises you one thing and gives you another; nor some title-page authors, who promise a great deal, and produce nothing at all.

(Fielding [1742] 1986: 99–100)

The reader is travelling along the text and, like a traveller, stops by the wayside to refresh himself (mentally). This metaphor extends to the inscriptions over inns as a metaphorical equivalent to chapter headings, but also as the table of contents for the next lap of the journey. From the process of reading as a peregrination along the sequence of words ('which tires the eye and fatigues the spirit'), the passage metonymically moves to the wayside inns in which travellers rest, and from there to inscriptions over the doorways of these inns, thereby slightly modifying the journey metaphor. In fact, this shift in perspective now serves to focus on the function of the chapter headings and the signified–referent relation of title to chapter. One fails to notice as a reader that the content of an innkeeper's inscription refers to the food provided at that inn, and does not concern the next stage of the journey over which one could skip if one disliked the prospect. Logically speaking, one cannot eliminate a section of one's journey, though one can forgo tasting the food, if it is not to one's liking, at the inn where one rests one's limbs. This extract allows us to observe how metonymy constrains the exploration of the metaphor into new inventive channels. *En route*, the text shifts from the first (journey) to the second (inns) source domain via a metonymy in the target domain:

target = chapters (→ chapter titles)
source 1 → metonymy → source 2

Fielding's metaphor of reading as a journey is superbly appropriate to narrative as temporal art determined by the reading process. It additionally ascribes Godly powers to the narrator persona, since the route is usually a given, whereas the text of a novel and its divisions clearly result from the author's creative and inventive energies.

★   ★   ★

A second issue in narratological analysis has been the question of attribution: who is responsible for a metaphor? In Fielding's case, this is easily answered since the foregrounded narrator persona explicitly, metanarratively, comments on his use of the image, analogizing travellers journeying and readers perusing narratives as well as chapter headings and inns (and, later, chapter titles and names of inns or menus displayed at their entry). The situation is much less obvious when one turns to novels in which the fictional world is focalized through the mind of one (or several) protagonist(s), as in the work of Virginia Woolf, James Joyce, D. H. Lawrence, Margaret Atwood, or Toni Morrison (and a host of other writers).

Take the following two passages from Woolf's *Mrs Dalloway* ([1925] 1983). The first gives us the brief life history of Septimus Warren Smith, of his aspirations to poetry, and then a view on him by his former employer:

> To look at, he might have been a clerk, but of the better sort; for he wore brown boots; his hands were educated; so, too, his profile – his angular, big-nosed, intelligent, sensitive profile; but not his lips altogether, for they were loose; and his eyes (as eyes tend to be), eyes merely; hazel, large; so that he was, on the whole, a border case, neither one thing nor the other; might end with a house at Purley and a motor car, or continue renting apartments in back streets all his life; one of those half-educated, self-educated men whose education is all learnt from books borrowed from public libraries, read in the evening after the day's work, on the advice of well-known authors consulted by letter.
>
> [...]
>
> London has swallowed up many millions of young men called Smith; thought nothing of fantastic Christian names like Septimus with which their parents have thought to distinguish them. Lodging off the Euston Road, there were experiences, again experiences, such as change a face in two years from a pink innocent oval to a face lean, contracted, hostile. But of all this what could the most observant of friends have said except what a gardener says when he opens the conservatory door in the morning and finds a new blossom on his plant: it has flowered; flowered from vanity, ambition, idealism, passion, loneliness, courage, laziness, the usual seeds, which all muddled up (in a room off the Euston Road), made him shy, and stammering, made him anxious to improve himself, made him fall in love with Miss Isabel Pole, lecturing in the Waterloo Road upon Shakespeare.

(Woolf [1925] 1983: 75–6)

Here, in the ironic juxtaposition of Smith's sordid existence as a clerk and his passionate espousal of art (figured as the flowering of a blossom, the love poem he writes 'at three o'clock in the morning' [ibid.: 77]), we get the moving story of the awkward young man and his adoration of Miss Pole, who 'ignoring the subject, [...] corrected [his love poems] in red ink' (ibid.: 76). Despite the unpromising circumstances of Smith's life off the Euston Road, his genius flourishes and is only cut off by his war service (ibid.: 77). The fictive gardener of the simile is not, one presumes, an image that Smith himself might have resorted to; could it be Miss Pole's, who opens the next paragraph with 'Was he not like Keats? she asked ...' (ibid.: 76) and who possibly envisages Smith's immersion in poetry as the process which 'lit in him such a fire as burns only once in a lifetime, without heat, flickering a red-gold flame infinitely ethereal and insubstantial over Miss Pole' (ibid.)? Although Miss Pole's association of Smith with Keats implies that she associates him with romanticism and poetic genius, the fact that her fire is 'without heat' seems to suggest that she does not love him; vainly, he may even have volunteered in order to impress Miss Pole ('He went to France to save an England which consisted almost entirely of Shakespeare's plays and Miss Isabel Pole in a green dress walking in a square' (ibid.: 77). Would she then have dreamed of him as a gardener raising a plant? We do not know. It makes most sense to discard such ascriptions of the imagery and to take it as part of the narrator's idiosyncratic and ironic phraseology.

The second passage starts with what is clearly Elizabeth Dalloway's perspective of her London bus as a pirate ship. Later Elizabeth's thoughts turn to her career, her ideals, and to life and death:

Suddenly Elizabeth stepped forward and most competently boarded the omnibus, in front of everybody. She took a seat on top. The impetuous creature – a pirate – started forward, sprang away; she had to hold the rail to steady herself, for a pirate it was, reckless, unscrupulous, bearing down ruthlessly, circumventing dangerously, boldly snatching a passenger, or ignoring a passenger, squeezing eel-like and arrogant in between, and then rushing insolently all sails spread up Whitehall. And did Elizabeth give one thought to poor Miss Kilman who loved her without jealousy, to whom she had been a fawn in the open, a moon in a glade? She was delighted to be free. The fresh air was so delicious. It had been so stuffy in the Army and Navy Stores. And now it was like riding, to be rushing up Whitehall; and to each movement of the omnibus the beautiful body in the fawn-coloured coat responded freely like a rider, like the figure-head of a ship, for the breeze slightly disarrayed her; the heat gave her cheeks the pallor of white painted wood; and her fine eyes, having no eyes to meet, gazed ahead, blank, bright, with the staring, incredible innocence of sculpture.

(Woolf [1925] 1983: 120–1)

In this passage the 'impetuous creature' of the omnibus belongs to Elizabeth's imagination. It is she who is experiencing the surge of the bus through traffic. Yet towards the end of the paragraph the phrase 'the beautiful body in the fawn-coloured coat' refers to Elizabeth from an external (Miss Kilman's?) perspective and compares her to a ship swaying in the breeze of the ocean. Here the narrator creeps in by the back door, comparing Elizabeth to a figurehead ('painted wood') and to a statue ('sculpture'). Later, Elizabeth is inspired by all the activity around her to take a profession, '[...] determined, whatever her mother might say, to become either a farmer or a doctor' (ibid.: 122):

> And it was much better to say nothing about it. It seemed so silly. It was the sort of thing that did sometimes happen, when one was alone – buildings without architects' names, crowds of people coming back from the city having more power than single clergymen in Kensington, than any of the books Miss Kilman had lent her, to stimulate what lay slumbrous, clumsy, and shy on the mind's sandy floor, to break surface, as a child suddenly stretches its arms; it was just that, perhaps, a sigh, a stretch of the arms, an impulse, a revelation, which has its effects for ever, and then down again it went to the sandy floor. She must go home. She must dress for dinner. But what was the time? – where was a clock?
>
> (Woolf [1925] 1983: 122)

Again, one starts and finishes with Elizabeth's free indirect thought, which leads one to assume that the central part of the paragraph must also be part of her consciousness; yet could she really think about the processes of inspiration like a force resident on 'the mind's sandy floor'? Further on, Elizabeth on Fleet Street encounters 'this voice, pouring endlessly year in, year out' (Woolf [1925] 1983: 123), and again one wonders whether the image is Elizabeth's or the narrator's (implied author's, Woolf's?). On the one hand, we have just heard that 'that uproar' (ibid.) was an unconscious experience: 'It was not conscious. There was no recognition in it of one's fortune, or fate [...]' (ibid.: 123). Elizabeth clearly thinks about all of this, but does she think about it consciously? Or is it the narrative voice we are hearing? And is it this voice, too, which echoes the 'voice, pouring endlessly year in, year out' and which 'would take whatever it might be; this vow; this van; this life; this procession; would wrap them all about and carry them on, as in the rough stream of a glacier the ice holds a splinter of bone, a blue petal, some oak trees, and rolls them on' (ibid.)? The voice (of life?) wraps up the world and its problems, but also its beauties, like a present, and preserves them as a glacier does a remnant of former ages, freezing the experience in epiphany. Although the following paragraph returns to Elizabeth's free indirect thought, the images in this paragraph cannot be ascribed to her with any certainty.

★ ★ ★

So far I have concentrated on two theoretical aspects touching on metaphor in novels – their common metonymic basis (a feature that can be found in poetic metaphors as well), and the evocation and attribution of voice that has been the focus of narratological study of metaphor in narrative.

As the examples from Virginia Woolf illustrate, the attribution issue is an extremely difficult one to resolve in some cases. In fact, positing a narratorial voice in these passages relies on the presence of an external perspective on the protagonist (Smith, Elizabeth) and on the presence of foregrounded metaphors such as that of the gardener watching a blossom emerge from the cactus. It is, therefore, perhaps not the most useful approach to concentrate on the issue of voice, on an attributional analysis. In the cited extracts from *Mrs Dalloway*, it seems much more fruitful to focus on the ironies in the passage, for instance on the way in which Septimus romantically produces love poems and finally a masterpiece, all as a result of his infatuation with his English teacher. Even more ironically, this poetic romanticism proves to be his undoing, first at his job and then, more seriously, by making him volunteer and, after some initial heroism at the front, turn into the depressive man who commits suicide. The fire of poetry breaks out despite his sordid living conditions on the Euston Road, but the even more sordid conditions of modern warfare are responsible for crushing that poetic bloom and ruining Septimus's life.

Likewise, Elizabeth, who ventures through London in the mental framework of a pirate, loves the flush of work and activity in the London streets and feels this hubbub to be sacred, preserving life at its most precious, allowing her to experience it as a wrapped-up present. With this, her evocation of London as eternal life in the process of becoming and renewing itself links back to her mother Clarissa's experiences of the city at the opening of the novel, with the morning 'fresh as issued to children on a beach' (Woolf [1925] 1983: 5). Elizabeth's epiphany therefore links with other metaphors and themes of the book. From that perspective, the person to whom a specific metaphor can be attributed is less important.

Comparable studies of imagery have been common in the analysis of Shakespeare's plays (Clemen 1951; Spurgeon 1952). Texts that teem with metaphors of whatever genre clearly lend themselves to an examination of their overall function and impact. When a work can be demonstrated to emphasize a particular semantic field as source domain for its metaphors, this provides a good route into the interpretation of the text. For instance, close analysis of the metaphors in Angela Carter's story 'The Erlking' (1979) suggests a reading of the story as an instance of the LOVE IS A PRISON trope (Fludernik, forthcoming; under review). Looking at such macro-structural effects of metaphor has been popular in the criticism of some authors such as Charles Dickens, Elfriede Jelinek, or Robert Musil (Biebuyck 1998; Martens 2006). What these studies demonstrate is the fact that some narratives are so imbued with metaphors that a literal reading of the text becomes difficult (what actually is being reported?). A good example of this would be the opening of Jeanette Winterson's (1994) *Art & Lies*:

> From a distance only the light is visible, a speeding gleaming horizontal angel, trumpet out on a hard bend. The note bells. The note bells the beauty of the stretching train that pulls the light in a long gold thread. It catches in the wheels, it flashes on the doors, that open and close, that open and close, in commuter rhythm.
>
> On the overcoats and briefcases, brooches and sighs, the light snags in rough-cut stones that stay unpolished. The man is busy, he hasn't time to see the light that burns his clothes and illuminates his face, the light pouring down his shoulders with biblical zeal. His book is a plate of glass.
>
> (Winterson 1994: 3)

It is extremely difficult to realize on a first reading that the protagonist, Handel, is actually sitting in the carriage of an underground train. We seem to be in a fantasy landscape, where the metaphorical and the literal cannot be disentangled: are we at the Apocalypse? In a nightmare? Metaphors are therefore not merely ornaments or rare rhetorical flourishes; they crucially model the narrative discourse and are inextricably knotted together with the semiotics of the text. Hence, a poetics of fiction ignores metaphor only at its peril.

The second point to underline in this context is the shift in attention that a study of narrative metaphor makes available to narratologists and novel critics alike. Novel criticism in the wake of literary modernism had centred on postmodern strategies of disruption – self-reflexivity, metafictionality, the breaking-up of spatial, temporal, plot- and character-related aspects of nineteenth-century realism. This emphasis in the description of literary developments since the 1920s has lost sight of a prominent feature of narrative texts before modernism, namely metaphor, and how metaphors in the Victorian novel strategically supported, but also undermined, the realist message. Ansgar Nünning in his work on metanarrative (Nünning 2001, 2004; see also Fludernik 2003) has argued that metanarrative, which is frequently interpreted as equivalent to metafiction and serves to disrupt the verisimilitude of realist texts, actually in many cases helps to evoke an illusion of narratorial mimesis, or mimesis of narration, and that it cannot, therefore, automatically be aligned with postmodernist disruptions of mimesis.

Similarly, what metaphor studies could do is to trace the central role of metaphor in the history of the novel, not just for nineteenth-century realism, and to analyse the various global functions of imagery in narratives period by period. Although studies of individual works or of particular authors have spent some effort on elucidating the importance of metaphor in a number of novels, an overall history of the place of metaphor in narrative remains as yet unwritten. A preference for metaphors, or an obvious reluctance to use them, clearly tells us something about the realist project of the author of that text, but it also elucidates the larger connection between realism and non-literal language. In fact, it might throw some very important light on realism's suppressed debt to fictionality and fictivity. Taking Eliot's ([1870–71] 1986) *Middlemarch* as an illustration, for instance, one could argue that the reader through the metaphors of water and dryness is immediately alerted on a sub-conscious level to the incompatibilities between Dorothea and Casaubon. Whereas Dorothea fondly imagines Casaubon's 'feelings' as 'a lake compared with [her] little pool' (I, iii; Eliot [1871–72] 1986: 47) and wants to pour her energies into Casaubon's project ('Into this soul-hunger as yet all her youth-ful passion was poured', [1871–72] 1986: 51), Casaubon himself admits that he is a dried-out rill coming alive only under the influence of Dorothea's overboarding intellectual passion: 'I have been little disposed to gather flow-ers that would wither in my hand, but now I shall pluck them with eagerness, to place them in your bosom' (1986: I, v, 73). As the narrator slyly notes, 'the frigid rhetoric at the end was as sincere as the bark of a dog, or the cawing of an amorous rook' (ibid.). Ironically, Casaubon's arid vapidity is hinted at even earlier when Dorothea negatively contrasts society's small talk with Casaubon's supposedly weighty conversation. As the narrative implies, she gets her impressions all wrong: Casaubon's ideas are like a 'stale bride-cake brought forth with an odour of cup-board' (1986: I, iii, 55). Echoing Miss Havisham in Dickens's (1860–61) *Great Expectations*, the combination of withered flower and stale cake sets the reader on a journey of associative discovery that ranges from sexually dry river beds to dessicated miserly scare-crow husbands to skeletons in the cupboard.

It is this connection between the virtual scenarios of metaphoric discourse and the fictional, invented scenes of the narrative plot that needs to be explored more fully and more theoretically in future research.

Wmatrix, Key Concepts and the Narrators in Julian Barnes's *Talking It Over*

BRIAN WALKER

1. Introduction

Talking It Over by Julian Barnes (1991) is a novel with a fairly familiar theme – a love triangle – that is told in rather an unusual way: there are nine first-person narrators. In this chapter, I investigate three of those narrators with the help of a relatively new corpus-analysis tool called Wmatrix (Rayson 2008) to guide my analysis, using its capacity to (a) automatically semantically annotate texts and (b) extend the notion of keyness to semantic categories (key concepts). I will show how key concepts can provide empirical evidence that supports intuitive responses to the three narrators as well as offer new and interpretively important data. My study also demonstrates that Wmatrix's semantic functionality can help with the stylistic analysis of a larger text (in this case a novel) by identifying themes within the text, and locating potentially important sections of text for further investigation that might have been missed by (the more established) keyword analysis, thus making Wmatrix a useful addition to the stylistician's tool-kit.

I will start with a short synopsis of *Talking It Over* and continue by briefly introducing Wmatrix (ibid.). I will then turn my attention to the three main narrators of the story (Stuart, Gillian, and Oliver) and my investigation of their narrations based on the semantic data provided for each of them by Wmatrix. The majority of the discussion will be devoted to Oliver because (a) the data for this narrator turns out to be particularly interesting, and (b) it also raises questions regarding some of the semantic categories Wmatrix uses, and its lexicon. Therefore, this section of the chapter in particular does not only demonstrate how Wmatrix can be used for stylistic analysis, but also represents, to some extent, a testing out of the software for this purpose (Leech 2008: 162–78, also tests out Wmatrix in an analysis of Virginia Woolf's 'The Mark on the Wall').

2. *Talking It Over*

Talking It Over tells the story of a love triangle through the accounts of nine narrators. Stuart, Gillian, and Oliver can be regarded as the three main narrators because: (a) they narrate substantially more of the story than the other six narrators (see Table 20.1 for word total details); and (b) they are also the characters involved in the love triangle, so are therefore the principle protagonists in the story. The six other narrators in the table are also characters in the story but are involved in a more peripheral way, in relation to one or other of the main characters. Mme Wyatt is Gillian's mother; Gordon Wyatt is Gillian's father; Mrs. Dyer is (for a short time) Oliver's landlady; Mme Rives is a French hotelier in a small village where Oliver and Gillian live for a while; Val is the ex-girlfriend of Stuart; and Michelle is an assistant in a florist's where Oliver buys some flowers for Gillian.

The narrators each take turns at telling the story, with most chapters consisting of more than one narratorial contribution. Each new contribution is signalled by the narrator's name appearing in bold type at the beginning of that section of narration.

Through the combined accounts of the narrators we learn how Stuart and Gillian meet, fall in love, and marry. Oliver, Stuart's best friend since secondary school, plays witness to the courtship, and accompanies the couple

Table 20.1: The number of words narrated by each narrator in *Talking It Over* (percentage totals are shown in brackets)

No.	Narrator	Words (%)
1	Oliver	26,588 (36.1)
2	Stuart	23,147 (31.5)
3	Gillian	17,496 (23.8)
4	Mme Wyatt	2771 (3.8)
5	Val	1485 (2.0)
6	Mme Rive	599 (0.8)
7	Michelle	515 (0.7)
8	Gordon Wyatt	478 (0.7)
9	Mrs Dyer	390 (0.5)
Totals		**73,469 (100)**

on a number of dates. However, on Stuart and Gillian's wedding day Oliver realizes that he has also fallen in love with Gillian. The story continues with Oliver, over the course of the next few months, trying to 'win' Gillian from Stuart and, eventually, Gillian finds herself falling in love with Oliver. Consequently, she and Stuart separate and get divorced (just months after they were married) and soon after, Oliver and Gillian get married and move to France. This is not the end of the story, but I will end this brief synopsis here in order not to spoil the enjoyment of anyone interested in reading the book. Suffice to say, *Talking It Over*, with its nine narrators, offers interesting data with regard to the interaction between narrator, character, and different points of view, because the story is told from a number of different perspectives, with different narrators often commenting on the same events. In this analysis, I will be focusing on my intuitions about Stuart, Gillian, and Oliver, as well as those provided by a number of critics, and I will be using Wmatrix to provide empirical support for or against some of those intuitions.

My initial impressions of the three main narrators are that Stuart seems a little unimaginative and comes across as being rather unadventurous, slightly boring, and lacking in confidence, especially with females. Oliver, on the other hand, appears to have more confidence, especially with the opposite sex. He is articulate and droll, and seems to be clever and well-read. Others who have written about the novel have made similar observations, describing Stuart as 'dull' (Guignery 2006: 73), 'unclever, unimaginative' (Moseley 1997: 140), 'stolid and unglamorous' (Pateman 2002: 54), and 'a plodder, teetering on the edge of full-blown wallyhood' (Heller 1991: 28), while Oliver is said to be 'flamboyant and erudite' (Pateman 2002: 54), 'dashing, quick [...] witty, cultivated, charming' (Moseley 1997: 125), 'foppish, learned, showy, precious' (Moseley 1997: 141), 'pedantic and self-centered' (Guignery 2006: 75), and 'a clever dick' (Heller 1991: 28).

Gillian, however, is not as easy to sum up as the two contrasting males in the story since we learn comparatively little about her. This is partly due to the rather reserved and guarded narratorial contributions she makes, particularly at the beginning of the novel. Indeed, in her first, very short, narration she states:

> 'Look, I just don't particularly think it's anyone's business. I really don't. I'm an ordinary, private person. I haven't got anything to say.'
>
> (Barnes 1991: 7–8)

The critics also write very little about Gillian, but the fact that she seems to hold back, and keep herself, and her emotions, to herself does not go unnoticed. For example, Levenson describes her as 'reticent and deliberate' (Levenson 1991: 44), while Moseley notes that she is self-protective (Moseley

1997: 139). Others describe her as 'sensible' (Humphreys 1991), and 'cool and opaque' (Heller 1991: 28). This could be part of a defence mechanism because, even though she is not shy and does on occasion assert her will, Gillian seems quite emotionally vulnerable.

In the love triangle in the story, therefore, Stuart and Oliver reside at opposite ends of a metaphorical scale of luminescence, while Gillian positions herself somewhere in the shadows. Moseley notes that Barnes's 'creation of these three very different voice-personalities is a matter of vocabulary, references, reticences, syntax, and cadence' (Moseley 1997: 140). Unfortunately, though, he does not expand on this and gives no specific examples. In this chapter, I explore more precisely some of the ways that impressions of these characters are created, using Wmatrix.

3. Wmatrix

Wmatrix (Rayson 2008) is a web-based corpus-analysis tool developed and located at Lancaster University. Texts (electronic versions in plain .txt format) are uploaded via the internet to the Wmatrix server using a web interface. During the upload process, the words in the text are organized and quantified in three different ways:

1. Lexically – basic frequency lists of all the words in a text are generated;
2. Grammatically – using the Constituent Likelihood Automatic Word-tagging System (CLAWS – see Garside 1987; Leech, Garside and Bryant 1994; Garside 1996; and Garside and Smith 1997) developed at the University Centre for Computer Corpus Research on Language (UCREL)[1] at Lancaster University. Every word in a text is assigned a tag denoting the grammatical category or part-of-speech (hereafter POS) to which it belongs. Frequency lists based on grammatical groupings of words are then generated;
3. Semantically – every word is assigned a semantic tag according to the UCREL Semantic Analysis System (USAS[2]) using a hierarchical framework of categorization. Frequency lists based on the semantic groupings of words are then generated.

Notice that the grammatical and semantic quantification performed by Wmatrix is still word-based – it counts the word forms within each grammatical or semantic grouping based on the tags it automatically assigns, so it is the number of words within a group that decides the groups ranking.

The semantic framework used by Wmatrix was based originally on McArthur's (1981) *Longman Lexicon of Contemporary English*, but has undergone many revisions during the development of USAS. Tags consist of an upper-case letter, which indicates the relevant general semantic field (of which there are 21; see Table 20.2), followed by a number, which indicates the first subdivision of that field. For example, the major semantic field of GOVERNMENT AND THE PUBLIC is designated by the letter G. This major field has three first subdivisions: GOVERNMENT, POLITICS AND ELECTIONS – labelled G1; CRIME, LAW AND ORDER – labelled G2; and WARFARE, DEFENCE AND THE ARMY – labelled G3. In some instances, finer subdivisions of the subfield are possible, in which case the first number is followed by a decimal point (or period) and another number. For example, the first subdivision of GOVERNMENT AND THE PUBLIC DOMAIN, (G1 – GOVERNMENT, POLITICS AND ELECTIONS) is further divided into: GOVERNMENT ETC. – which has the tag G1.1; and POLITICS – which is tagged G1.2. Through this type of subdivision, the 21 major semantic fields of the hierarchy expand to 232 finer semantic categories.

From the initial frequency lists produced by Wmatrix, comparisons are possible within the web-based environment. For example, the word-list from one text can be compared with the word-list from another text or reference corpus to produce a list of keywords, that is, words that are statistically 'overused' (or 'under-used', depending on the settings selected) in the first text. This type of comparison is nothing new, of course. Indeed, Mike Scott's *Wordsmith Tools* (Scott 2008) has a 'Keyword' facility which has been used, over the years, to good effect in many different studies (see, for example,

Table 20.2: The 21 top level categories of the USAS tag-set[3]

A GENERAL & ABSTRACT TERMS	B THE BODY & THE INDIVIDUAL	C ARTS & CRAFTS	E EMOTION	F FOOD & FARMING
G GOVERNMENT & PUBLIC	H ARCHITECTURE, HOUSING & THE HOME	I MONEY & COMMERCE (IN INDUSTRY)	K ENTERTAINMENT	L LIFE & LIVING THINGS
M MOVEMENT, LOCATION, TRAVEL, TRANSPORT	N NUMBERS & MEASUREMENT	O SUBSTANCES, MATERIALS, OBJECTS, EQUIPMENT	P EDUCATION	Q LANGUAGE & COMMUNICATION
S SOCIAL ACTIONS, STATES & PROCESSES	T TIME	W WORLD & ENVIRONMENT	X PSYCHOLOGICAL ACTIONS, STATES & PROCESSES	Y SCIENCE & TECHNOLOGY
Z NAMES & GRAMMAR				

Culpeper 2002; Stubbs 2005; O'Halloran 2007). However, by carrying out similar comparisons at the POS level and semantic level, Wmatrix is able to extend the notion of 'keyness' to grammatical categories (known as key POS) and semantic domains (known as key concepts). It is the latter that I will be discussing in this chapter, as this output offers an alternative and relatively new approach to the stylistic analysis of prose fiction.

4. Methodology

Common approaches in corpus linguistics involve (i) comparing a text or corpus with a large(r) reference corpus or (ii) comparing two similar-sized corpora. For my exploration of the three main narrators in *Talking It Over*, however, I make a number of text-internal comparisons, which is a slightly less common approach, successfully employed by Culpeper (2002) in his keywords analysis of characters in Shakespeare's *Romeo and Juliet*. Using this approach I compare the words of one narrator with the words of all the other narrators in the novel combined. To achieve this, I first created a separate text file for each of the three main narrators, so that I had one file containing all of Oliver's narratorial contributions, one containing all Stuart's, and one containing Gillian's. Secondly, three comparison files were created, the first file containing all the contributions of all the narrators except Oliver (therefore, the novel minus Oliver's narrations); the second containing all narrations except Stuart's, and the third containing all narrations except Gillian's. These six files were uploaded into Wmatrix, and a series of comparisons made: the file containing all Oliver's narrations was compared with the file that contained all narrations except Oliver's, and so on for Stuart and Gillian. These comparisons produced lists of keywords, key POS, and key concepts for each of the three main narrators. However, as I have already stated, I will be restricting my discussion here to key concepts, although from time to time I will mention the keyword output.

One issue with this narrator-comparison methodology is that the process of splitting up the different narrators means that an already relatively small data source (the novel) is being divided into several smaller data sets. Consequently, the frequencies for individual items in the keyword/POS/concept lists produced by Wmatrix can sometimes also be rather small, which can be an issue when applying statistical significance tests. The test Wmatrix uses to ascertain keyness is log-likelihood (LL), and keyword/POS/concept lists are ranked by LL value, with the highest values (and therefore most significant items) at the top of the lists. Often when using keyness lists, the analyst will decide a cut-off level of significance or keyness to shorten the list. With LL, there are various cut-off points indicating different levels of significance. Since I am using relatively small amounts of data for my comparisons,

I have followed the recommendations in Rayson et al. (2004) and used a fairly high LL cut-off of 10.83, which is significant at p-value[4] 0.001 (the standard social science p-value of 0.05 is 6.63 in LL terms). Using this cut-off level increased the level of confidence in the statistical reliability of the results, as well as greatly reducing the list of key concepts for each narrator, thus making my analytical task more manageable.

5. Analysis and discussion

In this section I will discuss the results from the semantic comparisons described above for each of the three main narrators. The output is presented in tables and shows, for the sake of completeness and comparison, all the key concepts with a LL of 10.83 and above. However, I will necessarily restrict my discussion to only one item from each of the tables.

5.1. Analysis of key concepts in Stuart's narration

Table 20.3 lists, in order of statistical significance, the key concepts in Stuart's narration; that is, the semantic categories which are statistically 'over used' by comparison with the other narrations in the novel. In columns 3 and 4, 'Total Words' refers to the total number of word forms that Wmatrix has grouped under a particular USAS category. The figures in brackets represent that number as a percentage of the total number of words in the file. So, for example, 4401, or 19.01 per cent of the words in Stuart's narration, are pronouns, whereas in the rest of the narrations combined, 8702 or 17.44 per cent of the words are pronouns.

Table 20.3: Key concepts in Stuart's narration when compared with the other narrations combined

No.	USAS category	Stuart: Total words (%)	Others: Total words (%)	LL
1	E4.2: DISCONTENT	22 (0.10)	7 (0.01)	23.85
2	I1: MONEY GENERALLY	60 (0.26)	53 (0.11)	22.09
3	Z8: PRONOUNS	4401 (19.01)	8702 (17.44)	21.72
4	F2: EXCESSIVE DRINKING	17 (0.07)	4 (0.01)	21.68
5	T2: TIME	100 (0.43)	120 (0.24)	18.15
6	A3: EXISTING	980 (4.23)	1799 (3.60)	16.15
7	S2.1: PEOPLE: FEMALE	65 (0.28)	71 (0.14)	15.25
8	S2: PEOPLE	101 (0.44)	135 (0.27)	12.80
9	I3.1: UNEMPLOYED	13 (0.06)	5 (0.01)	12.42

An initial glance at Table 20.3 finds key concepts that relate thematically to Stuart's story. Using a term adopted by Scott (2009) in his definition of keyness in the Wordsmith Tools online manual, they give a sense of the 'aboutness'[5] of Stuart's narration. For example, the category of MONEY GENERALLY ties in with Stuart having a job in a bank, and that he loans Oliver money on a number of occasions throughout the story. The categories of F2: EXCESSIVE DRINKING and S2.1: PEOPLE: FEMALE also seem relevant since Stuart begins drinking heavily when things go wrong between him and Gillian (and Oliver), and he talks about females throughout the novel. Initially, he tells us that he had little success with them when he was younger, he then goes on to talk a lot about Gillian, and later he speaks about the escort girls he uses post-Gillian. Even the most statistically significant category, E4.2: DISCONTENT, seems to fit in well with Stuart's circumstances, as he is likely to be very discontented when his wife leaves him for his best friend. However, while this list of key concepts is, to some extent, thematically revealing, further investigation is required to determine whether these categories assist us interpretively. Indeed, it is perhaps best to regard each key concept as a possibility for more focused analysis. After all, statistical significance (or statistical overuse) indicates only that differences in relative frequencies obtained by comparison do not occur by chance. The high log-likelihood value for E4.2: DISCONTENT for Stuart's narration merely suggests (albeit quite strongly) that the higher frequency of words that fall into the USAS E4.2 category in Stuart's narration when compared with the other narrations combined is not a fluke. The job of the analyst, therefore, is to discover whether the statistical significance translates to interpretive significance (see also Leech 2008: 163–4; Leech and Short 2007: 41). Of course, there will not always be a connection, and there will be some data that is more or less interesting than other data. This is perhaps true of all stylistic analysis.

When investigating key concepts, I find that a useful way to start is to examine the list of the word forms assigned by Wmatrix to a semantic category using concordance lines. In the first instance, this is a good way to check that all lexical items have been assigned correctly, because Wmatrix can make mistakes (USAS is currently 92 per cent accurate). It is also a good way to check whether there are any patterns of distribution of the word forms, or whether they tie in with important incidents in the story. We therefore must return to the text in order to consider whether each key concept is interpretively useful. However, as there is not enough space here to work down the whole list shown in Table 20.3, I will restrict my discussion of Stuart to the most significant category in his narration, E4.2: DISCONTENT.

Table 20.4 lists the word forms in the DISCONTENT category in Stuart's narration and shows that even though this is the most significant category in

Table 20.4: Word forms in the DISCONTENT category
in Stuart's narration

DISCONTENT words	Totals
disappointed	8
disappointment	5
disappointing	4
disappoint	2
disillusion	1
disillusioned	1
displeased	1
Overall Total	**22**

Stuart's narration by comparison, the number of words assigned to it is actually quite small – just 22. Moreover, none of the word forms presented in Table
20.4 appeared in the keyword list resulting from the comparison between
Stuart's narration and the other narrations. As I mentioned in the introduction, Wmatrix can be a useful addition to the stylistician's tool-kit, because key
concepts can sometimes highlight important themes in a text that might have
otherwise been missed if only keywords or word-frequencies had been investigated. As we will see, E4.2: DISCONTENT is a good example of this.

Table 20.4 shows that most of the word forms that are assigned to the E4.2
semantic group from Stuart's narration are forms of the lexeme *disappoint*.
By looking at the distribution of these items in the text, we find that the
majority of them appear in small clusters in two places in the novel. The first
cluster is in Chapter 5 – 'Everything Starts Here' – where Stuart states that
whatever happened in the past, before he married Gillian, no longer matters;
the marriage is his new starting point. He illustrates this by talking about a
number of things from his past including his (deceased) parents, and how he
felt he might be a disappointment to them (note: in this and other quotations
from *Talking it Over* used throughout this chapter, all words from a particular
semantic category are underlined):

> My parents were the type of parents who always seemed faintly <u>disappointed</u>
> by whatever it was you did, as if you were constantly letting them down in
> small ways [...] I could see my parents' point of view. I was a bit <u>disappointing</u>.
> I was a bit <u>disappointing</u> to myself.
>
> (Barnes 1991: 49–50)

Stuart goes on to say that now, this is no longer important:

> It's now now; it's not then any more. Then has gone away. It doesn't matter
> that I <u>disappointed</u> my parents. It doesn't matter that I <u>disappointed</u> myself.

It doesn't matter that I couldn't ever get myself across to other people. That was then [...].

(Barnes 1991: 52)

At this early point in the novel, Stuart is making a new start for himself. Marrying Gillian, who accepts him and loves him the way he is, enables him to see the negative feelings he had (and he suspected his parents had) about himself as irrelevant. While he does not say that he is trying to forget the past, he is apparently drawing a line under those feelings, and moving on.

Later on in the novel, however, after Gillian has left Stuart, there is a second cluster. In Chapter 16, '*De Consolatione Pecuniae*', in which Stuart is the only narrator, Stuart reflects on his divorce from Gillian, and Gillian's subsequent marriage to Oliver. It is here that the theme of 'disappointment' re-emerges, and we find that, in fact, it has never been far from Stuart's mind. He explains how he used to be afraid that he was disappointing Gillian:

You remember about my parents, how I always had the feeling that I was <u>disappointing</u> them? [...] I used to think that I was <u>disappointing</u> Gillian.

(Barnes 1991: 225-6)

From this disclosure we realize that while, in Chapter 5, Stuart declared that being a disappointment to himself and to his parents did not matter any more, the fear of being a disappointment lingered post-nuptially. However, as Stuart continues to reflect, we discover that his perspective on 'disappointment' has, in fact, shifted:

Then, a bit later, I began to realize that it wasn't me who'd <u>disappointed</u> her, it was they who'd <u>disappointed</u> me.

(Barnes 1991: 226)

'Disappointment' remains a central concern for Stuart, but rather than worrying about being a disappointment to his wife (and others), he is more concerned about not being disappointed. Consequently, Stuart's new approach to life is:

Get your <u>disappointment</u> in first. <u>Disappoint</u> them before they <u>disappoint</u> you.

(Barnes 1991: 226)

This is because he feels that he can no longer trust people, particularly females.

How did I know someone wasn't just waiting for me to become attached to them so that they could stab me with <u>disappointment</u>?

(Barnes 1991: 227)

This change in attitude toward other people is a sign of a change in Stuart's personality, and while being rather negative (and paranoid), it actually helps him to do well in his job in the bank. This is because instead of trusting people, he puts his trust in money, and he devotes himself to his work, which results in a promotion (and a move to the United States). The change in attitude and the shift of trust are also symptomatic of Stuart's altered perspective on love: he becomes either unwilling or emotionally incapable of expressing and feeling love. This leads him to use the services of escort girls, which allows him to keep sex and love completely separate.

5.2. Analysis of key concepts in Gillian's narration

Table 20.5 lists the semantic categories over-used in Gillian's narration when compared with the other narrations in the novel.

The table contains only five significant items above the 10.83 cut-off value. This is 44 per cent fewer than the nine shown in Stuart's table (Table 20.4) and, unlike Stuart's items, they seem less thematically relevant to her narration and appear, at first glance, to be less promising. Also, when I looked more closely at the top two over-used USAS categories in the table, I found that the most frequent word forms in z8: PRONOUNS are 'I' and 'he', and in Q2.1: SPEECH: COMMUNICATIVE 'said'. While these give an indication that Gillian, when compared to the other narrators, does more reporting of the words spoken by both her and others in her narration, these three lexical items are also keywords for Gillian, when her narration is compared to the other narrations at the individual word level. So, in the case of these two key concepts, we do not really gain anything from the semantic groupings and subsequent comparison. The other three over-used categories, however, offer more potential, containing word forms that, firstly, are not keywords, and, secondly, cluster at important moments in the story. Word forms from O1.2: SUBSTANCES AND MATERIALS: LIQUID cluster around Oliver giving Gillian a bunch of flowers and telling her for the first time that he loves her, while

Table 20.5: Key concepts in Gillian's narration when compared with the other narrations combined

No.	USAS category	Gillian: Total words (%)	Others: Total words (%)	LL
1	Z8: PRONOUNS	3406 (19.47)	9697 (17.45)	29.56
2	Q2.1: SPEECH: COMMUNICATIVE	245 (1.40)	513 (0.92)	27.25
3	O1.2: SUBSTANCES AND MATERIALS: LIQUID	28 (0.16)	28 (0.05)	17.74
4	X3.2: SOUND: QUIET	18 (0.10)	16 (0.03)	13.20
5	A5.3: EVALUATION: ACCURATE	22 (0.13)	26 (0.05)	10.92

Table 20.6: Word forms in the EVALUATION: ACCURATE category in Gillian's narration

ACCURATE *word forms*	*Totals*
right	11
properly	4
exact	1
correctly	1
correction	1
correct	1
corrected	1
accurately	1
accurate	1
Overall Total	**22**

those from X3.2: SOUND: QUIET cluster around Gillian's description of Oliver when he comes to watch her do her painting restoration work. As for words forms from A5.3: EVALUATION: ACCURATE, the fifth item in the table, I believe these help to develop Gillian's character further, and it is this I will discuss in the rest of this section.

Table 20.6 shows that *right* is the most frequent of the word forms that Wmatrix assigned to the A5.3 semantic category from Gillian's narrations.

Looking at the very first occurrence of *right*, which is from near to the beginning of the novel, in Gillian's third narratorial contribution, we can see that it seems important to her that the story is being told accurately:

I'm just making a small <u>correction</u>.

That's the trouble with talking it over like this. It never seems quite <u>right</u> to the person being talked about.

(Barnes 1991: 39)

Later, towards the end of the novel, Gillian shows that even choosing the correct word seems to matter to her:

I do have this fear. Is that the <u>right</u> word?
(Barnes 1991: 269)

Gillian's *fear* about getting it *right*, though, seems to extend beyond lexical choice and accuracy of account, and into how she sees life in general:

I remember thinking as we stood in the baggage hall, this is a bit like the rest of life. Two of us in a great mass of strangers, and various things to do that you've got to get <u>right</u>, like follow signs and collect your luggage.

(Barnes 1991: 76)

Gillian's account of what she was thinking while she and Stuart waited for their bags in the airport after returning from their honeymoon reveals that she believes life is about getting things *right*, doing things in the correct order, and following rules. However, when Oliver begins trying to win Gillian from Stuart, this belief begins to unravel because she is unsure about how to react and what is the right thing to do.

Oliver's pursuit of Gillian starts with him delivering a large bunch of flowers to her at home while Stuart is out at work. She initially dismisses this incident as erratic behaviour caused by stress due to Oliver recently losing his job. She takes time 'to think over <u>properly</u> what had happened' (ibid.: 92), which involves her imagining possible conversations with Stuart when he returns home from work that evening. She concludes that the flowers will turn Stuart against Oliver, jeopardizing their long friendship, and she believes that Oliver needs the full support of his friends while he sorts himself out. She decides, therefore, to keep the flowers a secret from Stuart, and to dispose of them. This moment marks the beginning of Gillian concealing Oliver's actions from Stuart, although she does it with, apparently, good intentions, and after due process of thought. She has decided on what she believes to be the *right* thing to do, and she is at this point, harking back to Levenson's (1991) description of Gillian, deliberate. Oliver, however, is persistent and continues by phoning her daily to tell her that he loves her. Gillian decides to hang up each time and, importantly, to carry on not telling Stuart. Oliver even secretly follows Gillian and Stuart to France when they go on a short weekend break. Gillian spots Oliver on the ferry during the homeward journey, but she does not tell Stuart about this either. She finds, therefore, that her carefully thought-through course of action is not working and is forcing her to conceal more and more from Stuart. She eventually admits to the reader, 'I don't know if I did the <u>right</u> thing' (Barnes 1991: 105), and she goes on to tell the reader, after Oliver phones again, soon after the trip:

> I keep trying to think whether I've ever encouraged him. I never intended to. Why do I feel guilty? It's not <u>right</u>. I haven't done anything.
>
> (Barnes 1991: 114)

Gillian seems frustrated: her deliberate course of action (or inaction) is backfiring. If life is simply about '... various things to do that you've got to get right' (ibid.: 76), then she must have got this wrong because she finds herself in a situation that is *not* right. What is more, she feels guilty about it. A few lines later we find out why, when she confesses, 'I feel guilty because I find Oliver attractive.' (ibid.: 114). At this moment we realize that Stuart has lost.

The word forms assigned to the A5.3: EVALUATION category in Gillian's narration highlight her use of *right*, and her concern about what is *right*, and doing the *right* thing. The A5.3 category is, therefore, not only statistically significant, but also interpretively significant, as it helps identify a pattern of behaviour that assists in the characterization of Gillian. This particular behaviour could also be linked to other important aspects of her narration. For example, Gillian reporting what she and others said more than other narrators (mentioned at the start of this section) could be another way in which she tries to tell the story as accurately as possible, adding further detail to a character that is not easily described.

We can see from the two analyses so far that, by comparing semantic categories, Wmatrix can focus our attention on a small group of word forms that individually were not statistically key by comparison. Bringing the words together in a list, as Wmatrix does, can create a focus for closer reading and draw attention to salient moments in a text.

5.3 Analysis of key concepts in Oliver's narration

Table 20.7 lists, in order of statistical significance, the over-used semantic categories for Oliver's narration when compared with the other narrations in the novel. We can see from the table, first of all, that Oliver's narration

Table 20.7: Key concepts in Oliver's narration when compared with the other narrations combined

No.	USAS category	Oliver: Total words (%)	Others: Total words (%)	LL
I	Z99: UNMATCHED	1319 (4.96)	602 (1.30)	822.32
2	B1: ANATOMY AND PHYSIOLOGY	307 (1.15)	339 (0.73)	33.42
3	Z5: GRAMMATICAL BIN	7294 (27.43)	11,700 (25.18)	32.84
4	L2: LIVING CREATURES: ANIMALS, BIRDS, ETC.	86 (0.32)	58 (0.12)	32.19
5	X2.4: INVESTIGATE, EXAMINE, TEST, SEARCH	52 (0.20)	24 (0.05)	32.04
6	O4.1: GENERAL APPEARANCE AND PHYSICAL PROPERTIES	54 (0.20)	31 (0.07)	25.68
7	K2: MUSIC AND RELATED	35 (0.13)	16 (0.03)	21.78
8	C1: ARTS AND CRAFTS	62 (0.23)	48 (0.10)	18.07
9	X2: MENTAL ACTIONS AND PROCESSES	18 (0.07)	6 (0.01)	14.83
10	Z3: OTHER PROPER NAMES	59 (0.22)	52 (0.11)	12.89
11	O4.3: COLOUR AND COLOUR PATTERNS	86 (0.32)	88 (0.19)	12.29
12	A1.7: CONSTRAINT	26 (0.10)	15 (0.03)	12.28
13	X3.3: SENSORY: TOUCH	17 (0.06)	7 (0.02)	11.73
14	G3: WARFARE, DEFENCE, AND THE ARMY; WEAPONS	32 (0.12)	22 (0.05)	11.60

contains more key concepts than the other two main narrations (almost three times more than Gillian's and 55 per cent more than Stuart's), and represents a very broad variety of semantic domains.

However, none of the key concepts appear to be thematically related to Oliver's story: falling in love with his best friend's wife; winning her from him; getting married to her; and moving to France. Anyone who has read the novel, though, will have noticed how Oliver 'decorates' his narration, as Moseley puts it, with 'far-fetched cultural allusions' (Moseley 1997: 141) some of which, as Guignery points out, are literary and musical (Guignery 2006: 76). He also shares with the reader his thoughts and theories about, for example, life in general ('Life is like invading Russia.' [Barnes 1991: 15]), and he frequently, as Stuart explains, 'just sort of zooms off' (ibid.: 2) into 'spiels' (ibid.) or, as Oliver calls them, 'riffs' (ibid.: 2, 79, 220), about anything and everything, whether it be marriage vows or time-share apartments. Consequently, Oliver's narration contains a broad range of topics, evidence of which we can see reflected in the relatively long list of key concepts, which offers statistical backing for these features of Oliver's narration.

We can also see from Table 20.7 that the first key concept in the list is highly statistically significant with an LL score of over 800, the largest LL by far of any key concept for any narrator. That Z99:UNMATCHED turns out to be so statistically key is rather interesting because it is not a semantic grouping at all, but the 'bin' into which Wmatrix puts all the word forms that it cannot assign to a specific semantic domain, because they are not in its lexicon and are therefore not recognized. The Wmatrix lexicon has, by and large, coped well in other research (e.g. Archer et al. 2009 analyse key concepts in Shakespeare's comedies and tragedies; Ho 2007 investigates two editions of a novel; and Nakano and Koyama 2005 investigate e-learning materials), but Table 20.7 shows that nearly 5 per cent of the word forms in Oliver's narration are UNMATCHED, compared with just 1.3 per cent of the word forms in all the other narrations. Thus, the vocabulary used by Oliver appears to be very different not only from that used by the other narrators, but also from that represented by Wmatrix's lexicon. Oliver's UNMATCHED category, therefore, demands further investigation, and for that reason, the rest of this section will concentrate on just that.

To understand Oliver's UNMATCHED category more fully, I undertook a manual analysis of the word forms it contained and found that they could be divided into seven broad categories. These are shown in Table 20.8[6] and reveal some initial patterns in Oliver's UNMATCHED word usage that provide a starting point for further investigation.

Looking first at 'English, general', we can see from Table 20.8 that it contains the largest number of Oliver's UNMATCHED items. Subsequent analysis

Table 20.8: Oliver's UNMATCHED word forms: seven initial categories

Category	Frequency (tokens)	%
English, general	514	39.0
Hyphenated	312	23.6
Foreign	218	16.5
Names	141	10.7
Slang	58	4.4
Nonce	46	3.5
Other	30	2.3
Totals	**1319**	**100**

Table 20.9: 'scientific', 'poetic/archaic', and 'unusual' English words from Oliver's UNMATCHED group

Grouping	Words
Scientific	Propanol, Isobutyraldehyde, Auscultatory, Embryonically, Xylene, Sulphurous, Spectroscopic, Pheromones, Pachydermatous, Wattage, Rhombus, Heliotropic, Corona, Deliquesce, Rectal, colonic, Faecal, Steatopygous, Pudendum, Gonads, Micturition, Ejaculatory, Jugular, Mucous, Cerebellum, Corporeal, Lactating, Tricep, Sputum, Subcutaneously, Salivating, Carcinogenic, Ganglion, Goitrous, Torpor, Propranolol, Salve
Poetic/archaic	atop, carven, danegeld, doff, hie, limpid, mayhap, milady, moidore, plashing, quaff, quailing, swain, sward, triste, trysting, bedewed, swaddle, lumpen, lilting, legman, laggardly, despoiling, carven, besmirched, bedizened, slaked, febrifuge, wist, yeoman, yore
Unusual	aestival, aestivate, afflatus, albid, apothegm, appurtenances, beagling, cadenza, carapace, cartologists, cerulean, costive, cravenly, crepuscular, culpability, decrepitude, dotards, effulgent, emasculates, etymological, fetid, fomenter, frangible, harridan, histrionics, hymeneal, inspissated, jocosity, lachrymose, miscegenation, munificent, oleaginous, prescient, quotidian, quiddity, rebarbatively, rubescent, saturnine, sempiternal, senescence, simulacrum, skirl, taciturn, umbrageous, valerian, vicissitudes

of the word forms in this initial grouping found that three smaller subgroups were possible: 'scientific', 'poetic/archaic', and 'unusual'. These subgroups, which are presented in Table 20.9, account for around 25 per cent of the total word forms in 'English, general', and from them we can see at a glance that Oliver's vocabulary is broad, varied, and contains many unusual items and scientific terms. We can relate this to Moseley's comments reported in Section 2, that the creation of 'different voice-personalities is a matter of vocabulary ...' (Moseley 1997: 140), but notice the analysis here clearly shows specific words that form part of Oliver's vocabulary and which help to create his 'different voice-personality'. The items shown in Table 20.9 suggest that Oliver regularly opts for less conventional, ostentatious, rare, or scientific words instead of choosing more obvious, commonly used alternatives which are probably perfectly adequate. By constructing Oliver's language in this way, Barnes is creating a narrator that shows off lexically, which relates back to the descriptions of Oliver being 'showy' and a 'clever dick', as well as 'erudite' and 'learned'.

Bringing these words together manually into these groupings helps provide a clearer picture of Oliver's lexical repertoire and Wmatrix, by not recognizing so many of the word forms in the narration and thus creating a relatively large UNMATCHED bin, helped us notice this feature of Oliver's vocabulary. What I wish to consider at this point is what would have happened to Oliver's key concept list if Wmatrix had managed to assign all the words in my 'English, general' category to appropriate USAS categories.[7] I will do this using the 'scientific' words as an example, because they match up with the USAS categories of Y1: SCIENCE AND TECHNOLOGY IN GENERAL, B1: THE BODY AND PHYSIOLOGY, B2: HEALTH AND DISEASE, and B3: MEDICINES AND MEDICAL TREATMENT. If the *scientific* word forms are added to the word forms Wmatrix automatically tagged with Y1, B1, B2, and B3, and the log-likelihoods are recalculated,[8] we find that the LL value for Y1 increases from 3.35 to 27.46, putting it in sixth position in the list of over-used items shown in Table 20.7, thus increasing the number of key concepts with a LL above 10.63 to 15. Recalculating B1 increases the log-likelihood from 33.42 to 55.35, making it more key without altering its rank. Amending B2 and B3, however, only increases the LL from 1.37 to 2.57, and from 0.59 to 3.02 respectively, which means that these concepts would still not be considered key.

We can see from this exercise that, by and large, if the Wmatrix lexicon were updated and Oliver's 'scientific' words assigned to appropriate categories, this aspect of Oliver's narration would still be highlighted. However, it is unlikely that the same would be true for the 'poetic/archaic' and 'unusual' word forms used by Oliver, because my manual categorizations are not semantic, but based instead on my own language intuitions, and they therefore do not correspond to any of the USAS categories. So, while the Wmatrix lexicon could be updated to include these lexical items, they would end up being dispersed across many semantic groups, and this aspect of Oliver's language would probably disappear off the 'empirical-radar'. It is arguably fortuitous, then, that in this case Oliver lexically 'outperformed' Wmatrix.

We can see from this that for the analyses of some texts, such as *Talking It Over*, a relatively limited 'standard' dictionary, rather than a large broad-ranging dictionary, might be more useful, because 'non-standard' language usage is then highlighted via the UNMATCHED bin. However, other investigations of more specialized texts might need a more specialized lexicon, otherwise too many words might be tagged as z99, thus rendering the results less than useful. Thus, a choice of Wmatrix lexicons might sometimes be useful, depending on the type of text being analysed.[9]

Turning now to the hyphenated words, this category simply includes any English words that are connected by a hyphen. Examples of such words (with some limited contextualization) include:

> rampant nut-eater
> hinge-creaking arthritis
> bone-snafflingly puppyish
> éclat-lacking
> dog-and-boning it
> assegai-wielding sociopath
> less-than-state-of-the-art spectacles

This love affair with hyphens is a sign of Oliver's creativity: he uses them inventively to form new units of meaning throughout the novel. This category also highlights that computer analysis of hyphenated word forms is problematic, because they are multi-word units that have meaning different from the meanings of the individual words. Wmatrix, therefore, did not know what to do with many of them, and since the use of hyphens in English is rather flexible, designing software to cope with all hyphen possibilities would, I imagine, be very difficult. In order for Wmatrix to classify hyphenated words, therefore, they have to be added manually to the lexicon. However, in a situation where someone is joining words by hyphen *willy-nilly*, as Oliver does, this would be a time-consuming task, which in any case might prove counterproductive. This is because, again, we have a case where it is better to see the evidence of idiosyncratic language usage grouped in such a way that it can be easily noticed and quantified.

'Foreign words' are here defined as any non-English words excluding foreign borrowings that are now well established in the English language. The languages Oliver makes use of, along with the number of word forms used, are given in Table 20.10, which shows that Oliver draws on a wide variety of different languages in his narration.

He seems better acquainted with some languages than others, but is particularly fond of French and, to a lesser extent, Italian. When you consider Oliver's partiality for certain types of wine and cuisine (following his marriage to Gillian, he chooses to have the 'wedding breakfast' in an Italian restaurant), this gives an indication of where his cultural allegiances lie. Oliver often weaves foreign words or phrases into his narration to form polyglot sentences and this could be seen as another way in which he shows off.

Table 20.10: Foreign words in
Oliver's narration

Origin	Tokens	%
French	130	60.00
Italian	40	18.60
Latin	27	11.62
German	12	5.58
Spanish	6	2.79
Afrikaans	1	0.47
Japanese	1	0.47
Greek	1	0.47
Total	**218**	**100**

The 'Names' category, in Table 20.7, includes words that I identified as proper nouns and is the only group from my initial classifications that matches a major USAS category (and associated subcategories). Many of the proper nouns used in Oliver's narration were not recognized as names by Wmatrix, hence their presence in the UNMATCHED bin, and in order to understand Oliver's use of names more clearly, I analysed the list of UNMATCHED items manually. I found that two further subgroupings were possible, which are presented in Table 20.11, and emphasize the particular types of name that Oliver refers to: (a) people, both real and characters from literature including Greek mythology; and (b) varieties of grape.

The names of composers and the famous names from cinema and photography that Oliver drops into his narration give yet another indication of his breadth of knowledge. Those from literature suggest that he is well-read, perhaps as a result of his university education. Those of varieties of grape relate to his interest in wines, which we are told about by Stuart, and to Oliver's apparent wish to be knowledgeable about such things. This perhaps tells us what sort of knowledge and behaviour he perceives to be desirable and/or valuable, and also relates to his 'showiness'. The names become points of reference that indicate, or attempt to indicate, a passing knowledge of many different cultural arenas.

Following this analysis, I manually assigned the UNMATCHED 'Names' items to the relevant USAS categories and found that 81 per cent of the words fit into Z1: PERSONAL NAMES, 5 per cent into Z2: GEOGRAPHICAL NAMES, and the rest (14 per cent) into Z3: OTHER PROPER NAMES. The new totals along with the recalculated LL values for these three categories[10] are presented in Table 20.12 and show that if Wmatrix had successfully categorized the names used in Oliver's narration, the significance of the Z1 and Z2 categories, when compared with the other narrators, would still have been below the 10.83 cut-off value.

Table 20.11: Some of the proper names used in Oliver's narration

People	Viticulture
Shostakovich, Schreker, Casanova, Cartier-Bresson, Halley, Berlitz, Voltaire, Kafka, Palladio, Poulenc, Rossini, Rimsky, Herod, Uccello, Oskar Werner, Orson Welles, Thalia, Ganymede, Orfeo, Mélisande, Pelléas, Patrodus, Morpheus, Tatyana, Tristan, Beowulf, Silenius, Lares, Goliath	shiraz, tempranillo, pinot noir, malbec, mourvèdre, cinsault, sercial, soave

Table 20.12: Recalculated LL scores for USAS categories Z1, Z2, and Z3

	Oliver		Others combined		
USAS category	Raw total	%	Raw Total	%	LL
Z1: PERSONAL NAMES	590	2.22	935	2.01	3.44
Z2: GEOGRAPHICAL NAMES	122	0.46	205	0.44	0.12
Z3: OTHER PROPER NAMES	79	0.30	66	0.14	19.58

Thus, in the case of Z1: PERSONAL NAMES, using statistical significance as a means of directing closer analysis of a text would have resulted in the references to literary characters in Oliver's narration not being highlighted. The more general category containing other proper names, which was already statistically significant (see item 10 in Table 20.7), would have a higher LL score of 19.58 (increasing from 12.89) and would have highlighted, for example, the references to viticulture. So, while a category containing relatively few items (Z3) is usefully shown to be highly significant, a category containing many more (interesting) items (Z1) is shown to be much less significant by comparison. Clearly, then, sometimes it is not the number of items that are in a category that is important, but the nature of the items. The USAS categories on this occasion do not help because proper names, as Oliver demonstrates, can come from many walks of life and the category is too broad to show this. However, developing new USAS categories to cope with all eventualities probably goes beyond what is reasonably possible. It is again fortunate, therefore, that many of the names used by Oliver were placed in the UNMATCHED bin.

My 'slang' category collects together word forms from Oliver's narration that are of a highly colloquial nature, and also includes taboo or swear-word forms, such as *wankpit*. The slang terms Oliver uses, shown in Table 20.13, seem to be a mixture from different cultures and different sections of society: *vamoose* and *mugwump* are perhaps more associated

Table 20.13: Slang word forms used by Oliver

Slang word forms
vamoose, bosh, corking, canoodle, mugwump, slammer, mucker, chivvying, filch, podge, wankpit, stiffy, pinkie, joshing, handjob, gusher, gasper, fartface, clodhopped, chuffer, brownnosed, bopping, bonky

with North American English; *bosh* and *corking* are British English slang with public-schoolboy associations; and *mucker* and *slammer* have working-class associations.

The nonce category mainly includes words that Oliver has created by compounding (e.g. *plodmobile*), affixation (e.g. *farouchely*), and conversion (e.g. *mugwumping*). These again show that creativity is part of Oliver's style and that word-class conversion is something at which Oliver appears to be very adept. While this feature of Oliver's narration did not go unnoticed when I read the novel (i.e. it is a deviant use of language that is foregrounded), this type of corpus analysis enables all instances of this feature to be quickly accessed and collected together, which helps in quantification, identification of patterns, and assessing interpretive relevance.

Some of the words created by Oliver use the names of real people as their stem, showing that not only does Oliver use names as points of reference, he also uses them ingeniously to describe, for example, the manner in which he does things, for example:

So I Nureyeved the front steps and flowed through the door in a single motion of Yale and Chubb.

(Barnes 1991: 46)

After coffee I announced myself eager for the fleecy crook of Morpheus' shoulder, and they buggered off. I gave them a three-minute start then Bogartishly gunned my heap.

(Barnes 1991: 116)

Both examples require the reader to possess certain cultural knowledge to appreciate what is meant by *Nureyeved* and *Bogartishly*, and it is not surprising, therefore, that Wmatrix placed these items in the 'bin'.

Finally, the 'Other' category shown in Table 20.6 collects together the remaining words that would not fit into the other groupings, for example instances of Oliver representing certain sounds in his narration, such as 'whoozh' or 'paf'. These perhaps give an indication of a sometimes fairly animated style of narration, but the frequencies are very low, and I will not be discussing them any further in this section.

The Wmatrix output for Oliver provides evidence to suggest the he is unusual semantically when compared with other narrators. It also indicates, using the Wmatrix lexicon as a yardstick, that Oliver is generally lexically unusual. The highly significant z99: UNMATCHED group that resulted from comparing Oliver's narration to the others turned out to be unexpectedly very useful because it (a) provided empirical evidence for some of the observations made about Oliver noted in Section 2; (b) helped to test out Wmatrix, raising questions concerning the USAS categories, and (c) demonstrated that an unexpected (or negative) result can sometimes turn out to be interesting and useful.

6. Summary and conclusion

In this chapter, I tested out the semantic functionality of Wmatrix by using its output (a) to guide my analysis of the three main narrators in *Talking It Over* and (b) to provide empirical evidence for subjective impressions about those narrators. The list of key concepts produced by Wmatrix by comparing each of the three main narrators helped to identify and quantify certain characteristics of each of those narrators arising from intuition and critical commentary of the novel. The most significant key concept for Stuart (E4.2: DISCONTENT) help to show that, at the start of the novel, he is concerned with not being a disappointment to others, but towards the end of the novel, after his divorce from Gillian, his main concern is for him not to be disappointed, thus indicating a shift in personality. Gillian's fifth key concept (A5.3: EVALUATION: ACCURATE) provided information about her character that I have so far not seen mentioned in any critical reviews of the novel. It indicated her concern with accuracy, that the details of her account are complete and correct, and about getting things right. Oliver's top key concept (z99: UNMATCHED) contains the word forms from his narration that Wmatrix could not match to a semantic category. This grouping contained scientific, archaic, poetic, foreign, hyphenated, nonce, and slang word forms that Oliver uses in his narration, and suggests that he has a comparatively broad vocabulary, containing both learned and colloquial words. The unusual, technical, and poetic words suggest knowledge of many different walks of life, and using these words in place of more commonplace alternatives could be seen as evidence of Oliver being showy and flamboyant. The list also showed that Oliver can be creative with language, and creativity is very much part of his style.

This chapter demonstrates, then, that Wmatrix can be useful in stylistic analysis, providing an objective and replicable method of investigation of the narrators of a novel. The USAS component made it possible to compare and contrast the narrators' language in a systematic way using a level of analysis that would have been extremely difficult and time-consuming to perform by hand. It produced empirical data that supported my intuitions, as well as those of various critics, about the three main narrators and, in the case of Gillian, offered new, interpretively relevant, information. It identified a key theme in Stuart's narration, and generally helped to highlight parts of a novel that were worthy of closer reading and further consideration. Importantly, in many instances, the insights that this 'semantically guided' closer reading provided would have been missed by individual or keyword analysis alone.

The analysis of Oliver's key concepts offered an unexpected test for Wmatrix, and demonstrated that the USAS categorizations were not always sufficiently detailed to tease out all aspects of Oliver's style of narration, and that further manual manipulation of the data was required. This showed that there is perhaps a case for expanding the semantic categories represented in the USAS system, to include, for example, foreign words or hyphenated words (even though, like PRONOUNS, these are not necessarily semantic domains). Other categories, such as proper names, are perhaps necessarily broad and would be more difficult (or impossible) to expand in a way that would cater for all possible eventualities, such as a narrator like Oliver. Indeed, if the Wmatrix lexicon and semantic categories represent some sort of standard then we can see, through the analysis of Oliver's narration, that it makes a useful measure against which language use can be compared. Connected to this is the issue concerning how the Wmatrix lexicon should be managed. Currently, it is updated and expanded as an ongoing process. Whether this is the best way to proceed, and whether there should be a fixed 'standard' lexicon (and what that standard should be) is still to be decided. Nevertheless, as this chapter has demonstrated, Wmatrix is a useful corpus tool, and as its functionality develops and expands, it will become increasingly useful for stylistic (and other) analysis.

Acknowledgement

I wish to thank Jane Demmen for her constructive criticism, detailed comments, and general help during the writing of this chapter.

NOTES

1. For further information about UCREL see http://www.comp.lancs.ac.uk/ucrel/
2. For further information about USAS, see http://www.comp.lancs.ac.uk/ucrel/usas/
3. In Table 20.2 and throughout the rest of this chapter, I will use SMALL CAPITALS when referring to particular USAS top level categories.

4. P-value is the probability of error or chance. The lower the p-value the less likely it is that the result is by chance or that accepting the result is incorrect.
5. 'Aboutness' is a term relating to topic or subject. It is discussed on the EAGLES (Expert Advisory Group on Language Engineering Standards) website in relation to Phillips (1983, 1989) and his work on determining topic through computer-assisted analysis of texts. See <http://www.ilc.cnr.it/EAGLES/texttyp/node21.html> (accessed 28/09/2009). See also Leech's comment concerning semantic level analysis and 'aboutness' (Leech 2008: 176).
6. I am not claiming the categories used here and later on in this section are perfect, but they are sufficient to illustrate the discussion.
7. To some extent, Wmatrix does now cope better with Oliver's narration because its lexicon has since been updated in light of Oliver's original unmatched list.
8. Before recalculating the LL, the unmatched 'bin' of the other narrators also had to be checked for words that could be reassigned to the Y1, B1, B2, and B3 categories.
9. This, to some extent, has been addressed, as it is possible for users to build their own lexicons within the Wmatrix environment.
10. Again, this involved checking the unmatched 'bin' for the other narrators combined, and reassigning any items that matched the Z1, Z2, and Z3 USAS categories before recalculating the LL values.

CHAPTER 21

Writing Presentation, the Epistolary Novel and Free Indirect Thought

Joe Bray

This chapter examines the representation of writing and reading in the eighteenth- and early nineteenth-century novel. Compared to the parallel discourses of speech and thought, the representation of writing has received little critical attention. This essay demonstrates that it is prevalent in a popular genre of the novel in the eighteenth century: the epistolary novel. The letter-writers of the two epistolary novels under investigation here, Samuel Richardson's (1753–54) *The History of Sir Charles Grandison* and Charlotte Smith's (1792) *Desmond*, quote copiously from each other's letters and represent the words of their correspondents with varying degrees of accuracy, often to distance themselves from accusations and criticism. This chapter argues that the way in which written words are read and responded to is also crucial in novels which, although not epistolary, contain letters. In Jane Austen's (1813) *Pride and Prejudice*, for example, the interpretation of letters is a major preoccupation. The increasingly detailed and sophisticated representation of reading within the novel necessitated the development of new narrative techniques for illuminating the reader's consciousness. It led in particular to the emergence of the style which was to dominate the subsequent history of the nineteenth- and twentieth-century novel, free indirect thought.

1. The neglect of writing presentation

Of the three scales of discourse presentation, that of writing has received the least critical attention. Semino and Short (2004: 47) point out that because in fictional texts 'the presentation of writing is not usually very central', in their original account of the discourse presentation scales 'Leech and Short (1981) had not felt the need to posit a separate set of categories for writing presentation', and that 'the same applies to all other studies of discourse presentation we are aware of, including those that focus on non-fictional texts'. In the most comprehensive recent study of free indirect discourse, for example, Fludernik (1993: 3) notes that 'speech and thought representation in (fictional) narrative is clearly a crucial issue in narrative poetics and for a variety of reasons', making no mention of writing representation. Throughout her book though, 'speech and thought (or consciousness)' often slides into the more encompassing 'discourse', which could include writing, as for example in the sentence 'The rendering of (others') speech and consciousness in the medium of language includes a variety of phenomena on very different levels of discourse production and a critical analysis of *representation* needs to distinguish between these levels and their various aspects of linguistic (re) production' (ibid.: 16).

Work on the Lancaster Speech, Writing and Thought Presentation Written Corpus of around 260,000 words of contemporary British English, divided equally among prose fiction, newspaper news stories, and (auto)biographies, has however revealed the need, in Semino and Short's (2004: 16) words, 'to systematically distinguish a third parallel presentation scale, writing presentation', to put alongside those of speech and thought presentation.[1] Though analysis of the corpus has confirmed that writing presentation is not very common in fiction, it does occur, according to Semino and Short (2004: 48), 'quite regularly in news reports and (auto)biography, and so the analysis of our corpus made us aware of the range of possible writing presentation forms'.

One of the key findings of the analysis of the Lancaster corpus, as reported by Semino and Short (ibid.), is that while 'the relative frequencies of writing presentation categories in the corpus are quite different from those that we found in relation to speech presentation on the one hand and thought presentation on the other [...] with relatively few exceptions, the forms and functions of writing presentation categories are very similar to those for speech presentation'. That is, direct writing (DW) was found to be similar in form and function to direct speech (DS), and indirect writing (IW) to indirect speech (IS), and so on. Semino and Short's explanation for this congruence across the two scales is that 'in both cases the original is (or purports to be) a piece of discourse, even though the medium is different. Indeed, it could be argued that writing presentation is "like speech presentation but more so", in the sense that canonical faithfulness claims associated with DS apply more strongly to DW, and that this strengthens the association of the various faithfulness claims with the different presentational categories on the writing presentation scale' (2004: 50). The strength of the 'faithfulness claims' of the writing categories is also emphasized by Short et al. (2002: 334), who argue that 'while faithfulness is fundamentally problematic in relation to thought presentation', it remains a pertinent criterion in the presentation of speech and, especially, writing: 'writing and speech are both in principle accessible to the reporter, but speech is only accessible at the moment of utterance, and so memory limitations intervene unless a recording is available. Writing, on the other hand, does not degrade rapidly over time, and is therefore usually available for reporters (and others) to check' (Short et al. 2002: 349). For Short et al. (2002: 334), the fact that each of the presentation scales has a different relationship to the notion of faithfulness is further evidence of the need to 'distinguish systematically among speech, thought and writing, and only use "discourse" when it is genuinely inclusive of its hyponyms'.

This chapter investigates the historical development of the presentation of writing by examining a fictional genre in which, as Semino and Short note, the quotation of writing is relatively frequent, at least in comparison to other types of fiction: the epistolary novel (2004: 47). This genre was at its height in the eighteenth century, when it developed techniques for the representation of speech and consciousness which greatly influenced the later history of the novel (see Bray 2003). Attention to two eighteenth-century epistolary novels, Samuel Richardson's (1753–54) *The History of Sir Charles Grandison* and Charlotte Smith's (1792) *Desmond*, reveals that the way writing is represented in this genre is no less sophisticated. Furthermore, comparison between the two texts suggests that the representation of both writing and reading within the epistolary novel may have developed during the latter half of the eighteenth century in ways which were important and far-reaching for the novel as a whole. This essay endorses the findings from the Lancaster corpus-based studies, as summarized in Semino and Short (2004), that the writing presentation scale has more in common with its counterpart for speech than that for thought, especially as regards claims to faithfulness to an anterior source. However, it also suggests that the increasingly complex representation of writing in the late eighteenth-century epistolary novel influenced the development of ways of representing consciousness in the novel, including one crucial stylistic technique which went on to dominate the nineteenth- and twentieth-century novel: free indirect thought (see also Busse, Chapter 2, this volume).

2. Writing and the epistolary novel I:
The History of Sir Charles Grandison

Samuel Richardson's third epistolary novel, *The History of Sir Charles Grandison*, was published in seven volumes between 1753 and 1754. In some ways it was written as a response to the reception of his second, the controversial *Clarissa; or The History of a Young Lady* (1747–48). Richardson was anxious in particular to counteract the unexpected sympathy many of his readers had felt for Lovelace, the rakish villain of *Clarissa*, by, as he puts it in his Preface, 'produc[ing] into public View the Character and Actions of a Man of TRUE HONOUR' ([1753–54] 1986: 4). In comparison with *Clarissa*, the structure of *Grandison* is also more complex, and the focus is less completely on the central heroine, in this case the reserved Harriet Byron. Instead Richardson presents a more diverse set of letter-writers and correspondences; Harriet not only writes letters to and receives them from her cousin Lucy Selby, but also her aunt Mrs Selby and her grandmother Mrs Shirley, and indeed various other members of her family, and later in the novel Sir Charles's sister Lady Grandison and other members of his family. Sir Charles's correspondence is also presented, especially in Volume III, where a series of letters to his friend Dr Bartlett detailing his adventures in Italy is shown by the latter to Harriet, who in turn incorporates and comments on them in her letters to Lucy.

Within this complicated structure, reports of letters and quotations of writing abound. In Letter XXXVI of Volume I, for example, Harriet, after summarizing letters she has received from her 'aunt Selby', 'my dearest grandmamma', Lucy's siblings Nancy and James, and her godfather Mr Deane, assures Lucy that she has not forgotten '*your* letter in the enumeration of the contents of the previous pacquet!', claiming that 'you and I, my dear, write for all to see what we write: And so I reserved yours to be last-mention'd' ([1753–54] 1986: 178). Lucy has apparently demanded that she tell her more about her new acquaintances Sir Charles and his sister:

> And so you expect the particular character and description of the persons of this more than amiable brother and sister. Need you to have told me that you do? And could you think that after having wasted so many quires of paper in giving you the characters of people, many of whom deserved not to be drawn out from the common crowd of mortals, I would forbear to give you those of persons who adorn the age in which they live, and even human nature?
>
> You don't question, you say, if I begin in their praises, but my gratitude will make me write in a *sublime stile*; so you phrase it; and are ready, you promise me, to take with allowance, all the fine things from me, which Mr. Reeves has already taught you to expect.
>
> (Richardson [1753–4] 1986: 178)

Various forms of writing presentation are apparent in this passage. The opening sentence is a representation of Lucy's words in her letter, as indicated by the next sentence: 'Need you to have told me that you do?' How close it is to Lucy's actual written words is a matter of debate; it could simply be a general summary of her letter (Narrator's Report of Writing). Alternatively, if Lucy's words were something like 'I expect you to tell me more about the character and appearance of Sir Charles and his sister', then this is an example of the category Narrator's Report of Writing Act, with Harriet reporting Lucy's request (this category is parallel to Narrator's Report of a Speech Act (NRSA) on the speech presentation scale). The sentence in the next paragraph may come nearer to Lucy's actual words, as indicated by 'you say', 'so you phrase it', and 'you promise me', with the reported writing in subordinate clauses and the first-person pronouns transposed to second-person, and vice versa. This is thus Indirect Writing (or IW), but with some direct quotation; the italicization of *'sublime stile'*, for example, suggests that these are actual words from Lucy's letter. As Parkes has shown, one of the earliest functions of italics was to mark quotations, especially scriptural ones, and during the course of the seventeenth century their quotative use spread to other types of text. In the eighteenth century they were gradually supplemented by quotation marks, which grew out of the ancient mark for indicating noteworthy passages from the Scriptures, the 'diple' (Parkes 1992: 52, 58; see also Bray 2000a: 108–9).

Unfortunately Lucy's original letter is not available for us to check the faithfulness of Harriet's representation of her words, though of course it would have been to Lucy (who like most eighteenth-century letter-writers would probably have kept a copy). On other occasions the 'anterior discourse' is accessible to the reader though, as it comes from a previous letter in the novel. In Letter XL of Volume I, for example, Mrs Selby tells Harriet that it has become obvious to them all that she is falling in love with Sir Charles. A few pages later, in Letter XLIV, Harriet replies to her aunt in a defensive, even angry tone, beginning by declaring that 'Indeed, my dear and ever-indulgent aunt Selby, you have given me pain; and yet I am very ungrateful, I believe to say so: But if I feel the pain (tho' perhaps I ought not) should I not own it?' (Richardson [1753–54] 1986: 217). Harriet then proceeds to quote passages from her aunt's letter, accusing her of letting her uncle write the most incriminating parts:

What *circumstances*, what *situation*, am I in, madam, that I cannot be mistress of myself? That shall turn my uncle's half-feared, tho' always agreeable raillery into *pity* for me?

'Over head and ears in the passion' – 'I to be on the hoping side; the gentleman on the triumphant' – 'It is impossible for you my friends to be aforehand with my inclinations' – 'A beginning love to be mentioned, in which one is willing to conceal one's self from one's self!' *Fires, Flames, Blazes* to follow! – *Gratitude* and *Love* to be spoken of as synonymous terms – Ah! my dear aunt, how could you let my uncle write such a letter, and then copy it, and send it to me as yours?

And yet some very tender strokes are in it, that *no man*, that hardly any-body but you among *women*, could write.

(Richardson [1753–54] 1986: 217)

Again there is a variety of different kinds of direct and indirect writing presentation here. Harriet's first question, for example, appears to quote the words 'circumstances' and 'situation' from her aunt's letter, as well as the suggestion that 'I cannot be mistress of myself', which may not have been expressed directly. This could therefore be seen as an example of the Narrator's Report of Writing, with some elements of direct quotation. At the start of the next paragraph Direct Writing predominates, with Harriet apparently quoting phrases from her aunt directly, though again the category is slightly mixed, as the pronouns and person are changed as they would be in Indirect Writing (e.g. in 'I to be on the hoping side; the gentleman on the triumphant', where Mrs Selby would have used 'you'). This time the faithfulness, or accuracy, of Harriet's representation of her aunt's words can be checked against their original, anterior source, Letter XL. Thus 'What *circumstances*, what *situation*, am I in, madam, that I cannot be mistress of myself?' is a reference to Mrs Selby's comment that 'But do we not see, my dearest child, that something has happened, within a very few days past, that must distance the hope of every one of your admirers, as they come to be acquainted with the circumstances and situation you are now in?' (Richardson [1753–54] 1986: 212), while 'That shall turn my uncle's half-feared, tho' always agreeable raillery into *pity* for me?' picks up on 'Your uncle's tenderness for you, on such a prospect, has made him suppress his inclination to railly you. He professes to pity you, my dear' (ibid.). While Harriet uses italics for '*circumstances*', '*situation*', and '*pity*', she adopts the relatively new quotation marks for longer phrases and sentences. 'Over head and ears in the passion', 'I to be on the hoping side; the gentleman on the triumphant', 'It is impossible for you my friends to be aforehand with my inclinations', and 'A beginning love to be mentioned, in which one is willing to conceal one's self from one's self!' are indeed all almost direct quotations from Mrs Selby's letter, though the first two come from her report of her husband's words, while the third and fourth slightly alter the passage 'By several hints in your letters, it is impossible, my dear, that we *can* be aforehand with your inclinations. Young women in a beginning love are always willing to conceal themselves from themselves' (Richardson [1753–54] 1986: 212). '*Fires, Flames, Blazes* to follow! – *Gratitude* and *Love* to be spoken of as synonymous terms' refers more loosely to the passage which follows immediately after:

[...] they are desirous to smother the fire, before they will call out for help, till it blazes, and frequently becomes too powerful to be extinguished by *any* help. They will call the passion by another name; as *gratitude* suppose: But, my

Harriet, gratitude so properly founded as yours is, can be but another name
for *love*.

(Richardson [1753–54] 1986: 212)

In this letter, then, Harriet adopts two different quotative techniques. She
uses italics to quote single words from her aunt's letter, while preferring the
new quotation marks for longer phrases or sentences. In each case, comparison with Letter XL reveals Harriet's faithfulness to her original, anterior
source; though she is certainly selecting from the letter for her own purposes,
arguably distorting it in the process, Harriet quotes her aunt's words accurately. This is true of other examples in the rest of the novel. In Letter X of
Volume II, for example, Harriet responds to two previous letters, from her
aunt and her grandmother, which again express their view that she is in love
with Sir Charles, and offer their sympathy. She is less defensive by now, and
more persuaded of the truth of their opinion. While she uses quotation marks
for passages from which 'I will endeavour to reap consolation [...] in the two
precious letters before me', such as ' "If you love, be not ashamed to own it to
us – The man is Sir Charles Grandison" ' and ' "Love is a natural passion" ',
she uses italics when picking out words and phrases from her relatives' letters.
Thus the opening of Mrs Selby's letter –

We are all extremely affected with your present situation. Such apparent struggles betwixt your natural openness of heart, and the confessions of a young, of
a new passion, and that so laudably founded, and so visibly encreasing – O my
Love, you must not affect reserves. They will sit very aukwardly upon a young
woman, who never knew what affectation and concealment were.

(Richardson [1753–54] 1986: 301)

– prompts this response:

To be charged so home, my dear aunt! – *Such apparent struggles* – And were
they, madam, so *very* apparent? – A *young*, a *new passion*! – And so *visibly
increasing*! – Pray, madam, if it be *so*, it is not at its height – And is it not, while
but in its progress, conquerable? – But have I been guilty of *affectation*? of
reserves? – If I have, my uncle has been very merciful to the *awkward* girl.

(Richardson [1753–54] 1986: 307)

In *Grandison* then, letter-writers often quote each other's written words as
they comment on or take issue with them. Especially in the early part of the
novel, the heroine Harriet Byron is eager to refute the insinuations of her
correspondents that she is falling in love with Sir Charles. As she responds
to their views, she incorporates their written words into her letters using a

variety of forms of writing presentation, as shown in the above examples, as well as two different quotative techniques. In each case she quotes the written words of others with a high degree of accuracy, as can often be checked by comparing her versions with the original letters given earlier in the novel. In other words, writing is represented faithfully and often very directly in *The History of Sir Charles Grandison*, as its many letter-writers quote each other frequently and copiously.

3. Writing and the epistolary novel II: *Desmond*

In Charlotte Smith's *Desmond* ([1792] 2001), on the other hand, the representation of writing is less immediate and accurate. Much of this epistolary novel is taken up with the correspondence between the hero Lionel Desmond and his friend E. Bethel, who repeatedly attempts to dissuade him from his romantic infatuation for a married woman, Geraldine Verney. In order to try and conquer his passion, Desmond makes a tour into France with Geraldine's brother Waverly, reporting back on the situation there in the aftermath of the French Revolution. Though he generally comments favourably on what he sees, his journey is hazardous and his itinerary ever-changing, and as a result he and Bethel often either do not receive the other's letters or send replies that cross confusingly. Their correspondence is further strained later in the novel when Desmond secretly follows Geraldine once she has separated from her husband, refusing in his evasive letters to his friend to reveal his exact location. As the rest of this section will demonstrate, the more fraught and uncertain nature of the epistolary exchanges in *Desmond* means that, in comparison with *Grandison*, quotations of writing are less immediate and less easily traceable to their anterior source.

As in *Grandison*, letter-writers in *Desmond* do quote frequently from each other's letters, though the quotations are often less direct. Take this example from Letter II of Volume I, in which Bethel replies to Desmond's Letter I, in which he announces his plan to travel to France with Waverly:

Yes! – you have really given an instance of extreme prudence – and, in consequence of it, you will, I think, have occasion to exert another virtue; which is by no means the most eminent among those you possess; the virtue of patience. – So! – you have really undertaken the delightful office of bear-leader – because the brother of your Geraldine cannot take care of himself – and this you call setting about your cure, while you continue to dispute, whether it be wise to be cured or no – and, while you argue that a passion for another man's wife may save you from abundance of vice and folly, you strengthen your argument to be sure wonderfully, by committing one of the greatest acts of folly in your power. – And as to vice, I hold it, my good friend, to be a great advance towards it, when you betray symptoms (which no woman can fail to under-stand) of this wild and romantic passion of yours, or, as you sentimentally term it, this ardent and pure attachment – an attachment and an arrangement, I think, are the terms now in use. I beg pardon if I do not always put them in the right place.

(Smith [1792] 2001: 52–3)

Some phrases here are clearly intended to refer back to Letter I, in which Desmond protests his continued love for Geraldine. Both 'this you call set-ting about your cure' and 'or, as you sentimentally term it, this ardent and pure attachment' seem to represent Desmond's actual words. Yet in fact in his letter Desmond refers to himself as 'a patient, who knows his disease to be incurable' (2001: 52), and writes separately of 'this attachment – which will end only with my life' and 'a passion, so pure and ardent as mine' (2001: 51, 52), never using the phrase 'this ardent and pure attachment'.

As the correspondence continues, Desmond continues to defend his pas-sion for Geraldine, often countering Bethel's jibes concerning his romantic ideals. In Letter V of Volume I, for example, he writes, 'You tell me, Bethel, that I vainly expect to meet the cultivated mind and polished manners of refined society, united with the simple and unpretending modesty of retired life, while the idea I have thus dressed up as a model of perfection, will embit-ter all my days – It will indeed! – But it is not the search that will occupy, or the *idea* that will persecute me – it is the reality, the living original of this *fair idea*, which I have found – and found in possession of another' (2001: 67). Again Desmond is clearly responding to a previous letter of Bethel's here, as indicated by the opening 'You tell me', though the exact form of words used by Bethel is not available, and hence it is impossible to know how accu-rately Desmond is representing his friend's words. What is evident though is his defiance, apparent here in the exclamation 'It will indeed!', followed by the adversative 'But'. Similarly in Letter XV Desmond rebuts forcefully his friend's suggestion that he could become attracted to another woman: 'What did I say to you, dear Bethel, in my letter of the 29th of August, that has given you occasion to rally me so unmercifully about Madame de Boisbelle; and to predict my *cure*, as you call it – I cannot now recollect the contents of that letter; but of this I am sure, that I never was more fondly attached to the lovely woman, from whom my destiny has divided me, than at this moment' (2001: 152), while in Letter X of Volume II he breaks off from his rage at Geraldine's ill-treatment by her husband with the words 'But if I continue in this strain, I shall get into those regions of heroics that are, you say, beyond the reach of your reasonable and calm comprehension' (2001: 202). In these two examples the 'as you call it' and 'you say' indicate that Desmond is again referring to his friend's letters, though again the accuracy of his representation is unclear, with only the italicized *'cure'* in Letter XV definitely signalling direct quotation.

In all these cases then, Bethel's original letters are not presented in the novel, so the possibility of checking the accuracy of Desmond's quotations is not available. There is thus a possibility that Desmond is in part responding not to specific accusations, but to the general tenor of his friend's criticism of his hopeless passion. That is, it is likely that Bethel has expressed the sentiment that his friend has created in Geraldine 'a model of perfection', which will 'embitter all my days', and that he tends when speaking of her to fly into 'regions of heroics' that are 'beyond the reach of your reasonable and calm comprehension' more than once, and not necessarily in these exact words. In the absence of actual letters from his friend, partly caused by his own somewhat chaotic travels in the novel, Desmond often responds in his letters to what he knows Bethel thinks, or would say, about his behaviour. Thus in Letter XVII of Volume III, for example, Desmond writes particularly gloomily of his apparently doomed love: 'Yet, I know, you will say I have lost nothing that I ever possessed; and that if I could once determine to look out for some other enjoyments than those my romantic fancy had described, I might yet find as reasonable a portion of happiness as any human being has a right to expect' (2001: 362), indicating through the words 'I know, you will say' that he is responding to imagined, rather than specific advice. In Letter XVI of Volume II Desmond makes the hypothetical quality of Bethel's accusations against him even more explicit, as he recounts how he concealed himself in the vicinity of Geraldine and her children, yet with 'no motive injurious either to my friendship towards you, or my more tender affection for Geraldine':

> 'How then,' you ask, 'were you concealed in her immediate neighbourhood, without any intention of either? – Incredible folly!' – Such, however, *were* my intentions. – I allow, if you please, all the folly; but I insist upon it, that there was no sort of harm in such a gratification as I proposed to myself, by which myself only (if romantic attachment can hurt a man) was alone likely to be hurt [...]

> (Smith [1792] 2001: 250)

The question and exclamation which Desmond imagines his friend writing in response to his revelation are thus examples of hypothetical writing, paralleling equivalent hypothetical categories on the speech and thought presentation scales. Semino et al. (1999) have investigated this hypothetical category further, linking it to possible worlds theory. Here the hypothetical writing shows Desmond's knowledge of his friend's likely reaction to his clandestine behaviour, as well as his own awareness of his foolishness. This example is thus far removed from the Direct Writing and examples of direct quotation in *Grandison*. Forty years later, the representation of writing in the episto-lary novel has, at least on the evidence of these two texts, become both less immediate and more imaginative. In *Desmond*, letter-writers do not simply quote each other's words back at them, but are capable of inventing them, and projecting their own anxieties on to their correspondents. The process of reading and responding to letters, in other words, has become as important as rendering the written words of the letter accurately, prefiguring the crucial role which letters would take in the development of the late eighteenth- and early nineteenth-century novel.

4. Reading letters and the representation of consciousness: *Pride and Prejudice*

Though the epistolary novel became less popular in the last decades of the eighteenth century, characters throughout the late eighteenth- and early nineteenth-century novel are constantly reading and interpreting letters. In this section I will focus on one novel in particular in which the reading of letters is crucial: Jane Austen's (1813) *Pride and Prejudice*, which according to several critics may have started out in draft in epistolary form.[2] Thirteen letters are given in full in the novel. Some of these are revealing of character; Elizabeth is appalled, for example, at Lydia's first letter after her elopement with Wickham: ' "Oh! thoughtless, thoughtless Lydia!" cried Elizabeth when she had finished it. "What a letter is this, to be written at such a moment" ' ([1813] 1996: 236). The two letters written by Mr Collins similarly display all his faults in full. After her father has read the first of them aloud to the family, Elizabeth gives another typically shrewd assessment of its writer: ' "He must be an oddity, I think," said she. "I cannot make him out. – There is some-thing very pompous in his stile." ' (ibid.: 56).

Thus although characters in *Pride and Prejudice* do not quote from letters or seek to imaginatively reconstruct them, they do spend a great deal of time reading and interpreting them. One letter in particular in the novel is cen-tral to the development of the plot and subject to much scrutiny. After his first rejection by Elizabeth, Darcy writes her a long letter defending himself against the two principal charges of which she has accused him: first that he has 'detached Mr Bingley from your sister', and second that in defiance of honour and humility he has 'ruined the immediate prosperity, and blasted the prospects of Mr Wickham' (ibid.: 162). In the first half of the letter he presents his behaviour with a complacency bordering on smugness: ' "On this subject I have nothing more to say, no other apology to offer. If I have wounded your sister's feelings, it was unknowingly done; and though the motives which governed me may to you very naturally appear insufficient, I have not yet learnt to condemn them"' (ibid.: 164). Even less introspection occurs in the second half of the letter as Darcy gives an account of his dealings with Wickham, laying before Elizabeth 'the whole of his connection with my family' (ibid.). This part of the letter is largely factual, as its writer indicates in conclusion: ' "This, madam, is a faithful narrative of every event in which we have been concerned together; and if you do not absolutely reject it as false, you will, I hope, acquit me henceforth of cruelty toward Mr. Wickham" ' (Austen [1813] 1996: 166).

Yet though this letter contains little internal debate or reflection, it prompts a great deal of both in its reader. Elizabeth's initial response to Darcy's self-justifications is confused: '... it may well be supposed how eagerly she went through them, and what a contrariety of emotion they excited. Her feelings as she read were scarcely to be defined' (ibid.: 168). Gradually as she re-reads the letter her feelings become clearer to herself. 'She read, and re-read with the closest attention' the part of the letter dealing with Wickham (ibid.: 169), slowly coming to a reassessment of his character. She tries to recollect 'some instance of goodness, some distinguished trait of integrity or benevolence, that might rescue him from the attacks of Mr. Darcy', but 'no such recollection befriended her' (ibid.). Instead her memory only serves to confirm Darcy's account:

> She perfectly remembered every thing that had passed in conversation between Wickham and herself, in their first evening at Mr. Philips's. Many of his expressions were still fresh in her memory. She was *now* struck with the impropriety of such communications to a stranger, and wondered it had escaped her before.
>
> (Austen [1813] 1996: 170)

Here the narrative style known as free indirect thought (or FIT) can be seen starting to emerge as Elizabeth remembers her first meeting with Wickham. While the third-person pronouns ('she', 'her') and past tense ('remembered', 'were') are retained, Elizabeth's perspective is suggested in the phrase 'the impropriety of such communications to a stranger'. Crucially, this last sentence also contains a commonly cited marker of the style: in Brinton's words, the 'co-temporality of narrative past tense with present and future time deictics' (1980: 367). Thus the past tense 'was', suggesting the narrator's perspective, is combined with the present time deictic 'now' in 'She was *now* struck'.[3]

After deciding that Darcy was 'entirely blameless' in his conduct with Wickham, Elizabeth turns to the second half of the letter dealing with her sister and Bingley:

> From herself to Jane – from Jane to Bingley, her thoughts were in a line which soon brought to her recollection that Mr. Darcy's explanation *there*, had appeared very insufficient; and she read it again. Widely different was the effect of a second perusal. – How could she deny that credit to his assertions, in one instance, which she had been obliged to give in the other?
>
> (Austen [1813] 1996: 171)

Again Elizabeth's re-reading leads her to re-evaluate Darcy's behaviour, and as she recollects his role in separating her sister and Bingley free indirect thought again emerges as her question is represented in the narrative: 'How could she deny that credit to his assertions, in one instance, which she had been obliged to give in the other?' This use of free indirect thought is an example of what Roger Gard describes as 'that flickering and subtle immediacy in representation of consciousness', which he calls 'one of Jane Austen's great gifts to the English novel' (1992: 56). It demonstrates that although she does not write a response, Darcy's letter provokes Elizabeth into a great deal of recollection and inner debate. She eventually comes to a complete reassessment of her past feelings concerning Darcy and Wickham: '"Pleased with the preference of one, and offended by the neglect of the other, on the very beginning of our acquaintance, I have courted prepossession and ignorance, and driven reason away, where either were concerned. Till this moment, I never knew myself"' (1996: 171).

5. Conclusion

In *Pride and Prejudice* then, as in Austen's other novels, the reading of letters is at least as crucial as the writing of them. While Darcy's letter of self-defence is relatively uninteresting in itself, it provokes a great deal of internal reflection and self-knowledge in its reader. Though Elizabeth does not quote passages from the letter, even to herself, the focus is on her response as she reads and re-reads it. Compared with the earlier eighteenth-century epistolary novels looked at in this chapter, in which characters quote, with varying degrees of directness, each other's written words, there is little or no representation of writing in Austen's novels. Instead letters are internalized within the consciousnesses of characters; Elizabeth wanders 'along the lane for two hours, giving way to every variety of thought; re-considering events, determining probabilities, and reconciling herself as well as she could, to a change so sudden and so important' (1996: 172). These 'varieties of thought' are in turn reflected in the narrative, as the style known as free indirect thought, so central to the development of the novel from Austen onwards, starts to emerge.

The depiction of reading within novels began to involve a psychological complexity that demanded a new technique for the representation of consciousness. The increasingly complex forms of writing presentation in the epistolary novel may have become relatively infrequent after the latter declined in popularity around the turn of the nineteenth century. Yet writing, and more especially reading, continued to provide fertile ground for stylistic innovation.

NOTES

1. Articles and chapters based on analysis of the corpus include Short, Semino and Culpeper (1996), Semino, Short, and Culpeper (1997), Semino, Short, and Wynne (1999), and Short, Wynne, and Semino (2002). A general summary of this work is given in Semino and Short (2004).
2. See, for example, Harding (1993: 465) and Southam (1964: 59).
3. For more on the form and function of FIT see Fludernik (1993); for its history and importance in the English novel see Cohn (1978) and Pascal (1977).

CHAPTER 22

'Appeased by the certitude': The Quiet Disintegration of the Paranoid Mind in *The Mustache*

JOANNA GAVINS

1. Clarity, comprehensiveness, and complexity

One would struggle to provide a more representative example of the typical impact of Mick Short's ideas over the last thirty years than the dominance across literary criticism, stylistics, and discourse analysis of the typology of speech and thought presentation originally outlined in Leech and Short (1981) (and subsequently tested and refined in Short 1996; Semino et al. 1997; and Semino and Short 2004). The appeal of this typology across a wide range of disciplines seems to lie equally in three parts: in its clarity; in its comprehensiveness; and in the added complexity it is able to lend broader enquiries into the construction of point of view in discourse (e.g. Fludernik 1993; Fowler 1986; Genette 1980; Simpson 1993). Of particular interest in this chapter is the light shed by Short et al.'s account of thought presentation onto our wider notions of literary focalization. Specifically, I examine the role played by free indirect discourse in the revelation of inner character in literary fiction through an analysis of Lanie Goodman's American-English translation of *La Moustache* by Emmanuel Carrère (1998). Idiosyncratic, anomalous, and stylistically deviant narratives have long been a source of fascination for stylisticians interested in literary point of view (see, for example, Fowler 1977; Gregoriou 2007; Leech and Short 1981; Semino and Swindlehurst 1996), and my interest in the peculiarities of *La Moustache* can be seen as part of this tradition. To date, no major critical work on the story has been published, although reviewers of the novel have described it variously as 'excruciating... [a novel which] sets forth the casual swiftness with which one's tenuous grip on reality can be lost forever' (Hawthorne 1997) and 'an allegory of the larger brutality which confronts our time: the narcissism which fails to flower into a new wholeness' (Couteau 1988). The analysis which follows examines the linguistic mechanisms through which this 'excruciating' effect is achieved. It also continues the recent cognitive trend in stylistic studies of point of view (e.g. Hoover 2004a; McIntyre 2005, 2006; Semino 2002, 2007), and seeks to extend traditional stylistic identification of moments of thought towards an understanding of the conceptual structures these moments entail. It is important to clarify from the outset that the conclusions I draw over the coming pages are not in any way intended as an account of the conceptual structures represented within the original French version of the text. The discussion below is not concerned with issues of linguistic, literary, or cultural translation, but with the style of Goodman's edition, *The Mustache* [*sic*], alone.

The framework I use for my analysis is text world theory (for fuller expositions see Gavins 2003, 2005a,b, 2007a,b; Hidalgo Downing 2000a,b, and c; Lahey 2006; Werth 1994, 1995a, b, and 1999). Here is where a further and, for me, far greater debt is owed to Mick Short's influence on stylistics. Had it not been for his forward thinking, his passionate commitment to innovation in stylistics, and his sheer hard work editing the original manuscript for *Text Worlds: Representing Conceptual Space in Discourse* (Werth 1999), text world theory simply would not exist in its current form as a vigorous, dynamic, and expanding approach to discourse analysis.

2. Building the world of *The Mustache*

The narrative structure of *The Mustache* progresses chronologically and appears, at least from its opening paragraphs, to be building a text-world along realist lines:

> 'What would you say if I shaved off my mustache?'
>
> Agnes, who was on the living room couch, flipping through a magazine, laughed and replied, 'That might be a good idea.'
>
> He smiled. Small islands of shaving cream sprinkled with little black hairs were floating on the water's surface in the bathtub, where he had been lingering.
>
> (Carrère 1998: 149)

The description of an unremarkable domestic scene here provides the reader with substantial information with which to construct a mental representation of the discourse. As with the majority of written fictional texts, the discourse-world in which this mental representation is produced is split, with the discourse participants, the author, and the reader, occupying separate spatio-temporal positions. In such cases, readers counteract the absence of a co-participant in their immediate environment by positioning the narrator of the fiction in a participatory role (see Gavins 2007a: 128–31). In order to construct a coherent mental representation of the text, readers must rely on the world-building and function-advancing information provided by the narrator of a third-person narrative as if this text-world entity were a discourse-world human being. Indeed, readers of literary fiction commonly 'flesh out' their mental representations of the narratorial voice by mapping their discourse-world knowledge of the real author of the text onto this fictional entity. Such activity creates an implied author figure in the fiction, whose presence may be asserted with varying strength in the course of the narrative through either the provision or lack of evaluative commentary on the events described. In a similar mapping of discourse-world knowledge, we may assume, although the exact time of the story is unspecified, that the events portrayed in the text-world are unfolding against a contemporary background (see Ryan's 1991 principle of minimal departure). The opening paragraph quoted above presents little challenge to this supposition, with none of its composite objects (a couch, a magazine, a bathtub, and so on) appearing out of place in our knowledge frames of everyday contemporary domestic existence.

The text-world also contains two characters, or *enactors*, to use Emmott's (1997) terminology (recently incorporated into text world theory in Gavins 2007a): a female, Agnes, and an unnamed male. It is this male enactor who provides the perspective through which the third-person narration of *The Mustache* becomes focalized. Simpson provides a useful framework through which such narratives can be understood:

> Category A narratives are defined as those which are narrated in the first person by a *participating character* within the story ... Category B narratives are somewhat more complex. They all possess a third-person narrative framework and are told by an invisible, 'disembodied', non-participating narrator ... Category B narratives, however, may be divided into two modes, depending on whether events are related outside or inside the consciousness of a particular character or characters. Where a third-person narrative is told from a 'floating' viewing position, outside that of any character, then it is said to be category B, in *Narratorial mode*. In this situation the only 'voice' is that of the narrator. If such a third-person narrative invokes the 'licence of omniscience' and moves, whether momentarily or for a prolonged period, into the active mind of a character, then that character becomes, to use the common label, the *Reflector* of fiction.
>
> (Simpson 1993: 55)

In Simpson's terms, then, the text of *The Mustache* is a category B narration in Reflector mode, and its narration remains fixed with the perspective of the unnamed male enactor throughout the novel. As the story
progresses, no explicit opinions or judgements are offered by the narrator on the unfolding events; a fact which becomes of crucial importance
to the construction of the 'excruciating' effect of the novel, as we shall
see later in this analysis. Typical of this kind of narration, the focalizer
forms the deictic centre of the text, a position which can be seen beginning to emerge in the opening lines of the novel with the use of definite
reference in the construction of the deictic space ('the couch', 'the water's
surface', 'the bathtub'). The narratorial voice, by contrast, falls into the
background of the discourse as a consequence of its silence and the text-
world it initially created becomes of less importance than the subsequent
worlds being constructed by the focalizer of the novel. This common literary phenomenon has been described as resulting in an 'empty text-world'
by Lahey (2005) (see also Gavins 2007a: 133–5). An enactor participating
directly in the narrative has now become the filter through which all the
world-building and function-advancing information required by the reader
must pass. This shift has important ontological consequences, which are
dealt with in text world theory through a distinction between *participant-
accessible* text-worlds and worlds which are only *enactor-accessible* (ibid.: 77).
Only those text-worlds created by the participants in the discourse-world
are fully accessible by other entities existing at the same ontological level.
These worlds are open to verification by those involved in the discourse
and their content is generally accepted by the other participants as reliable and true. Worlds created by enactors in the text-world, on the other
hand, cannot be verified for truth and reliability by the participants in the
discourse-world; these worlds exist at a separate and inaccessible ontological level. Having said this, and as already discussed above, readers of fictional discourse must frequently accept enactor-created worlds as though
they have been produced at the discourse-world level. In the absence of
the real-world author of the text as a co-participant in the immediate
discourse environment, fictional narrators often become the only access
point to essential text-world information. In fixed focalized narratives, a
further ontological layer is added to this conceptual structure. The world
which forms the main body of *The Mustache*, for instance, is in fact an
enactor-accessible focalized world, since it represents the point of view of
the reflector of events in the text-world. This world is embedded within
the enactor-accessible world of the third-person narration, the omniscient
but nevertheless fictional voice which gives the reader access to the reflector's perspective. The world created by this narrative voice is itself standing in for the participant-accessible text-world which would prototypically

occupy this level in face-to-face communication. The significance of this embedding of worlds for the reader's experience of the novel as a whole, and of the ontological remoteness of the main narrative world in particular, is explored further below.

According to Werth (1999: 221), the two instances of direct speech contained within the opening paragraphs of *The Mustache* also help to establish the focalizer's perspective, since they have the effect of changing the deictic parameters of the text-world, grouping temporal and spatial deictic markers around the speaking enactor, rather than around the participants in the discourse-world. In prototypical examples, direct speech functions to inject present-tense discourse into past-tense narration, generating a new world through a *world-switch*, in text world theory terms (Gavins 2007a: 48–50). In the lines of *The Mustache* quoted above, however, this process is complicated somewhat by the occurrence of a conditional construction within the direct speech. In traditional grammar, conditionals are divided into two components: the 'protasis' and the 'apodosis'. The protasis is the part of a conditional which sets up a theoretical situation and marks it as remote from actuality. The apodosis component, on the other hand, defines a situation which is consequent on the protasis. When the male enactor asks his wife, 'What would you say if I shaved off my mustache?', the conjunction 'if' in the protasis part of this conditional sets up a remote world in which the event described ('I shaved off my moustache') is realized. This world is embedded within the world-switch already created by the direct speech itself. Agnes's own response is modalized. Again, in text world theory terms, modalization is world-forming, since it can be seen to add an attitudinal layer to the discourse, expressing varying degrees of belief, desire, and obligation. When Agnes comments, then, that 'That might be a good idea', the epistemic modal 'might' expresses relatively weak epistemic commitment on her part. This creates a new epistemic modal-world (ibid.: 110) in which Agnes's attitude to her husband's suggestion to shave off his moustache can be conceptualized as remote and ambivalent.

3. Embedded worlds and emerging paranoia

Despite the apparently complex world-structures produced by the opening lines of the novel, the narrative of *The Mustache* initially presents the reader with few surprises. The worlds described above may seem numerous, but they progress coherently and cooperatively and are in no way out of the ordinary in literary discourse, in either number or nature. Agnes's departure to buy groceries, however, advances the plot to a new level, though this shift is by no means immediately evident in the unremarkable nature of her actions. With his wife gone, the protagonist ponders their recent conversation and the possibility of surprising her on her return:

> ... what if, when she came back upstairs, he surprised her by actually shaving off his mustache? She'd declared five minutes ago that it might be a good idea. But she couldn't have taken his question seriously, not anymore than usual. She liked him with a mustache, and besides, so did he, although after all this time he was no longer accustomed to a clean-shaven face; there was really no way of knowing. In any event, if they didn't like his new look, he could always let his mustache grow back.

(Carrère 1998: 151–2)

The tense of the narrative and its spatial location remain unchanged in this passage. However, as the protagonist is left alone in the apartment with his thoughts, a slip into free indirect thought emphasizes the focalized nature of the text. Figure 22.1 shows the multifaceted conceptual structure which develops around the inner thoughts and speculations which make up the free indirect style.

The epistemic modal-world which makes up the main body of the fixed focalized narrative is shown emerging from the empty text-world layer as a focalized world, marked FOC in the diagram. Since all focalization involves the portrayal, through various stylistic means, of an enactor's inner thoughts, it is classified as a type of epistemic modal-world in text world theory. A second epistemic modal-world, a hypothetical situation, is then embedded within the FOC world, as the protagonist considers what might happen if he were to shave off his moustache to surprise his wife. The origins of this world are marked in Figure 22.1 as HYP and a number of further worlds spring from within it. The focalizer's thoughts then flash back to Agnes's comments some minutes ago that shaving might be a good idea, creating another embedded world, shown in the diagram as an FBK frame. In this instance, the world's temporal parameters shift, indicated by the use of past perfect tense and resulting in a short-lived world-switch. The next sentence then contains some strong epistemic modality, as the protagonist decides that Agnes '*couldn't* have taken his question seriously', producing an embedded epistemic modal-world, marked EPS in the diagram. Further modality, this time boulomaic, is also evident in the sentence which follows, as we are told of both Agnes's and the protagonist's fondness of his moustache. Once again, the text is here filtered through an attitudinal position and the resulting new world exists remotely from the main narrative (see Gavins 2007a: 94). This new world is shown in Figure 22.1 as a BOUL frame. Finally, the conditional construction 'if they didn't like his new look, he could always

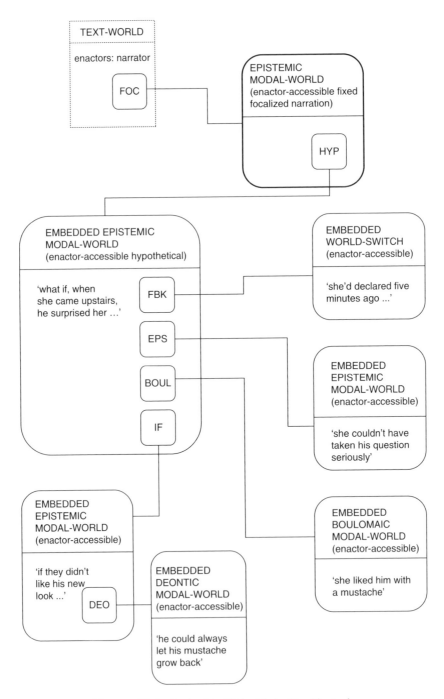

Figure 22.1: Embedded Worlds in *The Mustache*

let his mustache grow back', creates an epistemic modal-world, shown as an IF world embedded in the central hypothetical frame. Unlike the conditional examined in the direct speech in the opening paragraph of the novel, the apodosis portion of this construction is modalized, signified in this case by the deontic modal auxiliary 'could'. This sets up a further embedded modal-world, marked in Figure 22.1 as a DEO world within its containing IF frame.

At the end of this prolonged contemplation, the protagonist finally shaves off his moustache; another apparently unremarkable act, the eventual repercussions of which are only darkly hinted at as he awaits his wife's return 'with the distressing feeling that he was in a dentist's waiting room' (Carrère 1998: 155). His unease increases when Agnes's reaction to his new appearance fails to fit in with any of the hypothetical situations he has imagined while soaking in the bath. She simply unpacks her shopping, turns off the stereo, and the two of them leave for dinner at some friends' house, without her even mentioning the change. As the couple arrive at Serge and Veronique's building, another extended episode of free indirect thought allows the reader an additional insight into the protagonist's increasingly irritated and confused state of mind:

> Why was she pretending not to have noticed anything? Was it so she could retaliate with her own surprise to the one he'd arranged for her? But that was precisely what was so strange: she hadn't seemed surprised at all, not even for a second to regain her composure and put on a straight face... Of course, one could claim that he'd warned her, she'd even said laughingly that it would be a good idea. But that had obviously been in jest, a false answer to what was still, to his way of thinking, a false question.
>
> (Carrère 1998: 158–9)

Once again, a series of worlds are embedded within one another as the focalizer struggles to understand his wife's behaviour. Hypothetical worlds, for example, are created by the protagonist's wondering, 'Was it so she could retaliate ...?', as well as by his admission that 'one could claim that he'd warned her'. A number of modalized worlds also occur, created, for example, by the epistemic modality in the assertion that an earlier comment by his wife 'had *obviously* been in jest...'.

Crucially, as the occurrences of free indirect thought in the text increase to reflect the focalizing enactor's agitated state, no clues are provided for the reader by the third-person narrator about the accuracy, or otherwise, of the embedded worlds now being created at great frequency. The text-world level of the discourse remains silent and empty as the perspective of the protagonist continues to form the reader's only access point to the world-building and function-advancing information needed to process the text. A series of further remote worlds are then posited:

> Serge and Veronique were going to laugh, first at his new look, then at the practical joke Agnes had played on him, they'd laugh at his nervous irritation, which he planned to acknowledge, sparing no details, making himself look as if he were in a fog, and ridiculously grouchy, playing tit for tat.
>
> Unless... unless his opponent, who never ran out of ideas, was one step ahead of him and intended to let Serge and Veronique in on it... He imagined her in the middle of coaching Serge and Veronique at that moment, Veronique chortling with laughter, on the verge of hysteria from trying to act natural.
>
> (Carrère 1998: 159–60)

The first of these unrealized worlds is a hypothetical future situation (beginning 'Serge and Veronique *were going to* laugh') with different spatial and temporal parameters from those of its originating world. Interestingly, it is also considerably more detailed in its construction than those worlds which formed the protagonist's initial reaction to his wife's unexpected conduct, and it is unmodalized. Here, the focalizer seems confident in his predictions about Serge and Veronique's behaviour. Similar detail is provided in the further deictic alternation which follows it, embedded in the hypothetical construction 'Unless... unless his opponent, who never ran out of ideas, was one step ahead of him'. The contradictory content of the possibility he creates here, however, undermines his earlier confidence. In an instance of indirect thought, the protagonist goes on to imagine his wife coaching Serge and Veronique in their apartment. The reader's focus is allowed to relocate temporarily to a separate but concurrent scene, with the time-signature of the spatial shift matching that of the world from which it has sprung.

In the end, Serge and Veronique's behaviour during dinner seems to support the latter of the two hypotheticals contained within the extract above, as they too fail to mention any change in their friend's appearance. Their conduct, and the evidence it seems to provide for the focalizer, triggers a shift back to unmodalized narration:

> Serge and Veronique were in rare form. No supporting glances, no ostentatious display of discretion, they looked him straight in the eye, just as usual... During dinner the four of them talked about skiing, work, mutual friends, new films, so naturally that the joke began to lose its novelty.
>
> (Carrère 1998: 161)

The hypothetical wonderings of the previous passages are gone and the protagonist's opinions are presented in an epistemically non-modal form ('Serge and Veronique *were* in rare form', 'The game *was* played', and so on). His conclusions are obviously drawn – this is a joke, a game. The thoughts and feelings of the focalizer here form a simple subtext to the main narrative, as we are told that the joke is 'like those near-perfect pastiches', losing its appeal and making him feel 'like a child'.

As the evening draws to a close, despite his frequent provocations, the protagonist realizes that 'there would be no denouement, that the gag had stopped right there' (ibid.: 163), and his earlier irritation and confusion returns. During the car journey home, he finally confronts his wife and asks her directly if she has noticed anything different about his appearance. He becomes angry when Agnes claims not to know what he is talking about and refuses to admit that she has been playing a joke on her husband. An argument quickly escalates between the couple and it is during this extended fight that the significance of the fixed nature of the narration becomes most apparent. The positioning of what is an embedded enactor-accessible epistemic modal-world as the main text-world for the discourse means that, during the following exchange, the reader's empathy is firmly directed towards its focalizer as the only point of access to that world:

> She stammered, 'What's this story about a mustache?'
>
> 'Agnes,' he murmured, 'Agnes, I shaved it off. It's not important, it'll grow back. Look at me, Agnes. What's going on?'
>
> … 'You know very well that you never had a mustache. Stop it, please.' She was screaming. 'Please. It's ridiculous, please, you're scaring me, stop it. Why are you doing this?' Her voice trailed off in a whisper.
>
> (Carrère 1998: 170)

The reader sees Agnes's distress entirely from her husband's point of view, since no presentation of her inner thoughts is offered. Agnes's mind remains closed off and the focalization remains securely fixed with the main male enactor. The third-person narrator can once again be seen to be complicit in the creation of this effect, since once again no external evaluation of the protagonist's representation of events is given, as would be seen in a narrative in the 'narratorial' mode, in Simpson's (1993) terms.

It could be argued that the discrepancy between how Agnes seems to see the text-world and how her husband has presented it to the reader is significant enough to act at least as a *reminder* to the reader of the essentially enactor-accessible status of the narration so far. At one point Agnes even telephones Serge and Veronique to verify her case. However, though her obstinacy may begin to raise questions about the protagonist's reliability in the mind of the reader, the fact remains that he must be trusted as sole focalizer if any kind of mental representation of this story is to be built and maintained. Furthermore, the continuing, complicit silence of the omniscient narrator adds to the reader's confidence, since one might reasonably expect some sort of warning if the perspective of the main enactor was at fault in any way. Such trust is bolstered yet further by the production of the protagonist's own 'evidence' to support his claims. He hunts out some photographs of his and Agnes's last holiday in Java, in which he describes himself as appearing 'dressed in a batik shirt, his hair stuck to his forehead with sweat, smiling and mustached' (Carrère 1998: 174). Agnes simply hands the photos back to him, asking him, 'What do you want to prove?' (ibid.). Once again, the reader is encouraged to ignore the obvious ambiguity of this response by the protagonist's own acceptance of it as confirmation of his own perspective.

The protagonist remains confident in his thinking for most of that morning. The access granted to his inner thoughts reveals his conviction that Agnes has organized a conspiracy against him, a cruel practical joke in keeping with her mischievous personality. The protagonist's only uncertainty is his wife's motives for playing such a trick, but the modality of the majority of this section of the narrative remains categorical:

> [He] *decided to forget* the whole incident. He promised himself that *he wouldn't reproach her*, even if there was cause to do so. No, *there wouldn't be any cause. The case was closed. They wouldn't speak of it again.*
>
> (Carrère 1998: 182, my emphasis)

Once again, the focalizer's decisiveness is expressed through categorical constructions. On his arrival at work, however, a note of anxiety begins to resurface. None of his work colleagues mention the change in his appearance and, once again, he begins to hypothesize about their possible reasons. He speculates that Agnes may have called his work friends too and, while noting that his office is a busy place and his colleagues are overworked, he supposes that 'they might have said "Alright"' (ibid.: 184) and gone along with the joke. Some of the hypothetical worlds the protagonist constructs in this section of the novel have a stronger epistemic commitment attached to them than others (compare 'they *might have* said' with a later rationalization that 'upon his arrival, *surely* they would have shown their surprise' [ibid.]). This fluctuation provides a reminder of the real ontological status of the narration, and the conspiracy theory itself is also becoming less and less convincing as more people are drawn into the situation. The focalizer's own admission of this creates further epistemic distance between him and the reader.

As if in answer to the possibility of an increasingly doubtful reader in the discourse-world, the protagonist returns home and rummages through his dustbin, searching for the discarded remains of his moustache. He finds it and confronts Agnes again. Her reaction is as ambiguous as it was to his presentation of their holiday photos, as she comments that he has shown her, 'Hair...hair from your mustache. What do you want me to say?' (Carrère 1998: 194). Initially, her husband appears reassured of his own vindication, as he storms out of their bedroom and spends the night on the sofa. By morning, however, following a passionate reconciliation with Agnes, it seems that his true state of mind has changed little. Acute insecurity and paranoia are now evident in the occurrence of a series of conditional constructions, each setting up a hypothetical modal-world in which the focalizer is mentally ill: 'If things were actually what they seemed, he was suffering from hallucinations, maybe on the verge of a nervous breakdown' (ibid.: 204). Such explicit doubts may lead many readers to begin a re-evaluation of their mental representations of earlier scenes in the novel. Taking its terminology from Emmott (1997: 160), text world theory refers to such reassembly of text-world information to form a more coherent picture of events as *world-repair* (see Gavins 2007a: 141).

Determined to keep his fears from his friends and colleagues, the protagonist seeks an objective, external opinion by approaching a young woman in the street. He pretends, somewhat unconvincingly, to be blind and unsure whether the identity card he is carrying is his own. He asks the woman to verify whether the man in the photograph is wearing a moustache. When she says that he does, he responds, 'I don't have one!' and receives a further ambiguous reply, 'Yes, you do', from the young woman. This time, the protagonist does not miss the imprecision of the exchange, but becomes anxious when he tries to clarify what the woman means, opening his eyes and revealing his attempted deception. The woman becomes frightened and rushes away. A little later, as he calms down in a nearby café, the focalizer furthers the distance between himself and the reader by again admitting the possibility of a number of interpretations:

> He'd been unable to tell whether she was referring to the photo or to him as well, since he'd been standing right in front of her. But maybe she considered a mustache to be the black fuzz that during the last two days had started to grow on his upper lip. Maybe she didn't see that well. Or maybe he'd dreamed it, he'd never shaved off his mustache, it was still there, nice and thick.
>
> (Carrère 1998: 209)

Such paranoia has now become so prevalent in the text of *The Mustache* that it is worth examining how the worlds created by this narrative voice have been structured in more detail. Figure 22.2 (which also provides a more detailed breakdown of world-building [WB] and function-advancing [FA] information) shows how, on his arrival in the café, the protagonist's thoughts flash back to his meeting with the young woman on the street as he attempts

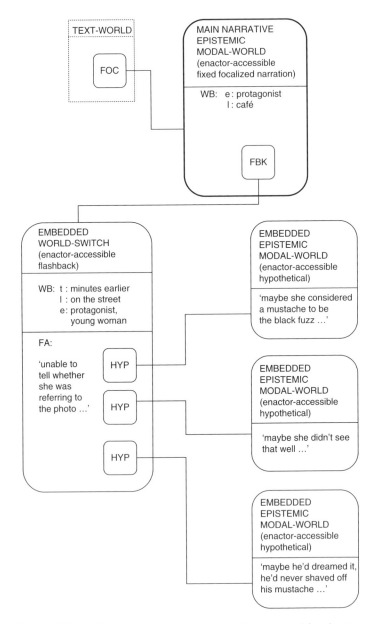

Figure 22.2: The conceptual structure of a paranoid focalization

to reconstruct his conversation with her. This is shown as an FBK world embedded within the epistemic modal-world of the main focalized narrative. Its temporal location (t) is five minutes earlier, its spatial location (l) is on the street, and its enactors (e) are the protagonist and the young woman. A series of hypotheticals then follow, each marked as a HYP frame in Figure 22.2, as the character considers a number of possible interpretations of the young woman's response to his questions.

The diagram makes clear the epistemic distance of this mental activity from the reader's discourse-world. As already discussed, in the first half of the novel the exclusive reader-focalizer relationship diverts the reader's attention from the logical inaccessibility of the main body of the narrative. As the story progresses and the protagonist becomes increasingly paranoid, however, his admission of his own mental instability presents a serious threat to any trust previously placed in his perspective by the reader. This does not mean, however, that the information provided by the focalizer necessarily ceases to be incremented into the reader's mental representation of the discourse. However paranoid and deluded the protagonist may prove to be, he remains the reader's only point of access to the text-world. It seems likely, then, that many readers may continue to sympathize with his distress and consider the numerous hypotheses he now presents as perfectly possible explanations for his situation.

Eventually, the protagonist decides to interpret the young woman's response to his questions as supporting his original belief that he used to have a moustache. His opinion does alter, however, on Agnes's role in the current confusion. He decides that it is, in fact, *she* who is mentally ill and he resolves to help her in any way he can, planning a quiet dinner out for them both later that evening. The modality of the narrative shifts accordingly:

> [T]he warning signs had made themselves clear: her flamboyant dishonesty, her excessive appetite for paradoxes, the stories on the phone, the brick walls, the radiators, the double personality, so sure of herself during the day, in the presence of a third person, and sobbing in his arms at night, like a child. He should have interpreted these warning signs earlier...he'd be there, always, and he'd always help her to be herself. He'd have to continue to behave that way, solid as a rock so she could lean on him.
>
> (Carrère 1998: 210–1)

The protagonist's conviction of his wife's instability is shown in his use of perception modality, 'the warning signs had made themselves *clear*', and his sense of duty in the deontic modality of the final sentences: '*He should have* interpreted these warning signs earlier', '*He'd have to* continue to behave that way', '*He couldn't* let himself be thrown off track'. Whether the reader now shares this point of view is debatable and, as before, external evaluation from the omniscient narrator remains absent. Nevertheless, access to the enactor's mind continues to be free and open, encouraging a close empathetic relationship between focalizer and reader, again helped by clear-cut instances of free indirect thought (e.g. 'he'd be there, always, and he'd always help her to be herself').

Further questions are raised by the events which take place during dinner, where the protagonist had planned to broach the subject of Agnes getting treatment for her mental illness. As he presents his identity card while paying for their meal, Agnes snatches it from him and scratches the photograph until the spot on his face where his moustache would be is completely removed. She then hands it back to him, accusing him of having defaced the card by drawing a moustache on it with a black marker. Throughout the ensuing fight the protagonist sticks to his conviction that Agnes is crazy, even explaining the black mark left by the photograph on her finger as having been put there deliberately before they went out. The modality of his narrative remains categorical as he attempts to deal with what he perceives as Agnes's elaborately destructive madness. When the couple return home, the protagonist attempts to close the matter once and for all by raising the issue of the photographs of Java he looked at earlier in the novel. Agnes simply responds: 'We've never been there.' (Carrère 1998: 238). The protagonist rushes to the bedroom to retrieve the photographs, which he finds are missing, so instead he throws a heap of other photographs in front of Agnes in which 'in every single one he was wearing a mustache' (ibid.). When, in the face of such conclusive evidence, Agnes clearly and calmly states, 'No you don't have a mustache ... in that picture or in any other' (ibid.), the protagonist performs a sudden and dramatic epistemic turnaround. He puts his trust entirely in his wife's perspective and concludes that *he* must be suffering a mental breakdown: 'It was, in fact, clear; all he could do now was be treated' (ibid.).

4. The quiet disintegration of the paranoid mind

The potential pitfalls of accepting an enactor-accessible modal-world as the basis for the mental representation of a discourse are quickly realized as the focalizer of *The Mustache* admits a version of his reality that he has fervently resisted up until this point. However, as I have emphasized throughout this analysis, the exclusive relationship so intimately constructed between the reader and the focalizer in this fixed focalized narration diverts our attention from the true logical status of the text so successfully that its worlds can be built upon even the shakiest of conceptual foundations. Hence in *The Mustache*, despite the mounting evidence of the focalizer's unreliability, despite the epistemic distance created by his own admissions of insecurity and his final acceptance of insanity, the empathetic relationship with the reader may nevertheless still prevail, even as the text-world disintegrates yet further.

Agnes offers to call her husband's parents and cancel a lunch they had planned. When the protagonist attempts to clarify the details of their arrangement a few moments later, however, she claims that she called only his mother: 'Your father died,' she said, 'last year.' (Carrère 1998: 242). His panic rising, the protagonist asks his wife to confirm the existence of a number of their other friends, his profession, her name, and her profession, before leaving their apartment and heading for his parents' house. He arrives in the street where he believes they live, only to discover that he cannot remember in which building or on which floor. This rapid final downward spiral eventually leads the protagonist to the airport, where he picks a flight at random and flees to Hong Kong. The dramatic geographical change is matched by a change in narratorial style, as the dizzying pace of the highly function-advancing Paris narration is replaced by a greater focus on world-building in the Far East:

> The traffic was flowing beneath arches of red lanterns with dragons on them. He walked aimlessly in the dense, indifferent crowd; there was a slightly stale odor of steamed vegetables, and at times, dried fish. Farther down, the stores became more luxurious. They mostly sold electronic equipment tax-free, and a large number of tourists were doing their shopping. He finally reached the end of the avenue, where there was a large square that opened onto the bay. Extending along the other side was a shimmering chaos of skyscrapers set against the side of a mountain, its peak obscured by the night fog.
>
> (Carrère 1998: 272)

Far more attention is paid now to constructing a realistic and believable physical environment in which the enactor exists. The spatial and temporal boundaries of the world are clearly and carefully established in much greater detail than for any of the scenes constructed in Paris. Though the surrounding streets of Hong Kong are full of hustle and bustle, the protagonist seems to have discovered a new form of inner tranquillity, signified by a striking reduction in mental activity. Although the text remains focalized through the same enactor, the recurrent slips into free indirect thought which characterized the narrative in Paris are no longer in evidence. He considers the problems he has left behind him relatively infrequently, settling quickly into a calm and highly structured new lifestyle. His days become based around routine: sleeping, waking, shaving, swimming, and repeated trips across the harbour on the local ferry. When the protagonist's opinions are presented, this is done either in epistemically non-modal categorical assertions (e.g. 'He wasn't crazy...nothing was in its right order' [Carrère 1998: 283]) or with positive epistemic commitment (e.g. 'he knew he was of sound mind' [ibid.]), backed up with perception modality (e.g. 'he now perceived that everything was more complicated' [ibid.]). The protagonist thus appears at ease with his fate: a solitary but solid existence, a regained sense of control.

Yet the roller-coaster ride of *The Mustache* is far from over, as the protagonist discovers on his return to the hotel one afternoon. He approaches the
hotel reception to find that his room key is missing. The receptionist informs
him that his wife is in their room and enquires if she didn't enjoy her swim
that morning. The protagonist enters his room to find Agnes lying on the
bed, suntanned, and reading a magazine, chatting as though she had been
there with him throughout his visit. Without speaking to her, he goes directly
to the bathroom, takes out his razor, and the following horrific scene then
occurs:

> His brain continued to function on its own, asking itself just how long it would
> continue to work, if it would carry on even further, before he lowered his arm
> to cut beyond the bone, to the bottom of his throat filled with blood... He
> sliced blindly, without feeling a thing, under his chin, from one ear to the
> other, his spirit alive until the last second, rising above the gurgle, the sudden
> jolt of his legs and stomach, alive and appeased by the certitude that now it was
> over, everything was back in place.
>
> (Carrère 1998: 318)

Perhaps most arresting about this final paragraph is the odd disjunction
which occurs between the enactor's mind and his body. Although he continues to focalize the text, remaining at its deictic centre, there is a complete
absence of presentation of the protagonist's thoughts here, in either direct or
indirect form. Some physical reaction to his injuries is reported, in 'without
feeling a thing', and 'the sudden jolt of his legs and stomach'. However, it is
his eerily disembodied brain which is described as functioning on its own and
'asking itself' questions. Furthermore, the neurological activity of the focalizing enactor becomes separated from his 'spirit' as he bleeds to death. In this
final sentence, it is made clear that it is this spirit which has been responsible
throughout the novel for the production of a multitudinous array of possible
worlds to explain the protagonist's increasingly terrifying predicament. The
predominant sense of panic and paranoia is suddenly vanished as the abundant hypothetical and conditional modal-worlds, used to play out the enactor's worst fears, are no longer needed and the entire complex conceptual
structure assembled to this end ultimately disintegrates. In death, thought is
made absent; the spirit is quiet, finally appeased.

CHAPTER 23

The Eleventh Checksheet of the Apocalypse

PETER STOCKWELL

1. The ten checksheets

In Mick Short's astonishingly rich and all-but-comprehensive *Exploring the Language of Poems, Plays and Prose* (1996), the new initiate into stylistics is led by the hand through a series of masterful expositions of the integration of language and literature. One of the beauties of stylistics is the swiftness of the journey from initial exploration to a capacity for undertaking original stylistic analysis, and this book represents the enabling spirit of the discipline. As a reward for understanding, and as a simple effective tool for further investigation, Short includes ten 'checksheets' which summarize the content of the book. These encourage stylistic explorers to ask themselves a set of questions that will guide them to look in the right places for the right things. Though each checksheet is fairly detailed, the broad outline of each is as follows:

Checksheet 1: Deviation, parallelism, and foregrounding
Checksheet 2: Style variation
Checksheet 3: Phonetic structure
Checksheet 4: Metrical structure
Checksheet 5: Discourse structure and speech realism
Checksheet 6: Turn-taking, speech acts, and politeness
Checksheet 7: Inferring meaning
Checksheet 8: Linguistic indicators of point of view
Checksheet 9: Speech and thought presentation
Checksheet 10: Style features of narrative description

Collected together like this, the subjects listed form a rough history of the development of stylistics itself. Normative patterns and departures from those patterns for defamiliarizing effects characterize the origins of the field in Russian formalism. Stylistic variation and phono-metrical patterning were the hallmark interests in the renaissance of stylistics in the 1960s. Meaningfulness moving from semantics to pragmatics was evident in the evolution of the field in the 1970s and early 1980s, and discourse analysis, ideological perspective, and perceptual and narratological concerns were features most popular with stylisticians into the 1990s and the turn of the millennium (see Carter and Stockwell 2008 for an anthology and survey.).

At each stage of development, of course, though the new insights were adopted enthusiastically by stylisticians, the preceding and more established tools remained available for use. As the discipline has evolved, this refinement of method and adaptation of new frameworks have given stylistics its progressive character. Throughout its history, researchers in stylistics have improved our methods (most recently thanks to the powerful tool of the computational analysis of large language corpora; see, for example, Walker's chapter in this volume), and adopted newly emerging fields of language study – not only from linguistics, but also from its various applied sub-branches and related fields of social theory, semiotics, hermeneutics, and psychology. Innovations from the interaction of these fields with stylistics improve the details in the checksheets listed above.

The latest innovation to be adopted widely by stylisticians has been cognitive poetics, and though the refocusing that is required in paying attention to cognitive science in stylistics has a potential impact across the ten checksheets, I believe there is an extra dimension that is brought into play. This requires an eleventh checksheet, one that concerns the schematic features of world-building, coherence, and texture. I will outline this eleventh domain of stylistics in this chapter.

2. A cognitive poetic dimension

Most of the historical development of stylistics has been characterized by an increasingly powerful analysis of meaningfulness (i.e. informativity) rather than experiential value (i.e. an affective and aesthetic dimension). Yet much of the readerly experience of a literary passage lies within the realm of impression and loose association – the aesthetic experience that stylistic analysis has addressed only with difficulty. Given the fact that the quality of a text-reading is in large part a stylistic matter, it is surprising that stylistics has not been more successful in the experiential domain until fairly recently. I call this felt experience the *texture* of the reading (Stockwell 2009c): the combined experiential quality of the reader's feelings occasioned by the patterning in the text itself. Texture – in my cognitive poetic understanding – is the integrated quality of what it feels like to read a particular text. (Note that this is a more precise and more psychologically based sense than the way that the term is used in systemic-functional linguistics: Halliday 2004).

This rediscovery of aesthetics alongside an interest in informativity is reflected in microcosm within cognitive poetics itself. Over the past two decades, the cognitive turn in literary study brought research into conceptual metaphor, deixis and perspective, mental spaces, schemas, and worlds – all focused on a richer account of how readers monitor and manage their knowledge about the fictional or lyrical representation that is being presented in the literary work. The richness of that rich account was a secondary or neglected matter (with a few honourable and pioneering exceptions: Tsur 1992, 2006; Miall 2005; Miall and Kuiken 2002).

One possible reason for this anomaly, as Louwerse and van Peer (2009) point out, is that, in spite of its stylistic ancestry at least outside the US, cognitive poetics has drawn more on cognitive psychology than on cognitive linguistics. Even the language-based ground of conceptual metaphor theory (Lakoff 1987; Lakoff and Johnson 1980, 1999) was more interested in idealized models and mappings rather than the stylistic realizations of metaphors. Most work revolved around mental spaces and parabolic projection (Fauconnier 1994, 1997; Turner 1996, 2006; Fauconnier and Turner 2002), worlds and schemas at an idealized level (Cook 1994; Cockcroft 2002; Stockwell 2003a, 2005), and a revivified interest in cognitive narratology (Herman 2004). Recent years have seen a turn to textual matters in renewed interest in deixis (McIntyre 2006), the more stylistic realization of worlds (Semino 1997; Gavins 2007b), and literary applications of cognitive grammar (Hamilton 2003, 2007; Stockwell 2009a, b).

Cognitive linguistics has largely developed below the clause level, in the form of different construction grammars (Goldberg 1995, 1996; Heine 1997; Croft 2001; Traugott and Dasher 2002), and Langacker's (2008) cognitive grammar itself. Text and discourse have been handled in terms of frames and schemas (Talmy 2000a, b), which have laid emphasis on psychological patterning rather than linguistic texture. However, it is entirely possible to adapt the principles of, say, Langacker's (2008) cognitive grammar to operate across linked clauses, clausal chains, text, and discourse. This will allow us, as stylisticians, to be able to discuss coherence as both meaningful and experiential discourse according to cognitive grammatical principles – I will sketch this out later in an apocalyptic analysis of end-of-the-world narratives as exemplars of textualized feelings of nostalgia and loss. Firstly, in the next section, I will outline the need for a schematic and world-based account in order to understand the readerly impact of personal knowledge.

3. Schematic features of world-building

All first-readings involve the deployment of readerly knowledge to a more-or-less unique or 'singular' (Attridge 2004) literary text. Where the work represents a realist and contemporary setting, a sense of familiarity arises because the schematic cultural knowledge of the reader closely matches the representation that is being evoked by the text. Where there is a degree of disjunction between the represented scenario and the reader's familiar experience, such a reader must draw down vicarious schemas experienced through literature or indirectly through other cultural media. For example, in reading a historical novel, readers will need to draw on knowledge frames that are not their own but have been encountered through other historical fiction, through their knowledge of history, and through their experiences of historical locations. Other, even more divergent scenarios in literary works might require quite radical adaptations of vicarious knowledge, or even a more imaginative and creative leap of schema. Surrealistic, absurdist, nonsensical, fantastic, supernatural, psychologically, or stylistically extremist writing will present such a challenge.

Schemas and worlds theories have been used largely for their propositional value as repositories of meaning and knowledge. However, schemas also have an aesthetic experiential dimension. The remembered feeling, the recollected tactile sense, the associated sensual, emotional and physical memories of an alluded experience are often also drawn down when a text imposes a schematic trigger that suggests these patterns of memory. This is obvious when the text is a meditation, a lyric, or a sutra, all of which focus on the subjective experience of the moment and establish a readerly relationship with the subject matter. However, even with texts that are prominently or stereotypically information-driven – such as crime thrillers, political narratives, or science fiction – the affective experiential dimension is always also present.

For example, every experience we have ever had of feeling fear and anxiety while being chased by an aggressive person or an antagonistic animal, and every similar example read about or seen on film or television, all these events form together an idealized personal schematic of chase-anxiety. This schematization of course will include the conceptual content of elements like the pursuer, the possibilities of hiding and running, the stages of progress through a journey, the speculation of what happens if you get caught, and so on. But the schema will also include the feelings of excitement, fear, sharpened awareness, and readiness for action that have their roots in physical manifestations of twitchiness, breathlessness, heart-racing, and agitation. The presence of these elements of the schema is what allows us to experience a chase narrative as thrilling and exciting, as visceral as well as conceptual. We are used to thinking of instantiating a schema as knowing its knowledge, but we must also think of an active schema as experiencing its experience afresh.

The same applies to other schematized forms of affective response: humour, wryness, arousal, fear, anxiety, pride, empathy, a sense of grittiness, a sense of compassion, a sense of disgust, a sense of loss, and so on. The last of these, for example, is invoked in several science-fiction narratives featuring the end of the world or the end of humanity. Science fiction is a genre usually known for its preference for conceptual content over emotion, but in fact there is a great deal of science fiction that aims for a combination of innovation in ideas as well as an exploration and evocation of speculative human experience. The first modern science-fiction novel (by Aldiss's 1988 reckoning), *Frankenstein* (Shelley 1818) includes an invitation to the reader to feel empathy with the monster: its loneliness is not only existential and philosophical but also emotional, inviting compassion. Mary Shelley developed this elegiac and existential blend in her 1826 novel, *The Last Man*, a fictionalized memorial to her dead husband in the form of a futuristic tale depicting the sole survivor in the year 2100 of a plague that has wiped out the rest of the human race.

Though there are many last-minute reprieves for the earth and humanity in science fiction – usually thanks to military prowess (Heinlein's *Starship Troopers*, 1960), scientific cleverness (Kneale's *Quatermass* television dramas, 1952–5), or accidental good fortune (Wells's *The War of the Worlds*, 1898) – there is also a long tradition of apocalyptic writing in which the endgame for humanity is played out to the last. These narratives tend to signal early on that the end is nigh, and then the desperate but futile actions of people to save their planet and themselves constitute the remainder of the novels. The tone is often elegiac, nostalgic, and mournful, as in perhaps the most famous example, Arthur C. Clarke's (1953) novel *Childhood's End*.

In brief, the story is set during the Cold War, which is brought to an abrupt end by the arrival of powerful alien spaceships that take position over the cities of earth. The benign aliens – the Overlords – bring war to an end, but also all human technological advances, including a ban on space exploration. After 60 years of utopia, human children begin to be born with telepathic and telekinetic powers, and the Overlords reveal their true purpose, which is to assist in the evolution of humanity towards an assimilation with the Overmind. This is a mystical, transcendental, cosmological entity composed of the final, post-material consciousness of evolved species. The Overlords – who resemble demons, a prospective echo of the future apocalypse embedded in cultural mythology – are incapable of joining the Overmind, and exist only to assist other species in this metamorphosis. As the human children become divergent from their parents, no more are born, and humanity withers away, to be replaced by this next form of being. A lone physicist,

Jan Rodricks, observes the transformation from the Overlords's ship, and is finally left on earth, the last man, transmitting his final thoughts to the departing Overlords:

> 'The buildings round me – the ground – the mountains – everything's like glass – *I can see through it*. Earth's dissolving – my weight has almost gone. [...]
>
> 'There goes the river. No change in the sky, though. I can hardly breathe. Strange to see the Moon still shining up there. I'm glad they left it, but it will be lonely now –
>
> 'The light! From *beneath* me – inside the Earth – shining upward, through the rocks, the ground, everything – growing brighter, brighter, blinding –'

★   ★   ★

> In a soundless concussion of light, Earth's core gave up its hoarded energies. For a little while the gravitational waves crossed and re-crossed the Solar System, disturbing ever so slightly the orbits of the planets. Then the Sun's remaining children pursued their ancient paths once more, as corks floating on a placid lake ride out the tiny ripples set in motion by a falling stone.
>
> There was nothing left of Earth.
>
> (Clarke 1956: 188)

The central realism of science fiction is maintained here: scenes are only described by observing characters; a sudden, intrusive omniscient narrator would be too God-like at this point. The first part of the passage is spoken aloud by the human, Rodricks. His breathlessness and fear are captured in the very short and ellipted clauses, punctuated by dashes and graphologically intensified with italics and exclamation marks. The moment of transcendence is prefaced with an upturning of the light not from above but from below, and a sequence of unconstrained comparatives: 'brighter, brighter'. There is no observed ending: the observing consciousness is blind (expressed in the moment as a present continuous participle), and then wordless (' "–" '). Transcendence cannot be described to us humans on this side of the evolutionary shift; it can only be gestured towards like this. The intervening paragraph break and the apt asterisk stars signal a shift in perspective to the listening Overlord, Karellen, on his ship speeding away from what is left of earth. The view here is his, though the perspective of Rodricks the physicist and Rodricks the human is echoed in the astronomical description of gravitational waves, and then in the metaphor of planets as children and the image of the stone rippling quiet water. The evolved alienness of the children who have transformed the earth into their energy source is invoked here, at the same time, as a simple, human-scale analogy.

Childhood's End is certainly an apocalyptic novel, but it is also intimate, nostalgic, and moving. This is achieved by rendering any potential violence and destruction through scientist characters who describe it as lucidly as possible. Rodricks does not witness the suicide of millions of adults, the pain at the loss of their children, the nuclear bomb clearances of the last adult human settlements. He is away on a relativistic round trip to the Overlords's star-system as the group-mind of Earth's children becomes more and more inhuman. The images and analogies he uses – like those above – draw on simple, universal, and basic schemas like motion, water, light, religious imagery, plants and animals, clouds and skies, days and nights, and so on across the novel. As a result, the readerly schemas required throughout the story are familiar and comfortable; in the context of the earth's destruction, this produces the strong feeling of nostalgia and loss as the book comes to a close. The final page stays with Karellen as he watches the solar system pass away behind him, and he goes on to assist another species towards the Overmind.

4. Stylistic features of the texture of worlds

Useful though world-based theories are, by definition they are most applicable at a macroscopic level rather than a microscopic textual level. When it comes to stylistic analysis at the textual level, there is a curious blind spot in the middle of the application of cognitive linguistics. Taking its cue from cognitive psychology, cognitive linguistics has adopted a top-down approach to schematization and world-building from above, and a bottom-up approach to grammar as an assembly of constructions from below. The problem for the stylistician interested in textuality and discourse is that these two perspectives do not meet up seamlessly in the middle. Most cognitive treatments of the discourse level are concerned with global processing of schemas, worlds, frames, scripts, scenarios, and other comparable and almost synonymous terms. Among these many frameworks, the only two which include a prominent textual aspect are text world theory (Werth 1999; Gavins 2007a) and, to a lesser extent, conceptual integration theory – especially in its earlier manifestation as the blending of mental spaces (Fauconnier and Turner 2002). From the opposite angle, cognitive grammar (as in Langacker 2008) sets out an account from phonology up to clause level, but then hands over responsibility for textual organization and discourse to the aforementioned frame and schema theories. The result is a lack of what we might call a genuine cognitive discourse grammar, analogous to the well-developed tradition in functional linguistics addressing features of textuality such as cohesion and coherence (see Halliday 2003).

However, the principled directions for developing this useful level of analysis are present in Langacker's (1993, 1995, 2001, 2008) own work. Langacker (1990, 1991: 13, 2008: 103, 355) and Talmy (1988, 2000a, b) describe the schematic content of clausal predications in terms of 'force dynamics', which they then generalize across complex and compound sentences, and frames of attention in text and discourse. As what they call a 'billiard-ball model', a clause is understood as comprising a prototypical agent which acts as an energy source, transmitting force along an action chain towards a prototypical patient. Agents and patients are typically grammaticalized as noun-phrases, and the action chain itself is usually grammaticalized as a verb-phrase predication (see also Evans and Green 2006: 42).

Figure 23.1 shows a schematic rendering of an action chain for the sentence 'The granite volumes enclosed them all', with energy transmitted from the figural trajector (TR) as agent to the grounded landmark (LM) in the patient role. In Langacker's (2008) cognitive grammar, the same event or state that is predicated can be construed in several different ways, depending on how the grammaticalized form stylistically encourages a reader to focus (or 'profile') different parts of the action chain. So, for example, in the sentence in Figure 23.1, the subject noun-phrase 'The granite volumes' is striking because it is highly agentive, highly active, definite, semantically interesting, governs an active material verb, and oddly gives an inanimate object animacy and precedence over humans ('them') – these are all features that make a strong figural attractor (Stockwell 2003b, 2009b,c). Other profiling patterns (such as the passive 'They were enclosed by the granite volumes', or the LM-focused 'The granite enclosed all of the people lying on the mountainside under the disappearing clouds') would provide different construals of the same event.

Of course, the readerly construal of the sentence must also be understood in context. This sentence is the end of the penultimate chapter in Greg Bear's (1987) apocalyptic novel *The Forge of God*. An alien race of planet-killers have fired two bullets of neutronium and anti-matter at the earth; when they spiral and collide at the planet's core, humanity will be destroyed. We have been warned about this by another, protector race of aliens, who document our

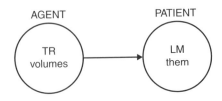

Figure 23.1: Profiling of an active verb in an action chain: 'The granite volumes enclosed them all'

civilization and save a handful of humans to set up an ark-colony on Mars, and hunt for the planet-killers in revenge: this is the domain of the sequel, *Anvil of Stars* (Bear 1992). In the following passage, an eye-witness account of earth's destruction is given by professor of geology Edward Shaw:

> He was past any expression of awe or wonder. What he was seeing could only be one thing: east of the Sierra Nevada, along the fault line drawn between the mountains formed by ages of wrinkling pressure, and the desert beyond, the continent was splitting, raising its jagged edge dozens of miles into the atmosphere.
>
> Edward did not need to do calculations to know this meant the end. Such energy – even if all other activity ceased – would be enough to smash all living things along the western edge of the continent, enough to change the entire face of North America.
>
> Acceleration in the pit of his stomach. *Going up.* His skin seemed to be boiling. *Going up.* Winds blew that threatened to lift them away. With the last of his strength, he held on to Betsy. He could not see Minelli for a moment, and then he opened his tingling eyes and saw against a muddy blue sky filled with stars – the atmosphere racing away above them – saw Minelli *standing*, smiling beatifically, arms raised, near the new rim of the point. He receded through walls of dust on a fresh-hewn leaf of granite, mouth open, shouting unheard into the overwhelming din.
>
> *Yosemite is gone. The Earth might be gone. I'm still thinking.* The only sensation Edward could feel, other than the endless acceleration, was Betsy's body against his own. He could hardly breathe.
>
> They no longer lay on the ground, but fell. Edward saw walls of rock, great fresh white revealed volumes on all sides – thousands of feet wide – and spinning trees and disintegrating clumps of dirt and even a small flying woman, yards away, face angelic, eyes closed, arms spread.
>
> It seemed an eternity before the light vanished.
>
> The granite volumes enclosed them all.
>
> (Bear 1987: 458)

As in the Arthur C. Clarke novel above, the witness is an expert, though here his narrative is thought-presentation rather than a spoken transmission. There is, too, a coda chapter in which the handful of saved humans on the spaceship watch the destruction of earth again from without. As in the Clarke passage, the observer's narration ends the moment before his death, which is (realistically) not articulated by the narrator.

There is not space here to mark up the action-chain dynamics of every clause in the passage, but overall there is a clear shift of profiling from the human as TR of an action chain towards the focusing of attention on the LM of the landscape, literally the ground in the passage, as it moves, rises up, and engulfs the human observers. In addition to the two main proto-roles of agent and patient, Langacker (1991: 282–91, 2008: 365) sets out several available roles for participants: a default *zero* role of mere existence where no energy is transmitted; the energetic roles of *agent, patient, instrument, experiencer,* and *mover*; an *absolute* role that resists the effects of energy transfer; and a *theme* role that summarizes the action chain. In the beginning of the passage, the profiling is very much on Edward as the experiencer of the scene. In context, we have followed this human consciousness for over 400 pages, so Edward is already a very strong figural attractor. However, as the passage continues, the focus of profiling is shifted stylistically towards the LM material, to the extent that as well as being the patient participant of Edward's experience, the ground becomes a mover in the grammar. Since ground usually does not do this, it is highly likely that a reader would shift profiling to the LM material. This shift is clearly signalled right at the beginning of the passage, where the TR 'What he was seeing' is de-profiled by its brevity, vagueness, and embedding of the human pronoun, in contrast to the strong profiling of the LM thanks to its specificity ('could only be one thing'), its precise locatives ('east of the Sierra Nevada, along the fault line drawn between the mountains formed by ages of wrinkling pressure, and the desert beyond'), its embedded active action-chain predications ('splitting, raising its jagged edge'), its voluminousness ('dozens of miles into the atmosphere'), and its overall textual length. Unusually for a grounded LM, the boundaries are profiled ('its jagged edge'), suggesting it is shifting to become a TR figure in its own right. (Prototypically, figures have edges, even absent figures [literary lacunae] which *only* have edges: see Stockwell 2009b).

The central paragraph continues this shift, with Minelli first appearing as a lacuna figure, defined by not being there ('He could not see Minelli for a moment'), and then he is there, a human figure but static ('standing, smiling'), but he is quickly de-profiled with a strong emphasis on the grounding LM: 'near the new rim of the point'. In the next sentence, he is minimally profiled as the pronoun 'He', and this TR is quickly diminished ('receded'), to place a strong focus on the large, new, active, metaphorically anomalous LM 'through walls of dust on a fresh-hewn leaf of granite'. The preceding TR becomes again a lacuna ('mouth open ... unheard') and the ground is large, specific, and noisy ('the overwhelming din').

Towards the end, though 'Edward' remains as the experiencer of the last substantial paragraph, all of the textual emphasis is end-focused towards the LM ground. By this time, the ground has shifted from being in patient role towards mover role, a much more active participation towards the proto-agency role. In 'they fell', the profiling falls on the action chain itself, deflecting agency from the actual agent and thus weakening it.

In describing the shifting patterns of action-chain profiling across the passage, I have necessarily moved into a discussion of textuality and texture. How textual cohesion works in cognitive grammar is a matter of the 'dominion' trace between clauses in the mind of the reader. In Langacker's (2008: 83) cognitive grammar, when an entity is mentioned, it creates a 'reference point' for further cohesion by co-referential 'targets'. On first mention, 'A particular reference point affords potential access to many different targets. Collectively, this set of potential targets constitute the reference point's *dominion*' (Langacker 2008: 83–4; my emphasis). In other words, the dominion of an entity or relationship can be regarded as a network of all of the linked and associated possibilities in the reader's stored experience that are most likely to be made available for subsequent cohesive targeting. In effect, dominion traces are linguistic specifications of schematic or world-based knowledge, derived from prior experience.

For example, the focalization of the passage above through a character who we know to be an expert geologist means that his fluent descriptions of geological features are both textually and texturally cohesive: 'Sierra Nevada', 'fault line', 'wrinkling pressure', 'calculations', 'leaf of granite', and so on. Each lexicalization of participant roles and action-chain predications prepare a set of possible mental paths that the reader has ready in order to process the next incoming text-sequence most efficiently. In Figure 23.2, these paths are represented by the dashed lines as a semantic and experiential cloud of possibilities radiating around an initial trajector.

Of course, only one or a few of these potentialities is actually textualized – the others remain untaken and gradually fade away. However, the impression of association and the quality of resonance created fleetingly by these untaken paths are felt as a richer reading experience than a plain denotational analysis might suggest.

In the passage, there are two broad reference points: the human figure and the landscape of the earth as ground; as the passage progresses, this reverses so that the human becomes the landmark and the earth fills the

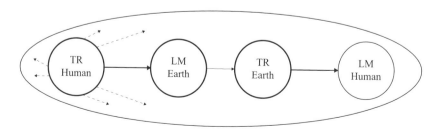

Figure 23.2: Dominion tracing in a passage from *The Forge of God*

TR of attention. Contrastively and conventionally, the passage sets human people on a smaller scale than the earth. As drawn in Figure 23.2, in the beginning, the examples of humans and their properties ('awe', 'wonder', 'tingling', 'smiling', and 'arms', 'mouth' 'body, 'face') are profiled more or less equally with the background earth. However, across the passage, this landmark becomes the trajector which moves above and around the humans, now landmarked. Furthermore, as sketched above in the action-chain profiling, the heavy attention (bolded in the diagram) is placed onto this TR earth rather than the humans (unbolded) who are about to be enclosed.

Described like this, the dominion chaining across the passage is very tightly cohesive and consequently feels coherent. Langacker (1995) describes such a sequence of reference points and dominions as defining a 'line of sight' through a text. However, there are some odd dominion paths lexicalized that pick up on thematic texture across the whole novel. For example, the religious allusion evident in the title of the book is a constant presence in dominion shaping throughout. Here in this end passage, the generally scientific register is interspersed with choices that are religious and locally surprising ('beatifi-cally, arms raised', 'face angelic, eyes closed, arms spread', and 'an eternity'), though they are more globally consistent. It is possible that these religious potentials in a reader's schema-network are more ready to be activated as a result of reading the novel by this point than they perhaps might otherwise be, so the religious sensibility can be regarded as a prominent aspect of the atmosphere of the novel. This is a shaping of dominion structure that the novel has enacted by its ending.

Within the dominion tracing, it is not difficult to extend the notion of action chaining beyond the clause to the force dynamics (Talmy 1988) at the textual level. In this violent passage in particular, the energy that is implicit in the LM earth gradually increases to the point at which the earth becomes profiled as TR. For the first two-thirds of the passage, there is a great deal of energy in the form of active and semantically violent predications. Where Edward is in a proto-agent role, he is usually figured as experiencer, though sight is the least agentive of experiencing roles – in the paragraph that begins in italics, even this weak experiencing becomes interior conscious thought, and then all he can do is 'breathe' and this is modalized and incompletely negated ('could hardly'). The strong action of the force across most of the passage pauses after this breath. 'It seemed an eternity before the light van-ished' minimizes the experiencer role by leaving the experiencer himself unlexicalized. 'It seemed' is merely an existential zero role, the experiencer implicit in the epistemic modal verb; 'the light vanished' is an absolute role – both of these stall the energy of the ongoing textual action chain, but only temporarily. After this brief lull, which acts as an emotional preparation, I think, the last sentence finally places the rock in strongly agentive TR position: 'The granite volumes enclosed' is definite, large and increasing in size, active, and agentive. There is of course a textual allusion in 'volumes' to the actual book that the reader is holding, as if to underline the physicality of being crushed to death.

5. The eleventh checksheet

The stylistic accounts set out above are sketches of what an applied cognitive discourse grammar might look like. I have adapted Langacker's cognitive grammar partly to allow an exploration of discourse-level features, but in the process I have tried to pay attention to the aesthetic effects of the reading experience. This approach has the potential to illuminate very clearly aspects of literary reading that emerge vaguely from discourse – things like atmosphere, tone, and a sense of richness and resonance. Because cognitive grammar makes a claim to be grounded in fundamental psychological experience and processes, its linkage of textual cohesion and coherence is motivated in a way that functional grammars are not. Crucially, the sort of analysis I have been sketching combines information-processing with the feeling of reading, into a holistic phenomenon I have been calling 'texture' (Stockwell 2009c).

Therefore it seems to me we are in a position to suggest an eleventh checksheet for stylistic analysis. It points the stylistician to the cognitive dimension, and invites questions concerning informational and aesthetic processing; it connects the impositions that the text provides with the dispositions that readers bring; and it is offered in the spirit of the original ten checksheets, for students and researchers to use as a means to a better understanding of literature.

Checksheet 11: Textural evocations of experience

Worlds

What is the world-structure as represented in the work?
What discourse world/schematic knowledge is being drawn on?
Are there many world-switches? What are the types of world-switch involved?

Force dynamics

How can you characterize the action chains in the text? How does the stylistic realization predispose a particular profiling and construal?
What are the participant roles and how are they significant?
How are the forces across the clauses chained across dominions?

Whole-text texture

What other cognitive poetic features can you discern?

How do these features contribute to your experience of the whole
   work?

Can you see connections between all eleven checksheets in order to
   advance the discipline of stylistics further?

CHAPTER 24

Multimodality: Extending the Stylistic Tool-Kit

Nina Nørgaard

1. Introduction

Since the 1960s, stylistics has developed into a broad and strong field of research, investigating how meaning is created through language in literature and other verbal texts. While thus providing analysts with a useful linguistic tool-kit they can draw on for systematic linguistic description and analysis of such texts, stylistics has as yet failed to develop adequate analytical tools for providing equally systematic analyses of texts which make use of further semiotic modes such as colour, layout, visual images, typography, and so on for their meaning-making.[1] Over the last two decades and more, technological and cultural developments have led to an increasing output of multimodal texts and hence an increasing need to extend the stylistic tool-kit to incorporate tools for dealing with multimodal semiosis. With a particular focus on literary stylistics, it is the aim of this chapter to sketch out and discuss a possible framework for the analysis of novels which employ several semiotic modes in their construction of meaning. The approach to multimodality applied to this end is the one proposed by, for example, Kress and Van Leeuwen (2001, 2006), Baldry and Thibault (2006), and others. Although this paradigm is still relatively new, with much territory yet to be explored and many adjustments to be made, its potential would seem promising from a stylistic perspective.

2. The social semiotic multimodal paradigm

The approach to multimodality advocated by Kress and Van Leeuwen (2001, 2006), Baldry and Thibault (2006), and others springs in essence from a specific branch of linguistics, that is, Michael Halliday's (1994) systemic functional linguistics (see Halliday 2004). Halliday views communication as social semiotics which means that language as well as other kinds of human meaning-making are seen as functional social practices which should be analysed in the social, cultural, and other contexts in which they occur, rather than investigated as phenomena separated from their context.

Central to Hallidayan thinking is the claim that language is structured to make not just one but *three* different major kinds of meaning and that these three types of meaning are made simultaneously. To uncover this semantic complexity of verbal semiosis, Halliday operates with what he calls the three metafunctions of language: the *experiential*,[2] the *interpersonal*, and the *textual* metafunction. Every utterance, be it written or spoken, makes experiential meanings (relating to how we represent experience), interpersonal meanings (to do with the relations between interlocutors), and textual meanings (relating to our organization of texts) – all at the same time.

For each metafunction, different grammatical systems of analysis are employed which enable the analyst to investigate how a given text linguistically constructs the three kinds of meaning mentioned above. Experiential meaning is analysed in terms of transitivity, focusing on how the experiential world of a given text is constructed as configurations of processes, participants, and circumstances. For the analysis of interpersonal meaning the most important grammatical systems employed are those of mood and modality. A mood analysis centres on speech functions and their lexico-grammatical realizations and what these reveal about the interpersonal relations between interlocutors. Modality, on the other hand, concerns the degree of speaker commitment to what is uttered in terms of probability, usuality, obligation, and inclination. Finally, textual meaning is examined in terms of cohesion and theme/rheme structures – systems which each in their own way help organize the experiential and interpersonal meanings expressed by the text and 'glue' the text together.

Inspired by Halliday's view of language, researchers with an interest in modes other than – or in addition to – verbal language have set out to develop equally consistent 'grammars' for these modes. Most prominent among the pioneering work within this new extended social semiotic paradigm are Kress and Van Leeuwen's *Reading Images: The Grammar of Visual Design* (1996) and O'Toole's *The Language of Displayed Art* (1994), but there soon followed other 'mono-modal' grammars of sound (Van Leeuwen 1999), colour (Kress and Van Leeuwen 2002), typography (Van Leeuwen 2005b, 2006), and so on. According to Kress and Van Leeuwen (2001: 2), 'common semiotic principles operate in and across different modes', and it would therefore make sense, it is argued, to try to develop a common terminology and ultimately a common grammar, designed to handle all these different modes and their interaction:

> We seek to break down the disciplinary boundaries between the study of language and the study of images, and we seek, as much as possible, to use compatible language, and compatible terminology to speak about both, for in actual communication the two, and indeed many others, come together to form integrated texts.
>
> (Kress and Van Leeuwen 2006: 177)

Appealing though these intentions may seem, the approach suggested is not entirely unproblematic. While the relatively direct application of Halliday's metafunctional approach to verbal language turned out to work quite well for visual language, its application to, for example, the mode of sound proved far more problematic, as acknowledged by Van Leeuwen himself in his concluding remarks in *Speech, Music, Sound* (1999: 189–93). In comparing his work on sound with that of visual communication he here concludes that:

> the method [i.e. the metafunctional approach] did not work as well with sound as it had with vision. The resources of sound simply did not seem as specialized as those of language and vision, and the mode of sound simply did not seem so clearly structured along metafunctional lines as language and visual communication.
>
> (Van Leeuwen 1999: 190)

Further research may reveal that similar reservations will have to be made in relation to other semiotic modes. The metafunctional approach should hence not be seen as a default tool for all analytical work, but is only to be employed when aspects of the object of analysis clearly qualify as either experiential, interpersonal, or textual/compositional[3] – and as combinations of these functions.

If the three metafunctions proved less universal than first assumed, other semiotic principles have turned out to work more truly across – and as combinations of – modes. *Framing* is one such principle which has so far proved a useful descriptive category in relation to visual images and page layout as well as in relation to the organization of three-dimensional space such as office design (cf., for example, Van Leeuwen 2005a: 6–24). Another cross-modal principle is that of *modality*, as will be demonstrated by my analysis below.

Although the search for common semiotic principles and a common descriptive terminology would seem a noble cause with promising potential, great care should clearly be taken not to force common concepts onto semiotic material that does not naturally accommodate such an approach. In my view, the advantage of a multimodal grammar is thus not necessarily a strict

standardization of our descriptive categories, but rather the wish to acknowledge the significance of all the different modes that go into a given instance
of meaning-making, as well as the attempt to develop ways of describing all
these modes and their interaction.

It is crucial to the understanding of multimodality that multimodal
meaning-construction is conceived, not as a simple sum of simultaneous realizations of separate layers of meaning (e.g. verbal language + tone of voice +
facial expression + gesture, and so on), but as a complex *interplay* of all these
semiotic resources which is meaningful in itself:

> Multimodal texts integrate selections from different semiotic resources to
> their principles of organization. ... These resources are not simply juxtaposed
> as separate modes of meaning making but are combined and integrated to
> form a complex whole which cannot be reduced to, or explained in terms of
> the mere sum of its separate parts.
>
> (Baldry and Thibault 2006: 18)

Even though the term 'multimodality' appears to entail the existence of 'mono-
modes' – as does much of the 'mono-modal' research done in the field so far – it
should furthermore be noted that, strictly speaking, mono-modes do not exist.
Even printed verbal language is multimodal, since it consists of a visual side,
that is, typography, as well as what I refer to as 'wording' (in order to be able to
distinguish between the two).[4] For ease of analysis, however, mono-modes are
useful theoretical and methodological abstractions which allow us to dissect
our object of analysis into manageable parts before we embark on examining
how these parts interact in the construction of the multimodal text. Although
arguably not faithfully in line with multimodal thinking, this is nevertheless
also the approach I choose to take in my analysis below.

In *Multimodal Discourse*, Kress and Van Leeuwen (2001) take stock of their
previous work and decide to cut the cake differently. The result of this is a
slightly different approach to multimodality which considers meaning-making as a process involving four different strata, or levels of articulation, which
are semiotic in their own right: *discourse, design, production,* and *distribution.*
That these different levels of articulation are also relevant to the meaning
produced by literature is indicated by the following remark by Zadie Smith
on editing a collection of short stories by different authors:

> As editor, I have tried to retain the individuality of each piece by leaving them,
> by and large, little changed. There is, however, an element of their character
> that has been removed: the fonts. Publishers standardize fonts to suit the style
> of the house, but when writers deliver their stories by e-mail, each font tells its
> own story. There are quite a few writers in this volume who use variations on
> the nostalgic American Typewriter font (and they are all American), as if the

ink were really wet and the press still hot. We have two users of the elegant, melancholic Didot font (both British), and a writer who centres the text in one long, thin strip down the page, like a newspaper column (and uses Georgia, a font that has an academic flavour). Some writers size their text in a gigantic 18. Others are more at home in a tiny 10. There are many strange, precise and seemingly intimate tics that disappear upon publication: paragraphs separated by pictorial symbols, titles designed just so, outsized speech marks, centred dialogue, uncentred paragraphs, no paragraphs at all. It seems a shame to lose these idiosyncratic layouts and their subtle effects.

(Smith 2007: viii).

Here, the production of the book clearly adds[5] a layer of signification through its standardization of the meanings created by means of typography and layout. Another example is that of the meaning-making involved in the production and distribution of Michael Ende's (1979) *Die unendliche Geschichte* (*The Neverending Story*). An important aspect of this novel is created by its use of respectively red and green typography for the two narrative strands of which it consists. Nonetheless, the meaning thus created typographically when the story was first published has subsequently been overridden – and hence changed – by a wish to produce and sell cheap paperback editions of the novel. While still available in the bookshop, most current editions of Ende's novel are set in black type only.

Obviously, the limited space granted here does not allow me to conduct a comprehensive multimodal analysis of a literary narrative. Instead, the aim of section three below is to provide a brief survey of some of the elements of a novel which, with its use of photographic images, newspaper clippings, drawings, school reports, and so on, explicitly invite a multimodal analysis – as well as of some of the tools available for analysis within the social semiotic multimodal paradigm. The text selected for analysis is Alexander Masters's ([2005] 2006) biographical novel, *Stuart. A Life Backwards*, which traces the life of a homeless man, Stuart Shorter, from his death at the age of 33 back to his childhood, pivoting around Stuart's own question 'What murdered the boy I was?' (Masters [2005] 2006: 6). My analysis will focus in particular on modes which are typically ignored in literary stylistics, while paying less attention to the mode of wording.[6]

3. Multimodal analysis of literary texts – an appetizer

3.1. *Typography*

With a few exceptions (e.g. Levenston 1992; Van Peer 1993; Bray 2000), typography is often overlooked in literary analysis, nor is it a mode to which readers typically pay much attention in their reading of narrative fiction.[7] This does not mean that the visual side of printed verbal language is not semiotic, however, but merely indicates that the typography seen in most literature is so conventionalized that readers usually do not notice. Other literary texts experiment more explicitly with the meaning-potential of the visual side of language, and the new technologies involved in book production in recent years obviously allow a larger extent of such typographic experimentation. Whether conventional or experimental, typography appears to deserve a more prominent place in our stylistic analysis of literature if we aim to capture all the stylistic features that go into the semiosis of the text.

It should be mentioned that I use 'typography' in a very broad sense of the word, stretching from printed typography via calligraphy to handwriting, since a number of common semiotic principles appear to be at play when it comes to decoding the visual side of language regardless of its source of production.

Inspired by work done in linguistics, Van Leeuwen (2006) calls for a grammar of typography and proposes the following system of *distinctive features* applicable to the analysis of typography: *weight* (regular ↔ bold), *expansion* (narrow ↔ wide), *slope* (sloping ↔ upright), *curvature* (angular ↔ rounded), *connectivity* (connected ↔ disconnected), *orientation* (horizontal orientation ↔ vertical orientation), and *regularity* (regular ↔ irregular). Although the list must be seen as preliminary[8] and quite possibly in need of additional categories such as, for example, *colour*, *surface*, and *edge*, it nevertheless provides the analyst with a consistent terminology for describing a given typeface in terms of the distinctive features[9] which set it apart from other typefaces.

In addition to his list of distinctive typographical features, Van Leeuwen (2005a, b) furthermore suggests that a number of common semiotic principles are at play in typographic meaning-making, namely *metaphor* and *connotation*. While I am largely inspired by Van Leeuwen's approach in this respect, certain reservations have made me argue elsewhere for the application of three alternative categories (Nørgaard 2009), which I will here extend to four: *index*, *icon*, *symbol*, and *discursive import*. The semiotic principles of index, icon, and symbol I have adopted from Peirce via Mollerup's work on logotypes (1999). The concept of discursive import, on the other hand, is retained from Van Leeuwen's work on typography (e.g. 2005a, b). Index, icon, and symbol are dealt with in the present section, while discursive import will be touched upon in Section 3.4.

In Masters's novel, parts of the meaning-making is clearly created typographically. At one point, for instance, the novel contains facsimile reproductions of a number of entries from Stuart's diary (Masters [2005] 2006: 159–61). This is a fairly simple example of typographic indexical meaning. The meaning-potential of the index resides in a basically physical and/or causal relation between the typographical signifier and the signified, as in the archetypal examples of smoke and fire, and between a footprint and the person who made the footprint. In a similar way, the look of the novel's fac-simile reproduction of writing from Stuart's diary entries evokes the material origin of its own coming into being and is likely to be seen as a fairly direct trace of Stuart, thereby helping to authenticate his existence to the readers. The mimesis at play here can be well described by means of the concept of *modality*.[10] While borrowed from linguistics, modality is seen by Kress and Van Leeuwen as a multimodal principle applicable also to modes other than verbal language. In visual terms, modality concerns the 'truth value' of a given representation – that is, the question of 'as how true' or 'as how real' something is represented. Like linguistic modality, visual modality is hence concerned with interpersonal 'colouring' and belongs to the interpersonal metafunction. Stuart's handwriting is an example of *high modality* in the sense that 'what we see is what we would have seen if we had been there' (cf. Van Leeuwen's definition of modality 2005a: 160–77).

If also concerned with Stuart's handwriting, the typographical meaning of the following passage from his diary seems iconic rather than indexical: '"Monday: ADDanBRocK's." "Tuesday: QuiSt going to Vist VoLanteR Service's. ASK for NAME & ADReSS For AwarD organation"' (Masters [2005] 2006: 10). An icon is a sign whose signifier resembles or imitates that which is signified which appears to be the semiotic principle at play in this example where Masters tries to imitate Stuart's handwriting through printed typography. Like the example above, a certain sense of authenticity is also created here, since the odd typographic mixture of upper- and lower-case letters mimics the irregularity of Stuart's handwriting and his rather arbi-trary use of capitals, and is thereby visually closer to the text originally pro-duced by Stuart than more conventional typographic choices. Nevertheless, the modality involved here is clearly lower than that of the previous example and does not qualify as convincingly as 'what we would have seen if we had been there'. Although the passage may give us an impression of an aspect of Stuart's handwriting, readers are unlikely to interpret it as an indexical trace of Stuart.

Other examples of typographic iconicity occur when the visual salience of italics is used to construct a different kind of salience, namely emphasis on word meaning, or when the visual salience of majuscules is employed to cre-ate the meaning of sonic salience, that is, of someone shouting (see Nørgaard 2009 for more examples of indexical and iconic typographic meaning).

The last semiotic principle to be mentioned in this section is that of the symbol. According to Peirce, a symbol is an arbitrary sign with no motivated, natural, relationship between signifier and signified (or between 'representa-men' and 'object' in Peirce's terms, cf. Mollerup 1999: 78). It would thus seem tempting to employ this principle to account for the kind of meaning created by the use of plain black typeface in literary narratives. If we do so, however, we should be aware that although the meaning of plain black typography may be determined by convention, this convention has actually evolved naturally (rather than arbitrarily) over time from motivations in production such as the affordances of the printing technology available, questions of economic viability, and so on More importantly perhaps, it should be noted that rather than being without semiotic significance, conventional black typeface in literary narratives is just as semiotic as more fanciful uses of typography. Plain black typography simply creates the meaning of 'typographically conventional'.

3.2. Layout

The modes of layout and typography are often very closely related in the process of meaning-making – at times so much so that analysts tend to treat the two together under the heading of 'typography' (cf., for example, Van Peer 1993). While acknowledging the significance of the intimate interplay of typography and layout, it does, in my view, make good sense to distinguish between the two as different semiotic modes: typography as the way the letterforms of a given typeface look in terms of shape, size, colour, and surface; and layout as the overall spatial page design of a given text, including visual elements such as line spacing and alignment, but also the placement of non-verbal visual features such as graphic elements, visual images, blank spaces, and so on, and the internal organization and linking of all these elements.

As with typography, readers seldom pay much attention to the meaning of layout in their reading of narrative fiction. The organization of such texts into, for example, chapters, paragraphs, and sentences framed by the white space of margins is so conventionalized that we hardly notice its existence. However, a quick commutation test, involving the (imagined) removal of these visual aspects of the text soon reveals their signifying potential. The question is, how do we best capture and describe the mode of layout in narrative fiction within a multimodal framework?

In Kress and Van Leeuwen's work on visual communication, the concept of *information value* plays a significant role in the description of compositional meaning. They argue that the grammar of visual communication resembles the grammar of verbal language in terms of a left-right distribution of meaning, with material situated to the left in a composition tending to be understood as Given information and material to the right as New information. Another compositional principle of Kress and Van Leeuwen's grammar involves a tendency to understand the top part of a visual composition as Ideal ('the idealized or generalized essence of the information') and the bottom part as Real (i.e. more specific details and/or more down-to-earth information) (Kress and Van Leeuwen 1996: 193–4). A third principle of composition applies to images and layouts which consist of a central element (Centre) and other elements which are represented as marginal (Margin) in relation to the Centre. Even if we disregard the problematic confusion of form and (ideological) function involved in Kress and Van Leeuwen's concepts and labels here,[11] these compositional principles do not seem particularly operational for the analysis of the layout of narrative fiction. There might, of course, be a sense in which Masters's footnotes to his narrative about Stuart (e.g. Masters [2005] 2006: 5, 48, 86, 176) may be seen as Real or at least marginal (Margin) and less important than the main narrative, yet the overall meaning of the visual layout of his text on the page clearly cannot be adequately described in terms of Given/New, Ideal/Real, or Centre/Margin.

The concept of *framing* seems more productive here,[12] but is not unproblematic either. Framing is a resource for visually connecting and disconnecting elements in a composition. In Masters's novel, the use of extended whitespace (i.e. broader margins) around certain parts of the text clearly frames these text passages and thereby helps to construct them as somehow different from the surrounding text. A good example of this occurs on page 101 where the framing of 21 lines by extended margins multimodally constructs the meaning of 'newspaper article' in combination with the modes of typography (e.g. large size and boldface for headlines) and wording. On a previous page, the same combination of modes is employed to create the meaning of 'recipe' (Masters [2005] 2006: 31). The difference between the two passages springs most essentially from the mode of wording, since the lexico-grammatical choices involved in the two passages result in lexical sets and speech functions typical of different genres. In addition to this, another layout feature further distinguishes the recipe from the newspaper text in that the first half of the former text makes use of the visual layout employed for lists (here the list of ingredients), whereas the latter consists of continuous prose only.

While the framing mentioned above clearly plays a part in the multimodal construction of narrative meaning in the passages in question, the meaning constructed by the general margins of the text seems less straightforward in terms of their framing function if we merely consider framing a means of connecting and disconnecting elements. In narrative fiction, the white frame around the text of a given page adds to the readability of the text, which would decrease considerably if the text ran from the right-hand edge of the page to the left-hand edge as well as from top to bottom. Just imagine the difficulty of reading the text of a two-page spread! In addition to matters of readability, margins also result from technological needs, since printing right to the edge of the page causes technical difficulties, and since a certain amount of page without text is needed for the binding of the novel. In these respects, the meaning of the general margins of a novel must hence be seen as meanings articulated at the production stratum of semiosis with a view to distribution and consumption (i.e. readability). Although visually disconnecting the text of one page from that of the next, the framing constituted by the general margins of the text is typically not semiotic at the narrative level, where the word meaning of the text on one page is not semantically disconnected from the text on the next page, indicated also by the fact that page breaks may occur in the middle of a sentence. When employing the concept of framing in our multimodal stylistic analysis of novels it is thus important to realize that this semiotic resource works at different levels and creates different kinds of meaning.

This being said, it should be noted that other novelists make use of framing for different effects. In Coetzee's *Diary of a Bad Year* (2007), for instance, each page is divided into three sections by means of two black horizontal framing lines which interact with the frames of the margins in interesting ways. But that is a different story to be told elsewhere.

3.3. *Visual images*

When it comes to the analysis of visual images, multimodal theory has much to offer to the stylistic tool-kit. In Kress and Van Leeuwen's 'grammar of visual design' we find operational methodologies for analysing visually expressed experiential, interpersonal, and compositional meanings. Some of the systems resemble those of Halliday's grammar of verbal language; others are systems that are more specific to the visual mode. The visual analysis of experiential meaning focuses on the visual realization of transitivity patterns in terms of represented participants, processes, and circumstances. Interpersonal meaning centres on the positioning of the viewer and is analysed in terms of gaze, size of frame/social distance, perspective, and modality. And compositional meaning (i.e. Halliday's textual meaning) is concerned with information structure, framing, linking, and salience. Since a comprehensive analysis of all these features is beyond the scope of the present chapter, the aim of the following is to examine an aspect of visual meaning that would seem particularly pertinent in an analysis of a literary narrative based on real-life people and events – namely the concept of modality.

As briefly mentioned above, modality is a semiotic resource for expressing 'as how true' or 'as how real' a given representation should be taken. In visual images, modality can be realized by different elements such as articulation of detail, articulation of background, colour saturation, colour modulation, colour differentiation, depth of articulation, articulation of light and shadow, and articulation of tone (cf., for example, Van Leeuwen 2005a: 167). In general terms, a photographic representation in natural colours with full articulation of detail, background, light, and shadow will (today) be seen as an example of high modality, whereas manipulation of some of these modality markers would lead to lower modality. The absence of background setting in an otherwise naturalistic photographic image of a tree would thus result in lower modality than an image where such background details are articulated, as would an image of the tree with no articulation of light and shadow or with little colour modulation. It should be mentioned that the modality of a given image depends on the coding orientation of the image and the communicative context in which it occurs and that different reality (and modality) principles consequently apply to texts with, for example, respectively a technological and a naturalistic coding orientation (cf. Kress and Van Leeuwen 1996: 170).

In Masters's novel, naturalistic photographic images are inserted into the main narrative as well as into the *post scriptum* of the book which consists of further information about Stuart, the novel, and the author. Most of these images are photographic portraits of individuals (mainly Stuart), as well as a couple of images displaying Stuart with a group of schoolmates and Stuart campaigning for the homeless. With their high naturalistic modality, these photographs clearly function to add to the authenticity of the narrative into which they are inserted. Through them, the reader is provided with photographic evidence that the characters in the book actually existed. More surprising for the context of a biographical narrative is the occurrence of Masters's own line drawings of various situations from the book. With the low modality of their cartoon-like nature, these drawings form a strong visual contrast to the photographic images mentioned above and clash more generally with the kinds of illustration we expect to encounter in contemporary biography. While the insertion of Masters's drawings might thus seem an odd choice for the genre – perhaps even visually undermining some of the narrative's authenticity – they fit in nicely with the strain of humour that runs through the novel. Notwithstanding the basically rather depressing subject matter of the life story of a homeless, periodically mentally disturbed drug addict, Masters has an eye for the potential humour of the various situations he describes. This is an aspect of the novel which makes the story easier to digest and combines well with the drawings, thus arguably creating a certain verbal-visual coherence.

3.4. The book cover

With the stylistic analysis of the text thus extended to go beyond wording by including other modes such as typography, layout, and visual images, a further extension of the analysis appears to invite itself: What is the meaning

created by the book cover? And how does it participate in the construction of
the overall meaning of the book?

The book cover (of my paperback version) of Masters's novel consists of a
photographic image of a boy and the non-diegetic (i.e. superimposed) verbal
text of the title, author name, and information about book awards and the
like. The experiential meaning of the photographic image is simple: a boy
engaged in the process of smiling with almost no circumstantial information about setting apart from a rather anonymous whitish background. Such
choices seem fairly conventional and may be interpreted as indicative that the
likely focus of the novel will be on an individual, that is, the boy we see on
the cover. The compositional and interpersonal choices realized by the photographic image on the cover are more intriguing. Most prominent is the atypi-
cal compositional cropping of the image which leaves the viewer with only a
view of parts of the boy's torso and the lower part of his face, cut just below
the eyes. This compositional choice results in close interpersonal distance
between the viewer and the represented participant (i.e. a close-up), but also
leaves us with a very unconventional interpersonal meaning for a portrait,
namely that of an ellipted gaze. In addition to being a rather odd interpersonal choice which is likely to leave the viewer with a sense that something
is not quite right, the ellipted gaze functions to anonymize the photograph.
In terms of set-up and pay-off relations, the visual set-up of the ellipted gaze
appears to create expectations of a pay-off to do with the identity (and personal character perhaps) of the person in the photograph.

On the inside of the cover we find a photographic image that 'rhymes' with
that on the outside in several respects – experientially, interpersonally, as
well as compositionally (cf. Kress and Van Leeuwen 1996: 216–17 on *visual
rhyme*). This image is also a portrait, composed very similarly to the cover
image, yet differing significantly in three salient respects. Experientially, the
stubble clearly constructs the participant of the second image as older than
the boy on the cover, and the process of smiling is replaced by a sulky look. In
addition to these two experiential differences, interpersonal selections within
the mode of colour differ markedly in that there is a strong contrast between
the dark (but authentic, high modality) colours of the image of what turns
out to be Stuart as an adult, and the brightness of the colour added in photographic post-production to the originally black and white (or faded colour
image) of Stuart as a boy. The low modality of the colour of the cover image is
clearly signification articulated at the level of production of the novel, and the
resultant contrast between the relatively bright and colourful image of Stuart
as a boy and the darker image of him as an adult may well be interpreted as
indicative of the contents of the narrative.

From a multimodal perspective, the typography on the cover also partici-
pates in the construction of the meaning of the book. Here the text is set

with a typeface that looks like handwriting, most prominently because of the distinctive features of curvature (rounded rather than [machine-like] angular forms), regularity (irregular characters, as well as irregularity of the strokes of which they consist), sloping (some letters, for example, 'f' and 'x', slope to the left whereas others, for example, 'r' and 't', display a slight slope to the right), and connectivity (some instances of connection, especially in the subtitle and the recommendation by The *Daily Mail*). Unlike the handwriting discussed in Section 3.1 above, the typeface employed on the book cover is probably unlikely to be interpreted as an indexical 'trace' of Stuart. As a matter of fact, closer scrutiny reveals that despite the overall irregularity of the writing, the individual letters are so regular – they are, in fact, identical – that the text is unlikely to have been produced by human hand, but is simply set in a typeface constructed to resemble handwriting. This is arguably an example of typographic discursive import where typographic signs – and their associated meanings – are imported into a context where they did not previously belong. In the case of Masters's cover, meanings such as 'human' and 'personal' appear to be imported into a context, that is, the book cover, where handwriting is the exception.

Seeing that the analysis of Masters's book cover above is just an analysis of the cover of the edition of the novel that happens to be on my own bookshelf, it would make sense to consider whether – and to what extent – a different cover would change the meaning of the book. If not exactly radically changing the overall narrative of the novel, the cover indisputably plays a certain role in our decoding of the text, in particular impacting on our first steps into the narrative. From a social semiotic multimodal perspective, one might even ultimately wish to consider the possible meanings created by the materiality of the book, by examining factors such as the quality of the paper, the binding, and the cover. While the materiality of the book is unlikely to articulate meanings as distinct as, for example, that of the cover, it is arguably not entirely without meaning either.

The inclusion into our analysis of meanings such as those constructed by the book cover and the materiality of the book, as well as of different meanings articulated at the level of production, inevitably leaves us with a less stable object of analysis than the written verbal text traditionally subjected to stylistic analysis. In a discussion of what should preferably be the stylistic object of analysis in the case of drama, Short (1981) suggests that the stylistician focus on the dramatic text itself as a more stable object of analysis than performance. McIntyre (2008: 310–1), on the other hand, argues that 'to ignore the performance element is to produce an impoverished stylistic analysis' and points to film versions of drama as an opening for conducting multimodal stylistic analyses of drama in performance. From a social semiotic multimodal perspective, I will argue that although the lack of stability of a given 'text' – be it a drama performance, a novel, or any other type of text – may result in different signification, all versions of these 'texts' are equally worthy of analysis. In the case of literature, the meaning of the cheap black-and-white version of Ende's novel clearly differs from that of the colour edition, yet the reader is left to decode the version at hand, no matter what meanings were intended by Ende in the process of encoding. The key thing is, of course, to make clear what version of a text is being analysed, so that the analysis can theoretically be falsified.

4. Conclusion

While Masters's novel briefly analysed above is a biographical narrative which makes use of authentic material such as photographs, posters, newspaper clippings, diary entries, and so on for its meaning-making, similar multimodal constructions of meaning also occur in narratives which are entirely fictional, like Jonathan Safran Foer's (2005) *Extremely Loud and Incredibly Close*. When embarking on a stylistic analysis of novels as explicitly multimodal as Masters's and Foer's novels, it obviously makes good sense to extend the stylistic tool-kit to contain tools designed to deal with multimodal meaning-making. Since all communication is multimodal, however, such tools may even be employed for the analysis of more conventional novels, though clearly to a smaller extent.

On the cover of Kress and Van Leeuwen's (2001) *Multimodal Discourse* it is proclaimed that the book presents 'an approach to social discourse in which colour plays a role equal to language', and time and again it is argued by the multimodal community that verbal language is gradually losing its status as a mode of communication as other modes such as visual images and sound increase in importance. While realizing that such claims are probably logical – and perhaps necessary – 'political' statements made by a new theoretical and methodological paradigm which is trying to find its feet in a rather crowded field of research, I humbly suggest that verbal language does, in fact, (still) have a special status in human communication, just as it has a special status in even the most explicitly multimodal novels today.[13] I thus believe it important to distinguish between the fact that all semiotic modes are in principle equally worthy of analysis and theorization, and the fact that such worthiness does not necessarily correspond to the prominence and importance of the mode in question in a given act of communication.

With the aim of multimodal theory thus being to acknowledge the equal status of all the semiotic modes that go into communication, it may seem somewhat ironic that the main proponents of the paradigm have selected a *linguistic* theory as the point of departure for their 'multimodal grammar'. From a stylistic perspective, the advantages of this would appear to be several. Most importantly, the linguistic foundation of multimodal theory is likely to lead to multimodal analysis that 'matches a traditional stylistic analysis in terms of level of detail', as called for by McIntyre (2008: 309). In addition to this, the extension of the Hallidayan approach to verbal language, to handle further modes of meaning, would seem to provide the analyst with a consistent methodology and terminology for dealing with multimodal meaning-making. The possible disadvantages of the approach should not be ignored, however. As mentioned previously, it is thus of utmost importance that analysts do not force given categories onto material that does not naturally accommodate these categories, and that they are willing to constantly question and test the paradigm and its ability to truly explore the meaning-potential of multimodal communication, as done, for instance, by Bateman (2008) in his work on multimodality and genre.

Because multimodal stylistics is a new field of research and the attempt to systematize the analysis of modes not usually analysed in stylistics is just as novel, the near future might see a tendency of research in the field to focus extensively on modes other than the wording of written verbal language. As a matter of fact, the present study as well as much of my previous work in the field are good examples of this (cf., for example, Nørgaard 2009, 2010). The reasons for this imbalance are obvious. First of all, to do a comprehensive multimodal analysis of even a medium-sized multisemiotic text is in itself a substantial task. It will thus often be impossible to cover in detail all modes and their interaction in less space than what is provided by the length of a book (and a long one at that). Secondly, much has already been said – and said well – in stylistics about verbal language, while other modes have been explored far less. Seeing that these other modes are relatively unexplored in stylistics, it is clearly tempting to dive into the novelty of this area. However, in order for our analyses to qualify as 'stylistics', it is important that we do not forget verbal language altogether, thus throwing out the baby with the bathwater. If we do not actually perform the multimodal algebra of adding 1 to 1, we will neither see, nor demonstrate to others, how the sum is more than 2.

NOTES

1. A few exceptions are exploratory work done in the field by Gibbons (2010), McIntyre (2008), Nørgaard (2009, 2010), and Simpson and Montgomery (1995).
2. Alternatively, 'ideational'.
3. In a visual context, the term 'compositional meaning' is used for referring to the types of meaning referred to as 'textual' in relation to verbal language.
4. I here follow Halliday's (e.g. 1994) use of 'wording' which refers to the combination of the lexis and grammar of verbal language.

5. It might be argued that signification is *removed* rather than *added*, though, in actual fact, the removal of meaning is meaning-making too.

6. For a more extensive treatment of the mode of wording from a Hallidayan perspective, see Nørgaard (2003).

7. While presently unable to prove this claim empirically for lack of research in the field, I assume that very few readers pay attention to the visual side of the printed verbal text of a typographically conventional novel or notice whether it is set in, for example, Palatino or Minion.

8. Van Leeuwen himself explicitly calls his work 'a first attempt at identifying the distinctive features of typography' and refers to the list as 'a provisional list' (2006: 147). A number of adjustments are suggested in Nørgaard (2009), among them a change of terminology to avoid the confusion that might otherwise be caused by employing the term 'regular' to refer to a feature of *weight* as well as of *regularity*.

9. While Van Leeuwen's choice of term, 'distinctive features', is clearly inspired by phonology and reflects a wish to be equally systematic in the approach to typography, the choice may be criticized as imprecise. Where distinctive features in phonology are minimal contrastive units of binary values which are either present or absent, the contrast involved in many of Van Leeuwen's distinctive features of typography is not binary but gradual.

10. Not to be confused with the concept of *mode*.

11. Cf., for example, Bateman's critical discussion of Kress and Van Leeuwen's categories (Bateman 2008: 43–53).

12. Another semiotic resource of significance to layout is that of *linking* (cf. Van Leeuwen 2005a: 219–47) which scarcity of space has forced me to leave out here.

13. I here disregard graphic novels, which I consider a radically different genre.

Corpus Approaches to Prose Fiction: Civility and Body Language in *Pride and Prejudice*

Michaela Mahlberg and Catherine Smith

1. Introduction

The present chapter focuses on prose fiction, and, more specifically, on the analysis of novels. Short (1996: 255) points out that 'the novel is probably the most difficult genre to analyse stylistically', one reason for this being its length. A close analysis is only possible for short extracts. 'Analysing a long novel in close stylistic detail could take a lifetime' (ibid.). Corpus linguistic methodologies can be seen as a means to support and facilitate the stylistic analysis of such 'long' texts. Corpus linguistics is an area of linguistics that only started to develop with the availability of computers as it uses computational tools to support the analysis of language. The term 'corpus' refers to a collection of computer-readable texts. Corpora are normally large, that is, containing many millions of words. Computer tools make it possible to quantify linguistic phenomena and arrive at generalizations about the behaviour of words and constructions across a range of texts. In the study of general corpora, literary texts only play a minor role. Individual qualities of a literary text are not of interest to a corpus linguist aiming to find general language patterns. When general corpora contain novels, it is not their idiosyncratic features that receive attention, but the cumulative picture that is created by prose fiction – as a subsection of a larger sample of the language. Corpus tools can identify a variety of linguistic patterns. When patterns are captured in quantitative terms, the more data available the more reliable the

449

description is. Compared to a corpus, a novel of about 200,000 words is a relatively small language sample. So the way in which corpus tools are applicable to the analysis of prose fiction differs to some extent from techniques that are applied to large corpora. The term 'corpus stylistics' has come to be used to refer to an emerging field that aims to combine questions from literary stylistics with approaches from corpus linguistics (for an overview see Mahlberg 2009). In contrast to some of the more computational approaches to stylistics, such as stylometry, one may want to see methods in corpus stylistics mainly as complementing interpretation and detailed manual analysis.

This chapter aims to illustrate some corpus methodologies that can support the stylistic analysis of prose fiction. The chapter argues that the value of applying such corpus methods depends on the links that can be made between quantitative data and thematic arguments and interpretations. Therefore, the chapter has two main analytical parts. Section 2 looks at three corpus methodological approaches: keywords, concordances, and intratextual comparisons. Section 3 then takes a thematic starting point. It shows how the methods illustrated in Section 2 link in with the discussion of thematic arguments. The text we analyse is Jane Austen's novel *Pride and Prejudice* (1813). The e-text was downloaded from *Project Gutenberg*.[1] Critics have highlighted that social expectations play an important role for how the characters in the novel behave, and in particular for the misunderstandings between characters. We focus specifically on the concept of 'civility' that Emsley (2005) discusses in the context of the virtues illustrated in Austen's fiction. Additionally, we look at body language that Korte (1997) highlights as having thematic relevance in *Pride and Prejudice*. We show how social expectations of civility are linked with examples of body language. The division into Sections 2 and 3 also aims to illustrate the benefit of combining different methods.

2. Critical mass – examples of corpus methodologies for stylistic analysis

Procedures that can be carried out by standard concordance packages typically include the creation of word lists, the display of words and their contexts in the form of concordances, and the comparison of frequencies in one text (or corpus) with another text (or corpus). Such methods focus on formal features of texts based on frequencies and patterns of words. An underlying principle for the analysis of such quantitative data is the observation that repeated patterns of words indicate repeated meaning relationships. The relationship between meanings and patterns makes it necessary to have sufficient data. Unless there is a certain number of repetitions it is difficult to establish a pattern or characterize meanings. Thus, for the study of individual texts, not all types of formal patterns can be found in all texts or are equally useful starting points for a detailed analysis. The following sections illustrate three different methods that draw on quantitative information to identify starting points for closer linguistic analysis. Section 2.1 exemplifies keywords and Section 2.2 illustrates a concordance example. These two sections illustrate corpus methods that are commonly used without necessarily looking at literary texts. Section 2.3 makes use of corpus annotation to investigate different ways in which language is used within a single text. It illustrates how methods from corpus linguistics can be applied to investigate specific questions relevant to literary stylistics.

2.1. Keywords – the 'civility' group

The keywords procedure enables the comparison of a single text with a reference corpus. To exemplify the method, we compare *Pride and Prejudice* (henceforth *PrPr*) with a reference corpus containing 18 novels by 18 nineteenth-century authors (not including Austen). The reference corpus contains about 2.8 million words, *PrPr* contains about 120,000 words. Keywords are those words that are relatively more frequent in *PrPr* than in the reference corpus. Table 25.1 shows the first 10 keywords, generated with *WordSmith Tools* (Scott 2008). The keywords are ordered according to their 'keyness', that is, a statistical measure for the difference in relative frequency of a word in *PrPr* and in the reference corpus. The table also gives the absolute frequency of the keywords in the novel (column '*PrPr* Freq.') and in the reference corpus (column 'RC. Freq.').

The first keywords are all names. When we go further down the list, the first ten words that are not names are given in Table 25.2. We find grammatical

Table 25.1: First ten keywords for a comparison of *PrPr* with a nineteenth-century reference corpus

N	Keyword	PrPr Freq.	RC. Freq.	Keyness
1	ELIZABETH	597	105	3230.62
2	DARCY	374	0	2388.87
3	BENNET	294	0	1877.69
4	BINGLEY	257	5	1592.24
5	WICKHAM	162	0	1034.48
6	COLLINS	156	2	974.87
7	JANE	264	505	739.07
8	LYDIA	133	28	702.84
9	LIZZY	95	2	587.27
10	LONGBOURN	88	0	561.89

Table 25.2: First ten keywords that are not names (*PrPr* compared to a nineteenth-century reference corpus)

N	Keyword	PrPr Freq.	RC. Freq.	Keyness
12	HER	2224	30,402	517.07
14	MR	786	7499	451.6
16	SHE	1710	22,919	423.36
19	SISTER	178	566	365.38
25	BE	1241	17,225	272.09
26	NOT	1429	20,859	260.12
27	SOON	216	1276	252.31
37	SUCH	389	3969	194.91
38	CIVILITY	42	23	185.61
40	SISTERS	76	188	184.10

words, where *her* and *she* are in line with the fact that the novel has a female protagonist, a temporal adverb (*soon*), both the singular and the plural form of the noun *sister*, which can possibly point to both the Bennett sisters, as well as Bingley's sister, and the noun *civility*, which we will investigate in more detail in Section 2.2. The number of words that result from a keyword comparison depends on the cut-off that is set for the significance measure. With a maximum p value of 0.00001, for instance, we get a list of 369 positive keywords, that is words that are relatively more frequent in *PrPr* than in the reference corpus.

In the introduction we outlined that one advantage of a corpus approach to prose fiction is the possibility to cover a whole text – an impossible task for manual analysis. Keywords do cover the whole text, but the overview they provide is initially quantitative. A list of 369 words does not constitute an analysis. Options to proceed in a keyword analysis are to investigate individual words in detail or to start by identifying groups of keywords. The first option again may require selections to be made, as a detailed analysis of keywords in context can be very time-consuming. At the same time, it can also bring up various strands for further analysis. For the second option – the identification of groups of keywords – there are again different possibilities. With the help of the tool Wmatrix (Rayson 2008), a key comparison can be conducted on the basis of semantic tags. Each word in the text and in the reference corpus would initially be assigned a label as to the semantic field they belong to. The key comparison then works on the tags and yields key semantic domains containing words with the same tag.

Another way of grouping keywords is by going through the list and intuitively identifying groups. This method is illustrated by Fischer-Starcke (2009), who also investigates the novel *PrPr*. Fischer-Starcke conducts two keyword comparisons, one comparison with a reference corpus containing Austen's novels without *PrPr*, and one comparison with a corpus of 30 novels that are seen as contemporary with *PrPr*. Fischer-Starcke shows that different reference corpora can result in different keyword lists. Her study also illustrates that intuitively identified groups of keywords can vary depending on how many keywords are there to fit into groups. In her first comparison, which yields 80 keywords, Fischer-Starcke has a category containing two words, *officers* and *regiment*, belonging to the field of 'military'. In the second comparison that yields 248 keywords, the category 'military' is less obvious and the noun *officers* is instead included among the words referring to men. This example shows that while corpus methods are useful to retrieve quantitative information and cover large amounts of data, corpus methods cannot replace detailed analyses and engagement with literary criticism. In Section 2.2 we will look at a concordance of the keyword *civility*, keyword number 38 in Table 25.2. While *civility* figures on both keyword lists in Fischer-Starcke (2009), the word is not covered by either of her two sets of semantic fields. In our list of 369 keywords there are also the word forms *civilities*, *civil*, and *politeness*, none of which occur in Fischer-Starcke's lists, which may be due to the difference in reference corpora, but also due to choosing a different p value. The words *civility*, *civilities*, *civil*, and *politeness* can be seen to form a group together with *behaviour*, *manner*, and *manners*. All are words that refer to the behaviour of characters. All are also keywords in both our study and in that of Fischer-Starcke (2009), but again in Fischer-Starcke do not seem to be assigned to any of the semantic groups.

2.2. *Concordances: Civility in context*

A concordance displays a 'node' word or search word with a specified amount of context to its left and to its right. Figure 25.1 shows all 42 occurrences of *civility*. The concordance is sorted in alphabetical order to the left of the node word. The most striking patterns in a concordance are normally verbatim repetitions of the same word around the node word, for instance, lines 4 and 5 show repetitions of *with cold civility* or in lines 40 and 41 we find *with the utmost civility*. There are also patterns with possessives such as *his*, *her*, or *Darcy's*, showing that civility characterizes a person or their behaviour. Civility can be seen as positive, when something is done with *great/greatest*, *utmost*, or *perfect* civility. However, civility can also be too much and become *obsequious*. Civility is not the same as being truly polite or friendly: it can be *cold*, *distant*, *formal* or even *sneering*. The fact that civility is part of social expectations is reflected in concordance lines that refer to civility 'allowing' something (line 1) or suggest that civility can be 'claimed' (14), 'owed' (29), or 'paid off in arrears' (22). The social expectations associated with civility can make people *sick* of it (27) and it seems civility can be used strategically

(28, *a stroke of civility*). The meanings that are illustrated in the concordance
are in line with how Emsley (2005: 90) defines 'civility': '[c]ivility is [...] ideally the outward manifestation of real goodness, politeness based on respect,
tolerance, and understanding'. However, in practice, it 'has a great deal to do
with decorum, with maintaining social niceties even when one does not feel
like being polite' (Emsley 2005: 91). So civilities can give the appearance of
goodness (ibid.: 94), but this appearance does not have to be a true reflection
of character, as is the case with Wickham. Darcy, in contrast, is truly good,
but needs to learn forms of civility in the course of the novel. When he first
proposes to Elizabeth his intentions are good, but the honesty with which

1	Elizabeth said as little to either as	civility	would allow, and sat down agai
2	med why, with so little _ endeavour _at	civility,	I am thus rejected. But it is
3	almost all, took place. Miss Bingley's	civility	to Elizabeth increased at last
4	ere better. She answered him with cold	civility.	He sat down for a few moment
5	, Madam,' said Miss Bingley, with cold	civility,	'that Miss Bennet will receive
6	and think with wonder, of Mr. Darcy's	civility,	and, above all, of his wishing
7	o speak, replied with an air of distant	civility.	Mr. Collins, however, was no
8	lied Darcy, 'was to show you, by every	civility	in my power, that I was not so
9	ot altered by his marriage; his formal	civility	was just what it had been, and
10	ly puzzled. Mrs. Bennet, with great	civility,	begged her ladyship to take s
11	r. Darcy invite him, with the greatest	civility,	to fish there as often as he
12	eeded no less in the real object of her	civility;	Mr. Darcy looked up. He was
13	g visitors, and of letting them see her	civility	towards himself and his wife,
14	e Miss Bennets were come away, when her	civility	was claimed towards Mr. Collin
15	g to anybody. At length, however, his	civility	was so far awakened as to inqui
16	s used to be free from them there; his	civility,	therefore, was most prompt in
17	hen, we have both, I hope, improved in	civility.'	'I cannot be so easily rec
18	rs. Bennet was mindful of her intended	civility,	and they were invited and enga
19	and was curious to know with how much	civility	on that lady's side the acquai
20	h; and they parted at last with mutual	civility,	and possibly a mutual desire o
21	sed to all the parading and obsequious	civility	of her husband. He bore it, h
22	retofore, and paid off every arrear of	civility	to Elizabeth. Pemberley was
23	roves? Has he deigned to add aught of	civility	to his ordinary style?--for I
24	eceived by Mrs. Bennet with a degree of	civility	which made her two daughters a
25	ceived them with all the forbearance of	civility,	and, at the request of the ge
26	may thank you, Eliza, for this piece of	civility.	Mr. Darcy would never have c
27	ss. The fact is, that you were sick of	civility,	of deference, of officious at
28	to her friends. This was a stroke of	civility	for which she was quite unprep
29	I am sure we owe him no such particular	civility	as to be obliged to say nothin
30	perfect composure, at least of perfect	civility.	She had instinctively turne
31	aw that he had lost none of his recent	civility;	and, to imitate his politeness
32	st opportunity of saying, with sneering	civility:	'Pray, Miss Eliza, are not
33	nt and the niece, that such a striking	civility	as Miss Darcy's in coming to s
34	r was amazing!--but to speak with such	civility,	to inquire after her family!
35	d; and Charlotte, detained first by the	civility	of Mr. Collins, whose inquirie
36	won; and Mr. Collins in describing the	civility	of Mr. and Mrs. Phillips, prote
37	she could hardly reply with tolerable	civility	to the polite inquiries which
38	e room, while Elizabeth tried to unite	civility	and truth in a few short senten
39	e room, and was assured with unwearying	civility	that they were perfectly needl
40	not only received him with the utmost	civility,	but even pointedly included hi
41	ention. He answered me with the utmost	civility,	and even paid me the complime
42	e rest of the day to Miss Lucas, whose	civility	in listening to him was a seaso

Figure 25.1: Concordance with all 42 occurrences of *civility* in *PrPr*

he expresses his thoughts anger Elizabeth. In this scene, both Darcy and Elizabeth accuse each other of being uncivil: Darcy for making his proposal sound to Elizabeth like an insult, and Elizabeth for *so little* endeavour *at civility* in rejecting Darcy (line 2 of the concordance in Figure 25.1) (cf. Emsley 2005: 92). The keyword *civility* thus relates to a major theme in the novel: characters have certain expectations of how good and bad characters would behave, and these expectations can lead to misunderstandings and misjudgements, especially when there is a mismatch between the outward civilities, or mere forms of behaviour, and the true virtues of a character.

2.3. Intratextual analysis

The keywords presented in Section 2.1 tell us something of the language used in *PrPr* as compared to other nineteenth-century novels. It is also possible to use the same technique to investigate the way language is used in different parts of the same text. Obvious parts of a novel are chapters. We could compare, for instance, the first chapter against the rest of the novel. Another way of looking at different parts of the text is to investigate different modes of speech, thought, and writing presentation. Semino and Short (2004) develop the model presented by Leech and Short ([1981] 2007) by conducting a large-scale corpus analysis. In order to be able to investigate discourse modes of the text using corpus methods, the features being studied need to be annotated in the electronic text. Semino and Short (2004) explain the challenges associated with such annotation that has to be added manually.[2] In the present study we take a much simpler and more limited approach that relies only on automatic annotation. For this study a script was used to annotate quoted speech in the text, based on the use of quotation marks and other punctuation indicators. While in this instance there has been no manual correction or checking of the final annotation, the initial script was developed using feedback from human correctors. The stretches of text identified by the script can be direct or free direct speech, but also thought or writing. A detailed distinction would need further manual analysis. It is only for reasons of brevity that at this point we refer to the annotated text as 'quoted speech'. In addition to quoted speech, the script also annotated 'suspensions' which are narrator interventions during a character's speech (these are examined further in Section 3.3 below).

The annotation is stored in XML (eXtensible Mark-up Language), which allows the text to be indexed and searched using tools which support XML files. For this project an XML search engine called Cheshire3 (www.cheshire3.org) was used to index and search the text. This application allows searches at various levels such as sentence and paragraph and also, because of the annotation in the corpus, within quotes or non-quotes as well as within suspensions. The

XML annotation and the Cheshire3 search tool currently being developed support investigations that can directly address questions of corpus stylistics in a way that more traditional corpus tools are not currently able to do. The development of specific tools to support corpus stylistic enquiry will be essential if the possibilities of the approach are to be fully explored. Figure 25.2 is a screenshot of a search for the word *civility* in quotes. The search reveals that only 8 of the 42 concordance lines displayed in Figure 25.1 occur in quotes.

The annotation also allows the study of language used in quotations compared to the rest of the novel. The keywords procedure outlined in Section 2.1 can be used taking the quotation sections as the text being studied, and the rest of the text as the reference corpus. This provides us with a list of words which are relatively more frequent in the 54,122 words of quotations in the novel than the 68,621 words of non-quoted material. Table 25.3 contains the first 10 keywords. As the quotations are very roughly equivalent to direct speech, it is not surprising that *I* and *you* are comparatively more frequent in quotes than in non-quoted text. If we go further down the list, another keyword that we find is *Lizzy*. Lizzy is a name used to describe the character Elizabeth Bennet but the fact that it is a keyword for quotations suggests that it is a name which is used by other characters in the novel rather than by the narrator. In addition, if we look at the negative keywords for quotations (i.e. the words which are relatively more frequent in non-quotes than in quotes) we find the name *Elizabeth*, which suggests that this form is used less frequently in conversations between characters and occurs more likely in the narration. Because of the simplified nature of the automatic annotation, these keywords obviously need further detailed

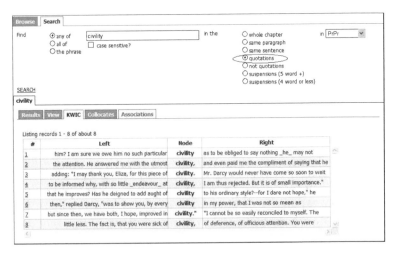

Figure 25.2: Screenshot of a search for *civility* in quotations in *PrPr*

Table 25.3: First ten keywords for a comparison of
quoted and non-quoted text in *PrPr*

N	Keyword	PrPr Freq.	RC. Freq.	Keyness
1	I	1967	101	2563.265
2	YOU	1317	40	1855.687
3	IS	820	40	1069.752
4	MY	670	49	798.4916
5	ME	418	29	503.8765
6	WILL	390	25	479.0421
7	YOUR	420	37	474.218
8	AM	312	5	465.3263
9	ARE	326	14	433.4259
10	HAVE	638	204	350.4709

analysis. Still, they indicate that proper names are worthwhile including in keywords analyses.[3]

3. Civility and body language – a thematic starting-point

Section 2 presents a more bottom-up approach, moving from patterns of words to thematic interpretations. This section starts at the other end, with top-down arguments. In *PrPr*, misunderstandings occur because the protagonists cannot talk openly about their feelings and do not have sufficient insight into the reasons and motives for the behaviour of others. For the way in which communication takes place or does not take place in the novel, body language plays an important role. Korte (1997: 152) claims that in *PrPr* 'problems of decoding body language contribute to the development of the central theme already indicated in the title of the novel'. We begin this section by linking Korte's (1997) arguments on body language in *PrPr* to our findings from the analysis of the word *civility* (Section 3.1). We then show how the selected examples given by Korte can be used as a basis for further lexical analyses of meanings in the novel (Section 3.2). Finally, we look at patterns in suspended quotations, as the context of speech appears to be a useful starting point in the search for body language (Section 3.3).

3.1. *Body language in* PrPr

Korte (1997: 31) argues that '[p]ride and prejudice prevent the protagonists from expressing their thoughts on important matters and they must instead rely on vague non-verbal signals'. This reliance on signals that can easily be misinterpreted causes misunderstandings in the novel. In the previous sections we have argued that the expectations that go with the concept of civility contribute to prejudice and the protagonists' misjudgements. It is not only pride and prejudice that affect the behaviour of the characters and the way they communicate. Social norms and expectations also have an impact. Thus civilities are related to body language as well as to the potential mismatch between formal behaviour and the true nature of a character. Korte (ibid.) uses the example below (1) to show that Elizabeth's assessment of the relationship between Wickham and Darcy is affected by her inability to correctly decode the body language between the two men. Korte (ibid.) points out that the question 'What could be the meaning of it?' highlights that Elizabeth does not fully understand the situation. The body language that Korte (1997) illustrates here is related to the concept of civility, as both characters try to be civil in spite of the underlying tensions between them.

> (1) Mr. Darcy corroborated it with a bow, and was beginning to determine not to fix his eyes on Elizabeth, when they were suddenly arrested by the sight of the stranger, and Elizabeth happening to see the countenance of both as they looked at each other, was all astonishment at the effect of the meeting. Both changed colour, one looked white, the other red. Mr. Wickham, after a few moments, touched his hat – a salutation which Mr. Darcy just deigned to return. *What could be the meaning of it?* It was impossible to imagine; it was impossible not to long to know.[4]
>
> (*PrPr*, Chapter 15)

The importance of behaviour, manners, and outward appearance is also reflected in the observations that characters make on others. Korte (1997: 200) quotes example (2) from the novel to illustrate the significance of looks, pointing out that '[w]ithin the social confines of the characters, most of whom belong to the gentry, the behaviour of every individual is carefully registered and analysed by the others' (ibid.: 199).

> (2) Mrs. Gardiner and Elizabeth talked of all that had occurred during their visit, as they returned, except what had particularly interested them both. *The looks and behaviour* of everybody they had seen were discussed, except of the person who had mostly engaged their attention.
>
> (*PrPr*, Chapter 45)

To illustrate the diverse messages that can be carried by looks and glances, Korte (ibid.) gives the example reproduced in (3). Here, Sir William's glance functions in place of speech, whereas Darcy's look does not seem to be intentional, but unconsciously reveals his reservations about a relationship between Bingley and Jane.

> (3) '[…] Allow me to say, however, that your fair partner does not disgrace you, and that I must hope to have this pleasure often repeated, especially when a certain desirable event, my dear Eliza (*glancing at her sister and Bingley*) shall take place. What congratulations will then flow in! I appeal to Mr. Darcy: […]'
>
> The latter part of this address was scarcely heard by Darcy; but Sir William's allusion to his friend seemed to strike him forcibly, and *his eyes were directed with a very serious expression towards* Bingley and Jane, who were dancing together.
>
> (PrPr, Chapter 18)

Eye behaviour can also function to communicate attitudes and opinions that would not be appropriate to be expressed in words, that is, civility would prevent them being spelled out. Korte (ibid.) illustrates with example (4) how Miss Bingley expresses her contempt for Elizabeth's family. The example also highlights that although civility plays an important role, formal behaviour does not necessarily match the characters' feelings.

> (4) Nothing but concern for Elizabeth could enable Bingley to keep his countenance. His sister was less delicate, and *directed her eyes towards* Mr. Darcy with a very expressive smile.
>
> (PrPr, Chapter 9)

Korte's (1997) examples provide links to the concordance analysis of civility in Section 2.2. We also want to point out two further aspects of her examples. Firstly, we look at lexical clues for body language and secondly, we discuss body language in relation to characters' speech.

3.2. Lexical clues for body language: the example of eyes

Body language can be realized in various ways. Without any clues as to what to search for, the topic is difficult to address with corpus methodology. Korte's (1997) examples can serve as a starting point to identify lexical clues as a basis for further searches. From the four examples in Section 3.1, we can extract a list of potential candidates for further concordances analyses (numbers in square brackets provide the number of occurrences in the four examples): *eyes* [3], *countenance* [2], *looked* [2], *look, behaviour, smile, expressive, expression, glancing*. Comparing examples (3) and (4), there are also two similar expressions: *his eyes were directed… towards* and *directed her eyes towards* ... which may suggest that Korte (1997) picked two examples of a repeatedly occurring pattern. The word *eyes* occurs 52 times in the novel. The concordance in Figure 25.3 displays the first half of the examples, sorted to the first 3 positions on the left of *eyes*. The concordance illustrates several patterns such as 'beautiful'/'fine' eyes to talk about the beauty of a woman, eyes that reveal a character's feelings as in 'eyes sparkled' or 'lifted up her eyes in amazement'. Equally, the word *eyes* occurs in patterns where characters avoid looking others in the eye: 'unable to lift up her eyes', 'dared not lift up her eyes'. Similar to the co-occurrences of 'directed ... eyes ... towards' that Korte cites are patterns with 'eyes were fixed on/turned toward' illustrating eye movement. As Korte shows, descriptions of eye movement make it possible to give insights into characters' feelings that cannot explicitly be expressed. One of the reasons for the inability to express certain thoughts and feelings are social expectations to which civility belongs. An example is the following one from chapter 54, another instance of the *turned towards* pattern. After Elizabeth has revised her attitude towards Darcy, she is hoping for an opportunity to speak to him at a party, but the two of them find themselves at different tables during a game of cards.

> (5) They were confined for the evening at different tables, and she had nothing
> to hope, but that *his eyes were so often turned towards her side of the room*, as to
> make him play as unsuccessfully as herself.
>
> (*PrPr*, Chapter 54)

Another pattern in the concordance that relates to thematic meanings is the metaphorical one of 'opening someone's eyes to a character': in line 22 below (Figure 25.3), Elizabeth is talking about opening Lydia's eyes to Wickham's character, and in the second part of the concordance (not reproduced in Figure 25.3 for reasons of space) there is an example referring to Darcy having his eyes opened to Wickham. The concordance search for *eyes* thus finds further examples relating to the theme of misunderstanding characters and only finding out their real nature in the course of the novel. The patterns to which a concordance points can help to follow up on observations based on individual examples. However, not every concordance line will necessarily contribute to the same picture. The example of *eyes* also shows another point. The word *eyes* is not a positive keyword, but a negative keyword; that is in *PrPr* it is comparatively less frequent than in the reference corpus. Still, a concordance for this negative keyword shows some relations to the keyword *civility* and points to thematic meanings. This underlines that corpus methods need to be complemented by qualitative analysis. Although keywords can be a useful starting point, even a thorough analysis of all keywords cannot be taken as pointing to everything that is thematically relevant.

```
 1       er could do justice to those beautiful eyes?' 'It would not be easy, indeed,
 2         eman, and a stranger.' Mrs. Bennet's eyes sparkled. 'A gentleman and a stran
 3       nt waited for an answer. Mrs. Bennet's eyes sparkled with pleasure, and she wa
 4       onger the first object; Miss Bingley's  eyes were instantly turned toward Darcy,
 5       verse of that young lady, whose bright eyes are also upbraiding me.' The lat
 6       instrument, how frequently Mr. Darcy's eyes were fixed on her. She hardly knew
 7      by the beautiful expression of her dark eyes. To this discovery succeeded some
 8       r, and she began her song. Elizabeth's  eyes were fixed on her with most painful
 9       all Miss Bingley's witticisms on _ fine eyes _ . Chapter 10 The day pa
10       ry great pleasure which a pair of fine eyes in the face of a pretty woman can
11       r affected your admiration of her fine eyes. ' 'Not at all,' he replied; 'the
12       the impulse of curiosity, she raised her eyes to his face, she as often found hi
13        ciety! But she had chosen it with her eyes open; and though evidently regretti
14        f the room. She followed him with her eyes, envied everyone to whom he spoke,
15          other sex.' Elizabeth lifted up her eyes in amazement, but was too much opp
16       h confusion, and unable to lift up her eyes. Had Miss Bingley known what pain
17       tions. Elizabeth dared not lift up her eyes. How Mr. Darcy looked, therefore,
18       sed, and without daring to lift up her eyes, till anxious curiosity carried the
19       semblance of Mr. Darcy, she turned  her eyes on the daughter, she could almost h
20       t was not often that she could turn her eyes on Mr. Darcy himself; but, wheneve
21       a smile of delight added lustre to  her eyes, as she thought for that space of t
22        Forster, the necessity of opening her eyes to his character never occurred to
23       and confused, scarcely dared lift her eyes to his face, and knew not what ans
24       ' replied Elizabeth, with tears in her eyes, 'that a sister's sense of decency
25      ke him,' she replied, with tears in her eyes, 'I love him. Indeed he has no im
26        out of the common way; and as for  her eyes, which have sometimes been called s
```

Figure 25.3: 26 of the 52 examples of eyes in *PrPr*

3.3. *Body language and speech: suspended quotations*

In this section we want to illustrate another option to find meanings related to body language and to the thematic concept of civility. We draw on the annotation described in Section 2.3 to find suspensions in *PrPr*. In this study, a 'suspension' is defined as a span of (narrator) text which interrupts a span of quoted speech (or thought, or writing). Following Lambert (1981),[5] only interruptions of five or more words are counted as suspensions. In addition, the suspension must be in the same orthographic sentence as the speech it interrupts. In other words, if a sentence ends in a section of text which falls between two quotations this is not considered to be a suspension. In example (6) below *said Mrs. Bennet to her husband* is such a suspension.

(6) 'If I can but see one of my daughters happily settled at Netherfield,' *said Mrs. Bennet to her husband*, 'and all the others equally well married, [...]'

This definition of suspensions means that in practice, most suspensions will be reporting clauses. But since the annotation only works on punctuation and not on grammatical categories, we use a surface-oriented definition. Also, as pointed out in Section 2.3, the annotation does not distinguish between speech, thought, and writing presentation. Although the annotation, which is still work in progress, has limitations, it is useful to find examples that can form the basis for the identification of functional categories. The motivation to look at suspensions as useful places to find examples of body language is that suspensions contain detail accompanying speech (or thought, or even writing presentation). In real life, there will always be body language accompanying speech. In narrative prose, it is impossible to describe all the body language that would occur in a real situation. It is often taken for granted, but it can also be added. When it is made explicit it serves a function in the narration. In *PrPr* we find 60 examples of suspensions. A manual analysis of these 60 examples yields 4 groups of suspension that fulfil different functions. These functions were identified by following the inductive principle that underlies a concordance analysis: examples that are similar are put into one group. The functional label assigned to the group then aims to capture the similarity between the examples. The groups that are found in the present study are 'speech organization', 'body language', 'narrator's interpretation of speech', and 'direct characterization'.[6]

(a) Speech organization

Suspensions that can be classified as organizing speech contain information that refers to aspects of turn-taking, for instance, example (6) above specifies both the speaker and the person she talks to, or example (7) below indicates that there was a pause. Example (7) also is a case that shows how the representation of speech in fiction differs from the transcription of natural speech. The pause that the example refers to actually took place before the *But what* is spoken, but is indicated at a later stage so that it interrupts the speech that does not contain a pause. The third example to illustrate the speech organization category, example (8), contains temporal information that puts the speech in the context of the ongoing actions of the characters.

> (7) 'But what,' *said she, after a pause,* 'can have been his motive? [...]'
> (8) 'I have been thinking it over again, Elizabeth,' *said her uncle, as they drove from the town;* 'and really, [...]'

(b) Body language

The category 'body language' covers examples where a body-part noun occurs in the suspension, as in example (9), but also cases of body movement and practical actions that accompany speech as in (10), as well as examples that describe voice quality and loudness (11). Example (9) is a straightforward example of body language in the sense that we find a body-part noun: *head*. In the example, the character's speech is supported by body language that can be described as 'gesture', that is, 'movements of individual body parts that are clearly delineated, for example, nodding, raising a hand, waving an arm', and such movements often seem to have a conventional meaning (Korte 1997: 38).

> (9) 'Ah!' *said Mrs. Bennet, shaking her head*, 'then she is better off than many girls. [...]'
> (10) 'And this,' *cried Darcy, as he walked with quick steps across the room*, 'is your opinion of me! [...]'

The body language in example (10) can be described as practical action. This type of body language can be seen on a continuum with actions that place the speech they accompany in the context of other ongoing activities of the characters, as in (8). The difference between the actions in (10) and (8) lies in the relationship between what happens and what is being said. Example (8) is the first sentence of chapter 43 so the information *as they drove from the town* serves to connect the chapter to the previous one, while at the same time it makes it possible to begin in the middle of a conversation. The primary function of the action in example (10), in contrast, is to accompany speech. Finally, an example that describes the tone, loudness, or way in which a character speaks is (11).

> (11) 'I am afraid, Mr. Darcy,' *observed Miss Bingley in a half whisper*, 'that this adventure has rather affected your admiration of her fine eyes.'

(c) Narrator's interpretation of speech

The third group of suspensions includes examples where the narrator evaluates and interprets how the characters say something. Instead of the 'showing' that prevails in the categories of speech organization and body language, the narrator is now 'telling' us how to interpret the characters' speech. In examples (12) and (13) it is the 'voice' or the 'tone' in which something is said that indicates the speaker's displeasure or the fact that she is angry. Similarly, in (14), by referring to *an air of awkward gallantry* the narrator provides an interpretation of a character's outward appearance.

> (12) '[...] Far be it from me,' *he presently continued, in a voice that marked his displeasure*, 'to resent [...]'

(13) 'Miss Bennet,' *replied her ladyship, in an angry tone,* [...]
(14) 'You are uniformly charming!' *cried he, with an air of awkward gallantry;* [...]

(d) Direct characterization

The final group of suspensions are examples of direct characterization. In example (15) the information in the suspension contrasts with what Elizabeth says: she is curious, although she acts as if she was not. In example (16), we are given information on how Mary likes to see herself.

(15) 'Oh! certainly,' *said Elizabeth, though burning with curiosity;* 'we will ask you no questions.'
(16) 'Pride,' *observed Mary, who piqued herself upon the solidity of her reflections,* 'is [...]'

With the four categories of suspensions we see a cline from the description of contexts in which characters are placed to explicit characterization. The categories of body language and narrator's interpretation of speech, for instance, differ in the following way. With examples of body language such as *Mrs. Bennet shaking her head*, the reader would be able to interpret the description themselves. In contrast, *with an air of awkward gallantry* does not give any information on what look, movement, or facial expression is taken as the basis for the interpretation presented by the narrator. However, it is clear that the four categories are not discrete.

The analysis of suspensions in *PrPr* shows several links to the thematic points made in earlier sections. In the concordance of *civility* above (Figure 25.1), line 5 (example 17 below) is an example of a suspension that falls into the category of narrator's interpretation of speech: Miss Bingley's words cannot be criticized on the basis of social expectations of politeness, but the adjective *cold* indicates that she is mainly formal and not good-natured.

(17) 'You may depend upon it, Madam,' *said Miss Bingley, with cold civility,* 'that Miss Bennet will receive every possible attention while she remains with us.'

Although only one of the 60 examples contains an explicit reference to civility, we also find other suspensions that link to the concept. Example (10) is from chapter 34, where Darcy declares his love for Elizabeth but they end up arguing because of the misconceptions that Elizabeth has about him. Darcy's walking reflects his emotional involvement in the increasingly heated exchange between him and Elizabeth. The suspension occurs in effect in a longer paragraph of speech that continues with (10a), where we find another suspension. In (10a) reference is made again to the walking, and more precisely to Darcy's stopping and turning. So the practical actions serve to indicate emotions and thereby support the speech.

(10a) This is the estimation in which you hold me! I thank you for explaining it so fully. My faults, according to this calculation, are heavy indeed! But perhaps,' *added he, stopping in his walk, and turning towards her,* 'these offen[c] es might have been overlooked, had not your pride been hurt by my honest confession of the scruples that had long prevented my forming any serious design. [...]'

(*PrPr*, Chapter 34)

In chapter 34, Darcy and Elizabeth argue, and each accuses the other of being uncivil (cf. Section 2.2). Emsley (2005: 92) highlights the proposal scene in chapter 34 as a 'crucial moment' where the anger of Elizabeth and Darcy is demonstrated. The anger of each is triggered by thinking the other is uncivil. Both struggle to contain their anger and behave in a civil way. When Elizabeth tells Darcy that she does not accepts his proposal, he becomes 'pale with anger' and he is 'struggling for the appearance of composure, and would not open his lips till he believed himself to have attained it'. Examples (10) and (10a) have to be seen in this context. As the conversation between Elizabeth and Darcy continues, his temper is rising and his walking across the room seems to be one way of trying to retain his calm.

The fact that we find the only two suspensions that occur in one paragraph in a crucial scene of the book relates to the functional relevance of suspensions. Suspensions are places that help to picture the synchronicity of speech and body language. At the same time, the fact that body language is described and not taken for granted gives it emphasis. This emphasis is even greater when two suspensions are related and show development in the behaviour of a character, as in examples (10) and (10a). Another point to consider, however, is how we can interpret such suspensions in terms of foregrounding. Our corpus methods take us to a crucial scene in the novel. But because the scene is so crucial we would not really need a computer to direct our attention to it. On the other hand, the suspension pattern seems to be one that a manual analysis would not necessarily pick up on. As Toolan (2009: 191) highlights when discussing corpus methods, 'it is not that textual obviousness alone is sufficient condition for something to be likely to be psychologically real for readers'. Although readers may not necessarily be aware of the same patterns that a computer helps to find, it is still possible that the patterns contribute to the perception of certain effects. In this sense corpus methods can complement the analysis of features that are obvious enough to be found without corpus methods.

4. Conclusions

The present chapter has shown a number of starting points for corpus stylistic analyses. The methods in Section 2 show how corpus tools can guide the way into a text. In all three cases, however, it is necessary to make certain choices: keyword comparisons need an appropriate reference corpus, and a keywords list has to be further interpreted to yield meaningful observations; concordance analyses focus on individual words, and need links to larger topics and themes; and finally intratextual comparisons need some motivation as to what is usefully compared or extracted with the help of annotation. The aim of Section 3 was to join the methods in Section 2 with more detailed thematic concerns of the novel. What we have shown in this article in terms of an analysis of the novel *Pride and Prejudice* is still necessarily a partial picture. Obviously, this is partly due to the limited space in an article, compared to a book-length study. Still, even a corpus approach cannot counter Short's (1996: 255) observation that the analysis of a novel 'could take a lifetime'. What we set out to show is that corpus methods can complement detailed textual analysis. Corpus methods are not to replace detailed textual analysis, and should not be seen in isolation from it. For instance, the fact that a word does not show as key (positive or negative) is not to say that it does not play a role in the creation of meaning in the text. Equally, concordances or searches for suspensions may retrieve data that is relevant to the question that guides our analysis, but at the same time the search may also yield a number of examples that do not seem directly relevant. It is for the analyst to assess how searches can be narrowed down and complemented with further methodological approaches.

An important aspect of the added value that corpus analyses bring to stylistic studies is the comparative nature of corpus work. The example of suspensions shows how similarities can be identified across the 60 examples of suspensions that would be very hard to find by reading through the text. The example of suspensions also highlights how corpus stylistic questions can and should have an impact on the tools that are available. Standard concordancing packages have thus far been uninterested in allowing the user to search within suspensions. Corpus stylisticians, however, can profit from software that is better tailored to the nature of the texts they want to analyse. Overall, it is important that the questions we aim to answer are not dictated by the corpus tools available to us. We have to create appropriate tools so that we can investigate the questions we want to ask.

NOTES

1. http://www.gutenberg.org/ (accessed: July 2006). Because we use an e-text, quoted examples do not have page references. However, longer examples contain references to chapters.
2. For a discussion of annotation for stylistic analysis see also McIntyre (2007b).
3. For the analysis of short stories, Toolan (2009) also shows the value of investigating name keywords in detail.
4. Italics in indented examples have been added for emphasis.
5. Lambert (1981) looks at suspended quotations in Dickens.
6. For an analysis of speech presentation in nineteenth-century fiction, see also Busse (forthcoming) and Busse (present volume).

CHAPTER 26

Non-literary Language: A Stylistic Investigation of the Cover Pages of the British Satirical Magazine *Private Eye*

BEATRIX BUSSE

1. Introduction

Although the focus of stylistic investigation has mainly, but not exclusively, been on literature, the research framework of stylistics, as well as its methodological and theoretical basis, can be fruitfully applied in the analysis of non-literary texts. The concept of foregrounding and the essential stylistic question of 'how a text means what it does' are crucial to the identification of meanings, styles, and discourses of non-literary texts. This potential grows further if one follows Fowler (1986) or Carter (2004) who argue that the distinction between literary and non-literary language needs to be questioned, and that literary language has to be seen on a continuum; that is, a cline of literariness. However, perhaps due to the fact that stylistics has for a long time wrongly, though almost exclusively, been associated with the identification of the style of an author and with the analysis of literature alone, stylistic applications to non-literary texts are not as numerous as those using literature as their source text of investigation. Nonetheless, the functional potential of stylistics for the analysis of language other than literature has lately been more prominently recognized and acknowledged outside of the stylistics community (e.g. Jeffries 2010a) due to findings in such fields as, for example, new historical stylistics, cognitive stylistics, corpus stylistics or multimodal stylistics.

In order to demonstrate the value of a stylistic approach to the analysis of non-literary texts, I will investigate stylistically the verbal and non-verbal strategies used on the cover pages of the British satirical magazine *Private Eye*. Launched in 1961 amid the British satire boom (see also Simpson 2003: 11), *Private Eye* is a fortnightly British satirical magazine, which satirizes political issues in Great Britain and worldwide, and targets, for example, politicians, royals, and other celebrities. On a diachronic dimension, it can be said that it provides its readers with a commentary on the social and political history of Great Britain and the world. Even though the magazine has been accused of, and sued for, some of its scurrilous and allegedly offensive 'news reporting' (see Simpson 2003: 168), it enjoys high popularity with its British and international readership. Many successful cartoonists and writers have contributed to it, and *Private Eye*'s columns, such as 'Eye TV', a mocking analysis of TV programmes, 'Colemanballs', a selection of linguistic blunders made by television and radio presenters (and analysed by Paul Simpson in 1993), and its parodies of newspaper articles, constitute some of its celebrated regular sections.

The cover pages combine linguistic und visual modes of presentation and, since its beginnings in October 1961, have functioned as means of 'setting the scene' for the respective issue or as a major satirical comment on Britain's or the world's political leaders, their actions and decisions, the lifestyle of the British royal family, and so on. My focus is on the question of how the constant transition from humour and biting (and at times bad-tempered and style-less) satire to political, social, cultural, and linguistic commentary is construed for the reader on these cover pages. Furthermore, I illustrate how these multimodal images are likely to trigger, in the reader, an understanding of which relevant contexts are to be invoked for interpretive purposes. I pursue a diachronic and synchronic, stylistic corpus-based investigation of the language used in the captions and headlines as well as in the speech-bubbles on the cover pages, from its beginnings to December 2008. This allows me to argue in terms of what are innovative and what are stable linguistic strategies or styles.

This analysis also includes an investigation of the visual or multimodal means of presentation in terms of the photograph used or the speaker(s) depicted. Within a broader framework, I will argue that the modes of representation chosen have textual, interpersonal, and experiential functions.

2. The corpus of cover pages of *Private Eye*

The linguistic corpus of the cover pages of *Private Eye* consists of the language used on those cover pages. The cover pages include the issues ranging from October 1961 to December 2008. The corpus contains 20,612 words. As can be seen in Figure 26.1, language may be used in speech-bubbles and in the captions of the cover page. Therefore, the corpus is subdivided into the language used in the speech-bubbles and that used in the captions. The speech-bubble corpus contains 13,160 words and the corpus consisting of the captions has 7452 words. These two corpora have been further subdivided into chronological periods of 10 years, ranging from 1961 to 1969, from 1970 to 1979, and so on.

In order to be able to establish the discourses of the language used on the cover pages of *Private Eye*, an 'objective' empirical text analysis is pursued. As part of this informed (textual) stylistic analysis, I draw on a corpus stylistic approach and apply the corpus comparison tool Wmatrix, developed by Paul Rayson (http://ucrel.lancs.ac.uk/wmatrix.html, Rayson 2008),[1] to the corpus of speech-bubbles and captions compiled from all the cover pages published from October 1961 to December 2008. The goal is to identify statistically prominent parts of speech and semantic fields, because Wmatrix is a tool for text comparison and investigates on various linguistic levels linguistic features for their statistical keyness (see also Culpeper 2002; Archer 2009; Walker this volume, for a fuller description). Admittedly, the assumption that word choice alone construes meaning stands on shaky ground, especially with regard to approaches which no longer favour the separation between lexis and grammar, but stress their interplay in pattern grammar (Hunston and Francis 2000) or lexical priming (Hoey 2005), for example. Yet, the application of statistical measurement through the use of Wmatrix may be supportive for, and stands in interaction with, the qualitative analyses pursued below.

A word prominently used in the first text will appear at the top of the list. In other words, the words in the keyness list are ordered according to their keyness value, calculated as a positive score of log-likelihood. Log-likelihood (LL) is a measure of significance, which can be compared to the chi-square test in the following way: 'Any score at or above 3.8 is significant to the level of $p < 0.05$ in chi-square terms; any score at or above 6.6 is significant to the level of $p < 0.01$' (Leech 2008: 165).

According to Leech (2008: 167), the reference corpus/corpora should be of the same period as the text to be investigated in order to permit a synchronic investigation (see also Toolan [2009: 16] for his discussion of the difficulties in determining a 'comparator corpus'; and Scott 2009a). Ideally, genre should be taken into account, but a comparison should also take place between the text and other genres. Leech favours what he calls a 'scatter-gun approach' (Leech 2008: 167) and opts for multiple comparison with the different reference corpora, but 'slight differences of period, genre and so on among alternative reference corpora are unlikely to make substantive differences to the results' (Leech 2008: 167). The reference corpus for both the headlines and captions in *Private Eye* is the *BNC sampler* written corpus. The speech-bubbles on the cover pages have been compared with the *BNC sampler* spoken subpart.

3. The multimodal design of the cover pages of *Private Eye* – interpersonal, experiential and textual narrative representations

3.1. *General layout of the cover pages of Private Eye*

The typical cover page of *Private Eye* usually looks as follows:

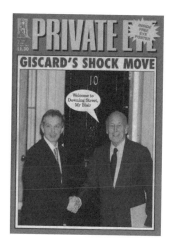

Figure 26.1: 'Giscard's shock move' (Issue 1081, 12 June 2003)

Within the framework of a multimodal analysis, these cover pages can be seen as acts of sign-making (Peirce 1931–58, Saussure 1916; Kress and Van Leeuwen 2006; see also Nørgaard, this volume). As stylisticians, we need to explore how these cover pages make use of the semiotic potential around them in order to take a particular stance and/or create humour and satire. Following Kress and Van Leeuwen (2006: 15), whose base is Hallidayan (1994, 2004) grammar (see Nørgaard, this volume, for a complete, but also critical description of their model), every semiotic system fulfils an 'ideational' function, a function of representing 'the world around and inside us', as well as an 'interpersonal' function, a function of enacting social interaction as social relations. All message entities – texts – also attempt to present a coherent 'world of the text', what Halliday calls the textual function – a world in which all the elements of the text cohere internally, and which itself coheres with its relevant environment. Semiotic modes are shaped by and reflect the intrinsic characteristics of the medium, but also the requirements, histories, and values of societies and their cultures (Kress and Van Leeuwen 2006: 35). To investigate the corpus of those cover pages from a multimodal perspective seems useful in order to be able to establish the intra- and intertextual norms, and what is innovative. At the same time, these observations need to be related to political, cultural, and linguistic developments of the respective time periods under investigation. However, caution is necessary. As Nørgaard (this volume, 436) puts it:

> [G]reat care should clearly be taken not to force common concepts onto semiotic material that does not naturally accommodate such an approach. In my view, the advantage of a multimodal grammar is thus not necessarily a strict standardization of our descriptive categories, but rather the wish to acknowledge the significance of all the different modes that go into a given instance of meaning-making as well as the attempt to develop ways of describing all these modes and their interaction.

Similar to how the different levels of language always interact when language is used, the different modes presented and used on these cover pages and how they are interpreted are interdependent in their meaning-making processes. For ease of understanding, however, a detailed and systematic analysis of the different modes used for those cover pages will be presented separately (see also Nørgaard, this volume).

An abstraction of the prototypical structure of the cover page is illustrated with the help of Figure 26.2 (see also Nørgaard, this volume, for her general emphasis on layout in multimodal discourse):

Figure 26.2: The structure of the prototypical *Private Eye* cover page

As Figure 26.2 shows, the name of the magazine *Private Eye* usually covers almost 25 per cent of the whole page and constitutes the eye-catching top of the page (on the top left-hand side you find the magazine's mascot 'Gnitty', which is apparently based on John Wells, one of the early founders). A similar function is fulfilled by the captions, which can usually be found underneath the magazine's name. In earlier issues from the 1970s and 1960s, however, they either did not appear at all or were printed at the bottom of the page as in Figure 26.3.

Figure 26.3: 'Come home, Baillie. All Is forgiven' (Issue 91, 11 June 1965)

Similar to the functions of the headlines, the captions introduce the topic of the issue, or inform the reader about and comment on what is presented in the photographs (while performing other functions, as will be shown below). The photograph usually takes up almost two-thirds of the A4 page. Strikingly, and this is another particularity of the covers, the photographs of, for example, celebrities, politicians, and royals contain speech-bubbles (sometimes even thought-bubbles) used to present direct speech.

The layout structure of the cover pages has not changed much in the course of the 40 years of the magazine's existence. This becomes apparent when comparing Figure 26.3, which shows a cover from 1965, to the cover in Figure 26.4 from 2000. One important alteration took place in 1998, however, when coloured photos began to replace black and white ones.

In Hoey's (2005) terms, the reader of *Private Eye* has been primed towards this layout on a textual, interpersonal, and experiential[2] level, that is, the reader expects this structure. Textually speaking, the layout creates coherence as the Western reader will follow the conventional reading path and probably move from top to bottom, that is, from the title of the page to the captions (Kress and Van Leeuwen 2006) as well as to processing the photograph, or from processing the photograph to the captions. Whether there is a

Figure 26.4: 'Loyal wedding souvenir' (Issue 1008, 11 August 2000)

language-first orientation, and whether the reader will read and process the captions and/or the speech-bubbles first before the photo is fully processed, would certainly have to be tested.

The world inside and around us – that is, the experiential function – is usually represented through the photograph and the language used, because both establish an anchor of the message and present an aspect of the world as experienced by humans. In Kress and Van Leeuwen's (2006: 47) terms, these 'participants' also have an experiential function as they participate in the presentation of objects and their relations in the world. Kress and Van Leeuwen (ibid.) distinguish between 'interactive participants' and 'represented particpants':

> The former are the participants in the act of communication – the participants who speak and listen or write and read, make images or view them, whereas the latter are the participants who constitute the subject matter of the communication; that is, the people, places, things [...] represented in and by the speech or writing or image, the participants about whom or which we are speaking or writing or producing images.

Since pictures can be interpreted as narrative (rather than conceptual) representations, we will see below that it may (even) be necessary to include in this model an additional discourse structure to that relating to the narrator and the reader.

Simpson (2003: 85) also uses a triadic structure that describes the subject positions involved in satirical discourse. Referring to an abstract set of 'subject placements' (Simpson 2003: 86), he distinguishes between *satirist* (the addresser), the *satirized* (the target), and the *satiree* (the addressee). These three

positions are interlinked 'by bonds that are in conflict and open to interrogation in satirical discourse' (ibid.).

The distinction between 'interactive participant' and 'represented participant', as well as between *satirist*, *satirized*, and *satiree*, helps explain the interpersonal function transferred by this layout. It also brings to mind Short's
model of the typical discourse structure that characterizes interaction in dramatic texts (see also McIntyre and Culpeper this volume):

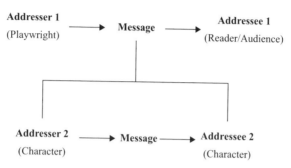

Figure 26.5: Discourse structure of dramatic texts (Short 1996)

According to Short, the first level depicted in Figure 26.5 deals with the writer
and the reader (or the audience of a play), whereas the second, embedded
level concerns the characters communicating with one another. As in drama,
the discourse structure presented on the cover pages of *Private Eye* has at least
two levels of interpersonal interaction. The first is that between the personali-
ties/figures in the photograph who appear to communicate with one another
through speech that is presented/projected (in Figure 26.1, quoted above, this
is Tony Blair and Valérie M. R. Giscard d'Estaing). As with drama, authors
of the cover pages of *Private Eye* transfer their meanings indirectly to the
reader by having their characters communicate with one another. But while
the playwright has more time in drama to inform the audience about who is
who in the play, the covers of *Private Eye* need a number of multimodal triggers in order to make meaning, and to enable the reader to understand what
the 'semiotic landscape' is about. Therefore, the second interpersonal discourse level, which is that between author/producer/editor of that cover page
and the reader, plays a crucial role.

The layout of the cover pages of *Private Eye* reflects and creates patterns of
representation through its multimodal modes of representation (experiential
function). It also creates patterns of interaction (the interpersonal function).
And, finally, it creates a message which coheres internally and externally. It has
already been hinted at that the cover pages also exploit conventional schemata to
create humour and satire. Therefore, it is useful to draw on some of the essential

linguistic approaches to satire, which additionally help us know how to interpret the visual and linguistic interplay on the cover pages of *Private Eye*.

Attardo (1997) and Attardo and Raskin (1991) elaborate on Raskin's (1985) semantic script theory of humour. According to Attardo (1997), a joke is structured in a linear way in order to capture the different phases of the joke's development. The concept of incongruity through script opposition remains the core of the joke's text. Stages in the production of a text are identified. They include:

a) The setup, which prepares the groundwork for the joke by establishing an accessible, neutral context, which is congruent with the receiver of the text. The elements occurring first will become part of the context, and will establish a framework of expectations against the scripts that appear afterwards and have to be processed (see Simpson 2003: 39).
b) Incongruity (or script opposition), the concept of which has been broadened to account for cognitive-psycholinguistic oppositions. There are two scripts: the first is highly accessible and based on a neutral concept; the second, the opposite script, is much less accessible and context-dependent (ibid.). Script opposition is somewhat like negation, because the receiver needs to have both in mind: the negated and the positive in order to process and understand it.
c) Resolution, which requires local, logical mechanisms and brings sense to an ambiguity (ibid.: 40).

It is obvious that the notion of script opposition also relates to typical stylistic ideas of creativity (as outlined by poetic effects and cognitive aspects of literary processing) and foregrounding.

In a similar way, Simpson (2003: 88), in addition to identifying the positions of the participants in a satirical event, elaborates on the concept of the satirical text itself. Two opposing discourse slots describe its make-up in discourse terms and its method of transmission in a discourse event. One is a prime (based on Emmott 1997), which is an intersemiotic quality and an echo of the discourse genre. It conveys a mediated message. One contextual frame becomes the focus of attention (Simpson 2003: 89) and the reader's main context. In addition, there is a dialectic (the discursive twist), which is text-internal (not intertextual) and positioned after the prime, almost like an antithesis. It may be achieved through the interplay of all levels of language and contexts.

3.2. The captions on the cover pages of Private Eye – some corpus-based observations

Within the overall layout, the captions, which refer to an important item of news, add to the creation of coherence and the top-down structure. Due to their position at the top of the page, conventionally, they will be read first. Experientially speaking, they also create a specific situation by means of the language that is used to refer to participants and circumstances. They form the setup (Attardo 1997) or the prime (Simpson 2003: 88, 168). The newspaper character of the captions and the general adherence to the style of newspapers superficially also aim at enlarging the degree of credibility. Also, from an interpersonal point of view, they address the hearer and help the reader to identify characters depicted in the photo. At the same time, they also comment on or stand in opposition to what the viewer can see in the photo. As such they go beyond functioning as a prime, but can also set the dialectic in motion, as will be illustrated below.

The key parts of speech and key semantic fields used in the captions have strong meaning-making potential. Many of the parts of speech prominently used in this corpus remain the same diachronically speaking when compared to the *BNC* sampler written, as can be seen in Table 26.1. To some extent, this is surprising because a hypothesis could have been that in order to create humour and satire, linguistic creativity is one prerequisite.[3]

Table 26.1 reveals that in all periods the captions of *Private Eye* are marked by a prominent use of nouns and noun phrases. The head of the noun phrase is either a proper name or a singular common noun, although for 2000–08 we find more common nouns. Examples are 'Loyal Wedding Souvenir' (Issue 1008, August 2000, see Figure 26.4), 'Prince Charles: A Nation Waits' (Issue 5, February 1962, Figure 26.6), or 'Blair's TUC Shock' (Issue 907, Sept. 1996, Figure 26.7).

Both in these headlines and captions, noun phrases are particularly useful tools for packaging information into very dense chunks. In addition, they appear more static and fixed than verbal constructions. Over-usage in terms of statistical keyness does not immediately lead to foregrounding and stylistic significance. But the high frequency of nouns and noun phrases supports the notion that the caption's function is to set the scene in terms of identifying the content of the photographs, the speakers, or the topic.

Verbs used in the third person are also frequently used in all periods. Because of the reference to persons or single common nouns, the captions contain either noun phrases alone or sentences with a noun phrase and a verb phrase, as in 'Blairy Halliwell entertains the troops' (Issue 1039, October 2001) illustrated in Figure 26.8.

Another very popular structure in the captions of the cover pages of *Private Eye* is the copular structure with the dummy *it*, as in 'Oh no, It's hymn!' (Issue 1028, May 2001, see Figure 26.9) or 'Yes, it's wedding balls!' (Issue 1032, July 2001, see Figure 26.10). Together with the use of interjections and the discourse marker *yes*, which become more frequent moving towards the 1990s, this shows a general trend towards colloquialization and oral style in

Table 26.1: Key parts of speech in the captions of the cover pages of *Private Eye* (comparison with the *BNC sampler written*)

	1961–69 parts of speech	Log-l.	1970–79 parts of speech	Log-l.	1980–89 parts of speech	Log-l.	1990–99 parts of speech	Log-l.	2000–08 parts of speech	Log-l.
1.	sgl. proper noun	170.85	sgl. proper noun	319.70	sgl. common noun	141.89	sgl. proper noun	111.00	sgl. common noun	144.66
2.	lexical verb	127.46	sgl. common noun	278.20	sgl. proper noun	130.79	sgl. common noun	106.80	sgl. proper noun	127.77
3.	sgl. common noun	91.37	-s form of lexical verb	212.58	lexical verb	66.42	lexical verb	88.10	lexical verb	112.86
4.	-s form of lexical verb	86.86	lexical verb	152.45	superl. adj.	53.54	interj.	64.57	genetive	48.60
5.	title	40.89	genetive	62.45	genetive	35.96	genetive	63.81	locative adv.	36.11
6.	temporal noun	24.48	temporal noun	39.27	adj.	23.53	superl. adj.	48.11	general superl. adj.	35.01
7.	poss. pers. pro.	22.92	title	34.12	lexical verb	23.22	adj.	45.67	interj.	30.01
8.	genetive	21.74	interj.	33.60	prep., adj.	16.00	lexical verb	30.74	adj.	25.25
9.	adv. locative	19.15	prep., adv.	24.22	temporal noun	14.76	temporal noun	25.80	temp. noun	19.43
10.	proper noun	12.51	sgl. letter	19.23	interj.	9.37	prep., adj.	21.66	lexical verb	16.55
11.	sgl. letter	10.41	general adj.	17.96	numeral noun	7.03	pl. proper noun	17.90	pl. proper noun	9.24

Figure 26.6: 'Prince Charles: A nation waits' (Issue 5, 27 February 1962)[4]

Figure 26.7: 'Blair's TUC shock' (Issue 907, 26 September 1996)

the written medium (Leech and Smith 2006), and how the magazine reacts to it.

We might therefore claim that, on the one hand, the headlines prototypically function as primes, and that the reader of the covers of *Private Eye* is – to

Figure 26.8: 'Blairy Halliwell entertains the troops' (Issue 1039, 19 October 2001)

Figure 26.9: 'Oh no, It's Hymn!' (Issue 1028, 31 May 2001)

Figure 26.10: 'Yes, it's wedding balls!' (Issue 1032, 26 July 2001)

use Hoey's (2005) terminology again – additionally primed towards these particular syntactic structures in the headlines.

Intratextual norms may nevertheless be broken up or particular items may be foregrounded so that the headlines in themselves play with scheme opposition, and with prime and dialectic. Therefore, it is not only the speech-bubbles that serve as triggers for the dialectic phase, but also the headlines. For example, often some morphemes of words are changed for comic effect, although the homophonic resemblance to the original is maintained. For example, 'Blairy Halliwell' used on the cover page depicted in Figure 26.8 contains the last name of the then prime minister, Tony Blair. The letter/morpheme 'y' of the first name and the last name 'Halliwell' alludes to the singer Geri Halliwell, who was popular during the 1990s as a member of the famous British girl-group 'The Spice Girls'. Halliwell was also appointed as a UN Goodwill Ambassador, knowledge of which adds a further element of satire to the cover. Blair is being likened to her and her role. The speech-bubble representing the song Blair sings is 'It's raining bombs! Hallelujah!' and refers to a song by the 'Weather Girls' called 'It's raining men!' The allusion to Tony Blair's singing is created by the iconic sign representing a musical chord: ' ♪ '. It is particularly cynical that the noun *men* is replaced here by the noun *bombs*, because the 'War on Terror' has caused many (male) victims. But let us go back to consider the captions first. The blend 'Blairy' merges two schemas. The scene is set during the 'War on Terror', that is, the war on Iraq immediately after the atrocities of 9/11. Tony Blair was criticized for Great Britain's participation in the war. 'Blairy Halliwell Entertains the Troops' illustrates that his crime in sending British men to war cannot be made up for by visiting the troops in their camps and entertaining them with music. Another schema is reversed here: during war-time, it has been a fairly common practice that famous female singers visit their country's troops (Marilyn Monroe had done so during the Second World War). The gender-reversal of this schema and Blair's attempt to cheer up his troops, pretending to be nothing more than a singer without political responsibilities, are heavily criticized and lead *ad absurdum* through renaming and repositioning him as 'Blairy Halliwell'. This adds to Tony Blair's recreation as a 'goodwill ambassador' by being likened to Geri Halliwell.

Table 26.2 illustrates the semantic fields referred to in the captions of the cover pages of *Private Eye*. There are also a number of stable factors here, which supports semantically what has been said about the priming function of these headlines. There is a continuous reference to *shock*, as in 'Imran/Goldsmith Wedding Shock' (Issue 872, May 1995) or 'Scott Report Shock' (Issue 892, February 1996). The overused grammatical strategy of drawing on noun phrases is semantically corroborated by the constant reference to personal names, hence celebrities, which set up the prime for the satirical

Table 26.2: Over-represented semantic fields in the captions of the cover pages of Private Eye compared with the BNC sampler written

	1961–69	Semantic f.	1970–79	Semantic f.	1980–89	Semantic f.	1990–99	Semantic f.	2000–08	Semantic f.
1.	243.79	personal names	411.92	personal names	279.16	fear/shock	138.91	personal names	169.74	personal names
2.	80.09	judgement of appearance: beautiful	163.05	fear/shock	142.55	personal names	134.81	fear/shock	107.31	fear/shock
3.	76.54	people: male	106.02	judgement of appearance: beautiful	83.59	time: new and young	98.19	time: new and young	65.02	time: new and young
4.	62.62	paper documents	81.47	unmatched	80.11	time: new and young	80.71	time: new and young	54.17	other proper names
5.	52.71	religion and the supernatural	77.07	people: male	49.81	detailed	48.89	other proper names	41.35	detailed
6.	49.09	sensory	66.78	religion and the supernatural	48.75	mental object: conceptual object	41.19	politics	37.90	politics
7.	47.33	unmatched	54.80	sensory	46.49	other proper names	39.46	happy	30.94	time: new and young
8.	47.27	sensory: sight	52.49	time: new and young	27.25	objects generally	34.74	closed; hiding/hidden	30.68	no obligation or necessity
9.	46.10	without clothes	51.15	other: proper names	22.94	unemployed	34.64	detailed	28.28	information technology and computing
10.	31.75	other proper names	48.58	closed; hiding/hidden	19.05	religion and the supernatural	31.80	no obligation or necessity	24.43	location and direction
11.	27.19	the media: newspapers	38.93	without clothes	18.56	closed; hiding/hidden	20.91	information technology	18.09	mental object: conceptual object
12.	25.71	anatomy and physiology	36.80	mental	16.60	disease	20.70	location and direction	14.42	geographical

discourse. The following list generated by Wmatrix from the 2000–08 captions indicates the range of people, place-names, or countries dealt with:

BLAIR
IRAQ
BROWN
SADDAM
BRITAIN
BUSH
US
GORDON
TONY
HARRY
HAGUE
CAMERON
AMERICA
HEATHROW
UN
TEX
WAYNE TOONEY
SADDAM BUTLER
THATCHER
CHERIE
BORIS
MICHAEL HOWARD
PAXMAN
BBC
EUROPE
BA
LONDON
NEW ORLEANS
GELDORF
NHS
ENGLAND
LORD LEVY
LEBANON
BLUNKETT
ULSTER
FALKLANDS
IRA
DIANA
CONWAY

FAYED
HARRY
ZIMBABWE
JUDAS
MUGABE
RUSSIA

In addition, the construction '(the) latest' is also overused and occurs under the semantic heading 'Time, new and young'. It adds to the immediate, newspaper style of the captions, as in 'Arms row latest' (Issue 950, May 1998).

It should be stressed, however, that many of the terms used are also often homographs or homophones, or polysemous words, and serve as both cohesive and disjunctive puns (Simpson 2003: 102). They often carry sexual allusions, as in 'Yes, It's Wedding Balls' (Issue 1032, July 2001, see Figure 26.10), where *balls* superficially refers to a festive ball. It replaces *bells* but also refers to Prince Charles's testicles and therefore his sexual potential. Furthermore, *balls* refers to complete nonsense, which may reinforce the magazine's view of the whole furore over Charles and Camilla getting married.

A large number of words could not be assigned by Wmatrix to any kind of semantic category (see also Walker, this volume, for details of this problem), but they seem to be particularly revealing in terms of the linguistic creative potential that has been applied to generate particular effects. For the 2000–08 captions the list generated by Wmatrix is as follows:

blunkett
dubya
palios
gotcha
PAXMAN
jowell
MADNESS
bush-brown
t5
instand
crunchmas
horreur
pisshead
CARE
rollover
xmas/new
four-page
non-election

bottom
SARS
wmd-day
94-page
conman
waiting-to-go-on-holiday
80–90–100
plotillo
byers
legover
Osama
at-a-glance

The words not identified by Wmatrix include (a) some new word-formations created by *Private Eye*, such as 'Plotillo', which refers to Michael Portillo, the former Tory leader, who is portrayed as someone who considers himself to be a clever 'plotter' of schemes (see Figure 26.11), (b) foreign words, such as 'horreur', (c) personal names such as 'Osama', which Wmatrix does not know, and (d) acronyms, such as 'SARS' (Severe Acute Respiratory Syndrome). At the same time, the authenticity of casual conversation is reinforced.

Figure 26.11: 'Yes – It's Plotillo' (Issue 1026, 3 May 2003)

To conclude, the language used in the captions shows stable features when seen from both a diachronic and a quantitative perspective. Specific thematic fields are also continuously referred to, with variations on particular themes and linguistic forms.

3.3. The photographs on the cover pages of Private Eye

The photos also carry interpersonal, textual, and experiential functions. They frequently present narrative representations (instead of conceptual presentations), in which participants are connected by a vector, that is, they are presented as doing something to or for each other (Kress and Van Leeuwen 2006: 59). Unfolding actions or processes of change are presented. For example, in Figure 26.13, two people are shaking hands. They are depicted as being in some kind of interaction, which is represented visually by those vectors indicating an orientation from one participant to the other. The represented participants also appear to be looking directly at the viewer, which constitutes an interpersonal link.

The photographs often show politicians, the royal family, or celebrities in action. The pictures are frequently personal, dynamic, and dramatic (as opposed to being static, and conceptual). The point here is that the cover pages use visual representations of these characters although the message could have been conveyed in linguistic form only. Generally speaking, the choice of photographs is also supposed to function as a means of enlarging the degree of credibility because they seem to be real representations of what has happened. The general assumption the cover pages play with is that photographs do not lie, that our sense of sight is more reliable than our sense of hearing, for example, and that usually seeing is associated with understanding. Nonetheless, we do have to remember that the photos are often taken out of their contexts and are certainly not made for the specific (satirical) purpose of appearing as a photograph on the cover pages of Private Eye. As such, they do not only serve as supplementing the verbal prime in the captions (Simpson 2003: 168), but are themselves visual onsets of the dialectic phase. Generally, we also have to keep in mind that those who use a camera may just not tell the whole truth. In addition, today there are computer programmes such as Photoshop, which can be used to manipulate photographs. Hence, there is a need to distinguish between the functions the photographs had originally, and how they are perceived now.

This also relates to another point Kress and Van Leeuwen (2006: 163) mention, namely the degree of modality of visual design, which describes how the author's stance is stressed in relation to culturally and historically determined standards. Modality aligns the producer and the reader with some statements, and distances him/her from others. Linguistic indicators of modality include modal verbs, such as *can, may*, or *should*, and stance adverbials such as *hopefully, really*, or *generally speaking*. Visually, modality can be expressed by means of colour, for example. In order to establish the effect of visual modality, a diachronic investigation is useful. For example, in the 1960s when the magazine was first launched, most of the photos were in black and white (see Figure 26.5), which was the standard then. Colour images would have been considered to be foregrounded.

Figure 26.12 shows the quantitative distribution of the various forms of visual design from a diachronic perspective. It differentiates between photographs, photo collages, and 'other', which refers to drawn images, for example. Visual modality is divided up between 'black and white', 'coloured', and 'tinted'. From the beginnings of the magazine until 2000 most of the photographs were printed in black and white. The number of colour photos is negligible for the first three periods. Since 1998, more cover pages have been in colour. Therefore, in comparison to the magazine's early years, coloured photos are no longer considered to be of high modality because they have become more frequent. Black and white photographs would show a higher modality than those in colour, while before black and white was the unmarked form.

What increases the modality in these photographs is the insertion of speech-bubbles, because this is usually not what is expected in photographs, although it is and has been the typical strategy on the cover pages of *Private Eye*. The speech-bubbles also fulfil both roles in the satirical discourse,

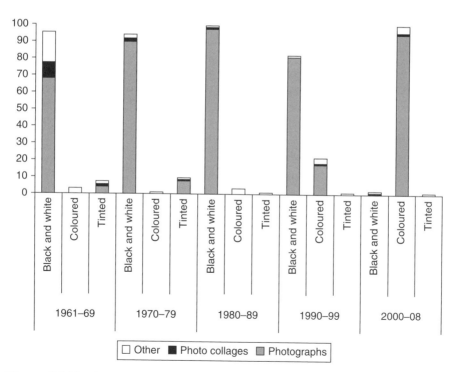

Figure 26.12: Overview of diachronic differences between visual modality (black and white, coloured, tinted) on the cover pages of *Private Eye* (raw figures)

that of prime and a dialectic, because of the commonly assumed functions of (free) direct speech presentation. Even though the assumption of faithful report for direct speech presentation has been refuted by Tannen (1989) as unrealistic, direct speech provides the words and grammatical structures claimed to have been used by the speaker to utter the propositional content and associated speech act. In addition, the speech act value and the propositional content of the utterance is presented. Presentation of the exact words of a character (Toolan 2001: 120) – with no apparent interference from the narrator – brings with it the effect of vividness, dramatization, and detail, and it characterizes the speaker. What we get is the colourful and idiosyncratic language of the character. Therefore, this mode of speech presentation appears at the character-oriented end of Leech and Short's ([1981]/2007) and Semino and Short's (2004) speech presentation model. Yet it should be kept in mind that the narrator is always present and that what the speaker says is still reported to some extent. These assumptions, in addition to alluding to the cartoon genre, are played with on the cover pages of the magazine (a strategy that is chosen by many satirical magazines), and interplay with the already described effect of the visual representations of the participants by means of photographs. They are equally dramatic, and frequently the narrative presentations create some kind of action.

In order to identify significant linguistic patterns of usage in the speech-bubbles, these have been compared to the *BNC* sampler spoken and the *BNC* sampler written subsections provided by Wmatrix. When compared to the *BNC* sampler written, it is striking that the speech-bubbles commonly adhere to many of the features of oral style, such as the use of first- and second-person pronouns as markers of interaction. This creates further authenticity and faithfulness of report of direct stretches of speech.

When compared with the spoken sub-corpus of the *BNC* sampler, the corpus of speech-bubbles shows an overusage of noun phrases that either use proper nouns or common nouns as heads (see Figure 26.1, for example), as illustrated by Table 26.3. These personal names set the scene and position the speaker within a particular situation, scenario, and frame.

Table 26.4 shows the frequently used semantic fields in the speech-bubbles. Terms from politics are also over-represented, and increase in frequency in the years leading up to the new millennium, which shows the preoccupation of the cover pages of *Private Eye* with political commentary and satire. For the speech-bubbles from the 1960s these include *fascists, republican, by-election*, and *labour*, and for the 1990s these are, for example, *vote, conservative, by-election*, and *Tory*.

The category 'in power' especially comprises forms of address, such as *Mr* or *Madam* (see Figure 26.1). The use of forms of address or vocative forms is a marker of orality and in addition to interpersonal functions of

Table 26.3: Key parts of speech in the speech-bubbles of the cover pages of *Private Eye*

	1961–69 parts of speech	Log-l.	1970–79 parts of speech	Log-l.	1980–89 parts of speech	Log-l.	1990–99 parts of speech	Log-l.	2000–08 parts of speech	Log-l.
1.	proper noun	63.62	proper noun	73.89	am	57.62	am	68.98	am	80.48
2.	formula	41.11	sgl. common noun	60.05	sgl. common noun	29.60	proper noun	39.46	hyph. number	59.78
3.	foreign word	23.61	foreign word	59.74	proper noun	29.46	Me	22.64	me	46.12
4.	am	21.73	am	43.33	title	23.51	adv.	21.43	-ing part.	23.30
5.	sgl. common noun	18.38	title	34.61	formula	20.32	poss. pro.	21.20	formula	20.92
6.	poss. pro.	15.86	us	34.01	for (prep.)	15.41	formula	20.24	sgl. common noun	19.81
7.	modal aux.	10.75	lexical verb	33.72	unit of measure	14.92	are	18.01	are	19.64
8.	adverb	10.07	adj.	27.00	adj.	13.83	sgl. common noun	15.87	I	18.75
9.	lexical verb	9.94	poss. pro.	22.72	lexical verb	13.43	numeral noun	14.85	lexical verb	17.26

Table 26.4: Key semantic fields in the speech-bubbles on the cover pages of *Private Eye* when compared to the BNC sampler spoken

	1961–69 Log-l.	Semantic f.	1970–79 Log-l.	Semantic f.	1980–89 Log-l.	Semantic f.	1990–99 Log-l.	Semantic f.	2000–08 Log-l.	Semantic f.
1.	50.06	personal names	170.59	other proper names	68.64	unemployed	47.21	politics	58.08	politics
2.	20.24	location and direction	59.79	government	56.76	in power	34.21	evaluation: false	28.62	happy
3.	19.30	anatomy and physiol.	41.30	sensory: sound	24.50	important	33.32	personal names	23.82	warfare, defence, and the army
4.	17.06	politics	36.10	personal names	23.97	politics	24.11	people: male	21.95	in power
5.	15.62	polite	35.24	anatomy and physiol.	23.79	government	20.82	time: future	21.87	people: male
6.	15.17	calm	28.53	geogr. names	20.17	anatomy and physiol.	20.52	unexpected	18.77	work and employment
7.	14.06	government	26.19	politics	17.34	religion and the supernatural	17.31	evaluation: inaccurate	18.51	sensory: sound
8.	13.36	worry	25.85	religion and the supernatural	15.91	geographical names	16.88	failure	18.40	time: future
9.	13.03	pers. relations	20.95	in power	15.80	location and direction	14.08	in power	18.16	safe
10.	12.42	geographical	19.18	sailing, swimming	14.63	happy	13.96	evaluation: bad	18.12	quantities: little
11.	11.81	in power	17.91	sound: loud	13.99	personal names	12.76	unemployed	16.29	failure

establishing a relationship and marking politeness, it may also have experiential and textual functions, as will be illustrated in the analysis of Figure 26.13 below. Geographical names are particularly frequent from the 1960s to the 1980s, and serve to create a locational background for the narrative depicted in the photograph.

Again, we can see that since its beginnings, there have been many more similar semantic fields used on the cover pages of the magazine *Private Eye* than different ones. I would also like to stress that on the cover pages of *Private Eye* 'verbal language does, in fact, (still) have a special status in human communication' (Nørgaard, this volume, 446), and satire functions 'through a layering of linguistic structures' (Simpson 2003: 102).

4. Case studies

4.1. *A multimodal reversal of schemata as strategies to create humour and satire*

These general remarks about the interplay between the visual and the linguistic presentations will help us to understand exactly why it is that the cover pages are satirical comments on, for example, political or royal actions.

In Figure 26.13, the captions identify the speaker who addresses Tony Blair. They serve as primes, but the reader also needs to draw on his or her cultural, political, or historical knowledge of genre to infer that 'Giscard' is Valérie M. R. Giscard d'Estaing. At the same time, it is a prerequisite that the viewer activates his/her political and historical knowledge of Valérie M. R. Giscard

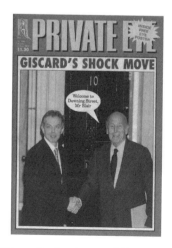

Figure 26.13: 'Giscard's shock move' (Issue 1081, 12 June 2003)

D'Estaing's role within the European Union. He was the president of the Convention on the Future of the European Union and adamantly fought for a European constitution, which, in turn, was heavily criticized by the British public. In order to make sense of the communicative event depicted in the photograph, readers also need to activate their 'welcome' schema, which is triggered by the greeting in the speech-bubble 'Welcome to Downing Street, Mr Blair'. A schema is a particular aspect of background knowledge of a particular event in the world. Schemas are triggered by headers or linguistic cues which invoke particular elements of the schema in question. Hence, the greeting in the picture activates the regular welcome schema through a precondition header. Typically, a welcome scene involves the movement of a guest to the place where the host welcomes the guest. Usually, a welcome scene also embraces positive emotions and pleasure on both sides. In Hoey's (2005) words, a welcome scene is pragmatically primed towards a happy occasion. Grammatically speaking, the construction *welcome to*, which is based on the predicative usage passing into an adjective (*OED* N[1], entry B. and C.), demonstrates the grammatical priming of this construction towards an interjection which here collocates with the vocative 'Mr Blair'. Although forms of address frequently collocate with welcome greetings, we have seen that the use of titles and so on is also a typical strategy used in the speech-bubbles on the cover pages to introduce the alleged status of the speakers, and to mark politeness. Note that here, however, Tony Blair is no longer addressed by his political role as the prime minister of Great Britain, but simply by *Mr*. Local headers refer to the fact that the welcome scene takes place at No. 10 Downing Street. This information is given by the iconic status of the sign '10' on the door in the photograph, which stands for the centre of Great Britain's government and the Prime Minister's home. Additional experiential reference is therefore given through this iconic sign as well as through the people interacting with one another, which can be represented by vectors moving from one character on the right to the character on the left. The persons directly looking into the camera, and by implicature into the face of the viewer, give further visual interpersonal clues. These semiotic modes, as well as the compositional arrangement, have the capacity to form texts and the presentation of a narrative.

The reader needs to make sense of these multimodal processes that take place within this schema, because in the image the two characters are presented as shaking hands, creating a conventional narrative representation of a welcome scene. But there is the rub. The scene that is described here deviates from our expectations on the experiential and interpersonal level because the role of the actor and the goal are changed on the visual and the linguistic levels. In other words, a foregrounding effect is created because the roles of the host and the guest are changed. The real host of No. 10 Downing Street,

Prime Minister Tony Blair, should welcome Valérie M. R. Giscard d'Estaing to his office/home. Hence, the clash generates meaning on the discourse level of reader–author. The change of roles is crucial to our interpretation of this scene.

A further schematic deviation takes place on the character–character discourse level. Although the characters do not seem to be particularly affected by this schematic clash, we need to take into consideration that a) this photo is taken out of its real context when Tony Blair welcomed Giscard d'Estaing, and b) because *Private Eye* is a satirical magazine, the originally assumed faithfulness claim of DS (Short 2007b: 231) – indicated by the speech-bubbles – does not hold. It cannot be assumed that the words are the words really used by the speaker, but the cover page with its use of direct speech in the speech-bubbles actually plays with the assumed notion of faithfulness, because the satirist pretends these to be the real words.

Nevertheless, with this in mind, we can open up the stylistician's tool-kit and take out the analytical tools to analyse speech and conversation. It is striking, for example, that Tony Blair is uncooperative in the Gricean sense and does not return Giscard d'Estaing's welcome. One reason for Blair's silence is given in the caption: 'Giscard's Shock Move.' Blair should be characterized as shocked by the European Union taking over Great Britain's centre of government and the prime minister's place of residence. As such, the captions also set the welcome schema back into place, because they describe the negative attitude of Blair and the whole nation to the alleged incorporation of Great Britain into the European Union. Yet, within the context of linguistic norms used in the captions we have seen that reference to the noun *shock* and the semantic field of *shock* is one stable linguistic strategy in the captions in the history of the cover pages of *Private Eye*.

4.2. Impoliteness and the destruction of the conventional metaphor LOVE IS A JOURNEY *to construe satire*

On the cover pages of *Private Eye*, royal life and scandals have been constant targets of satirical comment. Figure 26.14 illustrates *Private Eye*'s attitude to Camilla and Charles's wedding. It is also an example of how two turns – to use conversation analysis terminology – are represented as a communicative dyad on the cover of *Private Eye*.

Even though we are aware of Camilla and Charles's love story, let us here also very briefly describe the general associations evoked by the marriage scheme. It includes specific procedures, activated by specific conditions, such as the wish to get married, a happy couple, and, possibly, happy parents who are sympathetic to the aims of the couple, congratulations, salutes, and,

Figure 26.14: 'Eye salutes happy couple' (Issue 1130, 28 April 2005)

more abstractly, the implication of fidelity, and so on. Seemingly, *Private Eye* behaves accordingly by saluting 'the happy couple' – as expressed in the captions. But we immediately recognize that the congratulations are hyperbolic and ironic, and that the heading is in opposition to the photograph.

Leech (1983) has argued that there is a politeness principle alongside the cooperative principle (CP) in order to stabilize communication, and that within the interpersonal rhetoric we also have to include such second-order principles as irony and banter. The irony principle, he says, 'takes its place alongside the CP and the PP [Politeness Principle].' In being ironic, one exploits the PP by blatantly breaking a maxim of the CP in order to uphold the PP (Leech 1983: 82). We are anti-socially ironic at someone's expense, scoring by politeness that is obviously insincere. The use of the noun phrase 'happy couple', often stereotypically used to refer to a happy couple who have just got married, illustrates this irony. In addition, the caption cannot really function as a salute if it is ironic. The felicity conditions for a salutation are different. Note also the iconic but 'naff' wedding bells of the sort you would find on wedding invitation cards.

Let us look at the pragmatic structure of Charles's turn, again with the help of Searle's (1969, 1976) macro-classes of speech acts. The turn is multifunctional in terms of its illocutionary forces. It may be a *representative*, because Charles asserts and assumes that his mother will be equally sympathetic to their aims; it may also be an *expressive* because Charles allows us a view of his feelings; finally, it may also be a *directive*, that is, a kind of begging for acceptance and congratulation.

The choice of the personal pronoun *we* (rather than the actual mention of personal names) should indicate that for Charles the marriage to

Camilla, and the fact that the personal pronoun *we* refers to Camilla and him, is most natural (even though his facial expression rather conveys a certain disbelief that the marriage has really happened). He refers to the context by means of exophoric reference – the first mention of the referent by means of the personal pronoun, which, as opposed to pure deixis, is dependent on the context outside the text. Hence, the reader is asked to infer what is meant.

The adverbial of time *at last* can be understood as a conceptual (and orientational) metaphor by referring to a conceptual mapping between a source domain (journey) and a target domain (love), which describes LOVE IS A JOURNEY (Lakoff and Johnson 1980). This metaphor includes all the conventional associations: the couple has waited for so long, there have been stumbling blocks, but their love has been strong enough to survive the difficulties and they have finally tied the knot. This strategy is also used to distract from our knowledge of Charles's infidelity to Diana.

Notice that Camilla is not given a voice, and looks somewhat deranged. Charles and the Queen talk across her head, although her hat makes her appear slightly taller than she is. Of course, it was very windy that day, but she seems to cling to her headpiece as if it were a crown, symbolic of her newly acquired position.

What is the queen's retort? In her comic 'reply', which is supported by her somewhat acid facial features, she is presented as neither lovingly congratulating the couple, nor pretending to be a proud mother. Although Brenda – *Private Eye*'s nickname for the Queen – assumes that they are married to each other, her reply clearly implies that each has been married to another spouse before. So the adverbial *at last* in Charles's utterance assumes, further back in the chain of presuppositions, 'married at last'; but the Queen's completing and undercutting response more explicitly assumes 'to each other at last'. Therefore, the Queen also indirectly opens up the tragedy of the Charles, Camilla, and Diana triangle again by being implicitly uncooperative, impolite, and further naturalizing her own power as a Queen and a mother – and destroying the social relationship and identity which Charles has started to establish.

She is uncooperative because she flouts the maxims of the cooperative principle (Grice 1975): a) her contribution is not as informative as is required, b) she exploits the quality maxim by hyperbolically stressing what we know is true, c) from Charles's point of view it is not relevant to stress again who the couple is, and d) her turn is obscure and ambiguous. She does not complete the adjacency pair or meet the felicity conditions. She is ironic in that she clings to the PP by stressing the illocutionary act rather than the perlocutionary act (the effect on the hearer) and exploiting the CP: she does not congratulate them, and she alludes to Charles's infidelity.

She is presented as impolite, in public at least: her retort is a bald and unmitigated attack at Charles's negative and positive face. To enter into social relationships we have to acknowledge and to show an awareness of positive face, the need to be accepted and liked by others, and negative face, the need to be independent and have freedom of action.

In terms of Leech's (1983) PP, the Queen's utterance does not relate to the maxim of tact, because it does not minimize the cost to the hearer; it does not relate to the maxim of approbation, because she does not flatter or congratulate them; and it does not follow the maxim of sympathy, because she does not minimize antipathy between self and other.

Despite the humorous note transferred here, *Private Eye*, more satirically, also comments on the power and social relations the Queen assumes, and on her somewhat controlled callousness. *Private Eye* also lays bare the linguistic construal and linguistic naturalizations of these power relations, in which the relationship between the sign and its referent is no longer arbitrary. This is construed by other semiotic modes depicted in this narrative representation: that is, that of Charles's oddly defensive hand position and the 'buttoned up' body posture, which seems to go against the 'Happy Couple' facial expressions. In addition, their dresses are probably also a reason why this photo was chosen. While the grandmother queen, as opposed to the bride herself, dresses in bridal white, Camilla's costume is of matronly grey. Charles's dress is colour-coordinated with both.

5. Conclusions

This chapter has illustrated the stylistic potential for the analysis of non-literary texts. It has shown, from a synchronic and diachronic perspective, verbal and non-verbal interplay as a means of creating humour and satire on the cover pages of the satirical magazine *Private Eye*. Many of the linguistic and non-linguistic strategies on the cover pages have been identified as fairly stable in the course of the magazine's history, which stresses the need for diachronic investigation in stylistic research. I have only mentioned some multimodal issues that play a role in the creation of humour and satire on the cover pages and that have been suggested as part of the stylistician's tool-kit by, for example, Nørgaard (this volume, also offering a precise account including typography within the stylistician's multimodal tool-kit). This is but the tip of the investigation of the cover pages of *Private Eye*.

The major stylistic focus on how a text means and the relationship between what is foregrounded and what is conventional has helped to explain the reader's inferential processes. Multimodal discourse seems to be attractive here to both processing and selling/distribution of the magazines. These

covers may also make it easier for the receiver to understand certain strategies, because they multimodally build on the concept of repetition in terms
of a (familiar) prime that is given. Also, knowledge of the concept of genre
and the characters depicted on the pages are as important as contextual
knowledge.

NOTES

1. For further details on these tagging tools, see the UCREL website at Lancaster
   University: http://www.comp.lancs.ac.uk/ucrel/. I would like to thank Paul Rayson for
   giving me access to Wmatrix, and for his useful advice. All semantic labels have been
   checked in order to account for changes in meaning.
2. The term 'experiential' is often used interchangeably for the term 'ideational' in the
   ideational function of Halliday's (1994, 2004) grammar.
3. Also, Leech and Smith (2006) have illustrated quite a number of linguistic changes
   (in the use of modals, the use of the progressive etc.) in the time period between 1961
   and 1990. They stress that newspapers, to which the magazine *Private Eye* shows some
   similarities in structure (e.g. the headline and the captions), are particularly prone to
   change. Therefore, we might well have assumed that these captions would show linguistic change as well.
4. It should be stressed that the headline for this cover page appears in the picture itself
   and not at the top of the page below the name of the magazine.

AFTERWORD

CHAPTER 27

Stylistics, Linguistics and Literature: A Short Afterword

GEOFF HALL

Twenty years after the first edition of the journal *Language and Literature* appeared under the editorship of Mick Short, I am honoured to be following in the footsteps of Mick, Katie Wales, and then Paul Simpson, as fourth editor. I am excited to see what a thriving child Mick and others brought into the world, as witnessed by the preceding essays in this collection. At a PALA conference at Goldsmith's College, London, in 2000, Roy Harris of Oxford University asked in a plenary address that outraged some in the audience, 'When will stylistics grow up?' (The address was never published, to my knowledge). The argument was that stylistics had no distinct identity but was always dependent on developments in other areas. Stylistics needed linguistics and literature but linguistics and literature do not need stylistics, according to this argument. For me, the most salient point about Harris's plenary was, first, that many of the concerns Harris exhorted his audience to take up were in fact already central to stylistics practitioners' everyday research and thinking. But secondly, the fact that such charges could be brought at all strongly suggested we still had far to go in bringing the results of our research to the attention of a wider audience, in the academy at least. Cold-shouldered at the literary and linguistic parties, we had been talking too much to ourselves. Perhaps stylistics *has* grown up, but still needs a coming-of-age party to tell the world about it. This volume and this essay can be taken as part of that ongoing, necessarily protracted effort to convince our stuffy elders that we can safely stay out later at night now. In a few years we might even have something to talk about with each other. My generation, in Britain at least, was given well-intentioned advice to concentrate on either linguistics or literature (and certainly *not* the e-word, education) if we wanted a worthwhile career in a university. I am encouraged now to see that our own lean and hungry postgraduates have little or no awareness of that old debate, and look

with confidence for advancement based firmly on the merits of their published work, some of it represented here. Let me outline, then, some reasons
for this growing sense of confidence that many of us, at all levels, feel, by way
of a coda to this impressive collection.

Short's own career as stylistician in some ways models the progress that has
been made in the last 20 years. The early concern was with close description
of fragments and very short texts, with the interest very much in Jakobsonian
topics such as parallelism, deviation, and foregrounding. Arguably or implicitly the value or literariness of the text gobbet thrown to the students was
of secondary importance in this linguistically driven kind of activity. The
value and utility of such work, especially pedagogically, is celebrated by all
Mick's former students, and I can only regret till now that I was never one
of them – though perhaps this also gives me a kind of critical distance too,
to write a piece like this. We have all, colleagues as well as students, learned
and benefited so much from the checklists, the tool-box, and the like, which
Mick so systematically, clearly, and conscientiously developed. They are
indispensable. Teaching which assumes students can or will do this kind of
preliminary essential basic analysis is flawed, or wilfully closes its eyes to
the self-evident issues raised by more or less global changes of curriculum,
of social and cultural reading practices, and widening of student access in
recent decades. Encouragingly, a respected literary theorist and critic, Peter
Barry (2007), is now just one leading voice bemoaning the fact that students
can perceive the operations of power, race, gender, and all the rest in whatever text they are given, but seem unable to refer cogently to actual textual
features in support of these larger claims (or even perhaps to make them
more sophisticated!). We should note again though, as with Harris, Barry's
very imperfect but representatively limited awareness of what is going on in
stylistics today, which would obviously help him and his literary colleagues to
address these basic gaps in his students' skills – not to mention adding greater
conviction to their own partial analyses. Patterson (2009) lands on my desk as
I write this: an enthusiastic publisher clearly not aware of the old lang-lit split.
Patterson 'deploys keyword theory', an enthusiastic blurb tells us. It is a study
of 'keywords' in Milton by a leading Milton scholar, Professor Emeritus, Yale
University. There is surprisingly little on the methodology used for the study.
But these are not the keywords known to the corpus stylistician. They are keywords in the intuitive sense of Raymond Williams in the 1950s (see Williams
1976), and just in the same way a rather loosely correlated impressionistic
collection. I am a great admirer of Williams as a thinker, critic, and theorist,
indeed a key innovator in television studies and other modern developments
that he felt literature departments needed to study. Similarly, there are fascinating fragments of uncollected insight in this book. But it is disappointing
to find that Patterson's keywords are undefined and undefended in much the

same way nearly 50 years later: to an expert apparently they are self-evident, though there is no indication that even a Lion (Literature Online)/Chadwick Healey search has been attempted to validate these expert intuitions. Where exactly is the 'theory' in this? Haphazard examples are produced out of the hat in the 'best' lit-crit tradition. A 'Tools' section at the end of the book refers not to WordSmith (Scott 2008) or any such software, but to a 1972 'Concordance'. Christopher Ricks (another hero-critic of mine, undoubtedly, but with the same reservations) is the nearest we get to a stylistician's name in this book.[1] My own experience over the last 15 years or so as an MA literature supervisor and marker has been consistently to find myself asking 'How do you know that?' 'What exactly do you mean by that grand-sounding phrase?' This empirical cast of mind is what stylistics has taught me, and I believe it has made my own work more rigorous. It is to the detriment of research in literature departments that appeal to real-world evidence is still too often seen as irremediably grubby or incredibly naïve, or simply doesn't seem to be an issue. At the same time, I do not want to give up the concerns with the big issues, power, ideology, and the rest, which excite our students along with Barry or Patterson. I return to this a little later.

For at the same time as the checklists were being elaborated, many of us thankfully grabbing them to use in classes were nevertheless also increasingly worried by the modest 'ancillary' claims of Short and some of his co-workers for stylistics, apparently consigning stylistics to a permanent second rank of intellectual work: worthy, necessary, but rather dull and plodding – and so doomed to be ignored by literary colleagues like those cited above, or indicted by Harris, if somewhat anachronistically. Durant et al.'s (1988) response to Short and Breen in the 1988 *Critical Quarterly* pedagogy number stands renewed scrutiny today. Among other issues the Strathclyde group noted that the Lancaster 'Language and Style' course seemed content to take 'literature' as a given, handed down from literary colleagues, in no way interrogating what the literary might consist of, why some works are canonical and not others, or (say) where new media texts (at that time primarily film and television) stood in relation to the stylistics enterprise, even though that was almost the only game in town in literature departments at that time (Eagleton 1983, and others). Texts were of interest, but not reading. Why should stylistics not have anything to contribute to these larger issues too, or must it always stop just as the going got interesting? These problems have not entirely gone away despite the developments I will now enumerate, as witnessed by some telling reflections on the stylistics enterprise by one of its own strongest writers, Michael Stubbs, in *Applied Linguistics* in 2004:

A weak defence [Short's earliest position? GH]: a stylistic analysis tells us nothing that literary critics do not already know, but it allows us to describe things

more precisely. ... A stronger defence: a stylistic analysis tells us something new: it can discover features of a literary text which neither average readers nor expert literary critics have noticed. [Short's position now? GH] ... The strongest (?) defence: a systematic analysis not only describes new things, but also helps to explain readers' reactions to the text ...

(Stubbs 2004: 128)

That last strongest position is the one we should be aiming for if stylistics is to be interesting to a wider constituency, including the literature and media studies departments, cultural studies, and the rest – hence a need to extend our understandings of 'text' to discourse. For example, stylisticians seem less reluctant nowadays to confirm the inescapability of interpretation and evaluation in all they do. Interpretation and evaluation are of course central to literature departments' activities. As I detail in what follows, there are reasons to believe we are already more generally seeing the emergence of a more assertive and confident stylistics which will come to matter to a widening circle, hence the growing confidence I referred to earlier.

First, then, changing attitudes on the part of students and their teachers are immediately evident in demands for new English language 'A' levels, and notably in recent years for 'English Language and Literature' joint 'A' levels, in Britain. A rearguard still sees these as some kind of 'soft option' for 'illiterate' students (e.g. my daughter's 'A' level English coordinator, in a highly respected 'A' level centre). I am encouraged, again, however, to note that where my own institution, like many universities, still obliges me to ask incoming students on arrival whether they are looking for English Language or English Literature sections, or (another separate 'old' university section) 'Creative Writing', the students arriving this week are puzzled by the request: they are looking for 'English', which to them includes all of those and more. National government UK bench marks (QAA 2009) now recognize the diversity of 'English' as a subject in higher education with language and linguistics integral to its study. Not coincidentally, stylisticians like Katie Wales, Ron Carter, and Henry Widdowson have had significant input into these governmental publications, another sign of the new respect for our work. We should congratulate ourselves on these changes. Moving away from English, a cursory review of PALA membership, locations of conferences, and the identities of members, subscribers, and contributors to *Language and Literature*, all show how international the current high level of activity in stylistics has become.

Again, Short's own work, once criticized for its small-scale, fragmentary nature, has proceeded to look at whole texts and genres of text through his invaluable leading-edge research on corpus stylistics (Semino and Short 2004). Of course the taxonomies leak and have had to be modified and challenged. That is how research progresses in any discipline, the ongoing clarification of what we can't explain or account for. As heuristic tools rather than ontological claims (my own emphasis), this work on speech and thought representation is invaluable and (once again) should be more widely known beyond stylistics seminars. Students of Short's like McIntyre (2006, also 2008) have gone on to challenge the caution of earlier Short about discussing performance rather than texts, or film and other media rather than theatre – but so have later incarnations of Short! Again, it is now widely recognized among stylisticians, and so an even greater claim for the interest and value of the field, that 'creative' language use is widespread way beyond the confines of the literary text. Similarly, much language in literature is not obviously foregrounded (early stylistics privileged lyric poetry against the novel or other forms). 'Who is stylistics?' Short asked in 1996. We might ask in return 'Who foregrounded foregrounding, and why?' (Passives and deleted agents again!) More in perspective, 'deviation' is today widely understood not as the dominant feature of literature and the stylistician's key object of desire, but as just one kind of linguistic 'choice' (e.g. Carter and Stockwell 2008), where today the whole range of linguistic choices are seen as the stylistician's domain, and choice itself is understood with more contextual subtlety.

The strength or special claim of stylistics has always been to ask 'How does it work?' as well as, or even before, 'What does it mean?' (C.f., for example, Culler 1975 on Blake: 'We have enough damned interpretations already.') For me (naturally there are always other models being developed in a very active research area) this extends naturally into the key question of discourse analysis, the study of language in use: 'What's going on here?' Or as Malcolm Coulthard, who I *was* lucky enough to be taught by, trained us to ask: 'Why This Here?' How did this text come into being in just this form, and into this reader's hands at this time and place? Why? Why did this reader do this with it? Here we approach or even exceed Stubbs's most demanding criterion for a worthwhile stylistics. Because note, too, that we are moving with discourse analysis beyond speech acts and conversational exchanges, beyond the pragmatics of Widdowson or even of Verdonk, to a recognition that textual study is never sufficient by itself for understanding. (Compare the programmatic statements of, for example, Weber 1992). A worthwhile stylistics will map and explore the social and cultural imbrications of literary and other cultural and mediated uses of language. There is a need for connections, not to reciprocate the contempt and impatience of the literature and other departments. Thus there has been a 'social turn' but also a 'cognitive turn', which recognizes the need to investigate cognitive contexts, or at least the extent to which social contexts are also cognitive contexts, empirically investigatable, with much variation between individual readers of the same text. (C.f., van Dijk, 2008.) Textuality of course remains a key area of expertise for the stylistician but we must also now interest ourselves in real readers (Hall 2009), in non-linguistic features (Nørgaard 2010, this volume), contexts of all kinds in so far as they can be shown to contribute to the uptake and meaning of the linguistic features which we started looking at in the 1980s. 'Choices', again, is an area of social theory that has moved on immeasurably since Halliday and then Fairclough first used the term. Absences, silences, or other linguistic-ideological 'faultlines' (Sinfield 1992) are as much the advanced stylistician's concern as repetitions and other patterning.

In 1989, Carter and Simpson made a call for more 'discourse stylistics'. In 2002, Simpson and Hall were still lamenting discourse as a generally neglected area of stylistic activity despite some isolated studies of interest. Where (critical) discourse analysis has shown the way in integrating the study of textual features into more telling 'readings' of social and cultural meaning-making, stylistics needs similarly to develop its theoretical and practical endeavours. The call for textually grounded discussion of ideology, gender, and all the rest can begin with that work, for all the criticism that has been made of it.[2] The foundations for this activity and much subsequent work of importance in moving beyond stylistics, linguistics, and literature to an as yet unnameable discipline ('critical discourse stylistics' sounds clumsy to me; though see Jeffries 2010a on 'critical stylistics') are to be further developed by using Short's publications in our own writings and pedagogy. The evidence is in your hands now. I have already mentioned the importance of corpus stylistics today for anyone seriously interested in the language of literature. The work of Mahlberg literally startles with its obvious value and originality (see in particular Chapter 25, written with her colleague Catherine Smith). On multimodality, contributors like Nørgaard (Chapter 24) or McIntyre (Chapter 10) lead us into brave new textual worlds. Sylvia Adamson, or those who have worked with her such as Bray (Chapter 21), or Kytö and Romaine (2008), have shown that stylistics need not be nervous of bringing its procedures to bear on more historical texts than have been habitual. Jeffries excels here for her writings on schemata, as here, or elsewhere in critical linguistics and critical discourse analysis. These are some of my own favourites, but leaving aside that I now exceed my word limit, the point is the richness of this collection for any student of stylistics, linguistics, and literature.

An irony with which I close is that Mick Short is a board member of the 'English' national UK subject group. The subject groups promote good pedagogical practice in higher education teaching in various putatively 'different' subjects. I myself am at the same time a member of the wholly separate 'linguistics' subject group, even though we both label ourselves as working in stylistics. A pessimistic reading might say nothing has changed then. For our political masters, there is no 'stylistics' subject group, and English and linguistics have nothing to do with each other. But is the possibility of membership in notionally different groups like this a strength or a weakness? I would prefer to put before you the image of two moles, whose tunnels are about to join, in a projected *Language and Literature* issue and elsewhere, which already crumbles some of the surrounding fortifications. Parents can never quite believe their kids have grown up, can they?

NOTES

1. To be fair, Patterson's Introduction also mentions Corns (1990), an early linguistic computing study, though nothing much is subsequently done with his sometimes admittedly inconclusive statistics in the 'authorial style' tradition of *Literary and Linguistic Computing*. The study claims 'partly' (p. 55) to use Williams's concept, but the remainder of this 'partly' is never explicitly divulged as far as I can see, though there is some evidence of basic frequency counts (e.g. on p. 59).
2. Criticisms of CDA notably begin of course with Widdowson in *Language and Literature* (Widdowson 1995; 1996) – another coup for Short as its editor at the time! Then Stubbs (1998). More sophisticated criticism in more recent years has arguably come from CA – for example Tolson (2006). A sensible defence and rationale for ongoing and developing CDA work is offered in van Leeuwen (2006).

References

A Corpus of English Dialogues 1560–1760 (2006) Compiled under the supervision of Merja Kytö (Uppsala University) and Jonathan Culpeper (Lancaster University). [http://www.engelska.uu.se/corpus.html].

Adamson, S. (1994) 'From empathetic deixis to empathetic narrative: Stylisation and (de-)-subjectivisation as processes of language change', *Transactions of the Philological Society* 92(1): 55–88. Reprinted, with minor changes, in Wright, S. and Stein, D. (eds) (1995) *Subjectivity and Subjectivisation*, pp. 195–224. Cambridge: Cambridge University Press.

Adamson, S. (2001) 'The rise and fall of empathetic narrative', in van Peer, W. and Chatman, S. (eds) *New Perspectives on Narrative Perspective*, pp. 83–99. New York: State University of New York Press.

Adichie, C. N. (2006) *Half of a Yellow Sun*. London: Harper Perennial.

Albee, E. (1959; rpt. 1987, ed. 1995) 'The sandbox: A brief play in memory of my grandmother', in *The Zoo Story and Other Plays*, pp. 33–43. London: Penguin Books.

Albee, E. (1960; rpt. 1961, ed. 1995) 'The American dream: A play in one scene', in *The Zoo Story and Other Plays*, pp. 83–125. London: Penguin Books.

Albee, E. (1971) *Tiny Alice, Box and Quotations from Chairman Mao Tse-Tung*. Harmondsworth: Penguin Books.

Alderson, C. (2000) *Assessing Reading*. Cambridge: Cambridge University Press.

Alderson, J. C. and Short, M. (1989) 'Reading literature', in Short, M. (ed.) *Reading, Analysing and Teaching Literature*, pp. 72–119. Harlow: Longman.

Aldiss, B. (1988) *Trillion Year Spree: The History of Science Fiction* (with D. Wingrove). London: Paladin.

Alexander, M. (2006) *Cognitive-Linguistic Manipulation and Persuasion in Agatha Christie*. MPhil thesis: University of Glasgow.

Alexander, M. (2008) 'The lobster and the maid: Scenario-dependence and reader manipulation in Agatha Christie' [online]. *Proceedings of the Annual Conference of the Poetics and Linguistics Association (PALA)*. Available at: <http://www.pala.ac.uk/resources/proceedings/2008/alexander.pdf> [Accessed 1st January 2009].

Anderson, A., Garrod, S. C. and Sanford, A. J. (1983) 'The accessibility of pronominal antecedents as a function of episode shifts', *The Quarterly Journal of Experimental Psychology* 35: 427–40.

Anderson, E. R. (1998) *A Grammar of Iconism*. Madison, Teaneck: Fairleigh Dickinson University Press.

Anderson, S., (1921) 'The Egg' in *The Triumph of the Egg*, pp. 46–63. New York: Huebsch.

Anonymous (ed. 1956a; rpt. 1967) 'Cain and Abel', in Cawley, A. C. (ed.) *Everyman and Medieval Miracle Plays*, pp. 25–33. London: Dent; New York: Dutton (Everyman's Library).

Anonymous (ed. 1956b; rpt. 1967) 'The creation of Adam and Eve', in Cawley, A. C. (ed.) *Everyman and Medieval Miracle Plays*, pp. 11–16. London: Dent; New York: Dutton (Everyman's Library).

Anonymous (ed. 1956c; rpt. 1967) 'The creation, and the fall of Lucifer', in Cawley, A. C. (ed.) *Everyman and Medieval Miracle Plays*, pp. 1–9. London: Dent; New York: Dutton (Everyman's Library).

Anonymous (ed. 1956d; rpt. 1967) 'The fall of man', in Cawley, A. C. (ed.) *Everyman and Medieval Miracle Plays*, pp. 17–24. London: Dent; New York: Dutton (Everyman's Library).

Archer, D. (2007) 'Computer-assisted literary stylistics', in Lambrou, M. and Stockwell, P. (eds) *Contemporary Stylistics*, pp. 244–56. London; New York: Continuum.

Archer, D. (2009) 'Does frequency really matter?', in Archer, D. (ed.) *What's in a Word List? Investigating Word Frequency and Keyword Extraction*, pp. 1–16. Aldershot: Ashgate.

Archer, D., Culpeper, J. and Rayson, P. (2009) 'Love – "a familiar or a devil"? An exploration of key domains in Shakespeare's comedies and tragedies', in Archer, D. (ed.) *What's in a Word-List? Investigating Word Frequency and Keyword Extraction*, pp. 137–58. Aldershot: Ashgate.

Aristotle, trans. Hubbard, M. E. (1972; rpt. 1989) '*Poetics*', in Russell, D. A. and Winterbottom M. (eds) *Classical Literary Criticism*, pp. 51–90. Oxford; New York: Oxford University Press.

Attardo, S. (1997) 'The semantic foundations of cognitive theories of humor', in *Humor. International Journal of Humor Research* 10: 395–420.

Attardo, S. (2009) 'Salience of incongruities in humorous texts and their resolution', in Chrzanowska-Kluczewska, E. and Szpila, G. (eds) *In Search of (Non)Sense*, pp. 164–79. Newcastle-upon-Tyne: Cambridge Scholars Publishing.

Attardo, S. and Raskin, V. (1991) 'Script theory revis(it)ed: Joke similarity and joke representation model', *Humour* 4(3): 293–347.

Attridge, D. (1982) *The Rhythms of English Poetry.* London: Longman.

Attridge, D. (2004) *The Singularity of Literature.* London: Routledge.

Auerbach, E. (1953) *Mimesis: The Representation of Reality in Western Literature.* Princeton, NJ: Princeton University Press.

Austen, J. (1813) *Pride and Prejudice.* Whitehall: T. Egerton.

Austen, J. ([1813]1996) *Pride and Prejudice*, Ed. Jones, V. London: Penguin.

Austen, J. ([1816] 1985) *Emma.* Ed. Blythe, R. London: Penguin.

Austen, J. ([1817] 1985) *Northanger Abbey.* Ed. Henry Ehrenpreis, A. London: Penguin.

Austin, J. L. (1962) *How to Do Things with Words.* Oxford: Clarendon Press.

Baker, L. and Wagner, J. L. (1987) 'Evaluating information for truthfulness: The effects of logical subordination', *Memory and Cognition* 15(3): 247–55.

Bakhtin, M. M. (1984) in Holquist, M (ed.); Emerson, C. and Holquist, M. (trans.) *The Dialogic Imagination: Four Essays.* Austin, TX: University of Texas Press.

Baldry, A. and Thibault, P. J. (2006) *Multimodal Transcription and Text Analysis.* London; Oakville: Equinox.

Bally, C. (1909) *Traité de stylistique française.* Carl Winters.

Banfield, A. (1982) *Unspeakable Sentences.* London: Routledge.

Barcelona, A. (ed.) (2000) *Metaphor and Metonymy at the Crossroads. A Cognitive Perspective.* Topics in English Linguistics 30. Berlin: Mouton de Gruyter.

Barcelona, A. (2002) 'Clarifying and applying the notions of metaphor and metonymy within cognitive linguistics: an update', in Dirven, R. and Pörings, R. (eds) *Metaphor and Metonymy in Comparison and Contrast*, pp. 207–78. Berlin: Mouton de Gruyter.

Barnes, J. (1991) *Talking It Over.* London: Picador.

Barry, P. (2007) *Literature in Contexts.* Manchester: Manchester University Press.

Bartlett, F. C. (1932) *Remembering: A Study in Experimental and Social Psychology*. Cambridge: Cambridge University Press.

Barton, E. (1993) 'Evidentials, argumentation, and epistemological stance', *College English* 55: 745–69.

Barton, G. (1998) *Developing Poetry Skills*. Portsmouth: Heinemann.

Bateman, J. A. (2008) *Multimodality and Genre. A Foundation for the Systematic Analysis of Multimodal Documents*. Hampshire; New York: Palgrave MacMillan.

Beach, R. and Anson, C. M. (1992) 'Stance and intertextuality in written discourse', *Linguistics and Education* 4: 335–57.

Bear, G. (1987) *The Forge of God*. London: Victor Gollancz.

Bear, G. (1992) *Anvil of Stars*. London: Victor Gollancz.

Beckett, S. (1984) *Collected Shorter Plays*. New York: Grove Press.

Bentinck, A. (2001) *Romantic Imagery in the Works of Walter De La Mare*. Lewisham, New York: Edwin Mellen Press.

Berkeley, G. ([1732] 2007) *An Essay towards a New Theory of Vision*. Boston, MA: IndyPublish.com.

Berkowitz, G. M. (1992) *American Drama of the Twentieth Century*. New York: Longman.

Biber, D. and Finegan, E. (1988) 'Adverbial stance types in English', *Discourse Processes* 11: 1–34.

Biber, D. and Finegan, E. (1989) 'Styles of stance in English: Lexical and grammatical marking of evidentiality and affect', *Text* 9(1): 93–124.

Biber, D., Johannsson, S., Leech, G., Conrad, S. and Finegan, E. (1999) *Longman Grammar of Spoken and Written English*. London: Longman.

Biebuyck, B. (1998) *Die poetische Metapher: Ein Beitrag zur Theorie der Figürlichkeit*. Würzburg: Königshausen and Neumann.

Bigsby, C. W. E. (1992) *Modern American Drama, 1945–1990*. Cambridge: Cambridge University Press.

Black, E. (1993) 'Metaphor, simile and cognition in Golding's *The Inheritors*', *Language and Literature* 2(1): 37–48.

Boege, F. (1956) 'Sir Walter Besant: Novelist. Part one', *Nineteenth-Century Fiction* 10: 249–80.

Booth, W. ([1961] 1991) *The Rhetoric of Fiction*. Harmondsworth: Penguin.

Booth, W. C. (2005) 'Resurrection of the implied author: Why bother?', in Phelan, J. and Rabinowitz, P. J. (eds) *A Companion to Narrative Theory*, pp. 75–88. Oxford: Blackwell.

Bordwell, D. and Thompson, K. (1990) *Film Art: An Introduction*. 3rd edn. New York: McGraw-Hill.

Bousfield, D. (2007) '"Never a truer word said in jest": A pragmastylistic analysis of impoliteness as banter in *Henry IV, Part I*', in Lambrou, M. and P. Stockwell (eds) *Contemporary Stylistics*, pp. 209–20. London; New York: Continuum.

Bousfield, D. (2008) *Impoliteness in Interaction*. Amsterdam: John Benjamins.

Bradley, R. and Swartz, N. (1979) *Possible Worlds: An Introduction to Logic and Its Philosophy*. Oxford: Basil Blackwell.

Bransford, J. D. and Johnson, M. K. (1972) 'Contextual prerequisites for understanding: Some investigations of comprehension and recall', *Journal of Verbal Learning and Verbal Behaviour* 11: 717–26.

Brathwaite, R. (1620) *Essaies upon the Five Senses*. London: Whittaker.

Braunschneider, T. (2006) 'The lady and the lapdog: Mixed ethnicity in Constantinople, fashionable pets in Britain', in Palmeri, F. (ed.) *Humans and Other Animals in Eighteenth-Century British Culture. Representation, Hybridity, Ethics*, pp. 31–48. London: Ashgate.

Bray, J. (2000a) '"Attending to the *minute*": Richardson's revisions of italics in *Pamela*', in Bray, J., Handley, M. and Henry, A. C. (eds) *Ma(r)king the Text: The Presentation of Meaning on the Literary Page*, pp. 105–19. Aldershot: Ashgate.

Bray, J. (2000b) 'Signs in the text: The role of epigraphs, footnotes and typography in clarifying the narrator-character relationship', in Bray, J., Handley, M. and Henry. A. C. (eds), *Ma(r)king the Text: The Presentation of Meaning on the Literary Page*, pp. 26–34. Aldershot: Ashgate.

Bray, J. (2003) *The Epistolary Novel: Representations of consciousness.* London; New York: Routledge.

Breen, M. P. and Short, M. (1988) 'Alternative approaches in teaching stylistics to beginners', *Parlance* 1(2): 29–48.

Brinton, L. (1980) 'Represented perception: A study in narrative style', *Poetics* 9: 363–81.

Brinton, L. (2001) 'Historical discourse analysis', in Schiffrin, D., Tannen, D. and Hamilton, H. E. (eds) *Handbook of Discourse Analysis*, pp. 138–60. Oxford: Blackwell.

Brontë, C. ([1847] 1985) *Jane Eyre.* London: Penguin.

Brooks, C. and Warren, R. P. (eds) ([1938] 1976) *Understanding Poetry.* 4th edn. New York: Holt, Rinehart and Winston.

Brown, G. (1996) *Listening to Spoken English.* London, New York: Longman.

Brown, P. and Levinson, S. C. (1987) *Politeness: Some Universals in Language Usage.* Cambridge: Cambridge University Press.

Brown, R. and Gilman, A. (1989) 'Politeness theory and Shakespeare's four major tragedies', *Language and Society* 18: 159–212.

Brumfit, C. J. and Carter, R. (eds) (1986) *Literature and Language Teaching.* Oxford: Oxford University Press.

Burke, M. (2008) *The Oceanic Mind: A Study of Emotion in Literary Reading.* PhD thesis: University of Amsterdam.

Burrows, J. F. (1987) *Computation into Criticism.* Oxford: Clarendon Press.

Burrows, J. F. (1992) 'Computers and the study of literature', in Butler, C. S. (ed.) *Computers and Written Texts*, pp.167–204. Oxford: Blackwell.

Burton, D. (1980) *Dialogue and Discourse: A Sociolinguistic Approach to Modern Drama Dialogue and Naturally Occurring Conversation.* London: Routledge and Kegan Paul.

Busse, B. (2006a) 'Linguistic aspects of sensuality: A corpus-based approach to will-construing contexts in Shakespeare's works', in Houswitschka, C., Knappe, G. and Müller, A. (eds) *Anglistentag 2005 Bamberg Proceedings*, pp. 123–42. Trier: WVT 2006.

Busse, B. (2006b) *Vocative Constructions in the Language of Shakespeare.* Amsterdam: John Benjamins.

Busse, B. (2007) 'The stylistics of drama: *The Reign of King Edward III*', in Lambrou, M. and Stockwell, P. (eds) *Contemporary Stylistics*, pp. 232–43. London; New York: Continuum.

Busse, B. (2010) 'Adverbial expressions of stance in Early Modern "spoken" English', in J. Helbig (ed.) *Anglistentag 2009 Klagenfurt Proceedings*. Trier: WVT.

Busse, B. (forthcoming) *Speech, Writing and Thought Presentation in a Corpus of Nineteenth-Century Narrative Fiction.*

Busse, U. (2008) 'An inventory of directives in Shakespeare's *King Lear*' in Jucker, A. H. and Taavitsainen, I. (eds) *Speech Acts in the History of English*, pp. 85–114. Amsterdam; Philadelphia, PA: John Benjamins.

Calvo, C. (1992) 'Pronouns of address and social negotiation in *As You Like It*', *Language and Literature* 1: 5–27.

Cameron, N. (1990) *Collected Poems and Selected Translations,* ed. Warren Hope and Jonathan Barker. London: Anvil Press Poetry.

Carey, P. (2000) *True History of the Kelly Gang*. Brisbane: Faber and Faber.

Carey, P. (2006) *Theft*. Brisbane: Faber and Faber.

Carper, T. and Attridge, D. (2003) *Meter and Meaning: An Introduction to Rhythm in Poetry*. New York; London: Routledge.

Carrère, E. (1998) 'The mustache', (trans. Goodman, L.) in *Two By Carrère: Class Trip and The Mustache*. New York: Henry Holt, pp. 149–318 [first published in 1986 as *La Moustache*. Paris: P.O.L.].

Carter, R. (2004) *Language and Creativity: The Art of Common Talk*. London: Routledge.

Carter, R. and Long, M. N. (1987) *The Web of Words* Cambridge: Cambridge University Press.

Carter, R. and Long, M. N. (1991) *Teaching Literature* Harlow: Longman.

Carter, R. and McRae, J. (2001) *The Routledge History of Literature in English: Britain and Ireland*. London: Routledge.

Carter, R. and McRae, J. (eds) *Language, Literature and the Learner: Creative Classroom Practice*. London: Longman.

Carter, R. and Nash, W. (1990) *Seeing through Language*. Oxford: Blackwell.

Carter, R. and Simpson, P. (eds) (1989) *Language, Discourse and Literature. An Introductory Reader in Discourse Stylistics*. London: Unwin Hyman.

Carter, R. and Stockwell, P. (eds) (2008) *The Language and Literature Reader*. London: Routledge.

Ceci, L. G. (1983) 'The case for syntactic imagery', *College English* 45(5): 431–49.

Chafe, W. L. and Nichols, J. (eds) (1986) *Evidentiality: The Linguistic Coding of Epistemology*. Norwood, NJ: Ablex.

Chatman, S. (1978) *Story and Discourse: Narrative Structure in Fiction and Film*. Ithaca, NY: Cornell University Press.

Christie, A. ([1937] 1999) 'Yellow iris', in Christie, A. *Hercule Poirot: The Complete Short Stories*, pp. 609–22. London: Harper Collins.

Christie, A. ([1945] 1955) *Sparkling Cyanide*. London: Pan.

Clarke, A. C. (1953) *Childhood's End*. London: Ballantine Books.

Clarke, A. C. (1956) *Childhood's End*. Revised edn. London: Pan.

Clemen, W. H. (1951) *The Development of Shakespeare's Imagery*. London: Methuen.

Clement, R. and Sharp, D. (2003) 'Ngram and Bayesian classification of documents', *Literary and Linguistic Computing* 18: 423–47.

Cluysenaar, A. (1982) 'Formal meanings in three modern poems', *Dutch Quarterly Review of Anglo-American Letters* 12(4): 302–20.

Cockcroft, R. (2002) *Renaissance Rhetoric: Reconsidered Passion – The Interpretation of Affect in Early Modern Writing*. London: Palgrave Macmillan.

Cockcroft, R. and Cockcroft, S. (2005) *Persuading People: An Introduction to Rhetoric*. 2nd edn. Basingstoke; New York: Palgrave Macmillan.

Coetzee, J. M. (2007) *Diary of a Bad Year*. London: Harvill Secker.

Cohn, D. (1978) *Transparent Minds. Narrative Modes for Presenting Consciousness in Fiction*. Princeton, NJ: Princeton University Press.

Collie, J. and Slater, S. (1987) *Literature in the Language Classroom*. Cambridge: Cambridge University Press.

Collins, W. (1890) *Blind Love*. London: Chatto and Windus [online]. Available at: <http://ia311528.us.archive.org/0/items/blindlove00colluoft/blindlove00colluoft.pdf> [Accessed 18 March 2009].

Collins, W. (1900) *Blind Love*. The Works of Wilkie Collins. Vol. 28. New York: Peter Fenelon Collier [online]. Available at: <http://www.digitalpixels.org/jr/wc/blind/blind2.html> [Accessed 9 February 2009].

Collins, W. (2003) *Blind Love*, ed. Bachman, M. and Cox, D. Peterborough, Ont.: Broadview Press.

Conrad, J. (1900) *Lord Jim*. London: Blackwood.

Conrad, J. (1902) *Heart of Darkness*. London: Penguin.

Conrad, S. and D. Biber (2000) 'Adverbial marking of stance in speech and writing', in Huston, S. and Thompson, G. (eds) *Evaluation in Text: Authorial Stance and the Construction of Discourse*, pp. 56–73. New York: Oxford University Press.

Conradie, C. J. (2001) 'Structural iconicity: The English S- and OF-genitives' in Fischer, O. (ed.) *The Motivated Sign. Iconicity in Language and Literature 2*: 229–48. Amsterdam: John Benjamins.

Cook, G. (1994) *Discourse and Literature: The Interplay of Form and Mind*. Oxford: Oxford University Press.

Cook, G. (2000) *Language Play, Language Learning*. Oxford: Oxford University Press.

Cook, P. (1963) 'One leg too few', in Bennett, A., Cook, P., Miller, J. and Moore, D. (1987) *The Complete Beyond the Fringe*, pp. 148–50. London: Methuen.

Cooreman, A. and Sanford, A. J. (1996) *Focus and Syntactic Subordination in Discourse*. Human Communication Research Centre, Universities of Edinburgh and Glasgow [online]. Available at: <http://citeseer.ist.psu.edu/331528.html> [Accessed 14 December 2008].

Corcoran, N. (ed.) (2007) *The Cambridge Companion to Twentieth Century English Poetry*. Cambridge: Cambridge University Press.

Corns, T. (1990) *Milton's Language*. Oxford: Basil Blackwell.

Cosmides, L. and Tooby, J. (2000) 'Consider the source: The evolution of adaptations for decoupling metarepresentations', in Sperber, D. (ed.) *Metarepresentations: A Multidisciplinary Perspective*, pp. 53–116. New York: Oxford University Press.

Couteau, R. (1988) 'Book review: *The Mustache*, by Emmanuel Carrère', *Arete Magazine*, August/September.

Craig, H. and Kinney, A. (eds) (2009) *Shakespeare, Computers, and the Mystery of Authorship*. Cambridge: Cambridge University Press.

Crane, S. (1903) *The O'Ruddy*. New York: Frederick A. Stokes Company.

Crane, S. (1932) *Men, Women and Boats*. New York: The Modern Library [online]. Available at: <http://www.archive.org/stream/menwomenboatsedi00cranuoft/ men womenboatsedi00cranuoft_djvu.txt> [Accessed 18 March 2009].

Crane, S. (1971) 'The O'Ruddy', in Bowers, F. (ed.) *The University of Virginia Edition of the Works of Stephen Crane*. Vol. IV. Charlottesville, VA: University Press of Virginia.

Croft, W. (2001) *Radical Construction Grammar: Syntactic Theory in Typological Perspective*. Oxford: Oxford University Press.

Crystal, D. (1998) *Language Play*. Harmondsworth: Penguin.

Crystal, D. and Crystal, B. (2002) *Shakespeare's Words*. London: Penguin.

Crystal, D. and Davy, D. (1969) *Investigating English Style*. London: Longman.

Culler, J. (1975) *Structuralist Poetics*. London: Routledge and Kegan Paul.

Culpeper, J. (1998) '(Im)politeness in drama', in Verdonk, P., Short, M. and Culpeper, J. (eds) *Exploring the Language of Drama: From Text to Context*, pp. 83–95. London: Routledge.

Culpeper, J. (2001) *Language and Characterisation: People in Plays and Other Texts*. London: Longman.

Culpeper, J. (2002) 'Computers, language and characterisation: An analysis of six characters in *Romeo and Juliet*', in Melander-Marttala, U., Ostman, C. and Kytö, M. (eds) *Conversation in Life and in Literature: Papers from the ASLA Symposium, Association Suedoise de Linguistique Appliquée (ASLA)*, 15, pp. 11–30. Universitetstryckeriet: Uppsala.

Culpeper, J. (2005) 'Impoliteness and entertainment in the television quiz show: The Weakest Link', *Journal of Politeness Research: Language, Behaviour, Culture* 1: 35–72.

Culpeper, J. (2009a) 'Historical sociopragmatics: An introduction', *Journal of Historical Pragmatics* 10(2): 179–86.

Culpeper, J. (2009b) 'Keyness: Words, parts-of-speech and semantic categories in the character-talk of Shakespeare's *Romeo and Juliet*', *International Journal of Corpus Linguistics* 14(1): 29–59.

Culpeper, J. and Archer, D. (2008) 'Requests and directness in Early Modern English trial proceedings and play texts, 1640–1760', in Jucker, A. H. and Taavitsainen, I. (eds) *Speech Acts in the History of English*, pp. 45–84. Amsterdam and Philadelphia, PA: John Benjamins.

Culpeper, J. and McIntyre, D. (forthcoming 2010) 'Activity types and characterisation in dramatic discourse', in Schneider, R., Jannidis, F. and Eder, J. (eds) *Characters in Fictional Worlds: Interdisciplinary Perspectives*. Berlin: Mouton de Gruyter.

Culpeper, J., Short, M. and Verdonk, P. (eds) (1998) *Exploring the Language of Drama: From Text to Context*. Routledge: London.

Dancygier, B. (2005) 'Blending and narrative viewpoint: Jonathan Raban's travels through mental spaces', *Language and Literature* 14(2): 99–127.

Dancygier, B. and Sweetser, E. (2005) *Mental Spaces in Grammar: Conditional Constructions*. Cambridge: Cambridge University Press.

Darwin, C. ([1859] 1996) *The Origin of Species*, ed. Beer, G. Oxford: Oxford University Press.

Day Lewis, C. trans. (1940) *The Georgics of Virgil*. London: Jonathan Cape.

De la Mare, Walter (1912) *The Listeners and Other Poems*. London: Constable and Co.

De Quincey, T. ([1845] 1864) *Suspiria de Profundis* (published in one volume with Confessions of an English Opium-Eater). Boston, MA: Ticknor and Fields.

Dickens, C. ([1839] 1993) *Oliver Twist*, ed. Kaplan, F. New York; London: Norton.

Dickens, C. (1852–3) *Bleak House*. London and Aylesbury: Hazell, Watson and Viney.

Dickens, C. ([1860] 1999) *Great Expectations*, ed. Edgar Rosenberg. New York: Norton.

Dickens, C. (1861) *Great Expectations*. London: Chapman and Hall.

Dillon, G. L. (1978) *Language Processing and the Reading of Literature*. Bloomington, IN: Indiana University Press.

Dirven, R. and Pörings, R. (eds) (2002) *Metaphor and Metonymy in Comparison and Contrast*. Berlin: Mouton de Gruyter.

Doležel, L. (1998) *Heterocosmica: Fiction and Possible Worlds*. Baltimore and London: The John Hopkins University Press.

Douthwaite, J. (2000) *Towards a Linguistic Theory of Foregrounding*. Alessandria: Edizioni dell'Orso.

Doyle, R. (1998) *The Woman Who Walked into Doors*. London: Vintage Books.

Duffin, H. C. (1949) *Walter De La Mare: A Study of his Poetry*. London: Sidgwick and Jackson Ltd.

Durant, A. and Fabb, N. (1990) *Literary Studies in Action*. London: Routledge.

Durant, A., Mills, S. and Montgomery, M. (1988) 'Commentary on (1) "Putting stylistic analysis in its place"', *Critical Quarterly* 30(2): 21–3.

Eagleton, T. (1983) *Literary Theory*. Oxford: Blackwell.

Eagleton, T. (2007) *How to Read a Poem*. Oxford: Wiley Blackwell.

Eco, U. (1990) *The Limits of Interpretation*. Bloomington and Indianapolis, IN: Indiana University Press.

Edmondson, W. (1997) 'The role of literature in foreign language teaching and learning: Some valid assumptions and invalid arguments', *AILA Review* 12: 42–55.

Egidi, G. and Gerrig, R. (2006) 'Readers' experiences of characters' goals an actions', *Journal of Experimental Psychology: Learning, Memory and Cognition* 32(6): 1322–9.

Eliot, G. ([1871–2] 1986) *Middlemarch*, ed. Harvey, W. J. Harmondsworth: Penguin.

Eliot, G. ([1876] 1998) *Daniel Deronda*, ed. Handley, G. Oxford: Oxford University Press.

Emmott, C. (1997) *Narrative Comprehension: A Discourse Perspective*. Oxford: Oxford University Press.

Emmott, C. (2003) 'Reading for pleasure: A cognitive poetic analysis of "twists in the tale" and other plot reversals in narrative texts', in Gavins, J. and Steen, G. (eds) *Cognitive Poetics in Practice*, pp. 145–9. London: Routledge.

Emmott, C., Sanford, A. J. and Alexander, M. (forthcoming) 'Scenarios, characters' roles and plot status: Readers' assumptions and writers' manipulations of assumptions in narrative texts', in Eder, J., Jannidis, F. and Schneider, R. (eds) *Characters in Fictional Worlds: Interdisciplinary Perspectives*. Berlin/New York: Mouton de Gruyter.

Empson, W. E. (1953) *Seven Types of Ambiguity* (3rd edn). London: Chatto.

Emsley, S. (2005) *Jane Austen's Philosophy of the Virtues*. New York and Basingstoke: Palgrave Macmillan.

Ende, M. (1979) *Die Unendliche Geschichte* (Eng.: *The Neverending Story*). Germany: K. Thienemanns Verlag.

Enkvist, N. E. (1973) *Linguistic Stylistics*. Berlin: Mouton de Gruyter.

Evans, V. and Green, M. (2006) *Cognitive Linguistics: An Introduction*. Edinburgh: Edinburgh University Press.

Esslin, M. (1985) *The Theatre of the Absurd*. Harmondsworth: Penguin.

Fabb, N. and Halle, M. (2008) *Meter in Poetry*. Cambridge: Cambridge University Press.

Fairclough, N. (1989) *Language and Power*. Harlow: Longman.

Fairclough, N. (1992) *Critical Discourse Analysis*. Harlow: Longman.

Fairley, I. R. (1988) 'The reader's need for conventions', in van Peer, W. (ed.) *The Taming of the Text*, pp. 292–316. London: Routledge.

Falck, Colin (2003) *American and British Verse in the Twentieth Century: The Poetry that Matters*. Aldershot: Ashgate Publishing.

Fanthorpe, U. A. (1995) *Safe as Houses*. Calstock: Peterloo Poets.

Fauconnier, G. (1994) *Mental Spaces*. Cambridge: Cambridge University Press [original in French as *Espaces Mentaux* (1984) Paris: Editions de Minuit].

Fauconnier, G. (1997) *Mappings in Thought and Language*. Cambridge: Cambridge University Press.

Fauconnier, G. and Turner, M. (1996) 'Blending as a central process of grammar', in Goldberg, A. (ed.) *Conceptual Structure, Discourse, and Language*, pp. 113–31. Stanford, CA: Center for the Study of Language and Literature.

Fauconnier, G. and Turner, M. (2002) *The Way We Think: Conceptual Blending and the Mind's Hidden Complexities*. New York: Basic Books.

Ferguson, D. (1945) 'De La Mare's *The Listeners* and Housman's *On Wenlock Edge*', *The Explicator* 4(2) and (15): (n.p.).

Fielding, H. ([1742]1986) *Joseph Andrews,* ed. Brissenden, R. F. Harmondsworth: Penguin.

Fischer, O. (1999) 'On the role played by iconicity in grammaticalisation processes', in Nänny, M. and Fischer, O. (eds) *Form Miming Meaning*, pp. 345–74. Philadelphia, PA: John Benjamins Publishing Company.

Fischer, O. and Nänny, M. (eds) (2001) *The Motivated Sign: Iconicity in Language and Literature 2*. Philadelphia, PA, USA: John Benjamins Publishing Company.

Fischer-Starcke, B. (2006) 'The phraseology of Jane Austen's *Persuasion*: Phraseological units as carriers of meaning', *ICAME Journal* 30: 87–104.

Fischer-Starcke, B. (2009) 'Keywords and frequent phrases of Jane Austen's *Pride and Prejudice*: A corpus-stylistic analysis', *International Journal of Corpus Linguistics* 14(4): 492–523.

Fludernik, M. (1993) *The Fictions of Language and the Languages of Fiction: The Linguistic Representation of Speech and Consciousness*. London and New York: Routledge.

Fludernik, M. (2003) 'Metanarrative and metafictional poetry', *Poetica* 35: 1–39.

Fludernik, M. (2005) 'The metaphorics and metonymics of carcerality: Reflections on imprisonment as source and target domain in literary texts', *English Studies* 86(3): 226–44.

Fludernik, M. (forthcoming) 'The cage metaphor: Extending narratology into corpus studies and opening it to the analysis of imagery', in Heinen, S. and Sommer, R. (eds) *Narratology in the Age of Interdisciplinary Narrative Research*. Berlin: Mouton de Gruyter.

Fludernik, M. (forthcoming) *Carceral Topography and Metaphorics: Fact, Fiction, and Fantasy*.

Foer, J. S. (2005) *Extremely Loud and Incredibly Close*. Great Britain: Hamish Hamilton.

Fowles. J. (1963) *The Collector*. London: Jonathan Cape.

Fowler, R. (ed.) (1966a) *Essays on Style and Language*. London: Routledge.

Fowler, R. (1966) '"Prose rhythm" and metre', in Fowler, R. (ed.), *Essays on Styles in Language*, pp. 82–99. London: Routledge and Kegan Paul.

Fowler, R. (1977) *Linguistics and the Novel*. London: Methuen.

Fowler, R. (1986) *Linguistic Criticism*. Oxford: Oxford University Press.

Freud, S. (1919) 'The uncanny', in *The Complete Works of Sigmund Freud*, vol.17. London: Hogarth Press.

Friedman, N. (1967) 'Point of view in fiction: The development of a critical concept', in Stevick, P. (ed.) *The Theory of the Novel*, pp. 108–37. London: The Free Press.

Gabbard, L. P. (1982) 'Edward Albee's triptych on abandonment', in *Twentieth Century Literature* 28(1): 14–33.

Gard, R. (1992) *Jane Austen's Novels: The Art of Clarity*. New Haven, CT: Yale University Press.

Garside, R. (1987) 'The CLAWS word-tagging system', in Garside, R., Leech, G. and Sampson, G. (eds) *The Computational Analysis of English: A Corpus-based Approach*. London: Longman.

Garside, R. (1996) 'The robust tagging of unrestricted text: The BNC experience', in Thomas, J. and Short, M. (eds) *Using Corpora for Language Research: Studies in the Honour of Geoffrey Leech*, pp. 167–80. Longman: London.

Garside, R. and Smith, N. (1997) 'A hybrid grammatical tagger: CLAWS4', in Garside, R., Leech, G. and McEnery, A. (eds) *Corpus Annotation: Linguistic Information from Computer Text Corpora*, pp. 102–21. Longman: London.

Gaskell, E. ([1854] 2003) *North and South*, ed. Ingham, P. London: Penguin.

Gaskell, E. ([1863] 2006) '*Cousin Phillis*', in Hughes (ed.) *The Works of Elizabeth Gaskell*, vol. 4. London: Pickering and Chatto.

Gavins, J. (2003) 'Too much blague? An exploration of the text worlds of Donald Barthelme's *Snow White*', in Gavins, J. and Steen, G. (eds) *Cognitive Poetics in Practice*, pp. 129–44. London: Routledge.

Gavins, J. (2005a) '(Re)thinking modality: A text-world perspective', *Journal of Literary Semantics*, 34(2): 79–93.

Gavins, J. (2005b) 'Text world theory in literary practice', in Petterson, B., Polvinen, M. and Veivo, H. (eds) *Cognition in Literary Interpretation and Practice*, pp. 89–104. Helsinki: University of Helsinki Press.

Gavins, J. (2007a) '"And everyone and I stopped breathing": Familiarity and ambiguity in the text world of "The Lady Died"', in Lambrou, M. and Stockwell, P. (eds) *Contemporary Stylistics*, pp. 133–43. London: Routledge.

Gavins, J. (2007b) *Text World Theory: An Introduction*. Edinburgh: Edinburgh University Press.

Gavins, J. and Steen, G. (eds) (2003) *Cognitive Poetics in Practice*. London: Routledge.

Genette, G. (1980 [1972]) *Narrative Discourse*. Basil, New York: Blackwell, Cornell University Press.

Gerrig, R. (1993) *Experiencing Narrative Worlds*. New Haven, CT: Yale University Press.

Gibbons, A. (2010) '"I contain multitudes": Narrative multimodality and the book that bleeds', in Page, R. (ed.) *New Perspective on Narrative and Multimodality*, pp. 99–114. London: Routledge.

Gibbs, R. W. Jr. (1994) *The Poetics of Mind: Figurative Thought, Language and Understanding*. New York: Cambridge University Press.

Glucksberg, S. and Keysar, B. (1990) 'Understanding metaphorical comparisons: Beyond similarity', *Psychological Review* 97: 3–18.

Goatly, A. (1997) *The Language of Metaphors*. London: Routledge.

Goffman, E. (1967) *Interactional Ritual: Essays on Face-to-face Behavior*. Garden City, New York: Anchor Books.

Goffman, E. (1979) 'Footing', *Semiotica* 25(1–2): 1–29.

Goldberg, A. (1995) *Constructions: A Construction Grammar Approach to Argument Structure*. Chicago, IL: University of Chicago Press.

Goldberg, A. (ed.) (1996) *Conceptual Structure, Discourse, and Language*. Stanford, CA: CSLI Publications.

Gonzales-Berry, E. and Gynan, S. N. (1989) 'Chicano language', in Lomeli, F. A. and Shirley, C. R. (eds) *Dictionary of Literary Biography 82: Chicano Writers First Series*, pp. 304–8. Detroit: Gale Research.

Goossens, L. (1995) 'Metaphtonymy: The interaction of metaphor and metonymy in figurative expressions for linguistic actions', in Goossens, L. et al. (eds) *By Word of Mouth. Metaphor, Metonymy and Linguistic Action in a Cognitive Perspective*, pp. 159–74. Amsterdam: Benjamins.

Gower, R. (1986) 'Can stylistic analysis help the EFL learner to read literature?', *English Language Teaching Journal* 40(2): 125–30.

Graves, R. (1957) 'Introduction', *The Collected Poems of Norman Cameron*. London: Hogarth Press.

Greenblatt, S. (1988) *Shakespearean Negotiations: The Circulation of Social Energy in Renaissance England*. Berkeley, CA: University of California Press.

Gregoriou, C. (2007) *Deviance in Contemporary Crime Fiction*. Basingstoke: Palgrave Macmillan.

Grice, H. P. (1975) 'Logic and conversation', in Cole, P. and Morgan, J. (eds) *Syntax and Semantics 3: Speech Acts*, pp. 41–58. New York: Academic Press.

Grice, H. P. (1989) *Studies in the Way of Words*. Cambridge, MA: Harvard University Press.

Guignery, V. (2006) *The Fiction of Julian Barnes*. London: Palgrave Macmillan.

Guiraud, P. (1954) *La Stylistique*. PUF.

Gwynn, F. L. and Condee, R. W. (1954) 'De La Mare's *The Listeners*', *The Explicator* 12 (4) and (26): (n.p.).

Habermas, J. (1979) *Communication and the Evolution of Society*. Boston, MA: Beacon Press.

Haiman, J. (1980) 'The iconicity of grammar: Isomorphism and motivation', *Language* 56: 515–40.

Haiman, J. (ed.) (1985a) *Iconicity in Syntax*. Amsterdam: John Benjamins.

Haiman, J. (1985b) *Natural Syntax: Iconicity and Erosion*. Cambridge: Cambridge University Press.

Haining, P. (1990) *Agatha Christie: Murder in Four Acts*. London: Virgin Books.

Hakemulder, J. (2007) 'Tracing foregrounding in responses to film', *Language and Literature* 16(2): 125–40.

Halio, J. L. (1992) *The Tragedy of King Lear*. Cambridge: Cambridge University Press.

Hall, G. (2005) *Literature in Language Education*. London: Palgrave Macmillan.

Hall, G. (2009) 'Texts, readers – and real readers', *Language and Literature* 18(3): 331–7.

Halle, M. and Keyser, S. J. (1966) 'Chaucer and the study of poetry', *College English* 28: 187–219.

Halliday, M. A. K. (1971) 'Linguistic function and literary style: An inquiry into the language of William Golding's *The Inheritors*', in Chatman, S. (ed.) *Literary Style*, pp. 330–65. Oxford: Oxford University Press.

Halliday, M. A. K. (1978) *Language As Social Semiotic*. London: Edward Arnold.

Halliday, M. A. K. (1994) *An Introduction to Functional Grammar* (2nd edn). London, New York, Sydney, Auckland: Arnold.

Halliday, M. A. K. (2004) *An Introduction to Functional Grammar* (3rd edn) (with C. Matthiessen). London: Edward Arnold.

Hamilton, C. (2003) 'A cognitive grammar of *Hospital Barge* by Wilfred Owen', in Gavins, J. and Steen, G. (eds) *Cognitive Poetics in Practice*, pp. 55–65, London: Routledge.

Hamilton, C. (2007) 'The cognitive rhetoric of Arthur Miller's *The Crucible*', in Stockwell, P. and Lambrou, M. (eds) *Contemporary Stylistics*, pp. 221–31, London: Continuum.

Hamilton, I. (ed.) (1994) *The Oxford Companion to Twentieth Century Poetry in English*. Oxford: Oxford University Press.

Hanauer, D. (1999) 'Attention and literary education', *Language Awareness*, 8: 15–26.

Hanauer, D. (2001) 'The task of poetry reading and second language learning', *Applied Linguistics* 22(3): 295–323.

Hanauer, D. I. (2001) 'What we know about reading poetry: Theoretical positions and empirical research', in Schram, D. and Steen, G. (eds) *The Psychology and Sociology of Literature*, pp. 107–28. Amsterdam and Philadelphia, PA: John Benjamins Publishing Company.

Harding, D. W. (1993) 'The supposed letter form of *Sense and Sensibility*', *Notes and Queries* 40(4): 464–6.

Hardy, D. (2003) *Narrating Knowledge in Flannery O'Connor's Fiction*. Columbia: University of South Carolina Press.

Hardy, D. (2005) 'Towards a typology of narrative gaps: Knowledge gapping in Flannery O'Connor's fiction', *Language and Literature* 14(4): 363–75.

Hardy, T. ([1891] 1892) *Tess of the D'Urbervilles*. London: James R. Osgood and Co.

Hawthorne, M. (1997) 'Cold comfort', *New York Times*: 2 February 1997.

Hay, J. (2001) 'The pragmatics of humor support', *HUMOR: International Journal of Humor Research* 14(1): 55–82.

Heine, B. (1997) *Cognitive Foundations of Grammar*. Oxford: Oxford University Press.

Heinlein, R. (1960) *Starship Troopers*. New York: Putnam.

Heller, Z. (1991) 'The square and the other two sides', *The Independent*: 14 July 1991: 28.

Hemingway, E. (1927a) 'Hills like white elephants', in *Men without Women*. New York: Scribner.

Hemingway, E. (1927b) 'The killers', in *Scribner's Magazine*.

Herman, D. (2004) *Story Logic: Problems and Possibilities of Narrative*. Lincoln: University of Nebraska Press.

Herman, V. (1991) *Dramatic Discourse*. London: Routledge.

Hidalgo-Downing, L. (2000) *Negation, Text Worlds and Discourse: The Pragmatics of Fiction*. Stanford, CA: Ablex.

Hidalgo Downing, L. (2000a) 'Negation in discourse: A text-world approach to Joseph Heller's *Catch-22*', *Language and Literature* 9(4): 215–40.

Hidalgo Downing, L. (2000b) *Negation, Text-Worlds and Discourse: The Pragmatics of Fiction*. Stanford, CA: Ablex.

Hidalgo Downing, L. (2000c) 'Text world creation in advertising discourse', *Revista Alicantina de Estudios Ingleses*, 13: 67–88.

Higgins, C. (2008) 'The new Cicero', *The Guardian*: 26 November 2008.

Ho, Y. (2007) 'Investigating the key concept differences between the two editions of John Fowles's *The Magus* – a corpus semantic approach'. 27th International Conference of the Poetics and Linguistics Association (PALA), Kansai Gaidai University, Hirakata, Japan, 31 July–4 August.

Hoey, M. (2000) 'Persuasive rhetoric in linguistics: A stylistic study of some features of the language of Noam Chomsky', in Hunston, S. and Thompson, G. (eds) *Evaluation in Text: Authorial Stance and the Construction of Discourse*, pp. 28–37. Oxford: Oxford University Press.

Hoey, M. (2005) *Lexical Priming: A New Theory of Words and Language*. London: Routledge.

Holmes, J. (1988) 'Doubt and certainty in ESL textbooks', *Applied Linguistics* 9: 20–44.

Hoover, D. (1992) 'Not unless you ask nicely: The interpretative nexus beween analysis and information', *Literary and Linguistic Computing* 7: 91–109.

Hoover, D. (2001) 'Statistical stylistics and authorship attribution: An empirical investigation', *Literary and Linguistic Computing* 16: 421–44.

Hoover, D. (2004a) 'Altered texts, altered worlds, altered styles', *Language and Literature* 13(2): 99–118.

Hoover, D. (2004b) 'Testing Burrows's delta', *Literary and Linguistic Computing* 19: 453–75.

Hoover, D. (2006) 'All the way through: Testing for authorship in different frequency strata', *Literary and Linguistic Computing* 22: 27–47.

Hoover, D. (2007) 'Corpus stylistics, stylometry, and the styles of Henry James', *Style* 41: 174–203.

Hoover, D. (2008) 'Searching for style in modern American poetry', in Zyngier, S. et al. (eds) *Directions in Empirical Literary Studies: Essays in Honor of Willie van Peer*, pp. 211–27. Amsterdam: John Benjamins.

Hoover, D., Culpeper, J. and Louw, W. (forthcoming) *Approaches to Corpus Stylistics*. London: Routledge.

Hough, G. (1969) *Style and Stylistics*. London: Routledge and Kegan Paul.

Huerta, Jorge (1992) 'Introduction', in *Zoot Suit and Other Plays*, pp. 7–20. Houston, TX: Arte Público Press.

Hughes, C. (1976) *American Playwrights* 1945–75. London: Pitman Publishing.

Hughes, T. (1960) *Lupercal*. London: Faber and Faber.

Humphreys, J. (1991) 'He gave up smoking and irony', in *The New York Times* 13 October 1991. Available at: <http://www.nytimes.com/books/01/02/25/specials/barnes-talking.html> [Accessed 2 October 2009].

Hunston, S. and Francis, G. (2000) *Pattern Grammar. A Corpus-Driven Approach to the Lexical Grammer of English*. Studies in Corpus Linguistics 4. Amsterdam: John Benjamins.

Hunston, S. and Thompson, G. (eds) (2000) *Evaluation in Text: Authorial Stance and the Construction of Discourse*. New York: Oxford University Press.

Hunter, L. (2005) 'Echolocation, figuration and tellings: Rhetorical strategies in *Romeo and Juliet*', *Language and Literature* 14(3): 259–78.

Hyland, K. (1996) 'Writing without conviction? Hedging in science research articles', *Applied Linguistics* 17: 433–54.

Iser, W. (1971) 'Indeterminacy and the reader's response in prose fiction', in Hillis Miller, J. (ed.) *Aspects of Narrative*, pp. 1–45. New York: Columbia University Press.

Jacobs, A. and Jucker, A. H. (1995) 'The historical perspective in pragmatics', in Jucker, A. H. (ed.) *Historical Pragmatics: Pragmatic Developments in the History of English*, pp. 3–33. Amsterdam and Philadelphia, PA: John Benjamins.

Jahn, M. (2005) 'Focalization', in Herman, D., Jahn, M. and Ryan, M.-L. (eds) *The Routledge Encyclopedia of Narrative Theory*, pp. 173–7. London: Routledge.

Jakobson, R. (1956) 'Two aspects of language and two types of aphasic disturbances', in Jakobson, R. and Halle, M. (eds) *Fundamentals of Language*, pp. 69–96. Gravenhage: Mouton de Gruyter.

Jakobson, R. ([1958] 1987) 'Closing statement. Linguistics and poetics', in Pomorska, K. and Rudy, S. (eds) *Roman Jakobson. Language in Literature*, pp. 62–94. Cambridge, MA: The Belknap Press of Harvard University Press.

Jakobson, R. (1963) *Essais de linguistique générale*. Paris: Minuit.

Jakobson, R. (1990) 'Two aspects of language and two types of aphasic disturbances', in Waugh, L. R. and Monville-Burston, M. (eds) *On Language*, pp. 115–33. Cambridge, MA: Harvard University Press.

Jakobson, R. and Halle, M. (1956) *Fundamentals of Language*. The Hague: Mouton de Gruyter.

James, H. ([1902] 1998) *The Wings of a Dove,* ed. Brooks, P. Oxford: Oxford University Press.

James, H. (1904) *The Golden Bowl*. New York: Scribner.

James, H. ([1905] 1975) *A Portrait of a Lady,* ed. Bamberg, R. D. London: Norton.

Jeffries, L. (1993) *The Language of Twentieth Century Poetry*. Basingstoke: Palgrave Macmillan.

Jeffries, L. (2001) 'Schema theory and White Asparagus: Cultural multilingualism among readers of texts', *Language and Literature* 10(4): 325–43.

Jeffries, L. (2007) *Textual Construction of the Female Body*. Basingstoke: Palgrave Macmillan.

Jeffries, L. (2008) 'The role of style in reader-involvement: Deictic shifting in contemporary poems', *Journal of Literary Semantics* 37(1): 69–85.

Jeffries, L. (2010a) *Critical Stylistics. The Power of English*. Basingstoke: Palgrave Macmillan.

Jeffries, L. (2010b) *Opposition in Discourse*. London: Continuum.

Jeffries, L. and McIntyre, D. (2010) *Stylistics.* Cambridge: Cambridge University Press.

Johnson, M. (1987) *The Body in the Mind: The Bodily Basis of Meaning, Imagination and Reason*. Chicago, IL: University of Chicago Press.

Jones, G. R. (ed.) (1996) *The Nation's Favourite Poems*. London: BBC Books.

Joyce, J. ([1922] 1960) *Ulysses*. London: Bodley Head.

Kamermans, M. (2009) *Het Zien van het Onvoorspelde – Het Onvoorspelde van het Zien (Seeing the Unpredicted – The Unpredicted of Seeing)*. Amsterdam: Vossiuspers UvA.

Kantorowicz, E. H. ([1957] 1997) *The King's Two Bodies*. Princeton, NJ: Princeton University Press.

Kärkkäinen, E. (2003) *Epistemic Stance in English Conversation: A Description of its Interactional Functions, with a Focus on 'I think'*. Amsterdam: John Benjamins.

Kennedy, G. A. (1998) *Comparative Rhetoric*. New York and Oxford: Oxford University Press.

Kern, R. (2000) *Literacy and Language Teaching*. Oxford: Oxford University Press.

Kern-Stähler, A. (2005) 'Homer and the evolutionary scale: Interrelations between biology and literature in the writings of William Gladstone and Grant Allen', in Zwierlein, A.-J. (ed.) *Unmapped Countries: Biological Visions in Nineteenth Century Literature and Culture*, pp. 107–16. London: Anthem Press.

King, T. (2008) *Gendering of Men, 1600–1750: Queer Articulations*. Madison, WI: University of Wisconsin Press.

Kintgen. E. (1983) *The Perception of Poetry*. Indiana, IN: Indiana University Press.

Kneale, N. (1952–5) *The Quatermass Experiment; Quatermass II; Quatermass and the Pit*. London: BBC TV.

Knights, B. and Thurgar-Dawson, C. (2006) *Active Reading*. London: Continuum.

Knowles, G. (1974) 'The rhythm of English syllables'. *Lingua* 34: 115–47.

Kohnen, T. (2006) 'Historical corpus linguistics'. *Anglistik* 17(2): 73–91.

Kopytko, R. (1995) 'Linguistic politeness strategies in Shakespeare's plays' in Jucker, A. H. (ed.) *Historical Pragmatics*, pp. 515–40. Amsterdam: John Benjamins.

Korte, B. (1997) *Body Language in Literature*. Toronto: University of Toronto Press.

Lambert, M. (1981) *Dickens and the Suspended Quotation*. New Haven, CT and London: Yale University Press.

Kövecses, Z. (2002) *Metaphor: A Practical Introduction*. New York: Oxford University Press.

Kövecses, Z. (2006) *Language, Mind, and Culture*. Oxford: Oxford University Press.

Kövesces, Z. and G. Radden (1998) 'Metonymy: Developing a cognitive linguistic View', *Cognitive Linguistics* 9(1): 37–77.

Kramsch, C. (1993) *Context and Culture in Language Teaching*. Oxford: Oxford University Press.

Kramsch, C. and Kramsch, O. (2000) 'The avatars of literature in language study', *Modern Language Journal* 84: 533–73.

Kress, G. and Van Leeuwen, T. (1996) *Reading Images: The Grammar of Visual Design* (1st edn). London and New York: Routledge.

Kress, G. and Van Leeuwen, T. (2001) *Multimodal Discourse: The Modes and Media of Contemporary Communication*. London: Arnold.

Kress, G. and Van Leeuwen, T. (2002) 'Colour as a semiotic mode: Notes for a grammar of colour', *Visual Communication* 1(3): 343–68.

Kress, G. and Van Leeuwen, T. (2006) *Reading Images: The Grammar of Visual Design*, (2nd edn). London and New York: Routledge.

Kytö, M. and Romaine, S. (2008) "My dearest Minnykins': Style, gender and affect in nineteenth-century English letters', in Watson, G. (ed.) *The State of Stylistics*, pp. 229–63. Amsterdam: Rodopi.

Labov, W. (1972) *Language in the Inner City: Studies in the Black English Vernacular*. Philadelphia, PA: University of Pennsylvania Press.

Lahey, E. (2005) *Text World Landscapes and English-Canadian National Identity in the Poetry of Al Purdy, Alden Nowlan and Milton Acorn*. Unpublished PhD thesis: University of Nottingham.

Lahey, E. (2006) '(Re)thinking world-building: Locating the text-worlds of Canadian lyric poetry', *Journal of Literary Semantics* 35(2): 145–64.

Lakoff, G. (1987) *Women, Fire and Dangerous Things: What Categories Reveal about the Mind*. Chicago, IL: University of Chicago Press.

Lakoff, G. ([1993] 1995) 'The contemporary theory of metaphor', in Ortony, A. (ed.) *Metaphor and Thought* (2nd edn), pp. 202–51. Cambridge: Cambridge University Press.

Lakoff, G. and Johnson, M. (1980) *Metaphors We Live By*. Chicago, IL: University of Chicago Press.

Lakoff, G. and Johnson, M. (1999) *Philosophy in the Flesh: The Embodied Mind and Its Challenge to Western Thought*. New York: Basic Books.

Langacker, R. (1990) *Concept, Image and Symbol: The Cognitive Basis of Grammar*. Berlin: Mouton de Gruyter.

Langacker, R. (1991) *Foundations of Cognitive Grammar, Vol. II: Descriptive Application*. Stanford, CA: Stanford University Press.

Langacker, R. (1993) 'Reference-point constructions', *Cognitive Linguistics* 4: 1–38.

Langacker, R. (1995) 'Viewing in cognition and grammar', in Davis, P. W. (ed.) *Alternative Linguistics: Descriptive and Theoretical Models*, pp. 153–212, Amsterdam: John Benjamins.

Langacker, R. (2001) 'Discourse in cognitive grammar', *Cognitive Linguistics* 12(2): 143–88.

Langacker, R. (2008) *Cognitive Grammar: A Basic Introduction*. Oxford: Oxford University Press.

Langer, S. K. (1953) *Feeling and Form*. London: Routledge and Kegan Paul.

Leech, G. (1969) *A Linguistic Guide to English Poetry*. London: Longman.

Leech, G. (1983) *Principles of Pragmatics*. London: Longman.

Leech, G. (1985a) *English Grammar for Today: A New Introduction*. London: Macmillan.

Leech, G. (1985b) 'Stylistics' in Van Dijk, T. (ed.) *Discourse and Literature*, pp. 39–57. Amsterdam: John Benjamins.

Leech, G. (2008) *Language in Literature. Style and Foregrounding*. London: Longman

Leech, G., Garside, R. and Bryant, M. (1994) 'CLAWS4: The tagging of the British National Corpus', in *Proceedings of the 15th International Conference on Computational Linguistics (COLING 94)*, pp. 622–8. Kyoto, Japan.

Leech, G. and Short, M. ([1981] 2007) *Style in Fiction. A Linguistic Introduction to English Fictional Prose* (2nd edn). London: Pearson.

Leech, G. and Smith, N. (2006) 'Recent grammatical change in written English 1961–1992: Some preliminary findings of a comparison of American with British English', in Renouf, A. and Kehoe, A. (eds) *The Changing Face of Corpus Linguistics*, pp. 185–204. Amsterdam, Netherlands: Rodopi.

Lennard, John and Luckhurst, Mary (2002) *The Drama Handbook: A Guide to Reading Plays*. Oxford: Oxford University Press.

Levenson, M. (1991) 'Flaubert's Parrot: *Talking It Over* by Julian Barnes', *New Republic*: 16 December 1991: 42–5.

Levenston, E. A. (1992) *The Stuff of Literature: Physical Aspects of Texts and Their Relation to Literary Meaning*. New York: State University of New York Press.

Levin, S. R. (1962) *Linguistic Structures in Poetry*. The Hague: Mouton de Gruyter.

Levin, S. R. (1963) 'Deviation – statistical and determinate', *Lingua* 12: 276–90.

Levin, S. R. (1965) 'Internal and external deviation in poetry', *Word* 21: 225–37.

Levinson, S. C. ([1979] 1992) 'Activity types and language', in Drew, P. and Heritage, J. (eds) *Talk at Work*, pp. 66–100. Cambridge: Cambridge University Press.

Levorato, A. (2009) '"Be steady then, my countrymen, be firm, united and determined". Expressions of stance in the 1798–1800 Irish paper war.' *Journal of Historical Pragmatics* 10(1): 132–57.

Lewes, H. G. (1874–9) *Problems of Life and Mind*. Boston, MA: Houghton, Osgood and Co.

Lindauer, M. A. (2009) *Psyche and the Literary Muses*. Amsterdam and Philadelphia, PA: John Benjamins.

Lindemann, S. and Mauranen, A. (2001) '"It's just real messy": The occurrence and function of just in a corpus of academic speech', *English for Specific Purposes* 20: 459–75.

Locher, M. and Watts, R. (2005) 'Politeness theory and relational work', *Journal of Politeness Research* 1(1): 9–33.

Lodge, D. ([1977] 1988) *Modes of Modern Writing. Metaphor, Metonymy, and the Typology of Modern Literature*. Chicago, IL: The University of Chicago Press.

Louw, W. E. (2000) 'Contextual prosody theory: Bringing semantic prosodies to life', in Heffer, C. and Sauntson, H. (eds) *Words in Context*, pp. 48–94. Birmingham: Birmingham University Press.

Louwerse, M. and van Peer, W. (2009) 'How cognitive is cognitive poetics? Adding a symbolic approach to the embodied one', in Brône, G. and Vandaele, J. (eds) *Cognitive Poetics: Goals, Gains and Gaps*, Berlin: Mouton de Gruyter.

Lovecraft, H. P. ([1920] 2002) 'The statement of Randolph Carter', in *The Call of Cthulhu and Other Weird Stories*, pp.7–13. London: Penguin.

Lucas, J. (1986) *Modern English Poetry from Hardy to Hughes*. London: B. T. Batsford Ltd.

Mahlberg, M. (2006) 'Lexical cohesion: Corpus linguistic theory and its application in English language teaching', *International Journal of Corpus Linguistics* 11(3): 227–47.

Mahlberg, M. (2007a) 'Clusters, key clusters and local textual functions in Dickens', *Corpora* 2: 1–31.

Mahlberg, M. (2007b) 'A corpus stylistic perspective on Dickens' *Great Expectations*', in Lambrou, M. and Stockwell, P. (eds) *Contemporary Stylistics*, pp. 19–31. London: Continuum.

Mahlberg, M. (2007c) 'Corpus stylistics: Bridging the gap between linguistics and literary studies', in Hoey, M., Mahlberg, M., Stubbs, M. and Teubert, W. (eds) *Text, Discourse and Corpora. Theory and Analysis*, pp. 219–46. London: Continnum.

Mahlberg, M. (2007d) 'Review of *Investigating Dickens' Style: A Collocational Analysis* by M. Hori', *Language and Literature*, 16: 93–6.

Mahlberg, M. (2009) 'Corpus stylistics and the Pickwickian watering-pot', in Baker, P. (ed.) *Contemporary Corpus Linguistics*, pp. 47–63. London: Continuum.

Mair, C. (2006) *Twentieth-Century English*. Cambridge: Cambridge University Press.

Maley, A. (1999) *Short and Sweet: Short Texts and How to Use Them* Harmondsworth: Penguin.

Maley, A. and Moulding, S. (1985) *Poem into Poem*. Cambridge: Cambridge University Press.

Mandala, S. (2007) 'Solidarity and the Scoobies: An analysis of the –y suffix in the television series *Buffy the Vampire Slayer*', *Language and Literature* 16(1): 53–73.

Mansfield, K. (1921) 'Life of Ma Parker', in *Nation & the Athenaeum*.

Margolin, U. (2003) 'Cognitive science, the thinking mind, and literary narrative', in Herman, D. (ed.) *Narrative Theory and the Cognitive Sciences*, pp. 271–94. Stanford, CA: Center for the Study of Language and Information.

Martens, G. (2006) *Beobachtungen der Moderne*. Munich: Fink.

Martin, J. (2003) 'Negotiating heteroglossia: Social perspectives on evaluation', *Text* 23(2): 171–81.

Martin, J. R. and White, P. (2005) *The Language of Evaluation: Appraisal in English*. London: Palgrave Macmillan.

Masters, A. ([2005] 2006) *Stuart: A Life Backwards*. London, New York, Toronto, Sydney: Harper Perennial.

Mauranen, A. (2003) 'A good question: Expressing evaluation in academic speech', in Cortese, G. and Riley, P. (eds) *Domain-specific English: Textual Practices across Communities and Classrooms*, pp. 115–40. New York: Peter Lang.

McArthur, T. (1981) *Longman Lexicon of Contemporary English*. London: Longman

McCourt, F. (1996) *Angela's Ashes*. New York: Scribner.

McGough, R. (ed.) (2002) *100 Best Poems for Children Chosen by Children*. London: Puffin.

McGough, R. (ed.) (2001) *100 Best Poems for Children*. London: Puffin Books.

McHale, B. (1978) 'Free indirect discourse: A survey of recent accounts', *Poetics and Theory of Literature* 3: 235–87.

McHale, B. (2004) 'Narrative in poetry', in Herman, D., Jahn, M. and Ryan, M.-L. (eds) *Routledge Encyclopedia of Narrative Theory*, pp. 356–8. London: Routledge.

McIlwraith, A. K. (ed.) (1961) *Five Stuart Tragedies*. London: Oxford University Press.

McIntyre, D. (2003) 'Using foregrounding theory as a teaching methodology in a stylistics course', *Style* 37(1): 1–13.

McIntyre, D. (2004) 'Point of view in drama: A socio-pragmatic analysis of Dennis Potter's *Brimstone and Treacle*', *Language and Literature* 13(2): 139–60.

McIntyre, D. (2005) 'Logic, reality and mind style in Alan Bennett's *The Lady in the Van*', *Journal of Literary Semantics*, 34(1): 21–40.

McIntyre, D. (2006) *Point of View in Plays: A Cognitive Stylistic Approach to Viewpoint in Drama and Other Text-types*. Amsterdam: John Benjamins.

McIntyre, D. (2007a) 'Deixis, cognition and the construction of viewpoint', in Lambrou, M. and Stockwell, P. (eds) *Contemporary Stylistics*, pp. 118–30. London: Continuum.

McIntyre, D. (2007b) 'Trusting the text: Corpus linguistics and stylistics', *International Journal of Corpus Linguistics* 12(4): 565–77.

McIntyre, D. (2008) 'Integrating multimodal analysis and the stylistics of drama: A multimodal perspective on Ian McKellen's *Richard III*', *Language and Literature* 17(4): 309–34.

McKenna, W. and Antonia, A. (1996) '"A few simple words" of interior monologue in *Ulysses*: Reconfiguring the evidence', *Literary and Linguistic Computing* 11(2): 55–66.

McRae, J. and Vethamani, E. (1999) *Now Read On: A Course in Multicultural Reading*. London: Routledge.

Megroz, R. L. (1924) *Walter De La Mare*. London: Hodder and Stoughton.

Meisel, M. (2007) *How Plays Work: Reading and Performance*. Oxford: Oxford University Press.

Meredith, G. ([1859] 1968) *The Ordeal of Richard Feverel: The Works of George Meredith, Vol. 2*. New York: Russel and Russel.

Miall, D. S. (2005) 'Beyond interpretation: The cognitive significance of reading', in Veivo, H., Pettersson, B. and Polvinen, M. (eds) *Cognition and Literary Interpretation in Practice*, pp. 129–56. Helsinki: University of Helsinki Press.

Miall, D. S. and Kuiken, D. (2002) 'A feeling for fiction: Becoming what we behold', *Poetics* 30: 221–41.

Miller, A. (1955; rpt. 1970) 'A view from the bridge', in *A View from the Bridge, All My Sons*, pp. 8–85. Harmondsworth: Penguin Books.

Miller, A. (1972) *The Creation of the World and Other Business: A Play*. New York: The Viking Press.

Miller, A. (1978) *The Theater Essays of Arthur Miller*, ed. Robert A. Martin. Harmondsworth: Penguin Books.

Mills, S. (1995) *Feminist Stylistics*. Routledge: London.

Minitab (2005) Release 14. State College, PA: Minitab, Inc.

Minsky, M. (1975) 'A framework for representing knowledge', in Winston, P. H. (ed.) *The Psychology of Computer Vision*, pp. 211–77. New York: McGraw-Hill.

Mitchell, D. (2004) *Cloud Atlas*. London: Sceptre.

Mollerup, P. (1999) *Marks of Excellence*. Great Britain: Phaidon.

Morrison, B. and Motion, A. (eds) (1982) *The Penguin Book of Contemporary British Poetry*. London: Penguin.

Moseley, M. (1997) *Understanding Julian Barnes*. University of South Carolina Press: Columbia

Muir, K. (1994) *King Lear*. London: Routledge (The Arden Shakespeare).

Mukařovský, J. (1964) 'Standard language and poetic language', in Garvin, P. L. (ed. and trans.) *A Prague School Reader on Aesthetics, Literary Structure and Style*, pp. 17–30. Washington, D. C.: Georgetown University Press.

Müller, W. (1999) 'The iconic use of syntax in British and American fiction', in Nänny, M. and Fischer, O. (eds) *Form Miming Meaning*, pp. 393–408. Philadelphia, PA: John Benjamins Publishing Company.

Müller, W. (2001) 'Iconicity and rhetoric: A note on the iconic force of rhetorical figures in Shakespeare', in Fischer, O. and Nänny, M. (eds) *The Motivated Sign. Iconicity in Language and Literature 2*, pp. 305–22. Philadelphia, PA: John Benjamins Publishing Company.

Munkelt, M. and Busse, B. (2007) 'Aspects of Governance in Shakespeare's Edward III: The quest for personal and political identify', in Fielitz, S. (ed.) *Literature as History: History as Literature*, pp. 103–21. Frankfurt: Peter Lang.

Munro, A. (1986) 'Circle of prayer', in *The Progress of Love*. New York: Knopf.

Nakano, T. and Koyama, Y. (2005) 'E-learning materials development based on abstract analysis using web tools', in *Knowledge-Based Intelligent Information and Engineering Systems*. 9th International Conference, KES 2005, Melbourne, Australia, 14–16 September, *Proceedings, Part I*, pp. 794–800. LNCS 3681, Springer.

Nänny, M. and Fischer, O. (eds) (1999) *Form Miming Meaning*. Philadelphia, PA, USA: John Benjamins Publishing Company.

Nevalainen, T. and Raumolin-Brunberg, H. (2004) *Historical Sociolinguistics: Language Change in Tudor and Stuart England*. London: Longman.

Nørgaard, N. (2003) *Systemic Functional Linguistics and Literary Analysis: A Hallidayan Approach to Joyce – a Joycean Approach to Halliday*. Denmark: University Press of Southern Denmark.

Nørgaard, N. (2007) 'Disordered collarettes and uncovered tables: Negative polarity as a stylistic device in Joyce's *Two Gallants*', *Journal of Literary Semantics* 36: 35–52.

Nørgaard, N. (2009) 'The semiotics of typography in literary texts: A multimodal approach', *Orbis Litterarum* 64: 141–60.

Nørgaard, N. (2010) 'Multimodality and the literary text: Making sense of Safran Foer's *Extremely Loud and Incredibly Close*' in Page, R. (ed.) *New Perspectives on Narrative and Multimodality*, pp. 115–26. London and New York: Routledge.

Nostbakken, F. (1997) *Understanding MacBeth: A Student Casebook to Issues, Sources and Historical Documents*. Westport: Greenwood Press.

Nöth, W. (2001) 'Semiotic foundations of iconicity in language and literature', in Fischer, O. and Nänny, M. (eds) *The Motivated Sign. Iconicity in Language and Literature 2*, pp. 17–28. Philadelphia, PA: John Benjamins Publishing Company.

Nünning, A. (2001) 'Metanarration als Lakune der Erzähltheorie: Definition, Typologie und Grundriß einer Funktionsgeschichte metanarrativer Erzähleräußerungen', *Arbeiten aus Anglistik und Amerikanistik (AAA)* 26(2): 125–64.

Nünning, A. (2004) 'On metanarrative: Towards a definition, a typology and an outline of the functions of metanarrative commentary', in Pier, J. (ed.) *The Dynamics of Narrative Form. Studies in Anglo-American Narratology*, Narratologia 4, pp. 11–57. Berlin: Mouton de Gruyter.

O'Brien, F. (1996 [1941]) *The Poor Mouth: A Bad Story about the Hard Life*. (Published in Irish as *An Beal Bocht*). Dublin: The Dalkey Press.

O'Donnell, B. (1970) *An Analysis of Prose Style to Determine Authorship: The O'Ruddy, A Novel by Stephen Crane and Robert Barr*. Studies in General and Comparative Literature, Vol. 4. The Hague: Mouton de Gruyter.

O'Halloran, K. (2007) 'The subconscious in James Joyce's "Eveline": A corpus stylistic analysis that chews on the "fish hook"', *Language and Literature* 16(3): 227–44.

O'Toole, M. (1994) *The Language of Displayed Art*. London: Leicester University Press.

Oatley, K. (2001) 'Shakespeare's invention of theatre as simulation that runs on minds', *Empirical Studies of the Arts*, 19: 27–45.

Oatley, K. (2003) 'Writingandreading: The future of cognitive poetics', in Steen, G. and Gavins, J. (eds) *Cognitive Poetics in Practice*, pp. 161–73. London: Routledge.

Oatley, K. (2008) 'The mind's flight simulator', *The Psychologist* 21: 1030–2.

Oatley, K. (2009) 'Such stuff as dreams: The psychology of fiction' Plenary lecture to the Poetics and Linguistics Association, Wednesday 29 July, Middelburg, Holland.

Ochs, E. (ed.) (1989) *The Pragmatics of Affect*. Special issue of *Text* 9.

OED [Oxford English Dictionary] Available at: <http://www.oed.com >[Accessed 8 January 2010].

Ohmann, R. (1964) 'Generative grammars and the concept of literary style', *Word* 20: 423–39.

Oncins-Martínez, J. L. (2006) 'Notes on the metaphorical basis of sexual language in Early Modern English' in Vázquez-González et al. (eds) *The Historical Linguistics-Cognitive Linguistics Interface*. Huelva: University of Huelva Press.

Opas, L. L. and F. J. Tweedie (1999) 'The magic carpet ride: Reader involvement in Romantic fiction', *Literary and Linguistic Computing* 14(1): 89–101.

Opas, L. L. and F. J. Tweedie (2000) 'Come into my world: Styles of stance in detective and romantic fiction.' Poster. ALLC-ACH2000. Glasgow, UK.

Page, N. (1973) *Speech in the English Novel*. London: Longman.

Panther, K.-U. and Radden, G. (eds) (1999) *Metonymy in Language and Thought*. Amsterdam: John Benjamins.

Panther, K.-U. and Thornburg, L. L. (eds) (2004) *Metonymy and Pragmatic Inferencing*. Amsterdam: John Benjamins.

Paolucci, A. (1986) 'Albee and the restructuring of the Modern stage', *Studies in American Drama, 1945–Present* 1: 4–16.

Paran, A. (2006) *Literature in Teaching and Learning*. Case Studies in TESOL Practice. Alexandria, Va, TESOL.

Parkes, M. (1992) *Pause and Effect: An Introduction to the History of Punctuation in the West*. Aldershot: Scolar Press.

Pascal, R. (1977) *The Dual Voice*. Manchester: Manchester University Press.

PAST, [Paleontological Statistics]. Available at: <http://folk.uio.no/ohammer/past/> [Accessed 12 Febuary 2010].

Pateman, M. (2002) *Julian Barnes*. Tavistock: Northcote House Publishers Ltd.

Patterson, A. (2009) *Milton's Words*. New York: Oxford University Press.

Pavel, T. G. (1986) *Fictional Worlds*. Cambridge, Mass. and London: Harvard University Press.

Peirce, C. S. (1931–58) *Collected Papers*. Cambridge: Harvard University Press.

Peirce, C. S. (1960) *Collected Papers of Charles Sanders Peirce, Vol. 2*. Hartshorne, C. and Weiss, P. (eds) Cambridge, MA: Harvard University Press.

Persichetti, V. (1970) 'Vincent Persichetti', in Robert Stephen Hines (ed.) *The Orchestral Composer's Point of View*. (*Essays on Twentieth Century Music by Those Who Wrote It*), pp. 166–82. Norman, OK: University of Oklahoma Press.

Person, R. F. (1999) *Structure and Meaning in Conversation and Literature*. Lanham: University Press of America.

Pfister, M., trans. John Halliday (1988; rpt. 1993) *The Theory and Analysis of Drama*. Cambridge: Cambridge University Press.

Phelan, J. (2005) *Living to Tell about It*. Ithaca, NY: Cornell University Press.

Phillips, M. (1989) *Lexical Structure of Text*. Discourse Analysis Monographs 12. Birmingham: University of Birmingham.

Phillips, M. K. (1983) *Lexical Macrostructure in Science Text*. Unpublished PhD thesis: University of Birmingham.

Pierson, R. (1964) 'The meter of *The Listeners*', *English Studies* 45: 373–81.

Plummer, P. and Busse, B. (2007) 'Mick Short (Lancaster University) in discussion with Patricia Plummer (University of Mainz) and Beatrix Busse (University of Mainz)', *Anglistik* 18(1): 135–51.

Poos, D. and Simpson, R. (2002) 'Cross-disciplinary comparisons of hedging: Some findings from the Michigan Corpus of Academic Spoken English' in Reppen, R., Fitzmaurice, S. and Biber, D. (eds) *Using Corpora to Explore Linguistic Variation*, pp .3–21. Philadelphia, PA: John Benjamins.

Pope, R. (1994) *Textual Intervention: Critical and Creative Strategies for Literary Studies.* London: Routledge.

Pope, R. (2005) *Creativity: Theory, History, Practice.* Routledge: London.

Precht, K. (2003) 'Stance moods in spoken English: Evidentiality and affect in British and American conversation', *Text* 23(2): 239–57.

Priestley, J. B. (1947) *An Inspector Calls: A Play in Three Acts.* London: Heinemann.

Prince, G. ([1987] 2003) *A Dictionary of Narratology.* Lincoln: University of Nebraska Press.

Prince, G. (1988) 'The disnarrated', *Style* 22: 1–8.

Prince, G. (2005) 'Point of view (literary)', in Herman, D., Jahn, M and Ryan, M-L. (eds) *The Routledge Encyclopedia of Narrative Theory*, pp. 442–3. London: Routledge.

Prince, G. (2006) 'The disnarrated', in Herman, D., Jahn, M. and Ryan, M.-L. (eds) *The Routledge Encyclopaedia of Narrative Theory*, p. 118. New York: Routledge.

Psycho. U.S. (1960) Paramount Pictures. Writer: Joseph Stefano. Director: Alfred Hitchcock.

Punter, D. (2006) *Metaphor.* London: Routledge.

QAA (2009) English benchmarks website. Available at: <http://www.qaa.ac.uk/academicinfrastructure/benchmark/honours/english.asp#9> [Accessed 24 September 2009].

Quiller-Couch, Sir A. (ed.) (1939) *The New Oxford Book of English Verse* (2nd edn). Oxford: Oxford University Press.

Quirk, R., Greenbaum, S., Leech, G. and Svartvik, J. (1985) *A Comprehensive Grammar of the English Language.* London and New York: Longman.

Radway, J. A. (1984) *Reading the Romance.* Chapel-Hill, NC: University of North Carolina Press.

Rapp, D. N. and Gerrig, R. (2006) 'Predilections for narrative outcomes: The impact of story contexts and reader preferences', *Journal of Memory and Language* 54: 54–67.

Raskin, V. (1985) *Semantic Mechanisms of Humor.* Dordrecht/Boston/Lancaster: D. Reidel.

Rayson, P. (2004) 'Keywords are not enough', JAECS (Japan Association for English Corpus Studies), Chuo University, Tokyo, Japan, 27 November.

Rayson, P. (2008) *Wmatrix: A Web-based Corpus Processing Environment.* Computing Department, Lancaster University. Available at: <http://www.comp.lancs.ac.uk/ucrel/wmatrix/> [Accessed 9 October 2009].

Rayson, P., Berridge, D. and Francis, B. (2004) 'Extending the Cochran rule for comparison of word frequencies between corpora', in Purnelle, G., Fairon, C. and Dister, A. (eds) *Volume II of Le poids des mots: Proceedings of the 7th International Conference on Statistical Analysis of Textual Data* (JADT 2004), pp. 926–36. Louvain-la-Neuve, Belgium, 10–12 March. Presses Universitaires de Louvain.

Rea, P. W. and Irving, D. K. (2001) *Producing and Directing the Short Film and Video* (2nd edn). Woburn, MA: Focal Press.

Read, M. (ed.) (1997; rpt. 2001) *Classic FM's One Hundred Favourite Poems.* London: Hodder and Stoughton.

Reid, F. (1929) *Walter De La Mare: A Critical Study.* London: Faber and Faber.

Rhys Jones, G. (ed.) (1996; rpt. 2007) *The Nation's Favourite Poems.* London: BBC Books.

Richards, I. A. (1929) *Practical Criticism: A Study of Literary Judgement*. London: Kegan Paul.

Richards, I. A. ([1936] 1965) *The Philosophy of Rhetoric*. Oxford: Oxford University Press.

Richardson, J. (1973) 'Arthur Miller's Eden', *Commentary* 55(2): 83.

Richardson, S. ([1753–4]1986) *The History of Sir Charles Grandison*. Harris, J. (ed.) Oxford and New York: Oxford University Press.

Richter, V. (2009) 'Die große Erzählung vom Zufall: Charles Darwin hat Spuren auch in der englischen Literatur hinterlassen', *Neue Zürcher Zeitung*, 7-8 February, 2009: 31; B4.

Riddle Harding, J. (2007) 'Evaluative stance and counterfactuals in language and literature', *Language and Literature* 16(3): 263–80.

Rimmon-Kenan, S. ([1983] 2002) *Narrative Fiction*. London: Routledge.

Romaine, S. (1982) *On the Problem of Syntactic Variation and Pragmatic Meaning in Sociolinguistic Theory*. Cambridge: Cambridge University Press.

Ronen, R. (1994) *Possible Worlds in Literary Theory*. Cambridge: Cambridge University Press.

Rosolato, G. (1972) 'The voice and the literary myth', in Macksey, R. and Donato, E. (eds) *The Structuralist Controversy*, pp. 201–14. Baltimore, MD: Johns Hopkins University Press.

Rubik, R. and Widdowson, H. (2000) 'The stylistic intersection: On an integrated course in language and literature', *Arbeiten aus Anglistik und Amerikanistik* 25(1): 5–28.

Rubin, D. (1995) *Memory in Oral Traditions: The Cognitive Psychology of Epic, Ballads and Counting-out Rhymes*. New York: Oxford University Press.

Rudanko, J. (2006) 'Aggravated impoliteness and two types of speaker intention in an episode in Shakespeare's *Timon of Athens*', *Journal of Pragmatics* 38: 829–41.

Ryan, M. L. (1991) *Possible Worlds, Artificial Intelligence and Narrative Theory*. Bloomington and Indianapolis, IN: Indiana University Press.

Ryder, M. E. (2003) 'I met myself coming and going: (co?)-referential noun phrases and point of view in time travel stories', *Language and Literature* 12(3): 213–32.

Salgādo, G. (ed.) (1969) *Three Jacobean Tragedies*. Harmondsworth: Penguin.

Sanchez-Tranquilino, M. and Tagg, J. (1992) 'The pachuco's flayed hide: Mobility, identity, and buenas garras', in Grossberg, L., Nelson, C. and Treichler, P. A. (eds) *Cultural Studies*, pp. 556–70. London and New York: Routlegde.

Sanford, A. J. (2002) 'Context, attention and depth of processing during interpretation', *Mind and Language* 17(1/2): 188–206.

Sanford, A. J. and Garrod, S. C. (1981) *Understanding Written Language: Explorations in Comprehension beyond the Sentence*. Chichester: John Wiley.

Sanford, A. J. and Graesser, A. C. (eds) (2006) 'Shallow processing and underspecification', special issue of *Discourse Processes* 14(2).

Sanford, A. J. and Sturt, P. (2002) 'Depth of processing in language comprehension: Not noticing the evidence', *Trends in Cognitive Sciences* 6: 382–6.

Sanford, A. J. S., Sanford, A. J., Molle, J. and Emmott, C. (2006) 'Shallow processing and attention capture in written and spoken discourse', *Discourse Processes* 42(2): 109–30.

Sanford, A. J. and Garrod, S. C. (1998) 'The role of scenario mapping in text comprehension', *Discourse Processes* 26(2 and 3): 159–90.

Sarangi, S. (2000) 'Activity types, discourse types and interactional hybridity: the case of genetic counselling', in Sarangi, S. and Coulthard, M. (eds) *Discourse and Social Life*, pp. 1–27 London: Pearson.

Saussure, F. de (1916) *Cours de linguistique générale*. C. Bally and A. Sechehaye (eds). Lausanne and Paris: Payot. Trans. W. Baskin (1977) *Course in General Linguistics*. Glasgow: Fontana/Collins.

Scaggs, J. (2005) *Crime Fiction*. London and New York: Routledge.

Schank, R. C. (1982) *Dynamic Memory: A Theory of Reminding and Learning in Computers and People*. Cambridge: Cambridge University Press.

Schank, R. C. and Abelson, R. P. (1977) *Scripts, Plans, Goals and Understanding: An Enquiry into Human Knowledge Structures*. Hillsdale, NJ: Lawrence Erlbaum.

Scheibman, J. (2002) *Point of View and Grammar: Structural Patterns of Subjectivity in American-English Conversation*. Amsterdam: Rodopi.

Schifko, Peter (1979) 'Die Metonymie als universales sprachliches Strukturprinzip', *Grazer Linguistische Studien* 10: 240–64.

Scott Fitzgerald, F. ([1925] 1993) *The Great Gatsby*. Ware: Wordsworth.

Scott, M. (2004–6) *WordSmith Tools*. Version 4.0. Manual. Oxford: Oxford University Press. Available at: <http://www.lexically.net/downloads/version5/HTML/?keyness_definition.htm> [Accessed 1 October 2009].

Scott, M. (2008) *WordSmith Tools*. Version 5.0. Liverpool: Lexical Analysis Software.

Scott, M. (2009a) 'In search of a bad reference corpus', in Archer, D. (ed.) *What's in a Word List? Investigating Word Frequency and Keyword Extraction*, pp. 79–91. Aldershot: Ashgate.

Scott, M. (2009b) *Wordsmith Tools Help*. Liverpool: Lexical Analysis Software. [Accessed 28 September 2009].

Scott, M. and Tribble, C. (2006) *Textual Patterns: Key Words and Corpus Analysis in Language Education*. Amsterdam: John Benjamins.

Searle, J. R. (1969) *Speech Acts: An Essay in the Philosophy of Language*. Cambridge: Cambridge University Press.

Searle, J. R. (1971) 'What is a speech act?', in Searle, J. (ed.) *The Philosophy of Language*, pp. 39–53. Oxford: Oxford University Press.

Searle, J. R. (1975a) 'Indirect speech acts', in Cole, P. and Morgan, J. L. (eds) *Syntax and Semantics 3*, pp. 59–82. New York: Academic Press.

Searle, J. (1975b) 'The logical status of fictional discourse', *New Literary History* 6: 319–32.

Searle, John R. (1976) 'A Classification of Illocutionary Acts'. *Language in Society* 5: 1–23.

Semino, E. (1997) *Language and World Creation in Poems and Other Texts*. London: Longman.

Semino, E. (2001) 'On readings, literariness and schema theory: A reply to Jeffries', *Language and Literature* 10(4): 345–55.

Semino, E. (2002) 'A cognitive approach to mind style in narrative fiction', in Semino, E. and Culpeper, J. (eds) *Cognitive Stylistics: Language and Cognition in Text Analysis*, pp. 95–122. Amsterdam: John Benjamins.

Semino, E. (2007) 'Mind style twenty five years on', *Style* 41(2): 153–73.

Semino, E. (2008) *Metaphor in Discourse*. Cambridge: Cambridge University Press.

Semino, E. (2009) 'Text worlds', in Brône, G. and Vandaele, J. (eds) *Cognitive Poetics: Goals, Gains and Gaps*, pp .33–72. Berlin: Mouton de Gruyter.

Semino, E. and Culpeper J. (eds) (2002) *Cognitive Stylistics: Language and Cognition in Text Analysis*. Amsterdam: John Benjamins.

Semino, E. and Short, M. (2004) *Corpus Stylistics: Speech, Writing and Thought Presentation in a Corpus of English Writing*. London; New York: Routledge.

Semino, E. and Swindlehurst, K. (1996) 'Metaphor and mind style in Ken Kesey's *One Flew Over the Cuckoo's Nest*', *Style* 30(1): 143–66.

Semino, E., Short, M., and Culpeper, J. (1997) 'Using a corpus to test a model of speech and thought presentation', *Poetics* 25(1): 17–43.

Semino, E., Short, M. and Wynne, M. (1999) 'Hypothetical words and thoughts in contemporary British narratives', *Narrative* 7(3): 307–34.

Seyler, D. U. and Wilan, R. A. (1981) *Introduction to Literature*. California: Alfred.

Shakespeare, W. (1997) *The Riverside Shakespeare* (2nd edn). Ed. G. Blakemore Evans Boston, MA: Houghton Mifflin.

Shelley, M. ([1818] 2003) *Frankenstein*. London: Penguin.

Shelley, M. (1826) *The Last Man*. London: Henry Colburn.

Shen, D. (2001) 'Breaking conventional barriers: Transgressions of modes of focalization,' in Peer, W. van and Chatman, S. (eds) *New Perspectives on Narrative Perspective*, pp. 159–72. New York: SUNY.

Shen, D. (2002) 'Defence and challenge: Reflections on the relation between story and discourse', *Narrative* 10(3): 222–43.

Shen, D. (2003) 'Difference behind similarity: Focalization in third-person center of consciousness and first-person retrospective narration,' in Jacobs, C. and Sussman H. (eds) *Acts of Narrative*, pp. 81–92. Stanford, CA: Stanford University Press.

Shen, D. (2005a) 'How stylisticians draw on narratology: Approaches, advantages and disadvantages', *Style* 39 (4): 381–95.

Shen, D. (2005b) 'Mind-style', in Herman, D. et al. (eds) *The Routledge Encyclopedia of Narrative Theory*, pp. 311–12. London: Routledge.

Shen, D. (2005c) 'Story-discourse distinction', in Herman, D. et al. (eds) *The Routledge Encyclopedia of Narrative Theory*, pp. 566–8. London: Routledge.

Shen, D. (2005d) 'What narratology and stylistics can do for each other', in Phelan, J. and Rabinowitz, P. J. (eds) *A Companion to Narrative Theory*, pp. 136–49. Oxford: Blackwell.

Shen, D. (2007) 'Booth's *The Rhetoric of Fiction* and China's critical context', *Narrative* 15(2): 167–86.

Shen, D. and Xu, D. (2007) 'Intratextuality, extratextuality, intertextuality: Unreliability in autobiography versus fiction,' *Poetics Today* 28(1): 43–87.

Sherry, V. (2004) *The Great War and the Language of Modernism*. Oxford: Oxford University Press.

Shklovsky, V. (1917) 'Art as technique', English translation in Lodge, D. (ed.) (1988) *Modern Criticism and Theory. A Reader*, pp. 16–30. London and New York: Longman.

Short, M. (1981) 'Discourse analysis and the analysis of drama', *Applied Linguistics* 11(2): 180–202.

Short, M. (1988) 'Speech presentation, the novel and the press,' in van Peer, W. (ed.) *The Taming of the Text*, pp. 61–81. New York: Routledge.

Short, M. (1989a) 'Introduction', in Short, M. (ed.) *Reading, Analysing and Teaching Literature*, pp. 1–9. London: Longman.

Short, M. (ed.) (1989b) *Reading, Analysing and Teaching Literature*. Harlow: Longman.

Short, M. (1991) 'Discourse analysis in stylistics and literature pedagogy', *Annual Review of Applied Linguistics (ARAL)* 11: 181–95.

Short, M. (1993) 'Stylistics "upside down": Using stylistic analysis in the teaching of language and literature', *Textus* VI: 3–30.

Short, M. (1994) 'Mind style', in Asher, R. (ed.) *The Encyclopedia of Language and Linguistics*, pp. 2504–5. London: Pergamon.

Short, M. (1995) 'Understanding conversational undercurrents in *The Ebony Tower* by John Fowles' in Verdonk, P. and Weber, J-J. (eds) *Twentieth Century Fiction: From Text to Context*, pp. 45–62. Routledge: London.

Short, M. (1996) *Exploring the Language of Poems, Plays and Prose*. London: Longman.

Short, M. (1998) 'From dramatic text to dramatic performance', in Culpeper, J., Short, M. and Verdonk, P. (eds) *Exploring the Language of Drama: From Text to Context*, pp. 6–18. London: Routledge.

Short, M. (1999) 'Graphological deviation, style variation and point of view in *Marabou Stork Nightmares* by Irvine Welsh', *Journal of Literary Studies / Tyskrif ir Literatuur Wetenskap* 15(3/4): 305–23.

Short, M. (2007) 'Thought presentation twenty-five years on', *Style* 42(2): 227–43.

Short, M. and Breen, M. P. (1988a) 'Innovations in the teaching of literature: Putting stylistics in its place', *Critical Quarterly* 30(2): 1–8.

Short, M. and Breen, P. (1988b) 'Putting stylistic analysis in its place', *Critical Quarterly* 30(2): 3–10.

Short, M. and Candlin, C. (1989) 'Teaching study skills for English literature', in Short, M. (ed.) *Reading, Analysing and Teaching Literature*, pp. 178–203. London: Longman.

Short, M., Busse, B. and Plummer, P. (eds) (2006) *Language and Literature*. Special Issue: The Language and Style Pedagogical Investigations, 15(3): 219–328.

Short, M., Freeman, D., van Peer, W. and Simpson, P. (1998) 'Stylistics, criticism and mythrepresentation again: Squaring the circle with Ray Mackay's subjective solution for all problems', *Language and Literature* 7(1): 39–50.

Short, M., Semino, E. and Culpeper, J. (1996) 'Using a corpus for stylistics research: Speech and thought presentation', in Thomas, J. and Short, M. (eds) *Using Corpora in Language Research*, pp. 110–31. London: Longman.

Short, M., Wynne, M. and Semino, E. (2002) 'Revisiting the notion of faithfulness in discourse presentation using a corpus approach', *Language and Literature* 11(4): 325–55.

Sidney, P. ([1580] 1994) *The Old Arcadia*, ed. K. Duncan-Jones. Oxford: Oxford University Press.

Simon-Vandenbergen, A.-M. (2008) '*Almost certainly* and *most definitely*: degree modifiers and epistemic stance', *Journal of Pragmatics* 40: 1521–42.

Simpson, P. (1993) *Language, Ideology and Point of View*. London: Routledge.

Simpson, P. (1996) *Language Through Literature: An Introduction*. London: Routledge.

Simpson, P. (2003) *On the Discourse of Satire: Towards a Stylistic Model of Satirical Humour*. Amsterdam: John Benjamins.

Simpson, P. (2004) *Stylistics: A Resource Book for Students*. London: Routledge.

Simpson, P. (in preparation) '"That's not ironic, that's just stupid": A five-part pragmatic model of ironic discourse', mimeo, Queen's University Belfast.

Simpson, P. and Hall, G. (2002) 'Discourse analysis and stylistics', *Annual Review of Applied Linguistics (ARAL)*, pp. 136–49. New York; Cambridge: Cambridge University Press.

Simpson, P. and Hardy, D. (2008) 'American sentences: Terms, topics and techniques in stylistic analysis', in Stoneley, P. and Weinstein, C. (eds) *The Blackwell Concise Companion to American Fiction, 1900–1950*, pp. 113–31. Oxford: Blackwell.

Simpson, P. and Montgomery, M. (1995) 'Language, literature and film: The stylistics of Bernard MacLaverty's *Cal*', in Verdonk, P. and Weber, J. J. (eds) *Twentieth Century Fiction: From Text to Context*, pp. 138–64. London: Routledge.

Sinclair, J. (1966) 'Taking a poem to pieces', in Fowler, R. (ed.) *Essays on Style and Language*, pp. 68–81. London: Routledge and Kegan Paul.

Sinclair, J. (2003) *Reading Concordances: An Introduction*. Harlow: Longman.

Sinclair, J. (2004) *Trust the Text: Language, Corpus and Discourse*. London; New York: Routledge.

Sinclair, J. M. (1972) 'Lines about "Lines"', in Kachru, B. B. and Stahlke H. F. W. (eds) *Current Trends in Stylistics*. Edmonton, Alberta: Linguistic Research Inc.

Sinfield, A. (1992) *Faultlines. Cultural Materialism and the Politics of Dissident Reading*. Oxford: Clarendon.

Smith, C. ([1792] 2001) *Desmond,* ed. Blank, A. and Todd, J. Peterborough, Ontario: Broadview.

Smith, J. (2007) *Tarantino*. London: Virgin Books.

Smith, S. (1982) *Inviolable Voice: History and Twentieth-century Poetry*. Dublin: Gill and Macmillan Humanities Press.

Smith, Z. (2007) *The Book of Other People*. London; New York: Penguin.

Sorrentino, P. (2008) 'Stephen Crane's sources and allusions in "The Bride Comes to Yellow Sky" and "Moonlight on the Snow"', *American Literary Realism* 40: 52–65.

Southam, B. C. (1964) *Jane Austen's Literary Manuscripts: A Study of the Novelist's Development Through the Surviving Papers*. Oxford: Oxford University Press.

Spencer, H. R. ([1855] 1877) *Principles of Psychology*. New York: D. Appleton and Co.

Spencer, H. R. (1860) 'The social organism', *Westminster Review* 17: 90–121.

Spevack, M. (1963) *A Thesaurus of Shakespeare*. Hildesheim: Georg Olms Publishers.

Spitzer, L. (1948) *Linguistics and Literary History*. Princeton, NJ: Princeton University Press.

Spurgeon, C. F. E. (1952) *Shakespeare's Imagery and What It Tells Us*. Cambridge: Cambridge University Press.

Spurr, B. (1997) *Studying Poetry*. London: Macmillan Press.

Steffensen, M. S. and Joag-Dev, C. (1984) 'Cultural knowledge and reading', in Alderson, J. C. and Urquhart, A. H. (eds) *Reading in a Foreign Language*, pp. 48–64. London: Longman.

Stevenson, R. L. ([1886] 1993) *Strange Case of Dr Jekyll and Mr Hyde*. Milan: Guerini.

Stockwell, P. (2002) *Cognitive Poetics: An Introduction*. London: Routledge.

Stockwell, P. (2003a) 'Schema poetics and speculative cosmology', *Language and Literature* 12(3): 252–71.

Stockwell, P. (2003b) 'Surreal figures', in Gavins, J. and Steen, G. (eds) *Cognitive Poetics in Practice*, pp. 13–25, London: Routledge.

Stockwell, P. (2005) 'Schema theory: Stylistic applications', in Brown, K. (ed.) *The Encyclopedia of Language and Linguistics* (2nd edn). Oxford: Elsevier.

Stockwell, P. (2005b) 'Texture and identification', *EJES* 9(2): 143–53.

Stockwell, P. (2009a) 'Authenticity and creativity in reading lamentation', in Swann, J., Pope, R. and Carter, R. (eds) *Creativity in Language*. Palgrave Macmillan: Basingstoke.

Stockwell, P. (2009b) 'The cognitive poetics of literary resonance', *Language and Cognition* 1(1): 25–44.

Stockwell, P. (2009c) *Texture: A Cognitive Aesthetics of Reading*. Edinburgh: Edinburgh University Press.

Stockwell, P. (forthcoming) 'Authenticity and creativity in reading lamentation' in Swann, J, Pope, R. and Carter, R. (eds) *Creativity, Literature, Language: The State of the Art*. Palgrave: Macmillan Basingstoke.

Stubbs, M. (1998) 'Whorf's children: Critical comments on critical discourse analysis', in Ryan, A. and Wray, A. (eds) *Evolving Models of Language*. pp. 100–16. Clevedon: Multilingual Matters.

Stubbs, M. (2004) 'Review of Peter Verdonk, *Stylistics*, Oxford University Press, 2002', *Applied Linguistics* 25(1): 126–9.

Stubbs, M. (2005) 'Conrad in the computer: Examples of quantitative stylistic methods', *Language and Literature* 14(5): 5–24.

Studer, P. (2008) *Historical Corpus Stylistics. Media, Technology and Change*. London: Continuum.

Swales, J. M. and Burke, A. (2003) '"It's really fascinating work": Differences in evaluative adjectives across academic registers', in Leistyna, P. and Meyer C. F. (eds) *Corpus Analysis: Language Structure and Language Use*, pp. 1–18. New York: Rodopi.

Swan, J. (2002) '"Life without parole": Metaphor and discursive commitment', *Style* 36: 446–65.

Taavitsainen, I. and Fitzmaurice, S. (2007) 'Historical Pragmatics: What is it and how to do it', in Fitzmaurice, S. and Taavitsainen, I. (eds) *Methods in Historical Pragmatics*, pp. 11–36. Berlin: Mouton de Gruyter.

Tabakowska, E. (2005) 'Iconicity as a function of point of view', in Maeder, C. (ed.). *Outside-In – Inside-Out. Iconicity in Language and Literature 4*. Philadelphia, PA: John Benjamins.

Talib. I. (1992) 'Why not teach non-native English literature?', *English Language Teaching Journal* 46: 51–5.

Talib, I. (2002) *The Language of Postcolonial Literatures* London: Routledge.

Talmy, L. (1988) 'Force dynamics in language and cognition', *Cognitive Science* 12: 49–100.

Talmy, L. (2000a) *Toward a Cognitive Semantics. Vol. I: Concept Structuring Systems*. Cambridge: MIT Press.

Talmy, L. (2000b) *Toward a Cognitive Semantics. Vol. II: Typology and Process in Concept Structuring*. Cambridge: MIT Press.

Tamir-Ghez, N. (1979) 'The art of persuasion in Nabokov's *Lolita*', *Poetics Today* 1(1/2): 65–83.

Tannen, D. (1989) *Talking Voices: Repetition, Dialogue, and Imagery in Conversational Discourse*. Cambridge: Cambridge University Press.

Tarantino, Q. (1994) *Reservoir Dogs*. London: Faber and Faber.

Taylor, J. R. (2002) *Cognitive Grammar*. Oxford: Oxford University Press.

Thackeray, W. M. ([1847] 1994) *Vanity Fair*, ed. Shillingsburg. P. New York; London: Norton.

Thackeray, W. M. ([1847–8] 1961) *Vanity Fair*. London: Dent.

Thelen-Schaefer, I. (1992) *Mythos und Realität der Chicanos: Eine literarische Studie unter Berücksichtigung soziologischer Aspekte in den Romanen* Bless me, Ultima *von Rudolfo A. Anaya*, ... y no se lo tragó la tierra / ... and the earth did not devour him *von Tomas Rivera und* Generaciones y semblanzas *von Rolando Hinojosa*. Wien: Österreichischer Kunst- und Kulturverlag.

Thomas, J. (1995) *Meaning in Interaction*. London: Longman.

Thomas, J. and Short, M. (1996) *Using Corpora for Language Research*. London: Longman.

Thompson, G. and Hunston, S. (2000) 'Evaluation: An introduction', in Hunston, S. and Thompson, G. (eds) *Evaluation in Text: Authorial Stance and the Construction of Discourse*, pp. 1–27. Oxford: Oxford University Press.

Thompson, G. and Ye, Y. (1991) 'Evaluation in the reporting verbs used in academic papers', *Applied Linguistics* 12: 365–82.

Thomson, D. (2002) *The New Biographical Dictionary of Film* (4th edition). London: Little Brown.

Thomson, W. (1923) *The Rhythm of Speech*. Glasgow: Maclehose, Jackson and Co.

Tolson, A. (2006) *Media Talk. Spoken Discourse on TV and Radio*. Edinburgh: Edinburgh University Press.

Toolan, M. (1986) 'Poem, reader, response: Making sense with "Skunk Hour"', in Nicholson, C. and Chaterjee, R. (eds) *Tropic Crucible*. Singapore: Singapore University Press.

Toolan, M. (1997) *Language in Literature: An Introduction to Stylistics*. London: Hodder.

Toolan, M. (2001) *Narrative: A Critical Linguistic Introduction*. London: Routledge.

Toolan, M. (2007) 'Trust and text, text as trust', *International Journal of Corpus Linguistics*, 12(2): 265–284.

Toolan, M. (2009) *Narrative Progression in the Short Story: A Corpus Stylistic Approach*. Amsterdam; New York: John Benjamins.

Toolan, M. (forthcoming) 'Lost and found in the reading machine.' "Lost and found in the reading machine": Foreword for Zyngier, S., van Peer, W. and Viana, V. (eds) *Digital Learning: Methods and Technologies*. Hershey, PA: IGI Global.

Torne, J. P. (1965) 'Stylistics and generative grammars', *Journal of Linguistics* 1: 49–59.

Traugott, E. C. and Dasher, R. (2002) *Regularity in Semantic Change*. Cambridge: Cambridge University Press.

Tsur, R. (1992) *Toward a Theory of Cognitive Poetics*. Amsterdam: North-Holland.

Tsur, R. (2006) *'Kubla Khan' – Poetic Structure, Hypnotic Quality, and Cognitive Style: A Study in Mental, Vocal, and Critical Performance*. Amsterdam: John Benjamins.

Turner, M. (1991) *Reading Minds*. Princeton, NJ: Princeton University Press.

Turner, M. (1996) *The Literary Mind: The Origins of Thought and Language*. New York: Oxford University Press.

Turner, M. (2006) *The Artful Mind: Cognitive Science and the Riddle of Human Creativity*. Oxford: Oxford University Press.

Turner, M. and Fauconnier, G. (1999) 'A mechanism of creativity', *Poetics Today* 20(3): 397–418.

Uspensky, B. (1973) *A Poetics of Composition*. Trans. V. Savarin and S. Wittig. Berkeley, CA: University of California Press.

Valdez, Luis (1992) 'Zoot suit', in *Zoot Suit and Other Plays*, pp. 21–94. Houston: Arte Público Press.

van Dijk, T. A. (2008) *Discourse and Context: A Socio-cognitive Approach*. Cambridge: Cambridge University Press.

van Leeuwen, T. (1999) *Speech, Music, Sound*. London: Palgrave MacMillan.

van Leeuwen, T. (2005a) *Introducing Social Semiotics*. London; New York: Routledge.

van Leeuwen, T. (2005b) 'Typographic meaning', *Visual Communication* 4(2): 137–43.

van Leeuwen, T. (2006a) 'Critical discourse analysis', in Brown, K. (ed.) *Encyclopedia of Language and Linguistics* (2nd edn), pp. 290–4. Oxford: Elsevier.

van Leeuwen, T. (2006b) 'Towards a semiotics of typography', *Information Design Journal + Document Design* 14(2): 139–55.

van Peer, W. (1986) *Stylistics and Psychology: Investigations in Foregrounding*. London: Croom Helm.

van Peer, W. (1993) 'Typographic foregrounding', *Language and Literature* 2(1): 49–61.

Verdonk, P. (2002) *Stylistics* Oxford: Oxford University Press.

Verdonk, P. and Weber, J.-J. (1995) *Twentieth Century Fiction: From Text to Context*. Routledge: London.

Vickers, B. (1970) *Classical Rhetoric in English Poetry*. London: Macmillan.

Vipond, D. and Hunt, R. A. (1984) 'Point-driven understanding: Pragmatic and cognitive dimensions of literary reading', *Poetics* 13: 261–77.

Walder, D. (1987) *Ted Hughes*. Milton Keynes; Philadelphia, PA: Open University Press.

Wales, K. (1984) 'Dickens and interior monologue: The opening of *Edwin Drood* reconsidered', *Language and Style* 17: 234–50.

Wales, K. (1990) *A Dictionary of Stylistics*. Harlow: Longman.

Wales, K. (2001) *A Dictionary of Stylistics*. 2nd edition. London: Pearson.

Watson, G. and Zyngier, S. (eds) (2006) *Literature and Stylistics for Language Learners: Theory and Practice* Basingstoke: Palgrave Macmillan.

Wavell, A. P. (ed.) (1944, repr. 2007) *Other Men's Flowers*. London: Pimlico.

Weber, J.-J. (1992) *Critical Analysis of Fiction. Essays in Discourse Stylistics*. Amsterdam: Rodopi.

Weizman, E. (1985) 'Towards an analysis of opaque utterances: Hints as a request strategy', *Theoretical Linguistics* 12(1): 153–63.

Weizman, E. (1989) 'Requestive hints', in Blum-Kulka, S., Kasper, G. and J. House (eds) *Cross Cultural Pragmatics: Requests and Apologies*, pp. 71–95. Norwood, AJ: Ablex.

Wells, H. G. (1898) *The War of the Worlds*. London: William Heinemann.

Welsh, I. (1995) *Marabou Stork Nightmares*. New York: W. W. Norton.

Werth, P. (1994) 'Extended metaphor: A text world account', *Language and Literature*, 3(2): 79–103.

Werth, P. (1995a) 'How to build a world (in a lot less than six days and using only what's in your head)', in Green, K. (ed.) *New Essays on Deixis: Discourse, Narrative, Literature*, pp. 49–80. Amsterdam: Rodopi.

Werth, P. (1995b) '"World enough and time": Deictic space and the interpretation of prose', in Verdonk, P. and Weber, J. J. (eds) *Twentieth Century Fiction: From Text to Context*, pp. 181–205. London: Routledge.

Werth, P. (1999) *Text Worlds: Representing Conceptual Space in Discourse*. London: Longman.

Wertheim, S. (1997) *A Stephen Crane Encyclopedia*. Westport, CT: Greenwood Publishing Group. [online]. Available at: <https://ezproxy.library.nyu.edu/login?url= http://site.ebrary.com/lib/ nyulibrary/Doc?id=10017918> [Accessed 18 March 2009].

West, D. (2007) 'I. A. Richards' theory of metaphor: Between protocognitivism and poststructuralism', in Jeffries, L., McIntyre, D. and Bousfield, D. (eds) *Stylistics and Social Cognition*. Amsterdam: Rodopi.

Whistler, T. (1993, rev. 2003) *The Life of Walter De La Mare: Imagination of the Heart*. London: Duckworth.

White, P. (2003) 'Beyond modality and hedging: A dialogic view of the language of intersubjective stance', *Text* 23(2): 259–84.

Widdowson, H. G. (1975) *Stylistics and the Teaching of Literature*. Harlow: Longman.

Widdowson, H. G. (1992) *Practical Stylistics*. Oxford: Oxford University Press.

Widdowson, H. G. (1995) 'Discourse analysis: A critical view', *Language and Literature* 4(3): 157–72.

Widdowson, H. G. (1996) 'Reply to Fairclough: Discourse and interpretation: Conjectures and refutations', *Language and Literature* 5(1): 57–69.

Widdowson, H. G. (2004) *Text, Context, Pretext: Critical Issues in Discourse Analysis* Oxford: Blackwell.

Wilde, O. ([1890] 1969) 'The critic as artist', in Ellmann, R. (ed.) *The Artist as Critic. Critical Writings of Oscar Wilde*. New York: Random House.

Wilde, O. ([1890] 1994) *Picture of Dorian Gray*. London: Penguin.

Williams, J. (1985) *Reading Poetry: A Contextual Introduction*. London: Edward Arnold.

Williams, R. (1976) *Keywords*. London: Fontana.

Williams, T. (1947; 1959, rpt. 1969) 'The Glass Menagerie', in Browne, E. Martin (ed.) *Sweet Bird of Youth, A Streetcar Named Desire, The Glass Menagerie*, pp. 227–313. Harmondsworth: Penguin.

Winterson, J. (1994) *Art and Lies. A Piece for Three Voices and a Band*. London: Vintage.

Woolf, V. ([1925] 1983) *Mrs Dalloway*. London: Granada.

Woolf, V. (1927) *To the Lighthouse*. London: Hogarth Press.

Wynne, M. (ed.) (2005) *Developing Linguistic Corpora: A Guide to Good Practice*. Oxford: Oxbow Books.

Zinman, T. (2008) *Edward Albee*. Ann Arbor, MI: University of Michigan Press.

Zunshine, L. (2006) *Why We Read Fiction: Theory of Mind and the Novel*. Columbus, Ohio: Ohio State University Press.

Zwierlein, A.-J. (ed.) (2005) *Unmapped Countries. Biological Visions in Nineteenth-Century Literature*. London: Anthem Press.

Zyngier, S., Bortolussi, M., Chesnokova, A. and Auracher, J. (eds) (2008) *Directions in Empirical Literary Studies: In Honour of Willie van Peer*. Amsterdam: John Benjamins.

Index

537